D0713020

WOODPECKERS
of the WORLD

Gerard Gorman

WOODPECKERS *of the* WORLD

A Photographic Guide

Firefly Books

Published by Firefly Books Ltd. 2014

First printing

Publisher Cataloging-in-Publication Data (U.S.)

A CIP record for this title is available from the Library of Congress

Library and Archives Canada Cataloguing in Publication

A CIP record for this title is available from Library and Archives Canada

Published in the United States by
Firefly Books (U.S.) Inc.
P.O. Box 1338, Ellicott Station
Buffalo, New York 14205

Published in Canada by
Firefly Books Ltd.
50 Staples Avenue, Unit 1
Richmond Hill, Ontario L4B 0A7

Printed in China by C&C Offset Printing Co Ltd.

Conceived, designed, and produced by Christopher Helm, an imprint of Bloomsbury Publishing Plc,
50 Bedford Square, London WC1B 3DP.
Commissioning Editor: Jim Martin
Design by Julie Dando, Fluke Art

This book is produced using paper that is made from wood grown in managed sustainable forests. It is natural, renewable and recyclable. The logging and manufacturing processes conform to the environmental regulations of the country of origin.

CONTENTS

ACKNOWLEDGEMENTS

My travels in search of woodpeckers have seen me visit some of the world's most wonderful forests. In preparation for this book, my aim was to continue to gather as much first-hand field experience on as many species as possible. However, with well over 200 species and many subspecies to cover – some rare and/or found in difficult-to-access areas – this was always going to be a tall order, so I also examined museum collections and drew on the expertise of others. Very special thanks are due to Phil Brown, Simon Cook, James Eaton, Clive Mann, Chris Sharpe, Luis Fabio Silveira and Rick Wright, who read and improved sections of the text. I am also grateful to Anita Gamauf and Hans-Martin Berg (Naturhistorisches Museum Wien). Thanks also to: Danny Alder, Ken Allaire, Svetlana Annenkova, William Apraku, Nik Borrow, Diego Calderon, Laura Chazarreta, David Christie, Yoav Chudnoff, Ron Demey, Moussa Diop, Trevor Ellery, Tan Choo Eng, Andy Foster, Giraldo Alayon Garcia, Gonzalo Gonzalez, Sebastian Herzog, Thomas Hochebner, Rob Hutchinson, Tang Jun, Johnnie Kamugisha, Arturo Kirkconnell, Szabolcs Kókay, Steven Latta, Alexander Lees, Gabriel Leite, James Lowen, Gerald Mayr, Robert Niakor, Terry Oatley, Georges Olioso, Otte Ottema, Adam Riley, Glaucia del Rio, Amila Salgado, V. Santharam, Dave Sargeant, Andras Schmidt, Ann Sutton, Warwick Tarboton, Julio Salgado Velez, Pascal Villard, Tim Wacher and Stijn de Win. Tim Harris greatly improved my text and at Bloomsbury Jim Martin was a supportive editor. Finally, I must thank the talented photographers whose work illustrates this book.

◄ Female Black-rumped Flameback *Dinopium benghalense*. Allepey, Kerala, India (*John Holmes*).

► Woodpeckers appear in the legends and myths of many ancient cultures. For example, the Mayans believed that the red on the head of woodpeckers, such as this male Ladder-backed Woodpecker *Picoides scalaris,* appeared when the birds bled from wounds sustained whilst hacking into rocks to find hidden corn for humanity. Volcán Fuego, Mexico, March (*Gary Thoburn*).

INTRODUCTION

Woodpeckers are a family of near-passerines (the Picidae) in the order Piciformes. The Piciformes probably originated some 60 million years ago and includes some of the oldest avian lineages. The evolutionary history of woodpeckers and the relationships between them and other Piciformes remains unclear; however, recent DNA sequence analysis and morphological studies suggest that barbets (Capitonidae, Megalaimidae, Lybiidae, Semnornithidae), toucans (Ramphastidae) and particularly honeyguides (Indicatoridae) are relatives. Woodpeckers are the most species-rich of the Piciformes and probably became distinct from others in the order around 50 million years ago.

The picid fossil record is poor, but findings suggest that woodpeckers originated in Eurasia, before dispersing to North America and then South America. The earliest fossil, from the late Oligocene/early Miocene epoch (more than 25 million years ago), was discovered in central France and named *Piculoides saulcetensis.* The oldest New World fossil, from the Miocene (25–20 million years ago), is a contour feather in amber from Hispaniola. The oldest African fossil, from the Pliocene (5–3 million years ago), was unearthed in South Africa and named *Australopicus nelsonmandelai* in honour of Nelson Mandela. This picid is regarded as being more closely related to the *Celeus* and *Dryocopus,* which do not occur in Africa, than to any genus occurring on that continent. Woodpeckers as we know them today are probably around 5 million years old. They are usually divided into three subfamilies: Jynginae (wrynecks), Picumninae (piculets) and Picinae (true woodpeckers).

Woodpeckers appear in folklore and legends worldwide. Many North American Indian tribes considered woodpeckers to be prophets or medicine birds, associated with friendship and happiness, their drumming was linked to shamanism and their bills and feathers used in rituals and to adorn head-dresses and totem poles. In Mayan myth, a woodpecker is asked to tap on a rock to find where it is thinnest so that man can extract maize hidden within, but the bird was cut by flying stone and bled – and has ever since had a red nape. Woodpeckers have often been associated with security and fertility: in the Old World, Pan is said to have hatched from a woodpecker's egg, a woodpecker was believed to have joined the wolf in feeding the infants Romulus and Remus, the founders of Rome, and a curious tradition from the Peruvian Andes that lingers today maintains that the flesh of Andean Flickers helps nursing mothers produce more milk. In Greco-Roman mythology, the woodland King Picus was turned into a woodpecker by the enchantress Circe when he rejected her love. In many cultures woodpeckers have also been associated with fire, lightning, storms and destruction. Drumming was linked to thunder, the Greeks associating a woodpecker with Zeus, the Piceni tribes with Mars, and the Romans hailed woodpeckers as good omens in wartime.

When I was asked by Bloomsbury Publishing to work on this photographic guide, the timing was perfect. I had just finished a monograph *The Black Woodpecker* (Lynx Edicions, 2011) which had followed on from *Woodpeckers of Europe* (Bruce Coleman, 2004), and had already begun to accumulate data for a global project on these remarkable birds. During my research it soon became clear that many species of woodpecker are poorly-known, with questions on taxonomy, biology, behaviour, distribution and even existence remaining unanswered. I hope this book helps draw attention to these issues. Correspondence on any subjects relating to woodpeckers and/or to this book should addressed to the author c/o Bloomsbury Publishing. In particular, photographs of newly described or rare species and subspecies (especially those taxa which we were unable to obtain for this book), and of birds indulging in interesting behaviour, would be welcomed for future editions.

TAXONOMY

Woodpecker taxonomy is complex, with species limits sometimes unclear and many taxa hybridising. Classification has been somewhat untidy, with species and subspecies created and then rejected or moved to and fro between genera. Previously, most analysis was based on plumage, behaviour and ecology, or on morphology and anatomy. More recently, studies have focused on DNA sequences and suggest that in many aspects of plumage and ecology woodpeckers have undergone convergent evolution, arriving at similar solutions independently. Subsequently, subspecies are increasingly being granted full-species status and as studies continue, particularly on the piculets, this trend will continue. The conservation of woodpeckers (and indeed all animals) can be hindered by uncertainty in their taxonomic status, but fortunately conservation biologists are increasingly focusing on this issue.

There are many differing global and regional taxonomic checklists for birds. As taxonomy is man-made and on-going assessment of what constitutes a species and what does not varies, no single list is definitive. Sadly, the very existence of some species is also uncertain. Thus, a final figure for the number of woodpecker species on the planet is hard to ascertain. However, for works of this kind, decisions have to be made on which taxa to include and exclude. After synthesising the work of various international and regional taxonomic authorities and peer-reviewed papers – including Benz *et al.* (2006), Clements (2012), Collar (2011), Del-Rio *et al.* (2013), Dickinson (2003), Fuchs *et al.* (2008b), Gill & Donsker (2013), Moore *et al.* (2006), Rasmussen & Anderton (2005), Remsen *et al.* (2013), Tobias *et al.* (2010) and Webb & Moore (2005) – a total of 239 species have been included in this book. This compares with 214 species in Winkler, Christie & Nurney (1995) and 216 in *HBW* (2002). Some observers view recent taxonomic splits as exaggerated, others as too conservative, and thus the total of species included will please some and displease others.

Nomenclature

No overall agreement on which English vernacular names to use for many birds, including some woodpeckers, exists. Numerous woodpeckers have more than one English name, for example, the Asian flamebacks are often called 'goldenbacks' and Grey-headed Woodpecker is sometimes called Grey-faced Woodpecker. Alternative English names are given when relevant but the solution, when deciding exactly which species is being discussed, should be to refer to the scientific name of the species. The English names in this book mostly, but not entirely, follow the IOC World Bird List.

◀ The complex taxonomy of the Picidae is sometimes further convoluted by the inter-breeding of taxa. For example, this Little Woodpecker *Veniliornis passerinus* x Blood-coloured Woodpecker *Veniliornis sanguieus* is a not-uncommon hybrid in French Guiana (*Maxime Dechelle*).

DISTRIBUTION

Woodpeckers are globally quite widespread, being found from sea-level to high altitudes on every continent except Antarctica and Australia-Oceania. They are also absent from the Arctic, Greenland, Madagascar and Hawaii, though some (often endemics) are found on continental islands. The richest woodpecker diversity is in South America, followed by SE Asia, with Africa relatively poorly populated. The two wrynecks (Jynginae) have an exclusively Old World distribution, occurring in Europe, Asia and Africa. The piculets (Picumninae) have a pan-tropical distribution, with species in SE Asia, Africa and particularly South America. The true woodpeckers (Picinae) occur across the entire global range of the family.

Movements and migration

Very few woodpeckers undertake regular seasonal migrations; indeed, the majority of woodpeckers are highly sedentary. Most juvenile woodpeckers disperse before their first winter; exceptions include young Magellanic Woodpeckers which remain with their parents for up to four years.

Migrants include Eurasian Wryneck (most of the European population winters in Africa and Asian populations in India), Rufous-bellied Woodpecker (birds in NE China and SE Russia migrate to winter in S China), and Yellow-bellied Sapsuckers (breeding areas in Canada and northern USA are vacated in autumn for the warmer south-east, Central America and Caribbean). Northerly populations of Lewis's Woodpecker, Northern Flicker and Red-breasted, Red-naped and Williamson's Sapsuckers also move south in autumn to winter in the southern USA and Central America.

Nomadic and irregular movements of woodpeckers related to weather and food availability also occur. Territories are vacated when resources are scarce and areas where abundant food has become available are occupied, for example, when fire, storms or avalanches result in much dead timber and subsequently infestations of beetles, Black-backed and American and Eurasian Three-toed Woodpeckers will appear in numbers in such forests. In Eurasia, Great Spotted Woodpeckers move when northern conifer-seed crops fail and Red-headed Woodpeckers in North America respond in a similar way to shortages of mast. In addition, species that breed at high elevations may descend to lower areas in hard winters, but remain if weather and food resources are suitable.

► Eurasian Wryneck *Jynx torquilla* is one of the few woodpeckers that migrates over long distances. Most European breeders, for example, winter in sub-Saharan Africa. Romania, June (*Florian Andronache*).

ANATOMY AND MORPHOLOGY

Woodpeckers possess a range of anatomical adaptions that enable them to climb head-first up vertical tree-trunks, excavate cavities and drum on hard surfaces, and exploit ecological niches that are beyond most other birds. When a woodpecker drums, its skull can experience shocks in excess of 1200g (humans are usually left concussed at deceleration rates of under 100g). An adaptation unique to woodpeckers which functions as a shock-absorber, reducing pressure on the brain, is an inwardly curved maxilla, an overhang of spongy tissue between the upper mandible and skull. Avoidance of concussion is also aided by a long, sinewy apparatus of cartilage and bones inside the tongue called the hyoid. This remarkable structure can be retracted and extended and in retracted position is wrapped around the skull and fixed near the base of the upper mandible, which further helps absorb shock. A thick skull is situated above the line of the bill so that impacts are transmitted below the brain and a narrow space for cerebral fluid between the skull and the brain also reduces potentially damaging vibration. The inner ear resists damage by having a thick membrane. Other related features include strong limbs and claws, broad ribs and tough skin, muscles and tendons.

▲ Woodpeckers have evolved a wide range of anatomical features to support their generally arboreal lifestyle, such as a rigid tail, which is used to support the body when climbing and foraging. Even though it is hanging by its feet, this Acorn Woodpecker *Melanerpes formicivorus* still presses its tail against the seed-head upon which it is feeding. Texas, United States, March (*Dave Hawkins*).

True woodpeckers have robust bills; heavier than those of piculets and wrynecks. Species that forage terrestrially have longer and more decurved bills than the more arboreal species. The bill is hard but flexible (another shock-absorbing feature), typically broad-based, straight, dagger-shaped and chisel-tipped. Its importance is evident in that it is already large and developed on nestlings before their plumage appears. Nasal tufts catch fine debris during excavation and a nicitating membrane closes before impacts to protect the eye.

The tail feather shafts (rachis) of true woodpeckers are rigid and function as props to keep the body off the tree surface, the central pair being longest and toughest; wrynecks and piculets lack rigid tails. A large pygostile (last vertebrate bone) supports the tail and provides more support. Furthermore, a zygodactyl toe arrangement (two digits pointing forward, two backwards) is ideal for climbing. Another unique anatomical adaptation is a long barbed tongue (rigid and sharp for impaling prey, or flexible and sticky for licking up prey) that is retractable and partly prehensile and can be inserted into holes and crevices.

◄ Male White-bellied Woodpecker *Dryocopus javensis* in a classic pose. Note the impressive, dagger-like bill, huge claws gripping the tree-stump, and the stout tail, which is used as a prop to take the weight off the bird's body. Palawan, Philippines, January (*Carlo Benitez Gomez*).

Topography of a typical woodpecker

Woodpeckers vary greatly in size, from the tiny piculets (many are just 8cm long) to the Imperial Woodpecker (males reaching 60cm from bill-tip to tail-tip), however, the general structure of all species is similar.

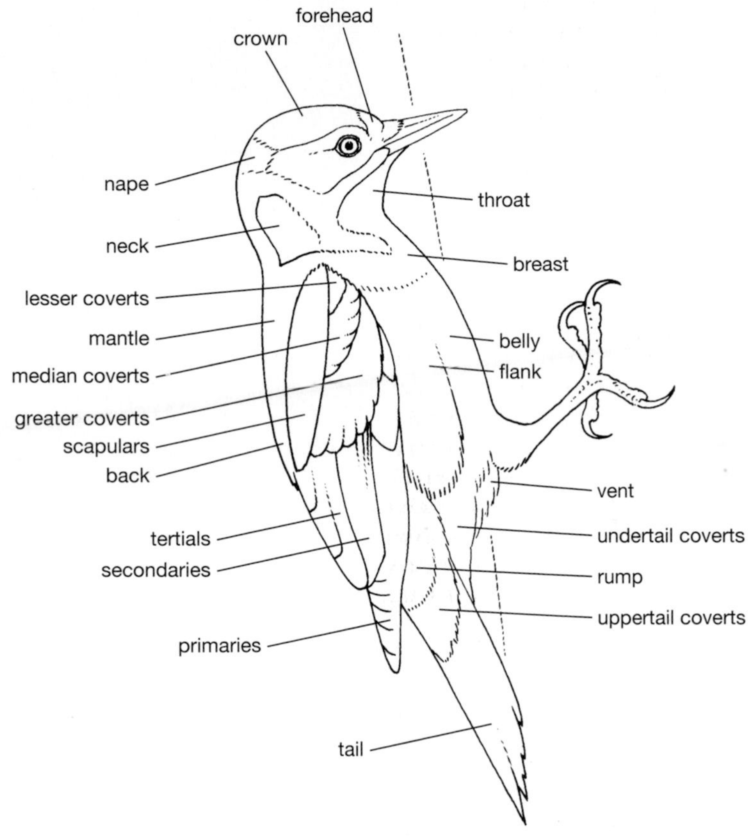

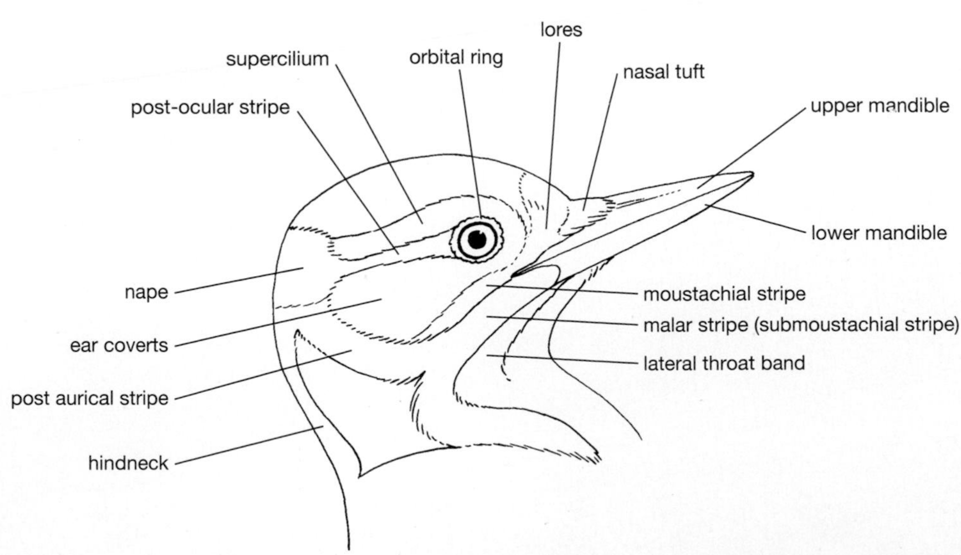

HABITAT

▲ A male Black-cheeked Woodpecker *Melanerpes pucherani* on a rotting snag. Dead and decaying timber is invariably rich with invertebrate life, and is thus an important element in the habitats of most woodpeckers. Atlantida, Honduras, February (*Greg R. Homel*).

Most woodpeckers are arboreal. Lowland tropical rainforests are home to the majority of species, but many other closed and open wooded habitats, from sea-level to the tree-line, are inhabited globally. Many woodpeckers are habitat specialists, with precise habitat needs; some are strongly associated with deciduous forests, others with coniferous, whilst some are associated with particular tree species. For example, in Europe Middle Spotted Woodpecker distribution is closely linked with the presence of old oakwoods whilst in North America the numbers of Acorn Woodpecker vary according to the abundance and even the fruiting of oaks. In tropical regions Rufous-headed, Kaempfer's, Pale-headed and Bamboo Woodpeckers and several piculets are associated with bamboo. Many flickers and *Picus* species occur in wooded grasslands, the likes of Bennett's, Fine-spotted and Nubian Woodpeckers in woodland savanna and Little Grey and Arabian Woodpeckers survive in sparsely wooded arid country. Gila, Ladder-backed and White-fronted Woodpeckers and Gilded Flicker are some that inhabit cacti-dotted deserts. However, across the world there are many adaptable species that can exploit man-made habitats such as plantations, orchards and urban parks and gardens. Such species are better able to adapt and bounce back after habitat loss. For example, in North America numbers of Pileated Woodpecker declined in the early 20th century following habitat loss, due in part to commercial tree felling; however, they have adapted to other habitats and new growth forest and numbers have recovered. Regardless, forest-dwelling species invariably need decaying or dead wood on which to forage. Remarkably, some woodpeckers are entirely terrestrial, having adapted to do without trees entirely; Ground Woodpecker in southern Africa and Andean Flicker in South America both inhabit treeless terrain such as rocky hillsides and montane grasslands.

▼ An anting Black Woodpecker *Dryocopus martius*. Anting is a specialised behaviour, where birds allow ants to swarm over them and squirt formic acid onto the plumage. The function of anting is unclear, but it is generally thought to be a form of 'comfort behaviour', the acid acting as a pesticide and fungicide. South Korea, April (*Un-Hoi Jung*).

BEHAVIOUR

Generalising on the behaviour of woodpeckers is difficult as a great variety of traits exists within the family and numerous exceptions to the more common ones also exist. However, the behaviour of all species is strongly mirrored in their morphology.

Most woodpeckers are feisty and aggressive to others of their kind, even to their partner during the breeding season. Indeed, some elements of antagonistic and courtships displays are very similar. Most disputes involve bill pointing, head swinging, wing spreading and flicking, noisy chases and bouts of aggressive calling or drumming. It is not unusual for rivals to 'freeze' for a while in an apparent stand-off before resuming their dispute. In serious conflicts, the formidable bill is jabbed at opponents, although actual full contact is rare. Such behaviour may also be employed against predators and nest-hole competitors. In most displays, coloured 'badges' on the head, wings or rump are invariably exhibited. Such badges are no doubt important in establishing sex in species where sexual dimorphism in plumage is minimal and they also probably illustrate the physical condition of individuals. Courtships displays typically involve raising the crown feathers or crest and fluttering flights. Mated pairs may touch bills, which is probably a form of symbolic feeding.

► A male Golden-cheeked Woodpecker *Melanerpes chrysogenys,* with his crown-feathers raised. Many woodpeckers, particularly males, have brightly coloured areas on the head that are erected and flaunted during courtship displays and conflicts. Jalisco, Mexico, December (*Greg R. Homel*).

Many species are generally solitary, usually only interacting to breed or when defending feeding sites, although in the tropics woodpeckers, including most piculets, are more likely to be seen in pairs. A few species migrate in groups and some, such as Magellanic Woodpecker in South America, Great Slaty Woodpecker in Asia and some species of *Melanerpes* and *Colaptes,* are gregarious, even social, living in extended family parties.

All woodpeckers are diurnal and usually roost overnight inside cavities, which may be specially made for this purpose or double as nest-holes. Most species roost alone, and will even oust relatives from their favoured roost hole, but some do roost communally with several individuals sleeping together in one cavity (e.g. Acorn and Magellanic Woodpeckers) or several individuals using a cluster of cavities (e.g. Greater Flameback, Red-cockaded and Grey-and-buff Woodpeckers). In SE Asia Grey-and-buff Woodpecker makes concentrations of numerous roost-holes that are much shallower than the holes made for nesting and are only used for roosting. In South America the Andean Flicker also commonly roosts communally in holes made in abandoned native huts and houses.

▲ Female (in the air) and male (on the ground) Syrian Woodpeckers *Dendrocopos syriacus,* engaged in a feisty encounter. When woodpeckers of the same species interact, it is often unclear whether they are indulging in courtship or in a dispute. Durankulak, Bulgaria, April (*Mladen Vasilev*).

A typical woodpecker day is spent foraging. Searching for food is, of course, more intense when there are nestlings to feed, but the overall time spent is generally less than that of birds that do not roost overnight in cavities. Food-rich resources, such as ant and termite colonies, beetle infested dead timber or a fruiting tree, can be revisited until the supply is exhausted and the non-social species defend such sites from other woodpeckers.

BREEDING

All woodpeckers breed in cavities. The majority nest in holes they have purposely excavated in trees (these species are the so-called primary cavity-excavators). Holes are usually made in living trees but in areas of soft or rotten wood surrounded by a harder shell. They are usually located high above ground level, though many piculets nest low down, and on smooth boughs or branches away from vegetation. However, some species, like Gilded Flicker and Ladder-backed Woodpecker, will nest in cacti while others, like Rufous and White-browed Piculets and Bamboo Woodpecker, in bamboo. Ground Woodpecker and Andean Flicker excavate cavities in earth banks and rocky slopes, Campo Flicker in termite mounds and Rufous Woodpeckers in arboreal ant nests. Others still will nest in fenceposts and utility poles, occupy man-provided nest-boxes and sometimes even create cavities in buildings.

A typical tree cavity consists of an entrance hole of about the same diameter as the woodpecker's body which leads to a wider vertical chamber. Successful nests may be reused. Material from outside the cavity is not used to form a nest, though wood chips from the

◄ A pair of copulating Scarlet-backed Woodpeckers *Veniliornis callonotus*. Most woodpeckers seem to be monogamous, although both polygamy and polyandry have been recorded. Further study may well reveal that non-monogamous pairings are not uncommon. Loja, Ecuador, August (*Dušan Brinkhuizen*).

▲ The secret life within the breeding chamber of a pair of Downy Woodpeckers *Picoides pubescens* revealed. Woodpecker eggs are white, and lie on only a few wood chips (a); hatchlings are naked and lack down (b); the eyes, beaks and limbs of nestlings develop relatively rapidly (c); woodpeckers are good parents, diligently feeding and brooding their young until they leave the security of the cavity (d). Minnesota, United States (*Stan Tekiela*).

walls of the chamber may litter the floor. The wrynecks and Antillean Piculet do not excavate their own cavities, but use those of other species or natural tree holes. Though they are often discreet around their nesting cavity, woodpeckers inextricably make no attempt to conceal the locations of their nesting holes by removing or hiding the debris that results from excavation. Wood-chips are usually simply tossed out from the hole and lie below the nesting tree where they are obvious evidence of a cavity above.

Most woodpeckers are monogamous breeders, although polygamy is known to occur in, for example, Lesser Spotted and Eurasian Three-toed Woodpeckers, and polyandry in West Indian Woodpecker and Northern Flicker. It is likely that non-monogamous pairings occur to a much greater extent than presumed. Cooperative breeding, often involving helpers at the nest, has been well-documented in species as diverse as Acorn, Red-cockaded, Ground and Great Slaty Woodpeckers.

As with most cavity breeders, woodpecker eggs are white and, though exceptions occur, woodpeckers lay just one clutch and raise only one brood annually. Average clutch size and incubation and fledging periods vary between species. Woodpeckers are also one of the few bird families where males incubate the eggs and brood nestlings overnight. In fact, males are involved extensively in the breeding period, doing most of the nest-hole excavation and often more incubation and feeding of the young than females. Both sexes work to keep the nesting chamber clean by removing the fecal sacs of nestlings, which are carried in the bill and (unlike woodchips) dropped away from the nesting tree. Nestlings are often noisy, begging for food with repeated chugging calls from deep within the chamber. Once out of the nest, most young woodpeckers must soon fend for themselves as parents can quickly lose interest in feeding them, though inevitably there are exceptions – adult Hispaniolan Woodpeckers continue to feed their offspring for several months and amongst the social species 'helpers' also assist in feeding their relatives. Cavity nests deter most predators, although arboreal snakes are an exception, and in Africa many woodpeckers have become the brood-hosts of honeyguides. Yet overall, like most cavity-breeding birds, woodpeckers have higher levels of breeding success than birds that nest in the open.

PLUMAGE AND MOULT

Woodpeckers range in colour from the drab to the gaudy. Numerous species have a basic plumage of green or brown, such as most piculets, the African *Campethera* and *Dendropicos*, the Eurasian *Picus* and many of the Neotropic *Piculus, Veniliornis* and *Celeus*. Many other species are mainly white, black, rufous or combinations of these, and many, particularly the *Dendrocopos*, are pied. Dull and pied plumage suggest camouflage, but a few species, such as the stunning Yellow-fronted and Black-headed Woodpeckers, are brightly coloured. Many species have a crest or at least a peaked or tufted crown. Crests are most prominent in large species, with those

◄ Many woodpeckers sport a crest of some kind, or at least a colourful face or head pattern, but few can rival the male Blond-crested Woodpecker *Celeus flavescens* when it comes to impressive head-gear. Itanhaem, Brazil, May (*Ronald Gruijters*).

▲ Most woodpeckers exhibit at least some sexual dimorphism in plumage; the presence or absence of red on the crown or face (especially in the malar region) is frequently the main point of difference. These are Nubian Woodpeckers *Campethera nubica*. Awassa, Ethiopia, October (*Ignacio Yufera*).

of Blond-crested and Magellanic Woodpeckers being particularly impressive. It is not unusual to find woodpeckers with worn areas of plumage in the breeding period – this is presumably due to birds repeatedly rubbing their feathers against the hard rim of their holes when entering and leaving the cavity.

Woodpeckers are unusual in that they lack down – even nestlings are naked. As woodpeckers are cavity breeders, data is limited for many species, but it seems that juveniles acquire most contour feathers whilst still in the nest, but moult these just prior to fledging. True woodpeckers have 10 primaries, 10-12 secondaries and 12 rectrices (tail feathers) although the outermost is usually reduced and hardly visible. Their moult regime has evolved in relation to their reproduction cycle and their foraging habits. Most adult woodpeckers undergo one main annual moult that begins as soon as breeding has ended. True woodpeckers do not have a pre-breeding moult, although the wrynecks have a partial one, and migratory species suspend their moult. Primaries are moulted sequentially (ascendant) from P1 and the secondaries from two centres (ascendantly from S1, ascendantly and descendantly from S8). The moult pattern of the tail of arboreal species is reversed – the two most rigid central feathers are moulted last, presumably so that birds can continue to scale and cling to trees during the moult.

Sexual dimorphism

The majority of woodpeckers are sexually dimorphic in plumage (males and females look different). This dimorphism usually involves the existence and extent of coloured (often red or yellow) areas on the crown, nape or in a malar stripe (the malar is an important plumage feature for many woodpeckers). Such coloured markings vary in extent, with males generally showing more colour than females, but for most species the differences are slight. Exceptions, where the sexes differ greatly, are Williamson's Sapsucker in North America and Orange-backed Woodpecker in south-east Asia. On the other hand, males and females of the two wrynecks, Red-breasted Sapsucker and Lewis's, Red-headed, Guadeloupe and Middle Spotted Woodpeckers, are sexually monochromatic (visually almost identical). In addition, there are also differences in size, weight and wing, tail and bill lengths between the sexes with males generally larger than females in true woodpeckers and the reverse in piculets. Such anatomical differences can be difficult to see in the field and relate to feeding ecology where the sexes use different foraging techniques and habitat niches.

► Although the differences in plumage between adults may be slight, the majority of woodpeckers are sexually dimorphic and separable in the field. The Red-headed Woodpecker *Melanerpes erythrocephalus* is one of the very few species in which adult males and females appear almost identical. United States, September (*Pete Morris*).

FOOD AND FORAGING

▲ The majority of woodpeckers are essentially insectivorous, although some are fairly frugivorous and there is generally a fair deal of opportunism when it comes to food. This female Crimson-crested Woodpecker *Campephilus melanoleucos* has captured a huge and protein-rich insect larva. Henri Pittier NP, Venezuela, November (*Pete Morris*).

Many woodpeckers live up to their name, pecking holes in wood to extract invertebrate prey, which are eaten as larvae, pupae and adults. Just how woodpeckers know where to open up timber to reach prey is not known, but it is likely that the high-frequency sounds produced by insects are detected and acted upon, though visual signs are probably also important. Some woodpeckers, such as the *Dryocopus*, will excavate large holes to expose Carpenter Ants, but a wide range of other foraging techniques are employed and food items taken by the various species: bark is scaled, crevices probed and foliage gleaned. Several species, including Red-naped Sapsucker and many of the *Melanerpes*, sally to take flying insects, with Lewis's Woodpecker a particularly expert flycatcher. Rufous Woodpecker and several *Celeus* species specialise in raiding the hive-like nests of arboreal ants, and in Africa termitaria are opened up by several of the *Campethera*. Some species seldom visit trees, foraging instead on the ground, often for terrestrial ants, or probing into soil for worms: the wrynecks, several *Colaptes*, *Campethera* and *Picus* species, and particularly Andean Flicker and the aptly-named Ground Woodpecker, are examples. Many species, particularly in the tropics, forage in association with other birds in mixed-species flocks (sometimes called bird-waves) with piculets and smaller woodpeckers taking prey flushed by larger species, whilst big woodpeckers such as flamebacks are often inadvertent 'beaters' for other birds. Some woodpeckers are food specialists, others generalists. Most are insectivorous, with over half of all species including ants in their diets and some preying almost exclusively on them, although many are omnivorous and a few mainly frugivorous eating fruit, berries, nuts, seeds and cambium, and sipping nectar. Woodpeckers remember productive feeding sites, returning repeatedly to them, and some species will defend them against rivals. They are opportunistic and inventive when foraging, frequenting bird-feeders for seed and

▼ A male Great Spotted Woodpecker *Dendrocopos major* (left) and a female Eurasian Three-toed Woodpecker *Picoides tridactylus* (right) face off on the same tree. Although conflicts do occur, subtle differences in habitat use and in what is eaten, and in how and where it is found, usually mean that several species can co-exist in one area. Luitemaa, Estonia, September (*Uku Paal*).

suet and taking advantage of seasonal food sources or sudden abundances such as a population explosion of beetles. Some species will supplement their main diet with bird eggs, nestlings, small rodents, lizards and even carrion. The sapsuckers, and several other species, drill small holes in trees and feed on the sap that oozes out, but also return to these sites to take the insects that are drawn to the sap.

Several species often forage in one habitat with minimal competition, but in tropical rainforests around a dozen species may co-exist in close proximity. Besides the fact that woodpecker species vary greatly in size, this is possible because different habitat resources are exploited, varying foraging techniques used and different food sought. Differences may either be obvious, for instance a species might specialise on a particular kind of insect or fruit, or they may be rather subtle. The height at which woodpeckers forage is also often significant: some feed in the canopy, others work tree trunks and some forage on logs or the ground itself. Methods of finding food vary, too, from boring and pecking into timber to working bark and to gleaning foliage for prey. Some species 'specialise' by being omnivorous generalists. Such niche and resource partitioning exists between species, but also often between the sexes of the same species. In most cases this involves different areas of a habitat being used and different sizes of prey being eaten. Ultimately, some overlap may occur in size, foraging methods and locations and in food, but generally detrimental competition is avoided.

▼ With its long, powerful bill, the Greater Flameback *Chrysocolaptes guttacristatus* is a good example of a woodpecker that has evolved the tools it needs to hack into and open up wood in order to extract insect prey. Karnataka, India, October (*Ram Mallya*).

▼ For most of the year the Black-rumped Flameback *Dinopium benghalense* feeds on invertebrates, but it readily exploits fruits and seeds when they are in season. Tamil Nadu, India, September (*Gnanaskandan Keshavabharathi*).

▼ The South American *Celeus* are omnivores that forage for insects, seeds and fruit. This female Blond-crested Woodpecker *C. flavescens* is feeding on ripe bananas, a favourite food. Itanhaem, Brazil, May (*Ronald Gruijters*).

A few woodpeckers use 'anvils' where food items such as nuts, cones and hard-bodied insects are wedged and processed. Anvils may be a simple natural crevice or notch in a tree or post, or a specially created and customised site. A few woodpeckers, in particular *Melanerpes* species, harvest and hoard invertebrate and plant food in stores – usually crevices and sometimes deliberately drilled holes in trees. Acorn Woodpecker is a particularly good example: specific oak trees may contain hundreds or even thousands of holes, each excavated to accommodate an acorn, and these trees will be defended by family groups.

▲ As their name implies, the sapsuckers are specialist feeders. They consume nutritional sap, which they acquire from wells drilled into the bark of suitable trees. This is a Red-breasted Sapsucker *Sphyrapicus ruber.* California, United States, February (*Johanna van de Woestijne*).

▲ A beakfull of ant grubs for the young of this Olivaceous Piculet *Picumnus olivaceus.* Costa Rica, April (*Noel Ureña*).

▼ The genus *Picus* includes many species that forage mainly on the ground. This female Streak-throated Woodpecker *Picus xanthopygaeus* is probing into and opening up a terrestrial termite mound. Tamil Nadu, India, April (*Gnanaskandan Keshavabharathi*).

▼ The woodpecker's bill is a multi-purpose tool. Here a male Crimson-breasted Woodpecker *Dendrocopos cathpharius* uses its bill as tweezers to extract an insect larva from its burrow in a thin branch. Bhutan, April (*James Eaton*).

FLIGHT

Many woodpeckers have an undulating flight pattern where rapid flapping is interspersed with deep bounds in a so-called 'typical woodpecker flight'. However, large species, such as the *Dryocopus*, fly on a straight, level trajectory, not unlike crows, many in the *Melanerpes* genus fly with a distinctive rowing wing-beat action, and the piculets usually fly in a rapid direct burst.

◄ The White Woodpecker *Melanerpes candidus* is typical of its genus in that it flies with deep, 'flapping' wing-beats, rather than in an undulating, bounding manner. Argentina, October (*Ramón Moller Jensen*).

▼ Woodpeckers often choose prominent, exposed vantage points from which to call and drum. This female Northern Flicker *Colaptes auratus* is announcing her presence from the top of a concrete utility-post. Zapata Swamp, Cuba, March (*Gerard Gorman*).

CALLS

Woodpecker calls tend to be much simpler in structure than those created by songbirds. The array of sounds given include sharp high-pitched notes, excited chattering, twittering and whistling, trills and rattles, repeated nasal churrs and far-carrying screams and wails. These are functional and often given by both sexes throughout the year, yet vary between and within species, with social species being especially vocal. Calls are contextual and relate to specific behavioural responses including alarm, territorial disputes and courtship, with many woodpecker species producing distinctive flight calls. Mated pairs may exchange quiet, low-pitched calls and nestlings produce incessant begging chugging noises from within the chamber; some also hiss when threatened. The frequencies of woodpecker vocalisations typically range between 1–2.5 kHz, ideal for transmission through densely wooded environments.

DRUMMING

Many species of woodpeckers and piculets use drumming as a mechanical means of communication. Unlike foraging or excavation work, drumming is a non-vocal sound produced by the bill being rapidly and repeatedly struck on a hard surface. Woodpecker drumming is most commonly associated with territorial behaviour in spring when it is especially important in communicating with conspecific rivals and potential mates. It functions as a form of song, with males tending to drum more than females. The sounds produced are comparatively simple and less complex than most passerine song. Drumming is species-specific and diagnostic, though roll length, number of beats, intervals between beats and cadence can vary between birds, suggesting that individual recognition is likely. It also probably supplies information on the condition of the drummer. Drumming is also performed when birds are alarmed; parents will urge young to leave the nesting cavity by gently drumming nearby; and some species drum from within the nesting cavity. Not all species drum to the same extent: for instance, several of the *Campephilus* species produce simple double-raps rather than rolls, while others like wrynecks use vocalisations and never drum. The drumming repertoire of many species is poorly known and for some, particularly several piculets, it remains unclear whether they drum or not.

Demonstrative tapping (as distinct from the irregular sounds resulting from excavating or foraging) is also used by most woodpeckers, even those that do not truly drum, to communicate by the nesting site.

Wing-beating is another form of mechanical communication. Many large woodpeckers produce deliberate swishing or flapping noises with their wings when in display or near the nest. Cuban Green Woodpeckers make whirring sounds with their wings when arriving at the nesting cavity to alert their sitting mate.

▲ An adult male Great Spotted Woodpecker *Dendrocopos major* drums on a tree stump. Kent, UK, March (*David Tipling*).

THE IMPORTANCE OF WOODPECKERS

Woodpeckers have a fairly universal appeal, usually fascinating those who see them at work, and are generally regarded in a positive light. However, they are occasionally viewed as pests. Some individuals habitually hack holes in wooden utility poles and buildings, annoying electricity companies and home-owners alike. In Israel Syrian Woodpeckers are sometimes culled because they peck into polyethylene irrigation pipes, and fruit-growers worldwide often dislike woodpeckers because they raid their crops. Yet overall such damage is negligible when compared to the harm humankind inflicts upon woodpeckers and the places where they live.

Pest Control

Studies worldwide have revealed the important role woodpeckers perform as natural controllers of forest insect pests. American and Eurasian Three-toed Woodpeckers regulate spruce bark-beetle populations and Hairy and Downy Woodpeckers are important natural controllers of the red oak borer beetle. In Israel, Syrian Woodpecker is the sole natural predator of eucalyptus boring-beetles and in Indian coffee plantations Rufous Woodpecker is beneficial as it predates the ants which nurture harmful mealy bugs.

▼ A male Eurasian Three-toed Woodpecker *Picoides tridactylus* with a bark-beetle larva. The key role that many woodpeckers play as natural forest-pest controllers is increasingly understood and appreciated. Stuhleck, Austria, June (*Otto Samwald*).

◀ Tengmalm's Owl *Aegolius funereus* in an old Black Woodpecker *Dryocopus martius* hole. In parts of its range, this secondary cavity-nesting owl is highly dependent upon large woodpeckers for breeding sites. Hohenberg, Austria, May (*Thomas Hochebner*).

Indicators and keystones

An indicator species is one that illustrates the quality of a habitat by its presence. Woodpeckers are good indicators of the diversity and health of wooded habitats. They are particularly suitable as indicators because they are diurnal and usually sedentary, making them arguably better indicators than migratory birds, which are affected by conditions elsewhere. Many woodpeckers can also be considered keystone species – animals that play an important overall role in an ecosystem – as other wildlife benefits from their cavities. A lack of tree cavities can hinder secondary cavity-users (species that use holes as breeding or sleeping sites, but which cannot excavate them themselves) such as some ducks, owls, doves, parrots, toucans, hornbills, trogons, starlings, swallows, tityras, flycatchers and also invertebrates and mammals. Locally, populations of some species can even be determined by woodpecker cavity availability. Woodpecker holes are generally in great demand and in some regions alien species, such as European Starlings in the USA, can negatively affect breeding woodpeckers by usurping their cavities.

▼ Hispaniolan Trogan *Priotelus roseigaster* using an old Hispaniolan Woodpecker *Melanerpes striatus* hole. This endemic trogan is unable to excavate its own nesting sites and, unless a natural tree hole can be found, relies upon the woodpecker for cavities. Dominican Republic (*Dax Román*).

▼ A Yellow-rumped Warbler *Dendroica coronata* poaches sap from a sapsucker well. Besides warblers, hummingbirds may also take advantage of this food resource, which is unwittingly provided by the sapsuckers. California, United States, February (*Johanna van de Woestijne*).

Technology

The incredible shock-absorbing features that woodpeckers have evolved (see Anatomy and morphology) have proved increasingly valuable in modern technology. The g-forces that woodpeckers experience when drumming and excavating are much stronger than those which humans can tolerate and scientists have attempted to replicate the attributes that allow woodpeckers to sustain such forces. The protective shells of 'black-box' flight recorders and various electronic devices and crash-helmets have all been modelled on woodpecker heads and skulls.

Conservation

Many woodpeckers are under threat. This is invariably linked to the degradation or total loss of wooded habitats. In particular, species in the rainforests of Brazil and Indonesia continue to suffer from excessive logging and clearance for farmland and 'development'. In other areas, woodpeckers are under pressure from unsuitable forestry methods. So-called 'close-to-nature' forest management is crucial for many boreal species. Alarmingly, with the exception of a few common and high-profile species, knowledge of the population trends and ecological needs of most woodpeckers is limited and even the existence of some species is uncertain. Yet all is not doom and gloom: there are losers, but also winners. Some species are thriving, especially those that have adapted to use man-made habitats, and woodpeckers that favour open habitats can benefit from some forest fragmentation. Few conservation projects specifically focus on woodpeckers; rather they are protected when their habitats are conserved. Clearly, besides being worthy of study and protection for their own sake, the conservation of woodpeckers and the places they inhabit directly relates to the viability of many other wildlife species.

▼ The range of Red-cockaded Woodpecker *Picoides borealis* has shrunk considerably, and is now fragmented into around 30 populations dotted throughout the south-eastern United States. However, this bird is the subject of intense conservation effort and numbers are slowly increasing. United States, September (*Pete Morris*).

NOTES ON THE SPECIES ACCOUNTS

Names English, scientific and (if applicable) alternative English names are given for every species.

Photographs The photographs in this book are not included merely to enliven the text; they are integral to the work. They have been chosen to illustrate particular plumages or behaviour. The photo captions also supplement the information contained in the text; species (and where relevant, the subspecies), location, date and the photographer's name are included. Occasionally such details were unavailable.

Identification Description of males, females and often juveniles with pertinent and diagnostic features are given. Overall length is given in centimeters. Note that in the field birds will invariably appear shorter than the lengths listed, as measurements have often been taken from museum specimens that have been laid out and measured from the tip of the bill to the end of the tail. The identification text should be used in conjunction with the adjacent photographs.

Vocalisations Transcribing bird sounds is problematic. Interpretations differ and phonetic renditions and mnemonic descriptions are subjective. There is no substitute for real sounds and listening to recordings is advised. However, despite being approximations, transcriptions can be useful pointers and so are included.

Drumming Descriptions of this mechanical form of communication are given for as many species as possible. However, despite drumming being unique to woodpeckers, detailed information is often lacking and for some species it is still unclear whether they actually drum or not. Hence, this is a subject where data for future editions would be welcome.

Status The conservation status categories of the International Union for Conservation of Nature and Natural Resources Red List of Threatened Species (IUCN) are given for all species at risk: Near Threatened (NT), Vulnerable (VU), Endangered (EN) and Critically Endangered (CR). Some recently described taxa have not yet been assigned an IUCN category. Population figures and trends are derived from various local and international sources including BirdLife's Data Zone. However, population data for many taxa is scant and the status of some uncertain.

Habitat An overview of the habitat and vegetation types that each species most often frequents is detailed.

Range Global distribution is outlined and altitudinal limits noted where known. The text should be used in conjunction with the adjacent map.

Map The distribution maps in this book are based on numerous sources. The scale of the maps means that local detail cannot be shown and only a general area illustrated. Most maps show one colour, green, which indicates resident range. A few maps show blue, for winter range, and yellow for summer range. Question marks indicate areas where occurrence is uncertain and information lacking.

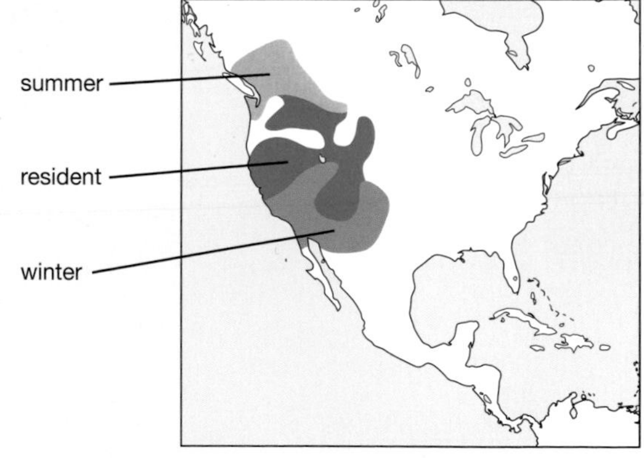

Taxonomy and variation The various races of polytypic species are listed with the range of occurrence and racial differences, where known, described. Species with no races are described as 'monotypic'. Non-racial differences, such as morphs and regional variants, are also covered.

Similar species Other woodpeckers, and sometimes other birds, with which the species may be confused, and the key points in distinguishing them, are mentioned. Generally, only sympatric species are described.

Food and foraging Information on the food and foraging techniques of many woodpecker species is lacking. Where known, they are included and commented upon.

Note on literature consulted For reasons of space and to avoid repetition, references are not listed at the end of each species account; rather a bibliography of literature consulted is included at the end of the book. Three important works, *Woodpeckers of the World* (Short 1982), *Woodpeckers* (Winkler, Christie & Nurney 1995) and *Handbook of the Birds of the World* 7 (Winkler & Christie 2002), were important resources. Many regional field guides, monographs and numerous scientific papers and articles were also consulted, but for most species no specific monographs or studies exist. Various sources were used when compiling the vocalisations and drumming descriptions. In addition to my own recordings and those of colleagues, two on-line resources, the Cornell Lab of Ornithology's Macaulay Library archive and Xeno-Canto, proved valuable.

▲ A male Pale-billed Woodpecker *Campephilus guatemalensis* arrives at the nest with food for its young. Atlantida, Honduras, March (*Greg R. Homel*).

JYNX

An Old World genus of two species which only overlap in a few areas of Africa, when Eurasian Wryneck arrives to winter and meets the resident Red-throated Wryneck. In many respects wrynecks are atypical picids, resembling certain large warblers or small shrikes in structure and nightjars in terms of their cryptic plumage. Wrynecks are perching, rather than climbing, birds; they do not drum and they lack most of the morphological adaptations that true woodpeckers have evolved. They have relatively thin, weak bills and soft tails, and do not excavate their own holes but use natural cavities and those made by barbets and other woodpeckers. Wrynecks take their vernacular name from their habit of rotating their necks and twisting their heads awry when threatened. Interestingly this snake-like movement is often accompanied by a hissing call and may be a defensive, anti-predator strategy.

Red-throated Wryneck *Jynx ruficollis*, adult. KwaZulu-Natal, South Africa, March (*Hugh Chittenden*).

1. EURASIAN WRYNECK
Jynx torquilla

L 16–19cm

Other name Northern Wryneck

Identification Slim, atypical woodpecker, with a sharp, weak bill and short rounded wings. Long rounded tail comprises a third of overall length. Cryptically patterned with mosaic of brown and grey tones. Crown to rump and tail mostly grey, finely speckled dark. Chocolate band from crown to back. Broad brown post-ocular stripe continues across ear-coverts onto neck-sides. Cheek to chest buff, finely barred brown. Tail has four blackish bands. Breast to vent cream, dotted with dark streaks and chevrons. Wings brown with darker flight feathers dotted rufous and buff. Legs greyish-brown. Iris chestnut. Sexes alike: male more rufous and yellowish below. Juvenile much like adult but duller, with cream rump, greyer throat, more white bars and fewer, but bolder, black bars on tail; streaks below rather than chevrons.

Vocalisations Very vocal in spring, calling vociferously from exposed perches. Song of 10–20 loud, whining *tu* or *quee* notes, whole phrase rising in pitch, though pitch of each note falls. Song reminiscent of smaller falcons. Less strident version after pair-formation. Contact calls include cooing *gruu*. Alarm calls soft or harsh *tek, tak* or *tyuk* notes, undulating in pitch, often in series. Nestlings make zizzing and hissing noises.

Drumming Does not drum, but may tap by nest-hole.

Status Not considered threatened, though has declined in parts of Europe due to degradation and loss of habitats. Persists in intensively farmed areas where open ground with abundant ants remains.

Habitat Warm, dry, open deciduous or mixed woodlands, wooded pastures, meadows, fallow-land, dunes, parkland, orchards, vineyards, plantations and gardens. Three main factors important: high densities of ants; open bare ground or short grass for foraging; and cavities for nesting. On migration, areas used are often almost treeless, such as montane farmland and deserts.

Range True migrant. Breeds mainly within Palearctic, wintering further south. In warmer regions some resident. Sea-level to mountains. Prone to vagrancy.

Taxonomy and variation Six very similar races: ***torquilla*** (Europe to the Caucausus; wintering Africa); ***sarudnyi*** (W Siberia; winters S. Asia); ***chinensis*** (E Siberia, NE China; winters S. Asia); ***himalayana*** (NW Himalayas; winters lowland India) typically heavily barred below; ***tschusii*** (Corsica, Sardinia, Sicily, mainland Italy, W Balkans; winters Mediterranean and Africa, e.g. Ethiopia, Eritrea) underparts and tail dark, throat and chest heavily barred, mantle and crown with bold black flecks, flanks barred rather than scaled; ***mauretanica*** (mostly resident in N Africa) is small and pale.

Similar species Always lacks rufous of Red-throated Wryneck; barred rather than streaked below. Ranges of the two meet in Africa, particularly Ethiopia, in winter.

Food and foraging Mainly small, terrestrial ants, in all stages. Prey is mostly gleaned and lapped up from surfaces. Also, other invertebrates, berries and sometimes cavity-nesting songbird eggs and nestlings.

◄ Adult Eurasian Wryneck; the sexes are usually impossible to separate in the field (*Roman Teteruk*).

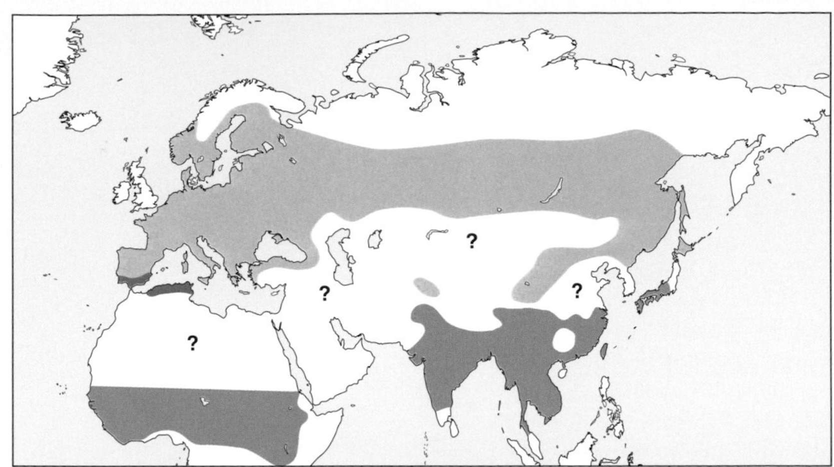

▼ Eurasian Wrynecks feed mainly on the ground, lapping up ants with a long sticky tongue that, unlike those of most other woodpeckers, lacks barbs. Norfolk, England, April (*Neil Bowman*).

▼ Like all picids, wrynecks strive to keep their nesting chamber clean. This adult is removing the faecal sacs of its young, which will be dropped away from the cavity.

▼ Juvenile Eurasian Wrynecks soon resemble their parents, though they are more compact and have an even weaker bill. Neuchatel, Switzerland, June (*Jean-Lou Zimmerman*).

2. RED-THROATED WRYNECK
Jynx ruficollis

L 18–19cm

Other names Rufous-necked Wryneck, Red-breasted Wryneck

Identification Slim, long-tailed, cryptically marked. Forages mainly terrestrially, hopping with tail cocked. Fine greyish bill. Chin to chest rufous. Breast and belly cream or white, streaked chocolate. Flanks, vent and undertail washed dusky-cinnamon. Pale underwing barred brown, rufous and buff. Primaries chocolate, boldly barred rufous. Scapulars spotted black. Upperparts, from crown to uppertail-coverts, grey-brown, finely mottled and vermiculated black. Variable dark streak from crown to mantle. Grey-brown tail barred black. Uppertail barred black and white; white bars narrow. Rump, uppertail-coverts, wing-coverts and tertials finely marked. Pale lower cheek and dusky ear-coverts barred buff and brown. Whitish malar area finely barred chocolate. Iris brown. Legs brown-olive. Sexes alike. Juveniles darker, more heavily barred above, lightly barred below, less rufous.

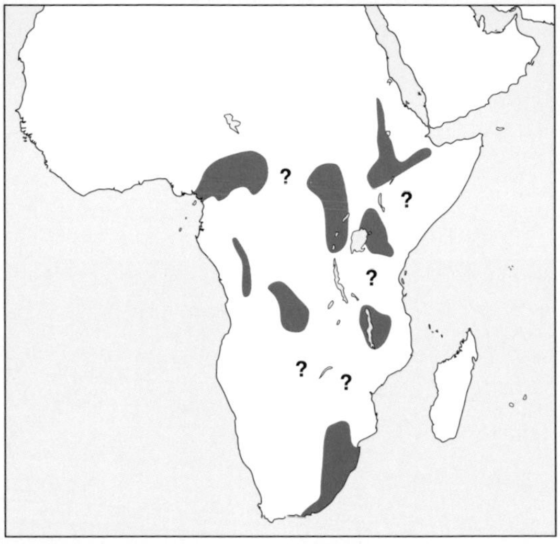

Vocalisations Calls from prominent perch such as snag or fence-post. Song a series of up to 10, loud, falcon-like *kweek, kwik, kwee* or *quee* notes. Variant series of *yeea* or *pyee* notes repeated after short pauses. Females make lower-pitched *uit-uit-uit-uit*. Drawn-out *krok* in displays. Alarms include a soft *klik* and repeated, scolding *peegh*.

◀ Adult Red-throated Wryneck; the sexes are alike, both with a red throat and chest, which Eurasian Wryneck *Jynx torquilla* never shows. KwaZulu-Natal, South Africa, January (*Hugh Chittenden*).

◄ Like its close Eurasian relative, Red-throated Wryneck has a long, flexible, sticky tongue, which lacks barbs and is ideal for licking up ants and termites. KwaZulu-Natal, South Africa, October (*Gary Upfold*).

▼ Adult Red-throated Wryneck with a beakfull of invertebrate prey at the nest-hole entrance. Wrynecks do not excavate their own cavities, but use natural holes or old ones of other woodpeckers or barbets. KwaZulu-Natal, South Africa, January (*Gary Upfold*).

Drumming Does not drum, but taps demonstratively by the nest.

Status Locally often common, though numbers unpredictable and sometimes inexplicably absent from seemingly suitable habitat.

Habitat Open wooded grasslands, acacia savanna, bush, forest edges. Also secondary woodlands, plantations, farmland, parks and gardens.

Range Sub-Saharan Africa. Largely resident, but fragmented distribution: northernmost populations in Sudan, Ethiopia, Eritrea; southernmost in South Africa. Sometimes nomadic, some altitudinal movements but not migratory. Lowlands and up to 3300m.

Taxonomy and variation Three races, differing in extent and intensity of rufous areas and upperpart colour. Nominate ***ruficollis*** (SE Gabon to SW and E Uganda, S Sudan, SW Kenya, N Tanzania, N Angola, NW Zambia, Mozambique, Swaziland, E South Africa) has rufous extending to chin; ***aequatorialis*** (Ethiopian uplands) most rufous, often to lower breast and flanks, sometimes on belly; ***pulchricollis*** (SE Nigeria, Cameroon to S Sudan and NW Uganda) warmer brown, less grey below, chest often chestnut, chin finely barred brown and white, lower belly and vent often rufous.

Similar species Like slightly smaller Eurasian Wryneck, with which it overlaps in winter in, for example, Ethiopia's Rift Valley. Eurasian greyer above, buffer below, never rufous, with dark eye streak.

Food and foraging Mainly terrestrial ants and termites in all stages, gleaned and lapped up with long sticky tongue.

PICUMNUS

This genus includes the smallest of the picids. All occur in the tropics, and all but one in South America. Only a handful of the currently recognised 27 species have been studied in any detail, and many taxonomic relationships remain unclear; species and subspecies limits are often vague and a re-evaluation of the whole genus is needed. In addition, the breeding biology of most piculets remains a mystery: this is worrying, as some species are threatened by deforestation. Though piculets have long tongues, they differ from true woodpeckers in having short, soft tails, which are seldom used for support. They are tiny, agile and acrobatic, often hanging upside-down from vegetation and feeding at the very ends of twigs. Piculets also perch across branches in songbird fashion. They are often first located by their trilling calls, surprisingly loud and fast drumming, or rapid pecking and drilling noises made when foraging. Although often solitary, many will associate in mixed-species flocks, invariably foraging busily at all levels.

Speckle-chested Piculet *Picumnus steindachneri*, adult male. San Martin, Peru, November (*Gerard Gorman*).

3. SPECKLED PICULET
Picumnus innominatus

L 10cm

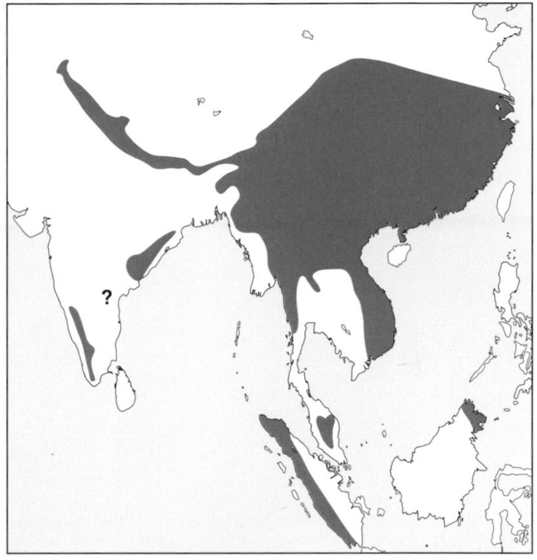

Identification Plain grey or olive crown. Broad blackish post-auricular stripe, pale post-ocular stripe, blackish malar on white face. Lores buff. White chin and throat often with yellow hue, sometimes spotted black. Plain buff to olive above. Buff or white below boldly spotted black, flanks with dark chevrons, heart-shapes or bars, lower belly often unmarked. Most of upperwing brown, with greenish-yellow on secondaries sometimes creating pale panel. Underwing grey or buff, slightly spotted black. In flight wings can appear unmarked. Short, square-ended tail black, central and outer feather pairs mostly white. Short bluish-black bill. Iris brownish, greyish-blue orbital ring. Legs grey. Sexes differ slightly: male has small ochre, orange or rufous forehead patch flecked black, which female lacks, being grey or green. Juveniles like adult female but drabber with pale bill.

Vocalisations Often vocal. Territorial song is a rapid, high-pitched, trilling, peeping *ti-ti-ti* and squeaky *sik-*

◄ Adult male of the race *malayorum*. This southern race is usually darker on the crown than the northern nominate. Goa, India, December (*Amit Bandeker*).

sik-sik series, first and last notes softer. Single, short, shrill *tsik* or *tsit* notes and agitated, high-pitched, chattering *chitititititi* alarm.

Drumming Often surprisingly loud, between 2–5-second rolls, with precise, solid strikes of even tempo. Drumming sounds tinny or knocking, depending upon substrate.

Status Often locally common, but rare in N Borneo. Overall considered stable, though population data lacking.

Habitat Wet and dry, open, pure deciduous and deciduous-evergreen tropical forests and jungle. Also thickets with saplings, bushes, creepers, vines and bamboo.

Range SE Asia. From Afghanistan to China, Indochina and Thai-Malay Peninsula. Isolated populations in S India, Sumatra and Borneo. Sea-level to around 3000m in the Himalayas. Resident and sedentary.

Taxonomy and variation Relationship to Neotropical piculets unclear. Three races: ***innominatus*** (NE Afghanistan, N Pakistan, N India, Nepal, SE Tibet to Assam); ***malayorum*** (India S of nominate, SW China, Indochina to Sumatra, N Borneo) like nominate though smaller, darker on crown, more heavily spotted below; ***chinensis*** (C, E and S China) largest race, richer brown or cinnamon from forehead to mantle, facial stripes darker brown, bolder spotting below.

Similar species None; the only *Picumnus* in Asia.

Food and foraging Invertebrates. Hawks for flying prey and frequently joins mixed-species flocks.

▲ Adult female nominate. Females of all races lack the coloured forehead patch of males. Himachal Pradesh, India, June (*Gaurav Sharma*).

◄ Speckled Piculets of the race *chinensis* are ochre or cinnamon on the crown. Sichuan, China, November (*John & Jemi Holmes*).

4. BAR-BREASTED PICULET
Picumnus aurifrons

L 7.5–8cm

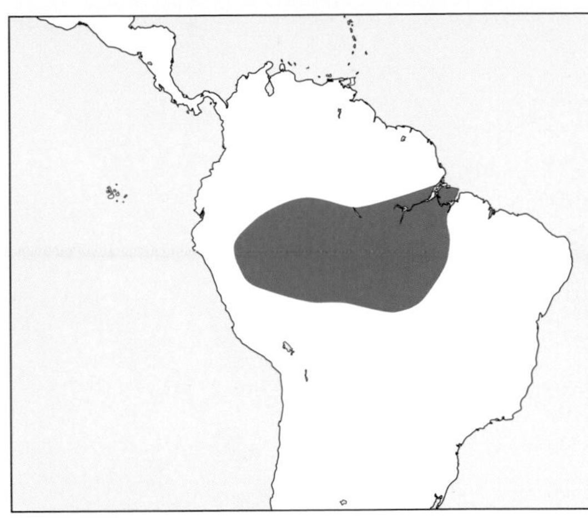

Other names Gold-fronted or Golden-fronted Piculet (yellow-crowned races).

Identification Yellowish-green above, mantle and back usually plain. Wings olive-brown with chocolate flight feathers edged yellow, tertials and coverts edged greenish. Underwing-coverts yellowish. Cream underparts flushed yellow, chest and breast barred blackish, belly and flanks streaked. Uppertail black, central feather pair with pale inner webs. Mostly brown crown and nape, with sparse but bold white spotting. Lores yellowish, ear-coverts greyish-brown. Faint white post-ocular line. Pale chin and throat with fine bars or chevrons at sides. Orbital ring grey, iris brown. Bluish-grey bill, lower mandible base paler. Legs grey. Sexes differ slightly: male forecrown flecked (can look solid) yellow, orange or red (depending on race); female lacks this colour. Juveniles overall browner, belly streaking lighter, crown brown and streaked or blotched pale not spotted.

Vocalisations Thin, high-pitched, falling *tsirrrit-tsit-tsit* or *tsi-tse-tsu,* very like Golden-spangled Piculet and recalling some hummingbirds. Sharp, metallic, single or repeated *seep* or *seet* notes. Whistling *see-see-suw* like Lafresnaye's Piculet.

Drumming Level-pitched, quickly repeated 2–4-second rolls.

Status Uncommon. Little-studied, with trends unknown. Given small size and habitat used, probably

▼ Male nominate Bar-breasted Piculet; note the yellow on the forecrown. All piculets are agile foragers; this one is in a typical 'hanging' pose. Claudia, Mato Grosso, Brazil, February (*Valdir Hobus*).

▼ Male *wallacii*. This race is also yellow on the forecrown, but it is paler below and less marked overall than the nominate. Amazonas, Brazil, January (*Nick Athanas*).

▲ Female nominate Bar-breasted Piculet. Females of all races lack the colourful forecrown markings of the males. Rio Roosevelt, Amazonas, Brazil, November (*Andy and Gill Swash*).

overlooked – e.g. *borbae* race is rarely seen as it occurs in a remote flooded region.

Habitat Rainforest, *terra firme, várzea,* bamboo thickets. Often in clearings and at edges. Also secondary growth and fragmented forests.

Range South America. Amazonia, S of the Equator, from extreme S of Colombia into Peru, Bolivia and Brazil S of Amazon. Resident and sedentary. Mainly lowlands, to 1250m.

Taxonomy and variation Seven races, but taxonomy complex, some arbitary, others probably warrant species status: ***aurifrons*** (Brazil: S Amazonas, Rondonia, N Mato Grosso in upper Madeira-Tapajós basin, extreme N Bolivia) male yellow on forecrown; ***flavifrons*** (NE Peru, extreme S Colombia, W Brazil) lightly barred on mantle, hardly barred on breast, belly boldly spotted, male yellow on forecrown; ***juruanus*** (E Peru, most of Bolivia, W Brazil) male has orange or red tips in forecrown; ***purusianus*** (W Brazil: upper River Purus) dark, boldly barred black below, male yellow on forecrown; ***wallacii*** (W Brazil: middle-lower River Purus to lower River Madeira) pale below, breast faintly barred, belly spotted, mantle hardly barred, male yellow on forecrown; ***borbae*** (C Brazil: lower River Madeira to lower River Tapajós); yellowish on underparts, breast boldly barred dark, male has orange or red tips in forecrown; ***transfasciatus*** (E Brazil: River Tapajós to River Tocantins) most heavily barred above and on breast, male forecrown yellow.

Similar species Fine-barred and Lafresnaye's Piculets both barred on belly.

Food and foraging Invertebrates, but information lacking. Hangs sideways from slender twigs and vines, often in mixed-species flocks.

► Besides racial differences, many piculets exhibit individual variation in plumage. This nominate female is particularly boldly marked. Claudia, Mato Grosso, Brazil, February (*Valdir Hobus*).

5. LAFRESNAYE'S PICULET

Picumnus lafresnayi

L 9–10cm

Identification Rather plain. Upperparts and wings olive-brown barred green or yellow. Olive-brown crown and nape dotted or streaked white. Lores pale. Slight white post-ocular stripe. Dusky ear-coverts streaked brown. Underparts buff or white with bold, black, brown or green barring, broadest on lower flanks, sometimes absent from belly. Chin and throat buff, finely barred black. Primaries olive-brown, upper-wing-coverts paler greenish-brown with yellowish edges. Most of underwing brown with darker barring on yellowish coverts. Uppertail black, two central feathers white on inner webs, outer tail feathers mostly white. Short, dark bill. Orbital ring grey, iris brown. Legs greyish. Sexes differ slightly: male speckled red, orange or yellow on forecrown (depending on race), white spotted elsewhere on brownish crown; crown of female brown. Juveniles overall duller and irregularly barred below.

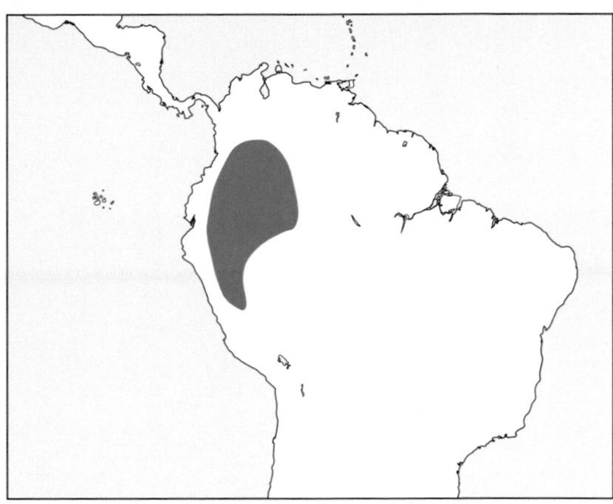

Vocalisations Often quiet. Subtle single *seep* note and high-pitched *tseeyt-tsit*. Song a slow, falling series usually of three evenly pitched notes, *seep-seep-seep* or *seet-seet-seet*, recalling Orange-fronted Plushcrown.

Drumming May not drum, or perhaps only rarely, but information lacking.

Status Common to uncommon. Poorly known; information on numbers and trends lacking. Easily overlooked.

Habitat Edges and clearings in dense, humid, tropical rainforest and thickets, particularly *terra firme* and *várzea*. Also parkland and gardens by forest.

Range South America. W Amazonia, between the Solimoes and Negro rivers and W of the Orinoco to the E Andean slope. Parts of SE Colombia, E Ecuador and NE Peru. Also an isolated population in Brazil. Mainly lowlands, but to around 1800m. Resident and sedentary.

Taxonomy and variation Four races. Nominate ***lafresnayi*** (SE Colombia, E Ecuador, N Peru) most boldly barred above, males speckled red on forecrown (other races usually yellow); ***pusillus*** (Brazil: mid-Amazonia E to the Rio Negro) male forecrown colour variable, rufous tones above, narrower and paler barring below; ***taczanowskii*** (NE and NC Peru) most yellow below, darkest on crown; ***punctifrons*** (E Peru) has darkest ear-coverts and narrow black bars below.

◄ Adult male Lafresnaye's Piculet of race *pusillus*. Forecrown colour of this small race varies; this bird's is red, others may be orange or yellow. Iranduba, Amazonas, Brazil, July (*Marcelo Barreiros*).

Similar species Most like Orinoco Piculet (which overlaps in SE Colombia and is sometimes considered conspecific), but paler on ear-coverts and crown, mantle light green and back barred yellow. Nominate male has red forecrown streaks: races with yellow do not meet Orinoco. Females alike. Bar-breasted Piculet streaked on belly. Golden-spangled Piculet race *undulatus* similar, but spotted on back.

Food and foraging Termites, arboreal ants and other small invertebrates, but little information. Frequently in mixed-species flocks, feeding unobtrusively from mid-level to the canopy.

► Adult female nominate. Lack of colour on the forecrown separates females from males, although some males may be minimally marked there. Moyobamba, Peru. November (*Gerard Gorman*).

6. ORINOCO PICULET
Picumnus pumilus

L 9cm

◄ Adult male Orinoco Piculet. The sexes hardly differ in plumage and are often difficult to separate in the field. This male shows a few yellow flecks on the forecrown. Vaupes, Colombia, June (*Nick Athanas*).

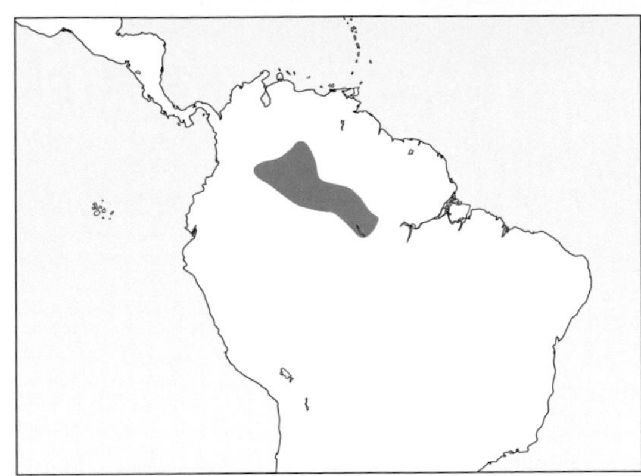

Identification Upperparts and wings olive-brown, plain or lightly barred tawny. Primaries and secondaries brown tipped with green, wing-coverts and tertials warmer brown with yellow or green edges. Underwing greyish with yellowish-cream coverts subtly barred brown. Underparts cream or buff, strongly barred chocolate from chin to vent, barring widest lower down. Uppertail black, central two tail feathers with white inner webs, outer feather pairs with white sub-terminal area. Thin white post-ocular stripe. Chocolate ear-coverts sometimes speckled white. Lores buff. Dark bill paler at base. Orbital ring bluish-grey, iris brownish. Legs grey. Sexes differ slightly: male has faint yellow streaks or spots on forecrown, white spotting on rest of brownish crown; female lacks yellow, all crown spotted white. Juveniles duller, greener above, with irregular, broken barring below, crown streaked buff.

Vocalisations Thin, sharp, double *seep-seep* or *seet-seet*. Song a faster, warbling, trilling series of similar notes.

Drumming May not drum, or perhaps only rarely, but information lacking.

Status Uncommon. A poorly known Orinoquian and Amazonian rainforest species. Range-restricted, probably under threat from deforestation.

Habitat Humid open rainforest, gallery forest, thickets, wooded savanna.

Range South America. Local in E Colombia and NW Brazil, almost entirely N of Equator. Likely to occur in adjacent S Venezuela, but no confirmed records. Resident and probably sedentary. Sea-level to 500m.

Taxonomy and variation Monotypic. Some individuals lack barring on central belly. Brown nape sometimes flecked yellow.

Similar species Slightly larger, paler Lafresnaye's Piculet has paler ear-coverts, barred back and lacks yellow on nape. Male has yellow rather than red forecrown streaks of nominate Lafresnaye's. Females alike. Golden-spangled Piculet race *undulatus* has bold white spots on nape and dark spots on back.

Food and foraging Termites, arboreal ants and probably other small invertebrates. Forages at all levels, but often in mixed-species flocks in canopy.

► Adult female Orinoco Piculet. Female Lafresnaye's Piculet *Picumnus lafresnayi* is very similar, and care should be taken with identification where the two overlap in SE Colombia. Vichada, Inirida, Colombia, May (*J. Dunning*).

7. GOLDEN-SPANGLED PICULET
Picumnus exilis

L 9–10cm

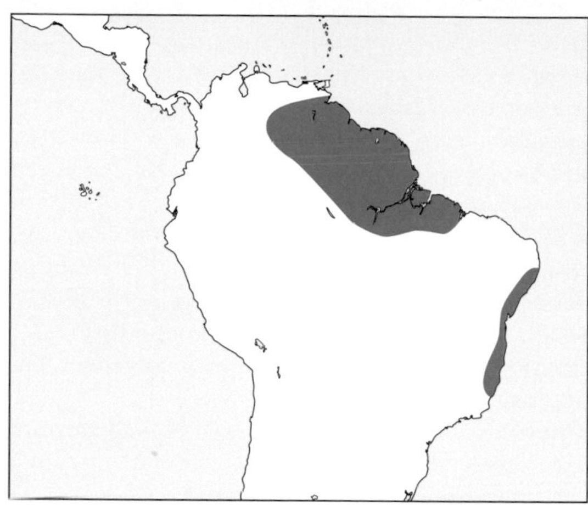

Identification Variable in plumage but most buff or white below, heavily barred black or grey with bars on lower belly often broken. Yellowish, greenish or brownish above, with rufous hue, mantle scaled black and yellow. Wing-coverts olive, variably marked with white spots and black crescents, flight feathers green or brown edged yellow, tertials with black sub-marginal marks. Underwing brown and white. Most of tail chocolate, central feather pair with white inner webs, outer three feather pairs with white sub-terminal marks. Buffy ear-coverts and cheeks finely barred black. Slight white post-ocular stripe. Malar and lores buff, pale chin and throat finely barred black. Iris variably yellow to brown, orbital ring grey. Legs bluish-grey. Lower mandible grey, upper black. Sexes differ slightly: both have black crown and nape spotted white, but male has red or orange forecrown which female lacks. Female also yellower and more densely barred below. Juveniles overall duller with olive crown flecked buff and less defined makings on paler underparts.

Vocalisations Falling high-pitched *seep* or *seet* notes in series, slow and fast trills and thin, high-pitched, falling *tsirrrit-tsit-tsit* or *tsi-tse-tsu*, very like Bar-breasted Piculet and other close relatives. Sharp *tsilit* and *tsirrrr* also described.

Drumming Produces rapid, staccato rolls. Precise details lacking.

Status Often common locally, but population data sparse. Probably declining due to loss of rainforest.

Habitat Rainforest, tall humid forest, cloud-forest,

▼ Adult male *undulatus* Golden-spangled Piculet. Currently regarded as a race, this taxon may well be a distinct species. French Guiana, March (*Michel Giraud-Audine*).

wooded savanna, riverine woods, bamboo thickets, cane-breaks, coastal forests and mangroves. Also secondary forest and more open woodlands.

Range South America. From extreme E Colombia through Venezuela to the Guianas and NE Brazil. Mostly lowlands, but to 1900m. Resident and sedentary.

Taxonomy and variation Racial limits unclear and ongoing study suggests five distinct species may exist as follows: ***P. exilis*** (EC Brazil: S from São Francisco River, in Atlantic Forest in Bahia and Sergipe) is distinct with diagnostic yellow-golden tones above and below, dark round spots on back, wing-coverts and prominent dark spots or chevrons with pale bars on covert centres. Some birds dark on belly rather than barred. ***P. undulatus*** (E Colombia, SE Venezuela, N Brazil, NW Guyana, S to the Rio Negro, W to the Orninoco) is relatively large, pale below, variably but usually boldly barred grey, richer olive-brown above with black and white spotting forming bars, male streaked red, orange or yellowish on crown, juveniles with olivaceous spots on a dusky head; ***clarus*** race in E Venezuela has narrower, broken bars on chest and flanks, belly spotted, yellower or greener above and male streaked orange on forecrown. ***P. buffoni*** (E Guyana to NE Brazil: Pará and Maranhão. One population E of Tocantins River and one N towards the Guianian Shield along the N bank of the Amazon, W to the Rio Branco and Roraima savannas) is variable, but usually olive above with black-edged white spots above and on wing-coverts and spots or bars on pale underparts, males have scarlet or orange on crown, juveniles have dusky crown with olive spots or bars. ***P. pernambucensis*** (coastal NE Brazil, N from São Francisco River in Alagoas, Pernambuco and Paraiba) is very distinct, variable white or buff below finely and extensively barred, plain olive-green above lacking spots on back and wing-coverts, boldly barred dark below, males with orange or red forecrown. Some birds spotted white on wing-coverts, some brownish above; juveniles may show olivaceous flecking on the head rather than white. ***P. obsoletus*** (NE Venezuela: Monagas, Delta Amacuro and Sucre, and islands in the Orinoco Delta) varies from buff to white below with often indistinct, sometimes absent, dark spotting. Some individuals have broken bars on the throat and chest.

Similar species Bar-breasted Piculet is less well marked above, throat pale. Black-dotted Piculet is greener above with boldly spotted (not barred) black on paler underparts. Orinoco and Lafresnaye's Piculets lack spotting on back.

Food and foraging Arboreal ants, and probably termites. Often solitary, but will forage in pairs and regularly joins mixed-species flocks from mid-levels to the canopy. Explores thinner, outermost branches and foliage and is then relatively conspicuous.

► Adult female *undulatus*. Females of all races lack the red or orange forecrown-patch of males. French Guiana, July (*Maxime Dechelle*).

8. BLACK-DOTTED PICULET
Picumnus nigropunctatus

L 9–10cm

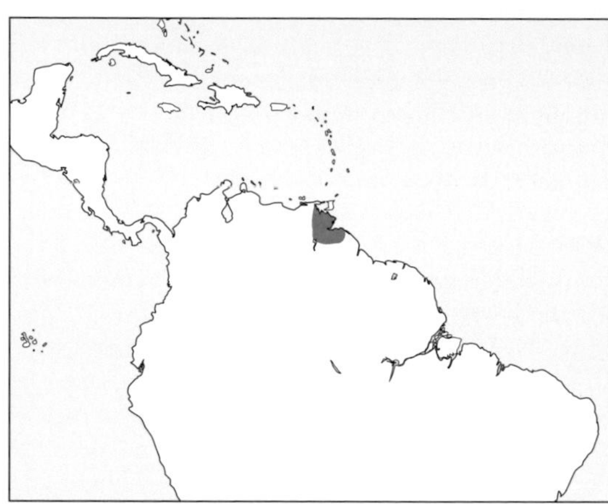

Other name Black-spotted Piculet
Identification Breast, belly and flanks subtle pale yellow, sparsely spotted black; undertail-coverts with faint crescents. Brown above with buff and olive tones and black spots or ovals on the mantle. Wings brown, feather edges buff. Central and upper outer tail feathers white. Ear-coverts brownish, spotted white. Variable, slight white flecks behind and above eyes. Lores, cheeks and neck-sides whitish flecked blackish; pale throat barred black. Bill and legs grey. Iris chocolate. Sexes differ slightly: males have black crown flecked white at rear, red at front; females lack red, with black crown flecked white. Juvenile plumage not adequately known.
Vocalisations Song 2–4 well spaced, thin, high-

▼ Adult male Black-dotted Piculet. This poorly known species is found only in coastal NW Venezuela. Cano Colorado, Venezuela, April (*Pete Morris*).

pitched *seeeet, seeep, tsee* or *tseest* notes, each slightly lower than previous. Single notes probably function as contact calls.

Drumming Occasionally produces strident, rhythmic rolls linked in a series of around 10 seconds.

Status Range-restricted and little studied, but fairly common in Orinoco and San Juan river deltas. Conservation category not yet assigned by IUCN.

Habitat Humid and wet lowland, coastal tropical forest and thickets, bushy secondary growth, mangroves, *várzea* and *terra firme*. Often by water courses and locally in hedgerows on cattle ranches.

Range South America. Endemic to NW Venezuela: Orinoco, San Juan and Amacuro deltas and coastal lowlands from Sucre to NE Monagas. Sea-level to 100m. Resident and sedentary.

Taxonomy and variation Monotypic. Birds in SE Sucre may have fine barring on the chest. Some individuals show a scaly throat and buff underparts, rather than yellow.

Similar species Differs from nominate Golden-spangled Piculet in black-dotted, rather than barred or streaked, breast and belly. Birds with buffy underparts might suggest Scaled Piculet, though that species clearly scaled below.

Food and foraging Presumably arboreal ants, termites and other small invertebrates, but precise information lacking.

▼ Adult female Black-dotted Piculet. A lightly marked individual. Sucre, Venezuela, January (*Fredrik Sahlin*).

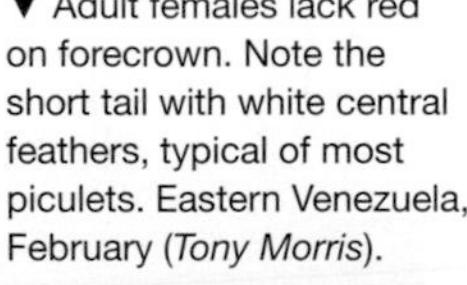

▼ Adult females lack red on forecrown. Note the short tail with white central feathers, typical of most piculets. Eastern Venezuela, February (*Tony Morris*).

9. ECUADORIAN PICULET
Picumnus sclateri

L 8–9cm

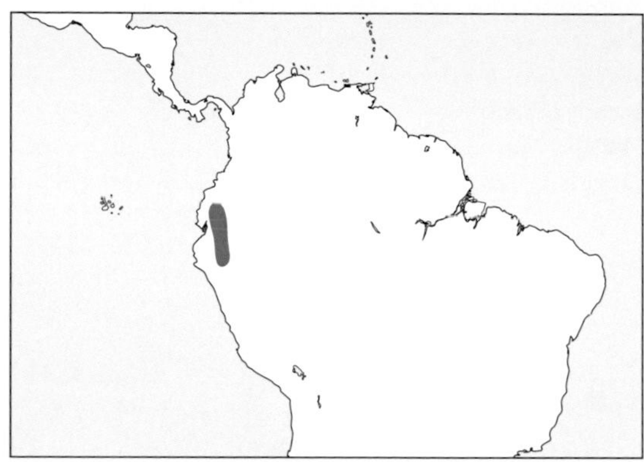

Identification Greyish-brown above, gently barred darker. Underparts white with chin, throat and breast barred black or brown, flanks and belly streaked boldly black, undertail-coverts barred. Uppertail dusky grey to brown, central two tail feathers white on inner webs, outer three pairs more white. Brown wing-coverts with pale tips. Tertials also tipped white. Underwing pale with coverts barred grey. Black crown and nape strikingly spotted white. Short, faint, white post-ocular stripe. Dusky ear-coverts streaked white. Lores white. Bill black with grey base. Iris brown-black. Legs grey. Sexes alike: male has subtle yellow spots or streaks on forecrown and white spotting on rest of black crown;

▼ Adult male nominate. Sexual dimorphism is minimal in Ecuadorian Piculet, with the yellow forecrown flecks of the males often hardly visible. Macara, Ecuador, August (*Wim de Groot*).

female lacks yellow. Juveniles overall duller with less defined markings and off-white spots or streaks on crown.

Vocalisations Often silent. High-pitched double *tseee-tsuit* or *tseee-up*. Single or double, thin, rising, *tseeet, sweet* or *seet* notes. Relatively slow, falling, trilling series of 3–7 *swee* notes.

Drumming Occasionally drums, but precise details lacking.

Status Locally common to uncommon. Considered stable overall, but limited in range and population trends and ecology largely unknown.

Habitat Tropical arid woodlands, forest edges, shrub and thorn thickets, cactus scrub and in SW Ecuador damp upland deciduous forests. Also abandoned, overgrown coffee plantations.

Range South America. Restricted to Pacific slope of the Andes, S of Equator, in W Ecuador and (despite vernacular name) NW Peru. Mainly lowlands, from sea-level up to around 2100m. Resident and probably sedentary.

Taxonomy and variation Three races: ***sclateri*** (SW Ecuador, extreme NW Peru) barred black below; ***parvistriatus*** (W Ecuador: Manabi S to Guayas) paler, greyer, less marked below with fine, weak barring and spotting; ***porcullae*** (NW Peru: C Piura to N Lambayeque) has boldest barring from throat to breast, heaviest streaking on belly and flanks.

Similar species Sympatric *harterti* race of Olivaceous Piculet has cinnamon or chestnut ear-coverts, and occurs in more humid habitats.

Food and foraging Presumably small insects, but information lacking. Rather skulking, tending to forage at lower levels and in understorey.

▼ Adult female *porcullae*; the darkest and mast heavily marked below of the three described races. Piura, Peru, July (*Niels Poul Dreyer*).

10. SCALED PICULET
Picumnus squamulatus

L 8–9cm

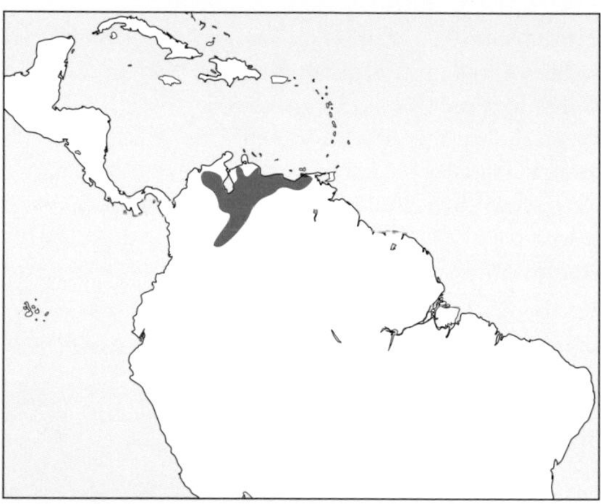

Identification Tan or olive above with dark feather tips and paler sub-terminal marks creating scaling, especially on mantle. Underparts white, heavily scaled black or brown on breast and flanks, fading on belly, vent and undertail. Chin and throat white, gently barred greyish-brown. Uppertail brown or black, two central tail feathers broadly tipped white on inner webs, outer pairs boldly marked white. Wing-coverts brown edged black, flight feathers brown, secondaries and tertials edged yellow. Underwing brownish with white coverts. Slight white post-ocular stripe, dusky-brown ear-coverts spotted white. Chocolate hindneck finely spotted white, indistinct pale malar with grey or brown feather tips. Lores pale. Iris brown. Legs greyish-olive. Bill blackish, lower mandible paler, yellow at base.

◄ Adult male *rohli* Scaled Piculet. The forecrown colour of males can vary from red to orange to yellow. Aragua, Venezuela, October (*Nick Athanas*).

Sexes differ slightly: male has black crown and nape, streaked red or orange at front, spotted white at rear; female lacks red. Juveniles plainer on head, darker above, weakly marked below.

Vocalisations Commonly a burst of staccato, twittering, *t't't't't't see-see-seep* notes, slowing at the end – recalling an *Amazilia* hummingbird. Song a falling, trilling series of 3–6 (occasionally more), thin, high-pitched, *seep, zeep* or *seet* notes, also delivered singly.

Drumming Adjacent territory holders frequently drum. Typically, 3–4 discrete but rapid rolls of 4–10 strikes each, with a brief gap between each roll. Often irregular, varying in pitch and speed.

Status Common locally in Venezuela. Considered stable, but population data lacking. Perhaps overlooked.

Habitat Damp and dry tropical forests, gallery forest, deciduous woodland edges, thickets and secondary growth. Also grasslands, farmland, parks and gardens where there are scattered trees, tangled undergrowth and vines.

Range South America. Parts of Colombia and Venezuela. Apparently extending range southwards into wetter regions, probably in response to deforestation. From sea-level to 1900m. Resident and sedentary.

Taxonomy and variation Five races, though some disputed. Nominate ***squamulatus*** (from NE to S Colombia: Arauca S to Huila, Meta and Cauca) heavily scaled above and below; ***rohli*** (NE Colombia: Santa Marta to Boyaca; N Venezuela: Zulia to W Sucre and Monagas) brighter, yellower above, weakly scaled below, brownish nape, male sometimes spotted yellow or ochre on forecrown rather than red; ***lovejoyi*** (extreme NW Venezuela: NW Zulia) greyer above, relatively lightly scaled below, male with yellow forecrown marks; ***apurensis*** (NC Venezuela: Apure, Guarico, Anzoategui) whiter below, weakly scaled, often appears unmarked; ***obsoletus*** (extreme NE Venezuela: Orinoco Delta to Delta Amacuro and E Sucre) more yellow-green above, buff or yellow below with fine scaling and dark dots rather than chevrons.

Similar species Race *apurensis* easily confused with White-bellied Piculet as both are plain below.

Food and foraging Small invertebrates. Forages on saplings, twigs, vines and in undergrowth, alone or in pairs.

► Female *rohli* Scaled Piculet. Females of all races are drab and are often only vaguely scaled below. Magdalena, Colombia, March (*Nick Athanas*).

11. WHITE-BELLIED PICULET
Picumnus spilogaster

L 9–10cm

Identification Tiny, but large for the genus. Underparts cream or white (except *pallidus* – see below), throat and chest broadly barred black, breast less barred, bars often broken, belly spotted black, flanks variably scaled (depending on race). Olive-brown above, finely barred grey. Brown flight feathers edged buff or cinnamon, especially secondaries and tertials, occasionally almost forming a pale panel. Wing-coverts olive-brown, edged pale. Greyish underwing with white coverts. Uppertail brown, central feather pair white on inner webs, outer two pairs with white stripe on outer webs, tips brown. Neck-sides finely barred white. Dusky ear-coverts gently barred and scaled white. Lores buff. Pale chin, throat and malar area variably barred brown or black. Bill grey, tip darker. Iris brown. Legs greyish-olive. Sexes differ slightly: male has red tips to black forecrown feathers, sometimes forming a patch, and black hindcrown dotted or streaked white; female lacks red, with black forecrown dotted white, hindcrown streaked. Juveniles of both sexes well marked overall, spotted and barred, buffer below than adults with brown crown which usually lacks spots.

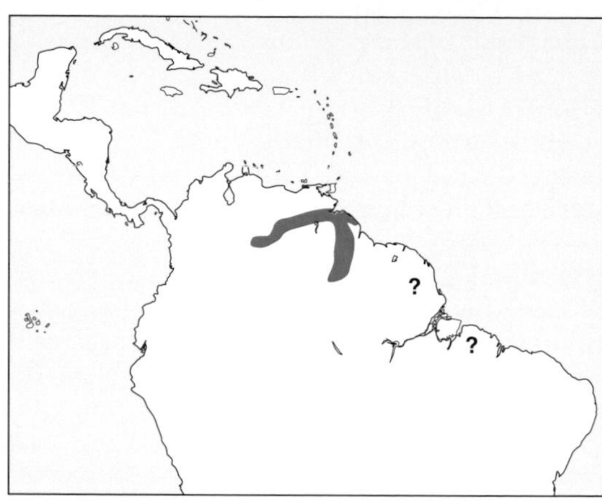

Vocalisations Thin, high-pitched, descending, whistling, trilling *zi-zi-zi-zi*. Relatively slow (very similar to, but possibly longer than those of close relatives at 3–5 seconds), composed of 12–15 notes, recalling Plain Xenops. Also high-pitched *ti* notes when agitated.
Drumming Occasional, brief, rapid rolls produced.
Status VU. Recently upgraded as its Amazonian

►Adult male White-bellied Piculet of the nominate race. The red forecrown on the male is variable in extent; sometimes just a few feather tips or, as on this individual, forming a distinct patch. Boa Vista, Roraima, Brazil, August (*Anselmo d' Affonseca*).

▲ Adult female nominate. Females show no red on crown. Boa Vista, Roraima, Brazil, August (*Anselmo d' Affonseca*).

habitat continues to disappear. In some areas common, but uncommon in, for example, Venezuela.

Habitat Rainforest, gallery forest, drier deciduous forest, thickets with vines and creepers. Also *llanos*, forest edges, partially cleared forest, wooded savanna, mangroves.

Range South America. Probably found in three separate areas: C Venezuela, N Brazil and Guyana. Mostly lowlands, sea-level to 100m. Resident, possibly some local seasonal movements.

Taxonomy and variation Three races currently recognised: ***spilogaster*** (Guyana; Roraima, N Brazil); ***orinocensis*** (C and E Venezuela: SE Apure to Amacuro Delta) is distinct, clean white below, only throat slightly barred, spotting darker above and scaled cinnamon, most white in tail; ***pallidus*** (NE Brazil, near Belém) is very different from other two races: males have heart-spotted breasts and females barred down to the upper belly. This taxon 'Pará Piculet' should perhaps not be assigned to *spilogaster* and may actually be a hybrid between Arrowhead and Spotted Piculets and is the subject of an ongoing genetic study.

Similar species Slightly larger Arrowhead Piculet more marked above and scaled below. White-barred Piculet very boldly barred below. Beware Scaled Piculet race *apurensis* (in S Llanos, Venezuela) which is rather plain below. Nominate resembles Black-dotted Piculet.

Food and foraging Unknown, but presumably takes small invertebrates.

► Adult male *orinocensis*. Delta Amacuro, Venezuela, October (*Nick Athanas*).

12. ARROWHEAD PICULET
Picumnus minutissimus

L 9–10cm

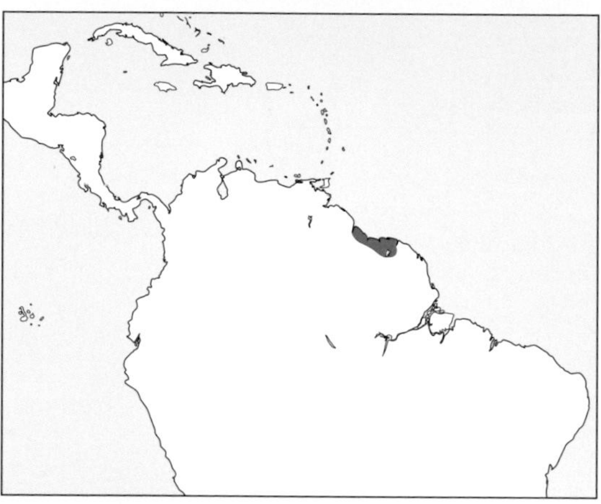

Other name Guianan Piculet

Identification Mostly olive-brown above with black centres to some feathers and white feather-tips on mantle. Rump often darkly barred. Underparts white with brown or black feather-tips (arrowheads) creating subtly scaled appearance. Scales larger on belly than chest. White chin, throat and malar finely barred black. Mostly brown or black tail, central feathers white and outer two pairs with an angled white stripe on outer webs. Upper-coverts sometimes barred. Flight feathers brown, secondaries and tertials edged white or buff on outer webs. Olive-brown wing-coverts edged white. Underwing grey to brown, coverts brown and white. Ear-coverts and cheeks brown, with fine pale markings. Small white post-ocular line, lores yellow or

◀ Adult male Arrowhead Piculet. Note the dark 'arrowheads' on the feathers of the underparts. Peperpot, Surinam, January (*Jean-Louis Rousselle*).

buff. Short greyish bill, paler at base of lower mandible. Iris colour variably yellow, red or brown, orbital ring grey. Legs greyish-green. Sexes differ slightly: male has black crown streaked or spotted red at the front, often creating solid patch, and spotted white at the rear; female lacks red, with black crown spotted white. Female also has shorter bill and longer tail and wings, though these differences hard to judge in the field. Juvenile browner above, barred black, plainer, less marked below and has brown rather than black crown that largely lacks spots.

Vocalisations Song a trilling, sometimes more ticking, series of 10–14 thin *it-it-it* notes. Sometimes a stronger, shrill *kee-kee-kee* or *tjeek-tjeek-tjeek*. Various excited, twittering noises when in dispute or threatened.

Drumming May not drum, or perhaps only rarely, but information lacking.

Status NT, but actually common in Paramaribo and coastal habitats in Surinam. Rarer in the savanna belt.

Habitat Wet lowland forests, coastal, riparian and wetland woodlands, mangroves, plantations, secondary and disturbed forest, even urban gardens.

Range South America. Contrary to much of the literature, it is probably endemic to Surinam, where it is found mostly in lowlands along Atlantic coast. Sight records from elsewhere are disputed and specimens lacking. Resident and sedentary.

Taxonomy and variation Monotypic. White-bellied Piculet *pallidus* has been treated as race of this species. Taxonomy needs revision.

Similar species Superficially similar White-bellied Piculet does not overlap. White-barred Piculet is barred, not scaled, below.

Food and foraging Ants, beetles and other small invertebrates. Agile and active, foraging on twigs, vines and in bushes.

▲ Adult male Arrowhead Piculet. The black-and-white tail common to most piculets is clearly seen here. Galibi, Surinam, February (*J. Dunning*).

▼ Adult female. Arrowhead Piculet is highly restricted in range, and is probably endemic to Surinam. Peperpot Nature Park, Surinam, July (*Jean-Louis Rousselle*).

13. SPOTTED PICULET
Picumnus pygmaeus

L 10cm

Identification Distinctive. Warm chestnut-brown overall. Mantle, scapulars and back variably dotted with white-tipped black spots. Rump lighter brown. Uppertail blacker with central feather pair white on inner webs. Outer two tail feathers white before the tip, undertail paler. Throat to belly and flanks rufous-brown; belly usually lighter with large, bold white spots. Neck-sides and lower cheeks barred white. Flight feathers chocolate, secondaries and tertials edged and tipped buff to cinnamon. Brown wing-coverts edged and tipped white. Underwing pale brown, coverts paler, even whitish. Chocolate ear-coverts and cheeks dotted white. Slight white crescent sometimes above eyes. Lores buff. Short, black bill with bluish-grey base. Iris brown. Legs greyish. Sexes alike. Male has black crown

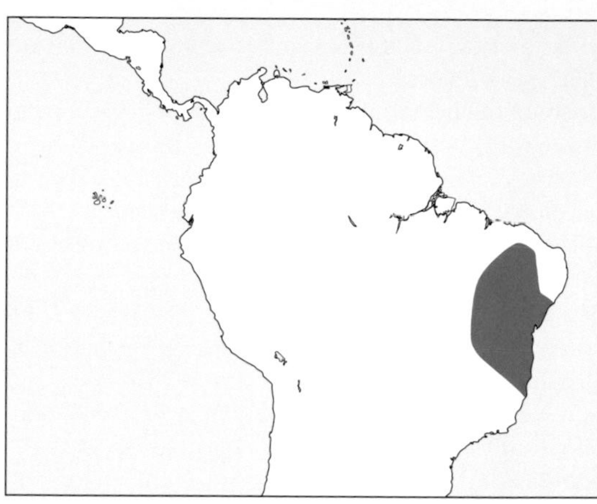

▼ Adult male Spotted Piculet. This is a particularly well-marked individual with a distinct red forecrown-patch. Maracas, Bahia, Brazil, June (*Marcelo Barreiros*).

and nape, streaked red at the front, often forming a solid patch, spotted white at the rear. Female lacks red, having white-spotted black crown and nape. Male also generally has white heart-shapes or spots below black dots on the breast, whilst females have barred breasts and unbarred lower bellies. Juvenile has plain or less spotted brown crown.

Vocalisations Squeaky, trilling, high-pitched, falling, two-second *tsirrrr-tsi-tsi-tsi* or *ttrrrruh* song, very like White-barred and other related piculets. Also thin, sharp *seep* calls.

Drumming Presumably drums, but perhaps only rarely, though information lacking.

Status Locally fairly common. Range-restricted and poorly known, perhaps overlooked, but seems adaptable and not considered threatened.

Habitat Arid, open lowland deciduous forest, wooded savanna, *caatinga*, thickets and coastal mangroves. Now also occupies extensively human-modified landscapes and abandoned degraded pastures, young secondary forests and exotic plantations including eucalyptus.

Range South America. Endemic to NE Brazil: Pará, Maranhão, Piaui, Pernambuco, Bahia and extreme N Minas Gerais. Sea-level to around 800m. Resident and mainly sedentary, but spreading westwards towards Amazonia

Taxonomy and variation Monotypic. Rather variable, some birds having little or no spotting above.

Similar species None within range.

Food and foraging Presumably small invertebrates – precise information lacking. Often forages low down, joins mixed-species flocks, but rather unobtrusive.

▼ Adult female Spotted Piculets lack read on the head. This Brazilian endemic is unmistakable within its range. Maracas, Bahia, Brazil, June (*Marcelo Barreiros*).

14. SPECKLE-CHESTED PICULET
Picumnus steindachneri

L 8.5–10cm

Identification Distinctive, heavily marked, mostly black, grey and white. Upperparts grey-brown with lighter feather fringes creating scales and bars. Black chest and breast marked with bold, white drop-shapes. Belly, flanks and undertail-coverts barred black and white. Uppertail blackish with central feather pair white along inner webs. Outer two tail feathers have white sub-terminal band. Wings brown with pale grey or white edges and tips, especially on secondaries and tertials. Underwing tan with white coverts. White fleck behind eye. Ear-coverts black, flecked white. Neck-sides barred black and white. Chin and throat white with black fringes. Lores buff. Bluish-black bill, base paler. Iris dark. Legs grey. Sexes alike: male has black crown spotted red at the front, white at the rear; female lacks red, having black crown spotted white. Juvenile more like adult female.

Vocalisations Song a fast, thin, falling, insect-like trilling *tree-e-e-e-e-e-e*. Gentle piping contact notes.

Drumming May not truly drum, though rattling and tapping sounds made during foraging.

Status EN. Range-restricted, declining and threatened by loss and degradation of habitat, main reasons being legal and illegal logging and clearance of forests for pastures and coffee plantations. However, seemingly adaptable, occurring in secondary and degraded habitats.

Habitat Montane rainforest, especially with epiphytes, vines and mixed tree and bamboo stands. Also wet thickets and tall secondary growth in cultivated areas.

Range South America. Endemic to N Peru. Currently known from a few areas on the E Andean slope in Amazonas and San Martin departments, particularly along the Rio Huallaga and tributaries. In N, reaches E of Abra Patricia, NW of Moyobamba, along the Rio Mayo; in S, around La Rivera. Possibly overlooked and perhaps present in relatively unexplored adjacent areas. Usually above 1000m to around 2500m. Resident, probably sedentary.

Taxonomy and variation Monotypic. Variation slight.

Similar species Like Ocellated Piculet in crown and upperpart colour and markings, but does not overlap. Lafresnaye's Piculet yellower below, more olive above, but does not overlap either.

Food and foraging Presumably small invertebrates, but little information. Single birds and pairs often join mixed-species flocks. Usually forages from mid-storey to canopy level.

► Adult female. Found only in the uplands of N Peru, Speckle-chested Piculet is unmistakable within its range. Afluentes, San Martin, Peru, November (*Gerard Gorman*).

◄ Adult male Speckle-chested Piculet. The small area of red on the forecrown separates males from females. Afluentes, San Martin, Peru, November (*Gerard Gorman*).

15. VÁRZEA PICULET
Picumnus varzeae

L 8–9cm

Identification Distinctive warm chestnut or chocolate overall. Underparts variable shades of brown, sometimes with olive hue, with indistinct black-and-white bars/chevrons. Chin and throat chocolate with fine white markings. Ear-coverts, cheeks and neck spotted and scaled black and white. Lores white, speckled black. Nape, mantle and back chocolate, often with olive tinge, and sometimes slightly barred dark. Uppertail rich brown with central two feathers mostly white, outer two feather pairs white before tip. Undertail-coverts less marked. Upperwing and coverts tan with subtle paler edges, which are broader on the secondaries and tertials. Iris brown. Black bill with bluish-grey base to lower mandible. Legs bluish-grey. Sexes differ slightly: male has varying amount of red on black fore- and mid-crown, often forming solid patch, rest of crown dotted white; female lacks red, having black crown spotted white. Juvenile more barred below.

Vocalisations High-pitched, falling, trilling *tsirrrr* and thin, sharp *seep* calls, very much like Spotted and White-barred Piculets.

Drumming Probably drums, but information lacking.

Status EN. Range-restricted and poorly known. More study on all aspects of its natural history urgently needed as deforestation and hydro-electric projects in Amazonia pose serious threats.

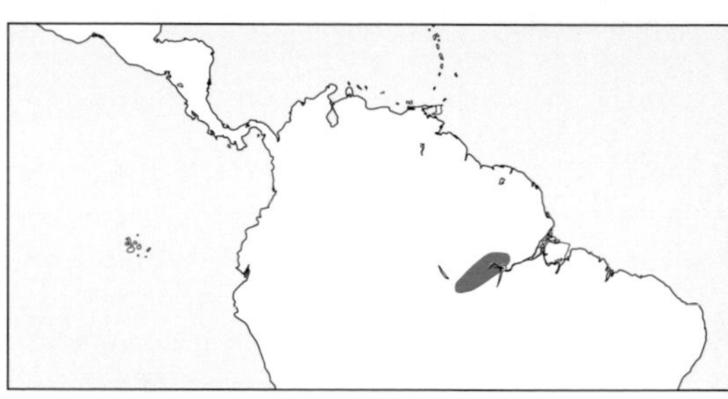

Habitat Low-lying floodplains, riverine, swamp and *várzea* forests, thickets and wooded islands – all with dense undergrowth.

Range South America. Endemic to Brazil's Lower Amazon Basin. Occurs in relatively small region between the confluences of the Amazon, Rio Negro, Rio Trombetas and Rio Tapajos. Resident and sedentary.

Taxonomy and variation Monotypic. Underpart and face patterns vary individually. Some birds have yellowish base to the lower mandible.

Similar species All other piculets within range are pale below. Apparently hybridises with White-barred Piculet.

Food and foraging Presumably small invertebrates, but information lacking.

◄ ▲ Adult male (left) and adult female Varzea Piculet. When alarmed or excited, male piculets will raise their coloured crown feathers. Varzea Piculet is the only *Picumnus* with dark underparts within its small range. Parintins, Amazonas State, Brazil, December (*Anselmo d'Affonseca*).

16. WHITE-BARRED PICULET
Picumnus cirratus

L 9–10cm

Identification Tan or olive above, faintly barred pale. White/cream below, heavily barred black; barring finest on chest, broadest on belly and flanks. Uppertail chocolate, central tail feather-pair white, outer pairs black with white inner sub-terminal area. Flight feathers chocolate, coverts edged pale, creating faint scaling. Underwing tan, coverts paler. Ear-coverts and cheeks olive-brown, lightly barred black. Slight white lines above and/or behind eye, bordering ear-coverts (depending on race). Chin, throat and lower cheeks buff or white, finely barred black. Nasal tufts buff. Black bill with bluish base to lower mandible. Iris chestnut, orbital ring bluish-grey. Legs grey. Sexes differ slightly: male spotted red on forecrown, sometimes creating patch, rest of crown black, dotted white; female lacks red. Juveniles overall darker, more barred above, boldest barring below, lacks crown spotting, bill pale.

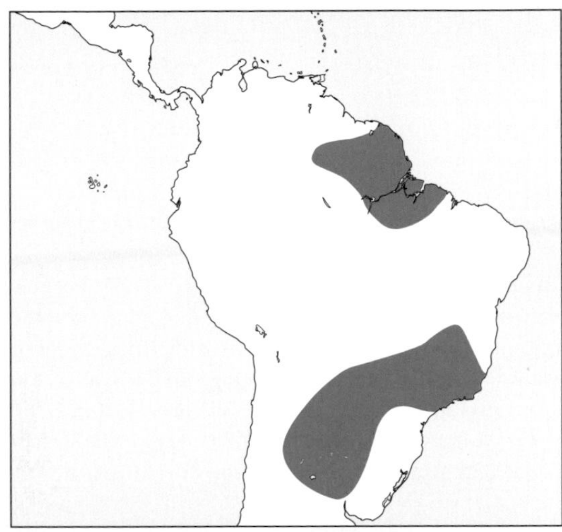

► Adult male White-barred Piculet, probably *pilcomayensis*, although the markings on the underparts are atypical. The amount of red on the crown of males varies individually. San Lorenzo, Salta, Argentina, December (*Nick Athanas*).

Vocalisations Rapid, shrill, high-pitched, falling, trilling *tsirrrrrrr,* very like Spotted and other related piculets. Brief, sharp *tsik* and *tsirik* notes. Also cricket-like cheeps and chirps.

Drumming Surprisingly loud, somewhat staccato, rolls produced.

Status Common and widespread, even found in down-town gardens in São Paulo and other cities.

Habitat Variety of lowland and upland, wet and drier, tropical woodlands: thickets, scrub, wooded savanna, shrub, bamboo stands, gallery forests, overgrown gardens, parks, invariably with vines and creepers.

Range South America. Two separate populations: around the Equator, locally in Guyana, NW French Guiana and N Brazil; further south in parts of Argentina, Bolivia, Paraguay and SE Brazil. Sea-level to 2200m. Resident and sedentary.

Taxonomy and variation Taxonomic relationships between races and with other species unclear; some taxa possibly full species. Plumage differences concern mantle colour, degree of markings and extent of red on crown in males. Currently six races: ***cirratus*** (SE Brazil, E Paraguay); ***confusus*** (SW Guyana, NW French Guiana, N Brazil) lacks white lines above ear-coverts, has heavily barred throat, pale feather fringes on dark mantle; ***macconnelli*** (NE Brazil: E Amazonia) has dark ear-coverts often spotted white, thick dark barring over malar, throat and chest, lacks white around eye (possibly a distinct species); ***thamnophiloides*** (Andes: SE Bolivia and NW Argentina) pale overall, appears washed-out, light grey above, plain below, bars tending to chevrons; ***tucumanus*** (NC Argentina) also greyish above, throat buff, wide-spaced black bars on belly, indistinct lines around eye, male has red restricted to forecrown; ***pilcomayensis*** (SE Bolivia, Paraguay, NE Argentina) often greyish, tightly barred black and white below, white line above ear-coverts. Last three races together sometimes considered separate species 'Pilcomayo Piculet'.

Similar species Within range most like Ochre-collared or Golden-spangled Piculets, but never has cinnamon tones of former, nor yellow or green of latter. Other sympatic piculets plain or scaled below. Apparently interbreeds with Várzea, Ocellated, Ochre-collared and White-wedged Piculets.

Food and foraging Various small insects, especially in larval stage. Follows ant-swarms, often solitary, but joins mixed-species foraging flocks.

▼ Adult female White-barred Piculet. This is the nominate, but a lightly marked individual. Bahia Negra, Paraguay, February (*Andrea Ferreira*).

▲ A juvenile. Note the pale bill and lack of white spotting on the black crown. Cordoba, Argentina, November (*Robert Güller*).

► A pair of White-barred Piculets. The female is on the left, the male with the red forecrown to the right. Argentina, November (*Ramón Moller Jensen*).

17. OCELLATED PICULET
Picumnus dorbignyanus

L 9–10cm

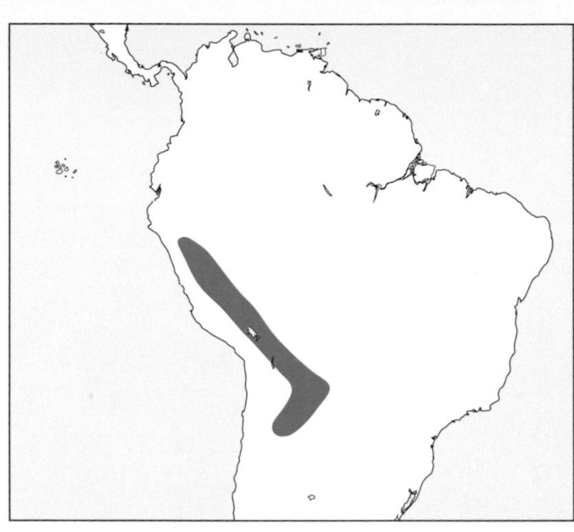

Identification Grey-brown above, flecked with pale feather tips and some black feather centres. Hindneck greyish, throat scaled. Mostly white below, with dark feather centres and shafts creating chevrons on chest and breast. Belly often more buff, plain or faintly barred. Flanks with dark spots or chevrons. Flight feathers tipped and edged buff, wing-coverts edged pale. Underwing pale greyish-brown, coverts whiter. Tail mostly black or brown, central feather pair white, outer two pairs white before tip. Ear-coverts dusky, gently streaked white, bordered above by slight white post-ocular line. Pale malar area. Lores and nasal tufts buff. Black bill with bluish-grey base. Iris black/brown, orbital ring grey. Legs greyish. Sexes alike: male has black crown, streaked red at front, spotted white at sides and on nape; female lacks red. Juvenile darker

▼ Adult male Ocellated Piculet of the nominate race. Note the scaling on the chest and the bright orange forecrown. Cochabamba, Bolivia, November (*Glenn Bartley*).

▼ Adult male nominate. Relationships between this species and other piculets remain unclear. Cochabamba, Bolivia, November (*Glenn Bartley*).

overall, finely barred below and on mantle.

Vocalisations High-pitched, shrill, whistling, trilling *tree-e-e-e-e-e-e*, delivered at varying speeds, usually falling away. Also single cricket-like cheeps and chirps.

Drumming May not drum, or perhaps only rarely, but information lacking.

Status Often rather localised, being rare or common. Population data lacking, but overall not considered threatened.

Habitat Andean rainforest and secondary humid foothill forests. Often found among bushy undergrowth, epiphytes, vines and creepers.

Range South America. Restricted to E Andes and foothills in Peru, Bolivia and Argentina, usually between 800–2500m. Resident, though some may move to lower elevations in winter.

Taxonomy and variation Two races: ***dorbignyanus*** (C Bolivia in La Paz, Cochabamba and Santa Cruz; NW Argentina in Jujuy and Salta regions) and ***jelskii*** (Peru: E Andean slope), which has bolder black markings on the breast, fewer on the belly, more delicate flank streaking and slightly shorter tail than nominate, although this hard to judge in the field.

Similar species White-wedged Piculet has darker mantle and lacks bold flank and lower belly markings. White-barred Piculet has bars, not chevrons, below (*thamnophiloides* in NW Argentina may have chevrons). Has been lumped with White-barred and Ochre-collared Piculets and known to interbreed with the latter as well as White-wedged Piculet. Similar Speckle-chested Piculet does not overlap in range.

Food and foraging Presumably small invertebrates, but precise information lacking. Often in mixed-species foraging flocks.

▲◄ Adult female Ocellated Piculet. This is race *jelskii* from the eastern Andean slope of Peru which has bolder streaks on the chest but is cleaner on the belly. Machu Picchu, Peru, October (*Lars Petersson*).

▲Adult female of the nominate race. Cochabamba, Bolivia, November (*Glenn Bartley*).

◄ Adult female nominate foraging on a lichen-strewn branch. Compare the barring on the belly with race *jelskii* above. Cochabamba, Bolivia, November (*Glenn Bartley*).

18. OCHRE-COLLARED PICULET
Picumnus temminckii

L 9–10cm

Identification Distinct cinnamon neck-sides and hindneck form 'ochre collar'. Brownish above, mantle sometimes slightly barred by pale feather edges. White or cream below, often cinnamon or buff on flanks and lower belly, heavily and boldly barred black. Bars broader on belly and undertail-coverts than on throat. Flight feathers chocolate; coverts tan, edged buff. Underwing tan with white coverts. Central two tail feathers white on inner webs; outer two pairs black with white inner webs before tip. Brown or buff ear-coverts and cheeks bordered above by slight white post-ocular line. Lower cheeks, chin and throat white, subtly barred black. Iris brown, orbital ring greyish. Lores and nasal tufts buff. Gently curved black bill, bluish-grey at base. Legs grey. Sexes alike: male has black forecrown flecked red, sometimes forming solid patch, rest of crown black, spotted white; female lacks

▼ Adult male Ochre-collared Piculet. The amount of red on the forecrown is highly variable. Itanhaem, Brazil, November (*Ronald Gruijters*).

◄ Adult female. The ochre hindneck, which shows well on this individual, is diagnostic of this species. Itanhaem, Brazil, November (Ronald Gruijters).

▼ A pair of Ochre-collared Piculets; the female, lacking red on the crown, is behind. Itanhaem, Brazil, November (Ronald Gruijters)

red having white-spotted black crown. Juvenile darker with bolder but looser black barring.

Vocalisations Shrill, high-pitched, whistling, trilling *tsirrrrt* or *trrrrruh* of varying length that usually falls away. Also a sharp *si-si-si* or *see-see-see.*

Drumming Series of loud, solid volleys of varying lengths (1–3 seconds), staccato and irregular.

Status Fairly common locally. Not considered threatened, though little studied and population data lacking.

Habitat Mainly lowland rainforest with understorey of vines and bamboo. Sometimes humid thickets, tall scrub, shrubland, gardens and parks, even in large cities.

Range South America. Southern Atlantic rainforest region: Brazil, E Paraguay and Misiones, NE Argentina. Sea-level to 800m. Resident and sedentary.

Taxonomy and variation Monotypic. Sometimes lumped with White-barred Piculet.

Similar species White-barred Piculet lacks ochre collar. Beware of possible hybrids from interbreeding with White-barred and other piculets. Some calls very similar to White-barred Piculet.

Food and foraging Small invertebrates such as ants and beetle larvae. Often forages in vines, undergrowth and on twigs and saplings.

19. WHITE-WEDGED PICULET
Picumnus albosquamatus

L 10–11cm

Identification Very variable. Brownish-olive above with bold white feather tips on mantle. Ear-coverts dusky. White dots and slight line behind eye. Lores and nasal tufts buff. Malar and throat scaled black and white. Underparts from throat to upper belly white or buff, heavily scaled with black chevrons. Flanks and lower belly plainer. Brown tail with white central feather pair; outer pairs with white sub-terminal area. Flight feathers brown; secondaries and tertials edged buff or white; coverts edged pale. Underwing tan. Iris brown, orbital ring grey. Bill blackish with pale yellow base to lower mandible. Legs greyish. Sexes alike: males have red fore- and mid-crown, hindcrown black, spotted white; females lack red, having black or brown crown, spotted white. Juvenile more like adult female, lacking red, but crown lighter brown.

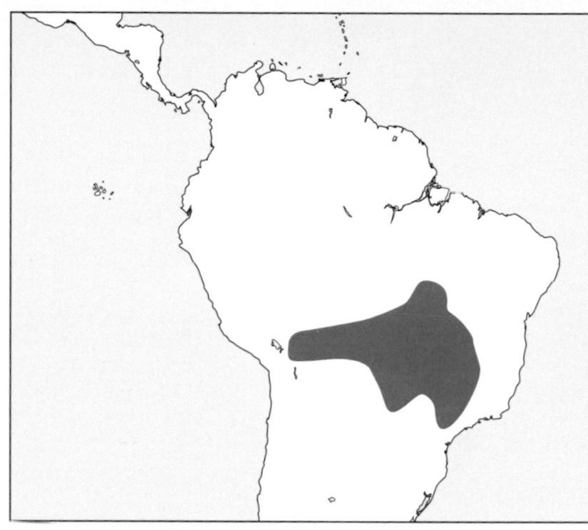

▼ Adult male White-wedged Piculet. Brasília, Brazil, December (*Flavio Cruvinel Brandao*).

Vocalisations High-pitched, wavering, tinkling, falling series of *ti* or *tee* notes and a trilling *tsirrrr*, repeated after brief pauses.

Drumming Reported to drum occasionally, but details lacking.

Status Fairly common in the Pantanal. Not considered threatened, though little studied and population data sparse.

Habitat Damp, open, lowland and foothill deciduous forests, riverine woodlands, thickets, dry wooded savanna and *cerrado*.

Range South America. Occurs in parts of Bolivia, N Paraguay and S Brazil. From sea-level to 2100m. Resident and probably sedentary.

Taxonomy and variation Two races: ***albosquamatus*** (N and E Bolivia, N Paraguay, and SW Brazil: Pantanal) is scaled black below; ***guttifer*** (E and C Brazil: S Pará and Maranhão to S and E Mato Grosso and W São Paulo) larger, ear-coverts darker, mantle and wing-coverts spotted white, more tightly marked below, often blackish on throat and chest, dark spots on belly (can look all-black), male with more red on crown than nominate. Subspecies *guttifer* sometimes treated as distinct species 'Guttate Piculet'.

Similar species Ocellated Piculet more boldly marked below. White-barred Piculet is uniformly barred below. Similar Arrowhead Piculet does not overlap in range. Known to hybridise with Ocellated, Ochre-collared and White-barred Piculets.

Food and foraging Presumably small invertebrates but specific information lacking.

► Adult female White-wedged Piculet of race *guttifer*; this is the larger of the two races. Minas Gerais, Brazil, October (*Nick Athanas*).

◄ This female White-wedged Piculet displays the agility for which the genus *Picumnus* is noted. Brasília, Brazil, December (*Flavio Cruvinel Brandao*).

20. RUSTY-NECKED PICULET

Picumnus fuscus

L 9–10cm

Identification Distinctive, but despite vernacular name, neck often tawny or buff rather than rusty. Throat buffy, ear-coverts browner, lower cheeks finely barred. Slight, broken pale line behind eye. Lores and nasal tufts buff. Brownish-olive above with ochre hue. Underparts warm tawny or buff, scaled or gently barred on breast, flanks with cinnamon tones. Upperwings chocolate, coverts edged paler, underwing tan. Tail chocolate, central feather-pair white, undertail-coverts paler. Iris chestnut, orbital ring greyish. Bill blackish with paler base. Legs pinkish-grey. Sexes differ slightly: male has reddish or orange streaks on top of otherwise black crown; female has plain black crown. Juveniles have browner crown and are less marked below.

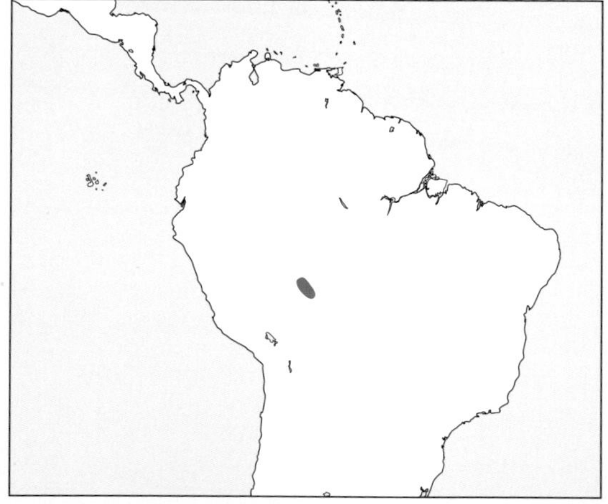

Vocalisations Strident series of clear, thin *seep* or *tssep* notes.

Drumming Probably drums but information lacking.

Status Recently downgraded from NT when found to be locally common. Nevertheless, very poorly known and range-restricted. Habitat used is probably threatened by deforestation and encroaching development.

Habitat Apparently attached to flooded lowland riparian forests (*várzea*) with an understorey of vines and bamboo.

Range South America. Range-restricted, confined to remote Amazonia in Santa Cruz and Beni departments (along Rio Guapore) in NE Bolivia, and Rondonia in extreme W Mato Grosso, SW Brazil. Resident and probably sedentary.

Taxonomy and variation Monotypic. Variation slight.

Similar species None within range.

Food and foraging Presumably small invertebrates but information lacking.

21. RUFOUS-BREASTED PICULET
Picumnus rufiventris

L 9–10cm

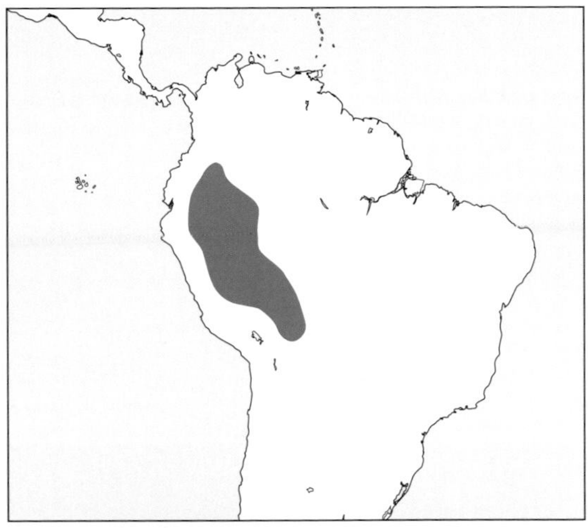

Identification Distinctive, being plain rufous below. Face rich red, ear-coverts and neck ochre or cinnamon. Variable thin white post-ocular line. Mantle, back and wings olive with rufous or cinnamon hue. Rump rufous. Wings mostly brown with grey, olive and cinnamon tones; underwing-coverts reddish. Uppertail brown, central feather pair cinnamon on outer webs. Lores and nasal tufts white, tipped black. Iris chestnut, orbital ring bluish-grey. Bill blackish, base of lower mandible paler. Legs grey. Sexes differ slightly: male has red streaks on black crown, rear and sides dotted white; female lacks red, having white-dotted crown and streaked nape. Juvenile drabber, less rufous with brown forecrown scaled buff.

Vocalisations Relatively slow, weak, lisping, high-pitched *sheep*, *seep* or *tseep* notes in series. Often just two

► Adult female Rufous-breasted Piculet of race *grandis*; this race often has yellowish tones above. Pantiacolla Lodge, Manu, Peru, September (*Glenn Bartley*).

notes uttered, but up to six. Also sharper, single, more whistling *seeep*. Rapid *tsit-tsit-tsit,* often in flight, and thin, falling *tseeyt-tseeyt-tsit*.

Drumming Regularly produces between 2–8 rapid, strong bursts of variable pitch but level speed and volume, in a stop-start series.

Status Overall population considered stable, but patchily distributed and probably declining due to deforestation in the Amazon Basin. Considered scarce in Ecuador, more common in Colombia, uncommon in Peru, but possibly overlooked.

Habitat Mainly lowland tropical riverine forests, *várzea*, humid *terra firme* and swamps, with thick undergrowth of vines, creepers and bamboo. Also in drier areas, secondary growth, clearings with scattered trees, sometimes degraded forests and around settlements.

Range South America. W Amazonia, mostly S of Equator, from E Andean slope in Colombia, Ecuador, Peru, Bolivia and Brazil, but not continuous, often localised. Sea-level to 1500m, often below 400m. Resident, presumably sedentary.

Taxonomy and variation Three races: ***rufiventris*** (E Colombia, E Ecuador, NE Peru, W Amazonian Brazil); ***grandis*** (E Peru to SW Amazonian Brazil) lighter below, yellower above and larger than nominate, males more red on crown; ***brunneifrons*** (N and C Bolivia) browner, more chestnut above and with more white markings on the crown.

Similar species Most like Tawny and Chestnut Piculets, though neither overlap in range.

Food and foraging Presumably small invertebrates but information lacking. Forages low in thickets, undergrowth and vine tangles, frequently in mixed-species foraging flocks.

▼ Adult female Rufous-breasted Piculet. Hummingbird Lodge, Peru, January (*Saturnino Llactahuaman Lastra*).

22. OCHRACEOUS PICULET
Picumnus limae

L 9–10cm

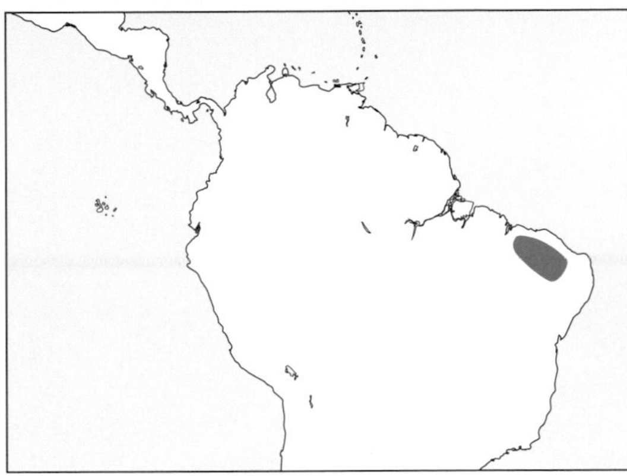

Identification Rather plain overall. Pale grey below. Throat and chest gently mottled or streaked white or buff. Tan above. Ear-coverts richer brown, malar area mottled white. Lores and nasal tufts white or buff. Broken white line behind eye, white fleck above. Malar area cream, lightly barred. Hindneck buff or rufous. Wings brown, coverts edged buff, underwing pale brown. Uppertail brown, central feather pair white. Iris chestnut, orbital ring grey. Bill grey or black. Legs grey. Sexes differ slightly: male has black crown and nape spotted and streaked red at the front, often forming patch, spotted white at the rear; female lacks red, being all dotted white. Juvenile has paler, yellowish bill.

Vocalisations Very thin, high-pitched *seeer-seeer* or *sirr-sirr-sirr*, reminiscent of some hummingbirds. A piercing, but rather musical *tee-tee-tee-titiwi*.

Drumming Simple, short bursts of level speed and pitch.

Status LC (Least Concern). One of the few picids that has had its conservation status downgraded (from VU). However, has certainly declined as vast areas of suitable forest have been lost within its range, and fragmentation is a problem. However, population now considered greater than previously thought as seems able to adapt to degraded and man-influenced habitats.

Habitat Mostly wet wooded habitats such as damp semi-deciduous forest, but also drier tall *caatinga* scrub, wooded savanna, thickets, cane-breaks and degraded and/or urban woodlands such as forest edge with introduced bamboo and abandoned orchards.

Range South America. Endemic to NE Brazil: Ibiapaba, Baturite, Aratanha, Ceara and Rio Grande do Norte. Probably more common and widespread than believed as recently found to occupy secondary habitats. Sea-level to 1000m. Resident and sedentary.

► Adult male Ochraceous Piculet, with crown feathers raised in alarm. NE Brazil, December (*Pete Morris*).

Taxonomy and variation Monotypic. Some individuals faintly barred on belly and flanks. Birds in Ceara often appear darker below.

Similar species Most like Plain-breasted Piculet but does not overlap in range. Birds with darker underparts might suggest Tawny Piculet.

Food and foraging Presumably small invertebrates but information lacking.

▼ A pair of Ochraceous Piculets. The male with the red forecrown is to the right, the female is on the left. Ceara, Brazil, November (*Andy & Gill Swash*).

23. TAWNY PICULET
Picumnus fulvescens

L 10cm

Identification Rather plain. Fulvous below, sometimes faintly streaked white on breast, heavier on belly and flanks. Throat cream or buff. Upperparts plain brown with buffy tones. Cheek and neck tawny or rusty, ear-coverts browner. Variable white moustachial streak and mottled malar area. Slight white lines or flecks above and behind eye. Lores and nasal tufts buff or white. Wings brown, coverts edges pale. Uppertail blackish, central tail feathers white. Bill bluish-grey, black at tip. Legs grey. Iris chestnut, orbital ring bluish-grey. Sexes differ slightly: male has black crown streaked red on fore and centre, sometimes forming patch, spotted white on rear; female lacks red, with black crown spotted white.

Vocalisations Rapid, high-pitched, trilling *see-see-see-sisi-wi*. Falling, hesitant series of repeated *driee* notes that trail off.

Drumming Said to drum occasionally, but exact details unavailable.

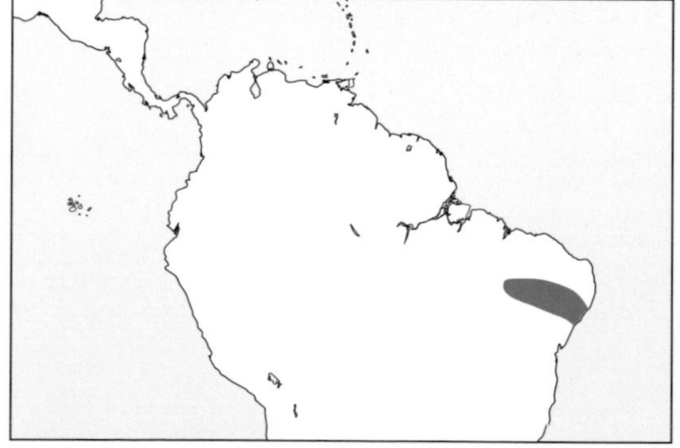

Status NT. Scarce. A range of human activities impact on its habitat including logging (particularly in Alagoas and Pernambuco), clearance for pasture, sugarcane and other plantations, wood harvesting and road building, but seems to be adaptable and probably more common and widespread than believed.

▲ Adult male Tawny Piculet. Within its range this species is largely unmistakable – no other plain brown piculets occur. Alagoas, Brazil, November (*Andy & Gill Swash*).

► Adult female. This rare Brazilan endemic continues to be threatened by the loss and degradation of wooded habitats. Pernambuco, Brazil, July (*Nick Athanas*).

Habitat Damp or dry tropical deciduous and semi-deciduous forest, particularly Atlantic rainforest. Also *caatinga*, palm groves, savanna, scrub, secondary forest and new growth.

Range South America. Endemic to NE Brazil (Piaui, Ceara, Paraiba, Bahia, Pernambuco, Alagoas and Sergipe). Mainly lowlands, but to around 1000m. Distribution not as fragmented as previously thought, as recently found in 'new' areas. Resident and probably sedentary.

Taxonomy and variation Monotypic. Formerly treated as a race of Ochraceous Piculet. Some birds very pale below. Some females heavily streaked.

Similar species Other plain brown species like Rufous-breasted, Rusty-necked and Chestnut Piculets do not overlap in range. Birds with paler underparts may suggest Ochraceous Piculet.

Food and foraging Presumably small invertebrates but information lacking.

24. MOTTLED PICULET
Picumnus nebulosus

L 10–11cm

Identification Ear-coverts, cheek, neck and nape buff or brown, forming broad collar. Crown often tufted, crested at rear. White fleck and/or spot behind eye. Malar area white, gently barred black. Throat finely barred black and white. Mantle and back plain tan with rusty hue. Chest and breast blotched rufous-brown. Belly and flanks rusty, tawny or buff, streaked and mottled black. Vent paler. Wings brownish with paler feather margins, particularly on secondaries; underwing paler. Uppertail black, central tail feathers white, outer feathers streaked white. Iris brown, orbital ring grey. Bill black with paler base. Legs greyish. Sexes alike: male streaked red on black forecrown, sometimes forming a patch, with white spots on rest of crown; female lacks red, having all crown spotted white. Juvenile similar to adult female, but crown chocolate streaked buff, throat pale and underparts less marked.

◀ Adult male Mottled Piculet. Unmistakable within its range. Tacuarembo, Brazil, March (*Santiago Carvalho*).

Vocalisations Simple, repeated *cheep* or *seep* notes, also linked into brief trilling series. A humming *tsewrewt-si-si-si* also described. Alarm a sharp, cricket-like whistling note.

Drumming Staccato, broken, irregular bursts of 2–4 strikes, repeated after short pauses. Particularly loud on bamboo.

Status NT. Uncommon. Little studied but probably declining due to destruction of its forest habitat by burning, mining, road building and conversion to farmland and plantations.

Habitat Atlantic rainforest and lowland *Araucaria* forest with dense understorey. Also riverine forest, wooded savanna, thickets, scrub, bamboo stands and cane-breaks. Recorded also in fragmented and degraded woodland patches.

Range South America. Restricted to and localised in SE Brazil (from Parana to Rio Grande do Sul), E Paraguay, NE Argentina (Misiones and Corrientes) and Uruguay. Mainly lowlands, but to 1400m. Resident and probably sedentary.

Taxonomy and variation Monotypic. Slight individual variation.

Similar species Similar relatives like Olivaceous Piculet do not overlap in range.

Food and foraging Presumably small invertebrates but information lacking. Joins mixed-species flocks, often foraging low down on twigs, vines and bamboo stalks.

▲ Adult male Mottled Piculet. The red forecrown feathers can form a patch or merely a few tips. Rio Grande do Sul, Brazil, February (*Cláudio Timm*).

◄ Adult female Mottled Piculet, with raised crown feathers creating a tufted appearance. Santa Catarina, Brazil, January (*João Quental*).

25. PLAIN-BREASTED PICULET
Picumnus castelnau

L 8–9cm

Identification Rather plain and drab. Unmarked, clean white or buff below; flanks and belly sometimes browner. Olive, brown or grey above, gently scaled or barred white with buffy tones. Wings brownish, inner flight feathers edged yellowish-green, underwing greyish-brown. Uppertail brown, central tail feathers white. Nape and hindneck finely scaled or barred olive, grey or white. Dusky ear-coverts scaled greyish. Lores buffy. Throat and lower cheeks buff or white. Pale streak above and behind eye. Iris chestnut, orbital ring pinkish-buff. Legs grey. Bill blackish, lower mandible paler at base. Sexes differ slightly: male has all-black crown speckled red or orange; female lacks red having distinctive plain black crown and less scaling on nape. Juvenile more like adult female, lacking red, but slightly barred above and below.

Vocalisations Rapid, high-pitched, weak, thin trilling *tree-e-e-e-e-e-e*. Repeated every 20–40 seconds, falling in pitch and fading in volume after first few notes.

Drumming Occasionally drums in irregular, short, staccato bursts.

Status Common on islands in Upper Amazon and its tributaries, uncommon elsewhere. Information limited but suspected to be in decline, though like many other piculets seems to be adaptable.

Habitat More open, tropical, wet lowland forests, *várzea*, riparian forest, swamps and thickets. Often in stands of young *Cecropia* and *Mimosa* trees. In some areas also secondary growth forest away from rivers and degraded forests, wooded pastures, even gardens.

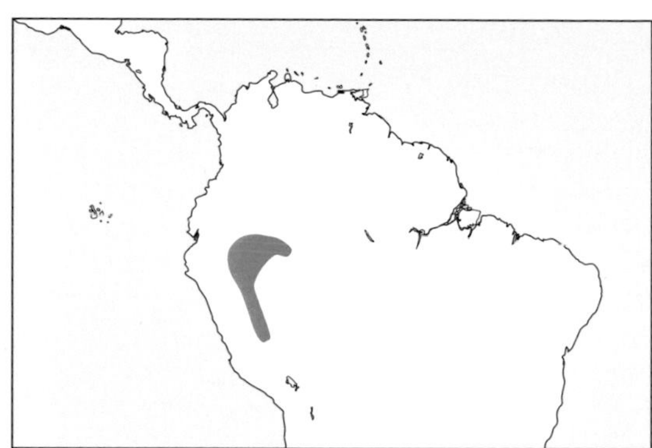

Range South America. E of the Andes, in W of the Amazon Basin, mainly along the Rio Ucayali in Peru, and W Brazil, extreme SE Colombia, possibly SE Ecuador. Rather localised. Mostly lowlands, but to around 1000m. Resident and probably sedentary.

Taxonomy and variation Monotypic. Some birds have faint moustachial line and/or faint barring on belly.

Similar species Within range rather distinct. Fine-barred Piculet (which may overlap) is yellowish below, barred grey, slightly barred above, spotted white on the nape and female has spotted crown. Bar-breasted Piculet is more olive above, yellower and very marked below. Similar Ochraceous Piculet does not overlap.

Food and foraging Presumably small invertebrates but information lacking. Usually forages inconspicuously from the canopy to mid-levels, occasionally descends to understorey. Often in mixed-species flocks.

◄◄ Adult male Plain-breasted Piculet. This is a typical individual with unmarked underparts, although some may be slightly barred. Iquitos, Peru, December (*Joe Fuhrman*).

◄ Adult female Plain-breasted Piculet lacks the reddish orange crown-spotting of the male and, unlike many other female *Picumnus*, also lacks white crown-spotting. Iquitos, Peru, December (*Joe Fuhrman*).

26. FINE-BARRED PICULET
Picumnus subtilis

L 9–10cm

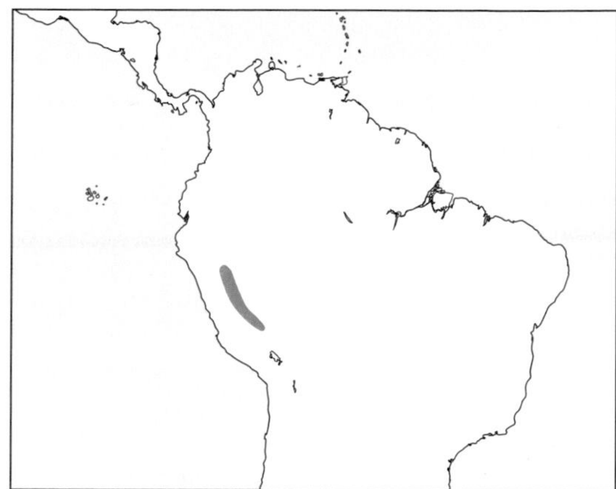

Identification White or buff below, very finely barred grey or olive on breast and flanks; belly usually plain. Chin and throat cream. Olive-green back and mantle subtly barred grey or brown. Tail brown, central feather-pair white on inner webs, outer pair with white sub-terminal patch. Black nape boldly spotted white. Ear-coverts and neck-sides gently barred olive and white. Faint buff malar barred darker. Lores and nasal tufts buffy. Brownish wings, flight feathers and coverts edged yellow or beige. Underwing tan. Iris chestnut, orbital ring grey. Legs olive-brown. Bill black, base of lower mandible bluish-grey. Sexes differ slightly: male has black crown dotted and speckled orange or red, spotted white at rear; female lacks red having black crown flecked or spotted white. Juvenile more barred below, both sexes with chocolate crown, flecked buff.
Vocalisations Series of 4–8 sharp, thin, high-pitched *see-see-see* or *seet-seet-seet* notes, usually falling, but sometimes starting slow before speeding up. Also repeated, quiet, warbling, squeaky notes.
Drumming Strong, repeated (2–6) bursts of level pitch and volume. Rather irregular, rolls often broken, slowing, ending with distinct strikes.
Status Fairly common locally in Peru. Considered stable overall, though range-restricted and poorly known.
Habitat Rainforest, damp woods, bamboo thickets, *terra firme*, riverine woods, rural gardens and parks.
Range South America. Andean foothills of SE Peru (until recently considered endemic to here) and from adjacent W Brazil: Loreto to Cusco and Madre de Dios, and along Rio Purus, Acre. Not continuous between these areas, but possibly overlooked. Lowlands and up to 1100m. Resident, probably sedentary.
Taxonomy and variation Monotypic. Variation slight.
Similar species Sympatric Bar-breasted Piculet more heavily barred on breast and striped on belly. Plain-breasted Piculet (possibly sympatric) is unbarred below, nape barred rather than spotted and female lacks crown spotting.
Food and foraging Presumably small invertebrates, but information lacking. Forages from mid-level to canopy, singly, in pairs and in mixed-species flocks.

► Adult female Fine-barred Piculet. The sexes are very similar, with the male having red or orange on the forecrown. Both images Atalaya, Peru, November (*Joel N. Rosenthal*).

27. OLIVACEOUS PICULET
Picumnus olivaceus

L 8.5–10cm

Identification Plain olive-brown with yellowish hue above. Olive or buff chest and breast, cream flanks and belly streaked olive-brown. Blackish outer tail, central feather-pair buff. Brown wings edged yellow or green, coverts edged buff. Underwing brown or grey, coverts paler. Cheeks, ear-coverts, throat and neck cinnamon or buff, scaled dusky-brown. Iris brown, orbital ring bluish-grey. White flecks around eye. Lores pale. Bill grey or black. Legs bluish-grey or olive. Sexes alike: both with chocolate crown and nape finely dotted white, but male has forecrown flecked red, ochre or gold (depending on race), which female lacks. Juvenile like female but browner, heavier marked below and lacks white on crown.

Vocalisations Simple, fast, high-pitched, falling trilling and twittering. Shrill versions recall Yellow-faced Grassquit. Single or double, sharp, chirping *ssip, tip, seet, seep* or *peep* notes.

Drumming May not drum, or perhaps only rarely, but information lacking.

Status Often common locally. Population data scant, but considered stable.

▼ Adult male Olivaceous Piculet, probably of race *dimotus*: there is much variation in crown colour in this species. Cano Negro, Costa Rica, October (*Dave Hawkins*).

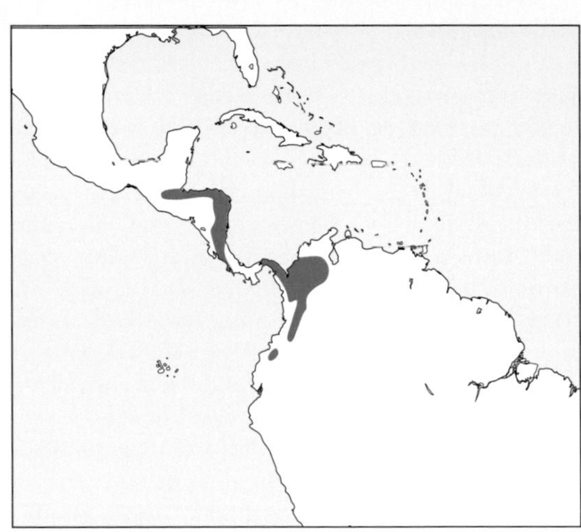

Habitat Rainforest, cloud-forest, damp deciduous forest and thickets. Also more open shrub woodland, wooded savanna and pastures, plantations, even gardens, with vines and creepers.

Range C and NW South America. Northernmost piculet in the Americas. From Guatemala to NW Peru, but discontinuous, occurring in three main areas: Caribbean slope in E Guatemala, Honduras, Nicaragua and N Costa Rica; S Costa Rica into Panama, Colombia and NW Venezuela; Ecuador and NW Peru. In Venezuela *eisenmanni* and *tachirensis* are montane species (700–2500m), whereas W Ecuadorian *harterti* occurs in lowlands and foothills. Resident and sedentary.

Taxonomy and variation Seven races, subtly different in colour: ***olivaceus*** (Colombia: W Andes) male is reddish on forecrown; ***dimotus*** (E Guatemala, N Honduras, E Nicaragua) palest below, male forecrown yellow, red or ochre; ***flavotinctus*** (Costa Rica, Panama, extreme NW Colombia: N Chocó) is olivaceous, male forecrown yellow; ***malleolus*** (N Colombia) also olivaceous, male forecrown usually yellowish; ***eisenmanni*** (NW Venezuela, adjacent Colombia) most yellow, male forecrown yellow or ochre; ***tachirensis*** (Colombia: E Andes, adjacent SW Venezuela) darkest green above, most marked below, male forecrown yellow or ochre; ***harterti*** (SW Colombia, W Ecuador, extreme NW Peru) is small, dark above with chestnut ear-coverts, male fore-crown variably yellow, gold or orange.

Similar species Greyish Piculet lacks yellow tones above and is paler below. Other similar piculets do not overlap in range. Beware xenops species.

Food and foraging Arboreal ants and termites, beetles and other invertebrates in all stages. Often in family parties and mixed-species flocks. Though not shy, usually forages inconspicuously in low tangled vegetation, gleaning and extracting prey from timber.

▲ Adult male *harterti*: note the golden-orange forecrown. This indiviudal is particularly plain below. Buenaventura, Ecuador, August (*Wim de Groot*).

▲► Adult female *flavotinctus*. Crown colour varies in males, but females of all races show only white spotting. Costa Rica, April (*Noel Ureña*).

► A family of *flavotinctus* Olivaceous Piculets, around the nesthole in a snag. Costa Rica, April (*Noel Ureña*).

28. GREYISH PICULET
Picumnus granadensis

L 9–10cm

Identification Relatively unmarked. Greyish or white underparts finely streaked grey or brown. Flanks smudged brown. Olive, brown or grey above. Lores white. Cheek, malar area and throat cream with dark spotting. Dusky or rusty ear-coverts (but variable, minimal on some birds, missing on others) with some fine white streaks. Grey-brown neck sides also finely spotted or flecked white. Grey-brown wings edged buff/yellow on coverts. Uppertail brownish; central feather-pair white, outer pairs blackish. Underwing greyish-brown. Iris brown, orbital ring bluish-grey. Bill black. Legs greyish. Sexes alike: male has black crown finely spotted yellow and white; female crown lacks yellow. Juvenile darker, smudged and streaked grey below.

Vocalisations Utters a quiet, weak, thin, high but level-pitched trilling of variable speed that trails off at the end.

Drumming Presumably drums, but information lacking.

Status Uncommon, range-restricted and poorly known. Not considered threatened, but probably affected by deforestation.

Habitat Rainforest edges and drier open deciduous forest. Also wooded savanna, thickets, scrub, secondary growth with vines and creepers, sometimes damper, humid forests. In the Cauca Valley found in remnant dry forest patches and hedges between pastures.

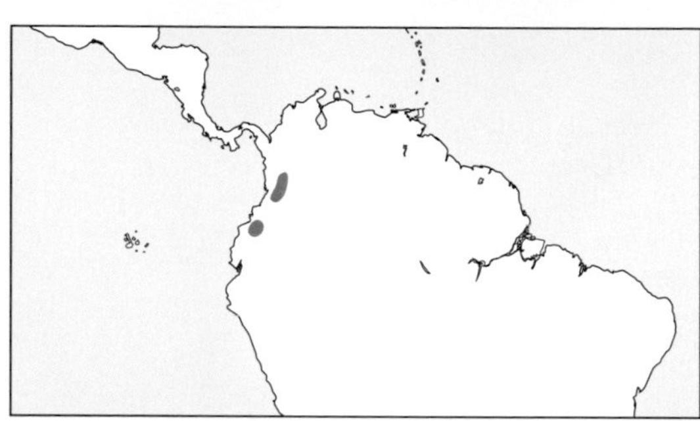

Range South America. Endemic to interior slopes in W and C Andean forests in Colombia. Mainly in Cauca River Valley, as far N as S Antioquia, S to Narino in Patia River Valley. Usually between 800–2200m. Resident and sedentary, though may be occupying new areas as displaced from original habitat by logging.

Taxonomy and variation Two races: ***granadensis*** (W Colombia) is plain white below; ***antioquensis*** (NW Andean Colombia) more streaked on belly and flanks, greyer above.

Similar species Differs from Olivaceous Piculet in whitish underparts and greyer, less olive, upperparts – but unclear if, and where, these species meet.

Food and foraging Presumably invertebrates but information lacking.

◄◄ Adult male Greyish Piculet, nominate race. Some males show hardly any yellow on the forecrown and good views are often needed to sex birds in the field. Laguna de Sonso, Colombia, December (*Pete Morris*).

◄ Adult female nominate; this race is plainer below than *antioquensis*. Manazales, Colombia, January (*Adam Riley*).

29. CHESTNUT PICULET
Picumnus cinnamomeus

L 9–10cm

Identification Distinctive. Overall rufous, chestnut or cinnamon (depending on race). Upperwings and tail chocolate with paler edges; underwing cream or grey. Central tail feathers buff. Forehead and lores buff, yellow or cinnamon. Bill black. Iris chestnut, orbital ring buff or grey. Legs grey to pinkish. Sexes differ slightly: male has gold or yellow streaks on black crown, white spots on nape; female has mid-crown to nape spotted boldly white. Juvenile plumage not adequately known.

Vocalisations Rather silent, but does utter weak, high, thin notes, often three in quick succession. Song a rapid, falling trilling series of *tititititi* notes recalling Scaled Piculet but more like Crested Spinetail. Also more chirping, warbling notes in series.

Drumming Typically, several rattling, rapid, level-pitched 1–2-second rolls strung together with short breaks between. Not hesitant like Scaled Piculet.

Status Uncommon in Venezuela, more common in Colombia. Population numbers and trends unknown.

Habitat Mainly dry tropical forests, but also mangroves, more open forest, lowland thorny scrub, wooded grasslands, even coffee plantations.

Range South America. Confined to extreme N of continent in NE Colombia and NW Venezuela. Sea-level to about 300m. Resident and sedentary.

Taxonomy and variation Four races, differing mainly in forehead and body colour: ***cinnamomeus*** (coastal N Colombia: S to Cauca and Magdalena valleys) palest, cinnamon not rufous, yellow forehead runs onto crown; ***persaturatus*** (Bolivar, NC Colombia) darkest, chestnut overall, wings edged buff, female spotted white on most of crown; ***perijanus*** (NW Venezuela: N shore of Lake Maracaibo) brownish, forecrown buff, crown heavily streaked buff or yellow, female crown very spotted; ***venezuelensis*** (W Venezuela: S and E shores of Lake Maracaibo) is chestnut, forehead cinnamon or pinkish, male has fine white streaks on nape, female's nape plain black.

Similar species None. Unmistakable.

Food and foraging Insectivorous. Forages alone, in family parties and in mixed-species flocks, in tangles of vines and other vegetation at all levels.

► Adult male Chestnut Piculet. Within its small range, this species cannot be mistaken for any other piculet. La Guajira, Colombia, March (*Pete Morris*).

►► Adult female Chestnut Piculet lacks yellow on the crown. La Guajira, Colombia, March (*Pete Morris*).

White-browed Piculet *Sasia ochracea*, adult female at the nest hole. Thailand (*Boonchuay Promjiam*).

SASIA

Three Old World species, one in Africa, two in Asia. Though geographically separated, these tiny species are similar in many aspects of behaviour and share some distinct morphological features such as an obvious orbital ring of flesh and a round cross-section of the upper mandible. Yet, some unusual morphological differences also exist: the two Asian species have 10 tail feathers and three toes, lacking the first toe, while the African has eight tail feathers and four toes, with the first digit thin and reduced. Taxonomical relationships with the *Picumnus* species remain unclear.

30. AFRICAN PICULET
Sasia africana

L 9cm

Identification Appears top-heavy and tailless. Green-olive above, tinged yellow on back. Dusky from throat to vent, belly often paler. Face greyish, ear-coverts darker, slightly streaked. Lores blackish. Thin white brow line, behind and above rear of eye. Slight horizontal fleck (white above, black underneath) below ear-coverts. Iris red, prominent orbital ring pink, red or purple. Short, rounded chocolate tail feathers edged olive. Upperwing dark green, fringed yellow, primaries browner, underwing whiter. Black bill, lower mandible paler. Legs reddish or purple. Sexes differ slightly: male has chestnut, red or orange forehead and forecrown, slightly larger female lacks this. Juvenile most like female, but with duller red legs and orbital ring, brown iris, rusty-brown feather-tips on ear-coverts and throat, greyer breast, belly and flanks with grey and buff tones above.

Vocalisations Rapid but often weak, high-pitched, piercing, tinkling, trilling: *ti-ti-ti-t-ti* and *tsiririririr*. Likened to sounds made by some bats and insects, even to breaking glass.

Drumming Taps when foraging, but does not seem to drum.

Status Data sparse but overall considered stable, though has probably declined in some areas.

Habitat Lowland, tropical, damp and wetter primary, secondary and gallery forests. Forages in tangled, dense undergrowth, even grass-layer.

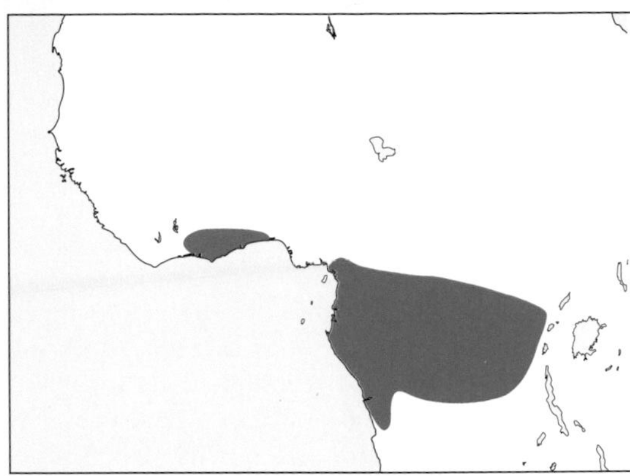

Range Africa. Mainly in western equatorial countries, including Liberia, Ivory Coast, Ghana, Cameroon, Equatorial Guinea, Central African Republic, Congo, Gabon and W Uganda (Bwamba/Semliki Valley). Also NW Angola and isolated populations perhaps elsewhere. Sea-level to 1000m. Resident, possibly dispersive.

Taxonomy and variation Monotypic. Formerly placed in monospecific genus *Verreauxia*. Variation slight.

Similar species None. Only piculet in Africa.

Food and foraging Mostly small arboreal insect larvae, especially wood-boring beetles. Bores into twigs and splits stems to extract prey. Two or three birds often forage together, usually low down.

► Adult male African Piculets have coloured foreheads; this one is orange. Sanaga River, Cameroon, March (*Lars Petersson*).

►► Adult female lacks the bright colour on the forehead. Sanaga River, Cameroon, March (*Lars Petersson*).

31. RUFOUS PICULET

Sasia abnormis

L 9cm

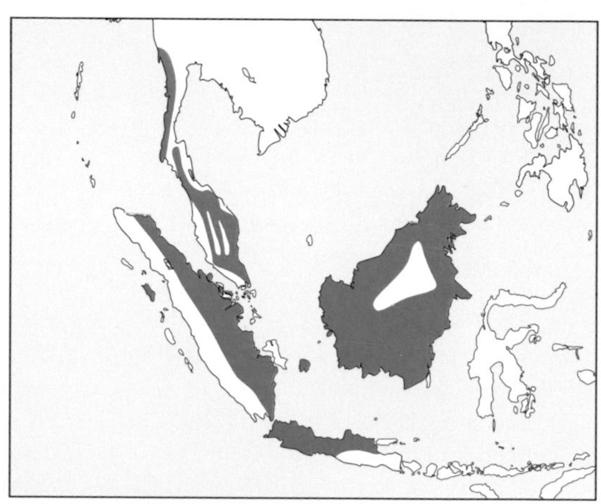

Identification Brightly coloured. Short-winged and appears tailless. Mostly green above with bronze tones. Rufous, orange or cinnamon below, breast sometimes washed golden. Forehead and forecrown mustard-yellow; nape, mantle and back olive with yellowish tones. Rump rufous. Face and neck-sides orange or rufous, ear-coverts duskier. Underparts plain orange to rufous; flanks paler, yellowish. Black uppertail edged olive. Primaries brownish with rufous inner-webs, darker outer webs; coverts olive-brown; secondaries and tertials edged yellowish. Underwing buff with some cinnamon on primaries. Upper mandible blackish, lower distinctive lemon-yellow. Iris reddish. Distinctive pink or purple orbital ring. Legs orange to mustard. Sexes differ slightly: male has gold or yellow

◄ Adult male Rufous Piculet has brighter gold or yellow on the forehead than the female. Sabah, Borneo, Malaysia, August (*Doug Wechsler*).

forehead flecked reddish; female's orange or chestnut. Female also has slightly larger bill, longer wings and tail. Juvenile duller: grey or olive head and mantle, greyish-brown below, brown iris, grey orbital ring, black bill, yellowish legs.

Vocalisations Often vocal. Fast, loud, persistent, high-pitched, yapping *kih-kih-kih* or *kik-ik-ik-ik*. Various single or repeated chips and squeaks: *szit, tsit, tick, tsik, pik*. Alarm call a series of slower but sharp *kip, kep* or *chip* notes.

Drumming Rapid, 1–1.5-second rattling volley of clearly spaced strikes. Starts fast, slows, ends in double strikes. Impressively loud, especially when drumming bamboo.

Status Common locally. Presumed stable. Has declined in some areas, such as the Sundas, due to heavy logging.

Habitat Variety of dense, damp, swampy, secondary-growth forests and thickets, with dead and rotting timber, tangles of vines, creepers, shrubs, saplings, rattan and bamboo. Often by streams. Not typically in primary forest.

Range SE Asia. From S Burma (Myanmar) through Thai-Malay Peninsula to the Greater Sundas. Mostly lowlands and hill country, but up to around 1600m in Borneo. Resident and sedentary.

Taxonomy and variation Two races: ***abnormis*** (most of range from the Thai-Malay Peninsula, to Sumatra, Borneo, Java, Bali and other islands); and ***magnirostris*** (Nias Island, off W Sumatra), which is heavier and longer-billed than nominate.

Similar species Differs from White-browed Piculet (range overlaps in N. of range) in yellow lower mandible, rufous above eye, lack of post-ocular stripe and darker rufous below.

Food and foraging Ants, termites, small beetles, spiders. Usually solitary, often restless, but sometimes in loose parties of up to six birds and in mixed-species flocks. Forages in bamboo, tangled vegetation and understorey by gleaning and boring holes.

▼ Adult female; note the orange forehead, rather than the gold or yellow of the male. Sepilok Forest Reserve, Borneo, Malaysia (*Chien Lee*).

32. WHITE-BROWED PICULET
Sasia ochracea

L 9–10cm

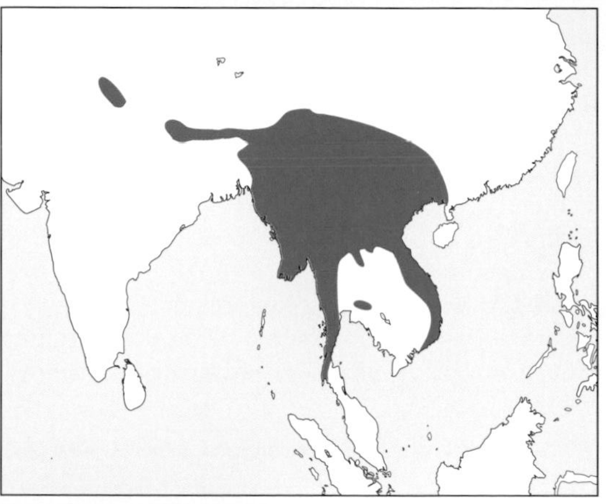

Other name Confusingly sometimes called Rufous Piculet (see *Sasia abnormis*).

Identification Appears tailless. Olive-green above with reddish or chestnut tinge. Rufous or cinnamon below, sometimes yellowish on flanks. Upperwing olive-brown; coverts tipped yellow; primaries edged buff; underwing grey or cream. Crown olive-green with rufous tones. White post-ocular mark (hence 'white-browed'), sometimes slight and indistinct. Lores rufous. Ear-coverts dusky-green. Striking red or pink orbital ring; iris red. Bill greyish. Legs orange or yellow; three-toed. Sexes differ slightly: male has small golden, orange or yellow forehead patch; female lacks this and orbital ring paler. Juveniles like respective adults but duller, greener above, greyish-green below.

◄ Adult male White-browed Piculet. Males have a dash of yellow within the russet forehead patch. This is the nominate. Thailand, March (*Chris Li*).

Vocalisations Speedy, high-pitched, nasal, trilling *chi-rrrrrrrrr* or *ti-iiiiiiii* that drops in pitch and tails off as it ends. A brief, single, shrill *chi, chik* or *tsik* and an inflected *chuick*.

Drumming Loud, rattling, rolls of 2–3 seconds each that start rapidly before fading and ending in 2–3 distinct strikes. Usually drums on bamboo, which produces a loud, tinny sound.

Status Occurs over large area and considered stable, but has declined locally due to loss of bamboo and other forests.

Habitat Understorey of damp or dry deciduous or mixed forests, jungle, thickets and scrub, particularly with vines and bamboo. Also woodlands near wetlands and disturbed forest.

Range SE Asia. From India through Nepal, Bangladesh, Bhutan, S China, Burma (Myanmar), Indochina and Thailand. From 250–2600m. Resident and sedentary.

Taxonomy and variation Three races: ***ochracea*** (Uttar Pradesh, N India, C Nepal to Thailand and Vietnam) has dark green crown and is deep rufous below; ***kinneari*** (S China, extreme N Vietnam) is darkest race; ***reichenowi*** (S Burma (Myanmar) into SW Thailand and Kra Isthmus) paler, more rufous above, orbital ring darker.

Similar species Differs from Rufous Piculet (overlaps in parts of Burma (Myanmar) and Thailand) in having white post-ocular mark, greyish lower bill and green crown extending lower to the eye. Also usually more rufous than Rufous with some reddish tips on the mantle and back.

Food and foraging Ants, small spiders, small bark beetles and other invertebrates in all stages. Often forages in pairs and mixed-species flocks, sometimes descending to the forest floor, even hopping with its tail cocked.

▼ Adult female White-browed Piculet. Note the greyish orbital ring and orange forecrown (*Boonchuay Promjiam*).

Male Antillean Piculet *Nesoctites micromegas*. Dominican Republic (*Dax Roman*).

NESOCTITES

A monospecific genus. The taxonomy of Antillean Piculet and its relationships with other picids remains unclear. Despite the name, anatomical studies suggest it is more closely related to true woodpeckers (Picinae) than to piculets (*Picumnus* or *Sasia*) and it is sometimes considered to be a link between the two. Often shy, skulking in dense understorey or tangles of vines, it usually first betrays its presence vocally. This species does not excavate cavities, but uses natural holes or the old holes of Hispaniolan Woodpecker.

33. ANTILLEAN PICULET
Nesoctites micromegas

L 14–16cm

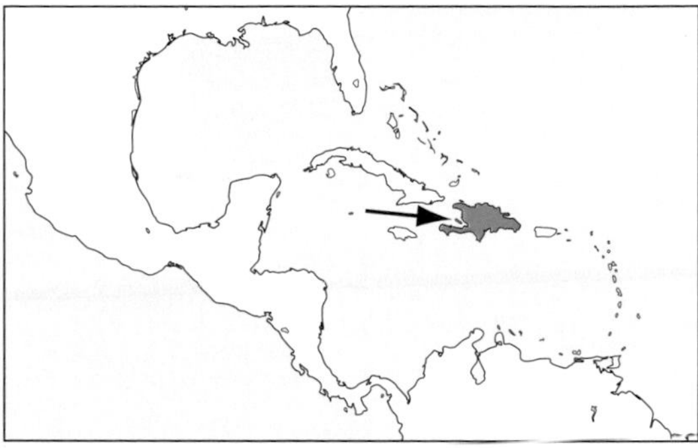

Identification Large and stocky for a 'piculet'. Olive-green above with bronze tones and some pale spots on the mantle. Wings green with paler feather tips and edges, primaries edged brownish, underwing paler. Buff or yellow below with variable dark flecks and streaks. Throat white, tinged yellow, usually with dark barring. Malar area lightly marked grey. Lores and nasal tufts buffy. Pale ear-coverts streaked olive. Neck-sides grey or olive, dotted white. Tail greenish with brownish tones. Bill blackish. Iris chestnut, orbital ring grey. Legs greyish-green. Sexes differ slightly: both sexes have yellow crowns, but male has bright orange or red patch on mid- to hind crown. Females larger and longer-billed than males. Juvenile duller green above, with duller yellow crown, males show some red, and barred rather than streaked below. Flies in a direct, non-bounding, manner.

Vocalisations Both sexes make a fast, loud, staccato *kuk-ki-ki-ki-ke-ku-kuk*. Also trilling, sometimes quite musical, *tu-tu-lu-feo* stressed on last squeaky syllable. Chattering *yeh-yeh-yeh* and weaker *wiii* notes in territorial confrontations. Single *pit* alarm note.

Drumming Probably does not drum.

Status Despite this classification, range-restricted, generally uncommon and declining. In Haiti threatened by deforestation, in the Dominican Republic less so as habitat destruction less drastic. Said to be common on Gonave Island but situation uncertain.

Habitat Mainly dry forests, but also moist tropical forests, pine forests, thorn and desert scrub, secondary

◄ Adult male Antillean Piculet. Males have red or orange on the mid-crown. La Vega, Dominican Republic, April (*Dax Roman*).

growth and wooded farmland; sometimes orchards, plantations and mangroves.

Range Endemic to Hispaniola. Sea-level to around 1800m, but mainly between 400–800m. Resident and sedentary.

Taxonomy and variation Two races: ***micromegas*** (Hispaniola: Haiti and Dominican Republic); and ***abbotti*** (Ile de la Gonave: off W Haiti) which is paler, greyer above, throat unbarred and less yellow on crown.

Similar species None. Unmistakable.

Food and foraging Omnivorous, foraging for ants, beetles, other insects and fruit. Often in pairs, gleaning prey in understorey and tangled mid-level vegetation and probing flowers, leaf-clusters and fruits rather than hacking into wood.

► The adult female lacks colour on the mid-crown. On average females are bigger than males. La Vega, Dominican Republic, July (*Dax Roman*).

▼Juvenile male Antillean Piculet. Young males show some red on the crown. La Vega, Dominican Republic, July (*Dax Roman*).

HEMICIRCUS

An Old World genus of two species, one occurring mainly in the Sundaic region of SE Asia, the other from India to Indochina. The overall taxonomic position of the *Hemicircus* within the Picidae is unresolved, but features such as a very short, rounded tail with relatively soft feathers suggest an intermediate position between the piculets and the true woodpeckers. Both species are dainty, agile, foraging by gleaning rather than boring and often in mixed-species flocks. A secretion on the back of these species, the precise purpose of which is unclear, can discolour their white rumps. Grey-and-buff Woodpecker roosts communally, specifically excavating clusters of shallow cavities in dead trees for this purpose.

Heart-spotted Woodpecker *Hemicircus canente*, adult male. Karnataka, India, March (*Ram Mallya*).

34. GREY-AND-BUFF WOODPECKER
Hemicircus concretus

L 13–14cm

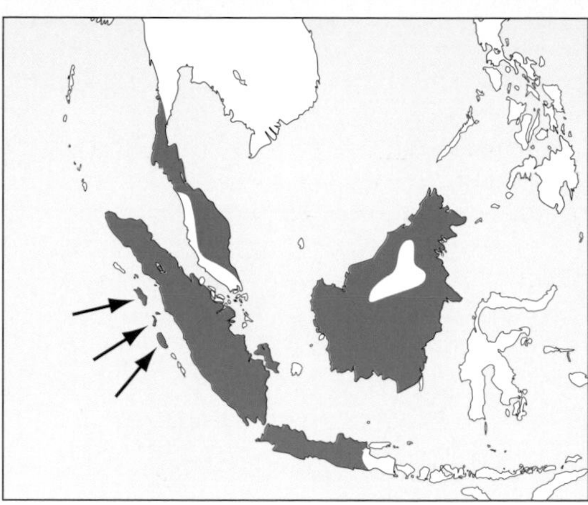

Identification Smaller of the two *Hemicircus*. Compact, rotund body with a short, rounded tail. Appears large headed due to thin neck and coned crest. Most of head plain grey with thin, wavy white line from malar onto neck and mantle. Nape white/cream. Plain grey below, sometimes faintly barred pale on flanks and undertail-coverts. Black above, feathers boldly edged and scaled buff or white. Black uppertail-coverts tipped white or cream. Rump also white or cream. Black flight feathers edged pale, secondaries subtly barred white. Black tertials edged whitish, sometimes more white than black, creating scales. Underwing dark, coverts barred white, buff at base of primaries. Relatively long, grey bill tipped black. Iris chestnut. Legs grey or brown. Sexes differ: male has red forehead, crown and crest (extent

▼ Adult male Grey-and-buff Woodpecker. Males of this race, *sordidus*, the more widespread of the two, have red on the crown but not on the crest. Johor, Malaysia, July (*Yap Kah Hue*).

depends on race); female lacks red (some rufous tips may show). Juvenile more marked, with large rufous or cinnamon feather edges above, buff barring or scaling below. Juvenile male cinnamon or orange on crown and crest; juvenile female usually buff, occasionally with some rufous.

Vocalisations Quite loud, sharp, sometimes squeaky, high-pitched, single *chik, tsip* or *pit* notes, made in flight or when perched. Double *ki-oo, ki-yow* or *kee-yew* notes during crest-raising display. Song a rapid trilling series of *tee-tee-ti* notes. Also rattling *ki-ki-ki* notes, whirring *chitter* during disputes and nervous chattering alarm.

Drumming Infrequent, feeble rolls produced.

Status Locally common, but declining in some regions due to deforestation. Extirpated from Singapore.

Habitat Edges, clearings and open evergreen rainforest, in some regions bamboo. Also plantations, wooded semi-urban or cultivated areas.

Range SE Asia. From Thai-Malay Peninsula, Indonesia and the Sundas. From lowlands to mid-elevations. Resident and sedentary.

Taxonomy and variation Two fairly distinct races. Male ***concretus*** (W and C Java) has all-red crest; ***sordidus*** (extreme S Burma (Myanmar), Thai-Malay Peninsula, Sumatra and nearby islands, Borneo) smaller, lighter grey, whiter on nape, male red only on crown with front of crest, tip and rear grey, juvenile with buffy crest and less marked above than nominate juvenile.

Similar species None. Some calls like Heart-spotted and Buff-rumped Woodpeckers.

Food and foraging Omnivorous, taking invertebrates and much fruit. Agile, often foraging in the canopy in groups and mixed-species flocks.

▼ Adult female *sordidus*. Note the grey crown and crest, lacking the red of the male. Johor, Malaysia, July (*Yap Kah Hue*).

35. HEART-SPOTTED WOODPECKER
Hemicircus canente

L 15–16cm

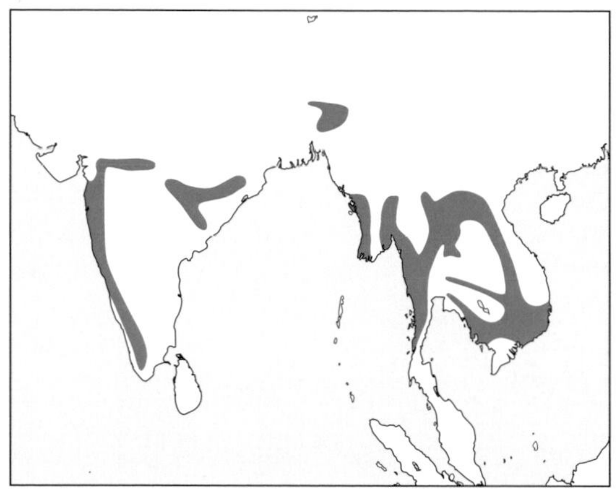

Identification Often described as 'toy-like', a term that aptly captures its jizz. Looks rotund and top-heavy due to prominent shaggy crest, slender neck and short rounded tail. When perched, tail largely obscured by folded wings so bird looks tailless. Pied, with white tertials, some coverts and scapulars marked with black heart-shapes (heart-spotted). Cream or white throat, collar and chest. Rest of underparts greyish. Undertail-coverts black, sometimes lightly barred pale. Black mantle, back and uppertail, sometimes slight barred white. Whitish rump and wing-linings obvious in flight. Relatively long, broad-based dark bill. Iris chestnut. Legs brownish with green hue. Sexes differ slightly: male has dark forehead and forecrown, speckled white; female's is plain cream or white. Crest black on both sexes. Juvenile most like adult female but with dark markings in white forecrown, pale edges in mantle feathers, darker below, white areas more buff.

Vocalisations Range of soft or harsh, fast or slow, nasal and squeaky notes. Pairs duet by the nest with fast, loud, sharp *twee* notes, repeated for up to a minute. Repeated, mewing, whining, inflected *ki-yew* or *ch-yew* alarm, recalling Ashy Drongo or small hawk. Drawn-out, grating *chur-r*. *Su-sie* during displays. Rasping, repeated *chirrick, kirrrick* or *karrick,* sometimes in fast series of three notes, *kirrrick-kirrrick-kirrrick*.

Drumming Rarely drums, making weak, quiet rolls.

Status Locally common or scarce. Overall population size and trends unknown. Probably extirpated from Bangladesh.

Habitat Humid, tropical deciduous and evergreen forest and jungle, often with teak and bamboo. Usually in open areas and at edges. Also lusher coffee plantations.

◄ Adult male Heart-spotted Woodpecker has a black forehead with the forecrown lightly speckled white. Thattakad, Kerala, India (*John Holmes*).

Range SE Asia. Occurs over large area, but thinly distributed. From W and NE India and possibly Bangladesh, through Burma (Myanmar) to Thailand and Indochina. Resident and sedentary. Mainly lowlands but to 1300m.

Taxonomy and variation Monotypic. Some slight clinal differences in size and individual variation in plumage. Males in W India may have smaller white spots on forecrown than those further east.

Similar species Most like sympatric Black-and-buff Woodpecker, but that species larger, finely barred pale on head, with white nape and dark throat, male with red malar, female dark on forecrown.

Food and foraging Termites, ants and various insect larvae. Typically active, foraging in pairs and mixed-species flocks, using varied techniques – gleaning, probing and pecking – to reach prey.

▲ A male Heart-spotted Woodpecker in a typical pose, perched sideways across a twig. Khao Yai NP, Thailand (*Ingo Waschkies*).

▲► Juvenile Heart-spotted Woodpecker. The forehead and forecrown are heavily speckled black and white. Karnataka, India, March (*Ram Mallya*).

► Adult female Heart-spotted Woodpecker has an unmarked white forehead and forecrown. Agumbe, Karnataka, India, October (*Shivashankar*).

MELANERPES

A New World genus with 24 small to medium species, *Melanerpes* includes some of the most colourful, conspicuous and vocal woodpeckers on the planet. Several are endemic to Caribbean islands, such as Guadeloupe, Puerto Rico, Jamaica and Hispaniola. Some, such as Acorn and Yellow-tufted Woodpeckers, are highly social, being cooperative breeders with complex clan-based breeding systems involving nest-helpers. Red-crowned and Hoffmann's Woodpeckers sometimes back into roost holes rather than entering head-first, a rare trait in woodpeckers. All have a non-bounding flight, with jay-like, rowing wing-beat actions. Many have very similar calls which can be hard to distinguish, but the different species vary in behaviour, morphology and plumage. Relatively little is known about the ecology of those occurring outside North America.

Yellow-fronted Woodpecker *Melanerpes flavifrons*, adult male. São Paulo, Brazil, August (*Wim de Groot*).

36. WHITE WOODPECKER
Melanerpes candidus

L 24–27cm

Identification Distinctive. Groups often flying over open country in processional lines of 5–10, with distinctly floppy wing-beats. Mostly black and white. Head, face, underparts and rump white, sometimes with buffy tones. Upperparts, wings and tail black. Wings mostly glossy black; flight feathers browner, underwing greyer. Tail mostly black with white upper-tail-coverts. Black stripe runs from eye to the nape and mantle. Thick yellow orbital ring forms striking 'goggles' around pale iris. Lores dusky. Long greyish bill, paler at base. Legs greyish. Sexes differ slightly: both have variable yellow belly-patch, but male also has yellow on breast and nape. Juvenile browner, with less glossy black, white areas more buff, yellow areas paler, orbital ring greyer and less distinct. On juvenile male yellow spreads onto the nape; female may also show some yellow on nape.

Vocalisations Very vocal. Groups are noisy, keeping in contact with chattering *kirr-kirr-kirr* or *cree-cree-cree-creek* calls, usually made in flight, recalling some *Sterna* terns. Loud, chirping, rolling or harsh, throaty *wheerrr-keerrr* notes. Also a loud slurred *ghirreh* or *kreer.*

Drumming May not drum, or perhaps only rarely, but information lacking.

Status Widespread and increasing as rather adaptable, occurring in urban areas, even cities like São Paulo, foraging in fruit plantations and tolerant to forest fragmentation.

Habitat Open dry tropical woodlands, forest edges and wooded savanna. Also wooded scrub, palm and orange groves, orchards, woodlots, mangroves, suburban areas with scattered large trees and plantations (including introduced species like eucalyptus and poplar).

Range South America. E of the Andes from Surinam, French Guiana, Brazil, SE Peru, Bolivia, Paraguay, Uruguay and N Argentina. Rather discontinuous within this vast area, but expanding range over logged areas of the Atlantic Forest. From sea-level to around

◄ Adult male White Woodpecker. The males have a variable amount of yellow on the nape and underparts. Brazil, June (*Jean Mayet*).

2000m. Resident but prone to wandering.
Taxonomy and variation Monotypic. Variation slight. Previously placed in genus *Leuconerpes*.
Similar species None: unmistakable.
Food and foraging Besides arboreal insects, occasionally sallies for prey and takes honey, much fruit, berries and seeds; it is a significant disperser of the last. Forages in noisy family parties.

► Adult female. Note the clean white underparts, although some individuals may exhibit a yellow flush on the belly. Itirapina, Brazil, June (*José Carlos Motta Junior*).

▼White Woodpecker in flight: note the deep wing-beat typical of the genus. Northern Argentina, October (*Ramón Moller Jensen*).

37. LEWIS'S WOODPECKER
Melanerpes lewis

L 26–29cm

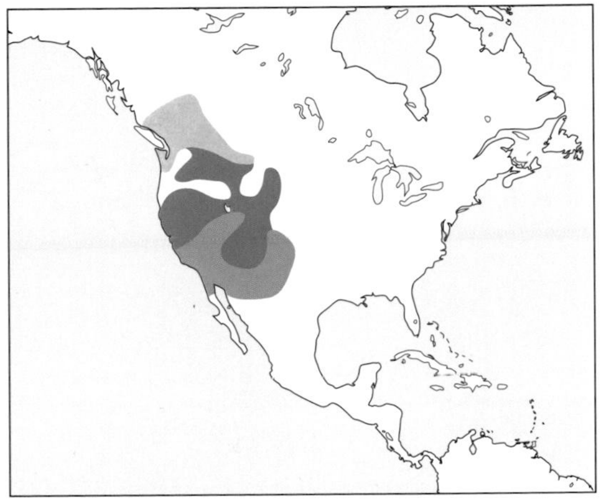

Identification Distinctive. Bulky, long-tailed, long-winged. Flight straight, flapping, corvid-like and flying birds looks all-dark. Crown, most of head and upperparts glossy bottle-green. Crimson lores, cheek and ocular area. Silver-grey nape, neck and chest form broad collar. Breast, belly and flanks salmon-pink, tinged silver. Wings and uppertail dark green, undertail darker. Some white occasionally on outer tail. Long grey-black bill. Iris chestnut. Legs bluish-grey. Sexes alike. Juvenile duller, less glossy, lacking red face and grey collar, minimal pink on often barred belly.

Vocalisations Rather silent. Male territorial song a short, rapidly repeated, series of 3–8 rough, muffled but harsh *churr* notes. Contact calls weak, sneeze-like *teef* and *kitsif*. Also a high-pitched, falling *rik-rik-rik,* and

► Adult Lewis's Woodpecker. This stunning species is one of the few woodpeckers that does not exhibit sexual dimorphism in plumage. Montana, United States, June (*Tom Reichner*).

dry, squeaky rattle and chatter, recalling European Starling. Male's alarm a single, soft, squeaking *yick*; female's is a two-syllable *yick-ik*.

Drumming Male's drum usually interspersed with *churr* calls. Relatively weak, subdued, medium-speed rolls, often ending with separated single knocks. Rarely drums outside breeding period. Females probably do not drum.

Status Uncommon in many areas because of habitat loss to farming, urbanisation and forestry management – particularly fire control and pesticide use. Despite local declines and overall steady decrease (since 1960s), not considered threatened.

Habitat Dry and damp, open deciduous temperate woodlands. Also riparian cottonwood stands. Post-burn pinewoods often important for breeding. In winter visits oak woods, nut-groves, plantations and orchards. Sea-level to 2800m.

Range North America. Breeding SW Canada and USA along western edge of Great Plains to New Mexico and Arizona, mirroring Ponderosa pine distribution. Some populations resident, others disperse according to food availability. Northernmost birds migratory; they gather in passage flocks, vacating breeding areas in late August and September, wintering in SW USA and NW Mexico and returning April and May.

Taxonomy and variation Monotypic. Variation slight.

Similar species Unmistakable. Migrant flocks suggest Pinyon Jays or crows rather than other woodpeckers.

Food and foraging An expert flycatcher. Patiently perches on snags and fence posts from where graceful sallies and glides are performed to take emerging adult insects. In winter turns to fruit, nuts and acorns, shelling hard items at anvils and storing them in crevices in tree-bark. Feisty disputes with Acorn and Red-headed Woodpeckers over such caches common. Also forages on the ground.

◄ Lewis's Woodpeckers are known to have suffered from habitat loss and degradation in many areas, and their conservation status warrants review. Okanagan Valley, British Columbia, Canada, June (*Glenn Bartley*).

38. GUADELOUPE WOODPECKER
Melanerpes herminieri

L 26–28cm

Identification Appears almost entirely glossy black, though actually subtly coloured with bluish hue above. Rufous or burgundy wash from throat to breast, yellow or orange on belly, sooty with brownish tones on flanks, vent, flight feathers and tail. None of these areas well-demarcated, colours merging. Iris chestnut. Legs bluish-grey. Long, narrow, dark bill. Sexes alike: the only island *Melanerpes* that does not exhibit sexual colour dimorphism. Main differences are in calls and bill size. Male's bill up to 20% longer than female's, longer than head width; female's bill and head equal in length. Juvenile like adult but less glossy, breast rusty-brown. Some juveniles show reddish crown feather tips and greyish iris.

Vocalisations Main *kwa* call uttered all year by both sexes, but pitched lower by male. Long *wa-hu* uttered by males, shorter *wa-ah* by females. Single *kra* or *ka* note, especially by young, to maintain contact, and produced in series when excited. Also up to 8 loud, harsh, double *ch-arrh* notes, a staccato *cht-cht-cht* and *kaykaykay* when in conflict, and *traytraytray* or *tratratra* to prompt nest change-overs. Fledglings beg for food with *tsii* or *tsi-sii* call.

Drumming Males drum regularly: slow rolls of on average 1.3 seconds each with 11 strikes per second. Females probably do not drum.

Status NT. Range-restricted; entire population of around 8500 pairs found on just two islands: about 82% on Basse-Terre, 18% on Grande-Terre. Although numbers have recently increased slightly on Grand-Terre, continued deforestation (due to construction and clearance for cultivation) means an overall decline and further isolation from larger Basse-Terre population is likely. This may ultimately affect the genetic pool. Has also suffered from predation by introduced rats and fungicide use in banana plantations.

Habitat Occurs in all wooded areas: evergreen, deciduous, mangroves, swamp-forest and coconut plantations.

Range Endemic to the Caribbean island of Guadeloupe, Lesser Antilles. From coast to tree line but most common at lower elevations. Absent from smaller offshore islands. Resident and sedentary, although one storm-blown bird recorded 80km away on Antigua.

Taxonomy and variation Monotypic. Birds on Basse-Terre slightly larger than those on Grande-Terre.

Similar species None: only woodpecker on Guadeloupe.

Food and foraging Omnivorous, eating insects, tree-frogs, anolis and much fruit, seeds and berries. Uses anvils to process large, hard prey.

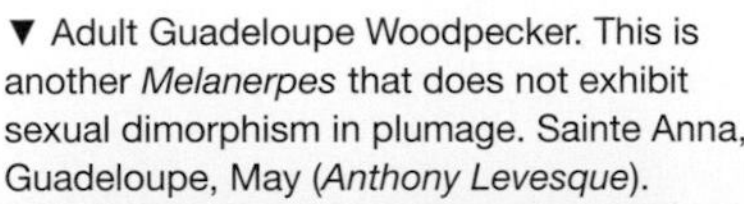

▼ Adult Guadeloupe Woodpecker. This is another *Melanerpes* that does not exhibit sexual dimorphism in plumage. Sainte Anna, Guadeloupe, May (*Anthony Levesque*).

▼ The relatively short bill of this individual suggests that it is a female. Le Gosier, Guadeloupe, June (*Anthony Levesque*).

39. PUERTO RICAN WOODPECKER

Melanerpes portoricensis

L 23–27cm

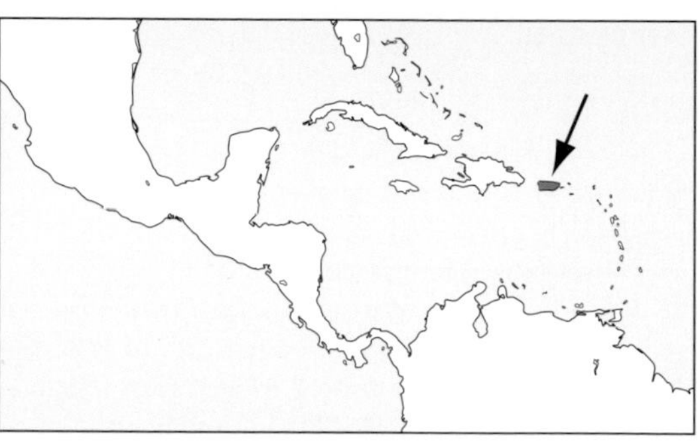

Identification Mantle and back blackish. Lower back and uppertail-coverts white. Crown and ear-coverts glossy bluish-black. Flanks and belly buff or tan. Chin, throat, lower cheeks and chest with varying amount of red. Forehead, lores and eye-ring white. Most of wings bluish-black; flight feathers browner, bluish on edges, white on inner webs of tertials, secondaries tipped white, underwing browner. Tail black with some white feather tips. Rump white. Iris chestnut. Long black bill. Legs grey. Sexes differ slightly: male has deep red throat, chest, breast and sometimes belly; smaller

▼Adult male Puerto Rican Woodpecker is more boldly coloured red below than the female. Puerto Rico, April (*Javier Hernández Ramos*).

female has brown or buff throat and lower cheek, only lightly flushed red below, sometimes orange or pink. Male also noticeably long-billed. Juvenile similar to adult female, but less glossy and with minimal red, usually more orange, on underparts. Some juvenile males may have red feather tips on crown.

Vocalisations Quite vocal with wide repertoire of harsh and squeaky calls, including a chicken-like *kuk,* a mewing note and a rolling *gurrr-gurrr.* Song a *wek, wek, wek-wek-wek, wek-wek* series that speeds up and increases in volume, faster when agitated.

Drumming Not an avid drummer. Rolls rapid but weak.

Status Fairly common locally. Considered stable, though range-restricted and has declined locally due to habitat loss. Now rare on Vieques Island. An important provider of cavities for non-excavating birds on Puerto Rico.

Habitat Typically wet, tropical forests, but occurs in most wooded areas including shade-coffee plantations, palm groves, mangroves, swamps, coconut groves, parks and suburban gardens.

Range Endemic to Puerto Rico, Greater Antilles. Widespread on main Puerto Rico island, local on Vieques. Sea-level to around 1000m. Resident and sedentary.

Taxonomy and variation Monotypic. Some variation in underpart colour intensity and extent.

Similar species Unmistakable, no other woodpeckers in range.

Food and foraging Omnivorous, feeding on invertebrates, especially beetles and ants, small lizards, geckos, frogs, seeds and fruits such as figs. Forages in loose groups. Sexes use different parts of trees: males usually low down, females from mid to canopy level.

▼ Adult female Puerto Rican Woodpecker. Besides being drabber, females are also shorter-billed than males. Puerto Rico, March (*Vaughan & Sveta Ashby*).

40. RED-HEADED WOODPECKER
Melanerpes erythrocephalus

L 20–24cm

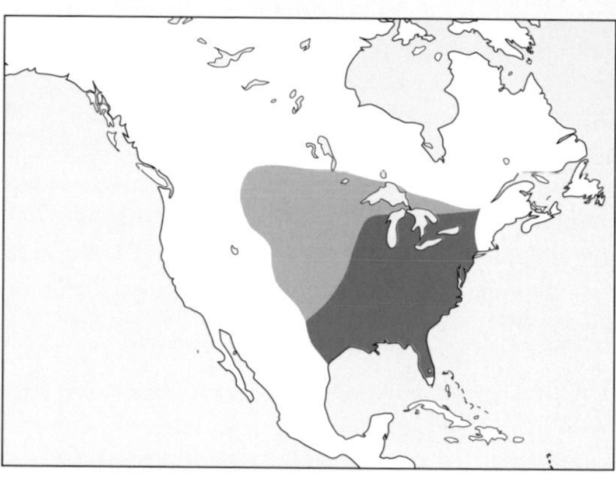

Identification Striking. Black and white body and bright crimson head, neck, throat and chest. Breast to vent white, often buffy over vent. Thin black line sometimes separates the red and white. Mantle, upper back and primaries glossy bluish-black. Lower back, rump and secondaries form a prominent snowy white area, obvious in flight. Primaries brownish. Central tail feathers black, outers with white margins and tips. Bill bluish-grey. Iris brown. Legs grey or olive. Sexes alike: slightly larger male has red hood extending further over nape. Juvenile drabber, brown and white, barred above including white secondaries, streaked or barred below, with minimal or no red.

Vocalisations Rapid, repeated, 5–8, sharp, feisty, squealing or cawing, *quiirr, queeark, queer* or *kweer,* sometimes *kwi-urr,* particularly when breeding. Weak, wheezing *queeah* or *queerp* and soft, dry, starling-like rattling *krrrrrr* contact calls. Also a shrill, rough *tchur* or *churr. Sterna* tern-like *scree* in conflicts. Repetitive, chattering *rrrr* at nest changeovers. Intimate *chrr* between pairs. Low-pitched *chug* in flight.

Drumming Both sexes drum. Brief, subdued rolls of 19–25 strikes per second. Often 2–3 well-spaced bursts in series. Pairs also indulge in slow demonstrative tapping at the nest.

Status NT. Population hard to estimate as thinly

▼ Red-headed Woodpecker – one of the most omnivorous and opportunistic of all woodpeckers. Eastern United States, June (*S & D & K Maslowski*).

◄ A pair of adult Red-headed Woodpeckers. The sexes are difficult to separate in the field. Ocean Springs, Mississippi, United States, September (*Dave Hawkins*).

▼ A juvenile Red-headed Woodpecker – very different to the adult, rather drab with a slight reddish blush to the forehead. New York City, United States, December (*Lloyd Spitalnik*).

distributed and naturally fluctuating according to food resources. But long-term decline clear, particularly in Florida and Great Lakes region, though it remains common in the W Midwest and on the Great Plains. Main threats are urbanisation and woodland change and loss. Somewhat adaptable, occupying new habitats such as parks and golf courses.

Habitat Open, sunny, mature woodlands, particularly oak, beech and burned pine forests. Also bur oak savanna, farmland, orchards, groves, plantations, riparian woods and swamps. Dead trees, snags and sparse undergrowth important.

Range North America. East of the Rockies, from SE Canada through C and E USA, to Atlantic and Gulf coasts as far as Florida and Texas. Mainly resident although many northern populations move south in winter whilst others are nomadic, responding to food availability.

Taxonomy and variation Monotypic. Sometimes orange or yellow tips in red hood and buff or pink wash to white areas.

Similar species None. Vocally similar to Red-bellied Woodpecker – and Great Crested Flycatcher *Myiarchus crinitus*.

Food and foraging Omnivorous, taking insects, nuts, fruit, corn and sap. An inventive forager, using anvils, expertly flycatching and eating songbird eggs and nestlings, and lizards and rodents on the ground. Maintains and aggressively defends food caches. Mast and stored acorns make up much of winter diet.

41. ACORN WOODPECKER

Melanerpes formicivorus

L 21–23cm

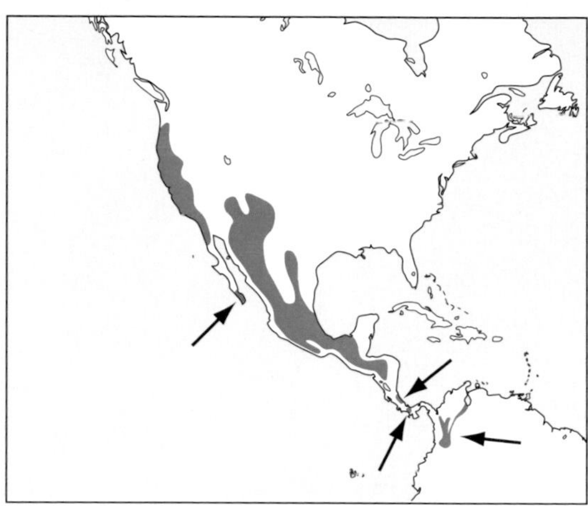

Identification Strikingly patterned. Bold facial markings often described as 'clownish': white or yellow iris, grey or black orbital ring, cream forehead connected to creamy cheeks and throat by narrow transloral band; black chin and nasal tufts form broad black patch at base of black bill. Chest black, breast white, white flanks streaked black. Belly and undertail-coverts mostly white, sometimes slightly streaked. Mantle, back and tail glossy black. White rump and primary patch obvious in flight. Sexes differ slightly: male has red crown; female red only on nape, or absent depending on race. Juvenile has red or orange crown resembling adult male; black areas dull, iris dark.

Vocalisations Raucous. Chattering, laughing calls include squeaky *ik-a,i k-a, ik-a* contact notes, mocking *yah a, wak-a* or *wick-a,* nasal *waaayk,* short *rrah* and longer *ahrr-ah-ah,* rising *quaay,* harsh *rack-up, rack-up* or *ratchet, ratchet,* loud *ja-cob, ja-cob, ja-cob* and a trilling *ddddrridrr* or higher-pitched *ddrreeerr.* Alarms include squealing notes and scratchy, drawn-out *karrit, krrrrit* or *krrrit-kut.* Cawing *urrrk* during disputes.

Drumming Slow, but accelerating rolls of 10–20 strikes. Sometimes interspersed with single knocks and taps.

Status Locally common. Overall probably stable, though local increases noted, as well as declines due to loss and degradation of oak woods.

Habitat Temperate and tropical, dry and humid, woodlands (especially oak and oak-pine). Also forest edges and clearings with scattered trees, wooded suburbs and gardens.

Range North and Central America. Disjunct from W USA (isolated population Edwards Plateau, Texas) to Colombia. Mostly resident; some migrate or wander north and east when acorn crops fail. Mainly mid elevations, sea-level in California to 3300m in Andes.

Taxonomy and variation Seven races: ***formicivorus*** (Arizona, New Mexico, W Texas to SE Mexico); ***bairdi*** (NW Oregon to N Baja California) large with solid black chest, flanks hardly streaked, bill longer and stouter than nominate; ***angustifrons*** (S Baja California) smallest race, proposed as distinct species 'Baja

◄ Adult male nominate Acorn Woodpecker; most of the crown is red. Hereford, Arizona, USA, April (*Dave Hawkins*).

► Adult female nominate. There is red on the hindcrown only; the mid-crown is black. Hereford, Arizona, United States, April (*Dave Hawkins*).

Woodpecker'; ***albeolus*** (S Mexico into Belize and NE Guatemala) throat very pale, plain below; ***lineatus*** (Guatemala. El Salvador, Honduras, N Nicaragua) heavily streaked below, primary patch large; ***striatipectus*** (Nicaragua, Costa Rica, W Panama) throat bright yellow, primary patch small; ***flavigula*** (Andean Colombia) heavily marked below, male has reduced red on the crown, female lacks red.

Similar species None. Unmistakable.

Food and foraging Omnivorous, taking flying insects, fruit, berries and seeds. Some populations (mainly in N), harvest and store acorns in multi-hole 'granaries' made in tree-trunks and buildings. Families create and share sap wells. Visits sugar-water feeders.

▲ Adult female nominate at a 'granary'. Such stores contain hundreds of acorns. Arizona, United States, June (*S & D & K Maslowski*).

◄ Adult male *flavigula*: note the buff throat and boldly marked underparts. Antioquia, Colombia, October (*Priscilla Burcher*).

42. YELLOW-TUFTED WOODPECKER
Melanerpes cruentatus

L 19–20cm

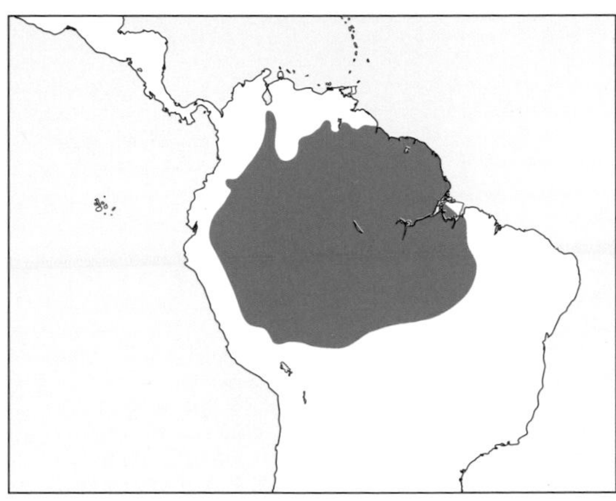

Identification Often conspicuous, sitting out in groups atop dead trees and snags. Throat, chest, cheeks, mantle, back and most of wings glossy bluish-black. Breast and belly red. Flanks and undertail-coverts white with black bars and chevrons. White rump and uppertail-coverts obvious in flight and when wings are spread in greeting after landing. Underwing barred black and white. Yellow iris and wide cream or yellow orbital ring striking. Black bill with greyer base. Legs greyish. Sexes of both morphs (see below) differ only slightly: males of both have red fore- and mid-crown which females lack. Juvenile browner above, greyer below with orange belly-patch; both sexes have red on crown. Juvenile yellow-tufted morph has less yellow on head than adult.

Vocalisations Noisy, several birds often calling together, with a falling, churring, chattering or rattling *cheer-eer-err* series, a series of (usually 9) *ih* or *trih* notes, a rising *trrrr-eh* and *churr-ee-ee*. Also double-syllable, grating, raucous, *aack-up, wrack-up* or *wik-up* repeated during interactions.

Drumming Not known to drum properly, but indulges in soft demonstrative tapping.

Status Often locally common. Adaptable and has probably benefited from forest fragmentation.

Habitat Open lowland rainforest, *terra firme* and *várzea*. Often in clearings, at edges and in burnt and degraded forests. Also settlements with tall dead trees and snags.

Range South America. Lowland E Colombia, adjacent W and S Venezuela, the Guianas, NE and Amazonian Brazil, E Ecuador, E Peru and E Bolivia. Typically from sea-level to 1200m, but up to 1500m in Ecuador. Resident and sedentary.

Taxonomy and variation Monotypic, but with two distinct morphs which differ mainly in head pattern. **Yellow-tufted morph** (mainly N and W) has variable yellow, buff or cream brow which extends to yellow or gold nape, sometimes projecting as tufts. Together with orbital rings these form impressive 'spectacles'. **Black-headed morph** (mainly Amazonian Brazil and E) lacks yellow on head. Male yellow-tufted often has larger red crown patch than black-headed. Extent of red belly very variable on both morphs. 'Hybrids' of the morphs may have irregular yellow brow.

Similar species None within range.

Food and foraging Omnivorous, taking insects (often flycatches in groups at dusk), and much fruit.

◄ Adult male Yellow-tufted Woodpecker. This is the 'yellow-tufted' morph, with crown feathers raised. French Guiana, May (*Michel Giraud-Audine*).

▼ Adult female of the 'yellow-tufted' morph. Females lack red on the crown. Peru, September (*Vaughan & Sveta Ashby*).

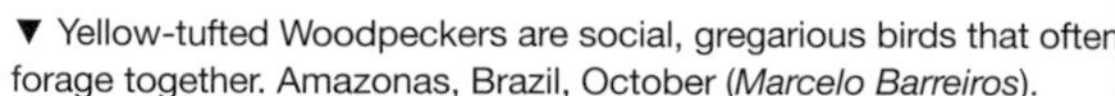

▼ Yellow-tufted Woodpeckers are social, gregarious birds that often forage together. Amazonas, Brazil, October (*Marcelo Barreiros*).

◄ The 'black-headed' morph is so-called because it lacks the conspicuous yellow tufts. El Pauji, Venezuela, February (*Lars Petersson*).

43. YELLOW-FRONTED WOODPECKER
Melanerpes flavifrons

L 17–19cm

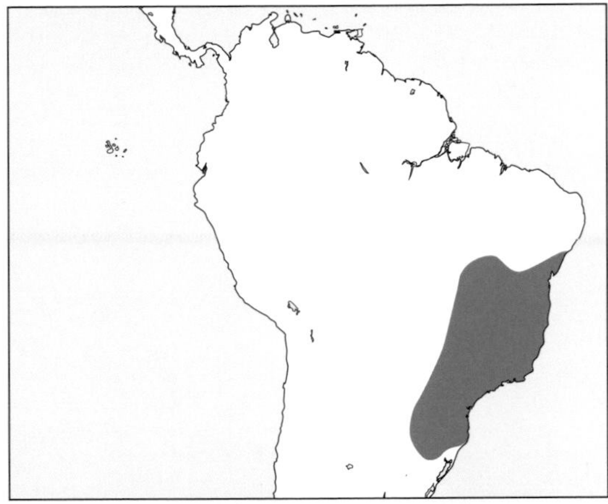

Identification Colourful. Mantle glossy black, streaked white, back and rump white. Uppertail black, some white bars on outer feathers, undertail browner. Breast grey or olive, belly red, flanks white or buff barred black. Upperwings glossy black, bluish tones on flight feathers, some white on secondaries and tertials, underwing brownish barred white. Forecrown, cheek, chin, throat and (sometimes) chest gold or yellow. Black mask runs from the bill and lores, around the eye, over the ear-coverts and continues down to the shoulder and mantle. Iris bluish-black, distinct yellow or orange orbital ring. Bill black. Legs olive-brown. Sexes differ: male has red from mid-crown to nape; female bluish-black crown. Juvenile less glossy, browner overall, with smaller and paler red belly-patch

► Adult male Yellow-fronted Woodpecker. Males of this stunning species have red crowns. Rio de Janiero State, Brazil, January (*Vaughan & Sveta Ashby*).

and brown iris. Juvenile male red on crown and nape, female with red mid-crown.

Vocalisations Often noisy, birds calling together. Greeting call an excited series of squeaky, liquid *chlit* notes. Rapid, raucous, rattling, repetitive *wutwut-wutwut, tweewetwee* and *kikikiki*. Calls piercing and chaotic when groups excited.

Drumming Brief, steady, level-pitched rolls, usually interspersed with calls.

Status Occurs over a large area and often fairly common. Reasonably adaptable and probably not threatened. A keystone species with its cavities used by parakeets and smaller toucans.

Habitat Open lowland and upland rainforest and gallery forest. Also palm groves, farmland with trees, orchards, wooded suburbs, secondary growth and degraded forests, often with tall post-fire trees.

Range E South America. Either side of the Equator in E and SE Brazil (Bahia, Goiás, SE Mato Grosso, Rio Grande do Sul), E Paraguay and NE Argentina (Misiones). Sea-level to 1800m. Resident and sedentary.

Taxonomy and variation Monotypic. Individual and regional differences in size, intensity of red belly-patch and orbital-ring colour. Some birds spotted black, others slightly barred, on white back. Birds in NW usually lighter below, with whiter breast and orange belly, than elsewhere.

Similar species None within range.

Food and foraging Highly frugivorous, even feeding fruit to its young. Visits feeders, uses anvils and stores both plant and insect food.

◄ Yellow-fronted Woodpeckers in a typical group pose. Misiones, Argentina, May (*Roberto Güller*).

► Female Yellow-fronted Woodpeckers lack red on the crown. Misiones, Argentina, July (*Nick Athanas*).

► Adult male Yellow-fronted Woodpecker, showing the white back and rump. Misiones, Argentina, July (*Roberto Güller*).

44. GOLDEN-NAPED WOODPECKER
Melanerpes chrysauchen

L 17–19cm

Identification Glossy black above with white panel or barring on mantle and back. Rump white. Throat, chest and breast yellow, buff or grey. Pale belly, flanks and undertail-coverts heavily barred black; barring often waved, forming chevrons. Red or orange belly-patch. Uppertail black, white on outer feathers, undertail chocolate. Wings-coverts bluish-black, primaries brownish tipped white, underwing browner. Lores, cheek and neck-sides pale. Bold black mask from eye runs over ear-coverts and down neck-sides. Forehead and nape gold/yellow. Slight white mark behind eye. Bill dark. Iris brown. Legs greyish-olive. Sexes differ: male has red or orange mid-crown; female lacks red,

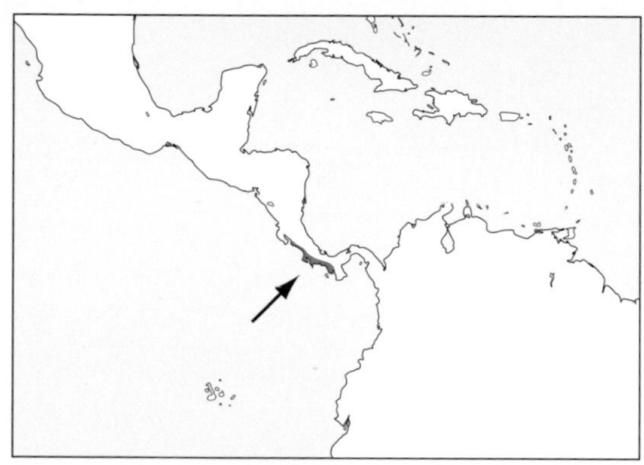

◀ Adult male Golden-naped Woodpecker has a red patch on the mid-crown. Carate, Costa Rica, April (*Jürgen Rekkers*).

having mostly gold or yellow crown with narrow black band across centre. Juvenile duller overall: black areas matt, paler yellow, belly-patch orange, markings below faded; both sexes with red feather-tips in crown.

Vocalisations Often noisy. A brief but loud, harsh, repeated, even-pitched, mocking trill. Short rattling *wret-wret-wret,* sometimes harsh, sometimes milder and more bubbling, and a falling *whikaka.* Loud vibrant *churrr* in displays and disputes.

Drumming Both sexes drum in breeding period, but few details.

Status Though fairly limited in range, and affected by rainforest loss, not considered threatened as seemingly adapts to disturbed habitats. Nowhere very common and often rather local.

Habitat Mainly open, humid, tall tropical forest. Uses edges of dense rainforest, thicker secondary growth, degraded stands and plantations adjacent to native forest.

Range Central America. Restricted to Pacific slope of SW Costa Rica and W Panama. Lowlands to 1500m. Resident and sedentary.

Taxonomy and variation Monotypic. Variation slight.

Similar species Like Black-cheeked and Beautiful Woodpeckers, but has yellow nape and range does not overlap with either.

Food and foraging Highly frugivorous, eating both wild and cultivated fruit (palm dates, figs, bananas, *Cecropia*) and visits feeders. Insects eaten include wood-boring beetles. Is an expert flycatcher, sallying high from snags, particularly at dusk, for winged termites. Forages in family groups.

► This species occurs only in parts of Costa Rica and Panama. The adult female lacks red on the crown. Sierpe River, Costa Rica, September (*Noel Ureña*).

45. BEAUTIFUL WOODPECKER
Melanerpes pulcher

L 17–19cm

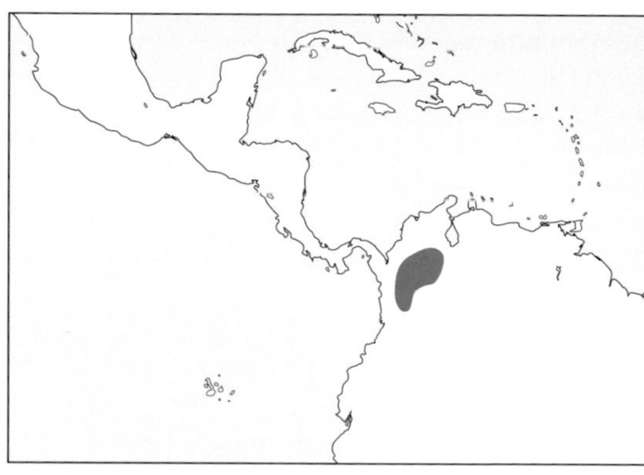

Identification Black mask formed by ocular area and ear-coverts extends down rear neck-sides to the mantle. Lores, cheek, chin, throat and chest plain cream or yellow. Breast, flanks and vent extensively barred black and white, red patch on mid-belly. White panel from mantle to rump, sometimes mottled black. Wings black with some white bars in flight feathers. Tail chocolate. Iris black. Bill dark. Legs greyish. Sexes differ slightly: male has gold or yellow forehead and nape and scarlet crown; female has yellow lores, black forecrown, red mid-crown and yellow nape.

Vocalisations Most commonly a distinctive loud call not unlike Great Kiskadee, sometimes squeaky, some-

▼ Adult male Beautiful Woodpecker has a red crown. This one has flung a piece of bark from the tree branch while in search of invertebrate food. San Luis, Antioquia, Colombia, June (*Félix Uribe*).

▼ An adult male Beautiful Woodpecker. This species is unmistakable, as similar *Melanerpes* do not occur within its small range. San Luis, Antioquia, Colombia, June (*Félix Uribe*).

times more throaty. Also a churring when agitated and harsh, rattling, mocking trills.

Drumming Both sexes may occasionally drum, but information lacking.

Status Considered stable overall, but this possibly optimistic as much forest has been lost within its range. Range-restricted and localised in Colombia.

Habitat Open, tall, humid or dry, tropical forest. Also plantations and, to a certain extent, fragmented and degraded forests.

Range South America. Endemic to lower elevations in the Magdalena Valley, Colombia. Mainly 400–1000m, but up to 1500m. Resident and sedentary.

Taxonomy and variation Monotypic. Colour of throat and chest varies from grey, to buff, to yellow. Red belly-patch variable in size and colour intensity.

Similar species Like Golden-naped (formerly treated as a race) and Black-cheeked Woodpeckers, but range does not overlap with either.

Food and foraging Quite frugivorous, taking figs, bananas, palm and *Cecropia* fruits. Usually forages unobtrusively in the canopy and sub-canopy. Also takes insects, hawking for winged prey.

▼ The female has less red on the crown than the male; it is restricted to the mid-crown. San Luis, Antioquia, Colombia, June (*Félix Uribe*).

46. BLACK-CHEEKED WOODPECKER

Melanerpes pucherani

L 17–19cm

Identification Striking. Black mantle and back finely barred white. Scapulars usually plain black. Lower back and rump white, sometimes barred blackish. Black wings barred and spotted white, some flight feathers tipped white. Underwing barred black and white. Forehead yellow, throat and neck buff. Chest buff or grey, breast to undertail-coverts cream or white with black chevrons and bars. Red belly and vent. Uppertail black with subtle white barring on central feathers, undertail buff to brown. Lores yellowish, chin and throat white or buff. Black around eye, ear-coverts, cheek and neck-sides. Variably sized white patch behind eye. Iris dark, orbital ring greyish. Bill black. Legs grey or olive. Sexes differ slightly: male has yellow forehead, red crown to nape; female grey or buff forehead, black crown often speckled white, red only at rear. Juvenile less glossy and browner, less white above, less and paler red on belly. Juvenile male has red crown but more orange nape; female has minimal red.

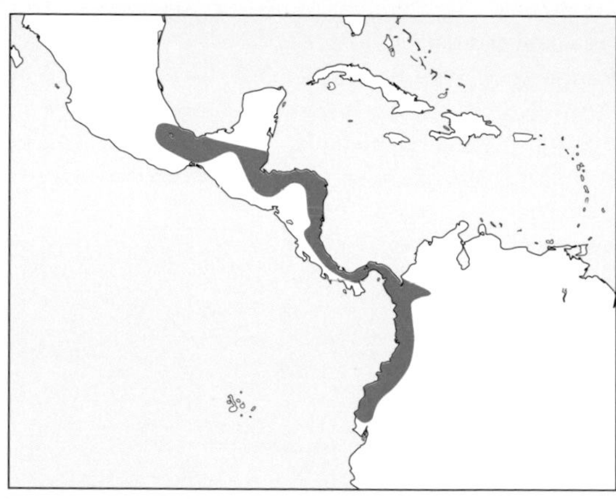

Vocalisations Quite vocal. Song a typical *Melanerpes* high (but level-pitched) rolling, trilling series of four-five *churrr, chirrr* or *cherrr* notes, very similar to Velasquez's Woodpecker. When harsher and briefer

▼ Adult male Black-cheeked Woodpecker has an all-red crown and nape. Rancho Naturalista, Costa Rica, October (*Dave Hawkins*).

recalls Black-billed Magpie. Sharper, nasal *kweh-eh-eh* and rolling *kwehrr-err-errr.* Also a shrill *chirriree* and loud *krrrr* and *whika-ka* notes.

Drumming Both sexes occasionally drum, though not avidly.

Status Often fairly common. May have benefited from forest fragmentation and establishment of plantations.

Habitat Mature humid forest, older secondary damp woodlands. Often in closed forest but also edges, clearings with scattered tall trees and snags. Also banana plantations, wooded settlements and gardens.

Range Central and South America. From S Mexico through Belize, Guatemala, Honduras, Nicaragua, Costa Rica, Panama into W Colombia and W Ecuador. Usually lowlands and foothills. Resident and sedentary, though a record from Tumbes NP, Peru, may indicate range expansion.

Taxonomy and variation Monotypic. Variation slight.

Similar species Golden-naped and Beautiful Woodpeckers do not overlap in range. Red-crowned Woodpecker lacks black on face.

Food and foraging Feeds on various invertebrates and flycatches, but very frugivorous, taking seeds, berries, nectar and both wild and cultivated fruit, especially palm fruit. Regarded as a pest by some growers. Often forages in family parties and joins mixed-species flocks.

▼ Adult female has red restricted to the nape and hindneck. Arenal, Costa Rica, May (*Dave Hawkins*).

▼ A pair of Black-cheeked Woodpeckers; the male is above, the female below. Arenal, Costa Rica, January (*Nick Athanas*).

47. WHITE-FRONTED WOODPECKER
Melanerpes cactorum

L 16–18cm

Identification Glossy black above with pale line running from white nape patch onto the back. Mostly plain grey to vinous below, barred dusky on lower flanks and vent. Bluish-black wings heavily barred white. Underwing browner. Uppertail black with white bars or spots, undertail browner. Black mask over eye and ear-coverts extends down neck-sides to mantle. Prominent white lores, forehead and forecrown (white-fronted). Lower cheeks whitish. Chin and throat white, buff or yellow. Iris chestnut. Bill dark. Legs greyish. Sexes very similar: males have small red patch on mid-crown (not always visible), which females lack. Juvenile duller black overall, more noticeably barred below; both sexes with some red or orange on the mid-crown.
Vocalisations Vocal and gregarious, families calling loudly together, often from top of cacti. Calls can be squeaky, yapping or harsh, fast or slow, depending on circumstances: *weep-weep-weep* or *weep-beep*. Single notes recall a child's squeaky toy. Also a high-pitched *wut-weetwut, wut-weetwut* when excited.

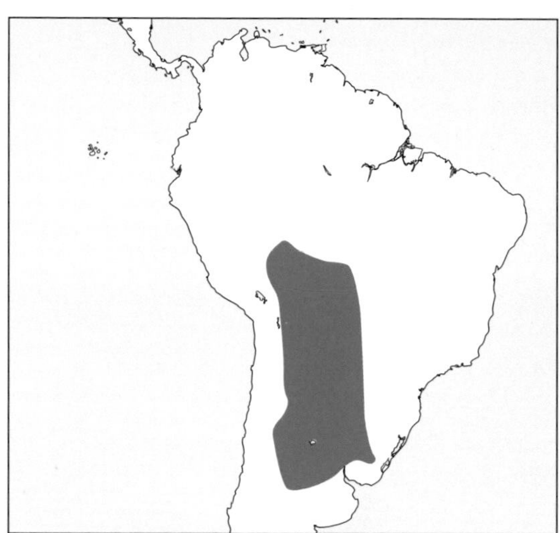

Drumming Not a regular drummer. Occasionally produces short rolls of variable speed and intensity, beginning or ending with distinct, slow heavy knocks or softer taps.
Status Common locally. Information sparse, but has large range and thus considered stable.
Habitat Tree, cactus and shrub-dotted deserts, savanna and arid areas such as the Chaco. Also gallery woodland, wooded pasture and palm groves.
Range South America. The heart of the continent S of the Equator in SE Peru, Bolivia, Uruguay, N Argentina, Paraguay and SW Brazil. Sea-level to 2500m. Resident and sedentary.
Taxonomy and variation Monotypic, but two colour morphs. Throat variably white or cream (mostly in S), yellow to golden (mostly in N). Primaries sometimes brownish.
Similar species None within range.
Food and foraging Sap is an important source of nutrition, especially in the dry season. Parties often feed together on single trees or shrubs, particularly mesquite, where wells have been specifically drilled. These sites are defended, but many other animals still benefit from the sap inadvertently provided. Also insects and fruit.

◄ Two adult white-throated morph White-fronted Woodpeckers. The sexes are very similar, and difficult to separate. Cordoba, Argentina, June (*Roberto Güller*).

▲ Adult of the yellow-throated morph. Omereque, Bolivia, November (*Dubi Shapiro*).

► Adult of the yellow-throated morph. Mato Grosso de Sul, Brazil, July (*Nick Athanas*).

48. HISPANIOLAN WOODPECKER

Melanerpes striatus

L 22–28cm

Identification Striking. Mostly buff, brown and olive below, flanks streaked dark. Blackish upperparts heavily and regularly barred green and gold. Rump greenish-yellow with some red feather tips. Forehead and supercilium grey or buff, ear-coverts darker grey, chin and throat grey. Rear neck striped black and white. Upperwings barred yellow or buff and black, underwing grey-brown with pale spots or bars, coverts olive. Uppertail blackish, uppertail-coverts red, undertail olive or grey. Iris gold. Legs greyish. Long bill grey-black, lower mandible paler. Sexes differ: male has red crown and nape, is noticeably larger and heavier than female and has a longer bill (around 20% longer); female has black crown, speckled white at the sides, and red only on nape. Juveniles of both sexes have black crown spotted white and red, more orange nape and dark iris.

Vocalisations Often vocal, producing a range of loud, yapping, squeaky, nasal and rolling calls. A series of repeated *waa* notes, simple *ta-a* when anxious, 3–5 distinctive *b-d-d-d-t* notes and a feisty *wup* alarm.

Drumming Rarely drums in true sense but demonstrative tapping done by the nest.

Status Locally common and widespread in the Dominican Republic. Deforestation and habitat destruction in Haiti probably detrimental. Although range-restricted, overall considered stable.

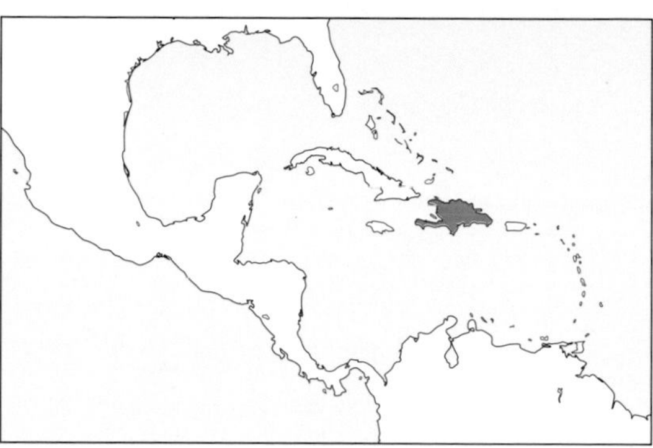

Habitat Most open wooded habitats: conifer and broadleaved, dry or damp. Uses mosaic forests but also coastal mangroves, swamps, plantations, cactus scrub, grasslands, palm stands in open country, wooded farmland and urban parks. Breeds in loose colonies (5–20+ pairs), several nests often in the same tree. A keystone species, its holes used by parrots, parakeets, trogons, Golden Swallow and Antillean Piculet.

Range Endemic to the Caribbean island of Hispaniola (Haiti and Dominican Republic) and adjacent Isla Beata. Resident and sedentary. Sea-level to around 2400m.

Taxonomy and variation Monotypic. Size differences concern the sexes. Worn birds have whiter barring above. Some birds have red feather-tips on belly.

Similar species None. Other picids on Hispaniola (Antillean Piculet and Yellow-bellied Sapsucker) not likely to be confused.

Food and foraging Omnivorous and inventive, taking ants, beetles, spiders, scorpions, lizards, fruit, seeds, corn and sap. This gregarious species forages at most levels in noisy groups. Will sally for winged prey and uses anvils to process hard or large food items. Sometimes considered a pest in orange and cocoa plantations.

◀ Adult male Hispaniolan Woodpecker. The male has an all-red crown, and a longer bill than the female. La Vega, Dominican Republic, June (*Dax Roman*).

► Adult female. Note the black crown, with red on the nape only. San Cristobal, Dominican Republic, March (*Dax Roman*).

▼ A pair of Hispaniolan Woodpeckers at their nest hole in a palm. The male is on the right, the female on the left. San Cristobal, Dominican Republic, March (*Dax Roman*).

▼ Juvenile Hispaniolan Woodpecker just prior to fledging; note the dark iris. Santo Domingo, Dominican Republic, February (*Dax Roman*).

49. JAMAICAN WOODPECKER

Melanerpes radiolatus

L 23–26cm

Identification Black above, finely barred white with greenish tones. Barring broadest on rump. Most of black wings also barred, primaries browner. Olive, grey or brown below with orange or rufous belly-patch. Flanks and undertail-coverts washed orange or yellow and barred black and white. Uppertail black with central feather pair finely barred white, outer feathers spotted. Lores yellow. Pale face, forehead, chin and throat merging into chest. Ear-coverts greyer. Iris reddish, orbital ring grey. Legs grey. Long black bill. Sexes differ: male has red crown and nape; female smaller, with greyish crown, red only on nape. Juvenile greyer below than adult, belly patch yellower, head pattern more or less like respective adult.

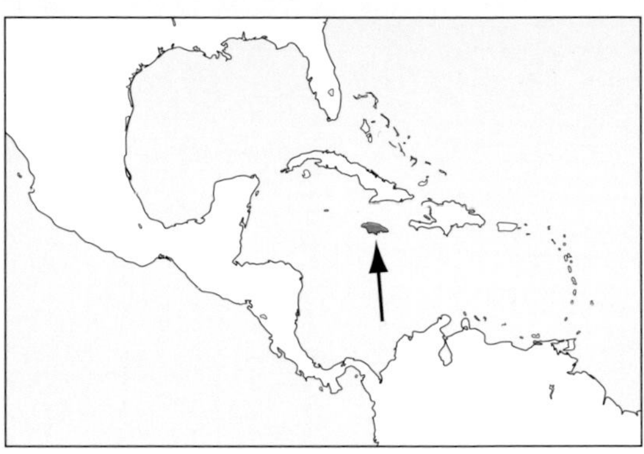

Vocalisations Rather vocal. A squawking, sometimes grating, *chee-ee-urp* (similar to Olive-throated Parakeet), *weecha-weecha* and faster *churp-churp-churp* in series or as separate notes. Softer *whirr-whirr* contact calls. Also loud, single or repeated *kaaa, kaaah, kao* and *krirr* notes.

Drumming Both sexes drum strongly in the breeding season. Besides rhythmic rolls, also a slower series of

▼ Adult male Jamaican Woodpecker. The males have a red crown, nape and hindneck. Port Royal Mountains, Jamaica, May (*Yves-Jacques Rey-Millet*).

demonstrative tapping produced near nest.

Status Range-restricted, confined to one island and decreasing in some areas due to habitat loss, but still fairly common and widespread.

Habitat Wide range of open and closed woodlands from humid and dry mountain forests to lowland coconut and palm groves, coffee, coconut and citrus plantations, mangroves, wooded pastures and farmland, and both rural and urban gardens. Unusually for a woodpecker, will raise 2 or 3 broods per year in the same cavity.

Range Endemic to Jamaica where sedentary. Sea-level to about 1800m.

Taxonomy and variation Monotypic. Variation slight. Birds in fresh plumage have greenish tinge below. Some females have buff crown.

Similar species None on Jamaica.

Food and foraging Omnivorous, taking fruits, nectar from flowering trees, various insects, snails, even lizards. Forages mainly in mid and upper levels of trees, often in vines, and probes bromeliads. Flycatches from treetops and uses anvils.

► Adult female Jamaican Woodpecker has a grey crown, with red only on the nape and hindneck. Montego Bay, Jamaica, May (*Yves-Jacques Rey-Millet*).

50. GOLDEN-CHEEKED WOODPECKER
Melanerpes chrysogenys

L 19–22cm

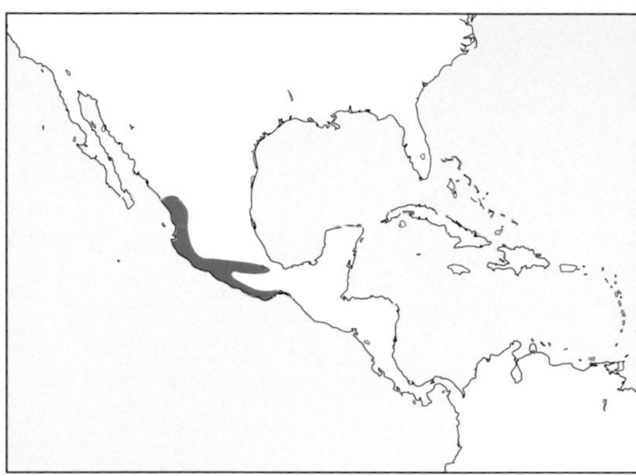

Identification Strikingly marked head: lores, cheek and chin yellowish, prominent black mask around reddish eye, orbital ring grey, forehead cream or buff, nape yellow, gold or orange. Heavily barred black and white above, particularly on rump and uppertail-coverts. Plain greyish-brown below with buff wash and orange or yellow belly-patch. Lower flanks and undertail-coverts barred black. Black upperwings barred white, broad white bar on primaries obvious in flight, coverts spotted white. Underwing brown with white barring. Black tail barred white, boldly on central feather pair. Bill black. Legs grey or green. Sexes differ: male has red (sometimes orange) crown; female greyish-brown

◄ Adult male Golden-cheeked Woodpecker of the *flavinuchus* race. The crown feathers are raised when alarmed or excited. Jalisco, Mexico, December (*Greg R. Homel*).

◀ The female lacks the bright red crown of the male. This is the race *flavinuchus*. Jalisco, Mexico, December (*Greg R. Homel*).

▼ Juvenile Golden-cheeked Woodpecker; duskier below than the adult, and the red and yellow areas are duller. This bird is of the race *flavinuchus*. Oaxaca, Mexico, March (*Nick Athanas*).

flecked black, sometimes orange or red on nape. Juvenile brownish above, greyer below than adult, with yellowish wash. Juveniles of both sexes have red on the head, but reduced and streaked black in females.

Vocalisations Quite vocal with various loud chattering, chirping, rattling and squeaky calls. Sharp, nasal *ki-di-dik* and *cheek-oo, cheek-oo*. A sneezing *ch-dik, ch-dik*. Harder, harsher, sneeze-like *keh-eh-eh-ehk* or *keh-i-heh-hek*, softer versions *keh-i-heh* or *kuh-uh-uh* or *churr-i-huh*. Also a drawn-out, churring, rolling series.

Drumming Said to drum occasionally, but details lacking.

Status Common locally. Range-restricted and poorly known, but seemingly not threatened and population considered stable.

Habitat Open, arid forest, woodlands and grasslands with scattered trees. Sometimes damper woods and more closed forests, and adapts to wooded coffee plantations and degraded forests.

Range Endemic to W Mexico. Widespread on the Pacific slope from sea-level to 1500m. Resident and sedentary.

Taxonomy and variation Two races: ***chrysogenys*** (NW Mexico: coastal lowlands from Sinaloa to Nayarit) has most yellow on face, males with red reaching nape; ***flavinuchus*** (SW Mexico: Jalisco to SE Puebla and E Oaxaca) is larger than nominate, greyer below, with less yellow on face, more on nape. Orange or yellow belly-patch varies in extent, but much overlap and differences in size and colour also clinal.

Similar species Co-occurring Golden-fronted, Gila and Grey-breasted Woodpeckers all paler below and on face, lacking black mask.

Food and foraging Seems to be fairly omnivorous, taking a range of insects, seeds and fruits, but details sparse. Often forages alone, sometimes in pairs, from mid to upper levels in trees.

51. GREY-BREASTED WOODPECKER

Melanerpes hypopolius

L 20–22cm

Identification Most of head, neck, throat, mantle and underparts plain smoky-grey. Forehead whitish. Ear-coverts and orbital area blackish with white eye-crescents. Faint pale malar. Lower flanks and undertail-coverts with black chevrons, belly with yellow patch. Heavily barred black and white above, white rump dotted or streaked black. Most of upperwing black, barred white, primaries less barred but tipped white, underwing greyish-brown barred white. Black uppertail barred or spotted white on central and outer feathers. Iris chestnut. Bill blackish. Legs grey. Sexes differ slightly: male has red patch on mid-crown and small rufous area below eye; female lacks red crown. Juvenile browner with diffuse barring above; both sexes have some red on crown.

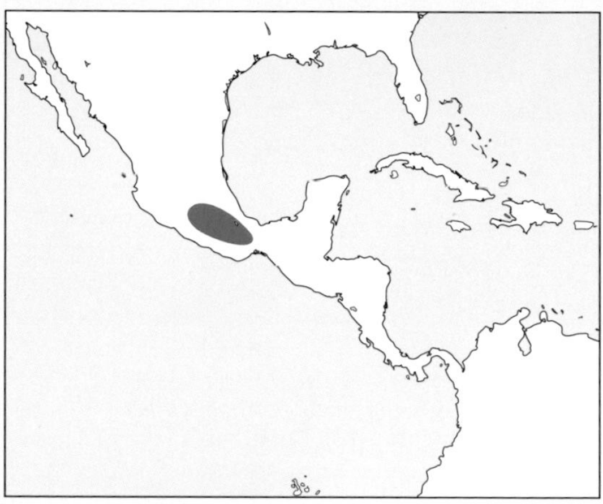

◄ Adult male Grey-breasted Woodpecker. The sexually diagnostic red crown-patch is just visible in this pose. Mexico, March (*Benito Hernández Leyva*).

Vocalisations Quite vocal with trilling, chattering and harsh rattling calls, including a repeated nasal *chuk, ke-hek* and *yek-a*. Also a gruff, low-pitched, churring *ch-i-i-ir*.

Drumming Produces loud, strident rolls in the breeding period.

Status Common locally in Oaxaca. Restricted to one region in one country, poorly known and population size probably relatively small, but not considered at risk.

Habitat Dry tropical scrub and semi-desert with cacti, wooded grasslands, cultivated land and open, montane woodlands. Avoids thick forest.

Range Endemic to SW Mexico. From N Guerrero and Morelos to Oaxaca. Between 900–2450m. Resident and sedentary.

Taxonomy and variation Monotypic. Some birds have faint reddish malar area, others lack red below eye. White barring on primaries can form patch.

Similar species Velasquez's Woodpecker is larger, paler, always lacks red below the eye, more coloured on the belly, males more red on crown and females have gold or orange nape.

Food and foraging Omnivorous, eating various invertebrates and cactus fruit. Rather social, often foraging in parties, at most levels including the ground. Regularly and expertly sallies for winged insects. Uses anvils and caches food.

▲ Adult male. Endemic to uplands in SW Mexico, the natural history of this species is largely unknown, but note that all three images here show birds on cacti. Cuernavaca, Mexico, July (*Dominic Mitchell*).

◀ The adult female Grey-breasted Woodpecker lacks red on the crown. Mexico, August (*Benito Hernández Leyva*).

52. YUCATAN WOODPECKER
Melanerpes pygmaeus

L 16–18cm

Other name Red-vented Woodpecker
Identification Black mantle, back and scapulars finely barred white. Rump and uppertail-coverts plain white. Plain grey below with olive tones and red or pink patch on lower belly and vent. Flanks and undertail-coverts barred blackish. Black upperwings barred white, primaries chocolate spotted white, underwing grey or brown barred white. Uppertail black, outer feather pairs with narrow white bars or spots, undertail greyer spotted white. Gold or yellow around bill-base, lores, nasal tufts and chin. Forecrown, face and throat grey. Iris reddish. Bill black. Legs grey. Sexes differ: male

◄ Adult male Yucatan Woodpecker has an all-red crown and nape and bright yellow on the face. This is race *rubricomus*. Calakmul, Campeche, Mexico, March (*Greg R. Homel*).

► Adult female nominate. The red is restricted to the nape, and there is less yellow on the face than in the male. Cozumel Island, Mexico, January (*Ernst Albegger*).

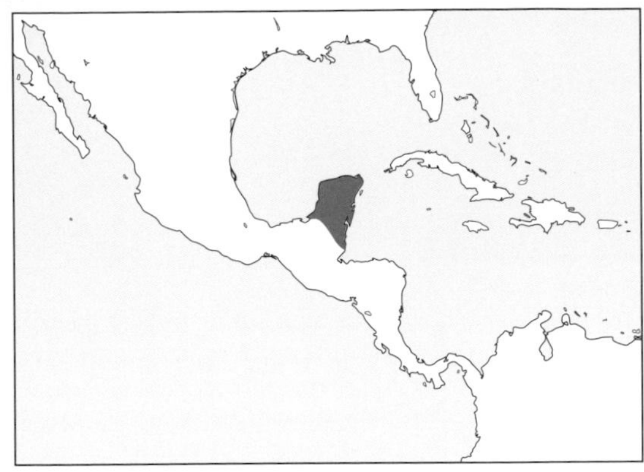

has red from mid-crown to nape; female red only on nape, crown grey, duller and less red on belly and less yellow on face. Juvenile duskier below, belly-patch pinker, male with red crown, female with blackish crown flecked red.

Vocalisations Often vocal. Rapid, strong, mocking, nasal or throaty *chuh-uh-uh-uh or cheh-cheh-cheh* or *keh-heh-heh-heh*. Softer, rolling *churr-r-r-r* or *purr-r-r-r*.

Drumming Solid, steady, level-pitched, repeated rolls, sometimes ending with several distinct single knocks.

Status Locally common. Overall population considered stable, but poorly known and island races could easily become vulnerable.

Habitat Mainly open, drier, tropical woodlands, often at edges and in clearings, and coastal scrub. To lesser extent, damper woods and degraded forests.

Range Central America. Yucatan Peninsula and Cozumel Island, Mexico, also Belize, NE Guatemala and Guanaja Island off Honduras. Mainly lowlands. Resident and sedentary.

Taxonomy and variation Three races: ***pygmaeus*** (Cozumel Island) dark grey below; ***rubricomus*** (Yucatan Peninsula, N Belize, NE Guatemala) palest below, less barred on flanks; ***tysoni*** (Guanaja Island, off N Honduras) dusky below, less yellow around bill, male with red crown separated from orange nape by grey or brown area, female with small, narrow red nape patch. Some birds have black barring on white uppertail-coverts. Amount and intensity of red on belly and yellow on face variable.

Similar species Sympatric Golden-fronted Woodpecker is larger with bigger bill, rufous nasal tufts, female with more red on nape. Very similar Red-crowned Woodpecker does not overlap.

Food and foraging Little information, but presumably omnivorous, taking invertebrates and plant matter as do its close relatives. Often forages low-down in trees and bushes.

53. RED-CROWNED WOODPECKER

Melanerpes rubricapillus

L 16–18cm

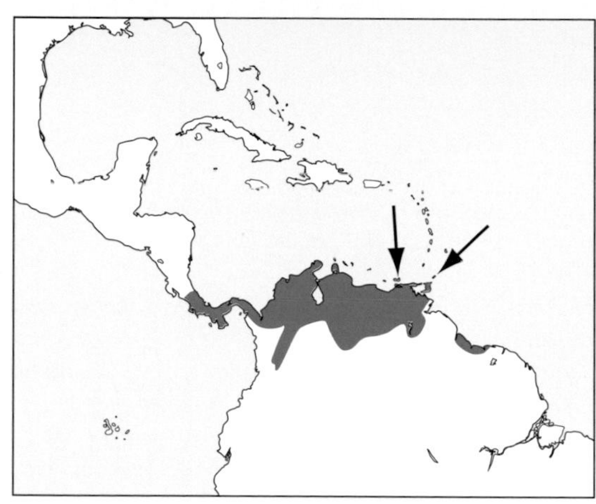

Identification Relatively short-tailed. Black above, evenly barred white. Rump and uppertail-coverts white. Black outer-tail barred white, central feather pair white with black tips. Plain olive, grey or buff below, lower flanks barred black. Variable pink, orange or red belly-patch. Most of upperwing black barred white, primaries browner, tipped white. Underwing brownish, barred white. Face grey. Nasal tufts and lores yellowish. Forehead buff or cream. Sometimes yellow on chin. Iris chestnut, orbital ring grey. Bill grey-black. Legs grey. Sexes differ: both have nape orange or red, but male has red crown, female pale crown. Male also has longer bill (*c.*10% longer). Juvenile duller overall, black areas browner, underparts faintly streaked, belly-patch and nape pink or yellow. Juvenile male has dull red crown,

▲ Adult male; the nominate is the palest and most widespread race. Colombia, January (*Robert Scanlon*).

◀ Adult male Red-crowned Woodpecker of the nominate race. Although both sexes have a reddish nape, males also have a red crown. Tobago, January (*Glenn Bartley*).

female variably barred dark crown with some rufous speckling.

Vocalisations Chattering, rattling, strident series of *churrr* or *krrrr* notes. Notes clearly spaced or rapidly merged. Also a more pleasant trilling version. Squeaky repeated *wicka* notes in displays or when alarmed.

Drumming Both sexes apparently occasionally drum, but details lacking.

Status Common locally. Not threatened and perhaps increasing as forest clearance creates more open, secondary habitats. Some island races less secure.

Habitat Tropical, open, drier, deciduous woodlands, gallery forest, thickets, mangroves. Also disturbed humid forests, savanna, thorn and cactus scrub, plantations, parks, gardens and even cities. Avoids dense forest.

Range C and N South America including some islands. From Costa Rica to Colombia, Venezuela and the Guianas. Mostly below 2000m. Resident and sedentary.

Taxonomy and variation Four races: ***rubricapillus*** (most of range from SW Costa Rica to C Colombia, N Venezuela, the Guianas, Tobago); ***subfusculus*** (Coiba Island: off SW Panama) darker, browner below than nominate; ***seductus*** (San Miguel del Rey Island: off SE Panama) dark on breast, female with very red nape; ***paraguanae*** (Paraguana Peninsula: NW Venezuela) has widest white bars above, golden belly-patch, buffy face; male more yellow on forehead and nape buff or rusty; female orange-brown on nape. Amount of red and buff on head and belly varies greatly, some individuals appearing washed-out.

Similar species Hoffmann's Woodpecker has yellow nape and belly, but beware hybrids in Costa Rica, which typically have red crown, orange nape and belly. Black-cheeked Woodpecker has dark face.

Food and foraging Omnivorous, feeding on invertebrates such as ants, beetles and spiders, as well as seeds, nuts, fruit, berries and nectar. Visits fruit feeders, uses anvils. Often forages in pairs.

▼ The female lacks red on the crown. This is a nominate. Panama, February (*Wim de Groot*).

54. GILA WOODPECKER
Melanerpes uropygialis

L 22–25cm

Identification Mantle and back barred black and white. White rump and uppertail-coverts lightly barred. Underparts from throat to vent plain grey, yellowish around vent. Wings barred and chequered black and white, white bases of primaries form patch that shows well in flight. White central tail feathers barred black, outers black spotted white. Plain milky-brown to grey face and nape, sometimes tinged yellow. Nasal tufts buff. Iris dark. Bill blackish. Legs greyish. Sexes differ slightly: male has red crown patch which female lacks, though some females have red feather-tips. Males larger and longer-billed, but this not obvious in field. Juvenile duller overall, white barring above tinged buff, throat slightly flecked, paler yellow on belly.

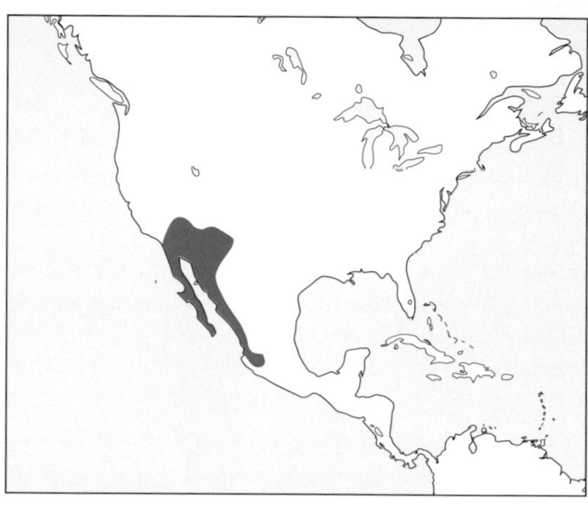

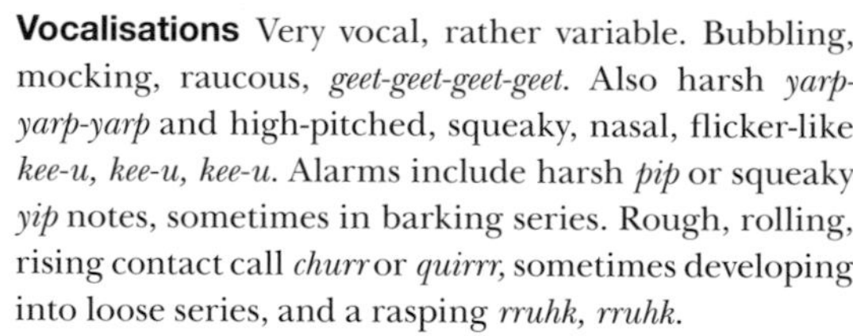

Vocalisations Very vocal, rather variable. Bubbling, mocking, raucous, *geet-geet-geet-geet*. Also harsh *yarp-yarp-yarp* and high-pitched, squeaky, nasal, flicker-like *kee-u, kee-u, kee-u*. Alarms include harsh *pip* or squeaky *yip* notes, sometimes in barking series. Rough, rolling, rising contact call *churr* or *quirrr,* sometimes developing into loose series, and a rasping *rruhk, rruhk*.

Drumming Infrequent, rather weak, but steady slow rolls, sometimes interspersed with calls.

Status Relatively common, but trends largely unknown. Probably stable overall, but has declined locally in California due to residential encroachment. In some areas under pressure from European Starlings usurping cavities.

Habitat Desert, especially with saguaro cactus. Also arid scrub, wooded watercourses, plantations, desert suburbs and settlements. Often excavates cavities in saguaro, but also palms or other trees. A keystone species; Elf Owl, Cactus Wren, Lucy's Warbler and other wildlife reuse its cavities.

Range North and Central America. From SW USA into Baja California and NW Mexico. Mainly lowlands, to 1600m in Mexico. Resident and mostly sedentary, some move northwards or to higher ground in winter.

Taxonomy and variation Four races: ***uropygialis*** (S California, Arizona, extreme S Nevada, extreme SW New Mexico into W Mexico); ***cardonensis*** (N and C Baja California) has wider barring and darker

◄ Adult male of nominate race. Note the red patch on the mid-crown. Arizona, United States, June (*Malcolm Schuyl*).

head than above; ***brewsteri*** (S Baja California) tightly barred above; ***fuscescens*** (NW Mexico) is dark. Birds on Tiburón Island, Gulf of California, paler than on mainland. Melanistic individuals regularly seen in SE Arizona. Note: individuals with purple faces have fed on saguaro fruit.

Similar species Velasquez's Woodpecker has coloured nape. Does not meet similar Grey-breasted Woodpecker.

Food and foraging Omnivorous and inventive. Takes insects, worms, lizards, songbird eggs and nestlings, nuts, berries, cactus fruit and corn. Visits feeders for oranges, suet, seeds and sugar water and stores acorns. Forages at all levels, often on the ground.

▲◄ Adult female Gila Woodpecker lacks red on the crown, and is overall slighter and shorter-billed than the male. Nominate race. Arizona, United States, April (*Judd Patterson*).

▲ Gila Woodpeckers often nest in a large saguaro cactus. Arizona, United States, June (*Malcolm Schuyl*).

◄ Both male and female juveniles are similar to the adult female, but they are duller and often with minimal yellow below. Arizona, United States, March (*Laura Stafford*).

55. HOFFMANN'S WOODPECKER

Melanerpes hoffmannii

L 18–20cm

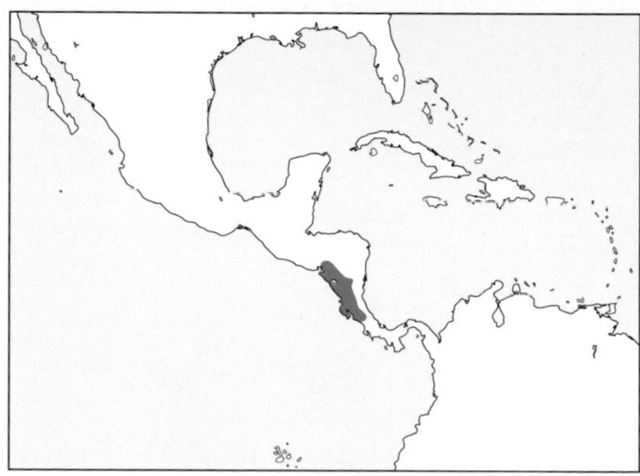

Identification Relatively short-tailed, subtly marked. Black above heavily barred white. Rump plain white. Face, ear-coverts, neck-sides and most of underparts pale greyish-buff. Flanks have yellow tones. Yellow, golden or orange belly-patch. Undertail and vent yellowish with dark bars and chevrons. Lores, nasal tufts, nape yellow to gold. Black upperwings barred white, primaries tipped white when fresh. Underwing barred brown and white. Uppertail black, central feather pair mostly white, outers black with some white barring. Iris reddish. Bill black. Legs grey. Sexes differ: male has orange or red mid-crown; female lacks red, having pale crown, and yellow areas often paler. Juveniles like respective adults, but duller with diffuse barring, washed-out yellow on belly and brown iris.

Vocalisations Often vocal. A raucous, harsh, rattling *chuurrrrr* of variable pitch and length, usually shrill, grating when alarmed. Also rapid, squeaky *witwitwit-witwit*. Song a softer, more pleasant, trilling.

Drumming Brief, about 1-second long, solid rolls made near nest.

Status Locally often common. Overall population and range increasing as forest clearance and fragmentation provides new open habitat.

◄ Adult male Hoffmann's Woodpecker. The male differs from the female in having a red patch on the crown. Rancho Naturalista, Costa Rica, December (*Dave Hawkins*).

Habitat Drier, open, lightly wooded terrain. Often in secondary growth, plantations, wooded pastures, farmsteads, settlements, gardens and parks.

Range Central America. From S Honduras through Nicaragua to C Costa Rica, largely on Pacific slope. Mainly lowlands, but to around 2000m. Resident and sedentary.

Taxonomy and variation Monotypic. Birds in Costa Rica with red crown, orange nape and orange belly are hybrids with Red-crowned Woodpecker.

Similar species Similar Red-crowned Woodpecker lacks yellow nape and belly. Differs from Velasquez's Woodpecker (interbreeds in Honduras) in smaller size and yellow nape.

Food and foraging Omnivorous. Takes ants, beetles and the like, but also figs, bananas, berries, *Cecropia* seeds, nectar, and often visits feeders. Forages mostly in trees, using various techniques.

▼ Adult female Hoffmann's Woodpecker has a pale grey crown; both sexes have a golden yellow nape. Rancho Solimar, Costa Rica, May (*Dave Hawkins*).

▼ Adult male. Although fairly restricted in range, this species is increasing as a result of anthopogenic habitat change. Arenal, Costa Rica, May (*Gérard Soury*).

56. GOLDEN-FRONTED WOODPECKER
Melanerpes aurifrons

L 22–26cm

Identification Barred black and white from mantle to lower back. White rump striking in flight. Tail mostly black with some white on outermost feathers. Plain grey below, often with yellow wash on belly. Face, ear-coverts and neck pale grey. Wings finely barred black and white, white base to primaries. Bill greyish. Iris reddish. Legs grey. Sexes differ: male has red mid-crown, golden or yellow nape, yellow lores and nasal tufts; female lacks red. Juvenile like adult female, but with streaked breast, crown sometimes tan.

Vocalisations Often noisy. Calls similar to, but generally louder and harsher than, equivalents of Gila and Red-bellied Woodpeckers. Contact calls include repeated clucking, chucking and croaking notes, harsh but steady *kirrrr,* grating *krrr* or *krr-r-r-r* and slower *kih-wrr* or *kih-wrr.* Cackling *kek-kek, check-eck, tsuka* and *wicka* alarms. Song a rolling, trilling series of *chuh* or *chah* notes. Simple *tig-tig* and gentle, low-pitched *grr* made by pairs.

Drumming Not an avid drummer. Males occasionally produce repeated 1-second rolls of medium tempo.

Status Locally common across range. Generally considered stable or increasing in the USA, though some local declines noted after a period of rapid increase. Its habit of excavating holes in telegraph poles led to culls in the USA in the late 19th and early 20th centuries.

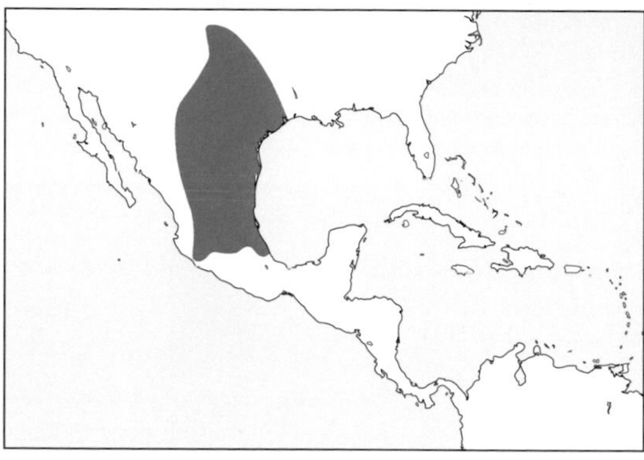

Habitat Arid, open woodland and scrub, particularly mesquite brush. Also oak-juniper savanna, riverine corridors, wooded grasslands, ranches, plantations and suburban parks and gardens.

Range North America. From S USA (extreme SW Oklahoma and Texas) into NE Mexico. Resident, but with a tendency to disperse. In the 20th century, US breeding range expanded 300km westwards in Texas and 400km to the N and NW into SW Oklahoma. Sea-level to 2500m.

◄ Adult male Golden-fronted Woodpecker. The male differs from the female in having a red patch on the crown. Mission, Texas, United States, February (*Dave Hawkins*).

Taxonomy and variation Monotypic. Individuals showing purple plumage have been stained by eating prickly-pear cactus.

Similar species Gila and Red-bellied Woodpeckers have white-barred tails and barred or speckled rumps. The latter, with which it hybridises, also has red on the nape.

Food and foraging Omnivorous, versatile, very frugivorous. Eats cactus fruits, berries, corn, nuts, seeds, as well as insects, spiders, songbird eggs, lizards and small mammals. Visits feeders and stores food. Forages at all levels.

► Adult male. This adaptable species is increasing its range across the southern United States. Mission, Texas, United States, February (*Dave Hawkins*).

▼ Adult female Golden-fronted Woodpecker lacks the red crown-patch of the male. Bentsen State Park, Texas, United States, February (*Dave Hawkins*).

57. VELASQUEZ'S WOODPECKER
Melanerpes santacruzi

L 22–26cm

Identification Very variable. All races barred black and white from mantle to lower back. Rump white. Tail mostly black with white dots on outer feathers. Plain grey below, with yellow, orange or red wash on belly, depending on race. Face, ear-coverts and neck pale grey. Wings finely barred black and white, white base to primaries on most. Bill greyish-black. Iris reddish. Legs grey. Sexes differ: male has red mid-crown, red/orange, gold or yellow nape; female lacks red on crown, nape colour varies. Juvenile more like adult female but duller, streaked below, and iris brownish.

Vocalisations Quite vocal. Most commonly a repeated loud, strident, level-pitched series of yapping, harsh notes, similar to Black-cheeked Woodpecker. Also a rolling, trembling, *pwurr-rr-rr*. Cackling *kek-kek-kek*

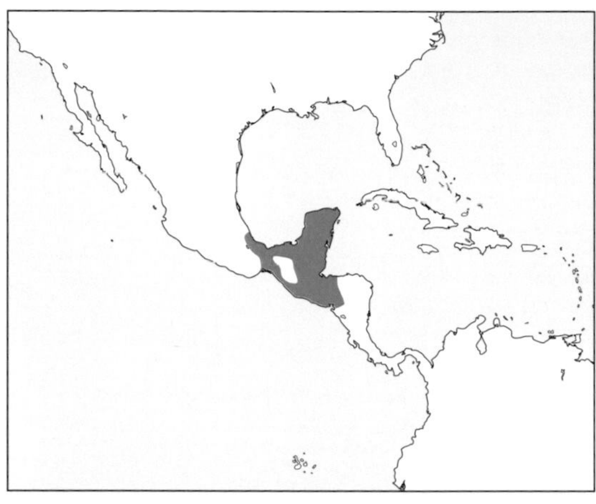

▲ Adult male *dubius*. Racial differences can be slight, but *dubius* usually has an orange or red belly and is very narrowly barred above. Yucatan Peninsula, Mexico, March (*Richard Tipton*).

◄ Adult male Velasquez's Woodpecker differs from the female in having a red crown. This is race *dubius*. Tikal, Guatemala, February (*Greg R. Homel*).

alarm and threat, plus nasal, repeated *ka-du-duk*.

Drumming Infrequent. Mainly done by males. Brief, repeated rolls of medium tempo, often ending with distinct, separated strikes.

Status Often locally common. Seems able to adapt to man-influenced habitats. Conservation category not assigned by the IUCN.

Habitat Dry, thorny scrub and brush with mesquite and cacti. Also tropical open, evergreen woodland, oak-juniper savanna, riparian corridors, pecan plantations and suburban parks and gardens.

Range Central America. From SE Mexico south to Nicaragua. Also islands off Honduras. Sea-level to around 2500m.

Taxonomy and variation In the early 20th century some of the current eleven races were considered distinct species, then grouped with Golden-fronted Woodpecker before being split and renamed once again. Further taxonomic changes possible: ***santacruzi*** (Chiapas, Mexico, to El Salvador, SW Honduras and NC Nicaragua) has buff or brown tones in mantle barring, buff or grey below, male has golden lores, greyish forecrown, red crown, red or orange nape, yellow belly; female golden lores and nape; ***grateloupensis*** (E Mexico: S Tamaulipas, C San Luis Potosi to E Puebla and C Veracruz) narrowly barred white above, lores red or gold; ***veraecrucis*** (E Mexico into NE Guatemala) is dark, tail with minimal white, lores, nape and belly red; ***dubius*** (Yucatan Peninsula, NE Guatemala and Belize) very finely barred white above; male has red lores, greyish forecrown, red crown and nape, red or orange belly; female lores red, nape orange or red; ***polygrammus*** (SW Mexico: SW Oaxaca into Chiapas) fairly broad white barring above, central tail feathers barred white; male has golden lores, greyish forecrown, red crown, orange or golden nape, yellow belly; female crown cream or grey, nape golden; ***hughlandi*** (Guatemala) broadly barred above; ***pauper*** (coastal N Honduras) narrowly barred above; ***leei*** (Cozumel Island: off Yucatan) has brown tones below, finely barred white on mantle, lower flanks and vent, rump barred, tail usually all black; male has red from lores to nape, deep red belly; ***turneffensis*** (Turneffe Islands: off Belize) broadly barred above, male's red areas tending to orange; ***insulanus*** (Utila Island: off N Honduras) has black tail, slight white supercilium and golden lores, male has all red crown, nape red or orange; ***canescens*** (Roatan and Barbareta islands: off N Honduras) is pale-faced, narrowly barred above, belly and nape red, male crown all red. Also pronounced regional differences in crown, nape, lores and vent colour and degree of barring above, and racial, intermediate and clinal variants in bill, tail and wing lengths.

Similar species Golden-cheeked Woodpecker has black around eye. Grey-breasted, Yucatan and Hoffman's Woodpeckers all smaller.

Food and foraging Omnivorous and versatile, taking wide range of invertebrates and plant matter. Forages from tree and cactus tops to the ground.

▲ Adult female Velasquez's Woodpecker lacks red on the crown. This bird is of the nominate race *santacruzi*. San Juan del Sur, Nicaragua, December (*Dan Polley*).

58. RED-BELLIED WOODPECKER
Melanerpes carolinus

L 24cm

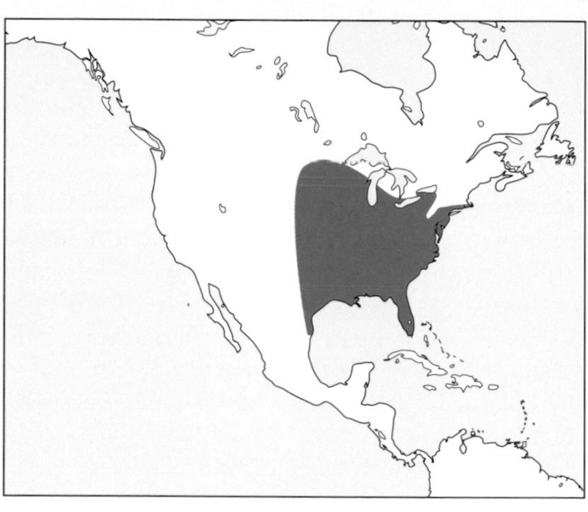

Identification Despite the name belly-patch is pinkish or orange and often faint. Barred black and white above. White uppertail-coverts and rump speckled black. Pale grey below, black chevrons on undertail-coverts. Wings barred black and white. White patch at base of primaries clear in flight. White central tail feathers barred black, outers black dotted white. Ear-coverts pale grey. Iris chestnut. Bill black. Legs greyish. Sexes differ: male has red or orange crown and nape, lores and cheek flushed pink or orange; female smaller, red only on nape, sometimes reddish feather-tips on crown and belly-patch can be minimal. Juveniles much like adults, but head dusky-brown, less or no red on crown, nape sometimes golden, iris brown.

Vocalisations Very vocal, except in summer. Various rattles and *wicka* notes. Loud, harsh or musical, gently rising *quirrr* or *kwirr* in series. Females utter flatter *quer.* Territorial *cha-aa-ah* made all year. Throaty contact *cha* note and scolding *cha-aa-aa. Kew-kew-kew* alarm, rolling single or double *churrr* in spring. Also *chig-chig, chiv-chiv* or *chiff-chiff* in slow series and faster *chig-chigchchchchch. Chee-wuck* in disputes. Single, low-pitched *chug* uttered in flight. Mated pairs exchange low-pitched *grr* sounds.

Drumming Both sexes drum, but not avidly. Even-pitched 1-second rolls of 16–19 strikes. Tempo steady, though may accelerate at the end. Rolls sometimes preceded by distinct knocks.

Status Locally common in SE, less so in NE and Great Plains. Increasing overall and expanding W and N.

Habitat Wide range occupied: damp, open pine, hardwood and mixed woodlands, swamps, savanna, farmland, orchards, plantations, parks and urban areas.

Range North America. Most common E of Great Plains, from SE Canada (Ontario) to SE USA (Florida, Texas). In last 50 years expanded to New England, Great Lakes and onto W Great Plains. Sea-level to 900m. Resident and mainly sedentary, N birds moving S in hard winters. Often appears outside usual range.

Taxonomy and variation Monotypic. Birds in S Florida smaller, with all-black central tail (recalling Golden-fronted) and less white on wings than in N;

◄ Adult male Red-bellied Woodpecker has an all-reddish-orange crown, and more colour on the face than the female. Milford, Michigan, United States, October (*Steve Gettle*).

males have brown forecrown, those further N red.

Similar species Golden-fronted Woodpecker lacks 'red' belly, has white rump and yellow nape. Hybrids occur in Texas and Oklahoma.

Food and foraging Omnivorous and opportunistic. Eats insects in all stages, spiders, fruit, berries, nuts, mast, nectar, sap, songbird eggs and nestlings, small mammals, reptiles and frogs. Visits feeders, uses anvils and caches food in trees, fence posts and utility poles.

◄ Adult female Red-bellied Woodpecker. Like many other *Melanerpes*, this species is highly omnivorous and an inventive forager. Venice, Florida, United States, March (*Dave Hawkins*).

▼ Adult female Red-bellied Woodpecker. Note that only the nape is red; the crown is greyish. Florida, United States, October (*Lesley van Loo*).

59. WEST INDIAN WOODPECKER
Melanerpes superciliaris

L 26–30cm

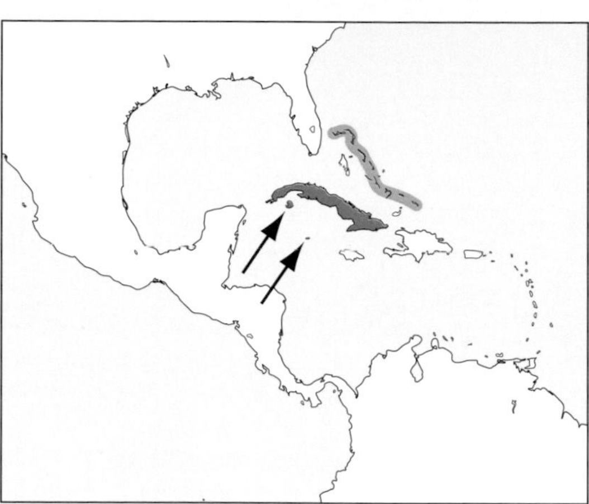

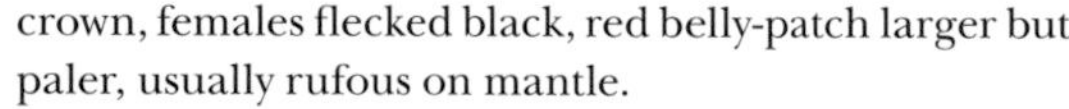

Other names In the Bahamas 'Bahaman Woodpecker', in Cayman Islands 'Cayman Woodpecker' and locally 'Red-head'.

Identification Upperparts and wings black, extensively barred buff or white. Rump narrowly barred, uppertail-coverts white with black chevrons. In flight white outerwing patches obvious. Underwing grey, coverts barred black and white. Uppertail black with bold white bars on central and outer feather pairs, undertail grey. Pale grey below, breast cinnamon, belly with red or orange patch, flanks with black chevrons. Throat and face pale grey with variable black around eye. Iris reddish. Long black bill. Legs greyish. Sexes differ: male red on crown and nape; female red only on nape with crown grey. Both juveniles have red on crown, females flecked black, red belly-patch larger but paler, usually rufous on mantle.

Vocalisations Range of loud, harsh, raucous, chattering calls. A high-pitched, repeated, churring *krruuu-krruu-kruu*. Also a lower-pitched *carrah-carrah-carrah* or *kkrraaa-kkrraaa,* a drawn-out *ke-ke-ke-ke-ke* and repeated *waa* notes.

Drumming Produces repeated short, solid rolls in the breeding period, birds sometimes duetting.

Status Abundant in Cuba, common on Grand Cayman and Abaco, rarer on San Salvador. Possibly extirpated from Grand Bahama after hurricanes devastated woodlands in 2004 and 2005. Range-restricted, scattered across several islands, but not threatened overall.

Habitat Typically dry, open scrub forests, but also palm groves, plantations, wooded swamps, mangroves, coastal and suburban woods, parks and gardens.

Range Caribbean. Cuba and adjacent isles, Grand Cayman, the Bahamas and the Turks and Caicos Islands. Sea-level to around 900m. Resident and sedentary.

Taxonomy and variation Five races: ***superciliaris*** (Cuba and adjacent islands) is largest race, most black around eye; ***nyeanus*** (Grand Bahama and San Salvador island) is smaller, darker below with greenish hue, nasal tufts dark and with minimal black behind eye;

◄ Adult male West Indian Woodpecker has an all-red crown. This race, *caymanensis*, lacks black around the eye. Grand Cayman, April (*Yves-Jacques Rey-Millet*).

▼ Adult female has red only on the nape, with grey on the crown. This bird is of the race *caymanensis*. Grand Cayman, March (*Yves-Jacques Rey-Millet*).

blakei (Great Abaco Island in N Bahamas) darker still, blacker around eye, greenish mantle, dark grey below and on face; ***murceus*** (Isla de Pinos, Cayo Largo, Cayo Real) is small with reduced red on nape; ***caymanensis*** (Grand Cayman) lacks black orbital area, is narrowly barred buff or yellowish above, female greyer on hind-crown: has been considered a distinct species.

Similar species None within range.

Food and foraging Omnivorous and opportunistic, besides invertebrates taking lizards, geckos, frogs, berries and fruit. Forages at all levels, including the ground. Uses anvils to process large and hard items.

► Adult male nominate. This race is very black around the eye. La Belen, Cuba, March (*Gerard Gorman*).

▼ A family of *caymanensis* West Indian Woodpeckers; the female is below, the male above, and a juvenile is in the cavity entrance. Grand Cayman, July (*Yves-Jacques Rey-Millet*).

SPHYRAPICUS

A New World genus of four species. All breed in North America and are, to varying degrees, migratory. Three (Yellow-bellied, Red-naped and Red-breasted Sapsuckers) resemble each other closely, have similar biology, calls and drumming and were previously considered conspecific. Hybridisation is common and this, along with racial and individual variation, can make identification difficult. Sapsuckers do indeed feed on sap (they lick it up rather than 'suck'), which they access by drilling rows of evenly spaced, shallow holes, called wells, in tree bark. Their diet also includes invertebrates, which visit the sap wells and become stuck, fruit, berries and nuts.

Williamson's Sapsucker *Sphyrapicus thyroides*, adult male. Wyoming, United States, July (*Mike Danzenbaker*).

60. WILLIAMSON'S SAPSUCKER

Sphyrapicus thyroideus

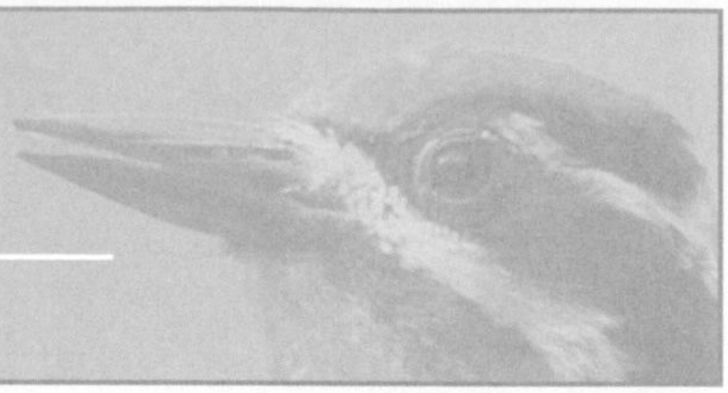

L 21–24cm

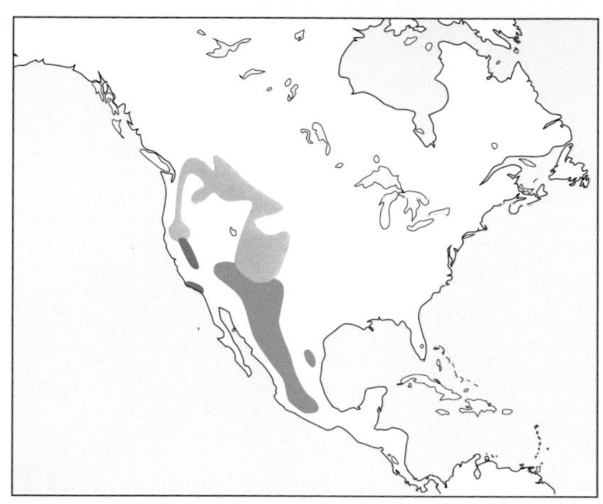

Identification Largest, most sexually dimorphic sapsucker. Both sexes have black chest band, yellow belly, white rump (obvious in flight), black bill, chestnut iris, greyish legs. Male black, white and yellow. Mostly unmarked glossy black upperparts and tail, often with bluish hue. Yellow from breast to vent, black flanks barred white. Wings black, spotted white on primaries, prominent white oval on coverts. Black head crossed by long white post-ocular and moustachial stripes, throat scarlet. Female much plainer, with tawny head, some streaking in malar area, buff or brown throat, brown upperparts and wings finely barred buff or white; less black below, dull yellow, sometimes barred. Also lacks white wing-patch and red throat, though some with orange or rufous feather-tips. Juvenile male resembles

◄ Adult male Williamson's Sapsucker. This is very different to the female, and to other sapsucker species. Race *nataliae.* Colorado, United States, October (*Rolf Nussbaumer*).

► In contrast to the male, the adult female is decidedly drab. Race *nataliae.* Wyoming, United States, June (*Ian Merrill*).

adult, but throat white. Juvenile female like adult, but less marked, lacking black chest band.

Vocalisations Mostly quiet outside breeding season. Plaintive mewing and soft chattering sounds. Clear, raptor-like *queeah* or *quee-ark* and slow *chh* contact calls. Scolding *churrr* alarm, undulating in pitch. Gruff, corvid-like *ca-haw* with high-pitched first syllable, sometimes ending in rapid trill, uttered in conflicts and courtship. Single or repeated *chyaah* or *cheeur* by territorial males, often interspersed with drums, female version higher-pitched. Also *pa-chik-a-wik*. Subdued *yuk, yuk, yuk* by nest.

Drumming Both sexes drum. Variable but distinctive, broken rolls of up to 3 seconds, beginning faster than other sapsuckers before slowing and ending with 3–8 solid knocks.

Status Considered stable, although steep declines locally due to intensive forestry.

Habitat Drier, open, mountain coniferous forests: spruce, fir, pines, especially ponderosa. Also mixed forest with aspen. Often winters at lower elevations in pine-oak-juniper forests. Oak-pine in Mexican uplands.

Range North and Central America. Breeds mostly 850–3500m in W and C North America. Isolated populations in Nevada and Baja California. Some migrate south in September-October to SW states (breeding and wintering ranges overlap) and Mexico, returning March-April. Females often winter farther south. California and Washington State populations sedentary. Some move altitudinally. Vagrant to eastern Great Plains.

Taxonomy and variation Two very similar races: ***thyroideus*** (British Columbia to N Baja California) and ***nataliae*** (SE British Columbia to the Rocky and Great Basin Mts, wintering Mexico). Latter has longer, heavier bill than nominate. Sometimes regarded as monotypic.

Similar species Could be mistaken for other sapsuckers in flight, but larger and not as similar to them as they are to each other. Females wintering in SW USA often confused with Gila Woodpecker.

Food and foraging Omnivorous, taking sap, phloem, cambium, fruit, berries and insects. Ants are important food for nestlings.

61. YELLOW-BELLIED SAPSUCKER
Sphyrapicus varius

L 20–22cm

Identification Mostly black and white with red crown. Striped head formed by black hindcrown, broad white post-ocular stripe to nape, broad black ear-covert band, white lores and moustache, black malar. Mantle and back heavily barred black and white. Black chest band, pale yellow breast and belly (not the only sapsucker with yellow below), flanks with black chevrons. Wings mostly black with white coverts forming long vertical panel. White rump obvious in flight. Mostly black tail, some white bars or spots on central and outer feathers. Bill blackish. Legs greyish. Iris chestnut. Sexes differ slightly: male has black-bordered red throat, female's throat white. Female's crown variably red, black or red and black; back usually black and buff rather than black and white. Juvenile distinct, scaled or mottled olive-brown, lacking red crown and throat (males may have some red) and black chest. Unlike relatives, juvenile plumage retained until winter.

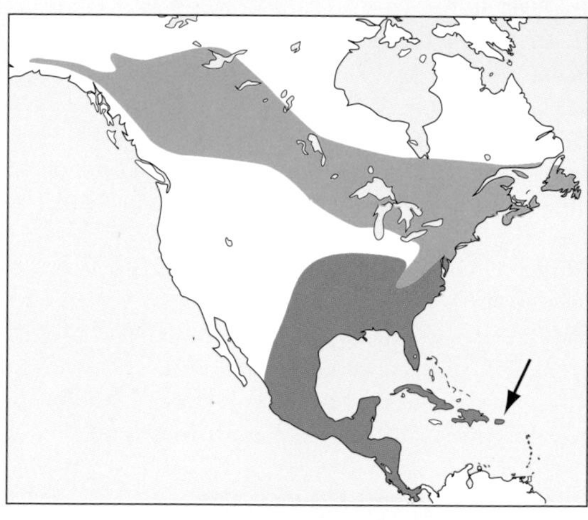

Vocalisations Nasal, whining, meowing *neeah, weeah, meeyay, meeww* or *mwee,* recalls Grey Catbird or small raptor. Male song a squealing series of 6–10 *quee-ark* or *kwee-urk.* Gentle *week* or *wurp* between mates, more emphatic *waa, chee-aa* or *quee-ah* alarms. Aggressive *juk* in conflicts, *geert* in flight, mewing *c-waan* when excited, shrill *quarr* when threatened. Hoarse, rattling *wik-a-wik-a* series.

Drumming Rhythmic, broken, knocking rolls of 1–2 seconds, beginning rapidly, then pausing, ending with 2–3 well-spaced single or double strikes. Females drum less than males.

Status Local declines and increases noted. Probably decreasing overall.

Habitat Breeds in open, mature, mixed forests, usually with aspen, birch and maple. Also younger forests, coniferous and riparian woods. On migration also uses orchards, plantations, coastal palm stands, scrub, parks and wooded suburbs.

Range North and Central America. Most northerly sapsucker. Breeding SE Alaska, across boreal Canada, NE USA and Appalachians. Isolated populations Tennessee and N Carolina. Migratory, almost whole

◀ Adult male Yellow-bellied Sapsucker. Note the red throat bordered by black. Jamaica, May (*Yves-Jacques Rey-Millet*).

population moving S in autumn, wintering SE USA through Mexico to Panama and Caribbean. Returns April-May. Sea-level to 3500m. Vagrant California, Colombia, Greenland, Iceland, Britain.

Taxonomy and variation Monotypic. Some females lack red crown. Birds in S Appalachians smaller and darker. Some may have red on nape.

Similar species Very like Red-naped Sapsucker (they hybridise in Canada) with some females and juveniles almost identical, but most lack red nape, brighter yellow below; male's throat enclosed by black. Calls also similar. Also apparently hybridises with Red-breasted Sapsucker.

Food and foraging Feeds mainly on tree sap taken from specially drilled, and defended, lines of wells (which hummingbirds also visit). Also phloem, fruit, berries, seeds, beetles and ants. Drills palm trees in wintering areas.

► Adult female Yellow-bellied Sapsucker. Note the white throat and reduced red on crown. Florida, United States, March (*Yves-Jacques Rey-Millet*).

▼ First-winter female, at her sap-wells. This young bird can be sexed, since first-winter male would show some red in the throat at this time of year. Bay of Pigs, Cuba, March (*Gerard Gorman*).

62. RED-NAPED SAPSUCKER
Sphyrapicus nuchalis

L 20–22cm

Identification Crown red, hindcrown black, nape red, rear of nape black. White stripe from lores across cheek and neck-sides to chest, thin white post-ocular line. Ear-coverts black. Broad black chest band, white or yellow from breast to vent. Flanks with dark flecks and chevrons. Black above, barred white. Rump white. Mostly black tail, some white on central and outermost feathers. Wings mostly black, large white patches on coverts, primaries tipped white. Bill blackish. Legs greyish. Iris blackish. Sexes similar: male has red chin and throat, female white chin or red mottled white and smaller red areas on head. Juvenile distinct, olive-brown overall, crown dark, throat buff.

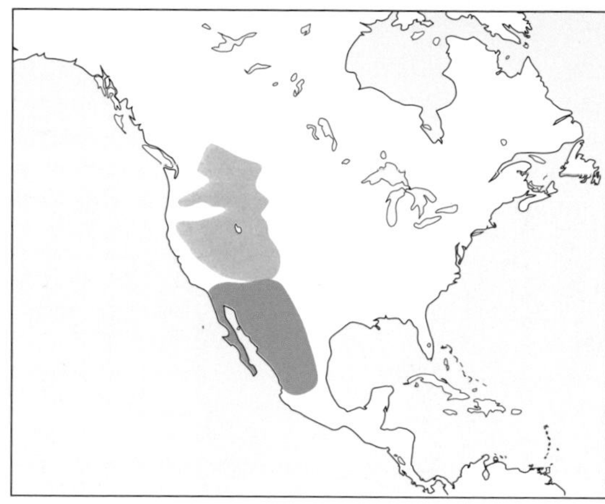

Vocalisations Rasping, chattering calls like Yellow-bellied Sapsucker. Plaintive, mewing *meeah*, soft, nasal, tooting notes. Male song up to 16 squealing *kwee-urk* notes. Alarm call a harsh, scolding *waa*.

Drumming Both sexes drum, males more so. Irregular, broken bursts of around 5–7 strikes, then brief pause before series of slower strikes ending in precise single or double knocks, lasting less than 2 seconds in total.

Status Fairly common, overall population probably stable. Local declines mainly due to forestry management and drought.

Habitat Breeds in open, fragmented, deciduous and coniferous forest, particularly fir, pine, spruce, larch, aspen, birch, willow. In winter also in oak, oak-pine, riparian woodlands, orchards, even gardens.

Range North and Central America. Breeds from British Columbia and Alberta, through the Rockies to New Mexico and Arizona. Isolated populations in S Dakota, Wyoming, Montana, E California, W Nevada. Sea-level to 3000m. Northern birds migrate S to winter, some to areas with sedentary populations, others to S Texas, S California, Mexico, sometimes Guatemala and Honduras. Females tend to winter further S than males.

Taxonomy and variation Monotypic. Previously lumped with Yellow-bellied Sapsucker. Both adults can lack red nape, some have red in black ear-coverts.

Similar species In some ways intermediate between

◄ The sexes are very similar in Red-naped Sapsucker. However, the red chin and extensive red on the crown indicate that this is an adult male. Colorado, United States, October.

Yellow-bellied and Red-breasted Sapsuckers. Hybridises with both, offspring with mixed features. Most like Yellow-bellied, but has red nape, larger red throat patch without clear black malar border, thinner white post-ocular stripe, less yellow below. Respective females and juveniles often inseparable, though difference in moult timings means birds retaining juvenile plumage after about October are Yellow-bellied.

Food and foraging Omnivorous, consuming sap, cambium, phloem, buds, berries, fruit, seeds, ants and other invertebrates. The most aerial sapsucker, often flycatching in breeding period.

▼ Adult female. Note the white chin and reduced red on the crown. Colorado, United States, October (*Rolf Nussbaumer*).

63. RED-BREASTED SAPSUCKER
Sphyrapicus ruber

L 20–22cm

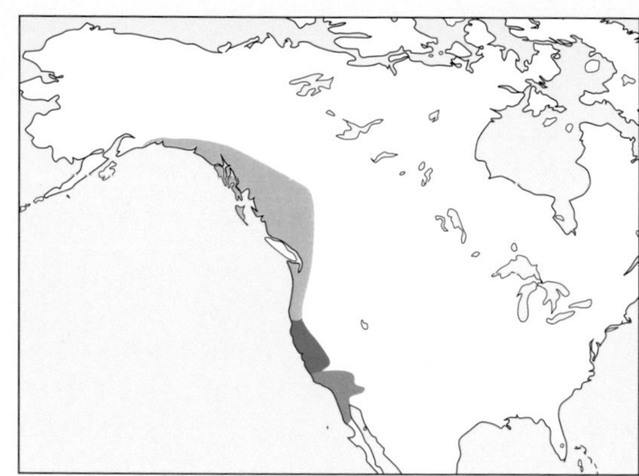

Identification Yellow, buff or white below, flanks flecked and streaked black. Black above with narrow rows of white, buff or gold spots. Black tail barred white on central feathers, outers edged white. Large white patches on wing-coverts. White rump obvious in flight. Lores white, variable white moustache depending on race. Black bill slightly upturned. Legs greyish. Iris chestnut. Sexes alike: both have red hood over head, nape and chest, but male often brighter, scarlet. Juvenilesdistinct until autumn, greyish below, brownish above, little if any red, plain back, rump barred.

Vocalisations Often silent outside breeding season. Various plaintive, whining, contact mews and chattering in flight, as other sapsuckers. Simple *waa* alarm note, also *puc*. Male song a series of nasal, squeaky, squealing *kwee-urk* or *quee-ark* notes. Harsh *wicka-wicka-wicka* in disputes.

Drumming Both sexes drum, females less so. Slow rolls with broken cadence and irregular length. Sequences usually around 1.5 seconds long, starting with around 22 rapid strikes per second, followed by slower, carefully spaced strikes.

▼ Adult Red-breasted Sapsucker of the nominate race. The sexes are generally indistinguishable in the field. Lake Selma, Oregon, United States, May. (*Steve Byland*).

Status Overall population probably stable, but local situations vary, e.g. increasing in Oregon, declining in California.

Habitat Open or thick, damp or dry, coniferous, deciduous and mixed upland forests. Also riparian woodlands, secondary growth and orchards. Conifers important for sap.

Range North America. Mainly Pacific Coast mountain ranges, from westernmost Canada into USA. Usually between 500–3000m. Northern birds are short-distance migrants, wintering as far S as Baja California. Others sedentary or move locally to lower elevations.

Taxonomy and variation Two races: ***ruber*** (coastal S Alaska to W Oregon) and ***daggetti*** (SW Oregon to Sierra Nevada: S California and W Nevada) which is slightly smaller than nominate, paler yellow below, duller red, less red on breast, more white on back and in flight feathers, with white lores continuing as long moustache and sometimes a white fleck behind eye. Previously lumped with Yellow-bellied Sapsucker.

Similar species Most (especially *daggetti*) like Red-naped Sapsucker but much redder and lacks black chest band. Juveniles very similar. Calls also alike (and Yellow-bellied Sapsucker). Hybridises with both, particularly Red-naped.

Food and foraging Makes and maintains its own wells, but also takes sap seeping from other tree wounds. Wild and cultivated fruit, berries, nuts, seeds, ants and other invertebrates also eaten.

► Adult Red-breasted Sapsucker. This is the California race, *daggetti*. Note the duller and less extensive red below than the nominate, and more white across the cheek (suggesting a moustache). San Francisco, California, United States, February (*Johanna van de Woestijne*).

Cuban Green Woodpecker *Xiphidiopicus percussus*. Adult male. Zapata Swamp, Cuba, March (*Gerard Gorman*).

XIPHIDIOPICUS

A monospecific genus endemic to Cuba and adjacent islands. Taxonomically fairly distinct, but relationships to other woodpeckers unclear; probably most closely related to *Melanerpes*. Often seen in pairs. Birds make deliberate whirring sounds with their wings when arriving at nest changeovers, in order to alert the sitting partner.

64. CUBAN GREEN WOODPECKER

Xiphidiopicus percussus

L 21–25cm

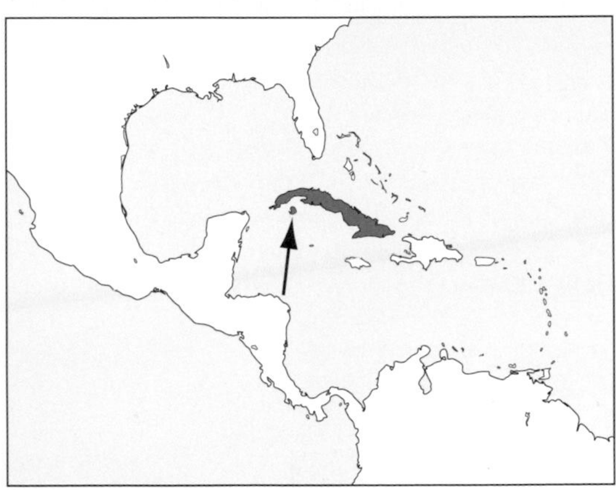

Identification Head and face mostly white with black post-ocular stripe. Olive-green with greyish tones above. Rump yellow, gently barred. Uppertail brown, central tail grey, outer feathers barred brown. Yellowish from breast to vent, flecked and streaked chocolate, whitish flanks heavily barred black. Chin black, red on throat and chest. Primaries and secondaries brown, broadly barred white. Underwing barred brown. Iris brown, orbital ring grey. Bill bluish-black. Legs greenish. Sexes differ: male larger with complete red shaggy crown from forehead to nape, female crown black streaked white, red only at rear and on nape. Both sexes raise their crown feathers when alarmed or excited. Juvenile overall duller than adult, more

► Adult male Cuban Green Woodpecker of the nominate race. Males have a complete red crown. Cuba, June (*Pete Morris*).

marked below, tail more barred, throat and chest chocolate, red on head restricted to crown stripe and some have red wash on mantle and/or orange on belly.

Vocalisations Most frequently a harsh, low-pitched *jorrr-jorrr-jorrr* (hence local name 'Jorre Jorre') or *gwurr-gwurr-gwurr.* Also a higher pitched *eh-eh-eh,* a repeated, nasal, two-note, mewing *ta-ha,* squealing, squawking *gwuk* and *chwet* notes.

Drumming Not known to drum.

Status Though restricted to one country, common, widespread and adaptable. Seemingly not threatened and considered stable.

Habitat Open and closed forests and woodlands of many types. Particularly damp deciduous, but also drier pine stands. Also mangroves, wooded farmland, palm groves, parks and gardens.

Range Endemic to Cuba, including many of its islets. Resident. Recorded on Hispaniola: probably storm-blown. Sea-level to 2000m.

Taxonomy and variation Two races, though others on smaller islands have been claimed. Much individual and regional variation in plumage and size, upland birds generally bigger. Nominate ***percussus*** (mainland Cuba, Sabana and Camaguey archipelagos); ***insulapinorum*** (Isle of Pines, Cantiles Keys, Jardines de la Reina archipelago) is smaller, paler yellow below, more barred on tail, less red on throat and chest than nominate. Some males have black in red crown, others have orange on belly.

Similar species None within range.

Food and foraging Mainly insectivorous, but also takes fruit and drinks flower nectar. Often forages in pairs, sometimes in parties of up to 5 birds, at most levels, often in epiphytes, creepers and vines.

◄ Adult female nominate. Females have a black forecrown, with red at the rear. Zapata Swamp, Cuba, March (*Gerard Gorman*).

Bennett's Woodpecker *Campethera bennetti*, adult male. Okavango, Botswana, October.

CAMPETHERA

An African genus of 12 small to medium-sized species, resident south of the Sahara. All are essentially green above with yellowish flight-feather shafts. The sexes mainly differ in crown and malar colour. Several species are very similar and difficult to separate. The *Campethera* are weak drummers, some species probably not drumming at all. Though not truly terrestrial, most readily forage on the ground; their body structure, with only a semi-stiffened tail, reflects this. They prey mainly on termites and particularly ants, which they lap up with their flexible and sticky (rather than sharp and harpoon-like) tongue.

65. FINE-SPOTTED WOODPECKER
Campethera punctuligera

L 21–22cm

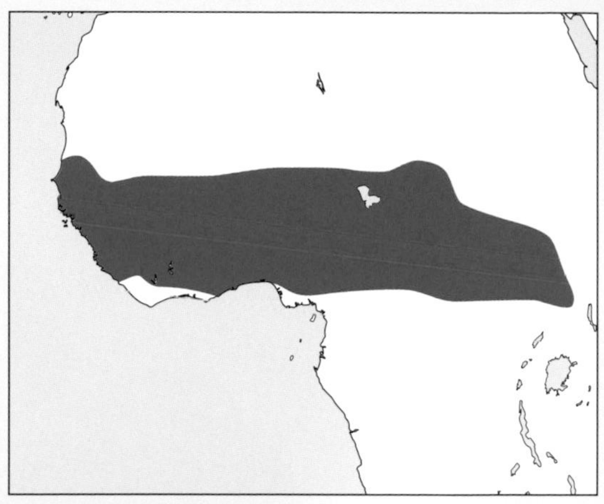

Identification Pale yellow or white below, finely and sparsely spotted black on chest, breast and flanks. Light green above with yellow spotting. Yellowish rump lightly barred. Ear-coverts off-white, blackish post-ocular stripe and broad white supercilium. White throat and cream neck finely spotted black. Olive wings barred yellow and cream on flight feathers; underwing yellowish with dark barring. Uppertail yellow barred olive-brown, feather shafts yellow. Iris pink or red, orbital ring grey. Bill grey. Legs greyish. Sexes differ: male has red crown, nape and malar, all variably flecked grey or black; female red only from hindcrown to nape, rest of crown black flecked white, faint black malar speckled white. Juvenile more like adult female in having plain black forecrown, but darker above,

◀ Adult male Fine-spotted Woodpecker nominate race. The red crown and touch of red in the malar stripe indicate a male. The Gambia, October (*Martin Goodey*).

more buff below, blacker malar and post-ocular stripes, duller iris and bluish legs.

Vocalisations Rather vocal, duets often performed by pairs. Repetitive, ringing *kip-kip-kip-kieeh-kieeh-kieeh*. Repeated, whining *peer* or *kweer* notes, not unlike a wryneck. Also a grating *nyaa-nyaa-nyaa, wik-wik-wik* and *tick-tick-tick* when agitated.

Drumming May not drum, or perhaps only rarely, but information lacking.

Status Widespread and fairly common. Little precise population data, but overall considered stable.

Habitat Lightly wooded dry savanna, bush and open grasslands with acacia and other trees. In some areas damp woodlands, more closed forest and palm groves.

Range Africa. Occurs across the heart of the continent, S of the Sahara, from SW Mauretania E to South Sudan and DR Congo. Mainly lowlands. Resident and sedentary.

Taxonomy and variation Two races: ***punctuligera*** (most of range from SW Mauritania and Senegambia E to SW Sudan and N DR Congo); and ***balia*** (South Sudan and NE DR Congo), which is whiter below, more clearly and widely spotted than nominate, female spotted, rather than streaked, white on forecrown. Some individuals finely barred dark on flanks.

Similar species Does not meet very similar Bennett's Woodpecker. May overlap with Nubian Woodpecker, which is browner, darker on cheeks and ear-coverts and more heavily marked below with larger spots. Golden-tailed Woodpecker is streaked below and more marked on the face.

Food and foraging Mainly ants and termites taken from trees, the ground and at their colonies (also excavates cavities in termitaria). Often forages in family groups, sometimes in mixed-species flocks.

▼ The black forecrown with red only at the rear and lack of red in the malar stripe indicates that this is a female Fine-spotted Woodpecker nominate race. The Gambia, October (*Bill Baston*).

66. BENNETT'S WOODPECKER

Campethera bennettii

L 18–20cm

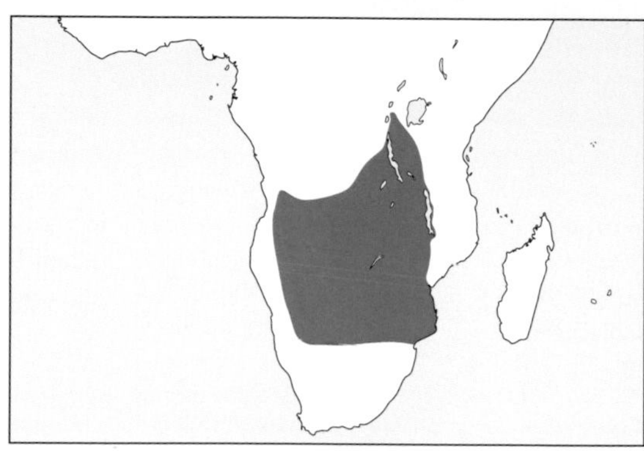

Identification Olive-brown above with pale yellow barring and spotting. Neck-sides white, spotted black. Yellowish or cream below with dark spots, tending to bars on flanks. Wings olive barred pale; primaries browner edged green. Uppertail buff or yellow; feather shafts yellow or gold. Undertail-coverts white spotted and barred dark; undertail yellow with black tip. Upper mandible grey, lower mandible paler. Legs grey-green. Iris red, orbital ring grey. Sexes differ: male has red crown and nape, red malar, cream throat speckled black at the centre and pale ear-coverts. Female yellower above, lacking red malar; red only on hind-crown; forecrown black spotted white; and distinct brown chin, throat and ear-coverts. Juvenile more like female, having black crown, but iris brown, and juvenile male has black malar.

Vocalisations Calls vary regionally. Commonly, a simple, single *churr* note and musical trilling, sometimes more throaty. A chattering, shrill, high-pitched *whirrr-itt-whrrr-itt,* often performed as duet. Territorial call a neighing *ddrahh, ddrahh, ddray-ay, ddray-ay, dray-ay*. Also a *wi-wi-wi-wi-wi*.

Drumming Seldom drums, only occasionally producing quiet rolls.

Status Fairly common overall. Common in the Okavango, uncommon in Tanzania. Considered stable, although local declines and population fragmentation has occurred due to woodland clearance for farming and creation of plantations.

Habitat Mature, damp and arid broadleaved woodlands, bush, savanna and parkland. Often in acacia and *miombo* (*Brachystegia*) and *mopane* woodlands. Avoids dense forest, plantations and non-native trees.

Range Africa. Mainly lowland savanna belt S of the Equator, in Congo, D.R.Congo, Rwanda, Burundi, Tanzania, Malawi, Mozambique, Zimbabwe, Botswana, South Africa, Swaziland, Namibia and Angola. Sea-level to 1600m. Resident and sedentary, perhaps nomadic in arid regions.

Taxonomy and variation Two races: ***bennettii*** (C Angola to SE DR Congo, Tanzania, Malawi and NE South Africa); and ***capricorni*** (S Angola to N Namibia, N Botswana and SW Zambia). Latter has whiter rump, more buff and plainer underparts, breast sometimes without spots; and females often darker on throat and ear-coverts than nominate. Birds in NW often very plain with peach hue below. Upperpart markings and tone vary between populations, e.g. in drier areas birds are usually drabber and paler.

◄ Adult male of the nominate race. Males have a complete red crown, red in the malar stripe and pale ear-coverts. Kruger NP, South Africa, August (*Martin Willis*).

Similar species Like sympatric Golden-tailed Woodpecker, though that species streaked not spotted below. Knysna Woodpecker darker, heavily blotched below. Nubian Woodpecker has larger and more spots on the breast and streaked face. Mombasa Woodpecker streaked not spotted below. Reichenow's Woodpecker has speckled throat and streaked ear-coverts.

Food and foraging Mostly ants and termites in all stages, often taken on the ground and at their colonies. More terrestrial than its relatives, foraging in short grass and on bare ground, though trees also visited. Sometimes feeds in family parties.

◄ Adult female nominate. Females have a distinctive brown ear-covert patch and throat, and red only on the hindcrown. Kruger NP, South Africa, August (*Ingo Waschkies*).

▼ Adult female *capricorni*. Differences between the two races are slight, with intergrades probably occurring. Khama Rhino Sanctuary, Botswana, March (*Vincent Grafhorst*).

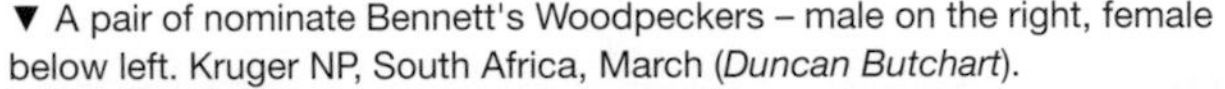

▼ A pair of nominate Bennett's Woodpeckers – male on the right, female below left. Kruger NP, South Africa, March (*Duncan Butchart*).

67. REICHENOW'S WOODPECKER
Campethera scriptoricauda

L 20–22cm

Other names Speckle-throated Woodpecker, Tanzanian Woodpecker.

Identification Olive-green above with pale spotting. White or buff below with large, bold olive or brown spots on chest and breast, belly to vent less spotted. White chin and throat speckled chocolate. Dark band behind eye merges into brown and white streaked ear-coverts. White supercilium. Wings dark green, flight feathers brownish barred buff or yellow; coverts spotted buff; underwing light green. Uppertail olive-brown, barred yellowish, feather shafts yellow. Iris dark red, orbital ring grey. Upper mandible greyish, lower yellowish at base. Legs grey, green or bluish. Sexes differ slightly: male has all-red crown, nape and malar, with dark flecks; female has red nape, black forecrown dotted white and indistinct dark malar flecked white. Juvenile more like adult female, lacking red forecrown, but spotting heavier above, less boldly spotted below.

Vocalisations Much like Bennett's Woodpecker. Repeated chattering *wi-wi-wi-wi* and a musical, trilling *churr.*

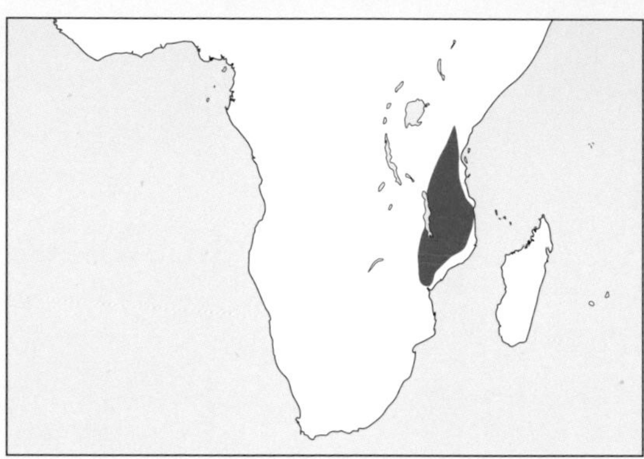

Drumming Said to occasionally drum softly, but details lacking.

Status Fairly common locally. Widespread in Mozambique, less so in Tanzania. Conservation category not assigned by the IUCN. Poorly known.

Habitat Various open, broadleaved woodlands, savanna, thorny bush and particularly *miombo* (*Brachystegia*) woodlands with a grassy understorey in which to forage.

Range Africa. Restricted to E and S Tanzania, S Malawi and N and C Mozambique. Resident and sedentary.

Taxonomy and variation Monotypic. Has been treated as a race of Bennett's Woodpecker, and also of both Fine-spotted and Nubian Woodpeckers.

Similar species Much like Bennett's, though male of that species has plain throat and smaller, finer spots below. Juveniles of both very similar. Golden-tailed is streaked not spotted below. Meets similar Nubian Woodpecker in N of range: that species darker, less spotted below and with plain throat.

Food and foraging Mostly ground-dwelling ants and termites: often forages terrestrially. Presumably other invertebrates taken, but details lacking.

◄ Reichenow's Woodpecker. As is typical for this genus, the red malar stripe and all-red crown indicate that this is a male. Chinizua, Mozambique, January (*Niall Perrins*).

◀ Adult female Reichenow's Woodpecker lacks red in both the malar stripe and the forecrown otherwise the sexes are simliar. Mikumi, Tanzania, November (*Nik Borrow*).

▼ Juvenile Reichenow's Woodpecker (probably a male as the malar is bold) resembles the adult female, but note the darker iris. Chinizua, Mozambique, January (*Niall Perrins*).

68. NUBIAN WOODPECKER
Campethera nubica

L 20–22cm

Identification Rather pale. Olive-brown above with heavy cream spotting and barring. Cheeks and ear-coverts dusky as densely streaked black and white. Bold white supercilium. Yellow around bill base. Throat white or cream. Breast white with bold dark spotting, flanks barred. Greenish wings barred white. Tail greenish-yellow barred brown, feather shafts bold gold. Iris pink or red, orbital ring grey. Bill greyish, tip darker. Legs grey or olive. Sexes differ: male has all-red crown and red malar streaked black; female has most of crown black spotted white, red only on nape and faint black malar speckled white. Juvenile more like adult female, having black crown and malar marked white, but darker, browner above, heavily spotted and barred below, variably flecked from throat to breast, iris greyish-brown.

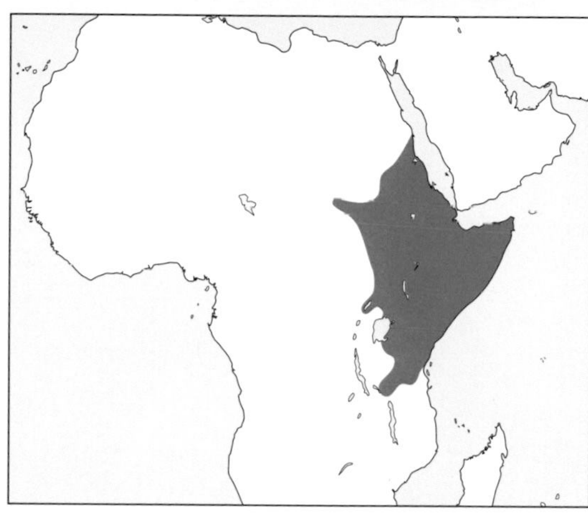

Vocalisations A loud, strident, ringing or piping, repeated series of *tyee, tee, yeee, weee* or *kieeh* or *kiee* notes. Notes often musical, sometimes a more metallic *tinkh*. Speed varies with mood, faster when excited, series often accelerating before ending slowly. Birds commonly engage in duets, one beginning, a second

▼ Adult male Nubian Woodpecker. Note the red malar stripe and all-red crown. Nominate race. Afar, Ethiopia, April (*Neil Bowman*)

soon joining in, synchronising accordingly. Also lower *kwick* and *kweek* notes.

Drumming Not an avid drummer, but information lacking.

Status Often locally common. Limited information, but overall population considered stable.

Habitat Various open, dry, lowland and upland woodlands, wooded savanna, bush country and scrub, particularly with acacia and euphorbia.

Range Africa. S of the Sahara, from Sudan in the N to Congo and Tanzania in the S, Somalia and the Horn in the E. Sea-level to around 2000m. Resident and sedentary.

Taxonomy and variation Two very similar races which intergrade: ***nubica*** (most of range: the Sudans, Ethiopia, Eritrea, W and N Somalia, inland Kenya, Uganda, NE DR Congo, SW Tanzania); and ***pallida*** (S and E Somalia, coastal Kenya), which is smaller, paler than nominate, less spotted below. Upland birds often darker, especially above, and heavier spotted below than lowland ones.

Similar species Beware other 'golden-tailed' woodpeckers. Mombasa and Golden-tailed Woodpeckers streaked below. Bennett's Woodpecker has speckled throat and yellow lower mandible. Green-backed Woodpecker smaller, with speckled throat, lacks bold malar. Meets very similar Reichenow's Woodpecker in south of range; that species more barred above and heavier spotted below. Calls similar to Fine-spotted Woodpecker.

Food and foraging Forages in trees, sometimes on the ground, for ants and termites. Spiders and beetles also taken. Not particularly gregarious; often feeds alone, though pairs keep in contact vocally.

▼ Adult female. Note the white-spotted black crown and malar stripe, with the bird having red only on the nape. Kenya, April (*Martin B. Withers*).

▼ Female Nubian Woodpecker in full voice. Birds often duet from a distance. Race *pallida*. Arusha, Tanzania, November (*Niall Perrins*)

▲ Adult female Nubian Woodpecker. This is the nominate race. Masai Mara, Kenya, August (*Eyal Bartov*).

69. GOLDEN-TAILED WOODPECKER
Campethera abingoni

L 20cm

Identification Despite English name, golden or yellow tail-feather shafts not diagnostic. Upperparts dull green, spotted or barred cream, especially on rump and uppertail. Pale chin and throat. Breast and flanks boldly streaked black, belly spotted. Creamy cheeks and ear-coverts streaked black. Iris reddish, orbital ring grey. Bill greyish, base greenish. Legs grey. Sexes differ: male has red malar, crown and nape, flecked grey; female lacks red malar (often a faint dark area flecked white), forecrown black spotted white, red only on nape. Juvenile like adult female, but more boldly marked below, greener above, white spots or flecks in faint malar, iris browner, darker.

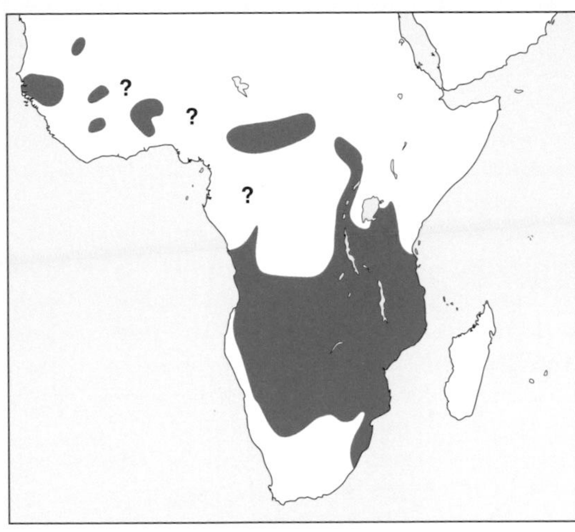

Vocalisations Repeated, loud, shrieking or squawking, nasal, drawn-out *wheeeeeaa, skweeeeeaa* or *k-heeeew.* Buzzing *creeeeew* or *creeee-aaw* variant. Slurred, undulating *tch-waaye,* first note harsh, second whining. Series of up to 12 *yaooaak-yaaaaak* notes. Rapid, rattling *weet-weet-wit-wit-wit* when agitated. Soft *pew* contact notes.

Drumming Slow, soft, weak rolls of up to 10 strikes over 1.5 seconds.

Status Widespread and often common locally. Overall considered stable.

Habitat Variety of open, arid or damp, lowland and upland, tropical broadleaved woodlands. Dry thickets, bush, particularly acacia savanna. Also riverine, *miombo* (*Brachystegia*), *mopane* and *karoo* woodlands. Avoids plantations but sometimes around settlements.

Range Africa. In savanna belt, mainly S of Equator to Mozambique and South Africa. Isolated populations include Gambia, Senegal, Ivory Coast. Mainly below 2000m. Resident, mainly sedentary though may wander.

◄ Adult male *anderssoni* Golden-tailed Woodpecker drilling into wood. Note the red malar stripe, which is the key to separating males from females as the extent of red on the crown varies. Modimolle, South Africa, December (*Warwick Tarboton*).

Taxonomy and variation Six races: ***abingoni*** (W DR Congo to W Tanzania, NE Namibia, NW Zambia, Zimbabwe, N Transvaal); ***chrysura*** (Senegambia to S Sudan, NE DR Congo, W Uganda: Bwamba lowlands) greener above, duskier below than nominate, ear-coverts streaked; ***kavirondensis*** (E Rwanda, N Tanzania, SW Kenya) olive-green above, pale below with narrow streaks, ear-coverts flecked; ***suahelica*** (N Tanzania to E Zimbabwe, Mozambique, N Swaziland) yellowish-green above; ***anderssoni*** (SW Angola, Namibia, SW Botswana and N Cape Provence and S Transvaal in South Africa) less green, greyish above, pale rump, often heavily marked below, throat and chest streaked blackish; ***constricta*** (S Swaziland, S Mozambique, Natal) dark green above.

Similar species Much like Bennett's Woodpecker, though that species spotted not streaked below, male lacking markings on cheeks and throat. Female Bennett's has brown cheeks and throat. Knysna Woodpecker darker below, heavily spotted rather than streaked, and has similar calls. Mombasa Woodpecker similar, but paler, less marked above.

Food and foraging Forages mainly for arboreal ants taken in all stages. Often in cover, usually low on tree trunks. Mainly solitary, sometimes in pairs; occasionally joined by smaller woodpeckers and other insectivorous birds.

▲ Adult female *anderssoni* Golden-tailed Woodpecker. Kruger NP, South Africa, July (*Robert Wienand*).

▼ Adult female Golden-tailed Woodpecker. Note the white-spotted forecrown and blackish malar stripe. The golden tail-shafts are obvious, but not diagnostic (*Stacey Ann Alberts*).

▼ Adult male of the nominate race *abingdoni*. Katanga, DR Congo, September (*Nigel Voaden*).

70. MOMBASA WOODPECKER
Campethera mombassica

L 20–22cm

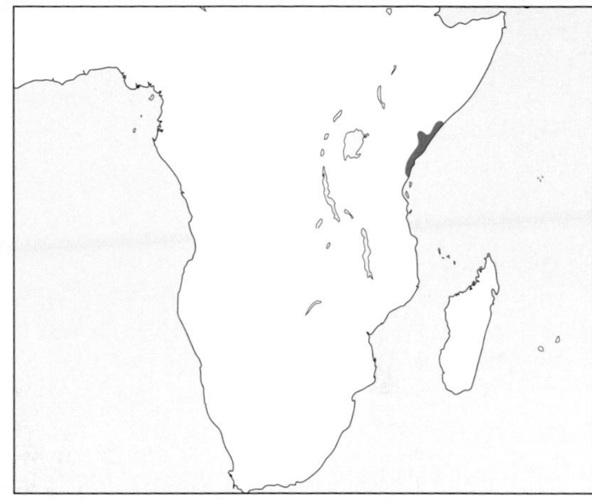

Identification Golden-green above with fine buff or yellow spotting which is often hardly noticeable from afar with birds appearing plain. Pale chin and throat. Cream or white below, flanks tinged yellow, boldly streaked chocolate, heavier on chest and breast than belly. Grey ear-coverts and cheeks heavily streaked black. White supercilium. Olive uppertail, outer feathers lightly barred brown/buff, feather shafts yellow, undertail browner. Wings green, flight feathers browner, lightly spotted white. Upper mandible grey, lower greenish. Legs greyish. Iris chestnut, orbital ring grey. Sexes differ: male has red crown and small malar, both streaked blackish; female blackish or olive crown speckled buff, red nape and dark malar. Juvenile more like adult female, but more boldly streaked below, duller green above and iris brown.

Vocalisations Nasal, accelerating *keeoank-yaaaank-yaaaank-yaaaank-yaank-yank-yank*, often ending with a *yuk* note. Repeated, trilling, rising *whirrrrrr* in series. A simple, sharp, slowly repeated *chip* note. Repeated, harsh, cawing *ghrrrrrk* and grating, throaty *drrrrdddt*.

Drumming May not drum, or perhaps only rarely, but information lacking.

Status Locally common or rare, possibly overlooked. Considered stable overall, though range-restricted. Clearance of woodland in some areas poses a threat.

Habitat Dry and damp mixed forest, particularly *Brachylaena* woodlands, bush and wooded savanna. Also riverine and coastal woodlands.

Range E Africa. Mostly coastal Kenya, but also adjacent S Somalia and NE Tanzania, S to Dar es Salaam, inland to E and W Usambaras. Mainly lowlands and

◄ Adult male Mombasa Woodpecker. There is a variable amount of red in the crown and malar stripe. Arabuko-Sokoke, Kenya, February (*Steve Garvie*).

foothills. Resident and sedentary.

Taxonomy and variation Monotypic. Formerly considered a race of Golden-tailed Woodpecker. Throat can be either spotted or streaked dark.

Similar species Golden-tailed Woodpecker (does not overlap in range) darker on back and throat, more heavily marked overall, barred on mantle and some calls different. Sympatric Nubian Woodpecker darker above, spotted not streaked below. Green-backed Woodpecker noticeably smaller.

Food and foraging Tends to feed unobtrusively on arboreal ants in foliage. Often solitary, but occasionally in mixed-species foraging flocks.

► Adult female Mombasa Woodpecker differs from the male in having red only on the nape, and none in the malar stripe. Masai Mara, Kenya, August (*Eyal Bartov*).

▼ Adult female Mombasa Woodpecker. Note the underpart streaking; Nubian Woodpecker is spotted. Sokoke Forest, Kenya, November (*Nik Borrow*).

71. KNYSNA WOODPECKER

Campethera notata

L 19–20cm

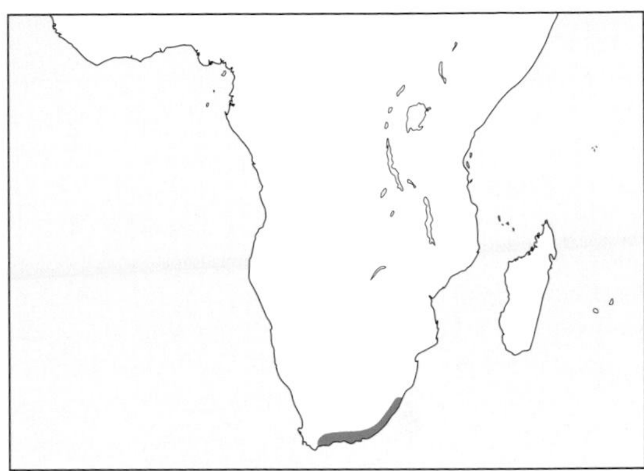

Identification Greenish above, finely dotted yellow. Rump and uppertail-coverts gently barred white. White, cream or buff below; chest, breast and flanks boldly dotted or blotched brown, less dense on belly. Uppertail olive-green, barred yellow, undertail buffy. Upperwings green, flight feathers browner with thin white bars, upper-coverts spotted and streaked pale, underwing paler. Face white or buff, heavily streaked, ear-coverts spotted. Chin, throat and neck-sides boldly spotted black. Lores cream or buff. Long, narrow white supercilium, flecked black. Iris red, orbital ring grey. Bill grey with darker tip. Legs greyish-green. Sexes differ: male has red crown, nape and malar, flecked

▼ Adult male Knysna Woodpecker has a red crown and malar stripe, with both red areas flecked black. Within its range, it is unmistakable. Eastern Cape, South Africa, November (*Warwick Tarboton*).

dark; female's crown chocolate spotted white or buff, red only on nape and faint black malar flecked white. Juvenile more like adult female, but less spotted and very green above, underparts markings bolder.

Vocalisations Fairly vocal. A simple, single, high-pitched whistling shriek, sometimes shrill, *pee*, perhaps *peeah*, *screee* or *wliee*, repeated after long pauses. Also harsher, croaking *kra-kra-kree-kree-kree-kree-kra-kra* and throaty *pree-pree-pree-pree* described. Triple-noted *weee-we-wi* and *yeh-he-het*.

Drumming May not drum, or perhaps only rarely, but information lacking.

Status NT. Generally uncommon. Surprisingly poorly known. Not considered declining, but small population (less than 5000 birds estimated), range-restricted and thinly distributed. Has suffered from clearance of woodlands for farmland, plantations and urbanisation.

Habitat Fairly broad range of more open evergreen woodlands. Typically in bushveld, scrub and thickets, especially with euphorbia and milkwood. Also riverine woods, drier wooded grasslands, savanna, even rural gardens. Some larger trees required for nesting, with introduced species and nest-boxes used.

Range South Africa. Endemic to the coastal plain, particularly on East Cape, but also N into S KwaZulu-Natal. Mostly lowlands, but also hilly country. Rather localised, resident and sedentary.

Taxonomy and variation Monotypic. Significant individual differences in markings and plumage tones. Back spotting sometimes forms bars; mantle sometimes with reddish hue. Birds in N of range often small, dark and very boldly spotted, sometimes regarded as a distinct race.

Similar species Same-sized close relative Golden-tailed Woodpecker (possibly overlaps at very NE of range) lighter overall, cleaner-faced and streaked brown below, not blotched. Does not meet any other *Campethera*.

Food and foraging Mainly arboreal ants, taken in all stages. Easily overlooked as usually forages unobtrusively, alone or in pairs. Occasionally in mixed-species foraging flocks.

▼ Adult female Knysna Woodpecker has a red nape, but lacks red on the crown and malar stripe. KwaZulu-Natal, South Africa, October (*Ronnie Potgieter*).

72. GREEN-BACKED WOODPECKER
Campethera cailliautii

L 15–17cm

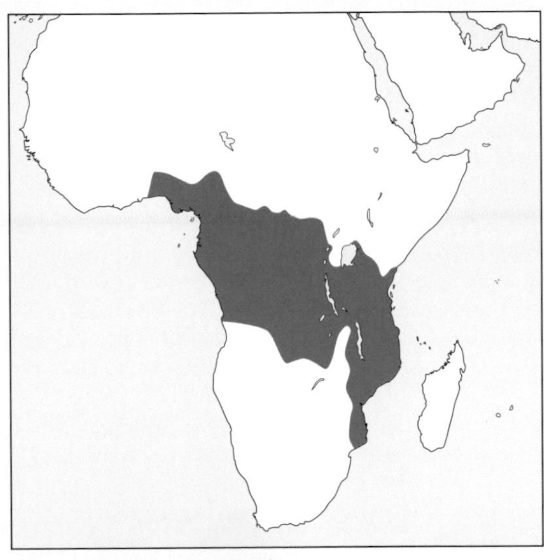

Identification Variably marked depending on race. Green above, faintly spotted yellow or cream. Buff or white below, boldly spotted black, especially on breast; flanks barred. Tail green with olive-brown shafts. Ear-coverts, neck and throat buff or cream speckled black. White supercilium. Iris chestnut, orbital ring grey. Short grey bill, tipped blackish. Legs grey or olive. Sexes differ: male has scarlet crown with dark flecks, nape brighter red; female mostly black crown spotted or speckled white, red only on nape. Juvenile more like female, though red slight or lacking and iris grey or brown.

Vocalisations An upwardly slurred *kiu-week* and *ke-wiu*, recalling a falcon, sometimes a softer kitten-like mewing. Fast series of around 20 *uweek, weet* or *pweet* notes. Also *wik-a, wik-a* and *tew-a, tew-a* in disputes. Nominate, *nyansae* and *loveridgei* utter high-pitched, wailing song of clear, repeated *wheeee, pwee, hee* or *kwee*

◀ Adult male Green-backed Woodpecker of race *permista*. This distinctive race has barred rather than spotted underparts. Nyasoso, Cameroon, March (*Lars Petersson*).

notes; *permista* makes series of shrill upwardly slurred *ke-wii* notes. Also harsh *grrrr* in disputes.

Drumming Soft, brief rolls of about 16 strikes per second.

Status Population considered stable. Often local, possibly overlooked. Loss of woodland to farmland a threat.

Habitat Varies across range. Both damp and drier open, tropical, broadleaved forests: riparian and flooded forest, bush, savanna, mature *miombo* (*Brachystegia*), coastal woodlands. In some regions palm groves, wooded settlements and gardens.

Range Africa. Across heart of continent, from S Sudan and Ethiopia to Mozambique. E to coastal Somalia and Kenya, W to Ghana. Mainly lowlands, but to 2100m. Resident, mostly sedentary, though some dispersal.

Taxonomy and variation Four races (first three spotted below and together sometimes regarded as separate species 'Little Spotted Woodpecker'): ***cailliautii*** (coastal S Somalia, Kenya to NE Tanzania and Zanzibar); ***nyansae*** (SW Ethiopia to SW Kenya, NW

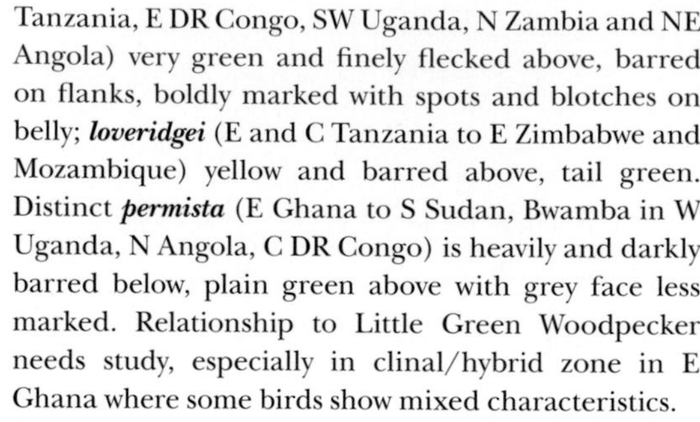

Tanzania, E DR Congo, SW Uganda, N Zambia and NE Angola) very green and finely flecked above, barred on flanks, boldly marked with spots and blotches on belly; ***loveridgei*** (E and C Tanzania to E Zimbabwe and Mozambique) yellow and barred above, tail green. Distinct ***permista*** (E Ghana to S Sudan, Bwamba in W Uganda, N Angola, C DR Congo) is heavily and darkly barred below, plain green above with grey face less marked. Relationship to Little Green Woodpecker needs study, especially in clinal/hybrid zone in E Ghana where some birds show mixed characteristics.

Similar species Much like Little Green Woodpecker, including calls, but female of latter lacks red nape. Cardinal Woodpecker has dark malar, yellow barring above rather than spotting, streaked not spotted below. Male Cardinal has brown forecrown, female brown nape. Larger Nubian and Mombasa Woodpeckers have prominent malars.

Food and foraging Arboreal ants and termites, usually taken at their colonies. Often forages in pairs and joins roving mixed-species flocks.

▼ Adult female *permista*. Females of all races only have red on the nape, while the males have a complete red crown. Lekoni, Gabon, August (*A. P. Leventis*).

▼ Adult female *loveridgei*. This is one of the races that is spotted below, rather than barred as in *permista*. Rio Savane, Mozambique, September (*Catherine Chatham*).

73. LITTLE GREEN WOODPECKER
Campethera maculosa

L 16cm

Identification Appears small-headed, thin-necked. Olive or bronze with golden tones above, rump gently barred dark. Face, ear-coverts, neck, throat and chest buff, densely mottled olive-brown. Indistinct cream supercilium, yellowish lores. Buff from breast to vent, boldly barred olive-brown. Uppertail black, outer feather pairs greener, shafts yellow (but not as obvious as on some relatives), undertail yellowish. Wings olive-brown, flight feathers barred buff, underwing cream or yellowish, slightly barred. Iris brown, orbital ring grey. Legs olive-grey. Bill olive or blackish, lower mandible paler, often bluish. Sexes differ: male has rufous crown, forecrown mixed with black; female has olive-brown crown and nape barred and flecked with buff or white. Juvenile brighter, greener above with pale streaking on mantle, paler and less barred below, iris darker.

Vocalisations Plaintive, prolonged *huweeeeh*, shorter, harsher *whee,* hard single *kewik* and repeated *teerweet* when agitated. Also a rapid series of 3–4 rising *teeay* notes.

Drumming May not drum, or perhaps only rarely, but information lacking.

Status Often common locally. Population trends largely unknown, but possibly increasing due to preference for open habitats and inadvertently benefitting from forest clearance.

Habitat Mainly tropical, damp, open, lowland primary and secondary forests. Also fragmented, mosaic and riverside forests, mangroves, partially logged areas, clearings with scattered trees, farm-bush and drier savanna.

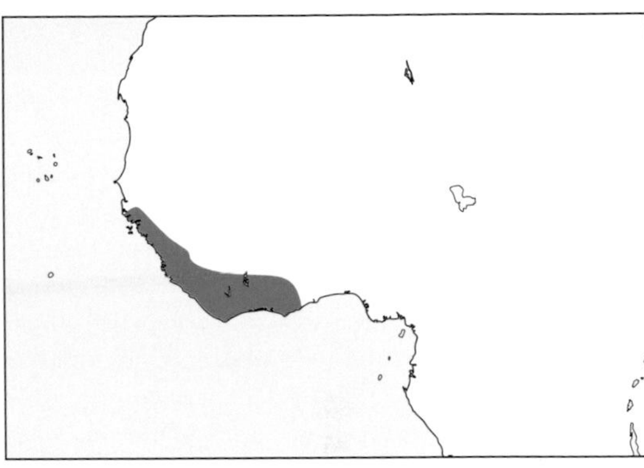

Range W Africa. In Senegambia, Guinea-Bissau, Guinea, Sierra Leone, Liberia, Ivory Coast, Ghana, but not continuous. Sea-level to around 1200m. Resident and probably sedentary.

Taxonomy and variation Monotypic. Females in particular can be spotted white and/or rufous on the mantle. Relationship to Green-backed Woodpecker needs study, especially in clinal/hybrid zone in E Ghana where some birds show mixed characteristics.

Similar species Like *permista* Green-backed Woodpecker, but that has whiter face, green tail, males have redder crown and females red nape. Calls of the two species also often indistinguishable.

Food and foraging Forages mainly for arboreal ants, particularly *Crematogaster* species. Sometimes forages with other birds, at all levels, but often in canopy. Will excavate nesting cavities in ant and termite nests.

► Adult male Little Green Woodpecker. Males have rufous crowns, which the females lack. Kakum NP, Ghana, January (*Lars Petersson*).

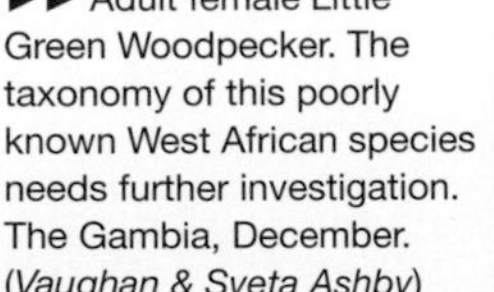

►► Adult female Little Green Woodpecker. The taxonomy of this poorly known West African species needs further investigation. The Gambia, December. (*Vaughan & Sveta Ashby*)

74. TULLBERG'S WOODPECKER
Campethera tullbergi

L 18–20cm

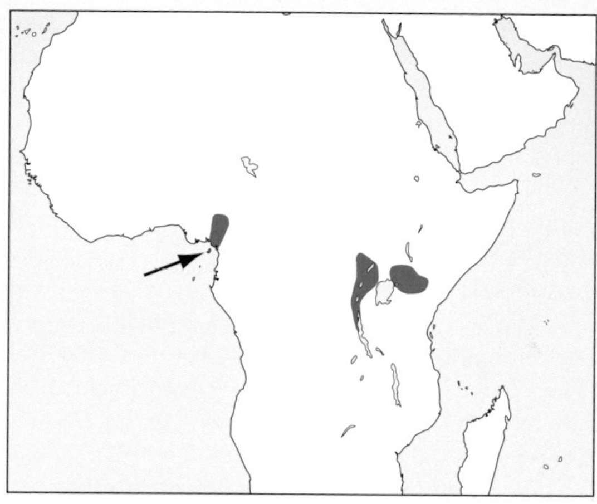

Other name Fine-banded Woodpecker (for two eastern races when considered a species).

Identification Subtly barred and spotted; from afar can appear unmarked. Mantle and back plain olive. Throat pale, cream or yellowish from chest to vent, heavily barred or spotted, depending upon race. Barring often broken into chevrons, especially on belly. Markings largest on flanks. Tail olive, undertail yellower. Duller greenish-brown wings with flight feathers edged yellow and red carpal patch or blotches (not always visible). Pale-grey face, ear-coverts, neck and throat finely dotted and vermiculated blackish. Bill grey, upper mandible slate, lower bluish-grey. Iris chestnut, orbital ring grey. Legs olive. Sexes differ: male has scarlet crown and nape, duller and mottled and smudged with black at front; female has red nape, black crown heavily spotted white. Juvenile more like adult female, but duller, grey-green with darker, heavier barring below, crown olive or black finely spotted white, iris brown.

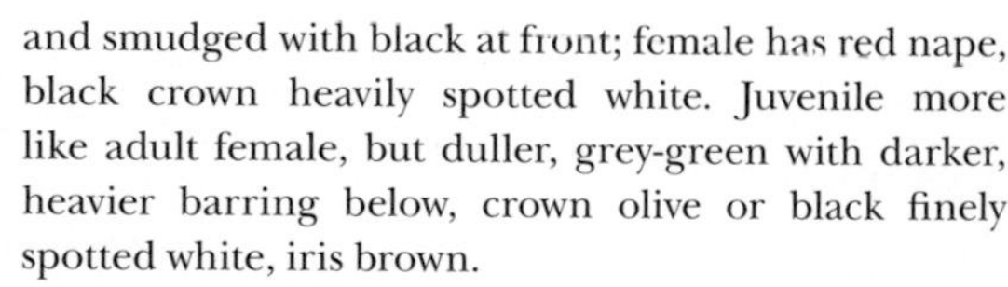

Vocalisations Remarkably silent. Known calls are simple, harsh, single or linked *kweek, kweeh* and *kreeer* notes.

Drumming Apparently drums occasionally, but details lacking.

Status Locally often common. Overall considered stable, but population data limited.

Habitat Essentially damp, tropical highland forests with standing dead trees.

Range Central Africa. Occurs in five separate areas: two in the east around the Equator and three in the west, in Nigeria, Cameroon and on Bioko Island. Usually between 1000–3000m. Resident and sedentary.

Taxonomy and variation Three races: ***tullbergi*** (upland SE Nigeria, W Cameroon, Bioko Island in Gulf of Guinea) is largest race and spotted not barred; ***taeniolaema*** (E DR Congo to Rwanda, SW Uganda, Burundi, W Tanzania, W Kenya) yellowish-olive above, rump sometimes barred pale, yellowish-green below finely barred black, female with reddish lores; ***hausburgi*** (Kenyan highlands E of Rift Valley, extreme

◄ Adult male Tullberg's Woodpecker. Note the red crown. This bird is from the eastern race *taeniolaema*, and is finely barred below. Kinari, Kenya, June (*Mike Barth*).

N Tanzania) buff or yellow, underpart barring wider, sometimes broken, bright green above. Last two barred races sometimes considered a distinct species.

Similar species No sympatric woodpecker has diagnostic red carpal area. Same-sized Brown-eared Woodpecker has brown ear-coverts, and is darker green and spotted below. Confusion with Olive Woodpecker perhaps possible when barred underparts are not seen.

Food and foraging Arboreal ants, caterpillars and other invertebrates. Canopy forager, often inconspicuous, working snags and probing in moss, lichen and leaf clusters. Sometimes descends to low levels when in mixed-species feeding flocks.

▲ Adult female *taeniolaema*. Females of all races are only red on the nape. Bwindi Impenetrable Forest, Uganda, February (*Adam Scott Kennedy*).

◄ Juvenile Tullberg's Woodpecker. This bird is of the western nominate race; note the spotting below. Bamenda, Cameroon, February (*Jaap van der Waarde*).

75. BUFF-SPOTTED WOODPECKER
Campethera nivosa

L 14–16cm

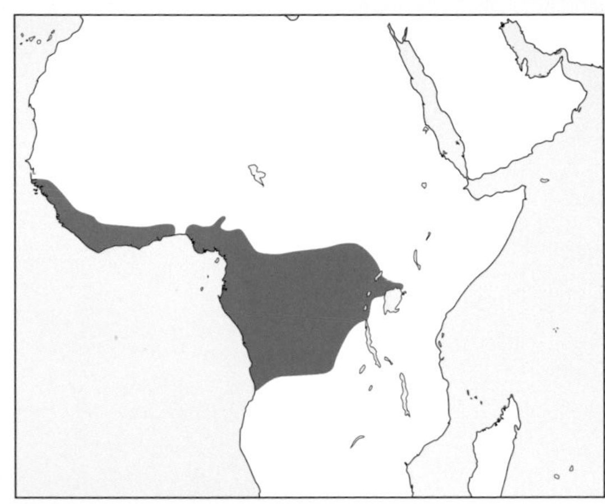

Identification Smallest in genus. Plain, dark olive above, often with bronze and yellowish tones. Chest and breast olive-green boldly spotted or blotched buff or white. Lower belly, vent and flanks barred cream. Tail brown. Wings mostly green with browner, pale-spotted primaries. White or buff face and ear-coverts finely streaked chocolate. Forehead and crown olive-brown. Buff throat and neck striped green. Small grey bill bluish at lower base. Iris reddish, orbital ring greyish. Legs olive. Sexes differ slightly: male has orange or red nape, which female lacks, being olive-brown. Juvenile more like adult female, lacking red nape, but greener above, browner below, barred rather than spotted, greyish crown and brown iris.

Vocalisations Often silent. Calls include a soft, dry,

◀ Adult male *herberti*. The sexes are very similar in this species; the red nape-patch indicates that this is a male. Bwindi Impenetrable Forest, Uganda, March (*Gerard Gorman*).

chk, chk, chk-chk, chk and rattling *dee-dee-dee* or *kee-kee-kee* trill which fades and falls away. A slurred, melancholic, falling *peeer, pheeu, preeew or wiurrrr* and a thin, whining, wailing *weeeooooo* that rises as it ends. *Te-te-te-te* contact notes, repeated rapidly in disputes,

Drumming Brief, rapid rolls of 3–6 strikes per second.

Status Population considered stable but data lacking. Not uncommon across much of vast range but, due to size, habits and habitat used, probably overlooked.

Habitat Wide range of dry and wet, upland and lowland tropical forests with dense understorey. Also secondary growth, gallery forests, wooded swamps, savanna, shrub-thickets, plantations, mangroves and rural gardens.

Range Africa. Mainly in mid-west, either side of the Equator, from Senegambia to Angola, E to W Kenya, though scattered. Isolated population on Bioko Island, Gulf of Guinea. On mainland usually below 1800m. Resident and sedentary.

Taxonomy and variation Four races: ***nivosa*** (Senegambia to Nigeria, Gabon, W DR Congo, NW Zambia, NW Angola); ***maxima*** (Ivory Coast) much like nominate but larger; ***poensis*** (Bioko Island) paler overall, more barred on chest and breast, tail and uppertail-coverts yellower; ***herberti*** (C African Republic, SW Sudan, E DR Congo, Rwanda, S and W Uganda, W Kenya: Mt Elgon, Kakamega and S Nandi Forests) lighter, greener above, buffer below, boldly spotted on breast, more barred on belly, undertail yellowish. Intergrades occur.

Similar species Sympatric Brown-eared Woodpecker larger and has dark ear-covert patch.

Food and foraging Forages at most levels in trees, bushes, vines, even low in undergrowth for termites and ants, particularly *Crematogaster* species. Nest-holes also often excavated in termitaria and arboreal ant nests. Joins mixed-species foraging flocks.

► Adult female nominate. This bird is probably not nesting in this old cavity, but is more likely foraging. Abuko Nature Reserve, The Gambia, November (*Vaughan & Sveta Ashby*).

76. BROWN-EARED WOODPECKER
Campethera caroli

L 18–19cm

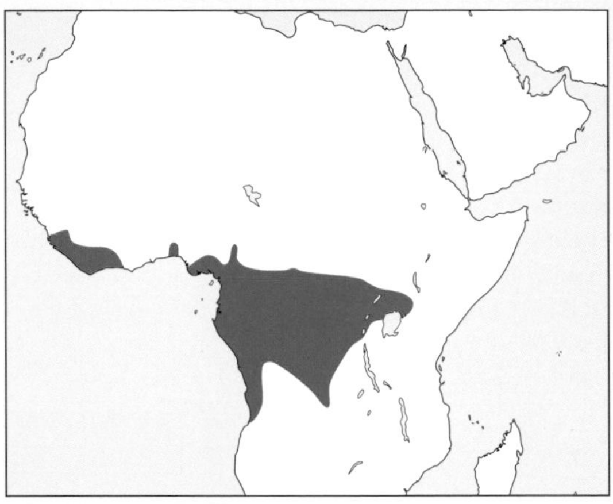

Identification Distinct chestnut-chocolate patch behind eye and over ear-coverts. Buff supercilium, speckled dark, extends above ear-covert patch to nape. Mantle, back and most of wings plain olive-brown. Underparts from breast to undertail olive-green, boldly spotted yellow, buff or white. Tail chocolate with some white dots on outer feathers. Face and throat dark olive heavily spotted or streaked white. Iris chestnut, orbital ring grey. Fairly long, bluish-grey bill, base tinged green. Legs olive. Sexes differ slightly: male has dark chocolate or olive forecrown and crimson hindcrown and nape, though this often confined to feather-tips; female lacks red, entire crown chocolate or olive. Juvenile more like female but greener above, ear-covert patch more rufous, sometimes pinkish, chin streaked,

▼ Adult female Brown-eared Woodpecker of the nominate race. Females lack red on the nape. Kakamega, Kenya, July (*Steve Garvie*).

underpart spotting paler but larger and more extensive, sometimes slightly barred.

Vocalisations Rather taciturn. Song a long, single, drawn-out, plaintive, melancholic or eerie, wailing *uwheeeeeu, huuweeeeuu* or *weeeeeeyu,* upwardly slurred before falling away. A low-pitched trilling *trrrrrrrrr,* high-pitched *trrree,* rapid *ttrrmmmup-trrrup,* sharp *prrrriiirrrii* and brief, throaty *kwaa-kwaa-kwaa.*

Drumming Infrequent drummer, occasionally producing subtle but solid rolls.

Status Occurs over a large range, but nowhere very common. Probably declining in some areas due to deforestation.

Habitat Mainly lowland, tropical, damp forests, particularly primary, dense stands with vines. Also thick secondary growth, wooded grasslands, shrub-thickets, gallery woodlands and plantations.

Range Africa. Core population in the mid-west around the Equator: Cameroon, Central African Republic, Gabon, Congo, Burundi, Rwanda, Uganda, NW Tanzania, W Kenya, to N Angola and Zambia. Also in scattered populations in the west from Guinea-Bissau and Guinea to Nigeria. Sea-level to around 1800m. Resident and sedentary.

Taxonomy and variation Two races: ***caroli*** (Benin to Nigeria, Cameroon, Angola, NW Zambia, Burundi, Rwanda, Congo, S and W Uganda, NW Tanzania, W Kenya: probably only Mt Elgon, Kakamega and S Nandi Forests) has bronze tones above and faint yellowish spotting on mantle; ***arizela*** (Guinea-Bissau, Sierra Leone to Ghana) olive-green above and below. Individuals sometimes stained green from tree algae.

Similar species Same-sized Tullberg's Woodpecker paler green, barred below and lacks dark ear-covert patch. Sympatric Buff-spotted Woodpecker smaller and also lacks ear-covert patch.

Food and foraging Usually forages for ants and other invertebrates in vines and tangled vegetation in the canopy, sometimes lower down. Often solitary, shy, but joins mixed-species foraging flocks.

▼ Adult female nominate. Though not uncommon locally, this often-silent forest species can be difficult to observe. Port-Gentil, Gabon, November (*Guillaume Passavy*).

GEOCOLAPTES

A monospecific genus. Ground Woodpecker is a truly terrestrial species, the only woodpecker in southern Africa that lives in largely treeless habitats, creating nesting and roosting burrows in earthen banks, road-cuts and between rocks. A gregarious species that lives in family clans, Ground Woodpecker also has an aspect of behaviour that may be unique among woodpeckers – a sentry perches on the highest nearby vantage point, a boulder or outcrop, looking for aerial predators while the rest of the group (or mate) forage on the ground. Sentry duty is commonly relieved at 10-minute intervals.

Adult female Ground Woodpecker. Note the lack of rufous in the malar area, and paler colours below. Sani Pass, Lesotho, October (*Ian Merrill*).

77. GROUND WOODPECKER
Geocolaptes olivaceus

L 25–30cm

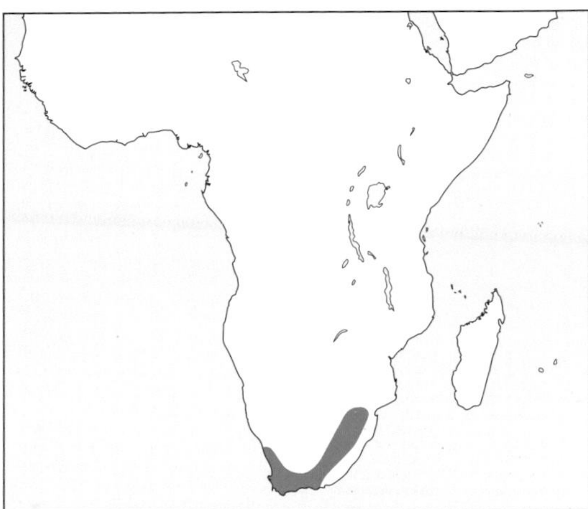

Identification Buff below, flushed red or pink from breast to vent, redder on belly and flanks, with some brownish barring. Greyish-brown above with pale spotting in fresh plumage. Red rump more obvious in flight. Uppertail-coverts brown, barred white. Crown, ear-coverts, neck and nape dusky grey, subtly mottled white. Chin and throat white. Upperwings brown, flight feathers barred whitish, coverts spotted or barred pale, tertials with green and bronze tones, underwing yellowish. Uppertail brown barred white, with yellow feather shafts; undertail lighter barred pale. Iris yellow/pinkish. Long slender dark bill. Legs grey. Sexes differ slightly: male has thin grey malar with reddish flecks; female lacks red in faint malar and has less red below and on rump. Juvenile similar to adult female, though red below pinker; often some rufous on the nape and white iris.

Vocalisations Rather vocal. Far-carrying, repeated, loud, ringing *ree-chick* and *peer-peer-peer, pee-o-pee-o* or *pee-aargh.* Softer versions uttered between family members. Greeting calls include falcon-like *krrreee* and *t-hew-kee* notes at nest and in displays.

▼ A pair of Ground Woodpeckers. The male is in front of the female. Western Cape, South Africa, October (*Callan Cohen*).

Drumming Probably does not drum.

Status Common locally. Overall considered stable. However, Ground Woodpeckers are easily heat stressed, showing marked heat-avoidance behaviour that suggests they are physiologically adapted to a cooler climate than that which presently prevails. In the event of increased global warming their future well-being may be threatened.

Habitat Rocky and boulder-strewn grassy slopes and ridges in mountains and hills. Often in Alpine-like grasslands close to surface water, avoiding very dry regions. Sometimes in areas with shrubs and scrub, but not overgrown terrain.

Range Southern Africa. Endemic to South Africa, Lesotho and Swaziland. Mainly between 600–2100m, but almost at sea-level in SW. Resident and mainly sedentary, though possibly makes seasonal movements in elevation.

Taxonomy and variation Monotypic. Two or three races sometimes claimed. Upland birds tend to be darkest. Birds in NE generally paler. Underpart colour sometimes tends to cinnamon. Some adult males have rufous tinge on the nape. Upperpart spotting may form bars.

Similar species Unique within range. More likely to be confused with a *Monticola* rock thrush than another woodpecker.

Food and foraging Forages in groups for terrestrial ants, taken in all stages, probing into their burrows. Also swishes aside debris in flicker-like manner. Seldom visits trees and then usually bare, dead ones or stumps.

▲ Adult male Ground Woodpecker. The sexes are very similar: the faint rufous in the malar area of this bird suggests that it is a male. Note the nest-hole is in a bank. Mpumalanga, South Africa, October (*Warwick Tarboton*).

► Ground Woodpeckers are social, gregarious birds. Western Cape, South Africa, August (*Warwick Tarboton*).

DENDROPICOS

An African genus of 15 small species found in sub-Saharan woodlands. All are basically green above with pale underparts, sometimes barred, and coloured rumps. Males have red or yellow on the crown, which females lack. Some species, such as Abyssinian, Stierling's and Elliot's Woodpeckers, have restricted ranges and are understudied. The taxonomy of this genus needs revisiting: three species (Bearded, Fire-bellied and Golden-crowned Woodpeckers) are sometimes grouped in another genus *Thripias*, while four (Elliot's, African Grey, Eastern Grey and Olive Woodpeckers) are sometimes placed in *Mesopicos*, and there is inconsistency between which species have been split and lumped.

African Grey Woodpecker *Dendropicos goertae*, adult male. Tarangire NP, Tanzania, October (*Ariadne Van Zandbergen*).

78. LITTLE GREY WOODPECKER
Dendropicos elachus

L 11–13cm

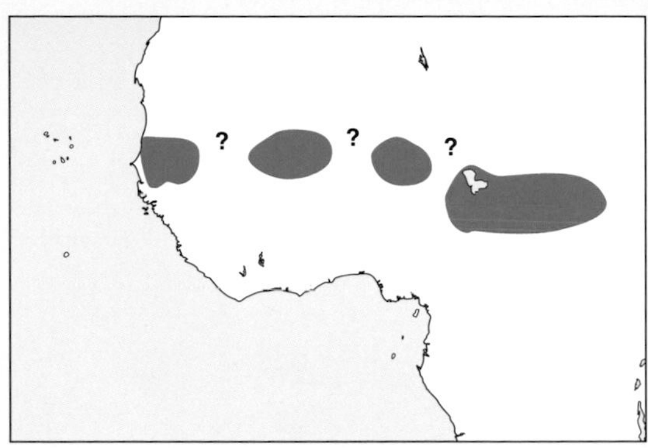

Other name Sahelian Woodpecker
Identification Rather pale, can look drab. Whitish supercilium, sub-ocular line and thin brown malar all indistinct. Ear-coverts brownish. Chin and throat white with fine dark streaking. White below, spotted or barred brown on breast, weaker on belly and flanks. Grey-brown above, barred pale. Red rump and uppertail-coverts show well in flight. Upperwings brown, coverts and edges barred white, shafts yellow, underwings white spotted brown. Rather short brown tail barred white. Bill grey, paler at base. Legs greyish-green. Iris brown. Sexes differ: male has red hindcrown and nape; female hindcrown and nape brownish. Juvenile duller, with paler yellow wing-feather shafts.
Vocalisations Rapid, harsh, rattling *kree* or *skree* notes in series, repeated up to 10 times – suggesting Cardinal Woodpecker call. A milder *tee-tee-tee* and low-pitched, whirring *wi-wi-wi-i-i-i* or *chi-chi-chi-chi*. Also a fast, loud *wi-wi-wik-wik-wik* rattle.
Drumming May not drum, or perhaps only rarely, but information lacking.
Status Nowhere common, often rare, occurring in low densities. Population trends largely unknown, but possibly declining.
Habitat Dry, open wooded grasslands and savanna, often in acacia thickets. Also oases, wadis and wooded waterways in semi-desert.
Range Africa. Scattered across the Sahel from SW Mauritania through Mali, Niger, N Cameroon, N Nigeria and Chad into W Sudan. Also disjunct population in Senegambia. Sea-level to around 1600m. Resident, probably sedentary.
Taxonomy and variation Monotypic. Newly moulted birds much darker, even brownish. Worn birds appear washed-out, with weaker head and face markings.
Similar species Paler and plainer than other small woodpeckers in its range. Brown-backed Woodpecker lacks red rump and has striped face.
Food and foraging Insects, particularly larvae. Forages on thinner branches in trees, but details limited.

◄◄ Adult male Little Grey Woodpecker. The red hindcrown separates males from females. Borno, Nigeria, October (*A. P. Leventis*).

◄ Adult female. This often inconspicuous species is poorly known, and may well be regularly overlooked outside its core range. Borno, Nigeria, October (*A. P. Leventis*).

79. SPECKLE-BREASTED WOODPECKER
Dendropicos poecilolaemus

L 14–15cm

Other name Uganda Spotted Woodpecker

Identification Greenish-yellowish overall. Buff and olive above with light, often faint, barring on back and uppertail-coverts. Rufous wash on rump when red feather-tips fresh. Wings mostly brownish with primaries barred or spotted yellow and coverts tipped buff. Pale buff or yellow below with chest finely, but distinctly, speckled grey or black. Belly vaguely streaked. Tail brownish with yellow feather shafts. Chin and throat white with fine dark flecks. Cheek and ear-coverts cream, gently streaked or spotted black. Faint, often indistinct, malar and moustache. Iris chestnut. Relatively long dark bill, sometimes tinged bluish. Legs grey or olive. Sexes differ: male has brownish forehead and forecrown, mid-crown to nape red; female lacks red, crown being entirely dark. Juvenile drabber with grey rather than yellow tones, minimal red on rump, faintly marked below, mantle slightly barred black, dusky behind eye, black nape and brown iris. Juveniles of both sexes have red on crown, more on male.

Vocalisations Hurried, dry, rattling *che-che-chi-chi-chichi* or *che-che-che-che-che;* harsher, chirping *chrrr-chrrr-chrrr;* and rapidly repeated, hard, double *ch-rit* or *k-ret* note.

Drumming May not drum, or perhaps only rarely, but information lacking.

Status Often locally common, but in Kenya, for example, rather uncommon. Little-studied, but population considered stable. Probably overlooked.

Habitat Mainly damp, open, tropical forests and woodlands. Also clearings with scattered trees and shrubs, riverine woods, drier savanna and wooded cultivated land. Persists in partially logged areas.

Range Africa. Heart of the continent, mainly N of the Equator. From southernmost Nigeria through S Chad, Cameroon, Congo, C African Republic, S Sudan, S and W Uganda and SW Kenya. From 700 to 2100m. Resident and sedentary.

Taxonomy and variation Monotypic. Slight individual variation.

Similar species Cardinal Woodpecker darker overall, much more boldly marked, streaked not speckled below and some races barred above. Other similar-sized sympatric species also streaked below.

Food and foraging Insects, particularly beetle larvae. Forages at forest edges, often in isolated bare trees, even in elephant grass. Often in pairs.

► Adult male Speckle-breasted Woodpecker. Red reaches from the mid-crown to the nape. The females lack the red. Kibale Forest, Uganda, July (*Rob Gipman*).

►► Adult female. Though not uncommon, Speckle-breasted Woodpecker is another African picid of which little is known. Kibale Forest, Uganda, July (*Graham Ekins*).

80. ABYSSINIAN WOODPECKER
Dendropicos abyssinicus

L 16cm

Other names Gold-mantled Woodpecker, Golden-backed Woodpecker

Identification Plain green mantle, back and scapulars with golden tones, sometimes a hint of rufous. In worn plumage mantle may appear mottled. Rump and uppertail-coverts red. White or cream below, heavily streaked brown or black. Well-marked face: lores dusky, broad white supercilium extending to nape, brown band over ear-coverts, brownish malar widening at rear, pale chin and throat streaked brownish. Brownish-green wings boldly spotted pale on outer-coverts, flight feathers barred buff. Underwing-coverts cream, lightly barred brown. Uppertail dark brown, narrowly barred white, undertail paler. Fine greyish bill. Legs grey. Iris chestnut. Sexes differ: male has scarlet from mid-crown to nape and brown or grey forecrown; female has brown crown, nape darker. Juvenile more like adult male as crown reddish, though less so on juvenile female, both sexes greener than adults above lacking golden tones, more densely streaked below, some barring on belly and rump pinkish.

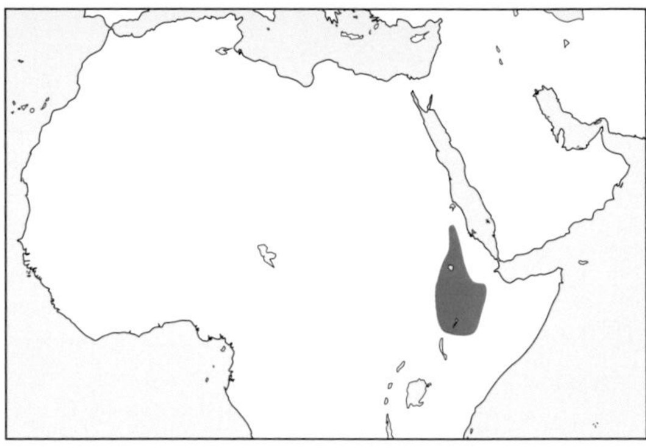

Vocalisations Not overly vocal. Series of high-pitched, fairly musical notes, sometimes bubbling, sometimes sharper, recalling some calls of Cardinal Woodpecker, but less rattling. Pairs often call together.

Drumming May not drum, or perhaps only rarely, but information lacking.

Status Little-studied, often elusive and conservation status needs reassessing as relatively restricted in range,

▼ Adult male Abyssinian Woodpecker is red from the mid-crown to the hindneck; females lack the red. Addis Ababa, Ethiopia, January (*Dave Semler & Marsha Steffen*).

seemingly nowhere common and probably declining as woodland continues to be cleared or replanted with alien trees.

Habitat Found in a range of upland, open, dry woodland and shrubland, particularly with euphorbia, juniper, fig, acacia and *Hagenia* trees. Also mixed broadleaved woods, wooded watercourses, scrub and damp high savanna. Also wooded urban areas, even cities like Addis Ababa.

Range East Africa. Endemic to the highlands of Ethiopia and Eritrea. From 1300m to 3250m. Resident and sedentary.

Taxonomy and variation Monotypic. Variation slight.

Similar species Cardinal Woodpecker slightly smaller, less yellow above, generally more strongly marked, not as washed-out. The two occur in C Ethiopia, but rarely meet as Abyssinian frequents higher elevations.

Food and foraging Various invertebrates, as well as seeds, nuts, berries and fruits. Forages unobtrusively in moss-clad trees, but information lacking.

► Adult male Abyssinian Woodpecker. Endemic to the uplands of Ethiopia and Eritrea, this species is under pressure from woodland clearance. Debre Libanos, Ethiopia, February (*David Beadle*).

▼ Adult female. Note the all-brown crown. Bale Mountains, Ethiopia, November (*Nik Borrow*).

81. CARDINAL WOODPECKER
Dendropicos fuscescens

L 13–16cm

Identification Green above, variably barred pale depending on race: some 'ladder-backed'. White or cream below, streaked black or brown. Green wings spotted white. Dark tail with yellow or golden shafts. Pale face, dark malar, ear-coverts and neck slightly streaked greyish-brown, forecrown brown. Iris reddish. Bill black, sometimes with bluish lower mandible. Legs grey or olive. Sexes differ: male has red mid-crown to nape; female lacks red, being chocolate. Juvenile duller overall, both sexes with mid-crown red (male more so), black hindcrown and nape. Iris grey or brown.

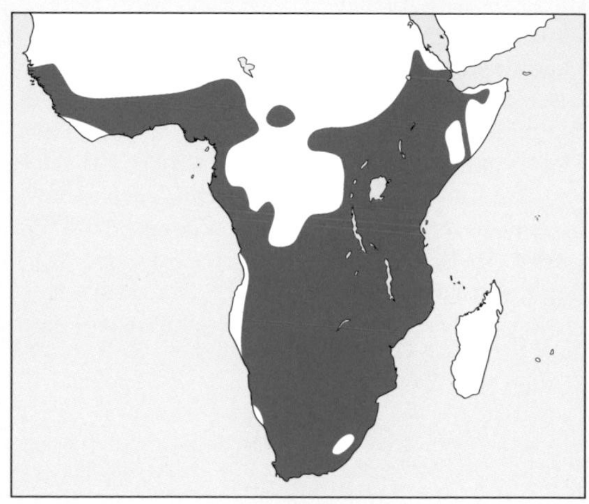

Vocalisations Range of buzzing, churring and trilling calls include high-pitched *krrek-krrek,* harsh *ti-ti-ti-ti, tri-tri-tri-trrrrr* or *kree-kree-kree* series; more chattering *chwi-chi-chi-chi-chi;* and rapid, sharp *kwik-ik-ik-ik* or

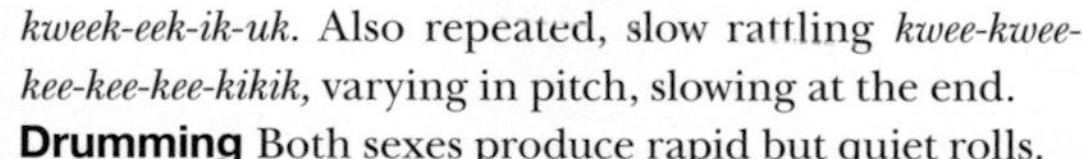

kweek-eek-ik-uk. Also repeated, slow rattling *kwee-kwee-kee-kee-kee-kikik,* varying in pitch, slowing at the end.

Drumming Both sexes produce rapid but quiet rolls.

Status Widespread, often common. Overall considered stable.

Habitat Wide range of open woodlands: forest edges, clearings, riverine woods, mangroves, shrubland, scrub, savanna, bushveld, *miombo* (*Brachystegia*), *mopane,* settlements, parks, gardens and plantations. Rainforest usually avoided, though *lepidus* is more of a forest bird.

Range Africa. Widespread in sub-Sahara, except in dense forests, as far as the Cape. Sea-level to 3500m. Resident and sedentary.

Taxonomy and variation Nine races, some distinctive in plumage and size: ***fuscescens*** (NC Namibia, Botswana, much of South Africa); ***lafresnayi*** (Senegambia and Sierra Leone to Nigeria) is greenish, faintly barred above, yellowish and lightly streaked below; ***sharpii*** (Cameroon E to South Sudan, S to N Angola) heavily streaked below; ***lepidus*** (eastern DR Congo to upland Ethiopia, much of Uganda, Rwanda, NW Tanzania and NE in Usambaras, WC Kenya) plain olive above, some with indistinct barring, narrowly streaked dark below; ***massaicus*** (S Ethiopia, NE Uganda, W Kenya

◄ Adult male Cardinal Woodpecker is red from the mid-crown to the nape; females lack red. This bird is of the coastal East African race *hartlaubi*. Maweni Farm, Tanzania, January (*Martin Goodey*).

N and E of highlands where *hemprichii* does not occur, N and C Tanzania) dark and ladder-backed, rather pied with narrow black and white barring, yellowish on rump and uppertail; ***hemprichii*** (lowland Ethiopia, Somalia, N and E Kenya, N Tanzania around Kilimanjaro, NE Uganda at Kideop) also dark and ladder-backed; ***centralis*** (N Namibia, E Angola, S DR Congo, Zambia, W Tanzania) brownish, barred yellowish above; ***hartlaubii*** (coastal S Kenya to most of Tanzania, Malawi, E Zambia, C Mozambique) small, pale, heavily but narrowly barred above, yellowish below; ***natalensis*** (Natal, Transvaal to C Mozambique) barred dark olive above, finely streaked below. Races *lafresnayi* and *lepidus* together sometimes considered separate species.

Similar species Abyssinian Woodpecker has red rump, brown malar and ear-covert band. Other similarly sized sympatric species have spotted underparts.

Food and foraging Mainly invertebrates (beetles, termites, locusts, caterpillars), with some fruits and seeds. An agile forager, often hanging from twigs and saplings, also in bushes, reeds, crops, but equally at home in large trees. Often in pairs and mixed-species flocks.

◀ Adult female nominate. Cardinal Woodpecker is one of the most widespread and common woodpeckers in Africa. Gauteng, South Africa, June (*Niall Perrins*).

▼ Adult female nominate. This small woodpecker is an agile, adaptable and omnivorous forager. Vumba, Zimbabwe, October (*Warwick Tarboton*).

82. GABON WOODPECKER
Dendropicos gabonensis

L 15–16cm

Identification Plain green above, some grey on mantle. Yellow or buff from chest to vent, boldly marked with large black or brown spots and blotches, lower flanks and undertail sometimes barred. White throat spotted and streaked brownish-black. Upperwing olive, flight feathers browner with white spots, underwing barred grey/white. Tail olive-brown. Pale face, ear-coverts and neck heavily streaked brown. Slight dark malar. Legs greyish-green. Bill grey or black. Iris reddish. Sexes differ: male has chocolate lores and forehead, red crown and nape with some dark streaks; female lacks red having all dark crown and nape. Juveniles of both sexes have red on mid-crown, are greener above than adults and have brown iris.

Vocalisations Rapid, strong, high-pitched, rattling or trilling *krititititititi*. Harsher, grating series of *trreee* and *kree* notes and a brief *breeep*. Also repeated, buzzing *zh-dzeeeep, dzheet* or *dzhaah* notes, very like Melancholy Woodpecker and not unlike Cardinal Woodpecker.

Drumming May not drum, or perhaps only rarely, but information lacking.

Status Varies locally from common to uncommon across range. Population data limited, but appears to be stable overall.

Habitat Damp lowland tropical forest, swamps, riverine forest. Often at edges, also in secondary growth, rural gardens, farmland and plantations. In drier wooded savanna in some areas.

Range W and C Africa. From S Nigeria E to Uganda, S to Angola. Sea-level to around 1400m. Resident and probably sedentary.

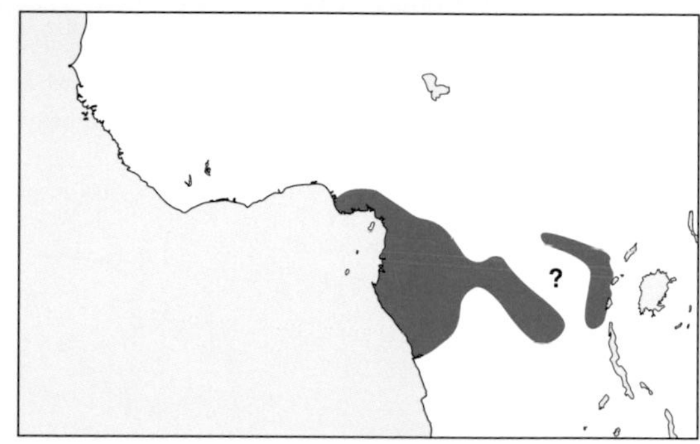

Taxonomy and variation Two races: ***gabonensis*** (S Cameroon to the Congos and W Uganda, S to N Angola); and ***reichenowi*** (S Nigeria, extreme SW Cameroon), which has more distinct malar, darker tail, bolder markings below, and is less streaked on face than nominate – appearing intermediate between *gabonensis* and Melancholy Woodpecker.

Similar species Melancholy Woodpecker is darker, bronze or green above, with solid dusky ear-covert patch, distinct malar, dark tail, plain neck-sides and bolder markings below – thus most like *reichenowi*.

Food and foraging Various invertebrates, particularly ants and wood-boring beetles. Forages in trees at all levels, in open areas and at forest edges, often in pairs.

◄◄ Adult male Gabon Woodpecker of the nominate race. Note the red crown and nape, which the females lack. This race is boldly spotted below. Ivindo, Gabon, November (*Adam Riley*).

◄ Adult female nominate. Note the streaked ear-coverts, unlike similar Melancholy Woodpecker. Sangha, Central African Republic, November (*Matthias Dehling*).

83. MELANCHOLY WOODPECKER

Dendropicos lugubris

L 15–18cm

Identification Appears short-tailed. Rather dark and dull overall with a marked face. Mantle and back plain olive-brown with bronze tones. Underparts buff, boldly marked with wavy, brown or olive streaks on breast, blotches on belly. Uppertail blackish, undertail greyer. Wings olive-brown edged bronze and barred or spotted on inner webs of flight feathers, underwing buff marked brown. Face cream or white with olive-brown malar, dusky ear-covert patch and white supercilium. Neck-sides and throat white with some brownish streaks and spots. Legs grey or olive. Bill greyish with paler base. Iris chestnut. Sexes differ: both have olive-brown crown, but males have red hindcrown and nape, which females lack having chocolate nape. Juveniles of both sexes have red crown patch and are lighter and greener above than adults.

Vocalisations A tinny trill and loud, harsh series of up to 12 *rrek* and *rrak* notes. Also a rapid, solid *bdddddd-d-it* or *br-r-r-r-r-r-r* and repeated, buzzing *zh-dzeeeep, dzheet* or *dzhaah* notes – very like Gabon Woodpecker and recalling Cardinal Woodpecker. In disputes utters low-pitched *pit* or *bit* notes.

Drumming Both sexes occasionally produce quiet, short, strident, level-pitched rolls.

Status Conservation category not assigned by the IUCN. Nowhere very common, but probably not threatened, though logging, mining and construction are ongoing in its rainforest habitat.

Habitat Clearings and edges in more open rainforest. Also secondary growth, farm-bush, swamps, riverine forest, plantations and rural gardens.

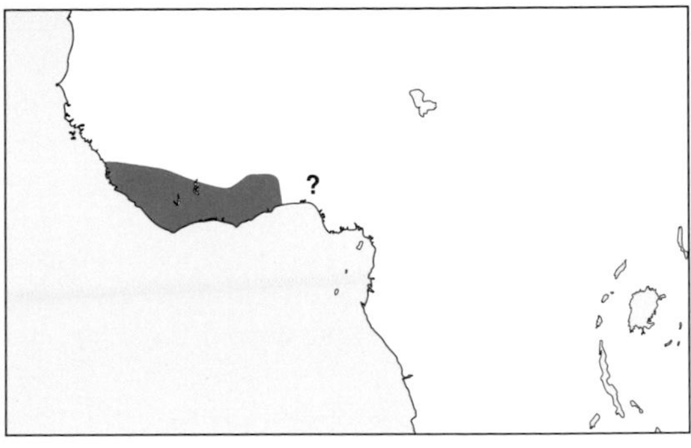

Range W Africa. Resident and sedentary in the Upper Guinea rainforests. Through Sierra Leone, Liberia, Ivory Coast, SE Ghana and Togo, but discontinuous. Mainly lowlands, to 1300m.

Taxonomy and variation Monotypic. Formerly treated as race of Gabon Woodpecker. Some individuals have faint light grey barring on mantle.

Similar species Gabon Woodpecker is paler green above, more spotted below, has lighter, browner tail and lacks bold dark ear-covert patch. But note that *reichenowi* race of Gabon Woodpecker is darker and so closer to Melancholy.

Food and foraging Various insects. Often forages in canopy, in family parties and mixed-species flocks.

► Adult male Melancholy Woodpecker. Note the red nape, which the females lack. Endemic to the Upper Guinea rainforests of West Africa. Freetown, Sierra Leone, November (*David Monticelli*).

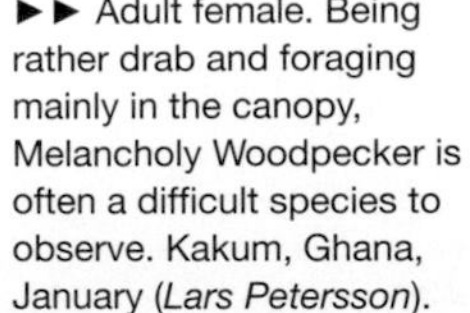

►► Adult female. Being rather drab and foraging mainly in the canopy, Melancholy Woodpecker is often a difficult species to observe. Kakum, Ghana, January (*Lars Petersson*).

84. STIERLING'S WOODPECKER
Dendropicos stierlingi

L 17–18cm

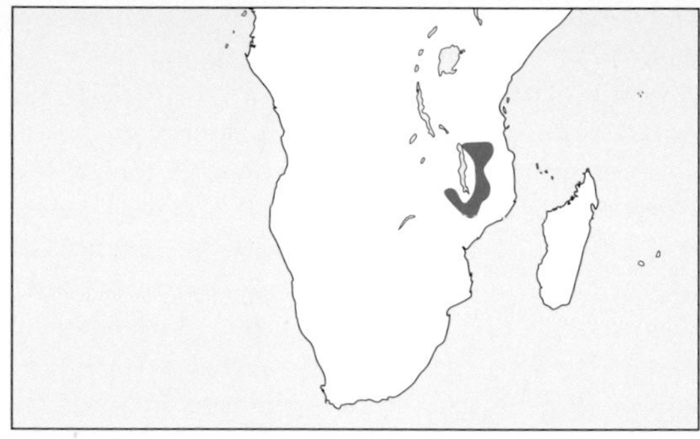

Identification Mantle, back, wings and tail all plain, unbarred, olive-brown. White or cream below, marked with brown streaks, scales and chevrons. Chin and throat white. Face and neck white, with bold chocolate post-ocular band crossing ear-coverts and thick brown malar continuing down to chest. Uppertail brown, tip buff, coverts lightly barred pale, undertail pale brown. Wings brown, outer-coverts edged olive, inner webs barred white, underwing white. Iris reddish. Bill greyish, base paler. Legs grey or olive. Sexes differ: male red from mid-crown to nape, forecrown brown; female lacks red, having brown crown streaked pale and blackish nape. Juvenile shows some red in mid-crown, has brown iris and is duller overall.

Vocalisations Loud, but low-pitched, sporadic, rattling *pi-di-di, da-da-da, da-da-da-da,* often interspersed with drumming. Also gentle, subtle, single or repeated, *pik* and *weep* notes. When agitated or alarmed a rattling *bdddt.*

Drumming Drums regularly in breeding season, indulging in prolonged bouts. Typically, loud, rapid (over 20 strikes per second) rolls.

Status NT. Generally uncommon and poorly known. Relatively range-restricted, occurs in low-densities, is often localised and possibly overlooked. Has declined in Malawi (and possibly elsewhere) due to clearance of woodland for firewood.

Habitat Closely associated with open, dry *miombo* (*Brachystegia*) woodlands. Avoids dense forest.

Range Africa. Rather scattered in S Tanzania, SW Malawi and N Mozambique. Lowlands to around 1500m. Resident and sedentary.

Taxonomy and variation Monotypic. In fresh plumage some individuals have reddish feather-tips on mantle and back.

Similar species None within range. Superficially like Bearded Woodpecker, particularly in head pattern, but obviously smaller and lacks the barred back and white-spotted forecrown of that species.

Food and foraging Insectivorous. Usually forages alone outside the breeding season, sometimes in pairs, working at higher levels in trees. Seldom joins mixed-species foraging flocks. Will sally for winged termites, but not as proficient at this as some other woodpeckers.

◄◄ Adult male Stierling's Woodpecker has a red crown, which the females lack. Dzalanyama Forest Reserve, Malawi, March (*Niall Perrins*).

◄ Adult female Stierling's Woodpecker. Found mainly in south-east Africa's dwindling *miombo* woodlands, this poorly known species is under threat. Dzalanyama Forest Reserve, Malawi, October (*Nik Borrow*).

85. BEARDED WOODPECKER
Dendropicos namaquus

L 24–26cm

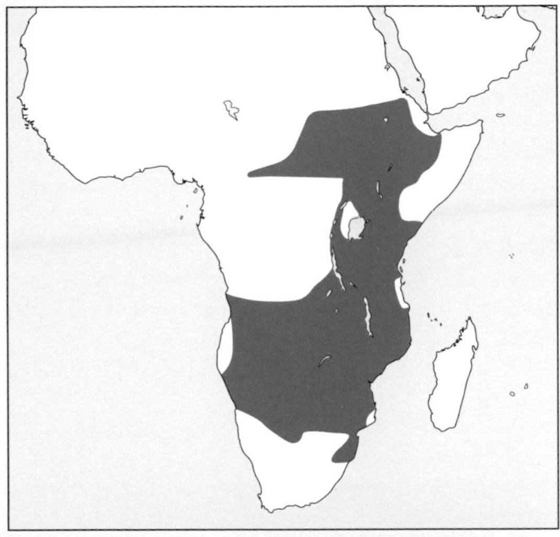

Identification One of Africa's largest woodpeckers. Rather dark body with boldly striped-faced. Black or brown behind eye and over ear-coverts. Black malar continues down onto chest. Black forehead and fore-crown speckled white. Solid black nape. Throat white. Dusky or olive below from chest to vent, with fine pale bars and chevrons. Upperparts and wings olive-brown, narrowly barred white. Rump and uppertail-coverts golden, tinged orange. Greenish tail lightly barred white with bold yellow shafts and tip. Long, grey bill. Iris chestnut. Legs greyish. Sexes differ: male has mid-crown to nape red; female lacks red. When sexes together shorter bill of female also evident. Juvenile less barred, greener above, iris grey or brown, both sexes having black, white and red on crown. Juvenile male may have more red than adult.

Vocalisations Loud, fast, repeated, trilling or rattling

► Adult male Bearded Woodpecker of the race *schoensis*. Males have a red crown, which females lack, and longer bills. Langano, Ethiopia, November (*Amano Samarpan*).

bursts of *wik, kwik or weet* notes in series – recalling Grey-headed Kingfisher. Noisy chattering *wickwickwick-wick-wick*. Variants include up to 7 *a-weet* and *chew-a* notes. Also drawn-out, falling, yelping *kree-kree-kree-kreekreekree*, accelerating at the end. Rather quiet outside breeding season.

Drumming Both sexes avid drummers. Loud, slow, almost mechanical rolls of around 12 staggered strikes per second, faltering towards the end and ending in several clear, solid knocks. Distinct and unmistakable within the range.

Status Not uncommon in mature woodlands, less so in open bush. Population data sparse but considered stable, although need for tall, dead trees has probably meant local declines, as these are often felled for firewood.

Habitat Dry bush and savanna, acacia, euphorbia, *mopane* and *miombo* (*Brachystegia*) thickets. Also tropical dry and damp woodlands, riverine woods, more open upland broadleaved forests. Drier areas with standing, dead, tall timber often favoured. Avoids plantations of exotic trees.

Range Africa. Mainly mid-east of continent, core range south of the Equator. From Sudan and Eritrea southwards to the East Cape, South Africa. Sea-level to 3000m. Resident and sedentary.

Taxonomy and variation Sometimes placed in genus *Thripias*. Three races: ***namaquus*** (W C African Republic into S Sudan, E DR Congo, SW Uganda, W and SE Kenya, Tanzania, Malawi, Zambia, Angola, Namibia); ***schoensis*** (Ethiopia to Somalia, N Kenya, NE and NW Uganda) smaller, browner above than nominate, spotted rather than barred below, with longer black facial stripes that meet on lower neck; ***coalescens*** (C and S Mozambique, Botswana, E South Africa) more olive above with barring broken, darker below with narrow bars tending to chevrons, tail coverts sometimes tipped red. Intergrades occur.

Similar species Most like Stierling's and Golden-crowned Woodpeckers, particularly in head markings, but former much smaller, latter not in same habitat and males never have red crown.

Food and foraging Range of invertebrates, but mostly beetle larvae. Forages at all levels, but often low on dead trees, stumps and logs. Once a productive site is found, will make repeated visits. Also takes small reptiles.

◀ Adult female *schoensis*. This race is spotted rather than barred on the breast, and browner above than the nominate. Langano, Ethiopia, November (*Amano Samarpan*).

▲ Adult male *coalescens*. This race is darkly and tightly barred on the chest and breast. Kruger NP, South Africa, October (*Dubi Shapiro*).

▲► Adult female nominate. Bearded Woodpecker is on average the largest *Dendropicos*, and is unlikely to be confused with any sympatric species. Lake Mburo, Uganda, March (*Gerard Gorman*).

► Juvenile *coalescens*. Both male and female juveniles have red on the crown. Nylsvley, South Africa, July (*Warwick Tarboton*).

86. GOLDEN-CROWNED WOODPECKER
Dendropicos xantholophus

L 22–25cm

Other name Yellow-crested Woodpecker

Identification Dark overall with boldly marked head. Mantle and back dull brownish-olive, usually plain, sometimes slightly barred. Yellowish rump and uppertail-coverts. Olive wings with slight pale barring on flight feathers. Tail chocolate. Brownish below, densely spotted buff or white on breast, barred on flanks and vent. Throat cream or white. Brown forehead, forecrown black lightly spotted white. Nape black. Black post-ocular and thin malar stripes, latter extending onto neck-sides. Iris dark red. Long bill; upper mandible darker, lower grey-green. Legs olive-grey. Sexes differ slightly: male has small golden or yellow crown patch (not always obvious until raised in displays or disputes), mottled and flecked black; female lacks yellow having entire crown and nape blackish. Juveniles of both sexes have some crown feathers tipped yellow, are drabber overall, more olive above, greyer below, less spotted and more barred.

Vocalisations Often vocal. Chattering calls include trilling, slurred, falling, repeated series of *kerrreee, kreeerr* or *kree* notes, often followed by excited, descending *kweek* or *kwi* notes. Single *dit* and double

▼ Adult male Golden-crowned Woodpecker. Unless the yellow crown-patch can be seen, separating males from females can be difficult. Sanaga River, Cameroon, March (*Lars Petersson*).

dit-it notes, sometimes developing into rapid purring series. Also loud *a-wik, a-wik, a-wik* and harsh *grrrrrr.*

Drumming Both sexes avid drummers. Distinctive loud, long rolls, which begin slowly before accelerating and finally fading.

Status Detailed population data lacking, but overall considered stable.

Habitat Dense, damp, primary and secondary tropical forests. Sometimes in drier forests and also cocoa and coffee plantations where large trees remain. Visits isolated tall trees at forest edges and in clearings.

Range Africa. W and C of the continent, around Equator. From Nigeria and SW Cameroon, E to S Sudan, S and W Uganda (including Mt Elgon) and W Kenya (Kakamega and N Nandi Forests), S through DR Congo to NW Angola. From 700 to around 2150m. Resident and sedentary.

Taxonomy and variation Monotypic. Sometimes placed in separate genera *Mesopicos* or *Thripias.* Variation slight.

Similar species Larger than all sympatric forest species. Same-sized Bearded Woodpecker has similar head markings, but lacks yellow on crown, has a barred back and rarely occurs in same habitat.

Food and foraging Insects, especially wood-boring beetle larvae. Forages from mid-levels to the canopy. Hacks into timber, scales bark, sometimes flycatches.

► Adult Golden-crowned Woodpecker. A touch of yellow on the crown of this bird suggests a male, however females may have some faint yellow feather-tips. Sanaga River, Cameroon, March (*Lars Petersson*).

◄ A recently fledged juvenile. Both male and female juveniles may show yellow in the crown until the first moult. Nyonie, Gabon, August (*A. P. Leventis*).

87. FIRE-BELLIED WOODPECKER
Dendropicos pyrrhogaster

L 24cm

Identification Head boldly marked. Face, neck and throat white with black malar that runs onto the chest and black post-ocular band and ear-coverts. Lores buff or white. Underparts white or cream, with bold black chevrons on the flanks and scarlet (fire-bellied) from centre of the breast to the vent. Mantle and back olive or bronze with some light barring and red feathers tips in fresh plumage. Rump and uppertail-coverts crimson. Uppertail blackish, undertail buff or greenish. Wings brownish, coverts olive or bronze with pale fringes, inner webs of flight feathers barred white, underwing white. Legs grey. Long grey bill with often paler lower mandible. Iris chestnut. Sexes differ: both have dark forehead, but male has red crown and nape; female crown all-black, less red below, shorter bill and longer tail – though latter two features often hard to judge. Juvenile browner, duller than adult, with less red below and iris brown. Juveniles of both sexes have some red on the crown, less so in females.

Vocalisations Short, squeaky, sometimes harder, *kweep, kwip, wip* or *week* contact notes. Similar notes linked into an accelerating, rattling *kwip-ib-ibibib* or *wip-wi-di-di-di-dit* series.

Drumming Both sexes drum frequently in dry season. Short, quickly repeated, loud or subdued, level-pitched volleys – one of the distinctive sounds of the forest. Speed varies from 14–38 strikes per second.

Status Common locally. Population data limited, but possibly increasing where forests have been selectively logged as prefers open forests. However, no room for complacency as West African forests are some of the most fragmented on the continent.

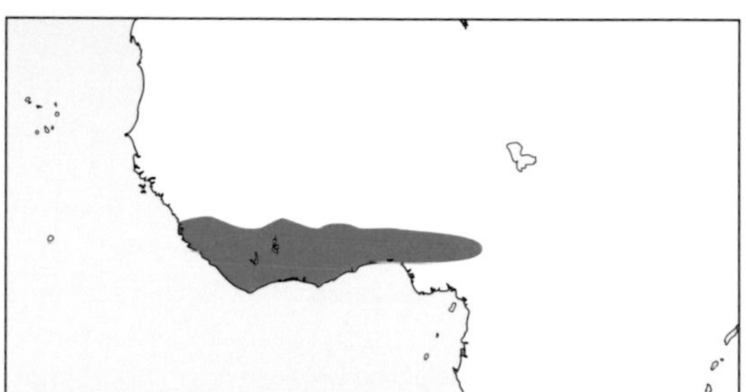

Habitat Edges, clearings and mosaic areas in lowland primary rainforest, invariably with some large dead trees. Also gallery forest, partially logged and degraded forests, farm-bush, old plantations and drier wooded savanna.

Range WC Africa. Upper Guinea Forests in Sierra Leone, S Mali, S Guinea, Liberia, Ivory Coast, Ghana, Togo, Benin, S Nigeria, as far E as N of Korup NP in SW Cameroon. Mainly lowlands and foothills. Resident and sedentary.

Taxonomy and variation Monotypic. Sometimes placed in genus *Thripias*. Some males buff on crown. Individual variation in extent and intensity of red on underparts.

Similar species None within range.

Food and foraging Insects, especially beetle larvae. Often in pairs and family groups, sometimes in association with other insectivorous birds. Usually forages in canopy, on snags and burnt trees, but will drop onto fallen timber.

◄◄ Adult male Fire-bellied Woodpecker. Both sexes are variably marked with red below, but only males have red on the crown. Kakum, Ghana, April (*Nik Borrow*).

◄ Adult female. If seen well, this often vocal species is unmistakable within its range. Kakum, Ghana, April (*Nik Borrow*).

88. ELLIOT'S WOODPECKER
Dendropicos elliotii

L 19–21cm

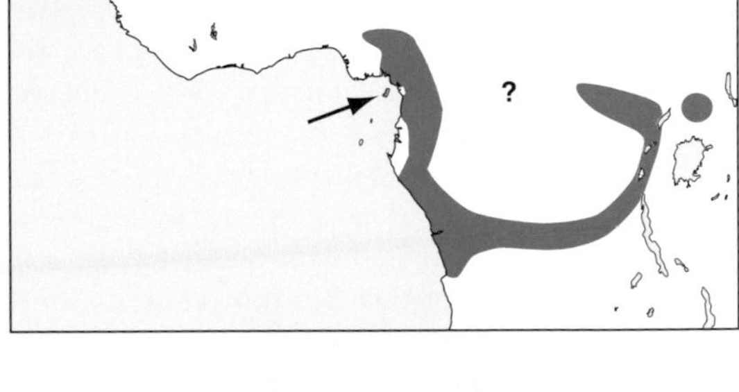

Other name Johnston's Woodpecker (when *johnstoni* race treated as species).

Identification Long-tailed, rather plain. Olive-green mantle, back and wings, with some brown or bronze tones, mostly unmarked. Underwing paler. Uppertail brownish, undertail yellowish. Buff or yellow below, streaked brown or olive. Chin and throat cream, finely streaked. Face, lores, forehead and ear-coverts plain buff or brown. Fine dark malar sometimes not discernible. Relatively long greyish bill, lower mandible and tip often yellowish. Iris reddish. Legs grey. Sexes differ: male has black forecrown, red from mid-crown to nape; female lacks red, entire crown black. Juvenile drabber, streaked below, with brown iris. Juvenile male has much of crown red, juvenile female red only at rear.

Vocalisations Remarkably taciturn and non-responsive. Known calls include a whining, nasal *weeeyu;* a shrill, harsh *kree-kree-kree, tree-tree-tree* or *bwe-bwe-bwe;* and a rattling, buzzing series of *churr* notes that rise and fall. Also an occasional more pleasant series of two-syllable *kiwik-kiwik-kiwik* notes.

Drumming Not an avid drummer. Occasionally produces slow, subtle rolls.

Status Locally common. Occurs over a large area, but rather fragmented and often absent from seemingly good habitat. Possibly overlooked. Data lacking but overall considered stable.

Habitat Varied across range. Mainly highland dense, damp, moss-clad, mature tropical forests. Nominate race also in some lowlands.

Range Africa. Occurs in a belt across the WC of the continent, around the Equator. From Nigeria E to Rwanda and Uganda, S to Angola, but discontinuous. Sea-level to about 2300m. Resident and sedentary.

Taxonomy and variation Sometimes placed in separate *Mesopicos* genus. Two races: ***elliotii*** (lowland Cameroon, Gabon, NW Angola, DR Congo, SW and E Uganda) has plain, olive-green face and ear-coverts and boldly streaked, brownish underparts; ***johnstoni*** (upland SE Nigeria, W Cameroon and Bioko Island, Gulf of Guinea) has paler face and mostly plain, or only faintly marked, buff or green underparts. Birds in NW Angola may have fine streaking below and are sometimes treated as another race *'gabela'*.

Similar species Most similarly sized sympatric green woodpeckers are not as plain, being more marked below and/or on the face.

Food and foraging Searches for insects from canopy to understorey, typically exploring leaf clusters, epiphytes and moss-clad boughs. Often in mixed-species foraging parties.

► Adult male Elliot's Woodpecker of the nominate race. Males have red from the mid-crown to the nape, which females lack. Bwindi Impenetrable Forest, Uganda. February (*Kristian Svensson*).

►► Adult female *johnstoni*. This mainly upland race has plainer underparts than the nominate. Mount Cameroon, Cameroon, March (*Lars Petersson*).

89. AFRICAN GREY WOODPECKER
Dendropicos goertae

L 19–20cm

Other name Grey Woodpecker

Identification Most of head, face and underparts plain grey. Plain green above. Scarlet rump and uppertail-coverts show well in flight. Wings olive, primaries browner, finely barred or spotted yellowish. Tail brown with outer feathers faintly barred buff. Grey below with, in most races, variable red, orange or yellow belly-patch. Iris chestnut. Long, pointed dark bill, lower mandible often greyer. Legs grey or olive. Sexes differ: male has red from mid-crown to nape; female lacks red, being totally grey-headed. Juvenile drabber, greener above, more barred below showing little or no red on belly, rump pinkish, with faint pale supercilium and grey iris; juveniles of both sexes have red on mid-crown, more so in male.

Vocalisations Very vocal. Commonly a loud, piercing *chwi-chwi-skew-skew-chree-chree-chree-chree-chree*, softer as it ends. Also a variable, vigorous, falling, shrill or

◄ Adult male nominate African Grey Woodpecker. Males have a bright red crown, which the females lack. Gunjur, The Gambia, October (*Martin Goodey*).

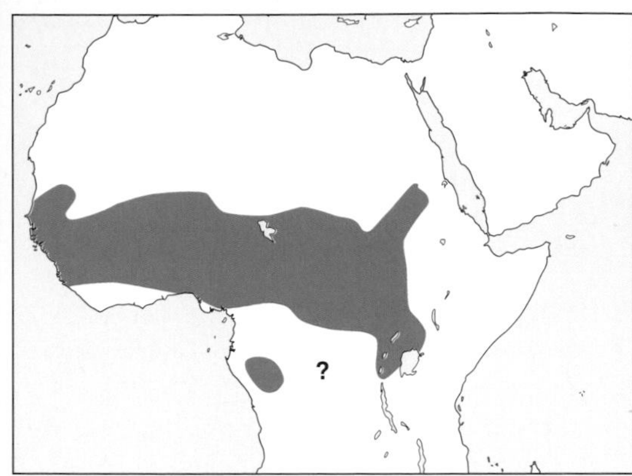

squealing *kwik-wik-wik-wi, skwi-skwi-skwi* or *kik-kik-kreet-kreet-kreet;* a weaker *ch-ch-reeek-reeek-reek;* and a rapid, rattling, high-pitched series of up to 30 *wik* notes. Also undulating, haphazard series of *weeka* or *week* notes and more musical, chirping or churring *trrree-tri-tree. pit-it* contact notes.

Drumming Drums infrequently, occasionally producing brief, tinny rolls.

Status Common across much of range. Data limited, but overall considered stable.

Habitat Various open, mainly arid woodlands: bush, savanna, thickets. In some regions damper woods, mangroves, cultivated land, pastures and settlements with trees, especially palms.

Range Africa. S of the Sahara, mostly N of Equator, but discontinuous. Through Sahel, from Mauritania E to Sudan and Eritrea, Kenya and Tanzania. In the W southwards to Angola. Sea-level to over 3000m. Resident, but some vagrant records. Mainly between 380–1820m.

Taxonomy and variation Sometimes placed in *Mesopicos* genus. Four races, differing mainly in belly-patch colour and extent. Nominate ***goertae*** (SW Mauritania, Senegambia to S Sudan, N DR Congo, Uganda, Rwanda, Burundi, NW Tanzania, W Kenya) lacks, or has minimal, belly-patch; ***koenigi*** (E Mali to Niger, Chad, W Sudan) much paler than nominate, face more flecked, wings and back barred pale, yellowish on belly, though this often indistinct; ***abessinicus*** (E Sudan, NW Ethiopia, Eritrea) also pale below with limited red on belly, dusky face and pale supercilium; ***meridionalis*** (S Gabon, Congo, NW Angola and SC DR Congo) brownish above, greyer below.

Similar species Formerly conspecific Eastern Grey Woodpecker has larger, redder belly-patch and mostly unbarred wings. Slightly smaller, stockier Olive Woodpecker is olive-green below, much darker overall and lacks tail barring. Interbreeds with both.

Food and foraging Ants, termites, beetle larvae and some nuts. Forages in trees, occasionally on ground; also flycatches. Somewhat opportunistic, e.g. recorded foraging for small crabs in mangroves.

▼ Adult female nominate. Although common across much of its range, little is known about the natural history of this woodpecker. Freetown, Sierra Leone, September (*David Monticelli*).

90. EASTERN GREY WOODPECKER
Dendropicos spodocephalus

L 19–20cm

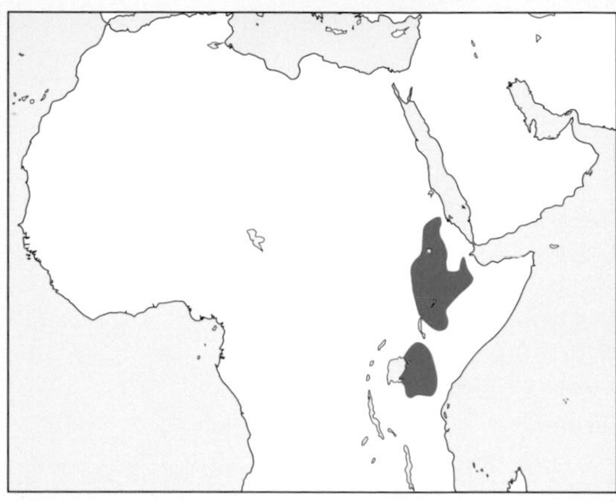

Other name Grey-headed Woodpecker (NB: Eurasian *Picus canus* also often called Grey-headed Woodpecker)
Identification Most of head, face and underparts plain grey. Ear-coverts duskier. Mostly green above; scarlet rump and uppertail-coverts prominent in flight. Grey below with red patch from belly to vent (can extend onto breast). Uppertail brown with outer feathers slightly barred off-white. Undertail brown with outer feathers barred buff or yellow. Wings green with browner flight feathers edged yellowish. Underwing barred dark and pale. Bill grey, lower mandible yellower. Iris chestnut. Legs greyish-green. Sexes differ: male has red from mid-crown to nape; female lacks red, having entirely grey head. Juvenile drabber, with belly-patch pinker; red on crown more extensive in male.
Vocalisations *Wik* notes in series. In disputes utters rapid *weeka-weeka-weeka* calls.
Drumming Drums very rarely, and details lacking.
Status Population data sparse, but locally often common and considered stable overall.
Habitat Wet upland forest, riverine woodland and scrubland.
Range E Africa. Extreme E of the Sudans, W and C

◄ Adult male Eastern Grey Woodpecker of the nominate race. Males have red on the crown; both sexes have red uppertail-coverts, which show well here. Wondo Genet, Ethiopia, November (*Vaughan & Sveta Ashby*).

Ethiopian highlands, extreme S Somalia (Somali-Masai region E of Wajaale Plains) and highlands of C and SW Kenya and NC Tanzania. Uplands to around 3000m. Resident and sedentary.

Taxonomy and variation Two similar races: ***spodocephalus*** (E Sudan, C and S Ethiopian highlands, S Somalia); and ***rhodeogaster*** (Central Kenyan highlands into NC Tanzania), which has larger red belly-patch, darker underparts and yellow dots on mantle. Formerly regarded as conspecific with Grey Woodpecker, and split often disputed.

Similar species Very like African Grey Woodpecker (previously treated as a race), but darker grey on head, bill paler, mantle and back lighter green, wings and tail less barred, belly-patch larger and redder. Olive Woodpecker much darker overall and green below. May interbreed with both.

Food and foraging Various invertebrates, spiders, centipedes, probably some plant matter. Forages in both live and dead trees, in pairs or alone. Occasionally hawks for winged prey.

► Adult female nominate. The female is truly grey-headed, lacking the red of the male. Langano, Ethiopia, January (*Paul Noakes*).

▼ Adult female nominate; female Eastern Grey can easily be confused with female African Grey Woodpecker *Dendropicos goertae*. Wondo Genet, Ethiopia, November (*Vaughan & Sveta Ashby*).

91. OLIVE WOODPECKER
Dendropicos griseocephalus

L 18–19cm

Identification Mostly plain but subtly marked. Dusky grey head and throat. Forehead and forecrown black. Dark grey and olive below, with golden tones and variably sized red-pink belly-patch (lacking in *kilimensis*). Olive above with golden and bronze tones. Scarlet rump and uppertail-coverts more obvious in flight. Wings brown with white spotted and barred flight feathers. Unbarred, blackish tail, some feathers edged

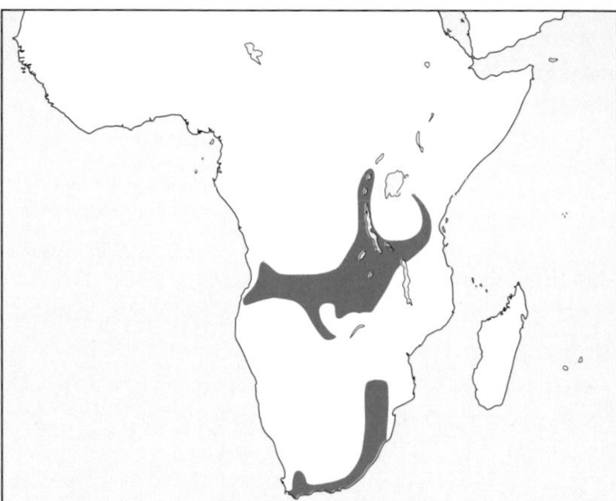

green. Upper mandible grey, lower sometimes bluish. Iris reddish. Legs greyish. Sexes differ: male has red from mid-crown to nape, mottled grey or black; female has all-grey head. Juvenile drabber, greener above, greyer below lacking yellow hues, some with pale flank barring, little or no red on belly, pinkish rump rather than red; both sexes have some red in black mottled or barred crown, more so in male.

Vocalisations Mocking, quivering *yeh-yeh-yeh-yeh* or *yeh-heh-heh-het;* repeated, rising *krrrreeee;* and nasal, whistling *whee-whee-whee.* Also a more pleasant, squeaky *week-week-week* or *tweet-tweet-tweet. Wat-chew, wat-chew* often delivered in flight. Also *pep-pep-pep* and *kiwi-kiwi-kiwi* contact notes and a disyllabic *wir-rit.* Loud *queek, tweet* and *tik* alarm notes.

Drumming Infrequently produces rapid but soft, subdued 1-second rolls.

Status Data limited but overall population considered stable. Often locally common.

Habitat Mainly damp, tropical, evergreen or mixed hill and mountain forests. Also riverine woods and drier areas like thickets, scrub, bushveld and sometimes gardens. Dead wood important, thus plantations avoided.

Range Africa. Almost entirely S of Equator. From DR Congo and Uganda to South Africa, though discontinuous. Resident and usually sedentary though some vagrant records. Sea-level to mountains, but

◄ Adult male nominate Olive Woodpecker. Note the red on the crown, which females lack. Both sexes have red uppertail-coverts. Wilderness NP, South Africa, August (*Ingo Waschkies*).

mainly between 450–3700m, depending upon forest cover.

Taxonomy and variation Sometimes placed in *Mesopicos*. Three races: ***griseocephalus*** (S Mozambique into South Africa: Natal, E Transvaal, Cape Province); ***ruwenzori*** (Namibia, Angola, Zambia, DR Congo, Burundi, Rwanda, SW Uganda, Tanzania and Malawi) has large red belly-patch, flanks sometimes barred white, more golden tones on breast and chest, primaries barred pale; ***kilimensis*** (Tanzanian mountains) lacks red on belly, grey breast lacks green and yellow tones.

Similar species Slightly bigger African Grey Woodpecker, with which it sometimes interbreeds, overall paler, grey below and with longer, barred tail. Juveniles of both sexes similar. More like Eastern Grey Woodpecker, which is paler and greyer and rarely overlaps.

Food and foraging Insects, especially beetles and ants. Usually forages in cover in trees, pecking and probing mossy, lichen-draped trees, moving actively on thinner branches. Often in pairs, sometimes family parties and in mixed-species flocks.

▼ Adult female *kilimensis*. Although not visible in this photograph, this race lacks red on the belly. West Usambara Mountains, Tanzania, August (*Adam Scott Kennedy*).

▼ Adult female nominate. This species inhabits lusher woodlands than the African Grey *Dendropicos goertae* and Eastern Grey *D. spodocephalus* Woodpeckers that it most resembles. Mbombela NR, South Africa, July (*Robert Wienand*).

92. BROWN-BACKED WOODPECKER
Dendropicos obsoletus

L 13–15cm

Identification Mainly brown and white. Plain brown mantle and back. White or cream below, variably streaked brown. Brown wings dotted white. Brown tail barred and spotted white. White face with large brown patch over ear-coverts and brown malar. Throat white. Fine bill; upper mandible dark, lower greyer. Iris reddish. Legs grey. Sexes differ: male has brown forecrown and red hindcrown and nape; female lacks red, having all-brown crown. Juvenile overall darker, often slightly barred below, both sexes with red in the crown, more so on male, iris dark.

Vocalisations Often silent. Strong, rapid, rattling, not unmusical *ki-ki-keew-keew, squee-squee-squee* or *chree-chree-chee* series that fades slightly. Also *krreet-krreet-krreet* or *kweek-week-week*. Chattering weak *chew* notes, various trills, single clicks and upslurred, falcon-like squeaks and squeals.

Drumming Drums regularly, but precise details lacking.

Status Often localised and uncommon. Overall population size and trends considered stable, though data limited.

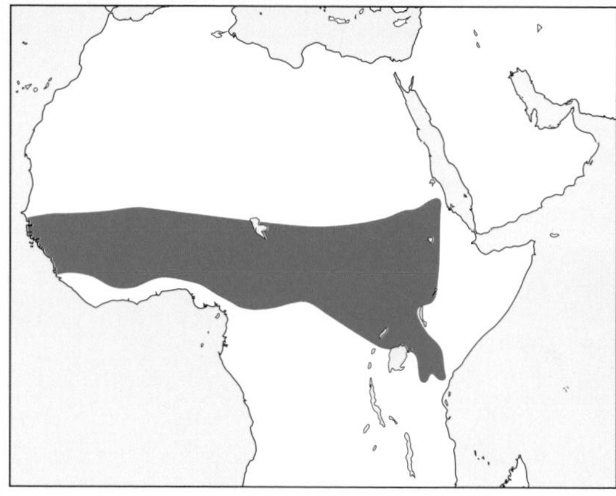

Habitat Varied dry, open, often sparsely wooded areas such as bush, savanna, scrubby hillsides, forest edges, gardens and wooded farmland.

◄ Adult male Brown-backed Woodpecker of the nominate race. Note the red on the crown, which females lack. Borgu, Nigeria, June (*A .P. Leventis*).

Range Africa. Through savanna and bush-belt of the sub-Sahara, mostly N of Equator. From Mauritania, Senegambia E to Eritrea, Ethiopia and Kenya, S to N Tanzania. Sea-level to 3000m. Resident but not entirely sedentary, nomadic movements noted.

Taxonomy and variation Previously in the *Dendrocopos* or *Picoides*. Four races differing in size, darkness of upperparts and extent of underpart streaking. Nominate ***obsoletus*** (Senegambia to the Sudans and Uganda S to Equator but not NE) is brown above, only lightly streaked below; ***heuglini*** (E Sudan, N Ethiopia, Eritrea) tan above, well-streaked below, wings only lightly spotted; ***ingens*** (C and S Ethiopia, NE Uganda, W and C Kenya and coast near Mombasa, N Tanzania at Loliondo) chocolate crown and upperparts, wings well-spotted, more heavily streaked below than nominate; ***crateri*** (N Tanzania: Crater Highlands to Nou Forest) largest, darkest race, blackish above; dense, dark streaking below often forms chest band.

Similar species Similar-sized Cardinal Woodpecker of *lepidus* race also has plain back, but olive not brown, lacks ear-cover patch and has yellow in tail.

Food and foraging Usually forages unobtrusively on twigs and small branches for invertebrates, especially larvae, fruit and berries. Often in mixed-species flocks.

▲ Adult female nominate. Although widespread and not uncommon, this is another unobtrusive African woodpecker of which little is actually known. Benoue, Cameroon, March (*Lars Petersson*).

◄ Adult female *heuglini*. This race has more streaks below than the nominate, but less spotting in the wings. Jemma Valley, Ethiopia, November (*Kristian Svensson*).

DENDROCOPOS

An Old World genus of 25 species with representatives in N Africa, Europe, the Middle East and Asia, as far as Japan and some SE Asian islands. They are essentially black and white and often called 'pied' woodpeckers. Most of these small to medium-sized woodpeckers are dark above with white barring and/or spotting, and pale underneath often with dark streaks. Many species have red on the ventral area and males have red on the head, which most females lack. Juveniles often have more red on the head than adults. Some species are very similar and attention should be paid in particular to face markings. Most fly in an undulating manner that fits the notion of 'typical woodpecker flight'. Some species have previously been included in *Picoides*.

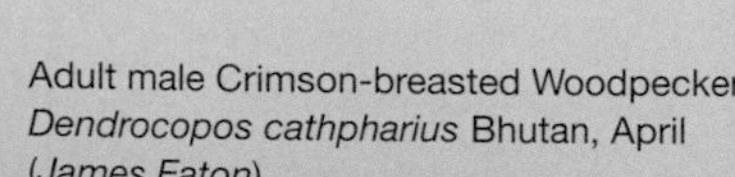

Adult male Crimson-breasted Woodpecker, *Dendrocopos cathpharius* Bhutan, April (*James Eaton*).

93. RUFOUS-BELLIED WOODPECKER
Dendrocopos hyperythrus

L 19–23cm

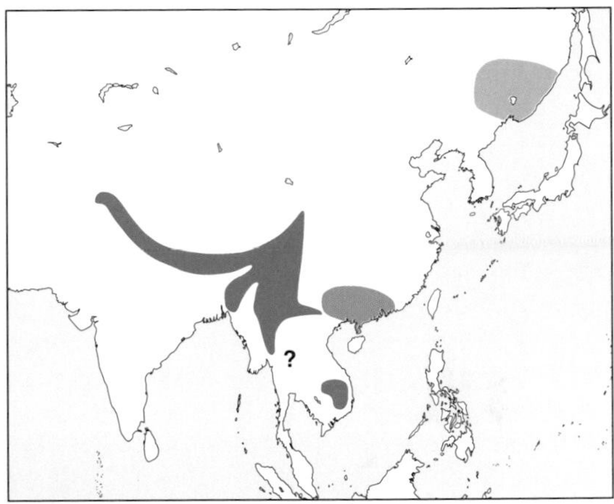

Identification Distinctive plain rufous or cinnamon ear-coverts, neck and underparts. Lower belly and lower flanks barred black and white, undertail-coverts and vent pink or red. Black mantle and wings barred white. Rump black. Uppertail black, outer two feather pairs spotted or barred white. Whitish lores, cheeks and supercilium. Thin, often negligible, dusky malar. Iris chestnut. Bill blackish, lower mandible paler. Legs grey or olive. Sexes differ: male has red from forecrown to nape; female crown black, heavily speckled white, sometimes with a few red tips, vent paler. Male also brighter rufous below. Juvenile duller, browner below spotted or barred black, upperparts spotted white, pale throat streaked black, face darkly mottled and

► Adult male Rufous-bellied Woodpecker of the race *marshalli*. With a red crown and vent and cinnamon-orange underparts, males of this species are among the most brightly coloured of all *Dendrocopos*. Uttarakhand, India, December (*Ingo Waschkies*).

streaked; both sexes have black crown spotted white, often streaked orange or red, less so on females.

Vocalisations Quite vocal, making a range of fast, chattering calls: high-pitched *tik-tik-tik;* excited *kirridick* or *kirritrick* wavering in pitch; rattling *chit-chit-chit-r-r-r-h;* and *twicca-twicca-wicca-wicca.* Alarm call a nervous *titi-r-r-r-r* and, when agitated, a rapid volley of harsh *ptikitititit* chatter.

Drumming Both sexes drum. Brief, understated roll that accelerates before dropping in pitch.

Status Rather thinly distributed and often uncommon. Probably declining due to habitat change and loss.

Habitat Varies across range. Mainly damp subtropical jungle and upland temperate coniferous, broadleaved and mixed forests.

Range SE Asia. Fragmented: breeds Himalayas, SE Russia and NE China (possibly NW Thailand) and Indochina. Most sedentary, though *subrufinus (*NE China and SE Russia) migrates to winter in S China (some in Tonkin, Vietnam). Occurs in Korea and vagrants, usually in September, have occurred in Hong Kong, Japan and Mongolia. From 500m to over 4000m. Altitudinal movements in Himalayas.

Taxonomy and variation Sometimes placed in the monospecific genus *Hypopicus.* Individual variation in underpart colour. Four races: ***hyperythrus*** (Nepal E to SE Tibet, Bhutan, SW China, Burma (Myanmar), Bangladesh); ***marshalli*** (NE Pakistan, Kashmir, N India) larger than nominate and more chestnut below, male has red crown extending onto neck; ***annamensis*** (E Thailand, Cambodia, Laos, S Vietnam) smaller but bill longer, less red on head; ***subrufinus*** (SE Russia, Ussuriland, Manchuria, wintering S China) larger, paler below, browner on face, vent pinkish.

Similar species None: unmistakable within range.

Food and foraging Insects, often arboreal ants. Usually forages alone. Also drills sap-wells, having favourite trees that are used for years – hence old alternative name 'Rufous-bellied Sapsucker'.

◄ The adult female has a black crown flecked white, and the rufous areas are less bright than on the male. This race, *subrufinus*, is migratory. Hebei, China, May (*Neil Bowman*).

94. SULAWESI WOODPECKER
Dendrocopos temminckii

L 13–14cm

Other names Sulawesi Pygmy Woodpecker, Celebes Pygmy Woodpecker

Identification Brown above, mantle with olive tones, finely barred white. Throat cream or grey, sometimes streaked. Underparts white or buff streaked greyish-brown, heaviest on chest and breast; lower flanks and undertail-coverts plainer. Lores, broad post-ocular line and cheek white. Forehead, ear-coverts and crown brown. Faint brown malar merges with chest barring. Wings chocolate, flight feathers barred white, coverts dotted. Brown tail barred pale. Iris chestnut. Bill black or grey. Legs grey or olive. Sexes differ slightly: male has red band from rear neck-side across white hindneck; female lacks red, having all white hindneck. Juvenile darker and less marked below.

Vocalisations Gentle, nasal, sometimes whistling, trilling *tirrrrrrr* of 1–2 seconds, slowing and falling slightly at the end. Also a harsher *geegeegeegee*.

Drumming Rather weak, brief rolls of around 0.5 seconds described.

Status Common locally. Considered stable, despite being poorly known. Deforestation ongoing within its range, but readily uses man-made and degraded habitats.

Habitat Edges of tall, primary, secondary and degraded forests. Also dry wooded savanna, damp woodlands, fruit, cacao and coffee plantations, farmland, settlements and partially logged areas.

Range Indonesia. Endemic to Sulawesi and some of its islands. From sea-level, but mainly between 800–2400m. Resident and sedentary. One of only two woodpeckers occurring south of Wallace's Line.

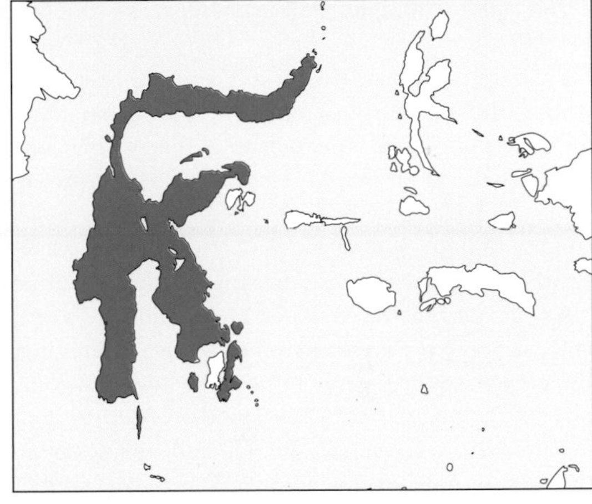

Taxonomy and variation Monotypic. Some regional differences in size, N birds said to be smaller than S ones. Crown sometimes flecked grey. Rump either white or buff, with brown bars or unbarred. Male's red hindneck variable in size and sometimes broken at centre.

Similar species Very like Sulu Woodpecker and browner races of Philippine Woodpecker, but does not overlap.

Food and foraging Presumably invertebrates and plant matter, but information lacking. Often in canopy and on high, thinner snags.

► Adult male Sulawesi Woodpecker. The red hindneck, which females lack, is not always as obvious as here. Sulawesi, Indonesia, September (*Kristian Svensson*).

►► Adult female. Endemic to the Sulawesi archipelago, where deforestation is rife, this species has fortunately been able to adapt to secondary habitats. Sulawesi, Indonesia, September (*Rob Hutchinson*).

95. PHILIPPINE WOODPECKER
Dendrocopos maculatus

L 13–14cm

Other name Philippine Pygmy Woodpecker

Identification Black or brown from nape to lower back, barred white on back and scapulars. Pale rump with dark bars or spots. White or buff from throat to undertail-coverts, breast with yellowish hue and spotted black or brown; flanks, belly and vent streaked. Wings chocolate, flight feathers finely barred white, coverts dotted. Tail black or brown barred white. Crown chocolate, lores cream, white post-ocular stripe reaches nape. Ear-coverts dark, cheek and chin white, malar black or brown often flecked white. Iris chestnut. Bill grey-black. Legs grey or olive. Sexes differ slightly: male has red patch on side of hindcrown, lacking in female. Female has longer bill, tail and wings, though these often hard to judge. Juvenile browner, duskier below and more barred above.

Vocalisations Commonly, 1–3 *chip, chilp* or *pilt* notes, also repeated in a harsh trilling, falling series of around 2 seconds. Grating, rattling alarm notes.

Drumming Reported to drum, but details unavailable.

Status Common locally. Population data scant, but considered stable.

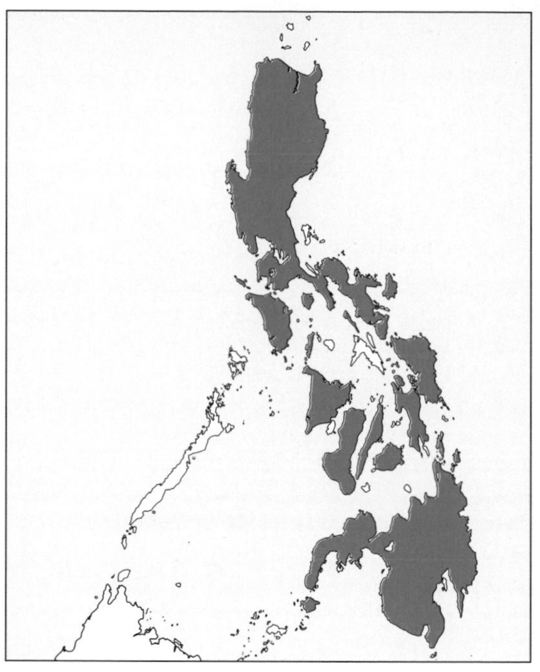

◄ Adult male nominate Philippine Woodpecker feeding a nestling. The sexes can be hard to separate in this species, as the red on the hindcrown of males is often slight. Negros, Philippines, April (*Clemn A. Macasiano Jr*).

Habitat Open lowland and upland humid tropical forests. Also cloud forests, riverine woods, drier forests, wooded grasslands, degraded forests and older plantations.

Range Endemic to Philippines, but not all islands. Sea-level to 2500m. Resident and sedentary.

Taxonomy and variation Five races; some are disputed and more study is needed: ***maculatus*** (Cebu, Guimaras, Negros, Panay, Gigantes) dark overall, tail mostly black, chocolate above heavily barred white, underparts streaked black or brown and buff, throat sides and chest white dotted black, blackish malar and long, white supercilium, male often has crown speckled red at rear; ***validirostris*** (Catanduanes, Lubang, Luzon, Marinduque, Mindoro) has darker upperparts than nominate, barred rump and white post-ocular band extending to nape, male with least red on head; ***menagei*** (Sibuyan) much like above; ***fulvifasciatus*** (Samar, Calicoan, Bohol, Basilan, Mindanao, Dinagat) is pied, blackish above boldly barred white, with plain white rump, most white in face and throat, buff chest and breast, tail mostly pale grey; ***leytensis*** (Leyte) much like previous.

Similar species Unmistakable; by far the smallest woodpecker in its range. Similar Sulawesi, Sulu and Brown-capped Woodpeckers do not overlap.

Food and foraging Arboreal ants and other invertebrates. Often forages at forest edges and in clearings, usually high up, but also in bushes and tall grass. Joins mixed-species feeding flocks.

▼ Adult female *validirostris*. This race has a particularly well-marked head pattern. Luzon, Philippines, October (*Alain Pascua*).

96. SULU WOODPECKER
Dendrocopos ramsayi

L 13–14cm

Other name Sulu Pygmy Woodpecker

Identification Mantle and back mostly plain brown, sometimes with golden tones and some white flecks or bars. Prominent white patch on lower back and rump. Buff or cream below with brown chest-band, variably edged yellow or gold at the sides, and only faintly streaked brown on the belly and flanks. Brown wings with small white bars on inner webs of primaries. Uppertail plain chocolate. Chin and throat white. Face white with dusky brown ear-coverts, broad white post-ocular stripe that reaches the nape and brownish malar. Iris reddish. Bill and legs greyish. Sexes differ: male has brown forecrown and red hindcrown and nape; female lacks red, having all-brown crown. Juvenile duskier below.

Vocalisations Fast staccato *kikikikikiki* that rises at the beginning. Lower-pitched than similar call of Philippine Woodpecker.

Drumming Probably drums, but details unavailable.

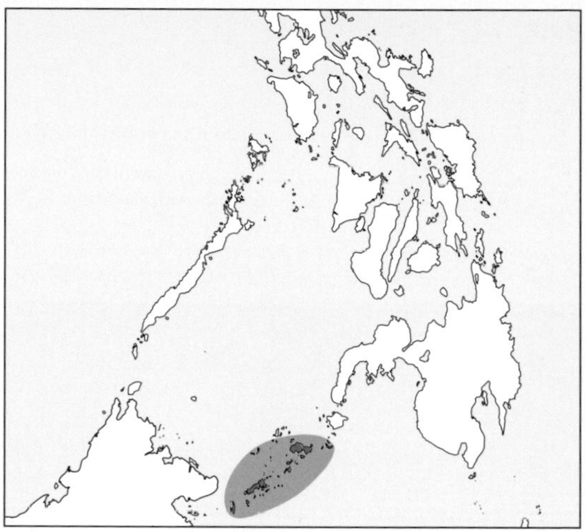

Status VU. Range-restricted and occurs on islands where native forest has been heavily logged and continues to be cleared. Despite being able to use degraded and secondary habitats, total deforestation is obviously detrimental and the already small population has declined.

Habitat Mainly edges and clearings in primary, damp, tropical, lowland forest. Sometimes in drier and partially felled forests, scrub, mangroves, plantations and wooded settlements.

Range Endemic to the Sulu Archipelago in the S Philippines. From sea-level to about 550m. Resident and sedentary.

Taxonomy and variation Formerly treated as a distinct species, then as a race of Philippine Woodpecker, and then split once again as geographically isolated and visually and vocally distinct. Two similar races described: ***ramsayi*** (Bongao, Jolo, Tawitawi, Sanga Sanga and Sibutu islands); and ***siasiensis*** (Siasi Island). Unclear whether it still occurs on all of these islands.

Similar species None: Sulawesi and Philippine Woodpeckers do not overlap in range.

Food and foraging Presumably invertebrates, but information lacking. Often forages high up in foliage and on snags. Joins mixed-species flocks.

◀ Adult male Sulu Woodpecker of the nominate race. Found on islands where deforestation is generally rampant, this little woodpecker is seriously threatened. Capual Island, Sulu, Philippines, October (*Bim Quemado*).

97. SUNDA WOODPECKER
Dendrocopos moluccensis

L 12–13cm

Other names Malaysian Pygmy Woodpecker, Sunda Pygmy Woodpecker

Identification Stripe-headed: plain brownish crown and nape, white face, bold brown band through eye and across ear-coverts and thinner brown malar continuing to the neck sides. Chocolate finely barred white above. Rump and uppertail-coverts white, barred brown. Underparts white or buff heavily streaked brown on chest and breast, less so lower down. Blackish wings barred and spotted white. Black tail spotted white on central feathers, outer feathers barred. Grey bill. Legs greyish. Iris brown. Sexes almost identical: male has slight, and often indistinct, reddish streak on side of hindcrown, lacking in female. Juvenile duller, browner and less streaked below, lower mandible pale with dark tip. Juvenile male has orange mark on side of hindcrown.

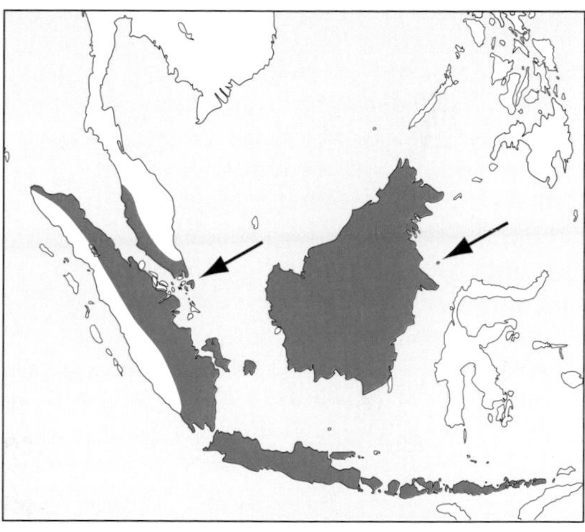

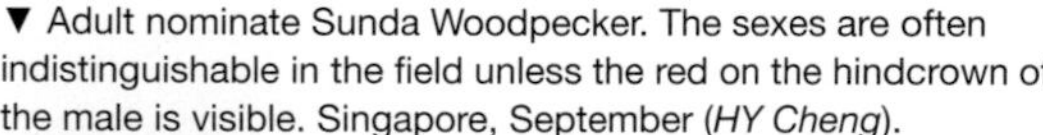

▼ Adult nominate Sunda Woodpecker. The sexes are often indistinguishable in the field unless the red on the hindcrown of the male is visible. Singapore, September (*HY Cheng*).

▼ Adult nominate Sunda Woodpecker – this is most probably a female, as the red hindcrown streak of a male would be visible in this pose. Sabah, Malaysia, January (*Neil Bowman*).

Vocalisations Often vocal. Sharp, high-pitched, trilling, repeated, *ki-ki-ki-ki-ki or pi-hi-hi-hi-hi,* usually pleasant, sometimes wheezing. Also churring, whirring *trrrrr-i-i* and *tjiep-tjiep-tjiep.*

Drumming Strong, rapid, even, high-pitched, 1-second rolls, repeated 6–8 times over a minute with silent pauses between each.

Status Locally common in Borneo, Peninsular Malaysia and Singapore. Probably increasing overall as adaptable, benefitting from forest fragmentation.

Habitat Deciduous tropical forest and woodland, coastal scrub and mangroves, particularly in Malaysia and Greater Sundas. Also parks, gardens, eucalyptus stands, cultivated land and plantations.

Range SE Asia. Peninsular Malaysia, Singapore, Greater Sundas and W Lesser Sundas. Recent records also from Thailand. One of only two woodpeckers south of Wallace's Line. Sea-level to 2200m, but mainly lowlands. In Lesser Sundas in lowlands and uplands, in Greater Sundas and Peninsular Malaysia lowlands. Resident and sedentary.

Taxonomy and variation Formerly considered a race of Brown-capped Woodpecker. Two races: ***moluccensis*** (Peninsular Malaysia, Singapore, Borneo, Sumatra, Java, Bali and Riau Archipelago); and ***grandis*** (Lesser Sundas: Lombok, Sumbawa, Komodo, Rinca, Flores, Pantar, Lomblen, Alor), which is larger than the nominate, more streaked and buffy below, rump less barred. Within *grandis,* birds on Alor are larger than those on Lombok, Sumbawa and Flores.

Similar species Differs from slightly larger Grey-capped Woodpecker by brown crown, bolder malar, darker upperparts and white underparts streaked darker. Very similar Brown-capped Woodpecker does not overlap in range.

Food and foraging Various insects, especially ants and beetles. Also fruit, berries and nectar. Usually works thin outer twigs and stems, gleaning rather than boring. Often in mixed-species foraging flocks.

▼ Adult male nominate Sunda Woodpecker with the red of the hindcrown exposed. Singapore, April (*Daniel Koh Swee Huat*).

▼ Adult Sunda Woodpecker of the race *grandis*. Komodo, Lesser Sunda Islands, Indonesia, June (*Ingo Waschkies*).

98. BROWN-CAPPED WOODPECKER
Dendrocopos nanus

L 13–14cm

Other names Brown-capped Pygmy Woodpecker, Indian Pygmy Woodpecker

Identification Dark overall, barred, streaked and striped white. Complete chocolate crown. Brown mantle and back finely barred or dotted white. Pale supercilium, broad brown post-auricular stripe continues down neck-sides to chest. Pale underparts faintly streaked brown on flanks and chest. Dark brown wings and tail barred or spotted white. Pale iris, reddish orbital ring. Bill and legs greyish. Sexes differ slightly: male has small reddish streak or patch on side of hindcrown, before nape, though this is often tiny and hard to see: female lacks this mark. Juvenile similar to adult female, though more streaked below.

Vocalisations Fast, chattering, tinny, rattling *click-r-*

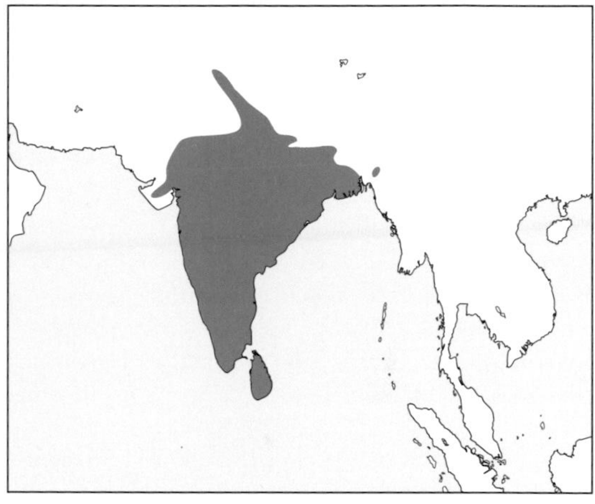

▼ Adult male nominate Brown-capped Woodpecker. The red hindcrown streak of the male is not always as obvious as on this individual. Koshi Tappu, Nepal, January (*Neil Bowman*).

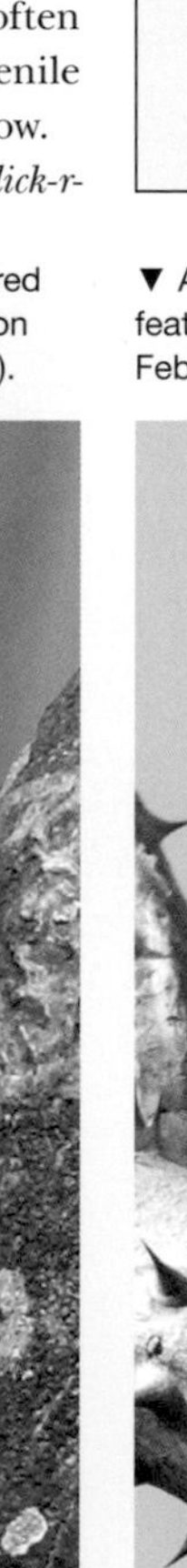

▼ Adult male nominate. When alert or agitated the crown feathers are raised, as in many woodpeckers. Goa, India, February (*Amano Samarpan*).

r or *tik-tik-tik-errrr*. A weaker, staccato, trilling *ti-ti-ti-ti* or *ki-ki-ki-ki* of around 1.5 seconds that rises in both volume and pitch. Churring, whirring *trrrr-i-i* and single, sharp high-pitched *pik*.

Drumming Rapid, long but weak roll. Drums persistently at start of breeding season.

Status Often quite common, but in some areas rather localised. Overall population possibly increasing as may benefit from forest fragmentation.

Habitat Open and dense, dry or damp, tall primary and secondary deciduous forest and woodland. Also bamboo thickets, mangroves, gardens, cultivated land and plantations.

Range Indian sub-continent and Sri Lanka. Sea-level to 1200m. Resident and sedentary.

Taxonomy and variation Four races, intermediates occur: ***nanus*** (most of India, Nepal, Bangladesh); ***hardwickii*** (C India) similar to nominate, possibly a cline; ***cinereigula*** (SW India) blacker crown and above than nominate, wings less marked; ***gymnopthalmos*** (Sri Lanka) blacker, more pied, cleaner, plainer white below.

Similar species Grey-capped Woodpecker slightly larger, blacker, more strongly marked below, less white in tail and lacks reddish orbital ring.

Food and foraging Omnivorous, taking insect larvae, ants, termites, fruit, berries and flower nectar. Mostly probes and gleans prey from twigs and saplings. Often in mixed-species foraging flocks.

▼ Adult female nominate. The sexes are often difficult to separate in the field, but there is clearly no red head-mark on this bird. Goa, India, February (*Amano Samarpan*).

▼ Adult male (left) and female (right) Brown-capped Woodpecker of the endemic Sri Lankan race *gymnopthalmus*. Racial differences are slight, but this race is generally paler below, darker above. Galawilawatta, Sri Lanka, June (*Uditha Hettige*).

99. PYGMY WOODPECKER
Dendrocopos kizuki

L 13–15cm

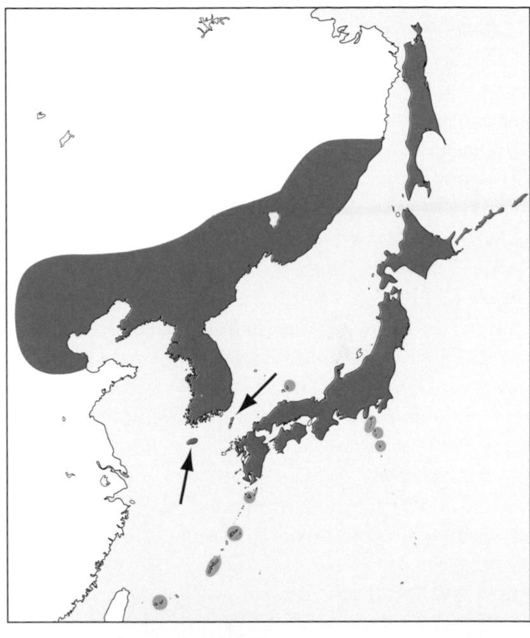

Other name Japanese Pygmy Woodpecker

Identification Brownish above, barred white on back. Underparts buff or white, brownish on upper flanks, chest sides smudged brown, breast and belly variably streaked. Blackish wings barred white. Tail blackish, outer feathers barred white. Ear-coverts brown. Lores, moustache, chin and throat white. Brown malar merges with brown or buff on chest sides. Brown from crown to mantle, rear neck-sides white. Small white post-ocular patch sometimes extends into a supercilium. Iris chestnut. Bill blackish. Legs grey. Sexes similar: males have tiny, often indistinct, red mark on side of nape, which females lack. Females have longer tail, wings and bill, though these hard to judge. Juveniles much like adults, though often streaked on the throat, bill pale and males with small red patch on mid-crown.

Vocalisations Very vocal, but limited vocabulary. Sharp, single or repeated *khit,* buzzing *kzzz-kzzz* and agitated *kikikiki.*

Drumming Produces brief, feeble, repeated rolls early in the breeding season.

► Adult male Pygmy Woodpecker of the race *nippon*. The small red mark on the head of this bird indicates it is a male. Honshu, Japan, May (*Tokio Sugiyama*).

Status Common over much of Japan, including smaller islands. Less common on mainland Asia. Often in secondary habitats and overall considered stable.

Habitat Wide range of coniferous and deciduous habitats used. Mainly lowland temperate forests, but also riverine, boreal and upland forests, parks, even city gardens.

Range Far East. SE Russia, Sakhalin, Kuril Islands, China, Korean Peninsula and Japanese archipelago. Sea-level to around 2100m. Resident and mostly sedentary, although seasonal altitudinal movements may occur.

Taxonomy and variation Sometimes placed in genus *Yungipicus*. Clinal differences, birds smaller, darker, more strongly marked from N to S. Racial taxonomy complex, four to 15 races described, including: ***kizuki*** (Kyushu, Japan); ***permutatus*** (NE China, SE Siberia, N Korea); ***seebohmi*** (E Siberia, Sakhalin, S Kuril Islands, Hokkaido); ***nippon*** (EC China, S Korea, Honshu); ***shikokuensis*** (SW Honshu and Shikoku); ***matsudairai*** (Yakushima and Izu); ***kotataki*** (Tsushima and Oki); ***amamii*** (Amani Oshima); ***nigrescens*** (Okinawa); ***orii*** (Iriomote). However, several races sometimes considered clines and lumped – e.g. N races grouped into ***ijimae***.

Similar species Coincides with Grey-capped Woodpecker in SE Siberia, E China and Korea, but slightly smaller and browner, especially on face. Beware Lesser Spotted Woodpecker in Hokkaido.

Food and foraging Arboreal invertebrates, especially caterpillars, aphids, spiders and ants. Also berries and presumably other plant matter. Usually in pairs and often in mixed-species flocks.

▼ Adult female *nippon*. Females always lack the red head-mark of males. Honshu, Japan, March (*Tadao Shimba*).

◄ Juvenile Pygmy Woodpecker. Note the pale bill. Miyake, Japan, June (*Tadao Shimba*).

100. GREY-CAPPED WOODPECKER
Dendrocopos canicapillus

L 13–15cm

Other names Grey-capped Pygmy, Grey-crowned Pygmy, Grey-headed Pygmy and Malabar Pygmy Woodpeckers

Identification Very variable. Black above, barred white. Buff underparts (in fresh plumage some yellowish), chest to belly streaked black. Wings black, coverts barred or spotted white, more on primaries. Uppertail black, white on outer feathers, undertail browner. White face with dark brown ear-coverts and post-auricular band continuing onto neck-sides. Faint brown malar. Crown grey, rear often darker. Lores and throat buff or white. Iris variably grey or brown; orbital ring grey. Bill blackish. Legs greyish. Sexes differ slightly: male has variably sized reddish streak on each side of hindcrown, although often hidden, which female lacks. Juvenile darker, more heavily marked below and with paler bill. Juvenile male may have more red or orange on the head than adult.

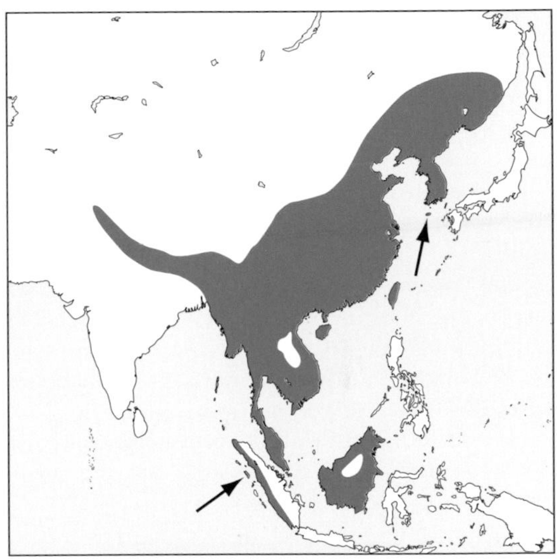

◄ Adult Grey-capped Woodpecker of the race *kaleensis*. Sexing birds is difficult unless a red mark can be seen on the side of the hindcrown. This race is heavily streaked below. Taiwan, January (*Ingo Waschkies*).

Vocalisations Fast chattering or rattling, high-pitched, *tit-tit-errr* or *tik-tik-tik-rrr* or *click-r-r-r* of up to 20 notes. Shorter, rolling *tr-r-r-p* and *chip-chip* with second note lower-pitched. Brief, sharp *kip, kik, chik, pik, pit* notes. Various *chirps* and *cheeps* and squeaky *kweek-kweek-kweek*.

Drumming Feeble, subdued rolls reported.

Status Generally common. Overall considered stable, but has declined in Singapore.

Habitat Wide range of mainly damp deciduous open forests and woodlands, sometimes drier coniferous. Also scrub, bamboo thickets, mangroves, farmland with scattered trees and gardens.

Range SE Asia and Far East. From Himalayan foothills to Pacific. Sea-level to about 2800m. Mainly resident and sedentary, though some seasonal altitudinal movements.

Taxonomy and variation Up to 15 races claimed, differing in plumage and size, with intergrades and clines possibly involved. Nominate ***canicapillus*** (Bangladesh, NE India, S Burma (Myanmar), Thailand and Laos) is short-tailed; ***doerriesi*** (SE Siberia, Manchuria and Korea) is largest and least-barred race, black above, white rump, much white in wing; ***scintilliceps*** (E China) has black back barred white, heavily streaked below; ***szetschuanensis*** (C China); ***omissus*** (WC China); ***nagamichii*** (E Yunnan to Fujian, China); ***obscurus*** (S Yunnan, China); ***kaleensis*** (Taiwan) larger than nominate, with blacker mantle, more buff and more streaked below; ***swinhoei*** (Hainan Island) pale below with much white in the wings; ***mitchellii*** (N Pakistan, NW India, Nepal) has large, dark ear-coverts, mantle barred white, outertail mostly white; ***semicoronatus*** (E Nepal, NE India) buff on cheeks and below, male's red mark large, touching nape; ***delacouri*** (SE Thailand, Cambodia and S Vietnam) heavily streaked below; ***auritus*** (SW Thailand and Malay Peninsula) dark, greyish chest band, central tail usually barred white; ***volzi*** (Sumatra and Riau Archipelago) has orange or gold belly; ***aurantiiventris*** (Borneo) smallest race, with distinct malar and often tinged orange below.

Similar species Brown-capped Woodpecker is slightly smaller, overall lighter, more washed-out, whiter in tail and has red orbital ring. Pygmy Woodpecker browner, less white in face and more barred above. Male Lesser Spotted Woodpecker has red crown.

Food and foraging Various invertebrates, seeds and berries. Agile, foraging at most levels, but often high, gleaning snags and outer limbs.

▲ Adult male *kaleensis*; note the tiny red fleck on the head. This race is very black above and buff below. Taiwan, January (*Gwo-Chiang Yang*).

◄ A juvenile Grey-capped Woodpecker. Note the pale bill. This race, *doerriesi*, shows much white in the wings. Beijing, China, February (*Martin Hale*).

101. LESSER SPOTTED WOODPECKER

Dendrocopos minor

L 14–16cm

Identification Smallest picid in Europe. Ladder-backed, variably barred black and white to rump. White or buff below, flanks and breast usually finely streaked black. Black wing-coverts tipped white. Black flight feathers boldly barred white. Central tail black; outer feathers white, slightly barred black. Nape, forehead and lores white or buff. Cheek, ear-coverts and throat white. Black malar runs to neck-side and joins black lateral neck stripe. Extent of black post-auricular stripe varies with race. Iris chestnut. Fine grey bill, base of lower mandible paler. Legs grey or olive. Sexes differ: male has red mid-crown; female lacks red. Juvenile duller, black areas tinged brownish, more finely streaked below, iris brown. Juvenile male has pink forecrown, female pale mottled black or grey.

Vocalisations Song a series of 8–16 loud, high-pitched, piping, decelerating *kee, gee* or *pee* notes – like small falcon. Alarm call a short, shrill *kik,* sometimes softer *pik.* Also single, squeaky *gig* and occasionally *chew-it,* not unlike Spotted Redshank. Contact call a clucking *chuck* or clicking *chik.*

Drumming Both sexes drum, males more so. Rapid, high-pitched bursts of even tempo. Typically 20–30 strikes over 1–2 seconds. Rather rattling, as often done on thin dry snags, and often faltering.

Status Locally common to rare. Has declined in some areas, drastically in Britain since 1980s. Reasons not entirely clear, but unsuitable management and loss of woodlands suspected.

Habitat Boreal and temperate deciduous woodlands. Also mixed deciduous-coniferous forests, riparian woods, orchards and parks. Persists in managed forests when some mature trees and snags remain.

Range Eurasia and N Africa. From Iberia and Britain to Kamchatka and Japan. As far south as Tunisia and Algeria, northwards to tree line. Resident, though weather and food-related irruptions occur.

Taxonomy and variation Thirteen races, several visually distinct. Also, clinal size and colour differences, particular whiteness of head. Nominate ***minor*** (Scandinavia to Urals) relatively long-tailed, long-winged with minimal flank streaking; ***kamtschatkensis*** (Urals to N Mongolia) largest and whitest race; ***immaculatus*** (Anadyr Basin and Kamchatka); ***amurensis*** (Lower Amur River Basin, NE China, NE Korea, Sakhalin, Hokkaido) often rather grey below; ***comminutus*** (England, Wales) greyish below, hardly streaked; ***hortorum*** (continental Europe) reduced white on back, dark below, flanks well streaked, outer-tail very barred, face buffy, throat and chest pinkish; ***buturlini*** (Iberia, S France, Italy, most of Balkans) dark, relatively short-winged; ***ledouci*** (NE Algeria, NW Tunisia) dark, buff not white and boldly streaked below; ***danfordi*** (most of Greece, European Turkey) dark, long post-auricular stripe often reaching nape; ***colchicus*** (Caucasus, Transcaucasia except SE) dark above, pale below; ***quadrifasciatus*** (SE Transcaucasia) has outer-tail boldly

► Adult male Lesser Spotted Woodpecker of race *hortorum*. Males have a red crown. Belgium, January (*Rudi Petitjean*).

barred black; ***hyrcanus*** (N Iran); ***morgani*** (NW Iran) has relatively long bill, broad black post-auricular line and bold black streaking below.

Similar species Nominate White-backed Woodpecker also ladder-backed, but much larger. In Far East beware similar-sized Grey-capped Woodpecker.

Food and foraging Highly insectivorous. Typically forages in canopy and on thin snags for aphids, caterpillars, spiders, woodlice and smaller beetles. Occasional plant matter includes berries. Also visits feeders.

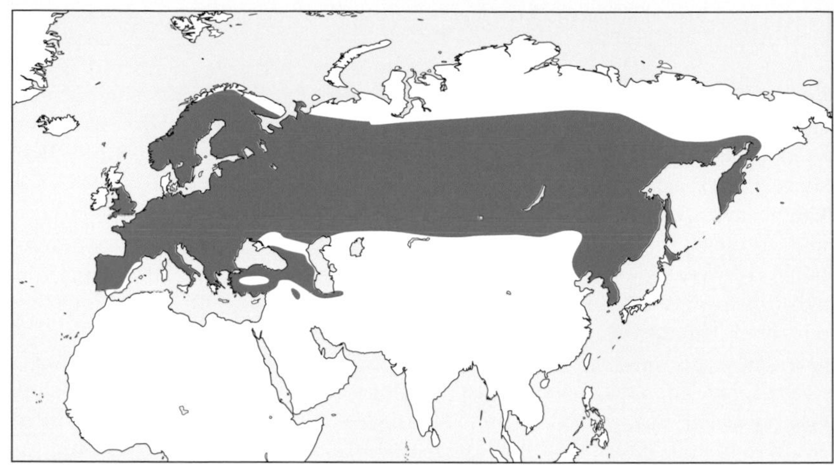

▼ Adult female *comminutus*. This race is only lightly streaked below. Adult females lack red on the crown, and are thus totally pied. Devon, UK, March (*Gary Thoburn*).

▼ Adult male *amurensis* delivering food to its young. Hokkaido, Japan, July (*Kazuyasu Kisaichi*).

102. FULVOUS-BREASTED WOODPECKER
Dendrocopos macei

L 18–21cm

Identification Buff below with brownish 'fulvous' hue. Chest dotted black, belly finely streaked, flanks lightly barred. Lower belly to undertail-coverts red. Black above, barred white on back to rump, mantle plain. Wings black, with coverts and primaries boldly barred white. Uppertail black, outer feathers barred white. Undertail boldly barred black and white. Lores, forehead, face, ear-coverts and throat buff or white. Black malar continues down neck-sides to meet black line from chest. Iris chestnut, thin orbital ring grey. Bill grey. Legs grey or olive. Sexes differ: male has dull red crown and nape finely streaked black; female has black crown and nape. Juvenile overall duller, pink rather than red on undertail and has larger white primary tips; both sexes streaked red on mid-crown, more so in male, but not as extensive as on adult male.

Vocalisations Rather vocal. Sudden, strong *tchick, tsik* or *skik,* sometimes harsh, sometimes more nasal and subtle, uttered singly or repeated. Rapid, excited series of *pik* or *pit* notes and milder, chattering *chika-chika-chika.* Also a 'growling' *kik-i-der.*

Drumming Subdued, weak 1–2-second rolls that gently accelerate before trailing off.

Status Locally common in India and Nepal. Overall population considered stable.

Habitat Open, damp, tropical mixed lowland and upland forests: often at edges. Also drier forests, bamboo, scrub, plantations, gardens, grasslands and farmland with tall trees.

Range SE Asia. Rather fragmented distribution, scattered from N Pakistan through N India to NW Burma (Myanmar). Sea-level to around 2800m. Resident and sedentary.

Taxonomy and variation Two races: ***macei*** (C Nepal, NE India, Bhutan, NW Burma (Myanmar) and Bangladesh); and ***westermani*** (N Pakistan, N India to W Nepal), which is larger than nominate with longer bill, wings and tail. Some birds have reddish hue on belly, some females brownish on forecrown.

Similar species Stripe-breasted Woodpecker is bigger, more boldly streaked below, more finely barred above, whiter on face and neck, males with red extending to nape. Brown-fronted Woodpecker also whiter and more streaked below, males red only on nape, females brownish on crown.

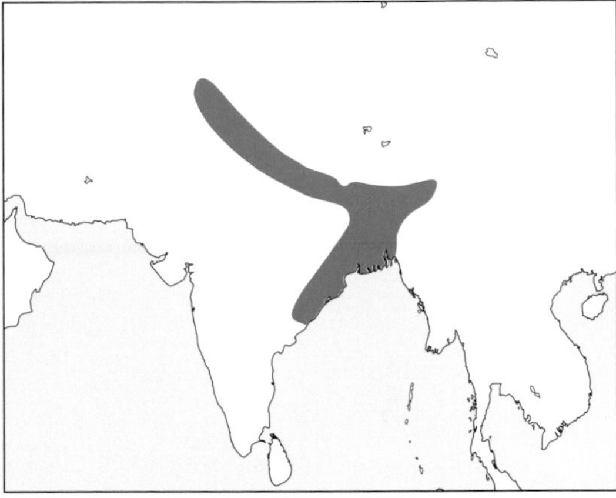

Food and foraging Arboreal insects, berries, fruit and nectar. Often in mixed-species flocks. Forages at mid to high levels in trees, on branches, trunks, foliage and bamboo, but opportunistic, even dropping to ground for ants and other prey.

► Adult male nominate Fulvous-breasted Woodpecker. Both sexes have a reddish ventral area, but males also have red on the crown. Assam, India, April (*Raj Kamal Phukan*).

► Adult female nominate. 'Fulvous' refers to the brownish wash on the underparts, but it is something of a misnomer as many other *Dendrocopos* have similar coloration. Assam, India, September (*Vijay Anand Ismavel*).

▼ Adult female nominate, displaying its agility while foraging. West Bengal, India, April (*Arijit Banerjee*).

103. FRECKLE-BREASTED WOODPECKER
Dendrocopos analis

L 16–18cm

Other names Spot-breasted Pied Woodpecker and Spot-breasted Woodpecker: NB: latter also used for *Colaptes punctigula* in South America.

Identification Ladder-backed, mantle less barred. Cream or buff below with prominent black spotting (freckles) on chest, sometimes forming a gorget. Vent pink or red. Black wings, uppertail-coverts and tail boldly barred white. Face and neck white, ear-coverts dusky, sometimes streaked brownish. Nape black. Black malar extends to neck-sides. Iris reddish, orbital ring grey. Bill and legs greyish. Sexes differ: male has dull red fore- and mid-crown, often streaked grey or black; female has blackish crown lacking red and is longer-winged and longer-tailed than male, though this hard to judge in the field. Juvenile has paler and reduced red-pink on vent and both sexes have some red in the crown, more so in male.

Vocalisations Slowly repeated, sharp *tsik* or *chik* notes and softer *tsip* or *chip,* sometimes developing into brief

► Adult male Freckle-breasted Woodpecker of the race *andamanensis*. Note the red crown mixed with grey. Large 'freckles' on the chest and breast are typical for this race. South Andaman Island, India, April (*Niranjan Sant*).

trill. A staccato 2-syllable *chu-ik* and shorter *kui*. Also loud, rising *kut-kut-kut* chatter and rapid, throaty, harsh, rattling series of up to a dozen *pik* or *pit* notes, beginning or ending with a separate single note.

Drumming Rather weak, 1–2-second rolls.

Status Locally common, but poorly known. Conservation category not assigned by the IUCN.

Habitat Open mature dry forest, secondary forest, wooded farmland, plantations, parks, gardens, mangroves and coastal scrub.

Range SE Asia. From Burma (Myanmar), through Indochina and Thailand, Java, Bali and the Andaman Islands. Lowlands to around 2000m. Resident and sedentary.

Taxonomy and variation Formerly treated as an eastern group of races of Fulvous-breasted Woodpecker. Three races: ***analis*** (Java, Bali and perhaps S. Sumatra) has pink vent, black nape, heavily spotted breast; ***andamanensis*** (Andaman Islands) is small, long-tailed, with paler bill, large black spots (even heart-shapes rather than freckles) on chest, reddish vent and obvious barring on the belly and flanks, male with red crown and nape, female with brown crown – this race geographically isolated, more a forest bird than mainland races, and may warrant full species status; ***longipennis*** (Burma (Myanmar), Thailand, Laos, Cambodia, S Vietnam) is pale buff below with bold broad markings, fine barring on flanks, vent and undertail-coverts reddish, central tail feathers mostly lacking white.

Similar species Fulvous-breasted Woodpecker is slightly larger, dark-billed, darker and streaked (not spotted) below, with plainer ear-coverts; male also red on nape. Stripe-breasted Woodpecker noticeably larger and has heavy streaks not freckles below.

Food and foraging Invertebrates, especially ants and termites, supplemented with fruit and berries. Usually feeds at mid to upper levels in trees.

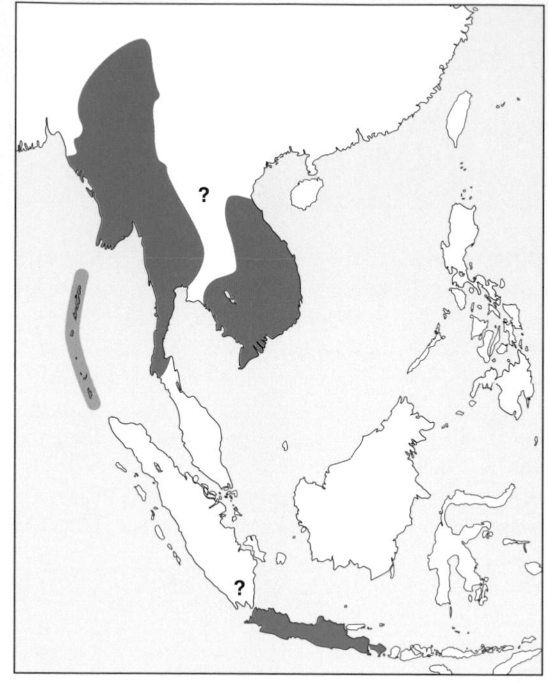

▲ Adult female nominate. Note all-black crown. Baluran, Java, Indonesia, April (*Lars Petersson*).

◄ Adult male *longipennis*. Southern Thailand, January (*Vaughan & Sveta Ashby*).

104. STRIPE-BREASTED WOODPECKER

Dendrocopos atratus

L 21–22cm

Identification Black back narrowly barred white, nape and mantle unbarred. Dusky buff or yellowish from throat to vent heavily streaked black. Undertail-coverts red. Wings black, primaries barred white, coverts spotted white. Uppertail black, outer feathers with some white dots or bars. Lores, cheeks and ear-coverts white. Bold black malar runs onto neck-sides and meets line from chest. Iris chestnut. Bill greyish. Legs bluish-grey. Sexes differ: male has crimson crown and nape with black flecks; female has black crown and nape. Juvenile greyer below with indistinct streaking, pink or orange rather than red undertail-coverts and larger white primary tips; juvenile male has dull red on crown, female some red flecks.

Vocalisations Loud, sudden *chip, chik, tchik* or *kyik*. Harsh, grating rattle and a more whinnying version.

Drumming May not drum, or perhaps only rarely, but information lacking.

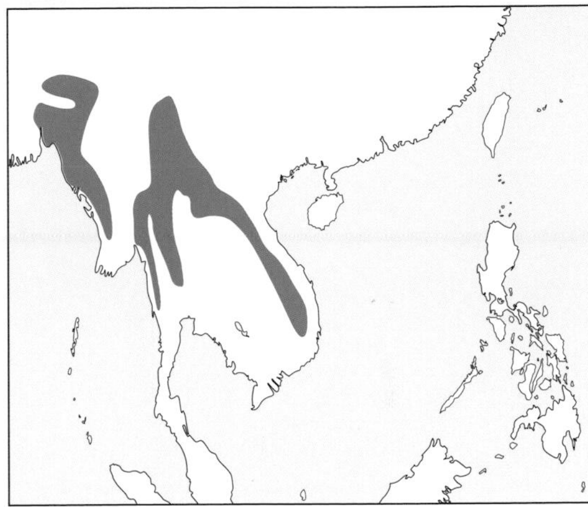

Status Common to uncommon. Often rather localised, but considered stable overall.

Habitat Upland open, damp deciduous and coniferous forests, especially oak and pine. Also drier wooded grasslands, farmland and degraded forests.

Range SE Asia. From extreme NE India through Bhutan, Burma (Myanmar) and SW China into Indochina and Thailand. Mainly between 800–2200m. Resident and sedentary.

Taxonomy and variation Two very similar races: ***atratus*** (most of range); and ***vietnamensis*** (Vietnam) – this race sometimes disputed. Some males have yellowish feathers in red crown.

Similar species Most like slightly smaller Fulvous-breasted and Freckle-breasted Woodpeckers, but has heavier, longer bill, whiter face and throat, heavier black streaks on yellower underparts, particularly on chest, unbarred mantle and narrower white barring on back. Red crown of male extends onto nape unlike on Fulvous-breasted and Freckle-breasted Woodpeckers.

Food and foraging Insectivorous. Mainly forages for arboreal ants and beetle larvae from mid-level to the canopy.

◄ Adult male Stripe-breasted Woodpecker. NE India, March (*Vaughan & Sveta Ashby*).

◀ Adult female nominate. Females can be mistaken for the very similar female Fulvous-breasted and Freckle-breasted Woodpeckers, but is found mostly at higher elevations than these two relatives. Doi Ang Kang, Thailand, March (*Ingo Waschkies*).

105. BROWN-FRONTED WOODPECKER

Dendrocopos auriceps

L 19–20cm

Identification Cinnamon or brown forehead and forecrown (brown-fronted). Face white with dusky-brownish cheeks and ear-coverts. White supercilium. Thin malar grey or brown at front, darker at rear, extending down to meet black line from chest sides. Chin and throat off-white. Chest to belly white or buff, boldly flecked and streaked chocolate. Pinkish lower belly, vent and undertail-coverts. Nape plain black; mantle and back black finely barred white; rump plain black. Chocolate primaries barred white; upperwing-coverts black; greater and median coverts marked white. Black uppertail with outer feathers barred or dotted white. Iris chestnut. Greyish bill and legs. Sexes differ: male has yellow mid crown and red or orange nape; female has dull mustard crown and lacks red nape (though sometimes tinged orange). Juvenile drabber overall, duskier below with washed-out pink vent. Napes of juvenile reflects adult of that sex, but not as strongly coloured. Juvenile male may have red feather tips on nape; crown of female very streaked.

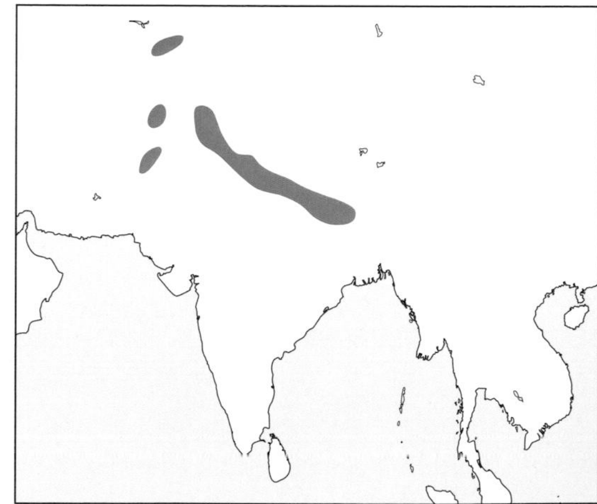

Vocalisations Fairly vocal. Rapid, chattering, wavering, rattling *chitter-chitter-chitter-rrr* series, prolonged when in dispute or as an alarm. Also various mewing calls, perhaps *tyu-week* or *tu-whit,* and a more nasal *tu-wic, tu-wic* repeated up to 10 times. Various short, shrill, high-pitched *pik, kik, chik, chip* notes, rapidly or slowly repeated. Also, more squeaky *chick* and *peek* notes.

Drumming Drums avidly early in the breeding season, but detailed information lacking.

Status Locally often common. Overall population probably stable, but few data.

Habitat Drier, upland, deciduous and coniferous (often pine) temperate forest. Also subtropical and degraded forests, wooded savanna and parkland.

Range South-central Asia. Rather restricted, from NE Afghanistan and Pakistan through Himalayan India to Nepal. Resident and essentially sedentary, though birds at higher altitudes (up to around 3100m in Nepal) may move lower in winter.

Taxonomy and variation Two similar races: ***auriceps*** (NE Afghanistan, N Pakistan, N India); and ***incognitus*** (C Nepal). Some clinal differences: birds in W on average largest. Also differences in crown colour and some birds unstreaked on belly.

Similar species Slightly smaller Yellow-crowned Woodpecker brighter yellow on crown, spotted not barred above and lacks dark malar and red vent. Similar-sized Fulvous-breasted Woodpecker less streaked below, never has yellow crown.

Food and foraging Supplements insect diet with fruits, nuts, berries and seeds. Tends to forage low on trees, at forest edges and in open, but seldom on ground. Often in mixed-species flocks.

► Adult male nominate. The bright yellow mid-crown and red nape of this bird indicate that it is a male. Uttarakhand, India, May (*Ishmeet Sanhai*).

▼ Adult female Brown-fronted Woodpecker has a yellowish crown but lacks red on the nape. This bird is of the nominate race. Uttaranchal, India, April (*Dolly Bhardwaj*).

▼ Juvenile Brown-fronted Woodpecker is much drabber than the adults. Uttarakhand, India, July (*Jitendra Bhatia*).

106. YELLOW-CROWNED WOODPECKER
Dendrocopos mahrattensis

L 17–19cm.

Other name Mahratta Woodpecker

Identification Brownish mantle, back and wing-coverts heavily spotted and barred white, creating a chequered pattern. Underparts cream or grey, often dusky, streaked brownish, particularly on flanks. Small rufous or orange belly-patch. Ventral area often lacks colour. White rump usually only seen in flight. Blackish primaries barred white. Black tail barred and spotted white. Light brown malar in otherwise dusky face, neck-sides with brownish patch. Throat white. Iris chestnut. Bill grey, lower mandible often paler. Legs greyish. Sexes differ: male has mustard-yellow crown and reddish nape (occasionally looks tufted); female lacks red, having brown-mustard crown and brownish nape, though sometimes with reddish flecks. Juvenile overall plainer, duller, browner above, less streaked below with pinkish belly-patch. Juveniles of both sexes have some orange or red on crown, more so in males.

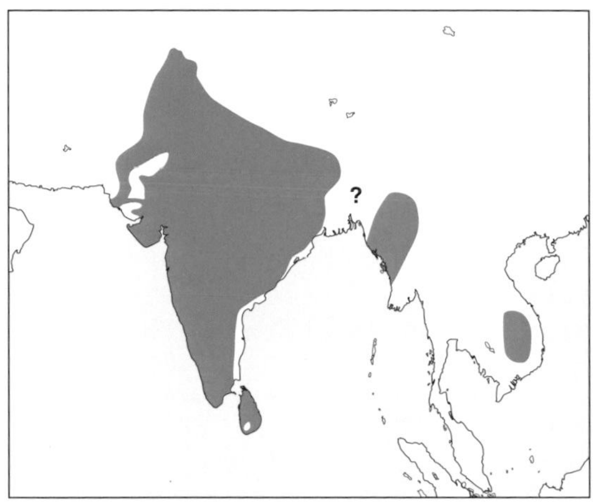

Vocalisations Not as vocal as most relatives. Calls include a soft *chip* and single high-pitched *kit, kik* and *klik* notes. Also a shrill *peek-peek,* rapidly repeated *kik-kik-kik-rrrrr* and a short, rapid, agitated version *kik-kur-kur.*

Drumming Fast, but weak, roll of even tempo produced.

Status Common locally in India and Sri Lanka, local and often uncommon in SE Asia. Overall considered stable.

Habitat Wide variety of arid habitats: dry open woodlands, tree-dotted savanna and semi-desert, parks, settlements, gardens, plantations, groves and farmland. Also damper woodlands, dry dipterocarp forests in Cambodia and euphorbia woods in Sri Lanka.

Range SE Asia. Widespread, but patchily distributed on the Indian subcontinent. Isolated populations in Sri Lanka and Indochina. Just one historical record from Thailand, though fairly common in adjacent N Cambodia. Sea-level to about 2000m, but mainly lowlands. Resident and sedentary.

Taxonomy and variation Two races: ***mahrattensis*** (India, Sri Lanka, Nepal, Bangladesh, Burma (Myanmar), SW China, E Cambodia, Vietnam, S Laos), and ***pallescens*** (E Pakistan, NW India). Latter paler, more washed-out, but more chequered above, less marked below and pink

◄ Adult male *pallescens* Yellow-crowned. The bright red nape-patch separates the male from the female. Race *pallescens* is paler and 'cleaner' than the nominate. Gujarat, India, January (*Arpit Deomurari*).

rather than red on belly. Birds in N generally lighter than in S. Some birds have brownish throat.

Similar species Brown-fronted Woodpecker (overlaps in N), may have similar crown pattern, but is less yellow on forehead, has distinct malar, is more barred above and has unbarred central tail feathers.

Food and foraging Mainly insects, especially beetle larvae and ants, supplemented with fruit and nectar. Forages mainly in trees, seldom on ground. Joins mixed-species flocks outside breeding period.

► Adult female *pallescens*. Both sexes have some red on the belly. Rajasthan, India, November (*Amano Samarpan*).

▼ Adult male nominate. The main confusion species, Brown-fronted Woodpecker, is sympatric in the north of the range. Tmatboey, Cambodia, November (*Con Foley*).

107. ARABIAN WOODPECKER
Dendrocopos dorae

L 18cm

Identification Rather plain overall. Grey or olive above. Paler below, from throat to vent, with red, orange or pink patch on mid-belly. Flanks lightly barred. Five or six white bars on brownish wings, most coverts tipped white. Uppertail mostly black with outer feathers barred white, undertail spotted or barred white. Most of head and face grey, orbital area dusky, ear-coverts faintly streaked. Iris dark. Bill and legs grey. Sexes differ: male has red on mid-crown and sometimes nape; female lacks red on head, has less white in wings and pinker belly-patch. Juvenile slightly streaked below with pink belly-patch, like adult female; juvenile male has orange on crown.

Vocalisations Rapid, accelerating, then falling *kek-kek-kek-ke-ke-kekekeke-ke-ke* rattle of 7–20 notes. Also *kik-kik-kik-kik,* like small falcon, and a slower, falling, mocking *keck-keck-keck-keck* or *kek-kek-kek-kek.* Contact calls between pair include a sharp *pweek-pit-pit-pit-pit.*

Drumming Males occasionally produce subdued, weak rolls. Females not known to drum.

Status VU. Locally common, but generally uncommon. Range-restricted, but widespread within its range. Population small (7500–10,000 individuals estimated). Possibly declining due to felling of trees for farmland, charcoal, firewood and fodder, and overgrazing. Promotion as a flagship species for protection of wildlife sites in Saudi Arabia proposed.

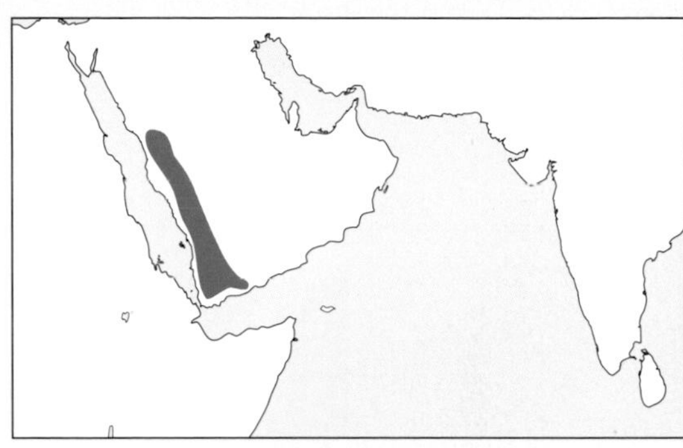

Habitat Mainly in dry acacia woods, but also visits juniper and tamarisk stands, wooded wadis, scrub and savanna, traditionally managed coffee plantations, date-palm and fig groves, old orchards and settlements with trees.

Range Endemic to Arabian Peninsula. Restricted to SW Saudi Arabia (most of population) and SW Yemen,

▼ Adult male Arabian Woodpecker. The male's small red crown-patch is the main difference between the sexes. Mahweet, Yemen, January (*Hanne & Jens Eriksen*).

occurring in wooded hills above the Red Sea. From almost sea-level to 2800m, but mainly between 1500–2000m. Resident, perhaps with some local, altitudinal movements.

Taxonomy and variation Monotypic. Differences minimal: some birds have golden or brownish tones, and extent and intensity of belly-patch varies.

Similar species None: only resident woodpecker in Arabia.

Food and foraging Mainly arboreal insects, particularly beetle larvae, ants and fig wasps, taken both by boring into wood and by gleaning foliage. Also descends to the ground in search of prey. Possibly takes sap and some fruit. Mostly forages alone.

▲ Adult female Arabian Woodpecker. Note lack of red on crown, but females also have less white in the wings than males. Mahweet, Yemen, January (*Hanne & Jens Eriksen*).

► Adult male Arabian Woodpecker busily preening. This Arabian endemic has evolved to live in very dry habitats, and does not overlap with any other woodpecker species. Mahweet, Yemen, January (*Hanne & Jens Eriksen*).

108. CRIMSON-BREASTED WOODPECKER
Dendrocopos cathpharius

L 17–18cm

Identification Variable crimson band across chest not always obvious, some also with black band. Chin and throat white. Buff or white underparts streaked black. Red or pink vent often faint. Plain black mantle, back and scapulars. Black wings with white patch on coverts, primaries with white spots or bars. Uppertail black, outer feathers barred white, undertail barred black and white. Forehead white, crown black, ear-coverts buff or white. Black malar extends to rear neck and meets black line from chest. Iris chestnut, orbital ring grey. Upper mandible mid-grey, lower paler. Legs greyish. Sexes differ: male has variably-sized red patch on nape which female lacks (though some golden or orange); female also less red on chest. Juvenile usually lacks red on chest, is less streaked below, paler, has reduced pink on vent and larger white primary tips; both sexes have orange or red on the nape, more extensive in males.

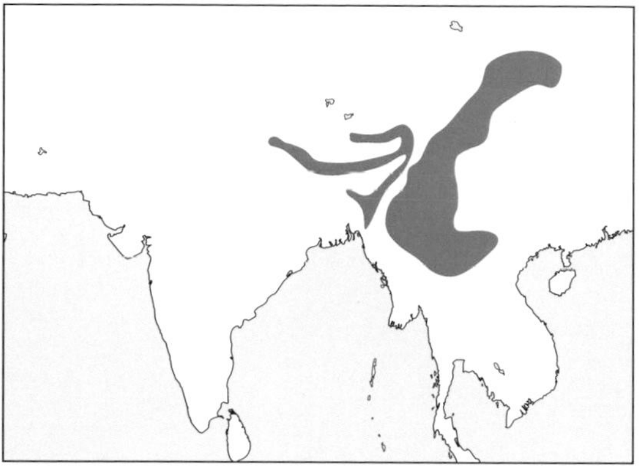

Vocalisations Loud, high-pitched, repeated *chip, tchik or skik* notes, sometimes linked in an intense, rapid, rattling, falling series. Also a shrill *kee-kee-kee.*

Drumming Subtle, short but fast roll of even-tempo that begins gently before increasing strongly.

Status Fairly common to rare. Overall population considered stable, but data lacking.

Habitat Various upland tropical broadleaved forests, especially with rhododendron, chestnut and some dead wood.

Range SE Asia. From NE India to China, Indochina and Thailand. From 700–3900m, but usually between 1200–3000m. Resident, probably sedentary.

Taxonomy and variation Six races with varying extent of red areas and underpart colour and markings. Nominate ***cathpharius*** (E Himalayas: Nepal and N Assam) often buff below, chest with minimal red and no black; ***ludlowi*** (SE Tibet) larger than nominate with more red on chest; ***pyrrhothorax*** (NE India, NW Burma (Myanmar), Bangladesh) much red and most black on chest, nape and undertail-coverts, but pale on underparts and face; ***pernyii*** (C and W China: NW Yunnan, Sichuan, Xinjiang N to Gansu) has red on head restricted to nape, red chest bordered by bold black below; ***innixus*** (NC and EC China) underparts less streaked, red chest bordered by black below previous race; ***tenebrosus*** (N Burma (Myanmar) to Thailand,

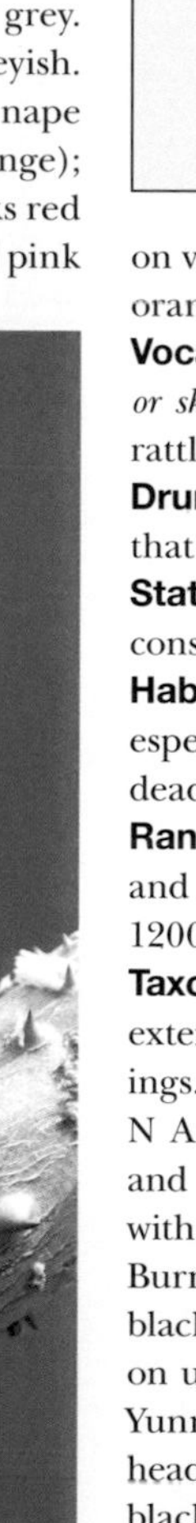

◀ Adult male nominate Crimson-breasted Woodpecker, with a beakfull of prey. Females lack the scarlet nape patch. Bhutan, April (*James Eaton*).

Laos, N Vietnam and Yunnan, China) is relatively small, heavily streaked with much black on chest.

Similar species Sympatric Darjeeling Woodpecker bigger, larger billed, lacks red on chest and yellow on neck.

Food and foraging Insects, particularly larvae, supplemented with nectar and probably other plant matter. Forages alone or in pairs, rarely in mixed flocks, low down on live and dead trees and in bushes. Often works outer twigs that larger relatives ignore.

▲ Adult female *pernyii*. There is more black on the chest in this race than in the nominate. Sichuan, China, October (*John Holmes*).

▲► Adult male nominate. The amount and intensity of red varies not only between races, but within populations. Bhutan, April (*James Eaton*).

► Adult female *innixus*. Females of all races are drabber than the males and lack the red nape. Hunan, China, June (*Jonathan Martinez*).

109. DARJEELING WOODPECKER
Dendrocopos darjellensis

L 24–25cm

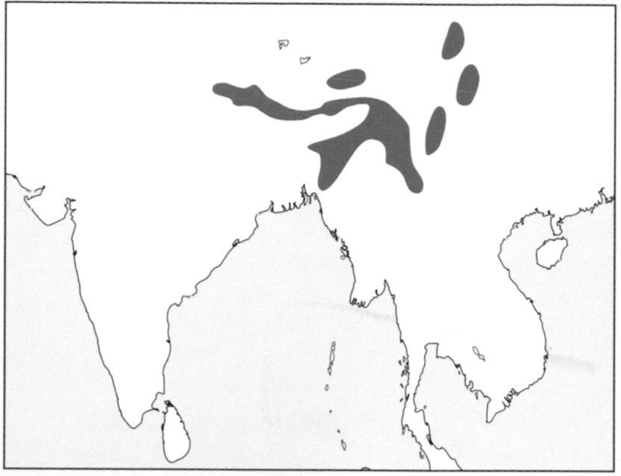

Identification Strikingly marked. Throat cream, chest and breast buff heavily streaked black, belly yellowish and flanks barred black. Undertail-coverts and vent red. Plain glossy black back and mantle. Wings chocolate with distinct white patch on coverts and thin barring on primaries. Uppertail black, outer feathers barred pale. Cheek and ear-coverts cream or greyish. Rear neck sides yellow, golden or orange. Lores and forehead white. Bold black malar extends down to meet black line from chest sides. Iris blackish or reddish. Bill black, lower mandible greyer. Legs greyish. Sexes differ: male has black crown and small red nape patch which female lacks. Juvenile lacks buff or yellow neck patch, has streaked throat, mottling rather than

◄ Adult male Darjeeling Woodpecker of the nominate race. Males are one of the more impressively plumaged *Dendrocopos*. Sichuan, China, May (*John Holmes*).

streaking below and pink vent; juvenile male has dull red crown, female has black crown with some red tips.

Vocalisations Sharp, single, harsh or squeaky *chip*, *tsik* or *pik* notes. Chattering or yapping, rattle series of same notes that wavers in pitch. Rattling or trilling *di-di-di-d-dddddt* and more strident *tchew-tchew-tchew.*

Drumming Short, repeated rolls of steady speed and volume, either level or falling in pitch.

Status Common locally in India and Nepal. Uncommon in China, N Burma (Myanmar) and N Vietnam. Overall population considered stable, but local declines as forests are felled for timber and firewood.

Habitat Tropical mature montane forests: coniferous, deciduous and mixed. Often at higher elevations than relatives in shrub zone.

Range SE Asia. Scattered from Nepal, NE India, Tibet to SW China and N Vietnam. Between 1500–4000m. Mainly resident, though possibly some seasonal altitudinal movements.

Taxonomy and variation Two very similar races: ***darjellensis*** (Nepal, NE India, Bhutan, N Burma (Myanmar) (Myanmar), SW China, N Vietnam); and ***desmursi*** (C China), which is sometimes disputed. Clinal differences in bill and overall size; W birds larger. Extent and colour of yellowish neck patch varies.

Similar species Great Spotted and Himalayan Woodpeckers similar in size and upperpart colour, but lack yellow neck patch and buff underparts. Crimson-breasted Woodpecker similar in several features but much smaller, lacks yellow neck patch and most have red on chest.

Food and foraging Insects, particularly wood-boring beetle larvae. Forages at all levels, on fallen logs, stumps, mossy boughs and trunks to the canopy. Sometimes in mixed-species flocks with songbirds, but perhaps not as often as relatives.

► Adult female nominate. Females lack the red nape, but are still beautifully marked. Bhutan, April (*Francesco Veronesi*).

110. MIDDLE SPOTTED WOODPECKER
Dendrocopos medius

L 20–22cm

Identification Ear-coverts, forehead, throat, neck and chest white or cream. Lores grey. Black post-auricular stripe ends before nape. Slight black malar. Black line down throat side to chest. White or buff below, sometimes yellowish on flanks, belly and leg feathering. Flanks and belly boldly streaked black. Lower belly to vent flushed pink. Mantle, back, rump and uppertail-coverts black. White oval scapular patches. Flight feathers black, dotted and barred white. Tail mostly black, outer two feathers white with black bars. Delicate grey bill. Legs greyish. Red iris often distinct in pale face. Sexes almost identical: both have red crown though male's protrudes slightly above the nape; female's not as bright, often orange or rusty at the rear.

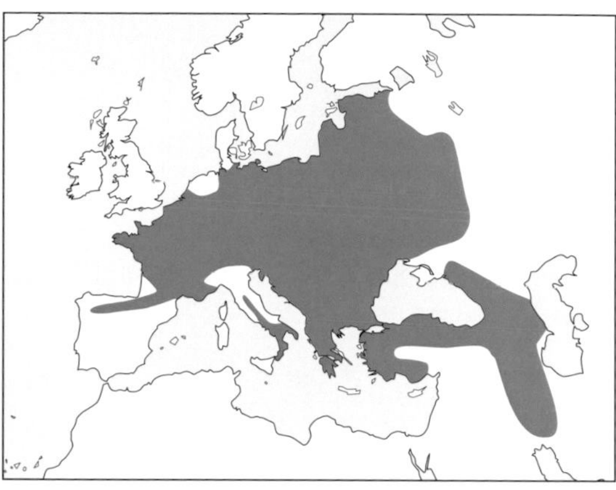

Juvenile less well marked; duller than adult, brownish on wings, face smudged grey, iris grey or brown.

Vocalisations Distinct, unlike those of relatives. Diagnostic song of up to 30 whining, meowing, almost painful *kwah, kvar* or *gwaar* notes. An excited, rattling *gi-ge-ge-ge-ge* or *kik-kek-kek-kek-kek* or *kvik-kvek-kvek-kvek*,first note high-pitched, recalling Red-footed Falcon. Harsh *chack-chack* alarm like Eurasian Blackbird. Also a single, soft, often feeble *kik* or *djug*.

Drumming Contrary to much of the literature, does drum, although very rarely and many probably never do. Rather, uses meowing song to declare territory.

Status After declines now increasing in some areas (eg. Estonia, Switzerland) but has declined where mature oak habitats have been lost or degraded. Extirpated from Sweden.

Habitat Mainly mature oak woodland. Also mixed deciduous forests with a high proportion of large oaks, parkland, wooded pasture, orchards, olive and chestnut groves, riparian woods with poplars, alders and willows, and ancient beech forests with high amounts of standing dead wood.

Range Western Palearctic. From Spain and France to Baltic States, W Russia and Balkans. As far E as Caucasus and Iran. Resident and sedentary.

Taxonomy and variation Four similar races: ***medius*** (NW Spain, Italy, Balkans, continental Europe, W

◄ Adult male nominate Middle Spotted Woodpecker. The sexes are often difficult to separate in the field, although this bird shows clearly that the red crown of the male does not fade at the rear. Lagenlois, Austria, February (*Thomas Hochebner*).

Russia, Ukraine); ***caucasicus*** (N Turkey, Caucasus, NW Iran); ***anatoliae*** (W and S Asia Minor); ***sanctijohannis*** (N Iraq, SW Iran). Differences in size and colour mainly clinal, N birds largest, palest and least streaked.

Similar species Adult Great Spotted and Syrian Woodpeckers similar, but larger, heavier-billed and either lack red on crown (female) or have red only on nape (male). Juveniles of those species most similar since they have all-red crown and pinkish ventral area, but both have thick black malar touching the bill and red crown has black border. White-backed Woodpecker is also streaked below, has pink vent and male has all-red crown, but back is barred.

Food and foraging Mainly bark and foliage-living insects and spiders. Prey gleaned from surfaces, does not bore deep into timber. Some sap, fruit, nuts and acorns taken. Usually forages from mid to high-levels, rarely on ground, seldom in mixed-species flocks.

▲ Pair of the race *anatoliae* at the nest hole. Female in foreground. Lesbos, Greece, March (*David Kjaer*).

◄ Adult female nominate Middle Spotted Woodpecker. Note that the red crown is tinged yellow and brown at the rear. Belgium, January (*Rudi Petitjean*).

111. WHITE-BACKED WOODPECKER
Dendrocopos leucotos

L 24–26cm

Identification Not as 'white-backed' as name suggests, amount of white varying. Nominate has white upper rump and lower back. Upper back glossy black, coverts barred white. White crescent-shaped area composed of lower scapulars, upper wing bars, lower back and upper rump, prominent in flight. Wings black with greater coverts dotted white. Flight feathers spotted or barred white. Most of tail black, outer feathers white, finely barred black. Vent and undertail-coverts pink, merging into white lower belly, flanks and legs. White or buff below, streaked black. Face and throat white, forehead and lores greyish. Black malar and post-auricular stripe meet on neck side. Black stripe runs from neck to chest. Long grey bill. Iris chestnut. Legs grey. Sexes differ: male has all-red crown, female black. Juvenile duller, tinged brown, white areas greyer, less pink below; juvenile male has red crown, female usually some red on forecrown.

Vocalisations Repeated, low-pitched, soft *tyuk, byuk, kuk* and *kok* notes, recalling Eurasian Blackbird. Also single, harder *gyig* or *gig.* When alarmed basic notes repeated in rapid series. Excited *weetcha-weetcha-wheetcha* in disputes. Pairs greet each other at the nest with *dyad-dyad* or *tchick.*

Drumming Both sexes drum, females less so. Drawn-out, accelerating rolls that trail off. Rolls around 2 seconds long, with about 30 strikes.

Status LC (Least Concern), but endangered in many parts of range, suffering from loss of old forests and intensive forestry methods.

Habitat Requires mature, old-growth deciduous or mixed forests with much rotten wood, especially standing dead trees. Only found in managed forests where nature-friendly management used.

Range Eurasia. Widespread from C Europe through boreal and taiga belt to Far East. Isolated populations on islands and south of main range. Resident and sedentary.

Taxonomy and variation Twelve races, some distinctive, particularly in back pattern and underpart colour. Several species probably involved: ***leucotos*** (N and C Europe through Russia, Siberia, Korea, NE China, Kamchatka and Sakhalin); ***uralensis*** (W Urals to Lake Baikal); ***lilfordi*** 'Lilford's Woodpecker' (Pyrenees, Apennines, S Balkans, Asia Minor and Caucasus) has narrow white wing-bars, heavy flecking below, extensive pink that reaches belly, and very 'ladder-backed' with barring on rump; ***subcirris*** (Hokkaido, Japan); ***stejnegeri*** (N Honshu, Japan) partly barred on rump, heavily marked below; both ***namiyei*** (S Honshu, Kyushu, Shikoku, Cheju-Do islands) and ***takahashii*** (Ullung Island, off E Korea) have buffy faces, less white in wings, very barred rumps and extensive pink

◀ Adult male nominate White-backed Woodpecker. Males of all races have red crowns, which females lack. Traisen, Austria, November (*Thomas Hochebner*).

or red below; ***owstoni*** (Amami-O-Shima Island, Japan) distinct 'Owston's Woodpecker', being large, almost all-black above with black breast band, heavy streaking below, minimal white in wings and reddish from vent to breast; ***quelpartensis*** (Jeju-do Island, off S Korea); ***tangi*** (Sichuan, W China) and ***fohkiensis*** (SE China, Fujian) both dark above and heavily flecked below; ***insularis*** (Taiwan) is smallest race with pink or red up onto belly.

Similar species All sympatric pied woodpeckers smaller. Those nearest in size lack barred back.

Food and foraging Highly insectivorous, only occasionally taking plant matter. Specialises in wood-boring beetle larvae, particularly longhorn species (*Coleoptera*) extracted from rotten timber. Other prey includes larvae of flies, carpenter moths and carpenter ants.

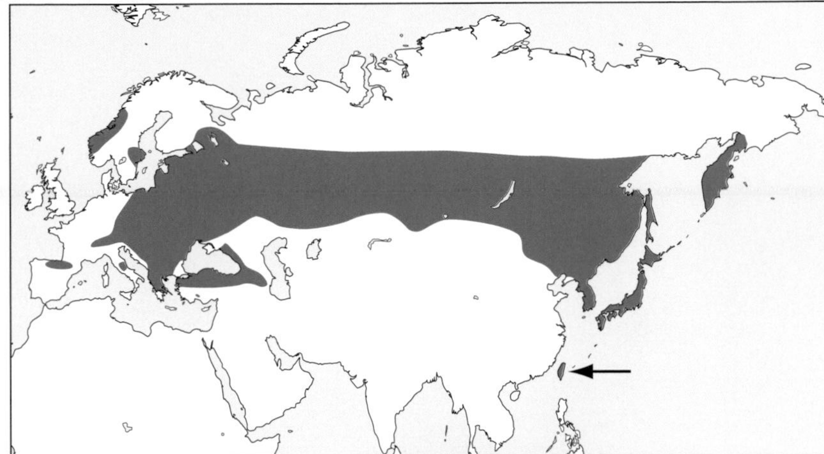

▼ Adult female nominate. Both sexes have pinkish undertail-coverts. Finland, December (*Tomi Muukkonen*).

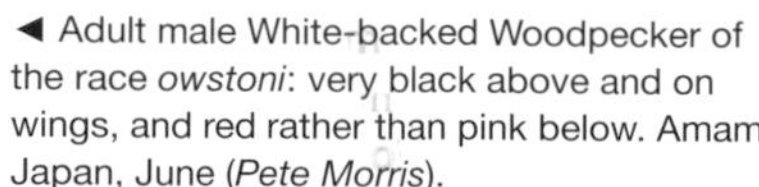
◄ Adult male White-backed Woodpecker of the race *owstoni*: very black above and on wings, and red rather than pink below. Amami, Japan, June (*Pete Morris*).

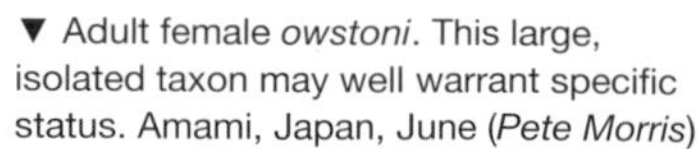
▼ Adult female *owstoni*. This large, isolated taxon may well warrant specific status. Amami, Japan, June (*Pete Morris*).

▼ Adult male *lilfordi*. This race is very 'ladder-backed', and heavily streaked below. Navarra, Spain, February (*José Ardaiz*)

► Adult male *tangi*. This is a dark race, with much black below. Sichuan, China, May (*James Eaton*).

112. OKINAWA WOODPECKER
Dendrocopos noguchii

L 31–35cm

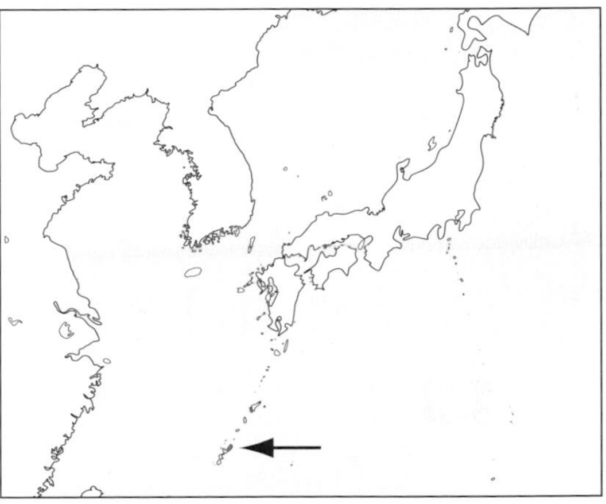

Other names Noguchi's Woodpecker, Pryer's Woodpecker

Identification Various shades of brown with rufous hues. Upperparts and wings chocolate, sometimes with faint reddish feather tips, especially on flight feathers. Reddish more evident on brown rump and darker uppertail-coverts. Primaries spotted or barred white. Underwing brown. Lores buff or brown, ear-coverts and neck-sides tan. Chocolate in malar region, but no distinct stripe. Throat and chest greyish-brown. Breast, belly and flanks brown, with dull reddish tones. Undertail brown with chestnut coverts. Long yellow or grey bill, broad at base. Iris chestnut. Legs grey. Sexes differ: male has deep red crown and nape flecked and streaked black; female lacks red, having dark brown crown. Juveniles like respective adults but overall greyer, duller, mostly lacking red tips. Juvenile male has less red on crown than adult.

Vocalisations Vocal most of year. Long, variable series of piping, whistling, sharp, *kyu* or *kwe* or *kup* notes. Single, whip-lashing *pwip* or *whit* when alarmed. A harder *kyo* or *kyu-kyu-kup* contact call and rattling *kyararara.* Nestlings make *pip* and *kyaa* sounds.

Drumming Accelerating, but often fairly slow 0.5–1.5-second rolls. Usually three rolls per minute.

Status CR. One of the rarest woodpeckers. In the 1930s was apparently close to extinction and by the 1990s probably fewer than 600 individuals alive. Today the total population may be as low as 100 pairs and is in real danger. Main threat has been habitat loss due to logging of mature forests, farming, golf-course construction and US military developments. With such small numbers, factors like natural disasters, disease, inbreeding and predation by feral cats, have become significant threats. Projects to save the species include purchasing key forests, planting corridors to link fragmented habitats, ending logging and providing nestboxes in young secondary forest.

Habitat Old-growth, damp, subtropical, evergreen broadleaved forest with tall trees and rotting timber. Such forest (at least 30 years old) is now mostly confined to hilltops. Nesting cavities often made in hollow *Castanopsis cuspidata* trees.

► Adult male Okinawa Woodpecker mainly differs from the female in having a red crown and nape. Okinawa, Japan, May (*Kenji Takehara*).

Range Endemic to Okinawa, Nansei Shoto (Ryukyu) islands, Japan. Localised, surviving mainly in the Yambaru Mts National Park (Mounts Ibu, Nishime-take and Lyu-take). Also occurs in some forested coastal areas. Resident and sedentary.

Taxonomy and variation Monotypic. Previously placed in a monospecific genus *Sapheopipo*. Slight individual variation.

Similar species None: unmistakable within range.

Food and foraging Beetle larvae, centipedes, spiders. Berries, seeds, acorns and nuts also taken. Sexes show significant differences in foraging niche, both searching dead and live tree-trunks and bamboo, but males also foraging on the ground, sweeping away leaf-litter and probing for soil-dwelling prey.

◄ Adult female Okinawa Woodpecker. A stunning image of one of the world's rarest woodpeckers. Okinawa, Japan, May (*Kenji Takehara*).

► A male Okinawa Woodpecker probes into foliage. The sexes differ in foraging methods and niches used. Okinawa, Japan, May (*Kenji Takehara*).

▼ A female Okinawa Woodpecker leaves its nest. Threats to this species' existence include the loss of forests to military and recreational developments. Okinawa, Japan, May (*Kenji Takehara*).

113. HIMALAYAN WOODPECKER
Dendrocopos himalayensis

L 23–25cm

Identification Unmarked glossy black back, mantle and nape. Plain white, cream or fulvous below, often with buffy hue. Undertail-coverts and vent red. Wings black with large white patch on the coverts and white bars on the primaries. Black tail with white on outermost feathers. Lores and forehead white or buff. Cheeks and ear-coverts white, sometimes dusky, enclosed by a vertical black post-auricular stripe which joins the black malar. Iris chestnut. Bill blackish. Legs greyish. Sexes differ: male has red crown, with some dark flecks, bordered by black on lower edge; female has black crown. Juvenile has duller black areas and pink vent, both sexes with some red or orange on crown, more so in male.

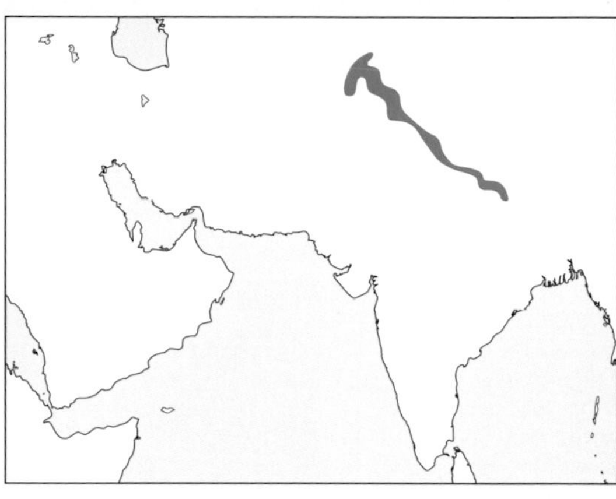

Vocalisations Series of crying *tri-tri-tri* calls; a high-pitched, fast *chisik-chisik;* and slower, ringing, evenly pitched *chupf-chupf.* Repeated series, slow or rapid, of squeaky *kwip* or *kwik* notes. Also hard, low-pitched *chuck* and single *kit* notes.

Drumming Short, rapid, rolls produced in breeding period, particularly by males.

Status Common locally. Population size and trends largely unknown, but considered stable.

Habitat Damp and dry upland coniferous and deciduous forests. Often in rhododendron.

Range Asia. Restricted to Himalayas and foothills in Afghanistan, Pakistan, India and Nepal. Between 1500–3200m. Usually at higher elevations than conjeners. Resident and mainly sedentary, perhaps some seasonal altitudinal movements.

Taxonomy and variation Two races that intergrade: ***himalayensis*** (N India: E Himachal Pradesh, Kashmir into W Nepal) is fulvous below; ***albescens*** (NE Afghanistan, N Pakistan into India: W Himachal Pradesh) is whiter below. In addition, amount of white in the tail varies; some birds have faint flank markings and some a black fleck behind the eye.

Similar species Darjeeling Woodpecker similar in size, but more boldly marked and coloured. Differs from smaller Sind Woodpecker (which it probably never meets) in facial pattern. White-winged

◄ Adult male Himalayan Woodpecker of the nominate race. Males have red on the crown, which females lack. Uttarakhand, India, June (*Soumyajit Nandy*).

Woodpecker (which might overlap in extreme NE Afghanistan) has more white in wing and more red below.

Food and foraging A generalist, taking both insects, sap and seeds in season. Uses anvils to process conifer cones. Invariably forages alone, mostly on trunks and larger branches, sometimes on ground. Occasionally in mixed flocks.

► Adult female nominate. This high-altitude species rarely overlaps with other similar-looking *Dendrocopos*. Uttarakhand, India, April (*Ishmeet Sahni*).

▼ A pair of Himalayan Woodpeckers, with the female above and male below. This is an unusual shot, as pairs seldom forage together nor drop to the ground. Western Himalayas, India, May (*Amano Samarpan*).

114. SIND WOODPECKER
Dendrocopos assimilis

L 20–22cm

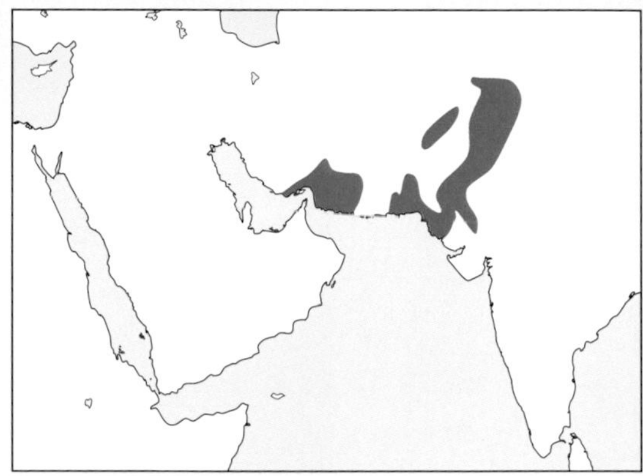

Identification Mostly white below, with faint greyish streaking on flanks. Vent and undertail-coverts red, colour sometimes extending onto belly. Plain glossy black back and mantle. Blackish wings boldly barred white on flight feathers, large white oval patches over scapulars and coverts. Tail black with outer two feather pairs barred white. Lores buff. Forehead, cheeks and ear-coverts white. Black malar extends to meet black area on neck-sides and line from chest. Iris chestnut. Legs greyish. Bill bluish-grey, lower mandible paler. Sexes differ slightly: male has red crown flecked and bordered by black; female crown all black. On juvenile white areas are duskier, black areas less glossy. Juveniles of both sexes have pinkish vent and red mid-crown (less so in female) with some dark flecking.

Vocalisations Loud, sharp *ptik*. Also a rather weak, high-pitched *chir-rir-rir-rirh* or *tr-r-r-r* and rapid, repeated *toi-whit, toi-whit, toi-whit.*

Drumming Both sexes produce loud, steady rolls.

Status Often common locally, though rather scattered. Widespread in Pakistan. Overall considered stable and adapts to secondary habitats.

Habitat Drier, subtropical open woodlands, thorn thickets, scrub, plantations, palm and olive groves, wadis, oases, settlements and gardens. Often in euphorbia, tamarisk, mulberry, pistachio and acacia trees.

Range SW Asia. Mostly Pakistan but also NW India and SE Iran. Mainly lowlands, but to 2000m. Resident and sedentary.

Taxonomy and variation Monotypic. Some birds have buff ear-coverts and/or underparts and some have minimal white in the tail.

Similar species Very like Syrian and White-winged Woodpeckers (may hybridise with the former in Iran, but does not overlap with the latter) though slightly smaller than both. Syrian male has red only on nape (though beware juvenile Syrian which has all-red crown).

Food and foraging Mainly carpenter ants and wood-boring beetle larvae. Presumably also some fruit and berries. Usually forages alone, low on smaller trees, saplings, stumps and logs.

◄◄ Adult male Sind Woodpecker. The male has a red crown, while that of the female is black. Baluchistan, Pakistan, May (*Ghulam Rasool*).

◄ Adult female. Sind Woodpecker inhabits arid, open woodlands, and secondary habitats such as groves and plantations. Iran, May (*Seyed Bubak Musavi*).

115. SYRIAN WOODPECKER
Dendrocopos syriacus

L 22–23cm

Identification Mostly black above, white or buff below, lightly streaked grey, especially on flanks. Undertail-coverts pink. Outer tail feathers black with some white spots. Lores buff, face white. Black malar meets lateral neck stripe below ear-coverts – no post-auricular stripe. Blacks wings with three lines of white spots on flight feathers, outer primaries tipped white. Large white oval scapular patches. Fine-tipped bill and legs greyish. Iris dark. Sexes differ: male has black crown and red nape patch; female lacks red. Juveniles of both sexes have all-red crown bordered black and variable pink or red gorget.

Vocalisations Contact calls include single, shrill, squeaky *chük, chik* or *dschik,* squeakier than Great Spotted Woodpecker. Also harder *gig, gug* or *pug.* Alarm calls include *kip,* often doubled *kip-kip* or *gipp-gipp,* in rapid series when excited, recalling Common Redshank. Also loud *kip kip kiririr kirir kirir kirir,* variable in length and pitch and *tyuk-tyuk-tyuk.* Aggressive, very squeaky *queeka-queeka-queeka* and rattling *queg-queg-queg-kreerirrrrr* in disputes. Repeated, gentle *kweep* or *kweek* notes during courtship.

Drumming Both sexes drum, and will duet from a distance. High-pitched accelerating 1-second rolls with 15–30 strikes, fading at the end.

Status Often common locally. Probably increasing. Sometimes viewed as a pest in plantations due to habit of pecking fruit and waterpipes.

Habitat Lightly wooded, drier areas. Often in urban and man-made habitats such as parks, gardens, vineyards, orchards, plantations. Avoids closed forest. Sea-level into foothills.

Range Mostly Western Palearctic. Rapidly colonised E and C Europe in the 20th century. Continued range expansion in most directions. Currently occurs in lowland Austria, Hungary, Czech Republic, Slovakia, Poland, Belarus, Russia and Ukraine. In S from Balkans through Turkey, Caucasus, Middle East, NE Egypt, Iraq and Iran.

Taxonomy and variation Monotypic. Three races sometimes claimed (*syriacus, transcaucasicus* and *milleri*) but all very similar and probably clines.

Similar species Differs from overlapping Great Spotted Woodpecker (hybrids occur) in pink rather than red undertail, lack of post-auricular stripe, mainly black outer-tail, lacking white on third rectrix, and on closed wing having larger but fewer white dots. Male Syrian has larger red nape patch. Juvenile best

► Adult male Syrian Woodpecker. The bright red nape patch separates the male from the female. Hungary, January (*Lee Mott*).

separated from Great Spotted by features mentioned above plus reddish chest band. Juvenile Syrian similar to Middle Spotted of all ages but larger, only faintly streaked below and less white in outer-tail. Male Sind Woodpecker has all-red crown.

Food and foraging Omnivorous. Various insects, earthworms, snails, fruit, berries, sap, seeds and nuts. Uses anvils.

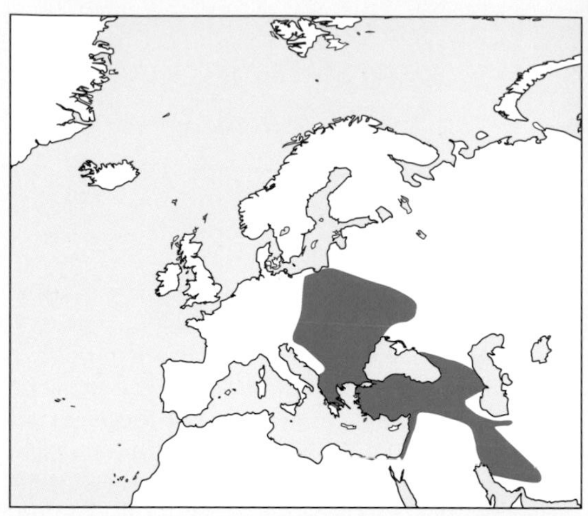

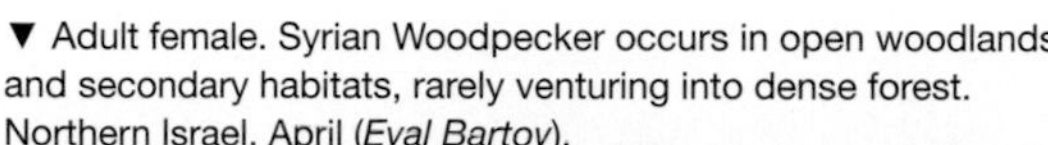

▼ Adult female. Syrian Woodpecker occurs in open woodlands and secondary habitats, rarely venturing into dense forest. Northern Israel, April (*Eyal Bartov*).

116. WHITE-WINGED WOODPECKER
Dendrocopos leucopterus

L 22–24cm

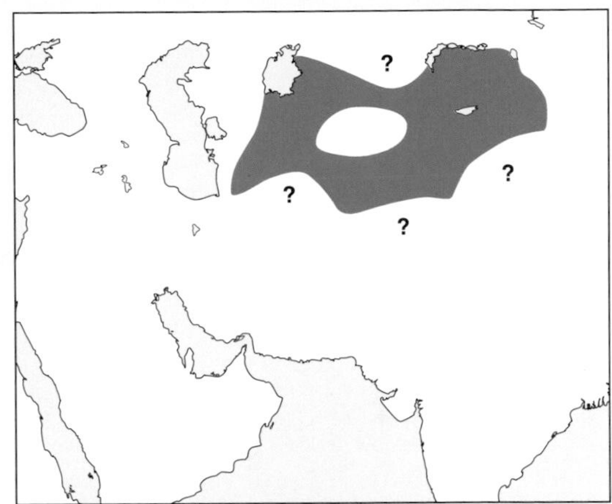

Identification Clean white below, sometimes tinged buff. Lower belly stained pink, undertail-coverts red. Glossy black above. Tail black with white on outer 2–3 feather pairs. Much white in wings (bars on primaries, secondaries and scapulars, tertials edged white) creating a long, large patch. Wide white forehead band. Broad black post-auricular, malar and neck stripes all meet on sides of neck to form large area of black: thus white neck patch is small. Ear-coverts white, crown black. Iris chestnut. Bill dark, lower mandible paler. Legs greyish. Sexes differ slightly: males have small red nape patch which females lack. Juvenile less glossy black, browner than adult, more buff below with some dark flank flecking, pink rather than red undertail-coverts, dark barring in the white wing patches

► Adult male White-winged Woodpecker. Note the small red nape patch. Almaty, Kazakhstan, June (*Vaughan & Sveta Ashby*).

▲ Adult male. This is another *Dendocopos* that inhabits open wooded areas rather than true forests. Kazakhstan, May (*Neil Bowman*).

and both sexes have some red on the crown, less so in female.

Vocalisations Harsh or squeaky, low-pitched *chyek, chik, kig* and *kick* notes: more like Syrian Woodpecker than Great Spotted. Also a raucous, rattling, chattering *chrerr-rrerr-trerr.*

Drumming Short, fast, rolls of even-tempo start strongly before fading.

Status Locally common. Overall population probably stable, though poorly known and situation in some countries uncertain.

Habitat Open wooded lowlands and foothills, often with birch, willows and turanga poplar. Semi-desert with saxaul trees, orchards, plantations, gardens, oases and riparian woods (which can run deep into deserts). In some regions upland broadleaved forests with juniper and fir. Frequents fruit and nut trees.

Range Central Asia. From the S and E shores of the Aral Sea in Kazakhstan and Uzbekistan to Tien Shan and Dzungarian Mts, Lake Balkhash region, Kyrgyzstan and into extreme W China. Also Turkmenistan, possibly NE Iran, NE Afghanistan and Tajikistan. Lowlands to 2500m. Resident, some nomadic.

Taxonomy and variation Monotypic. Variation slight, birds in Turkestan highlands may have less white in wing. Some birds in fresh plumage have pink on belly.

Similar species Only pied woodpecker over much of its range. Most like Great Spotted Woodpecker, which may overlap in some areas, but differs (from that and all other relatives) by having broader barring on wings and larger white scapular patches.

Food and foraging Ants, insects and molluscs, supplemented with plant matter.

▼ Adult female White-winged Woodpecker. Both sexes have red undertail-coverts, but the females lack the red nape of the males. Almaty, Kazakhstan, April (*Adam Riley*).

117. GREAT SPOTTED WOODPECKER
Dendrocopos major

L 21–23cm

Identification Mostly glossy black above, including crown. White outer scapulars and inner coverts form large ovals. Throat to belly white or buff, some races reddish on chest. Undertail-coverts and vent scarlet. Black malar joins black post-auricular stripe which reaches nape, enclosing white ear-coverts. Forehead and lores white or buff. Tail mostly black, outer feathers white dotted or barred black. Flight feathers black with 5–6 rows of white spots forming bars. Buff underwing-coverts spotted black. Dark bill, lower mandible paler. Iris red. Legs greyish. Sexes differ: male has red nape patch which female lacks. Both juveniles have red crown patch (larger on male) bordered black, white scapulars gently barred, post-auricular stripe often not touching nape, cheeks dusky, ventral region pinkish, sometimes dark or rufous chest band, brown iris.

Vocalisations Common call a loud, metallic, sharp, single, high-pitched *kik, tchik* or *chick.* Sometimes uttered twice or slowly repeated, about one per second. When agitated rapidly repeated. Also excited chattering *chett-chett-chett,* often ending with thrush-like rattle. Raucous *krraarraarrr* alarm. Nestlings noisy, producing incessant *vee-vee-vee, gay-gay-gay* and zizzing sounds.

Drumming Both sexes drum, but males more so. Typical rolls comprised of 10–16 strikes per second, accelerating before fading. Outside breeding season 3–4 bouts per minute, 8–10 in spring.

Status Common and widespread. Population secure and stable, perhaps increasing.

Habitat Generalist, occurring in wide variety of both dense and open coniferous, deciduous and mixed forests. Occupies natural and man-made habitats, from forests to parks, gardens and orchards. Highest densities in mature deciduous forests.

Range Palearctic. Most widespread woodpecker in the world. Occurs from British Isles across Europe through Asia to Japan. From Arctic tree-line to N Africa. Present on larger islands. Most populations sedentary, some irruptive. Vagrant to Hong Kong, Iceland and USA.

► Adult male Great Spotted Woodpecker of race *japonicus*. Males of all races differ from the females in having a red nape patch. Hokkaido, Japan, March (*Tadao Shimba*).

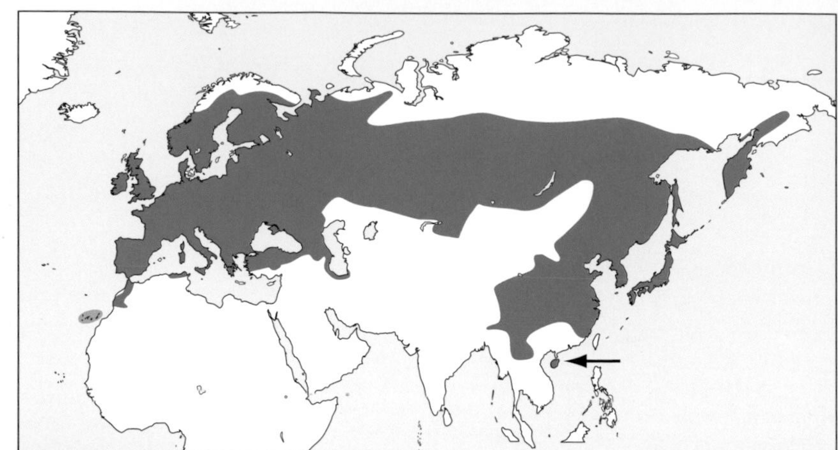

▼ Adult female *pinetorum*. The main confusion species in much of Europe is Syrian Woodpecker, but note here the black post-auricular stripe, white outer-tail and red undertail feathers. Olomouc, Czech Republic, March (*David Jirovsky*).

Taxonomy and variation Some races only arbitrarily described and recent phylogenetic analysis suggests the recognition of at least four different species: ***D. major*** in Eurasia and North Africa; ***D. poelzami*** in Iran-Azerbaijan; ***D. japonicus*** in Japan; and ***D. cabanisi*** in China. Populations in the Canary Islands, Algeria and Tunisia are visually distinct from those on mainland Europe and may also be different species. Up to 27 races have been claimed, usually on the basis of differences in measurements, underpart colour and extent of white on the wings. Some races very distinct, others less so. Northern races are larger, heavier-billed and cleaner below than southern ones. Described races include ***major*** (Scandinavia, N Europe to W Siberia); ***brevirostris*** (Siberia to N Manchuria and Mongolia); ***kamtschaticus*** (Kamchatka to Okhotsk Sea); ***anglicus*** (Britain); ***pinetorum*** (continental Europe); ***hispanus*** (Iberia); ***parroti*** (Corsica); ***harterti*** (Sardinia); ***italiae*** (Italy, W Slovenia); ***canariensis*** (Tenerife); ***thanneri*** (Gran Canaria); ***mauritanus*** (Morocco); ***numidus*** (N Algeria, Tunisia); ***candidus*** (E Balkans); ***paphlagoniae*** (N Turkey); ***tenuirostris*** (Caucasus into SW Asia); ***poelzami*** (Transcaucasia and S Caspian); ***japonicus*** (E Manchuria, Sakhalin, Kuril Islands, Japan, Korea); ***wulashanicus*** (Inner Mongolia); ***cabanisi*** (S Manchuria, E Burma (Myanmar), Indochina, Hainan Island); ***beicki*** (C China); ***mandarinus*** (S China, N Indochina); ***stresemanni*** (W China to N Burma (Myanmar), SE Tibet and NE India); ***hainanus*** (Hainan Island, China).

Similar species In Europe most like Syrian Woodpecker, which differs in having mostly black tail, pink vent and no post-auricular stripe (beware first-winter Great Spotted, which has incomplete post-auricular stripe). White-winged Woodpecker much whiter in wings.

Food and foraging Omnivorous, versatile, opportunistic. Main food varies locally. Takes wide range of invertebrates and plant matter: pine seeds, acorns, nuts, fruit, berries, sap. Readily visits feeders and creates anvils to process hard items.

◄▲ Adult male *stresemanni*: note the dusky ear-coverts and underparts. Qinghai, China, June (*James Eaton*).

▲ An adult male of the Tenerife race *canariensis*. This is one of several taxa that on-going studies suggest may warrant species status. Tenerife, May (*Elizabeth Barrett*).

◄ Adult male *anglicus*. Some authorities classify British birds as *pinetorum*, as in continental Europe. Warwickshire, UK, October (*Tony Hamblin*).

PICOIDES

All but one (Smoky-brown Woodpecker) of the 12 species in this genus occur in the Northern Hemisphere. The *Picoides* has been the subject of some taxonomic uncertainty, with several species shuffled between this genus and others, particularly *Dendrocopos* and *Veniliornis*. All are highly arboreal, rarely descending to the ground. Sexual dimorphism in foraging behaviour is particularly well illustrated in the *Picoides* with females tending to be smaller and using smaller trees, searching at greater heights, employing different techniques and taking smaller prey than males.

Black-backed Woodpecker *Picoides arcticus*, adult male. Oregon, United States, May (*Richard Tipton*).

118. LADDER-BACKED WOODPECKER
Picoides scalaris

L 16–18cm

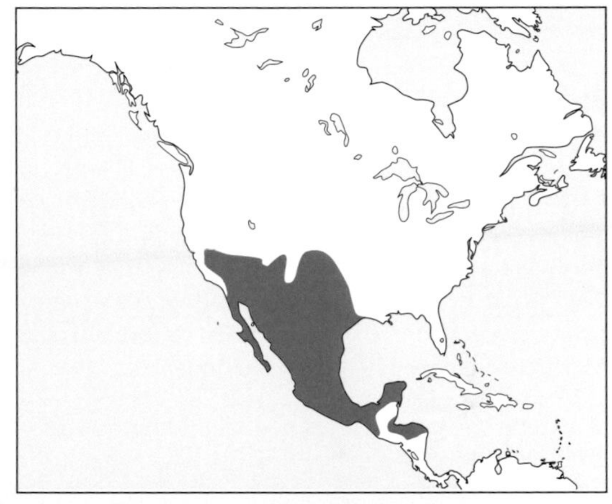

Identification Barred black and white (ladder-backed) above. Wings also barred. Buff or white below, breast weakly spotted. Flanks barred/streaked black. Uppertail black, bold white barring on outer three feather pairs. White or buff face crossed by black post-ocular and malar stripes which meet over the ear-coverts. Lores dusky. Bill blackish. Iris chestnut. Legs grey. Sexes differ: male has red crown, flecked black and white; female black with white spotting. Juvenile more barred and flecked brown below, both sexes with red mid-crown, more red in male.

Vocalisations Rattling series of 12–25 notes, ending with drop in pitch and grating sound: *kweek-week-weekweekweechrchr*. A louder, slower *kweek-kweek-kweek*

► Adult male Ladder-backed Woodpecker of race *cactophilus*. Males have a red crown, which the females lack. Arizona, United States, November (*Glenn Bartley*).

variant. Falling, whinnying *jee-jee-jee*. Sharp *peek*, *pwik*, *pik* or *chik* contact-alarm.

Drumming Rapid 1-second roll that slows and falls in pitch. Each roll around 28–30 strikes.

Status Often common, considered stable, though local declines noted, e.g. Edwards Plateau, Texas.

Habitat Desert and dry country with thorn scrub, agave, cacti, yucca, Joshua trees and mesquite brush. Also open piñon-juniper, willow, cottonwood, pine, oak and riparian woodlands, mangroves and around settlements.

Range North and Central America. From SW USA to NE Nicaragua. Resident, sedentary but some dispersal. Sea-level to 3000m.

Taxonomy and variation Nine races: ***scalaris*** (S Mexico: Veracruz and Chiapas); ***cactophilus*** (SW USA, NE Baja California and C Mexico) is large, with solid black malar, broad white bars above, white below dotted black; ***eremicus*** (N Baja California) is even larger, darker, dirtier overall, white barring finer, bill and tail long; ***lucasanus*** (S Baja California) is small, clean, barring above whiter; ***sinaloensis*** (coastal W Mexico) is dark on face, buff and heavily streaked below; ***soulei*** (Cerralvo Island, Mexico) also small; ***graysoni*** (Tres Marias Islands, Mexico) buff below, finely streaked; ***parvus*** (N Yucatan, Cozumel and Holbox Islands) also small, short-billed, blacker on back, belly barred, forehead black; ***leucoptilurus*** (Belize, Guatemala, El Salvador, Honduras and NE Nicaragua) is smallest race, dusky or buffy below with fewest markings.

Similar species Most like Nuttall's Woodpecker but more finely and evenly barred above, barred on mantle, more buff below with finer markings and broader white stripes on face and neck. Male Nuttall's red only on hindcrown and nape. Calls also similar, though Nuttall's rattle rises at the end. Rattling call perhaps most like that of Arizona Woodpecker.

Food and foraging Insects and cactus fruits. Forages by gleaning rather than excavating, in trees, bushes, cacti, mesquite, yuccas, agave and on ground.

▼ Adult female *cactophilus*. This race has a distinct dark malar stripe and spotting on the chest. Mission, Texas, United States, April (*Dave Hawkins*).

119. NUTTALL'S WOODPECKER
Picoides nuttallii

L 17–19cm

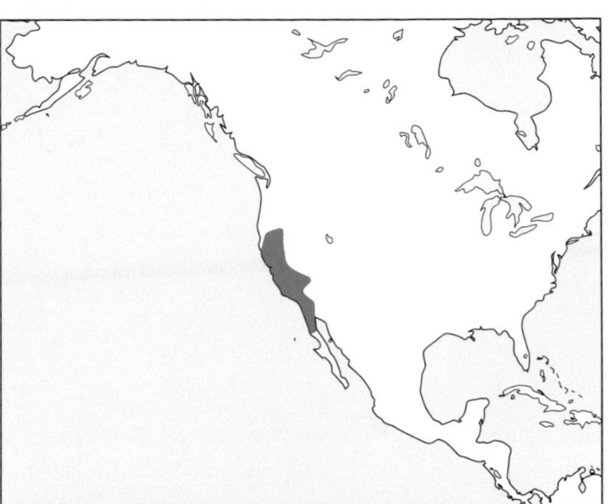

Identification Black and white 'ladder' back, but mantle solid black. Wings black, narrowly barred white. White or cream below, spotted and streaked, especially on flanks. Tail black, outer feathers dotted white. Face black and white: long, narrow white supercilium, black post-ocular stripe and ear-coverts, white cheek, thin black malar. Forehead buff, nasal tufts and throat white. Iris chestnut. Black-grey bill, lower mandible usually paler. Legs greyish. Sexes differ: male has black forecrown, scarlet hindcrown and nape; female has black crown flecked white. Juvenile plainer, less marked, white areas greyer, male with red centre-crown patch speckled white, female less red.

Vocalisations Low-pitched, rolling or rattling series of *prrrt* notes, usually 19–20 per second, often rising at end. Also longer trilling version *prrt-prrt-prrrrrrrrrrr.* A sharp *ka-teek,* loud, squealing *peek-peek-peek* or *kweek-kweek-kweek, wick-wick-wick* and *tew-tew-tew.* Contact calls include rising, sharp, single *pik* or *pit* and double *pik-ik, pit-it* or *kick-it,* also longer *pitikikik.*

Drumming Both sexes drum. Medium-paced, level-pitched, 1-second roll. About 20 strikes per second, tempo increasing. Active male birds may drum 20 times per minute.

Status Range-restricted but possibly increasing. Has moved into suburbs in some areas, but declined in others due to habitat loss to construction and agriculture.

Habitat Associated with dry, open oak woodland. Also found in mixed oak-chaparral and oak-conifer. Avoids deserts, though extends into them along riparian corridors.

Range USA (California) and Mexico (N Baja California). Sea-level to 2000m. Resident and mainly sedentary, some altitudinal movements in autumn to higher elevations. Vagrant to Oregon and Nevada.

Taxonomy and variation Monotypic. Variation slight.

Similar species Though rarely in same habitat, easily confused with Ladder-backed Woodpecker but broader barring on back, mantle unbarred, outer-tail whiter, white rather than buff nasal tufts and underparts. Male Nuttall's red only on hindcrown and nape.

► Adult male Nuttall's Woodpecker. Males differ from females in having a red hind-crown and nape-patch. California, United States, November (*Bob Steele*).

Some calls also similar, but Ladder-backed's rattle falls at the end, where Nuttall's rises. Hybridises with Ladder-backed and Downy Woodpeckers.

Food and foraging Usually a solitary forager that probes and gleans for insects, especially beetles, on twigs, foliage and in scrub. Acrobatic, sometimes hawks for flying insects. Also feeds on flower-buds, seeds, berries and takes sap from sapsucker wells.

◄ Adult female. Females lack red on the head and are thus totally pied, and very similar to female Ladder-backed Woodpecker: face and back patterns should be noted. California, United States, November (*Bob Steele*)

120. DOWNY WOODPECKER
Picoides pubescens

L 15–17cm

Identification Smallest woodpecker in N America. Pied, with black crown, broad white supercilium, black band across ear-coverts to nape, white moustache, black malar. White or buff below, usually unmarked. Black above, broad white stripe down back. Black wings variably spotted on upper coverts, barred on flight feathers. Nasal bristles white. Inner tail black, outer feathers white with black dots or bars. Short, delicate, dark bill. Iris chestnut. Legs greyish. Sexes differ: male has small red nape patch, which female lacks. Juvenile male has pinkish mid-crown, female mottled black and white, sometimes tinged pink; both duller overall, finely streaked black below.

Vocalisations Various soft single, rarely double, *pik, pit, kik* and *tsik* notes. Loud, multi-functional, whinnying *chick, chick, chick, chrr-rr rr* of 10–25 notes. Whistling, shrill *peep-peep-peep* or *peet-peet-peet* and rattling *tickirr*. Squeaky, rattling *twi-twi-twi, ki-ki-ki* or *kee-kee-kee* of 11–25 notes, beginning high-pitched then falling. Rapid *check* or *kweek* notes during courtship. Low *chirrr* at nest changeovers, harsher *chrr* or *tichrr* in conflicts.

Drumming Both sexes drum often in spring. Slow, even-pitched rolls of up to 2 seconds, with 15–18 strikes per second, decelerating at the end. Often several rolls in quick succession, 9–24 per minute, with brief pauses.

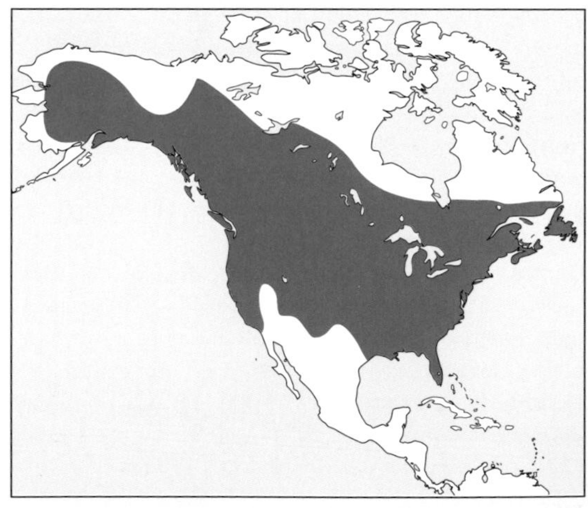

Status Locally common in E and S, uncommon in N and much of W. Overall stable, perhaps increasing, though some local declines. Has adapted to man-made habitats.

Habitat Variety of deciduous and mixed deciduous-

▲ Adult male *medianus*. The sexes can be difficult to separate in the field unless the male's small red nape-patch is seen. Minnesota, United States, June (*Kristian Svensson*).

conifer forests, often damp. Also orchards, parks, gardens.

Range North America. Most of continent south of tree line. Resident and mostly sedentary, though some disperse long distances. Sea-level to 2750m.

Taxonomy and variation Significant racial, clinal and individual differences. Undertail and head patterns often vary, some birds with white 'eyebrows' meeting on back of the head. Southern birds smaller, greyer below than northern. Seven races, plumage-wise often placed in three groups. Eastern group: ***pubescens*** (Kansas to S Virginia, E Texas to Florida) and ***medianus*** (C Alaska to Newfoundland and USA E of the Rockies, N of *pubescens*) very white. Rockies group: ***leucurus*** (SE Alaska to W Great Plains and SW states) and ***glacialis*** (SE Alaska) have less white in wings and more extensive black on head. Pacific group: ***fumidus*** (SW Canada, W Washington), ***gairdnerii*** (W Oregon to NW California) and ***turati*** (C Washington to inland S California) with NW birds tinged grey or brown above, grey or buff below, coastal birds darker with reduced white spotting on wing coverts and secondaries. Calls also differ regionally.

Similar species Like a small, short-billed Hairy Woodpecker, though oval neck patch larger, post-ocular stripe narrower, malar falls short of nape. Male has solid red nape patch, while on Hairy it may be split by a black line connecting the crown and nape.

Food and foraging Omnivorous and versatile, taking a range of insects (beetles, weevils, ants, aphids, caterpillars) as well as seeds, nuts, berries and corn. Forages at most levels, joins mixed foraging flocks and visits backyard feeders.

▼ Adult female nominate Downy Woodpecker. A plethora of subtle racial and individual differences in plumage exist across the range. Tennessee, United States, January (*Dave Hawkins*).

121. HAIRY WOODPECKER

Picoides villosus

L 17–26cm

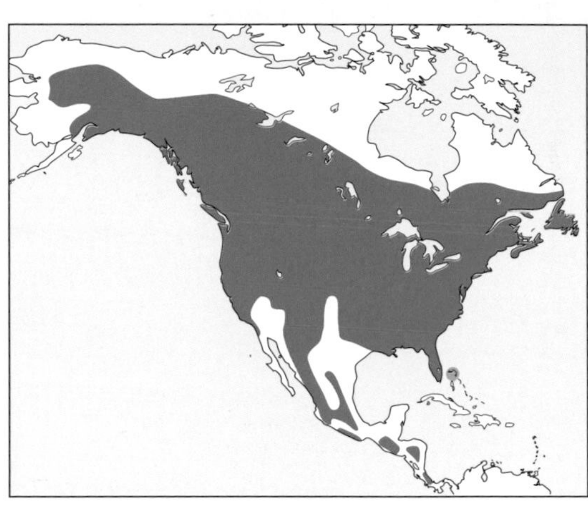

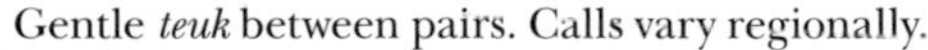

Identification Very variable. Name refers to large patch of coarse white feathers on its black back. Pied, with black crown, white supercilium, broad black band over ear-coverts, white moustache, thin black malar and white throat. Wings black, spotted white. White or buff below. Outer tail white, inner black. Stout, dark bill. Iris chestnut. Legs grey. Sexes differ: male has red nape patch which female lacks. Juvenile lightly barred below, black forehead spotted white, pale orbital ring, browner overall; juvenile male has red or orange crown.
Vocalisations Strong, sharp *keek, peek* or *speek*, sometimes *pee-ik* or squeaky *peech;* also linked in rapid, slurred series, sometimes *peek-rr-krr* or *cheerk.* High-pitched, trilling or rattling *queek* or *kweek* in series and whinnying *haan-haan-haan.* Squeaky *wicka* calls in conflicts. Gentle *teuk* between pairs. Calls vary regionally.
Drumming Both sexes drum. Rapid, buzzing 1-second rolls of 25–26 strikes, often slowing at the end. Pauses of 20 seconds or more between rolls.
Status Common in N. Probably increasing overall, though some local declines due to loss of mature forests.
Habitat Generalist, inhabiting open and closed, mature coniferous, deciduous and mixed woodlands. Also urban gardens and parks. Mainly deciduous habitats in N, pine in S and Bahamas, in C America also bamboo.
Range North and Central America. Pacific Coast to Atlantic from tree line. More fragmented in S (absent from much of Texas) and from Mexico to Panama. Also Bahamas. In SW USA and N Mexico, a high-mountain bird. Resident, mostly sedentary, but some dispersal S in autumn. Vagrant to Caribbean islands.
Taxonomy and variation Significant racial, clinal and individual differences in plumage and size. For instance, birds in Rockies and Pacific region have much black on wings. Fourteen races (though this debated): ***villosus*** (S Quebec and Nova Scotia to E North Dakota, Missouri, Virginia and C Texas); ***septentrionalis*** (SC Alaska, E to Quebec, S in the W to N Arizona, in the E to Virginia) largest, palest race; ***terraenovae*** (Newfoundland) minimal white above, flanks finely streaking black; ***sitkensis*** (SE Alaska,

◄ Adult male Hairy Woodpecker. Race *harrisi*: note the mostly black wings. Males have a red nape patch, which females lack. British Colombia, Canada, December (*Tom Middleton*).

N British Columbia) grey or brown face and below, minimal white on wings; ***picoideus*** (Queen Charlotte Islands) distinctive, dusky below, white back flecked black, often bold black barring on outer-tail; ***harrisi*** (W coast from C British Columbia to N California) grey-brown on face and underparts, reduced white on wings; ***audubonii*** (S Illinois to SE Virginia, E Texas and Gulf Coast) buffy-grey below, reduced white above; ***hyloscopus*** (W California to N Baja California) small, face clean white; ***orius*** (from S British Columbia to SE California, Utah and SW Texas) has less white above than boreal races, hardly spotted on wing coverts; ***icatus*** (SE Arizona and New Mexico through W Mexico to Jalisco) is small; ***jardinii*** (C and E Mexico) dusky or buff below; ***sanctorum*** (S Mexico to Costa Rica and W Panama) very small (some approaching Downy Woodpecker), darker, buff or cinnamon below; Bahaman ***piger*** (Grand Bahama, Mores and Abaco Island) and ***maynardi*** (New Province and Andros Island) are also small.

Similar species Downy Woodpecker usually visibly smaller, shorter-billed (shorter than head-length; Hairy's at least as long as head). Hairy has smaller white neck patch, black band over lower cheek runs further to rear. Male Hairy often has red nape patch split by vertical black line (especially in NE), Downy has solid red patch (Hairy in Central America may lack this line). Downy's calls weaker, flatter.

Food and foraging A key natural controller of forest beetles. Also takes caterpillars and spiders. Berries, nuts, acorns, conifer seeds and sap also consumed and feeders visited.

► Adult female Hairy Woodpecker. Nominate race: note the amount of white in the wing. Females lack red on the nape and so are totally pied. Illinois, United States (*Gerald Marella*).

122. ARIZONA WOODPECKER
Picoides arizonae

L 18–20cm

Identification Appears, stout and short-tailed. Mantle, back and rump plain rich brown. Underparts from throat to vent dull white, heavily blotched, spotted and flecked brown. Brown wings slightly barred or spotted pale. Undertail boldly barred brown and white, tail tip chocolate. Forehead and crown chocolate. Nasal tufts dull white. Distinct brown ear-coverts, white ear surrounds. Brown malar. Iris brown. Bill dark, paler at base. Legs grey. Sexes differ slightly: male has red nape, which female lacks. Juvenile duller overall, darker and more marked below, less white in tail. Juveniles of both sexes with some orange or red on mid-crown, more in male.

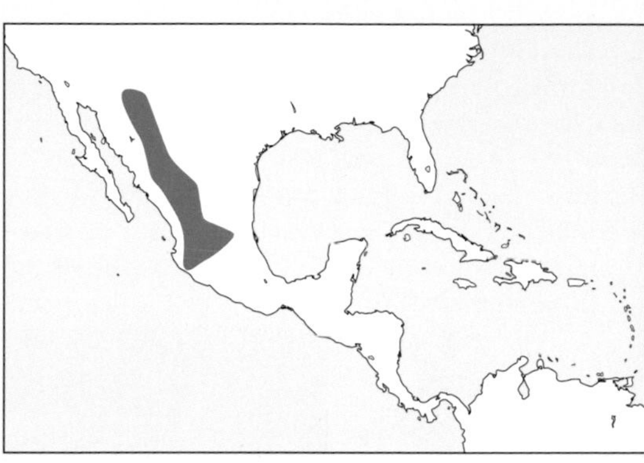

Vocalisations Often silent. Alarm a grating, screeching, rattling *keechrchrchr* of up to 30 double notes, recalling Ladder-backed Woodpecker. Multi-functional, loud, sharp, single or repeated *peep, peek* or *kweek* made all year recalls Hairy Woodpecker. Also a drawn-out, squeaky but sharp *keech,* 2–5 nasal *chriek-a* notes. Fast, twittering, rattling, series of mixed *qweek* and *wicka* notes. Gentle *tuk-tuk-tuk* uttered to prompt nest change-overs and as contact call.

Drumming Both sexes drum, males more so. Typically 3–4 rapid, level-pitched, steady-paced rolls per minute. When excited or challenged, up to a dozen per minute.

Status Population possibly increasing in very limited USA range. In parts of Mexico, probably declining as woodlands are felled for timber and cleared for farmland.

Habitat Dry montane evergreen oak, pine and mixed oak-pine woodlands. Also wet canyons with sycamore, maple, walnut and cottonwood.

Range Restricted to extreme SW USA (not only Arizona) and WC Mexico: Sierra Madre Occidental and S edge of Mexican Plateau. Mostly between 1200–2400m. Resident and essentially sedentary, though some move to slightly lower areas in winter.

Taxonomy and variation Formerly lumped with Strickland's Woodpecker, but split to species in 2000. Two races; ***arizonae*** (SE Arizona, SW New Mexico, NW

◄ Adult male Arizona Woodpecker of the nominate race. Males have a small red patch on the nape; otherwise the sexes are very similar. Arizona, United States, April (*Dave Hawkins*).

Mexico, S into Sinaloa and adjacent Durango, Mexico) and ***fraterculus*** (W Mexico: S Sinaloa and Durango, S to Michoacan), which has darker brown head and usually less white in outer tail. Some birds faintly barred white above are possibly hybrids with Strickland's Woodpecker.

Similar species Only woodpecker in USA with plain brown upperparts, so confusion there unlikely when bird seen well; some vocalisations resemble those of sympatric Hairy and Ladder-backed Woodpeckers. In Mexico very similar Strickland's Woodpecker shorter-billed, darker and barred above.

Food and foraging Insects, especially beetle larvae. Some fruit and acorns. Unobtrusive, usually foraging alone, occasionally in mixed-flocks. Also visits feeders for suet.

▲ Adult female nominate. As the only brown-and-white woodpecker in North America, confusion with other picids is unlikely. Arizona, United States, April (*Dave Hawkins*).

► Adult male nominate. The sexes seldom associate with each other outside the breeding season. Arizona, United States, April (*Dave Hawkins*)

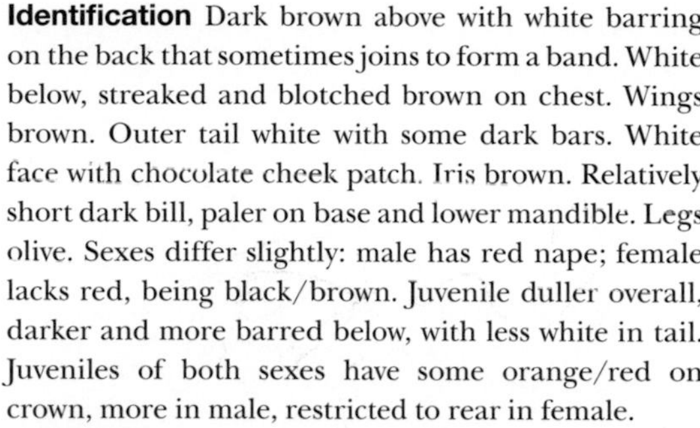

123. STRICKLAND'S WOODPECKER
Picoides stricklandi

L 18–19cm

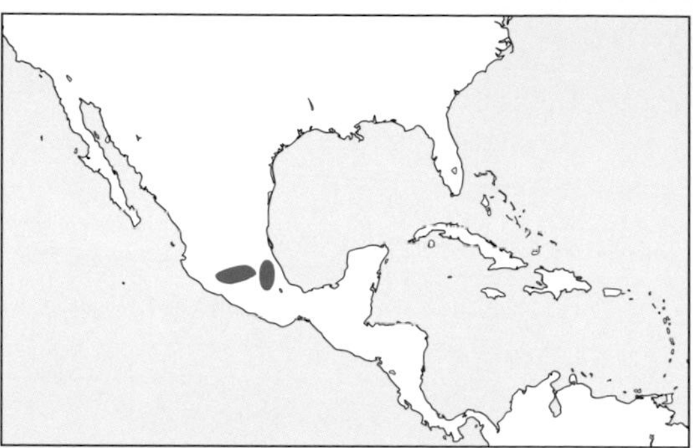

Identification Dark brown above with white barring on the back that sometimes joins to form a band. White below, streaked and blotched brown on chest. Wings brown. Outer tail white with some dark bars. White face with chocolate cheek patch. Iris brown. Relatively short dark bill, paler on base and lower mandible. Legs olive. Sexes differ slightly: male has red nape; female lacks red, being black/brown. Juvenile duller overall, darker and more barred below, with less white in tail. Juveniles of both sexes have some orange/red on crown, more in male, restricted to rear in female.

Vocalisations Distinctive, chattering, rattling *peep-chree-chree-chree-chree-chree*. Also single, sharp *peek* or *chiik*. Multi-functional *peep* note like that of Arizona Woodpecker.

Drumming Both sexes drum, male more so, but little information.

Status Range-restricted, poorly known and probably declining. Main threats are loss and fragmentation of forest to felling and over-grazing by livestock.

Habitat High-elevation tropical and temperate, open, humid, pine forests. Also mixed pine-fir-oak-alder.

Range Endemic to upland in C Mexico. Restricted and fragmented distribution in central volcano belt from E Michoacan to WC Veracruz and Puebla. Mainly uplands between 2500–4200m. Resident and sedentary.

Taxonomy and variation Monotypic. Formerly lumped, as nominate race, with two other races that now form Arizona Woodpecker. Barred birds may possibly be hybrids with most southerly occurring Arizona Woodpeckers, but more study needed.

Similar species Arizona Woodpecker (though ranges hardly coincide) is paler brown overall, mostly unbarred above, chest more spotted and less streaked, and longer-billed.

Food and foraging Mainly insects, especially beetle larvae. Some fruit and conifer seeds. Usually forages alone, occasionally joins mixed-species flocks.

◄ Adult male Strickland's Woodpecker. Darker and more barred above than Arizona Woodpecker, with which it was once considered conspecific. Morelos, Mexico, March (*Fernando Urbina Torres*).

124. RED-COCKADED WOODPECKER
Picoides borealis

L 20–22cm

Identification Distinctly barred black and white above. Rump plain black. Whitish below, belly and flanks spotted and flecked. Relatively long tail mostly black, outer feathers white with black dots. Blackish wings barred and spotted white. Central tail feathers black, outers white with some black dots. Crown solid black. Ear-coverts white. Black malar continues down onto chest sides. Slender bill grey. Iris chestnut. Legs greyish. Sexes very similar: male has inconspicuous red fleck (cockade) at the side of hindcrown, usually revealed only when excited; female lacks cockade. Juvenile distinct until autumn, dull black or brown with dusky ear-coverts and white-flecked forehead; some juveniles have red crown patch.

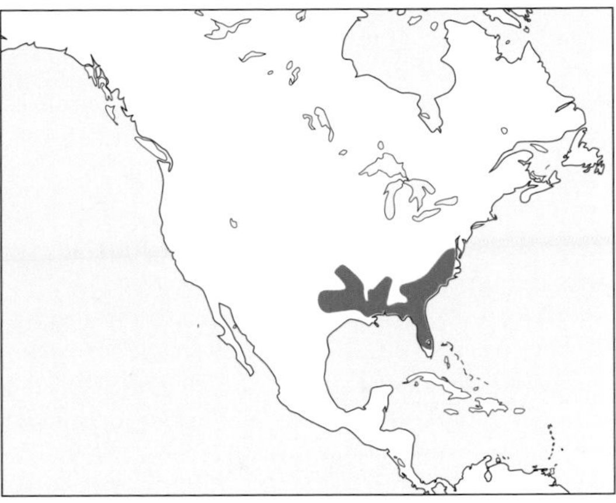

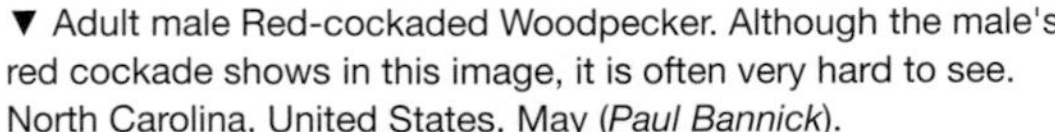

▼ Adult male Red-cockaded Woodpecker. Although the male's red cockade shows in this image, it is often very hard to see. North Carolina, United States, May (*Paul Bannick*).

▼ Adult male Red-cockaded Woodpecker. Note the ringed (banded) leg: this woodpecker is among most studied in the world. Florida, United States, May (*Judd Patterson*).

Vocalisations Fairly vocal. *Sklit, she-u* and *shurz* alarm calls. A sharp *churt,* rasping, nasal *shirrp* or *shrrit,* high-pitched, buzzing *tsick* and shrill, squeaky *kweeks,* in rapid, bubbling or trilling series when agitated. Also chattering *wicka* notes and a rattling, falling *shirrp-chrch-chrch-chrch.*

Drumming Paired birds occasionally drum, unattached males more often. Rolls produced on live pines are particularly quiet and dull.

Status NT. One of the most-studied woodpeckers. Most populations small, isolated and declining, due mainly to over-logging. Lives in small clans that breed cooperatively, monogamous pairs sometimes helped by a non-breeding (usually male) offspring. In 2000 an overall population of 11,000 birds estimated, limited to about 30 populations. Some have recovered after intense conservation measures including restoration of natural fire-regimes, understorey clearance, selective logging, habitat corridor creation, translocation of young females to clans lacking such and incentives to landowners to implement beneficial forest management. Current population estimated at maximum 15,000.

Habitat Specialised. Open, old-growth, fire-sustained pinewoods with sparse, savanna-like understorey. Mainly long-leaf, loblolly and short-leaf pinewoods, in some areas pine-oak and pine species including slash, Virginia, pond, and pitch pines. Excavates nest-holes in living trees, usually pines more than 100 years old with heart-rot. Small holes drilled around the entrance seep sap that deters predators such as snakes, hence trees with high resin flow needed.

Range Endemic to lowland SE USA. Originally distributed from Texas to Atlantic coast as far N as Maryland. Now fragmented, occurring in Arkansas, Alabama, Florida, Georgia, Kentucky, Louisiana, Mississippi, the Carolinas, Oklahoma, Tennessee, Texas and Virginia. Resident and essentially sedentary.

Taxonomy and variation Monotypic. Variation slight.

Similar species Bigger Hairy and smaller Downy Woodpecker have unbarred backs.

Food and foraging Forages for arboreal ants, spiders, bark-beetles and other invertebrates by scaling and flaking pines. Clans feed (and roost) together. Conifer seeds and berries also taken.

◄ Adult female at the nesting cavity with prey. This species has a complex and fascinating breeding biology. This individual is a member of a well-studied clan. North Carolina, United States, May (*Paul Bannick*).

125. WHITE-HEADED WOODPECKER
Picoides albolarvatus

L 22–24cm

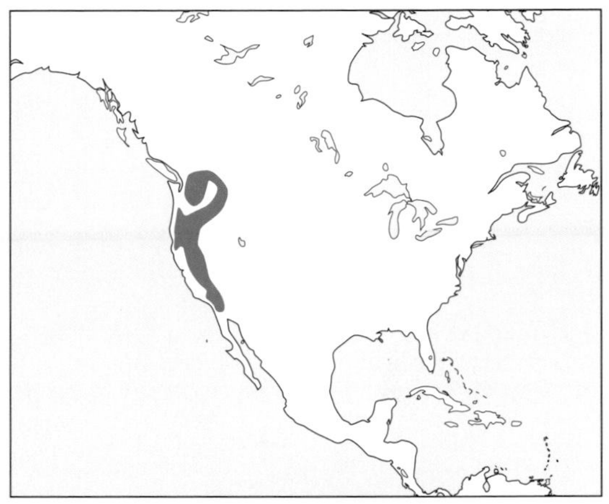

Identification Most of body, nape and tail black, with some glossy bluish tones. Forehead, forecrown, throat, face and chest white. Faint dark post-ocular line. Black wings with white in primaries forming patch, more obvious in flight. Iris chestnut. Bill and legs greyish. Sexes differ: male has red nape, female black. Juvenile browner, white wing-patch larger; male with orange or red patch on mid-crown, female usually lacks red.
Vocalisations Common call a sharp, metallic *peek-it* or *pi-tik,* sometimes *pee-de-dink.* Clicking, rattling, repeated, rapid series of *peek* or *kik* notes in disputes. Variants include *pee-dink, peek, peek, peek* and *pee-kikikikikik.* Also slow, squeaky but loud, repeated *kweek* notes. Gentle *chuf* and *tyet* made by mated pairs.
Drumming Both sexes drum, males more so. Medium-

► Adult male nominate White-headed Woodpecker. The small red nape-patch separates the male from the female. Oregon, United States, June (*Ginger Livingston Sanders*).

paced, 1-second rolls of 20 strikes per second. Variable, increasing or decreasing in tempo.

Status Overall considered stable, but range-restricted and absent from many apparently suitable areas. Has declined in Washington and now endangered in Canada, where scarce in British Columbia. Intensive forestry is main reason for decline, with clear-cutting, snag removal and fire suppression all being detrimental.

Habitat Upland conifer forests, particularly of mature ponderosa, Jeffrey, Coulter and sugar pines. Also mixed pine-fir-cedar-aspen forests and mature pine plantations.

Range North America. Confined to west of continent. Scattered populations from SW Canada into USA (Washington, Oregon, Idaho, California, W Nevada). Up to 3200m. Resident and mainly sedentary, although some descend to lower elevations in winter and dispersal of over 100km recorded, both probably prompted by poor food resources.

Taxonomy and variation Two similar races: ***albolarvatus*** (S British Columbia into W USA) and ***gravirostris*** (S California: mountains above Los Angeles and San Diego), which has longer bill and tail than nominate.

Similar species None: black body and white head unique in range.

Food and foraging Specialist in eating the seeds of large-coned pines; biggest items processed at an anvil (usually a bark crevice). Sap also consumed from specifically drilled and maintained wells, told from those of sapsuckers by larger size and tendency to be on only one side of tree. Insects also taken, but plant food relied upon in autumn and winter when prey is depleted. Feeders near forests visited.

► Juvenile male White-headed Woodpecker has red on the mid-crown, not on the nape as in the adult male. This is a nominate bird. California, United States, August (*Greg R. Homel*).

▼ Adult female nominate, feeding a well-grown male nestling (note the red on the head) at the cavity entrance. Oregon, United States, August (*Richard Tipton*).

126. SMOKY-BROWN WOODPECKER
Picoides fumigatus

L 16–18cm

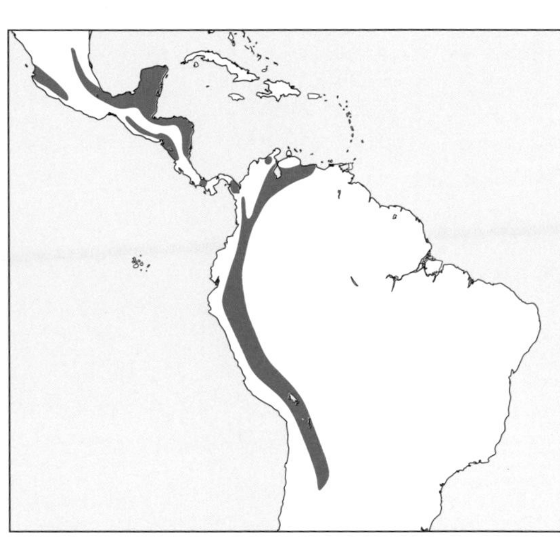

Identification Compact. Mostly plain brownish-olive. Face, ear-coverts, underparts and undertail-coverts paler than upperparts. Tail chocolate. Flight feathers slightly barred pale. Some rufous or ochre tones to mantle when fresh, tawny on scapulars. White or cream lores and sometimes ocular area. Dark or dusky malar. Iris dark. Bill and legs greyish. Sexes differ slightly: male has reddish crown and nape, flecked black; female usually lacks red, crown brownish (sometimes rufous at front), overall paler, rather drab. Juvenile very dull, even sooty, male with reduced reddish crown, female rufous on forecrown.

Vocalisations Characteristic song a buzzing, even-pitched, series of 10–20 *dze* notes with final note lower, and also described as a rolling *zur-zur-zur.* Various single, sharp *chip, chik, chak, chuk* notes, a softer *quip* and gruffer *kik* or *zick.* Similar notes linked in giggling, chattering series recalling Orange-chinned Parakeet, rapid when alarmed. Also squeaky *chika-chika* or *wicka-wicka* and high-pitched *keer-keer-keer.*

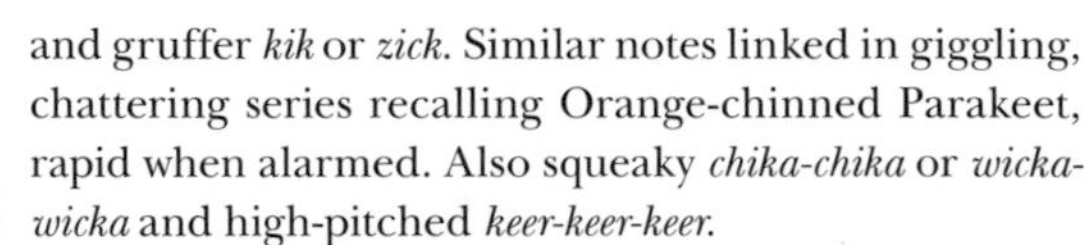

Drumming Brief, gentle, quiet, level-pitched, rapid 1-second rolls produced.

Status Occurs across large range and overall population considered stable, but densities thin and nowhere abundant.

Habitat Very varied across range. In Andes mainly tropical, mountain rainforest, *yungas,* cloud forest; in lowlands, particularly Central American, wet thickets, riparian woods, partially felled forest, even coffee plantations.

Range Mexico to Argentina. Only *Picoides* in southern hemisphere. In Andean region often at high elevations, sometimes at tree line. In Venezuela from 700–3000m. In Central America much lower. Resident and sedentary.

Taxonomy and variation Subject of taxonomic uncertainty, including previous inclusion in *Veniliornis.* Five current races: ***fumigatus*** (E Panama, Colombia, Ecuador, E Peru, Bolivia, NW Argentina); ***oleagineus*** (E Mexico) is long-winged with white supercilium and line above malar; ***sanguinolentus*** (C Mexico, Belize,

◄ Adult male nominate Smoky-brown Woodpecker. Males have a red crown, which is not always obvious and can be heavily flecked dark; otherwise the sexes are very similar. NW Ecuador, February (*Glenn Bartley*).

Guatemala, El Salvador, Honduras, Nicaragua, Costa Rica, W Panama) is short-winged and deep brown overall; ***reichenbachi*** (N Venezuela) is rather dull; ***obscuratus*** (SW Ecuador to NW Peru) is longest-winged and dark. Intergrades occur.

Similar species Distinct within range. Red-rumped Woodpecker greener above, barred below.

Food and foraging Forages low or high in shady thickets and tangled vegetation for insects, usually excavating for wood-boring beetle larvae. Often in unobtrusive pairs and joins mixed-species foraging flocks.

▼ Adult female nominate. Besides lacking red on the head, females also usually have duller brownish tones than the males. Pichincha, Ecuador, May (*Nick Athanas*).

127. EURASIAN THREE-TOED WOODPECKER
Picoides tridactylus

L 20–23cm

Identification Blunt-tailed, compact. Mostly black, chocolate and white. Variable, nominate described here. White back panel joined by white bars from sides of face. Throat white. White below; flanks and belly lightly barred or streaked greyish. Broad white post-ocular stripe runs to mantle. Broad black band over ear-coverts. Bold black malar reaches chest. Scapulars, lower back, rump and uppertail-coverts black or brown. Wings black or chocolate, coverts sometimes dotted white, primaries with bolder spots creating bars. Mostly black tail, outer feathers spotted white. Bill grey or black. Iris reddish. Legs grey, three toes. Sexes differ: male has black crown, flecked grey or white at the fore, yellow on mid-crown; female lacks yellow with all-grey crown. Juvenile less glossy, lightly barred grey, underparts more heavily barred, iris paler red. Juvenile male like adult, but with less yellow on crown; most juvenile females lack yellow, although some have a touch on forecrown.

Vocalisations Soft *bik* or *kip* and fluid *kjick* or *kyuk*, strung in rapid series *kipkipkipkipkip* when agitated. Rattling *kree-kree-kree*. A chugging, engine-like *watsch-watsch-watsch* during encounters.

Drumming Both sexes actively drum in spring. Rattling volleys start hesitantly before gathering speed and rhythm, but much variation. Typically about 1.3-second rolls long with 14–26 strikes.

Status Locally common during bark-beetle outbreaks, otherwise uncommon. Overall stable, but has declined locally in Finland, now rare on Hokkaido. Intensive forestry methods detrimental.

Habitat Mature boreal conifer and mixed old-growth forests with many dead or dying trees. Norway spruce favoured, but pine, fir, larch, birch, and locally beech, ash, alder, oak and hornbeam used.

Range Eurasia. Europe to Far East. Isolated populations in Alps, Balkans, Altai and Tien Shan Mts. Resident, but irrupts, invading areas where fire or storms have killed trees and beetle numbers increased. Lowlands to around 4000m.

Taxonomy and variation Formerly lumped with American Three-toed Woodpecker as single Northern Hemisphere species. Studies of DNA sequence divergence between Old and New World populations resulted in the split. Differences in morphology, calls and plumage, also. Wide racial and individual variations, mainly in face, back and underpart markings. Eight races: ***tridactylus*** (Fenno-Scandia, N Europe to S Urals, SE Siberia and NE China); ***alpinus*** (Alps, Carpathians, Balkans) has narrow white head stripes, white throat, rest of underparts streaked or barred chocolate, brownish rump dotted white, and most (but variable) with smaller, darkly barred white back

► Adult male Eurasian Three-toed Woodpecker of race *alpinus*. Males of all races have yellow on the crown, which the females lack. Stuhleck, Austria, June (*Otto Samwald*).

▲ Adult male nominate. Northern birds are generally paler than southern ones, but this is a particularly snowy-white individual. Northwest Finland, May (*Harri Taavetti*).

panel; ***crissoleucus*** (N Siberia: N Urals, N Mongolia, E Siberia) very white, plain on breast, flanks and belly streaked or barred; ***albidior*** (Kamtchatka) plain white back, clean white underparts; ***tianschanicus*** (E Kazakhstan, W China) white from throat to belly, flanks very barred; ***kurodai*** (NE China, N Korea) and ***inouyei*** (Hokkaido, Japan) like previous; ***funebris*** (C China) very dark, minimal white on back, blackish below barred and spotted white.

Similar species None: does not meet very similar American Three-toed Woodpecker.

Food and foraging Specialises in engraver and spruce bark-beetles (*Ips* and *Polygraphus* species) taken from dead standing trees. Also wood-boring beetles and other invertebrates. Leaves distinct markings on trunks which may relate to sap-sucking.

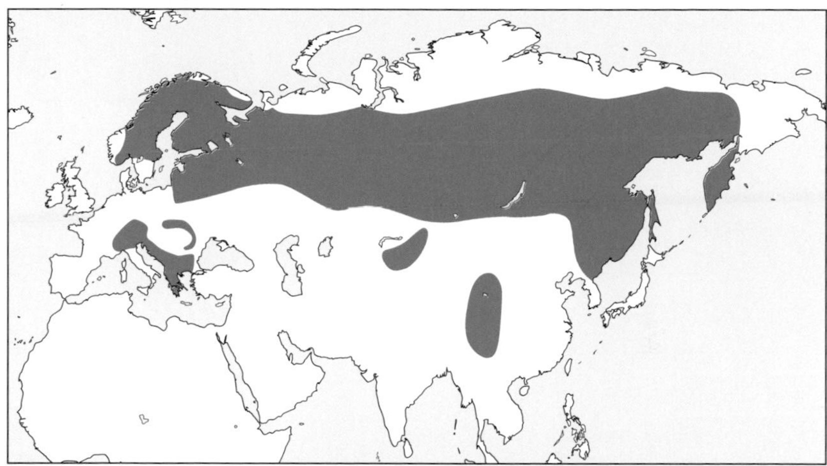

▼ Adult female *alpinus*. This southern European race is quite variable in plumage, but it is generally more darkly marked than the nominate to the north. Dürrenstein, Austria, June (*Otto Samwald*).

▼► Adult male *funebris*. A very dark race, with white spotting and barring on black underparts. Qinghai, China, July (*Paul Noakes*).

▲ Adult female nominate. Note the greyish crown. Northwest Finland, May (*Harri Taavetti*).

128. AMERICAN THREE-TOED WOODPECKER
Picoides dorsalis

L 20–22cm

Identification Compact, pied. Face striped: variable white supercilium, glossy black crown, ear-coverts and nape, white moustache, black malar. Bushy grey nasal tufts. Mainly black or chocolate above with white area on mantle and back variably barred black. White from throat to vent, barred black on flanks and undertail-coverts. Wings brownish, flecked and dotted white on primaries. Outer tail feathers white, inners black, undertail brown and white. Iris chestnut. Robust grey bill. Legs grey, three toes. Sexes differ: male has yellow forecrown flecked grey or white; female glossy black crown flecked grey or white. Juvenile duller black, iris grey or brown, male with mustard forehead patch, lacking or minimal on female.

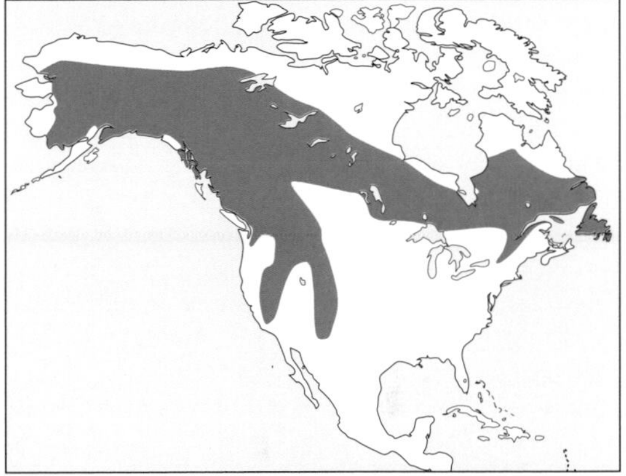

► Adult male *fasciatus* American Three-toed Woodpecker. There is yellow on the forecrown, which the female lacks. This race is very barred. British Columbia, Canada, June (*Glenn Bartley*).

Vocalisations Often silent, vocal mostly in early breeding period. Territorial calls include sharp, rattling *kli-kli-kli-kli,* uttered both in flight and at rest. Series of squeaky, whinnying *kweek* or *twitt* notes; very squeaky, rapid *wicka* when agitated. Contact calls high-pitched but flat *pwik, pik* or *kip.*

Drumming Both sexes drum. Steady rolls of clear knocks, accelerating before trailing off, lasting just over 1 second. Tempo varies according to situation, a fast version (c. 14 strikes per second) produced by birds in dispute.

Status Perhaps increasing, but modern forestry practices, including clear-cutting, fire suppression, removal of dead trees and pesticide use, have caused local declines.

Habitat Mature boreal coniferous forest, especially spruce, fir and lodgepole pine. Also swamp and taiga forest. In S, upland coniferous forests. Standing dead or dying trees always important. Avoids intensively managed forests.

Range North America. From Alaska and boreal Canada to mountains of W USA, New Mexico and Arizona. Up to 3350m. Resident, though irruptions occur when food scarce.

Taxonomy and variation Formerly lumped with Eurasian Three-toed Woodpecker as single Northern Hemisphere species. Three races. Plumage progressively darker from W to E, those in E Canada darkest. Amount of black barring on white back varies: ***dorsalis*** (Rockies from Montana to Nevada and New Mexico) has least black; ***bacatus*** (Alberta, Labrador, Newfoundland, to Minnesota and NE USA) most black, often minimal white; ***fasciatus*** (Alaska to Oregon, N Idaho and W Montana) evenly barred black and white.

Similar species Within range most like Black-backed Woodpecker, but that species larger, longer-billed and lacks white back and supercilium.

Food and foraging Important natural controller of bark and wood-boring beetles, invading dying forests where these insects explode in number after fire, storm damage or disease. Occasionally makes sap wells.

▲ Juvenile male *fasciatus* American Three-toed Woodpecker. Birds of this species can be sexed while still in the nest; the distinct yellow forecrown-patch indicates a male. Oregon, United States, July (*Stephen Shunk*).

◀ Adult female *fasciatus*. Note the burnt tree bark: this woodpecker seeks out and forages in fire-ravaged forests. British Columbia, Canada, June (*Glenn Bartley*).

129. BLACK-BACKED WOODPECKER
Picoides arcticus

L 23–25cm

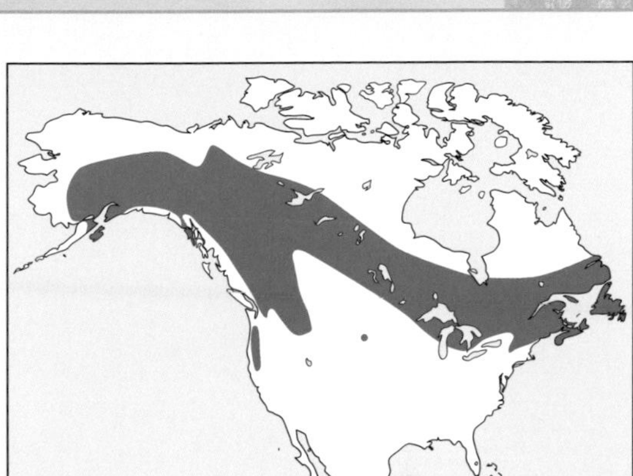

Identification Stocky, appears large-headed. Plain black above from head to rump. White below from throat to vent, flanks barred black. Wings black, primaries and secondaries lightly barred white. Tail mostly black, outer feathers white. Black face crossed by white stripe running from the lores below the ear-coverts. Iris reddish. Long grey bill. Legs grey, three toes. Sexes differ slightly: male has yellow central crown, female black. Juveniles of both sexes may have yellow or orange on crown; duller black above and more buffy below than adults.

Vocalisations Fairly vocal. Single *chet* note uttered year-round, often in flight, and a flat *kip*. A distinctive, rapid, grating, rattling, clicking series, beginning with a 'scream', ending in a rasping 'snarl', given in disputes. Fast, sharp, low-pitched double-click *pik-pik*. Single *wreo* used as greeting, *pet-pet-wreo* as an alarm. In spring, shorter rattling *kyik-ek* of up to 4 notes functions as beckoning call to a mate.

Drumming Both sexes drum. Drawn-out, level-pitched, accelerating 2-second rolls. Bursts often separated by 30–40 seconds. Females said to drum faster than males, producing more beats per roll.

Status Overall considered stable, though trends hard to judge due to natural population swings. Uncommon locally except when invasions occur. Suffers from forestry methods: removal of insect-infested trees, fire suppression and salvage logging.

Habitat Boreal, taiga and montane coniferous forests, particularly burnt stands with dead trees, snags and fallen timber. Often does not occupy an area until timber hosts the highest beetle densities, 2–3 years after a fire or storm.

Range North America. Boreal belt from Alaska through Canada S of tree-line to Nova Scotia. Southwards in W as far as California and Nevada, in E to Adirondack Mts, New York. Sea level to 3100m. Resident and non-migratory, but irrupts, leaving regular range in small parties. When food is scarce, winter irruptions also occur, even into urban areas.

Taxonomy and variation Monotypic. Variation slight.

Similar species Sympatric American Three-toed

► Adult male Black-backed Woodpecker. Males have a distinct patch of yellow on the crown; females lack yellow, and have a solid black crown. British Columbia, Canada, June (*Glenn Bartley*).

Woodpecker (particularly dark *bacatus* race) similar, but smaller, shorter-billed and barred black and white above. Male Black-backed has smaller, more solid yellow crown patch than male Three-toed. Female's plain black crown unlike paler, streaked crown of Three-toed.

Food and foraging A prey specialist that invades burnt conifer forests after outbreaks of wood-boring and bark-dwelling beetles. An effective natural controller of these insects. Pines are favoured. Also takes other invertebrates and some seeds and fruits.

◄ Adult female on a recently burnt tree: note lack of yellow. Like American Three-toed Woodpecker, this species invades forests in numbers after fires, once wood-boring beetle populations have increased. British Columbia, Canada, June (*Glenn Bartley*).

▼ Adult male Black-backed Woodpecker. Within its boreal range, this species is most similar to American Three-toed Woodpecker *Picoides dorsalis*, though it is larger, blacker and less streaked. Ontario, Canada, March (*Amanda Lahaie*).

VENILIORNIS

A New World genus of 14 species, all occurring in Latin America. Highly arboreal, they are often inconspicuous, foraging from mid-heights to canopy level in fast-moving mixed-species foraging flocks. The *Veniliornis* are small, mostly plain green or pied above (two species are very red) and variably barred below. Males have red on the crown, which females lack. There have been several exchanges of species between this genus and genus *Picoides.*

Little Woodpecker *Veniliornis passerinus*.
Adult female. Pantanal, Brazil (*Hermann Brehm*).

130. SCARLET-BACKED WOODPECKER
Veniliornis callonotus

L 13–15cm

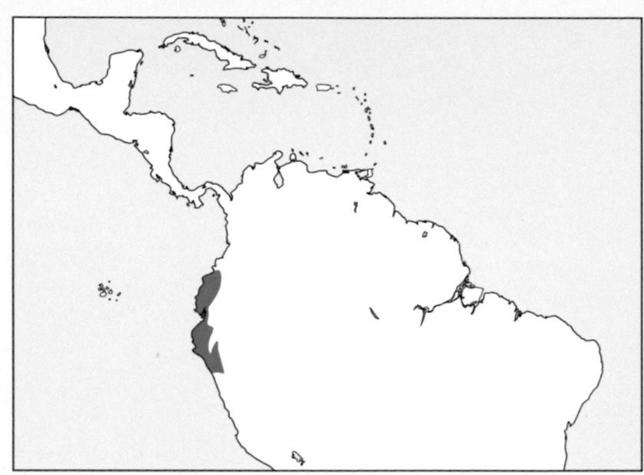

Identification Striking scarlet on upperparts and wings, with some brownish tones. Cream to white below, finely barred or mottled grey. Blackish tail barred white or buff on outer feathers. Wings mostly reddish, flight feathers browner. Ear-coverts and ocular area dusky-brown. Cheek, neck and throat white. Iris chestnut. Bill ivory or yellow, darker on tip and base. Legs greyish. Sexes differ: male has red crown and nape variably streaked black; female black from forehead to nape, sometimes with white tips on nape. Juvenile more like adult female, but buff below, mottled greenish-grey above. Juvenile male may have red on forecrown.

Vocalisations Fast, strident, high-pitched, 1–2-seconds-long rattling *keer-r-r-r-r-r-r-r*. Single, sharp *kik* and double *ki-dik*, often repeated in a rapid series. Sometimes a more liquid *quip* and *quip-ik*, also linked in a fast, bubbling series.

Drumming Several quickly repeated 1-second rolls.

Status Common locally in Ecuador and Peru, rarer in Colombia. Seems to be expanding into more humid forests, perhaps due to clearance of favoured arid habitats.

Habitat Dry, open deciduous woodlands, thickets, arid scrub and cactus country with scattered trees. Also degraded, fragmented forests and riparian woods.

Range South America. Restricted to parts of Colombia, Ecuador and NW Peru, but possibly spreading. Mainly lowlands and foothills, but to 1500m in Peru and 1800m in Ecuador. Resident and presumably sedentary.

Taxonomy and variation Two races: ***callonotus*** (SW Colombia, NW Ecuador) and ***major*** (SW Ecuador, NW Peru), which is more barred below, cleaner white behind distinct brown ear-covert patch, male with more black streaking in red crown than nominate. Some birds have a slight dark malar. Intergrades with mixed features occur.

Similar species None: a visually atypical *Veniliornis*. Main call recalls Golden-olive Woodpecker.

Food and foraging Presumably small invertebrates, but precise information lacking. Often in pairs or families, working in trees and scrub at most levels, usually on twigs and thinner outer limbs.

◄ Adult male Scarlet-backed Woodpecker of race *major*. Males of this species have a red crown flecked with black. Northern Peru, November (*Glenn Bartley*).

▲ Adult female Scarlet-backed Woodpecker. Females have an all-black crown. This bird is probably of race *major*, although this intergrades with the nominate in parts of southern Ecuador (indeed, this bird has features suggestive of both races). Macara, Ecuador, October (*Murray Cooper*).

► Adult male *major*. The most distinctive member of the genus – unmistakable. Bosque de Pomac, Peru, November (*Gerard Gorman*).

131. YELLOW-VENTED WOODPECKER
Veniliornis dignus

L 15–18cm

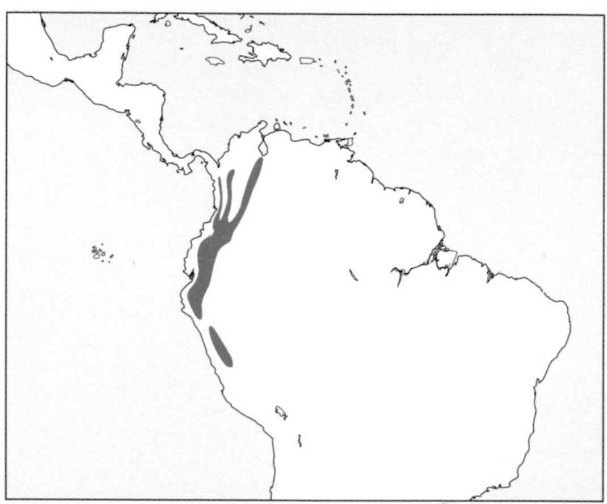

Identification Back olive-green with yellowish and bronze tones and red flecking. Olive rump and uppertail-coverts barred buff. Chest, breast and belly yellowish barred black, grey or olive. Undertail-coverts and vent plain yellow. Throat tightly barred black or grey. Ear-coverts dusky, bordered at rear by white post-ocular stripe, below by thin white moustachial line. Chin and throat finely barred black-and-white. Olive or brown wings with buff dots or streaks on upper-coverts, flight feathers browner, underwing barred brown, buff or white. Dark olive tail barred yellow on outer feathers, uppertail-coverts barred golden. Upper mandible dark grey, lower bluish-grey. Iris reddish. Legs grey. Sexes differ slightly: male has black-flecked red crown, nape and mantle; female red only from nape to mantle, crown blackish. Juvenile greener below, less yellow, both sexes with some red on crown.

Vocalisations Often quiet. Occasionally utters a weak, rapid, nasal, rattling *chrrrrrr*, *krrrrrr* or *keer-r-r-r-r-r*. Long trill, not unlike Golden-olive Woodpecker, but higher-pitched and faster. *Wicka-wicka* contact call recalls Red-rumped Woodpecker.

Drumming May not drum, or perhaps only rarely, but information lacking.

Status Scarce in Venezuela and Peru, uncommon in Ecuador, more common in Colombia. Population data lacking, but considered stable.

Habitat Tropical and subtropical, humid and wet, mossy, primary mountain forests, particularly cloud forest, above most other woodpeckers. In some areas mature or abandoned plantations.

Range South America. Upland Venezuela, E, W and C Andes in Colombia, Ecuador and Peru. From 1000m to 2700m, but mainly above 1700m. Resident and sedentary.

Taxonomy and variation Three races: ***dignus*** (extreme SW Venezuela, Colombia, N Ecuador) is long-billed, throat and breast barring tight and dark, lightly barred on uppertail-coverts; ***baezae*** (Ecuador: E Andean slope) is heavily and evenly barred below, paler on throat and relatively short-billed; ***valdizani*** (Peru: E Andean slope) is lightly barred on rump and has longest bill. White dots on wing coverts not always present.

Similar species Bar-bellied Woodpecker slightly larger, uniformly barred from chin to vent and generally at higher elevations.

Food and foraging Insects, but no detailed information. Usually forages discreetly on thinner limbs in cover and canopy. Often solitary, sometimes in pairs and loosely associates with mixed-species flocks.

► Adult female nominate. This poorly known species occurs mainly in northern Andean forests. Carchi, Ecuador, June (*Nick Athanas*).

◄ Adult male nominate Yellow-vented Woodpecker. Males differ from females in having the whole crown red, while females only have red at the rear. Cali, Colombia, February (*Peter Hawrylyshyn*).

132. BAR-BELLIED WOODPECKER
Veniliornis nigriceps

L 17–19cm

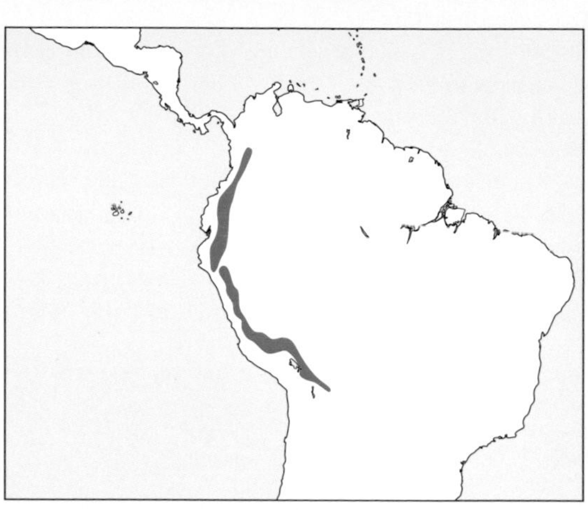

Identification Smoky-olive above, mottled bronze or reddish on mantle and back, rump spotted pale. Cream underparts variably barred dark olive or blackish, breast sometimes more ochre. Wings olive, brown or bronze, pale underwing barred brown. Uppertail black, outer two feathers barred white. Throat variably barred grey, buff or olive, neck-sides tinged golden. Ear-coverts dusky brown, finely streaked white. Slight, often indistinct, white moustachial streak. Short white supercilium, sometimes just a fleck. Iris chestnut; orbital ring grey. Bill greyish, base paler. Legs grey or olive. Sexes differ: male scarlet from forecrown to nape, flecked black; female lacks this red (although some rufous tips and golden tones may show), being all black. Juveniles more like adult male as both sexes have red on crown, less so on female; also greener overall and tail heavily barred.

Vocalisations Rather silent. Rising then falling, high-pitched *kree-kree-kree, kee-kee-kee* or *quee-quee-quee* of around 25 notes, recalling a small falcon. Fast, falling, chattering, sometimes trilling, described as *djeerdjeerd-jeer* and *kzzrrrr.* Repeated, squeaky, liquid *tuip* or *quip* notes and single, simple, soft *chik* or *chek* contact calls. Fast, repeated *wicka* series when excited.

Drumming Occasional, rapid, repeated, short rolls produced. Detailed information lacking.

Status Fairly common locally, but generally uncommon and thinly spread. Poorly known, perhaps overlooked, but overall population considered stable.

Habitat Temperate, humid or wet, cloud and elfin forests. Also upland stunted-growth forests, bamboo stands, *paramo* woods, thickets and cane-breaks, all with thick understorey.

Range South America. Restricted to Andes in Colombia, Ecuador, Peru and Bolivia. Between 2000–4000m, sometimes at tree-line. Resident and probably sedentary.

Taxonomy and variation Three races: ***nigriceps*** (Bolivian Andes: Cochabamba and W Santa Cruz) is tightly barred below; ***equifasciatus*** (Andes of N Colombia and Ecuador) has broad, clearly spaced

◄ Adult male Bar-bellied Woodpecker of the nominate race. The amount of black in the red crown of males varies greatly. Machu Picchu, Peru, January (*Greg Lavaty*).

blackish barring; ***pectoralis*** (Peruvian Andes) has broader dark and narrower pale barring. Females of last two races have dusky crown, nominate female's is blacker.

Similar species Differs from very similar, but smaller, Yellow-vented Woodpecker (mostly occurs at lower elevations) in being all-barred below. Dot-fronted Woodpecker hardly overlaps.

Food and foraging Presumably insects, but information lacking. Forages discreetly at all levels from the canopy to low in shrubs and undergrowth and is easily overlooked. Often in mixed-species flocks.

► Adult female Bar-bellied Woodpecker has a black crown. All females have rufous on the nape. This is the nominate. Machu Picchu, Peru, October (*Greg Lavaty*).

133. LITTLE WOODPECKER
Veniliornis passerinus

L 14–16cm

Identification Olive-green above with bronze tones and faint buff flecks. Wings green, median-coverts dotted white, flight feathers browner with some white bars. Dusky or olive below, finely barred buff or white. Undertail-coverts heavily barred white, grey or olive. Tail brown, outer feathers slightly barred buff. Face and ear-coverts dusky, neck faintly flecked pale. White moustachial line faint or absent on some races. Throat finely barred buff. Iris chestnut. Bill greyish. Legs greyish. Sexes differ: males red on crown, nape flecked grey; females lack red, crown grey dotted white. Both juveniles have red (less so on female) on white-dotted grey crown, pale iris and irregular barring below.

Vocalisations Rising, strident *ki-ki-ki* or *wi-wi-wi* series. Single, sharp *kik* and squeakier *kwip* notes. Sharp, rising, chattering *wuwuwuwiwiwi* and high-pitched rattling *wika-wika-wika*.

► Male Little Woodpeckers of all races differ from the adult females in having red on the crown. This bird is of the race *taeionotus*. Ceará, Brazil, July (*João Quental*).

Drumming Repeated, level-pitched, 1-second rolls produced.

Status Widespread and not uncommon overall, but perhaps declining locally due to deforestation.

Habitat Various forests used, including *várzea*, *caatinga*, gallery forests, bamboo, mangroves, plantations and degraded stands, in some regions drier savanna, gardens and cloud forest. In Amazonian Brazil usually in riverine secondary growth.

Range South America. Occurs over vast area from Colombia and Venezuela to Bolivia and Argentina. Sea-level to 1300m. Resident and sedentary.

Taxonomy and variation Nine races: ***passerinus*** (the Guianas, NE Brazil) has pale bill and narrow pale barring below; ***modestus*** (NE Venezuela) yellowish above, with clear white moustache and spotting on wings; ***fidelis*** (E Colombia, W Venezuela) also has moustache, yellowish tail barring and scalloped breast; ***diversus*** (N Brazil) has indistinct moustache, broad barring below, males with grey forecrown; ***agilis*** (E Ecuador, Peru, N Bolivia, W Brazil) has thin moustache and superciium; ***insignis*** (WC Brazil) is smallest race, lacks moustache, male has grey forecrown; ***tapujozensis*** (C Brazil) is yellowish above with rufous spots; ***taenionotus*** (E Brazil) is yellowish-green above speckled red, with broad barring below and large wing-covert spots; ***olivinus*** (S Brazil, Paraguay, S Bolivia, N Argentina) is largest race, male with red only on hind-crown and nape.

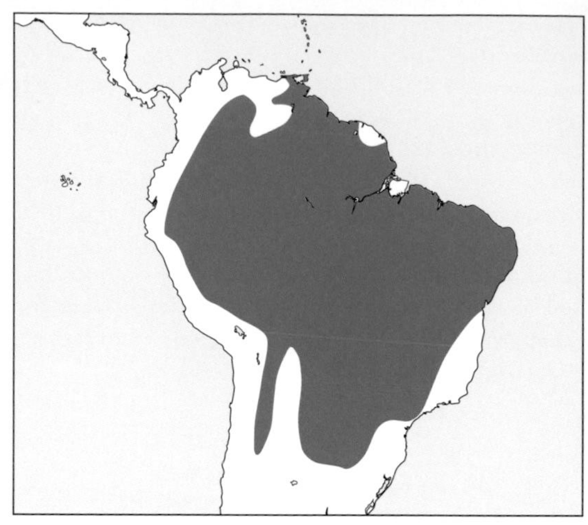

Similar species Dot-fronted Woodpecker larger, more spotted above and marked on face. Other similar relatives yellow on nape and neck.

Food and foraging Arboreal ants, termites, beetles and other invertebrates. Often unobtrusive, foraging at most levels, alone or in mixed-species flocks.

◄ Adult female Little Woodpecker lacks red, the crown being grey speckled with white. This is the nominate race. French Guiana, November (*Michel Giraud-Audine*).

▼ Adult male *olivinus*. The lack of yellow on the nape and neck helps separate this species from similar *Veniliornis*. Mato Grosso, Brazil (*Cláudio Timm*).

▲ Adult male; *olivinus* has the least red on the crown of all the races. Mato Grosso, Brazil (*Cláudio Timm*).

► Adult female *olivinus*. Little Woodpecker is the most widespread *Veniliornis*. Mato Grosso, Brazil (*Cláudio Timm*).

134. DOT-FRONTED WOODPECKER
Veniliornis frontalis

L 16–17cm

Identification Olive above, finely flecked buff or yellow. Throat to undertail-coverts greyish barred white, very fine on throat, broader below. Mostly olive upperwings dotted white on coverts, scapulars with pale spotting, primaries browner with buff barring and edges. Underwings barred grey or buff. Tail brown, lightly barred buff or yellow. Greyish ear-coverts, cheeks and neck sides densely streaked pale. Olive tail barred white. Forehead grey or olive spotted white. Fine white supercilium and moustachial stripe. Iris black or brown. Bill dark grey, lower mandible paler. Legs grey. Sexes differ: male has red crown flecked grey; female lacks red, having grey or olive crown mottled white. Juvenile greyer than adult, both sexes with red on crown, less on female.

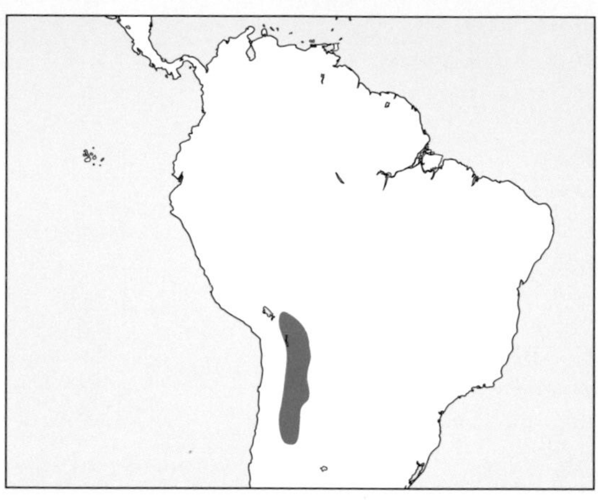

Vocalisations Single and repeated *yap* note, *pic* and *jik* in series and a harsher *wik*.

Drumming Short, solid, level-pitched, quickly repeated rolls produced.

Status Common locally. Population data lacking, but presumed stable.

Habitat Andean cloud-forest and subtropical forest. Also drier forests and wooded suburbs in foothills.

Range South America. Restricted to NW Argentina and S Bolivia. Andean foothills to around 2000m. Resident and mainly sedentary, though some altitudinal movements noted.

Taxonomy and variation Monotypic. Formerly lumped with Little Woodpecker. White facial lines sometimes indistinct.

Similar species Little Woodpecker slightly smaller, plainer above, less barred on tail.

Food and foraging Presumably insectivorous, like close relatives, but information lacking. Often forages low down.

▼ Adult male Dot-fronted Woodpecker, back and front. The red crown is marked with a variable amount of grey. The main confusion species is Little Woodpecker, which was formerly considered conspecific. Cachipampa, Salta, Argentina, November (*Graham Ekins*)

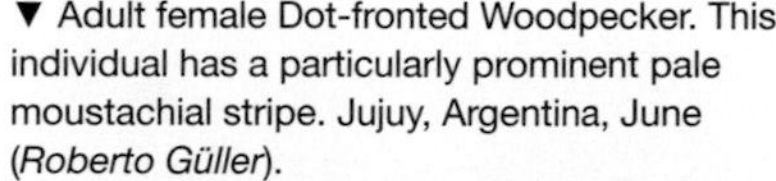

▼ Adult female Dot-fronted Woodpecker. This individual has a particularly prominent pale moustachial stripe. Jujuy, Argentina, June (*Roberto Güller*).

135. WHITE-SPOTTED WOODPECKER
Veniliornis spilogaster

L 17–19cm

Identification Rather even-toned overall. Dark olive below streaked white on throat, mottled on breast, barred on lower flanks, belly and vent. Olive above, barred and dotted yellow or buff. Green wing-coverts spotted white, browner flight feathers barred. Underwing barred brown and white. Olive-brown uppertail barred buff. Lores, face and throat paler; brownish ear-coverts streaked white. Long, thin, white supercilium extends onto olive neck-sides. White moustachial line from bill to neck-sides. Iris chestnut. Bill blackish or grey, yellowish base to lower mandible. Legs grey-olive. Sexes differ: male has blackish crown subtly streaked and speckled reddish and white; females lack red, having brownish crown dotted white. Female has shorter bill than male – sometimes noticeable in the field. Juvenile plainer, less marked above.

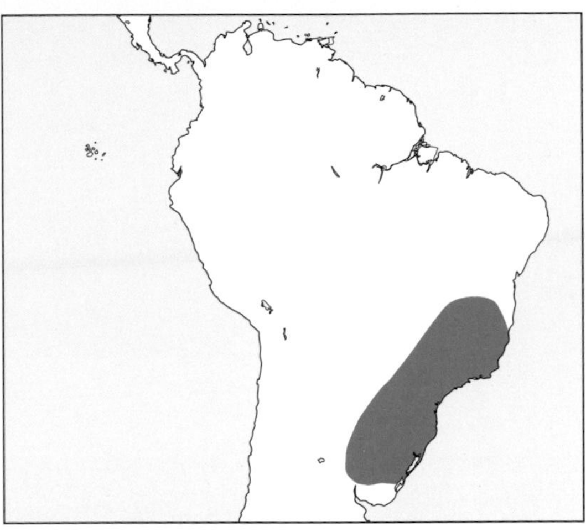

Vocalisations Fast or slowly repeated chattering notes. A harsh rattle and low-pitched *tjup-tjiddur, chip-ip* and *cheek-it*. Also single *pik* notes.

Drumming Short, rapid, level-pitched bursts, repeated after brief pauses.

Status Locally often common, even in cities like São Paulo. Population data lacking, but presumed to be stable.

Habitat Wide variety of woodlands occupied: rainforest edges, riverine forest, open humid woodland, parkland and to a lesser extent wooded savanna and drier forests.

Range South America. Confined to SE Brazil, SE Paraguay, Uruguay and extreme NE Argentina. Sea-level to around 2000m. Resident and sedentary.

Taxonomy and variation Monotypic. Occasional slight individual variation.

Similar species None within range, larger than Little Woodpecker.

Food and foraging Insects, especially beetle larvae. Also fruit and berries, so probably an important disperser of seeds.

◄ Adult male White-spotted Woodpeckers are not always as bright or well-marked as this stunning individual. Argentina, November (*Ramón Moller Jensen*).

◄ Adult female White-spotted Woodpecker lacks red, and is one of the plainer *Veniliornis*. Salto City, Uruguay, February (*Gonzalo Gonzalez*).

136. CHEQUERED WOODPECKER
Veniliornis mixtus

L 14–15cm

Identification Black or brown mantle and back spotted or barred (checkered) white. Underparts white, sometimes buff, sparsely streaked and scaled black. Wings and tail barred chocolate and white. White face with dusky brown ear-coverts forming a mask. Broad white supercilium. Thin, often broken, brown malar. Throat white, flecked brown. Iris chestnut. Bill grey with paler base. Legs grey. Sexes differ slightly: male has red or orange hindcrown and nape split by vertical black line and rest of crown black or brown faintly streaked white; female lacks red, having plain chocolate crown. Juvenile darker, more boldly marked below, both sexes with red on mid-crown but less red on female.

Vocalisations Sharp, high-pitched, rapid twittering *ti-ti-ti-ti* and a more bubbling *wutwitwitwitwih*. Also *wi-wi-wi-wi* and *kweh-weh-weh-weh-weh*. Single, soft *peek* notes.

Drumming Occasionally produces rapid, 1-second rolls, repeated after short pauses.

► Adult male Chequered Woodpecker of the nominate race. The small area of red visible on the hindcrown and the white-flecked crown indicate that this is a male. Buenos Aires, Argentina (*James Lowen*).

Status Often uncommon and local. Population data lacking, but presumed to be stable.

Habitat Mainly arid wooded savanna and *cerrado*. Also open, dry and damp woodlands, riverine woods, mesquite scrub, palm groves, roadside trees and urban parks.

Range South America. Brazil, Paraguay, Uruguay, Argentina and Bolivia. Sea-level to about 600m. Resident and sedentary.

Taxonomy and variation Previously in the *Picoides* but moved to current genus following molecular studies. Four races claimed, but some differences probably clinal, and study on limits needed: ***mixtus*** (N Argentina: Parana basin and most of Buenos Aires province); ***cancellatus*** (extreme E Bolivia, E Brazil, NE Paraguay, W Uruguay) browner than other races, with most white barring above, least marked and whitest below; ***malleator*** (Chaco region of N Argentina, Paraguay and SE Bolivia) has large dark ear-coverts patch, is boldly streaked below and barred on flanks; ***berlepschi*** (C Argentina: Córdoba S to Neuquen, Rio Negro and S of Buenos Aires Province) is dark with largest and darkest ear-covert patch. Some females are streaked pale on the crown, while some males have red feather tips.

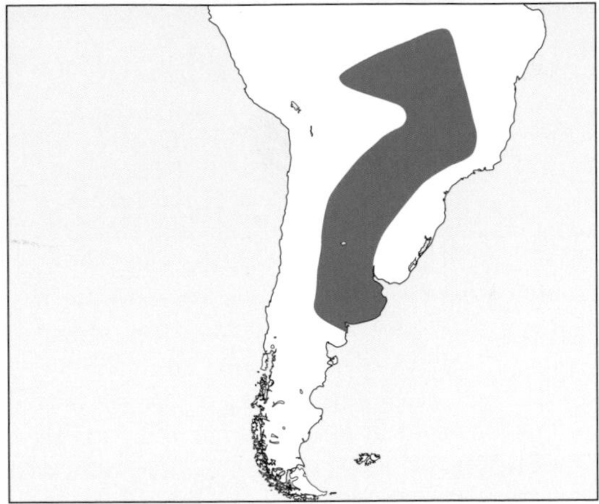

Similar species Striped Woodpecker is slightly larger and more pied, blacker above with more distinct white barring, more striped below, more boldly barred on the tail and dark ear-coverts are enclosed by white, but does not overlap in range.

Food and foraging Gleans insects from lower, thinner branches and twigs and in bushes. Also takes seeds, but precise information lacking.

▼ Adult female Chequered Woodpecker lacks red, and has an unstreaked dark brown crown. This is the nominate race. Entre Rios, Argentina, November (*Roberto Güller*).

▼ Adult male nominate. Within its range, this species cannot be confused with any other woodpecker. Buenos Aires, Argentina (*James Lowen*).

137. STRIPED WOODPECKER
Veniliornis lignarius

L 15–18cm

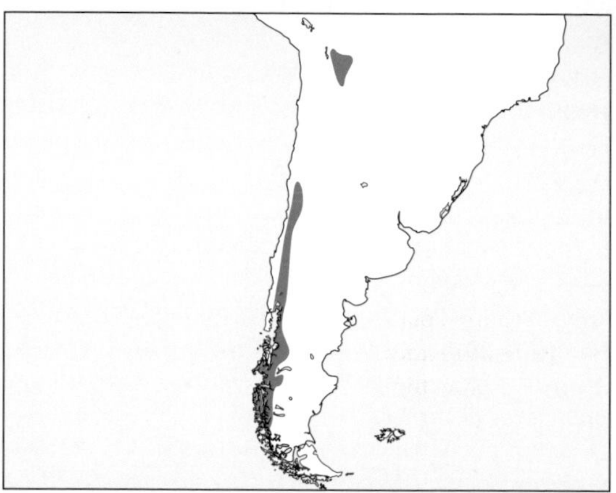

Identification Pied; barred above and striped below. Nape to back blackish, finely barred or scalloped cream or white. Underparts white or cream mostly streaked and scaled black on chest and breast, barred on buffy flanks and belly. Vent marked with black chevrons. Black wings barred white, coverts with bold spots. Tail chocolate barred buff or white. Black and white face pattern formed by dusky, brownish ear-coverts streaked white; dark but often indistinct malar flecked white; white streak across cheek; and broad white supercilium curves around ear-coverts to nape. Black crown spotted or streaked white. Throat white, flecked black. Iris chestnut. Bill black with paler base. Legs greyish. Sexes differ slightly: males have variable red or orange nape patch which females lack; females also usually lack white in crown. Juvenile browner, more boldly marked below, male with complete red crown, female with red crown patch.

Vocalisations Sudden, sharp, slowly repeated *pik* or *peek* and softer *chip* notes. A rapid mid- to low-pitched trilling (sometimes more rattling) song.

Drumming Level-pitched rolls, repeated after short pauses.

Status Widespread, but often uncommon. Considered stable, although population data scant.

Habitat Populations in the N inhabit dry scrub woodland in upland valleys and semi-desert with cacti; in the S in montane fairly open temperate deciduous forest, particularly of southern beech (*Nothofagus*), but also Mediterranean-type forest, chaparral, acacia scrub, degraded forests, wooded pastures and farmland, orchards, plantations and urban woods.

Range South America. Occurs in two separate areas divided by the high Andean plateau (Altiplano): in the N in C Bolivia and NW Argentina and in the S in Andean foothills in Patagonian Chile and Argentina. Resident and mostly sedentary though there may be local and elevational movements. Between 1600–4000m. Records of birds wintering in C Argentina probably refer to similar Chequered Woodpecker.

Taxonomy and variation Previously in *Picoides,* but moved to current genus following molecular studies. Treated as monotypic or as having two races separated by geography, altitude and climatic conditions; nominate ***lignarius*** in S (Patagonia) and ***puncticeps*** in N; the latter is smaller, shorter-billed, less boldly streaked below and scalloped rather than barred. Calls and habitats used also differ and study may reveal two distinct species.

Similar species Close relative and similarly marked Chequered Woodpecker is slightly smaller, browner and more lightly marked below, but does not overlap.

Food and foraging Invertebrates, but precise information lacking. Forages alone or in pairs, sometimes in mixed-species flocks.

► Adult female nominate. Note the lack of red on the unstreaked dark crown. Puerto Natales, Chile, January (*Gonzalo Gonzalez*).

◄ Adult male nominate Striped Woodpecker. The amount of reddish-orange on the nape of the males varies individually. Torres del Paine, Chile, January (*Gonzalo Gonzalez*).

138. BLOOD-COLOURED WOODPECKER

Veniliornis sanguineus

L 13–14cm

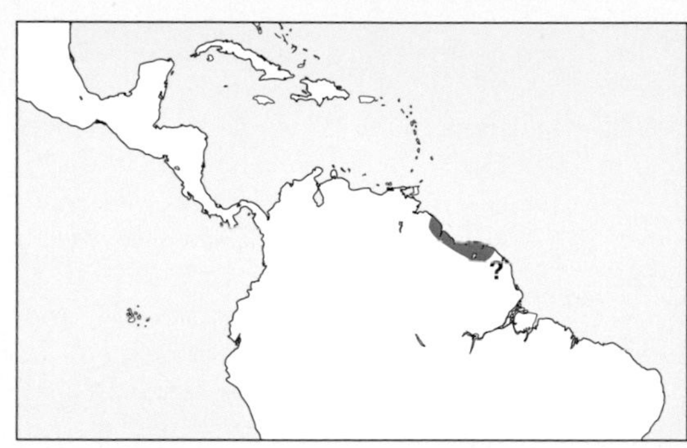

Identification Distinctive crimson mantle, back and rump, with some olive tones. Underparts grey or brown finely barred buff or white. Throat, face, ear-coverts and neck-sides brownish. Upperwings mostly red, with brown primaries, underwings barred white and brown. Tail chocolate. Iris chestnut. Bill pale. Legs greyish. Sexes differ: male has striking crimson crown and nape, flecked brown; female grey-brown crown mottled white. Juvenile much like adult, but browner.

Vocalisations Not overly vocal. A sharp, shrill *keek*, simple *chip* notes and a harsh rattle.

Drumming Both sexes produce level-pitched rolls in breeding season.

Status Fairly common. Range-restricted and population data scant, but seemingly stable.

Habitat Mangroves, swamp and riverine woodlands, *Curatella* savanna, coffee and cacao plantations, parks, sometimes gardens.

Range South America. Restricted to lowland coastal Guyana and Surinam. Occurrence in French Guiana unclear as hybrids with Little Woodpecker possibly involved. Resident and sedentary.

Taxonomy and variation Monotypic. Variable fine white flecking on ear-coverts. Individuals in worn plumage duller red. Birds with greenish wings probably Blood-coloured x Little Woodpecker hybrids.

Similar species None: unmistakable within range.

Food and foraging Invertebrates such as ants and beetles. Forages at all levels, but often low in shrubs, bushes and mangroves, alone or in pairs.

▲ Adult female is overall a duller rufous than the male, and has a greyish-brown crown with pale speckles. Peperpot Nature Park, Surinam, August (*Jean-Louis Rousselle*).

◄ Adult male Blood-coloured Woodpecker has a red crown, which the female lacks, and within its range is unmistakable. Abary River, Guyana, November (*Adam Riley*).

139. RED-RUMPED WOODPECKER
Veniliornis kirkii

L 15–16cm

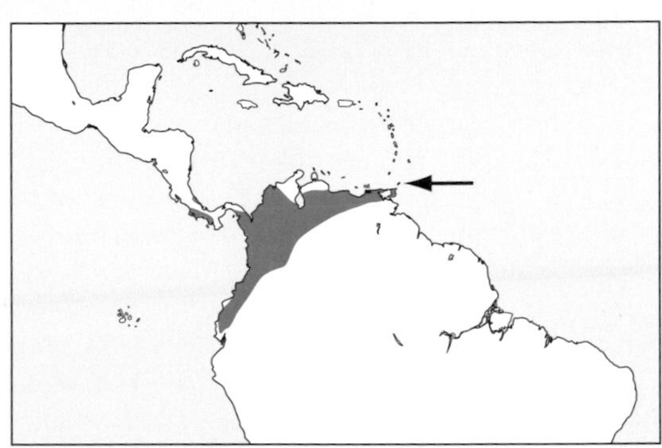

Identification Rump and uppertail-coverts crimson, but not always obvious. Olive above with yellow tones and reddish streaks. White or buff below extensively barred grey, olive or brown. Wings plain olive with some reddish tones on coverts. Tail olive-brown, variably barred white on outer feathers. Forehead dusky or buff. Dusky ear-coverts finely streaked buff. Chin and throat off-white. Nape olivaceous, yellow or golden. Bill blackish. Legs greyish. Iris chestnut. Sexes differ: males have red crown and nape streaked black; females have dusky crown finely scaled grey, nape only slightly yellow. Juvenile resemble adult

▲ Adult male Red-rumped Woodpecker of the race *cecilii*. The male is overall brighter than the female, with a red crown and yellower nape. Antioquia, Colombia, July (*Félix Uribe*).

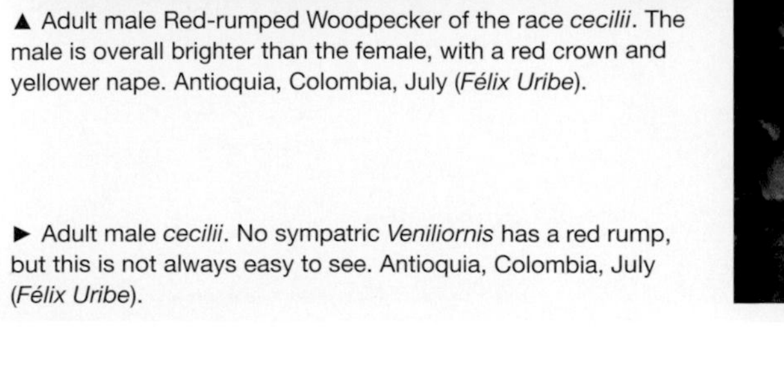

► Adult male *cecilii*. No sympatric *Veniliornis* has a red rump, but this is not always easy to see. Antioquia, Colombia, July (*Félix Uribe*).

male, both sexes with some red on crown but less in females.

Vocalisations Quite vocal. A low-pitched but loud, falling, nasal *keeer* or *kleee*, recalling Great Kiskadee. High-pitched, mewing *quee, kwee* and *kee* notes, sometimes *quee-yik, whik* or *kwik* often linked in series. Sharp, squeaky, repeated *trut* and *twit* notes.

Drumming Occasional, brief but solid, rapid rolls produced.

Status Common in Peru, Ecuador and E Panama; uncommon elsewhere, perhaps overlooked. Population size and trends largely unknown, but considered stable.

Habitat Range of open wet and dry habitats occupied: rainforest, gallery forest, mangroves, wooded savanna, thorn scrub with large trees, plantations, secondary growth, disturbed forest and suburban parks and gardens.

Range Central and South America. Mainly lowlands from SW Costa Rica and Panama into parts of N South America. Also Trinidad and Tobago. Mainly lowlands and foothills. Sea-level to 1900m. Resident and sedentary.

Taxonomy and variation Five races: ***kirkii*** (Trinidad, Tobago, Guyana, N Brazil, NE Venezuela: Paria Peninsula) is barred olive below; ***neglectus*** (SW Costa Rica, W Panama, Coiba Island) washed yellow above, dark on face, throat and chest and often lacking spotting on wing-coverts; ***cecilii*** (E Panama S to W Colombia, W Ecuador, extreme N Peru) is smallest race, minimally spotted on wings, most barred on tail; ***continentalis*** (N and W Venezuela) has broad black and white barring below, more yellow over nape; ***monticola*** (SE Venezuela: Mount Roraima and Cerro Uei-tepui) is largest race, with heavy dark barring below.

Similar species Within most of range most likely to be confused with Little Woodpecker, though that species never has red rump nor golden nape. Chocó Woodpecker also lacks red rump, has yellower nape and neck-sides and is more broadly barred below.

Food and foraging Wood-boring beetles and no doubt many other insects, but information lacking. Forages quietly, often in cover, from mid- to canopy level. Often in pairs and mixed-species parties.

▼ Adult female *cecilii*. Females can be rather drab, lacking red on the crown, and with the nape mustard rather than yellow. Colombia, March (*Robert Scanlon*).

140. RED-STAINED WOODPECKER
Veniliornis affinis

L 16–18cm

Identification Olive above, variably flushed or streaked rufous (red-stained) and gold or yellow. Buff or white below densely barred green or brown, broadest on belly and flanks. Tail olive-brown barred buff. Olive upperwing slightly marked red and yellow on coverts, flight feathers brownish, edged green or buff. Underwing barred brown and white. Variably barred pale throat. Ear-coverts and cheeks buff, streaked black. Neck-sides and nape orange, gold or yellow. Iris chestnut. Upper mandible blackish, lower grey. Legs grey or olive. Sexes differ: males have dark crown and nape streaked red; females have dusky crown lacking red and minimal red staining above. Juvenile more streaked, darker on face; both sexes with red on crown, less on female.

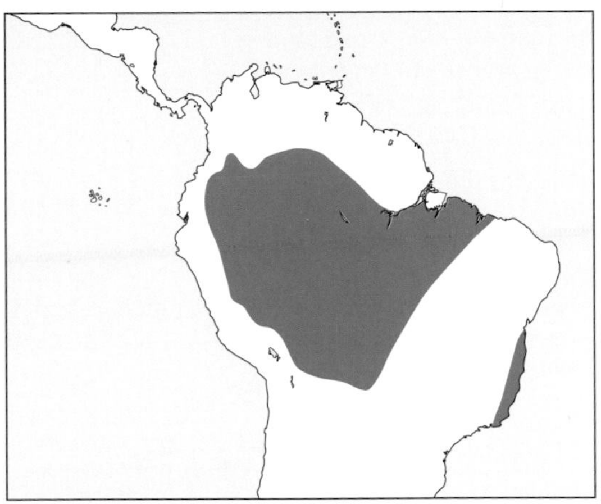

► Adult male nominate Red-stained Woodpecker. The extent of red on the crown varies from mere streaking to almost a solid cap. Alagoas, Brazil, July (*Nick Athanas*).

Vocalisations Often silent, but utters simple *kee-wick* notes in a rapid, trilling series, sometimes slower, like a squeaky bicycle wheel. Up to 14 clear *kee-kee-kee* (like Bat Falcon) or *kir-keer-keer-keer-keek* notes. Also high-pitched, nasal *ghi* or *kih* notes and soft trembling contact calls.

Drumming Both sexes produce repeated, rapid, steady, level-pitched rolls.

Status Fairly common in Ecuador, scarce in Colombia, uncommon in Peru and Venezuela. Common in *terra firme* in Brazil. Considered stable, but possibly declining due to deforestation.

Habitat Lowland tall rainforest, swamps and *terra firme*. In some areas riparian woodlands, *várzea*, drier thickets, scrub and shrub lands, secondary growth, degraded forests and plantations.

Range South America. From Colombia and Venezuela to Bolivia and Brazil, isolated population in coastal E Brazil. Mainly in lowlands and hilly country, to about 1300m. Resident and sedentary.

Taxonomy and variation Four races: ***affinis*** (E Brazil: Alagoas, E Bahia) has pale throat; ***orenocensis*** (SE Colombia, S Venezuela, N Brazil) greenish above with less red and yellow staining; ***hilaris*** (E Ecuador, E Peru, N Bolivia and W Mato Grosso, Brazil) is large, tinged bronze above, wing-coverts broadly tipped red, male red from forecrown; ***ruficeps*** (C and NE Brazil to Mato Grosso) also large, with bolder yellow streaks above and more red on wing-coverts. Some individuals lack yellow collar. Relationships with Golden-collared and Chocó Woodpeckers unclear.

Similar species Yellow-eared and Golden-collared Woodpeckers lack red above. Smaller Little Woodpecker lacks red and yellow on head and nape. Red-rumped and Chocó Woodpeckers do not overlap in range.

Food and foraging Invertebrates and fruit. Often forages in the canopy. Usually solitary, though joins mixed-species flocks and follows army-ants to take flushed prey.

▼ Adult male *hilaris*. Racial differences are slight, with variation also within populations. Tambopata Reserve, Peru, November (*Gerard Gorman*).

▼ Adult female nominate. Both sexes have red on the wing-coverts, but females lack red in the crown. Alagoas, Brazil, January (*Lars Petersson*).

141. CHOCÓ WOODPECKER
Veniliornis chocoensis

L 15–16cm

Identification Olive above, with bronze tones, mantle with rufous wash, back flecked and streaked yellow. Rump and uppertail-coverts barred yellow or green. Olive-green below, evenly and boldly barred white or buff on belly and flanks, more scaled on breast and chest. Buff throat densely barred greyish. Tail brownish, with yellow or green barring on outer feathers. Green upperwings spotted yellowish on coverts, primaries browner barred buff. Underwings barred cream and brown. Forehead and ear-coverts dusky olive or brown. Lores buff. Nape and rear neck-sides yellow. Iris chestnut. Upper mandible dark, lower pale grey. Legs greyish-olive. Sexes differ: male has scarlet crown flecked grey or black; female lacks red having dusky-olive crown. Juveniles of both sexes have red in crown, females less so.

Vocalisations Sharp *pik* and softer *quip* notes. Fast series of squeaky *wicka-wicka* notes and a gentle rattle.

Drumming Presumably drums, but information lacking.

Status NT. Uncommon and localised. Range-restricted and poorly known, and probably decreasing due to intense logging and clearance of forests for pasture, grazing, mining, building and plantations.

Habitat Wet, humid, evergreen, tropical forests.

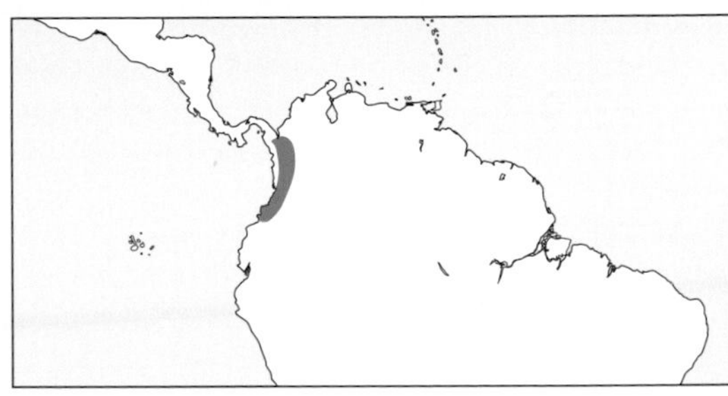

Range South America. Only occurs on the Pacific slope of W Colombia (from extreme W Antioquia and Chocó), S into adjacent NW Ecuador (Esmeraldas and Pichincha). Lowlands and foothills to about 1000m. Resident and sedentary.

Taxonomy and variation Monotypic. No notable variation. Formerly lumped with Golden-collared and Red-stained Woodpeckers.

Similar species Most like Red-stained Woodpecker, but does not overlap with it. Red-rumped Woodpecker, which does overlap, has whiter throat, less yellow on neck-sides and red rump.

Food and foraging Presumably invertebrates, but information lacking. Often forages alone in the subcanopy, sometimes joins mixed flocks.

► Adult male Chocó Woodpecker has a red crown, variably marked greyish or blackish; females lack the red. Esmeraldes, Ecuador, May (*Nick Athanas*).

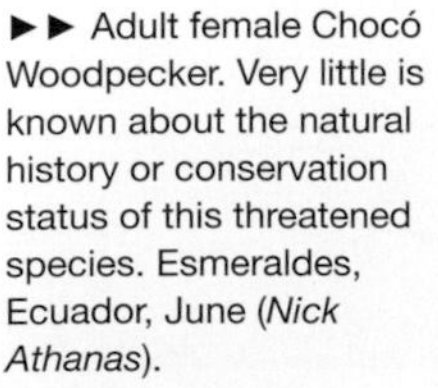

►► Adult female Chocó Woodpecker. Very little is known about the natural history or conservation status of this threatened species. Esmeraldes, Ecuador, June (*Nick Athanas*).

142. GOLDEN-COLLARED WOODPECKER
Veniliornis cassini

L 14–16cm

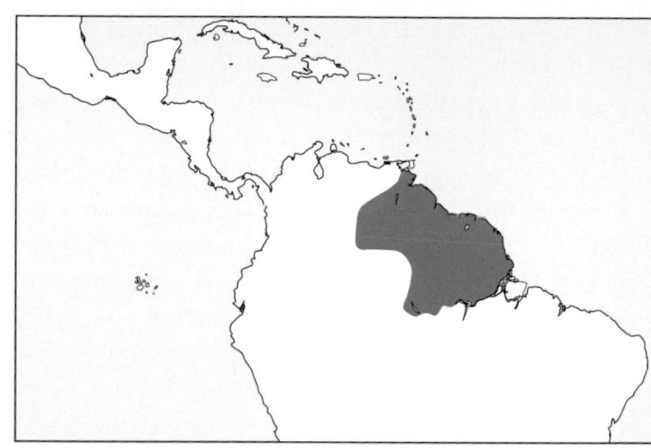

Identification Mantle and back olive with bronze hue and fine buff or yellow spotting. Most of upperwings olive, faintly dotted white or yellow on upper-coverts, flight feathers browner. Underwings barred brown and white. Underparts from throat to undertail-coverts densely barred black and white or buff, broadest on belly. Tail olive-brown with pale bars, more prominent on outer two feather-pairs. Lores buff or cinnamon. Ear-coverts dusky streaked black. Hindneck golden or yellow, flecked white. Bill grey. Legs greyish-blackish. Iris chestnut. Sexes differ: male has reddish crown and often ochre nape; female lacks red, having dusky-olive

▼ Adult male Golden-collared Woodpecker. Very similar to Red-stained Woodpecker, but smaller and lacking the rufous tones above. Imataca, Venezuela, February (*Lars Petersson*).

crown. Juvenile has less and duller yellow on the nape and a duskier face, and juveniles of both sexes have some red on the crown.

Vocalisations Level-pitched, rapid, trilling series of *khirr* notes lasting about 3 seconds long. Also a quieter, softer, upwardly slurred version. A level, high-pitched nasal rattling *drrrrrrrrrrrrrrr*. Contact call a meek *see-jhrrr-see-jhrrr*.

Drumming Steady, level-pitched rolls produced, often interspersed with calls.

Status Common locally. Population and other data lacking, as easily overlooked, but probably decreasing in areas where heavy deforestation continues.

Habitat Rainforest edges and clearings, *terra firme*, more open woodlands. Also adjacent secondary growth, wooded savanna and degraded forests.

Range NE South America: Colombia, E and SE Venezuela, the Guianas and Brazil N of Amazonia. Sea-level to 1500m. Resident and sedentary.

Taxonomy and variation Monotypic. Has been lumped with both Chocó and Red-stained Woodpeckers.

Similar species Very like Red-stained Woodpecker, but that species slightly larger, lacks yellow on wing-coverts, has reddish hue above and is less boldly barred below. Yellow-eared and Chocó Woodpeckers do not overlap.

Food and foraging Long-horned beetles, other arboreal insects and berries. Often in canopy, foraging alone or in pairs on creepers, vines and thinner branches and twigs. Joins mixed-species flocks.

▲ Adult male. The red crown is variably flecked with black, and the yellow 'collar' is variable in size. Imataca, Venezuela, February (*Lars Petersson*).

◄ Adult female in flight. Both sexes have a golden hindneck, but females lack red on the crown. French Guiana, September (*Maxime Dechelle*).

143. YELLOW-EARED WOODPECKER
Veniliornis maculifrons

L 15–17cm

Identification Olive-green above, finely spotted and barred yellow and grey. White or buff underparts barred greyish-green, fine on throat and chest, broader on breast, belly and lower flanks. Upperwings olive with white dots on upper-coverts, primaries browner with barred buff, underwing barred brown and white. Uppertail blackish barred cream or yellow; undertail boldly barred white. Lores cinnamon. Ear-coverts dusky olive, faintly streaked white. Pale throat and cheeks finely barred olive-brown. Nape and neck-sides gold or yellow. Thin pale moustache and supercilium. Iris dark. Bill bluish-grey. Legs grey. Sexes differ slightly: male has red from mid- to hindcrown with dark flecks, forecrown grey-black spotted white; female lacks red, having chocolate crown spotted white. Juvenile has dull yellow nape, more barring on back and mantle and a few red feathers on crown.

Vocalisations Slowly repeated harsh or squeaky chip notes and a high-pitched harsh or trilling rattle – the two often interspersed. Also a trembling, rising series, *u-u-u-u-u-u*.

Drumming May not drum, or perhaps only rarely, but information lacking.

Status Common locally, but range-restricted. Considered stable, but has probably declined as rainforest habitat has been heavily logged and degraded, though seemingly able to adapt to other habitats.

Habitat Lowland rainforest and upland forest edges and clearings, parks, plantations, secondary growth and degraded forest.

Range Endemic to SE Brazil. Occurs in Atlantic Forest and lowland forests from S Bahia, Espirito Santo to Rio de Janeiro and Minas Gerais. Sea-level to around 1300m. Resident and sedentary.

Taxonomy and variation Monotypic. Some birds have bronze hue above. Both supercilium and moustache can be indistinct. Males in worn plumage have less red on crown.

Similar species Slightly smaller Little Woodpecker lacks yellow. Most Red-stained Woodpeckers have red on wings, and males red on forecrown.

Food and foraging Insect larvae and presumably other invertebrates, but information lacking. Forages mainly in canopy, sometimes in mixed-species flocks.

▼ Adult male. Males have red on the hindcrown, which females lack, although its extent and intensity varies. Rio de Janeiro, Brazil, October (*Dario Sanches*).

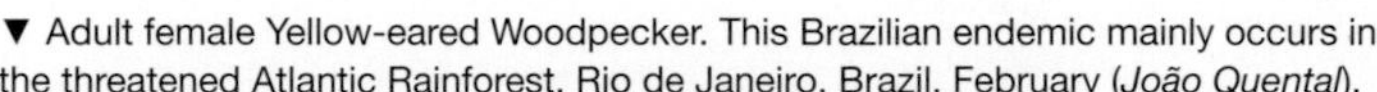

▼ Adult female Yellow-eared Woodpecker. This Brazilian endemic mainly occurs in the threatened Atlantic Rainforest. Rio de Janeiro, Brazil, February (*João Quental*).

Rufous-winged Woodpecker *Piculus simplex*, adult male. Heredia, Costa Rica, February (*Greg R. Homel*).

PICULUS

A genus of (currently) 12 species occurring in Central and South America, several having been previously considered conspecific. All are medium-sized with barred or spotted underparts and plain green-olive upperparts, often washed with red (extensively in Crimson-mantled Woodpecker). Facial patterns are crucial for identification. Mostly arboreal, the *Piculus* inhabit relatively dense forests and are often inconspicuous, their green plumage perhaps providing camouflage, foraging primarily at mid to high levels on branches and trunks. Several species have almost identical calls.

144. RUFOUS-WINGED WOODPECKER
Piculus simplex

L 18cm

Identification Despite English name, rufous in wings slight and not often obvious. Olive above with bronze tones and reddish wash on mantle. Chin to breast olive-green, breast with cream, beige or yellow dots and dark-tipped chevrons. Belly to undertail-coverts barred cream or beige and olive or brown. Most of upper wings green, flight feathers barred rufous or cinnamon, underwing-coverts rufous. Tail black with rufous tones. Ear-coverts olive, ocular area dusky. Iris pale, orbital ring grey or blue. Dark bill; lower mandible paler grey. Legs grey. Sexes differ: male has all-red crown, from lores to nape, and broad red malar; female has plain olive-brown crown, red only on nape, and lacks malar. Juvenile duller green overall, more mottled below, male red only from rear crown to nape.

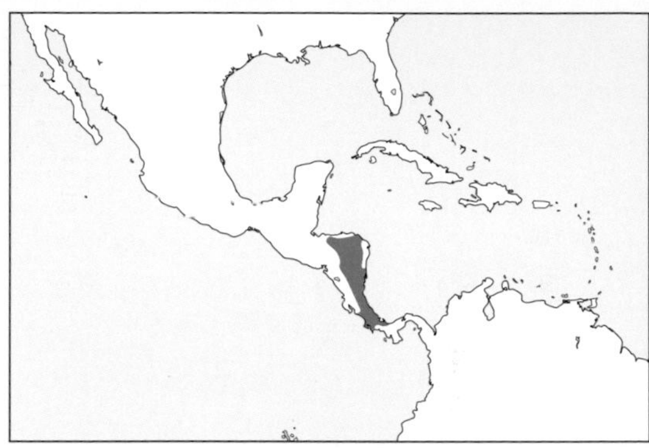

Vocalisations Strident, vigorous, nasal, repeated, high-pitched territorial song, *cheea-cheea-cheea,* usually harsh, like Brown Jay when delivered fast. A slower, high-pitched, sharp, nasal *deeeah,* recalling Great Kiskadee. Falling series of *heew* notes. Contact call, single or double, softer, whining, mewing note.

Drumming Repeated, even, gentle, 1-second rolls.

Status Rare in Panama, uncommon in Costa Rica. Poorly known, but considered stable overall, although probably declining as forest is felled.

Habitat Typically humid, lowland forest and wooded wetlands. To lesser extent forest edge and clearings in degraded forest, well-wooded parks and suburban gardens.

Range Central America. Restricted to E Honduras, Nicaragua, Costa Rica and W Panama. Mainly Caribbean slope, but also Pacific coast in places. Usually lowlands below 1000m. Resident and sedentary.

Taxonomy and variation Monotypic. Variation slight.

Similar species Most like Stripe-cheeked Woodpecker (probably does not overlap) but that species has marked throat and yellow moustache – beware some Rufous-winged juveniles that have yellow in malar area. Larger Golden-olive Woodpecker lacks rufous wings, has black crown, white face and barred throat.

Food and foraging Forages unobtrusively for ants, beetles and other insects in lush, mossy cover from mid-levels to the canopy. Outside breeding season usually solitary, sometimes in pairs and mixed-species feeding flocks.

◀ Adult male Rufous-winged Woodpecker has a complete red crown, nape and malar area; the female has red on the nape only. Heredia, Costa Rica, December (*Jim & Deva Burns*).

▲ Adult female Rufous-winged Woodpecker excavating a cavity. Heredia, Costa Rica, November (*David Seibel*).

145. STRIPE-CHEEKED WOODPECKER
Piculus callopterus

L 17cm

Identification Plain olive above with bronze tones. Rump barred olive or yellow. Throat and chest olive, boldly scaled buff, belly and flanks cream or buff, more widely barred green. Most of wings olive, primaries barred rufous or ochre. Underwings paler with cinnamon tones. Uppertail blackish with olive or cinnamon on outer feathers. Lores greenish. Chin mottled green. Ear-coverts and ocular area dusky. Buff or yellow moustachial line. Iris bluish-white (incorrectly shown dark in most books). Bill blackish with grey base. Legs grey. Sexes differ: male has red crown from forehead to nape, mottled grey, and long, broad red malar; female red only on nape, with dark grey crown and malar. Juvenile mottled rather than barred below; juveniles of both sexes more like adult female as lack red crown and malar.

Vocalisations A repeated two-note call, first note a nasal wheeze, second a sharp rising squeak, varying in pitch and rhythm. Repeated nasal, mewing and squeaky notes and yapping chatter in encounters and conflicts.

Drumming May not drum, or perhaps only rarely.

Status Uncommon and localised. Range-restricted, but considered stable and not threatened.

Habitat Typically in tropical, humid foothill forests.

Range Endemic to Panama. Scattered in the E to extreme eastern Darien Province – possibly in adjacent Colombia.

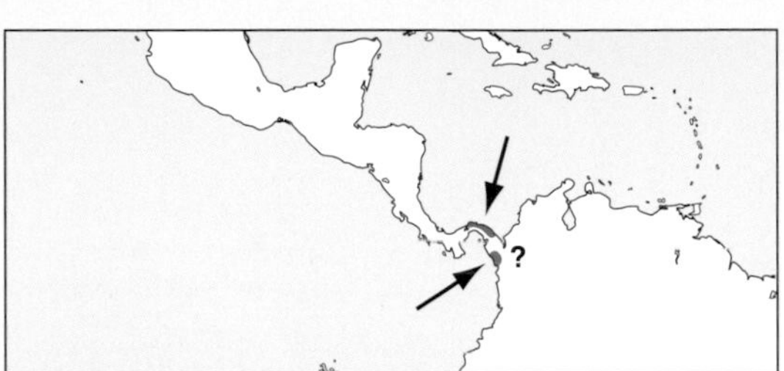

Isolated population in extreme E Cocle Province (Las Minas, on Caribbean slope N of El Valle de Anton) and records from W Panama (Altos del Maria) and W Colon Province – perhaps extending range westwards. Mainly 300–900m, but to 1200m.

Taxonomy and variation Monotypic. Formerly lumped with Rufous-winged and White-throated Woodpeckers.

Similar species Most like Rufous-winged Woodpecker (though does not overlap), but that species lacks yellow moustache (though sometimes present on juveniles). Sympatric Golden-yellow Woodpecker has similar face pattern, but is much larger, has yellow throat, lacks rufous primaries and differs in calls and habitat.

Food and foraging Arboreal ants and other invertebrates, but detailed information lacking. Forages at low and mid-levels, singly or in pairs, and joins mixed-species feeding flocks.

◄◄ Adult male Stripe-cheeked Woodpecker. In both sexes, the pale moustachial stripe helps separate from the similar Rufous-winged Woodpecker. Cerro Jefe, Panama, December (*Vaughan & Sveta Ashby*).

◄ Adult female. Females lack the red malar stripe of the males, and are only red on the nape. Panama, May (*Steve Bird*).

146. WHITE-THROATED WOODPECKER
Piculus leucolaemus

L 19–20cm

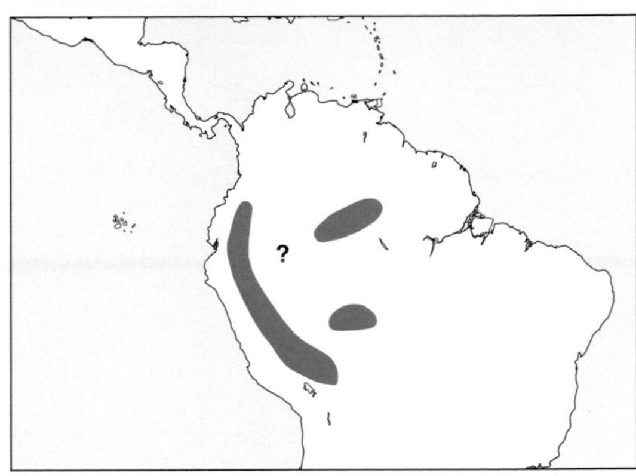

Identification Upperparts and most of wings plain olive-green with bronze tones. Flight feathers ochre or brown. Chest green smudged blackish; breast and belly white, scaled and barred olive, more scalloped on undertail-coverts. White chin and throat sometimes faintly streaked or speckled olive. Tail blackish or olive. Cheek greenish or yellow. Yellow moustachial streak continues below ear-coverts to neck sides. Dark green crescent over golden-washed ear-coverts. Crown slightly tufted at rear. Iris chestnut. Bill grey. Legs greyish. Sexes differ: male has long, broad red malar, scarlet crown and yellow streak above malar; female lacks red malar, having red only on nape, rest of crown green. Juvenile deeper green overall and lacks red crown and malar.

Vocalisations Often silent. Drawn-out single, sometimes double, falling, hoarse, rasping *psheeah, piisssh* or *shreer,* also described as *wheeeeee,* repeated after long pauses. Harsh, hissing *rahh-rahh-rahh, jahh-jahh-jahh* or *sraa-sraa-sraa* notes in series. Squeaky *wicka* notes when agitated.

Drumming Both sexes drum. Steady, level, repeated rolls of up to 2 seconds, often interspersed with calls.

Status Uncommon, possibly overlooked. Poorly

▼ Adult male White-throated Woodpecker has a completely red crown, nape and malar stripe. Afluentes, San Martin, Peru, November (*Gerard Gorman*).

▼ Adult male from below. In both sexes, the diagnostic pale throat helps separate it from other *Piculus* species. Afluentes, San Martin, Peru, November (*Gerard Gorman*).

known, population data lacking, but probably declining due to Amazonian deforestation.

Habitat Mainly tall humid and wet lowland forest: *várzea, terra firme*, riverine woods and swamps. Also secondary growth and older plantations.

Range South America. From parts of Colombia, E Ecuador to SE Peru and N Bolivia, with isolated populations in Amazonian Brazil. Sea-level to 1400m. Resident and sedentary.

Taxonomy and variation Monotypic. Variation slight. Formerly considered conspecific with Lita Woodpecker.

Similar species Yellow-throated Woodpecker has yellow ear-coverts and throat, males with smaller red malar. Lita Woodpecker has more yellow on head, particularly the female, and has dark throat, but ranges separated by the Andes.

Food and foraging Arboreal invertebrates, as close relatives, but information lacking. An inconspicuous forest forager, often in the canopy, usually solitary, but will join mixed-species flocks.

◄ Adult female White-throated Woodpecker is red only on the nape, with green in the malar area. Tarapoto, Peru, November (*Pete Morris*).

▼ Adult male at the nest hole. Although little is known about the conservation needs of this species, it is thought to be suffering from loss of its forest habitat. Tarapoto, Peru, November (*Pete Morris*).

147. LITA WOODPECKER
Piculus litae

L 17–18cm

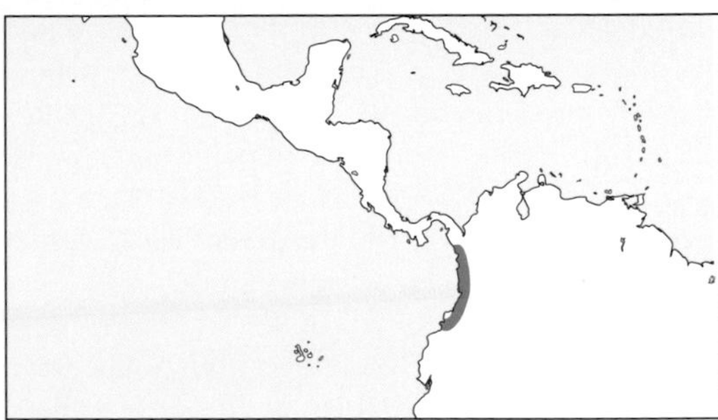

Identification Olive-green above with yellowish tones, rump darker green. Pale underparts heavily scaled buff, yellow or green on chest and breast, more barred on belly and flanks. Uppertail plain blackish-olive, undertail white barred black. Wings mostly green, primaries brown with ochre panel, underwing rusty. Ear-coverts, cheeks and neck-sides yellow. Both sexes have red malar. Throat blackish, faintly spotted white. Iris chestnut. Bill and legs bluish-grey. Sexes differ slightly: male has crimson crown from lores to nape; female red only on nape with crown yellow. Juvenile greener below, throat more streaked, face duller yellow and lacking red malar.

Vocalisations Slowly repeated, scratchy, drawn-out *peessh* or *shreeyr*. Sometimes rather hissing sound, like escaping steam, much like relatives. Also chattering notes in interactions.

Drumming Occasional, quiet, short rolls.

Status Uncommon. Range-restricted, poorly known and occurs in areas where deforestation continues, so conservation status needs review.

Habitat Damp, humid to wet, mature and secondary growth forests.

Range South America. Mainly restricted to lowlands and foothills on the Andean Pacific slope in NW Ecuador and W Colombia, reaching as far S as the Magdalena Valley in the east. Sea-level to 800m. Resident and sedentary.

Taxonomy and variation Monotypic. Subject of much taxonomic movement: formerly lumped with White-throated, Rufous-winged and Stripe-cheeked Woodpeckers. Amount and brightness of yellow on face varies.

Similar species White-throated Woodpecker is less yellow on head, with dark ear-coverts, pale throat, with females green on crown. Head pattern very like Yellow-throated Woodpecker. Neither overlaps.

Food and foraging Presumably arboreal invertebrates, as close relatives. Forages alone and in pairs, often in cover from mid-levels to canopy in smaller trees.

► Adult male Lita Woodpecker. Note the all-red crown; females are red only on the nape. Both sexes have a red malar. Esmeraldes, Ecuador, June (*Dušan Brinkhuizen*).

148. YELLOW-THROATED WOODPECKER

Piculus flavigula

L 18–22cm

Identification Well-marked head of bright yellow cheeks, ear-coverts and neck-sides. Olive-green above with yellow tones on mantle. Uppertail-coverts yellow. Underparts from chest to undertail-coverts white, heavily scaled or barred olive or blackish. Tail dark green. Most of upper-wings also green, flight feathers browner, ochre on inner webs. Underwings paler barred greenish. Iris brown. Bill blackish-grey. Legs grey. Sexes differ: male has all-red crown from lores to nape, flecked with dark feather bases; female red only on nape; crown streaked green, gold or yellow. Juvenile greener above, darker below, less yellow on face. Juvenile male has variable amount of red on crown, while female is greenish.

Vocalisations Often silent. Slowing, yapping, mocking *kee-kee-kee-kee* notes in series. Wheezing, hissing, hoarse, rising, double or single *psheeah*, *shreer* or *queer* notes, sometimes repeated after long pauses – like close relatives.

Drumming Steady, level-pitched rolls of up to 3 seconds.

Status Fairly common locally over most of range, but rare in Ecuador and uncommon in Peru and Bolivia.

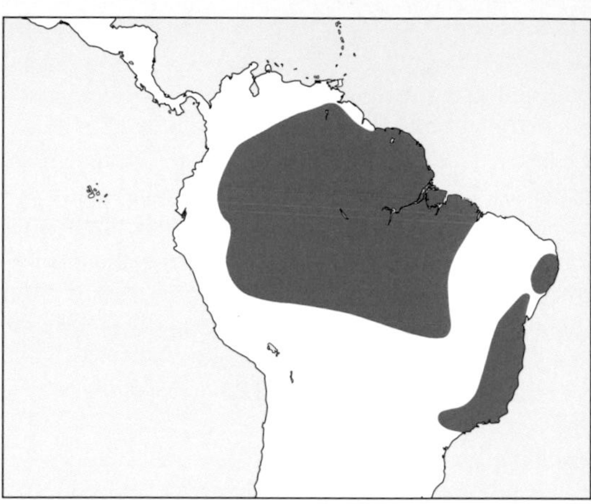

Probably declining in some regions due to deforestation.

Habitat Rainforest, riparian forest, tall damp *terra firme* and *várzea*, drier *caatinga* and savanna woodlands.

Range South America. Parts of Colombia, Venezuela, E Ecuador, the Guianas, Brazil, Bolivia and Peru. Lowlands and hilly country to 700m. Resident and sedentary.

Taxonomy and variation Three variably sized races, differing mainly in amount of red on males: ***flavigula*** (E Colombia to Venezuela, the Guianas, N Amazonian Brazil) has yellow throat, males show red malar; ***magnus*** (SE Colombia, Ecuador, Peru, N Bolivia and NE Brazil) also has yellow throat, males lack red malar; ***erythropis*** (E Brazil) smallest race, more barred below, males with red chin, throat and lower cheeks; females with some red on throat – possibly a distinct species as geographically isolated and found in different habitats from other races.

Similar species White-throated Woodpecker has much less yellow on face, white throat, male has bold red malar. Lita Woodpecker has black throat.

Food and foraging Mainly arboreal ants and termites. Forages from mid-levels to the canopy, often solitary, although joins mixed-species flocks.

◄ Adult male *erythropis* Yellow-throated Woodpecker. Note the distinctive red throat of this race. Bahia, Brazil, December (*Lars Petersson*).

▲ Adult female nominate. Females of all races have yellow crowns, with red only on the nape. Amazonia, Brazil, October (*Claus Meyer*).

149. GOLDEN-GREEN WOODPECKER
Piculus chrysochloros

L 18–21cm

Identification Olive-green above. Plain yellow or buff chin and throat. Ear-coverts dark olive. Tail olive-brown. Long yellow moustachial line extends below eye and ear-coverts to rear neck. Buff-yellow below barred greyish-olive. Iris bluish. Bill greyish, paler at base. Legs greyish. Sexes differ: male has red malar and crown to nape; female lacks red, having dark olive malar and crown. Juvenile male has orange or red crown and some green in red malar; juvenile female has greenish crown, with darker ear-coverts and malar.
Vocalisations Often silent. Screaming, falling, rasping *psheeah, shreeyr* or *shreer* note. Also a wailing, rising *rahh* or *schraah* in series. Squeaky *wicka-wicka-wicka* in disputes and displays.
Drumming Occasional, steady, 1-second rolls.
Status LC (Least Concern), but conservation status needs review following taxonomic changes. Poorly known and perhaps overlooked due to habits and habitats used, but probably fairly common overall, although uncommon in the Pantanal.
Habitat Varied humid lowland deciduous woods and rainforest: *caatinga*, tall *terra firme, várzea* and riparian woods. Also drier scrub, wooded savanna and pasture, degraded forest and palm groves.
Range South America. From NE Brazil, through the Caatinga, Cerrado and Pantanal regions to W Paraguay, N Argentina and the Chaco and Beni lowlands of Bolivia. Mainly lowlands. Resident and sedentary.

▼ Adult male Golden-green Woodpecker has a striking red crown and broad malar stripe. Bahia Negra, Paraguay, October (*Andrea Ferreira*).

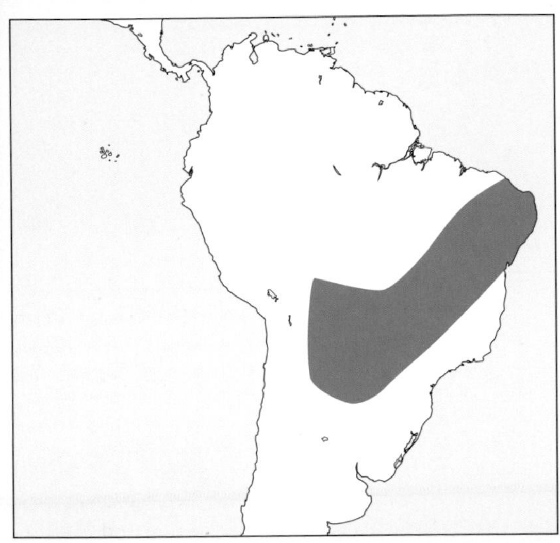

Taxonomy and variation Monotypic. Until recently was composed of nine races ranging over a vast area from Panama to Argentina, occurring in a variety of different wooded habitats. However, eight have been split to five species following a review of taxonomy and distribution, based on morphological and morphometric data. Another form, from the Tapajós-Tocantins river region, may also prove to be a distinct species.

Similar species Dot-throated Woodpecker overlaps in Pará state, but not in the same habitat, seemingly preferring *terra firme* forest whilst Golden-green occurs mainly in *cerrado*.

Food and foraging Mainly arboreal ants and termites, often raiding their nests or working dead wood. Forages at all levels from low-down to canopy, alone or in mixed-species flocks.

▲ Adult female Golden-green Woodpecker. Both sexes have a distinct long yellow stripe across the cheek, but females lack red. São Geraldo do Araguaia, Pará, Brazil, July (*Gabriel Leite*).

150. GOLDEN-YELLOW WOODPECKER
Piculus xanthochlorus

L 19–24cm

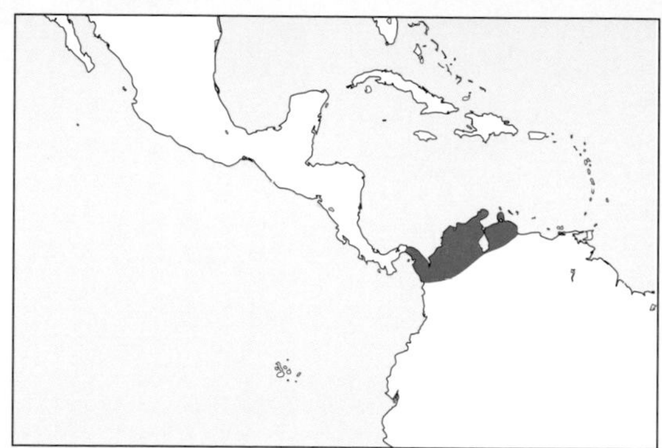

Identification Golden-green above, yellowish below finely barred olive. Wings greenish, tail olive-brown. Chin, throat and neck plain gold or yellow. Yellow supercilium. Ear-coverts light olive. Long yellow moustachial line extends below ear-coverts. Iris pale or bluish. Bill greyish, paler at base. Legs greyish. Sexes differ mainly in head pattern: male has scarlet crown to nape and red malar; female lacks red, having golden-yellow crown and greenish malar. Juvenile male has orange or red crown and mostly green malar with some red; juvenile female has duller yellow-green crown and darker ear-coverts and malar area.

Vocalisations Often silent. Occasional 1–3 falling, rasping or wheezing, raptor-like *shreer* or *wheerr* notes.

Drumming Presumably drums, perhaps rarely, but information lacking.

Status No official category assigned at time of writing. Poorly known and overlooked due to habits and habitats used, but perhaps fairly common.

Habitat Moist and dry tropical broadleaved forests. Varied humid lowland deciduous woods and rainforest: mangroves, swamps, *caatinga*, tall *terra firme*, *várzea*, riparian woods. Also drier scrub, wooded savanna and pasture, degraded forest and palm groves.

Range South America. From Panama, through N Andes in Colombia (Magdalena, Córdoba, Norte de Santander, La Guajira, Bolívar, Cesar and Antioquia) and NW Venezuela (Falcón, Zulia, Táchira). Mainly lowlands. Resident and sedentary.

Taxonomy and variation Monotypic. Formerly treated as race of Golden-green Woodpecker. Some males have slight yellow supercilium.

Similar species Stripe-cheeked Woodpecker is smaller, less yellow, with marked throat, rufous primaries; female has red nape and also differs in calls and habitat.

Food and foraging Arboreal ants and termites, often taken from nests, spiders and other small invertebrates. Often forages in mixed flocks in the canopy.

◄◄ Adult male Golden-yellow Woodpecker. The male's red crown is often raised and prominent. Barranquilla, Colombia, November (*Trevor Ellery*).

◄ Adult female lacks red. Note the long moustachial stripe, which is yellower than on Stripe-cheeked Woodpecker. Bayano Forest, Panama, September (*Jan Axel Cubilla*).

151. BAR-THROATED WOODPECKER
Piculus capistratus

L 24–27cm

Identification Olive-green above. Yellow below, boldly and evenly barred dark grey or olive. Chin and throat variably barred black or grey. Ear-coverts dark grey or olive. Tail olive-brown. Long yellow moustachial line extends below ear-coverts. Iris bluish. Bill greyish, paler at base. Legs greyish. Sexes differ: male has slight red malar and red crown to nape; female lacks red, having those areas dark olive. Juvenile male has orange or red crown and some green in malar.

Vocalisations Often silent. Occasional 1–3 falling, harsh, rasping or wheezing *shreeyr* notes.

Drumming Presumably drums, but information lacking.

Status No official category assigned at the time of writing. Poorly known due to habits and habitats used. Rare in Ecuador and Surinam, uncommon in Peru, Colombia, Guyana and French Guiana, but perhaps overlooked.

Habitat Tropical rainforest, particularly tall *terra firme*, also seasonally flooded *várzea* forests.

Range South America. N of the River Amazon in N Peru, E Ecuador, SE Colombia, S Venezuela, N Brazil and the Guianas. Mainly lowlands. Resident and sedentary.

Taxonomy and variation Two races claimed (though probably monotypic): ***capistratus*** (most of range) and ***guianensis*** (French Guiana). Formerly treated as races of Golden-green Woodpecker.

Similar species Within range, most like Yellow-throated Woodpecker, though that has yellow ear-coverts and neck-sides and scales rather than bars below.

Food and foraging Details lacking, but presumably mainly arboreal ants and termites as relatives. Often in mixed-species flocks.

► Adult male Bar-throated Woodpecker. Both sexes have a prominent yellow moustachial stripe, but the males have a red crown and malar stripe, which the females lack. Rupununi, Guyana, February (*Vaughan & Sveta Ashby*).

►► Adult female. The barring on the throat is much finer than on the rest of the underparts. Sucumbios, Ecuador, August (*Dušan Brinkhuizen*).

152. BELÉM WOODPECKER

Piculus paraensis

L 19–24cm

Identification Olive-green above. Chin, throat, neck plain golden. Ear-coverts light olive. Pale yellow below, broadly barred dark grey or olive. Tail olive-brown. Long yellow moustachial line extends below eye and ear-coverts. Iris bluish. Bill greyish, paler at base. Legs greyish. Sexes differ in head pattern: male has red crown to nape and yellow supercilium, some individuals lack red malar; female has yellowish-greenish crown. Juvenile male has orange or red crown; juvenile female has duller yellowish-green crown.

Vocalisations A level-pitched wheezing *shreeeyr.* Presumably also screaming, rasping notes like close relatives, but details scant.

Drumming Presumably drums, but information lacking.

Status Considered 'Endangered' on list of threatened species of Pará – where threatened with extinction. Very poorly known, but certainly uncommon and suffering from loss, fragmentation and degradation of remaining forest habitat.

Habitat Mainly well preserved *terra firme* forests, also seasonally-flooded *várzea* forests.

Range South America. Endemic to lowland NE Brazil: Belém Centre of Endemism, east of Tocantins River, in Pará and Maranhão states. Resident and sedentary.

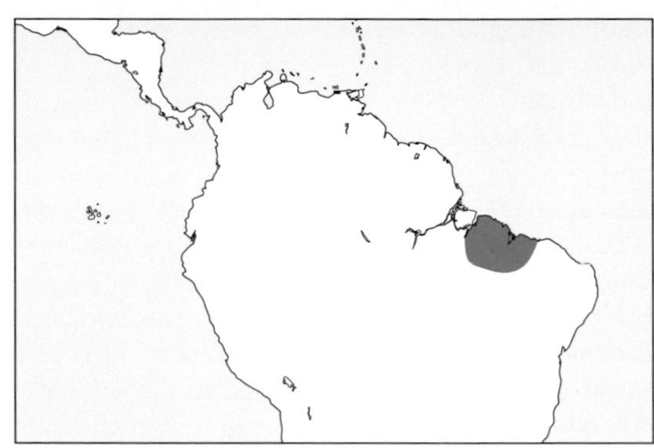

Taxonomy and variation Monotypic. Formerly treated as a race of Golden-green Woodpecker.

Similar species Sympatric Yellow-throated Woodpecker has yellow ear-coverts and neck-sides, scaling rather than barring below and male never has olive malar.

Food and foraging Presumably arboreal ants and termites, as relatives, but no data.

▼ Adult male Belém Woodpecker. Some individuals lack red in the malar stripe. Pará, Brazil, July (*Alex Lees*).

▼ Adult male Belém Woodpecker. A little-known and endangered woodpecker, endemic to the NE Brazilian states of Pará and Maranhão. Pará, Brazil, July (*Alex Lees*).

153. DOT-THROATED WOODPECKER
Piculus laemosticus

L 19–24cm

Identification Dark olive-green above. Light yellow below broadly and evenly barred grey or olive. Chin and throat buff with dark spotting. Ear-coverts dark greyish-olive. Tail olive-brown. Long, broad, yellow moustachial line extends below ear-coverts. Iris bluish. Bill greyish, paler at base. Legs greyish. Sexes differ slightly: male has red crown from lores to nape; female has dark olive crown. Both sexes have olive-green malars, although some males may show some red. Juvenile male has orange or red crown.

Vocalisations Often silent. Occasional 1–3 screaming, falling, wheezing and rasping *psheeah* or *shreer* notes.

Drumming Probably drums, but precise information lacking.

Status No official category assigned at time of writing. Poorly known, but considered uncommon. Perhaps overlooked due to habits and habitats occupied.

Habitat Rainforest and seasonally flooded *várzea* and *terre firme.*

Range South America. Amazonia S of the Amazon River to NW Brazil (N Mato Grosso) through Peru to N Bolivia. Mainly lowlands. Resident and sedentary.

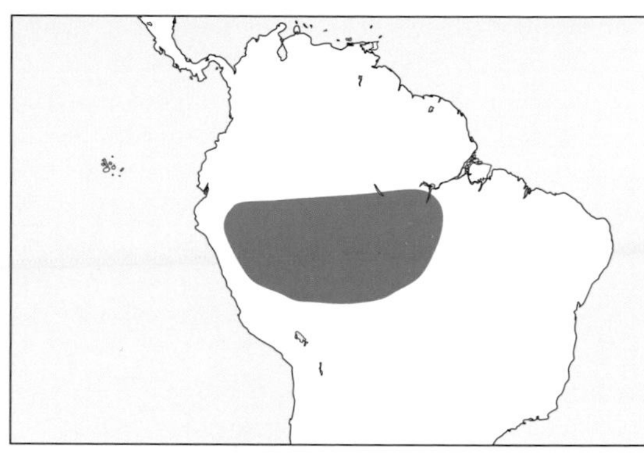

Taxonomy and variation Monotypic. Formerly treated as race of Golden-green Woodpecker. Rather variable, with some individuals having only a few spots on throat.

Similar species Golden-green Woodpecker overlaps in SE Pará state in Brazil, but not in same habitat, seemingly preferring *cerrado.*

Food and foraging Presumably arboreal ants and termites and other small invertebrates, as relatives. Associates with mixed-species flocks.

► Adult male Dot-throated Woodpecker. Males have a red crown and nape, which the females lack. The throat-spotting is highly variable. Mato Grosso, Brazil, December (*Christopher Borges*).

►► Adult female. Both sexes have a green malar region, and a clear yellow moustachial line. Mato Grosso, Brazil, September (*João Quental*).

154. ATLANTIC WOODPECKER
Piculus polyzonus

L 25–27cm

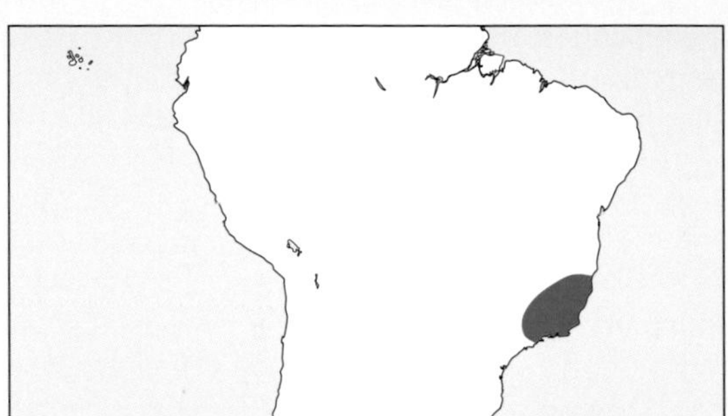

Identification Olive-green upperparts and wings. Underparts buff or yellow broadly and evenly barred dark olive. Tail olive-brown. Long, yellow moustachial line extends below eye and ear-coverts. Chin, throat, neck plain yellow. Ear-coverts dark greyish-olive. Iris pale, bluish. Bill greyish, paler at base. Legs greyish. Sexes differ in head pattern: male has red malar and crown to nape; female lacks red, having greenish malar and light olive crown. Juvenile male has orange or red crown and some green in malar.
Vocalisations Poorly known, but presumably screaming and falling wheezing and rasping notes like relatives.
Drumming Presumably drums, but information lacking.
Status No official category assigned at time of writing. Uncommon, range-restricted and very poorly known. Threatened due to deforestation and now very rare in Rio de Janeiro state. Farther north there are records from Una Biological Reserve.
Habitat Tall, dense, mature, wet (ombrophilous) forests.
Range Endemic to a relatively small area in old Atlantic Forest along the coast of SE Brazil in Espirito Santo and possibly Rio de Janeiro states – though overall distribution uncertain.
Taxonomy and variation Monotypic. Formerly treated as a race of Golden-green Woodpecker. Some females may be reddish on forehead and nape.
Similar species Yellow-browed Woodpecker is whiter below with cream-yellow supercilium. Very similar Golden-green Woodpecker is smaller, especially in wing length, but does not overlap.
Food and foraging Presumably arboreal ants, termites and other small invertebrates.

155. YELLOW-BROWED WOODPECKER
Piculus aurulentus

L 21–22cm

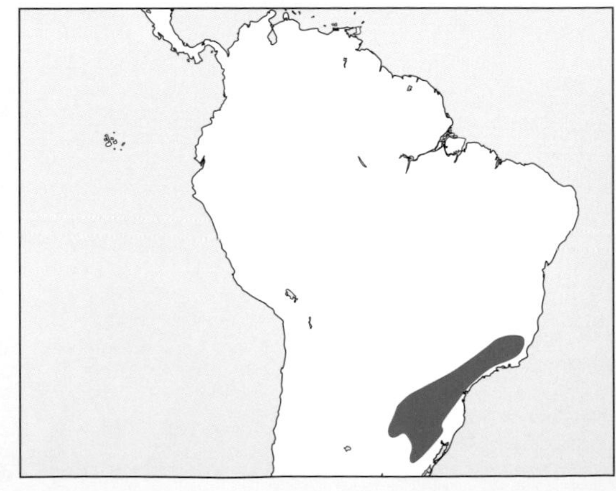

Other name White-browed Woodpecker
Identification Olive-green above with bronze tones. Underparts heavily barred white, buff or olive; barring narrow on breast, broader on belly and flanks. Upperwings olive with browner primaries and ochre or rufous panel, underwing rufous barred black. Tail blackish. Well-marked face with long fine cream-yellow supercilium that runs to nape, olive ear-coverts and ocular area, yellow band from lores to nape. Chin and throat yellow. Iris chestnut. Bill greyish. Legs greyish. Sexes differ slightly: male has all-red crown bordered by olive and red malar; female has green crown, red only on hindcrown and reduced red in malar. Juvenile much like adult, though greener overall.

Vocalisations Between 1–4 simple, slowly delivered, melancholic, piping notes, recalling a *Buteo*; also faster, longer version. A variably paced series of up to 15 high-pitched *wuh* notes. A wheeze, similar to other *Piculus* but not as frequent.

Drumming Occasional fast, solid, level-pitched rolls.

Status NT. Declining due to continued loss of rainforest. Rare in Argentina and Paraguay where logging has been intense. More common in upland forests in SE Brazil that have not been as heavily degraded. Besides logging, other threats are clearance for firewood, pasture and farmland.

Habitat Upland and lowland, humid, tropical forests. Sometimes drier forests and dense secondary growth.

Range South America. Restricted to the Atlantic Forest in SE Brazil (from Espírito Santo and Minas Gerais S to Rio Grande do Sul), NE Argentina (Misiones and NE Corrientes) and E Paraguay. Usually between 750–2000m in Brazil, but lower in Paraguay and Argentina. Resident and sedentary.

Taxonomy and variation Monotypic. Some birds have red on chin.

Similar species Atlantic Woodpecker lacks yellowish supercilium.

Food and foraging Mainly arboreal ants in all stages. Usually forages unobtrusively at mid-levels, alone, in loose pairs; often in mixed flocks in winter.

▲ Adult male Yellow-browed Woodpecker differs from the female in having all of the crown red. Rio de Janeiro, Brazil, September (*A. P. Leventis*).

◄ Adult male Yellow-browed Woodpecker. This fine woodpecker is threatened by habitat destruction. Santa Catarina, Brazil, May (*Dario Lins*).

▲ Adult female Yellow-browed Woodpecker has red on the nape as opposed to the whole crown, and a smaller area of red in the malar stripe than the male. Brazil, October (*Roger Tidman*).

Northern Flickers *Colaptes auratus*. United States, December (*Rob McKay*).

COLAPTES

A New World genus of 13 species, six known as 'flickers'. This genus has its highest diversity in South America, though two species occur in North America, and one is endemic to Cuba. They are generally social, gregarious birds of open country, even treeless landscapes, and rather terrestrial. Andean Flicker even excavates nesting burrows in earth banks, road-cuts, between rocks and walls of abandoned, or occasionally occupied, adobe buildings. The *Colaptes* are often placed in two groups: those that forage mostly on the ground, plus three more arboreal 'forest flickers', sometimes placed in a separate genus *Chrysoptilus*. Ants and termites often dominate their diet. The plumage coloration of the back is often brownish and their backs are invariably barred, which presumably provides camouflage when they are on the ground. The *Colaptes* woodpeckers are probably most closely related to those in genus *Piculus*.

156. GOLDEN-OLIVE WOODPECKER
Colaptes rubiginosus

L 19–24cm

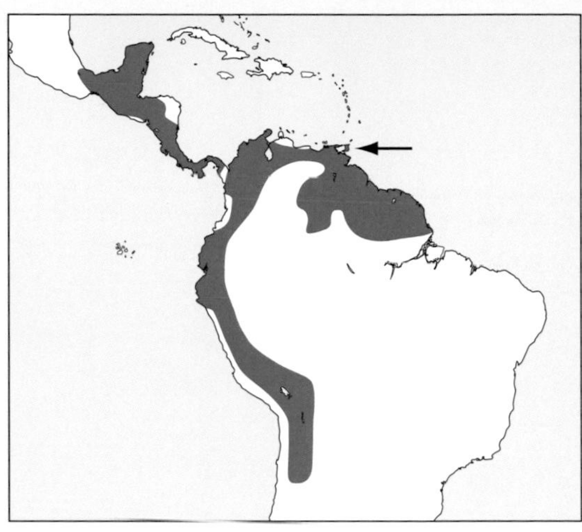

Identification Very variable and complex. Olive above, usually plain, sometimes slightly barred. Boldly barred blackish, green and yellow below, finely on throat and chest, broader below. Wings greenish-olive, shafts often yellowish. Undertail yellowish, uppertail browner. Face grey or buff, lightly barred at rear. Dark throat speckled white. Iris chestnut. Bill grey or black. Legs grey. Sexes differ: male has red malar and, depending on race, variable amount of red on crown, crown sides and nape; female lacks red malar, red only on nape. Juvenile more like adult male, but barring below vague and malar less distinct.

Vocalisations Vary regionally. Rising, explosive, loud series of *djeek or weeyk,* perhaps *wheeir* notes, often 2 per second, usually harsh, rattling, sometimes trilling or churring. Ringing, territorial *tree-tree-tree-tree.* Repeated, loud, piercing *greep, geep, dree* and *deeeeh.* Single, nasal, sharp, sometimes squeaky *k-yaah, kee-ah, chey-eh* or *kyow-n.* Bubbling *woick-woick-woick* in conflicts. Falling *pew,* dry *dzink,* rising *wink* and *ree,* buzzing *dzzet* and brief *dzert* notes.

Drumming Produces steady 1-second rolls, repeated after brief pauses. Sometimes clearly spaced knocks made rather than rapidly repeated strikes.

Status Common locally. Occurs over vast range and overall population considered stable.

Habitat Varied tropical humid and dry habitats: cloud forest, open upland and lowland oak-pine forests, wooded deltas, semi-desert with cactus and mesquite, scrub, mangroves, arable land, coffee and cocoa plantations, parks, wooded suburbs and gardens.

Range C and S America, also Trinidad and Tobago. Resident, mainly sedentary, recently expanded into Pará, Brazil. Sea-level to mountains.

Taxonomy and variation Previously in *Piculus.* Eighteen races differing in size, colour, markings and calls: ***rubiginosus*** (uplands in NC and NE Venezuela); ***yucatanensis*** (S Mexico to W Panama) has bronze wings and decreases in size from uplands to lowlands, male has red line from lores over eye; ***alleni*** (NE Colombia: Santa Marta Mts) large, bronze, golden or rufous above, rump plain, throat spotted white, barring narrow

◀ Adult male Golden-olive Woodpecker of the race *tucumanus*. Although the crown colour varies, males of all races differ from the females in having red in the malar stripe. Jujuy, Argentina, February (*Robert Güller*).

below; ***meridensis*** (NW Venezuela) golden-olive above, rump streaked, heavy white barring on chest, grey and yellow on breast, male has large red nape patch; ***tobagensis*** (Tobago) broadly barred greenish below; ***trinitatis*** (Trinidad) small, bill relatively slight, mask buff, bronze or olive above; ***deltanus*** (NE Venezuela: Delta Amacuro) also small, greenish above, large white throat spotting; ***paraquensis*** (SC Venezuelan uplands) large, mostly black crown, minimal red, bronze above; ***viridissimus*** (S Venezuela: Auyan-tepui plateau) large, back olive, mantle dusky, boldly barred blackish-grey and white below, ear-coverts barred blackish, throat black, male with little red on crown; ***guianae*** (E Venezuela, Guyana) dark olive back, barred heavily black below, black throat finely dotted buff, cheeks and crown dusky, malar reduced; ***nigriceps*** (Acari Mts of S Guyana, adjacent Surinam) male has minimal red on nape, female lacks red, crown black, bright green above; ***gularis*** (C and W Andes in Colombia) also large, pale below, male's crown almost all red, female

◄ Adult male *yucatanensis*. This race has the mid-crown grey bordered by a broad red band over the eye. Alajuela, Costa Rica, December (*Daniel Martínez A.*).

▼◄ Adult male *allenii*. This race is typically spotted white rather than streaked on the black throat. Santa Marta Mountains, Magdalena, Colombia, December (*Nick Athanas*).

▼ Adult male Golden-olive Woodpecker; this is probably race *chrysogaster* as the belly is unbarred and the crown mostly red, but racial differences can be vague. Aguascalientes, Peru, July (*Carlos Nazario Bocos*).

also very red; ***rubripileus*** (extreme SW Colombia to W Ecuador and NW Peru) has plain mantle, black barring below, male with grey centre to red crown; ***buenavistae*** (Andean foothills in E Colombia and E Ecuador) is large, rich bronze, rufous or olive above, heavily barred rump, green barring below, cheeks pale; ***coloratus*** (extreme SE Ecuador, NC Peru) golden-green above, bright yellow below, only flanks barred; ***chrysogaster*** (C Peru) plain bright yellow belly, rufous bronze tones above; ***canipileus*** (C and SE Bolivia) also yellow below but slightly barred; ***tucumanus*** (S Bolivia, NW Argentina) also large, but relatively thin-billed, olive above, whitish below.

Similar species Larger Bronze-winged Woodpecker has distinct calls. In Peru beware Black-necked Woodpecker.

Food and foraging Ants, termites, beetle larvae, some fruit and berries. Fairly arboreal, often in canopy, delving into leaf clusters, epiphytes, bromeliads, vine tangles; prey mostly gleaned. Sometimes in mixed-species foraging flocks.

◄ Adult female. This is probably race *gularis*, which is often very bronze on the wings and upperparts. Cali, Colombia, February (*Adam Riley*).

▼ Adult female Golden-olive Woodpeckers of the race *gularis* have much red on the crown. Colombia, February (*Robert Scanlon*).

157. GREY-CROWNED WOODPECKER
Colaptes auricularis

L 16–18cm

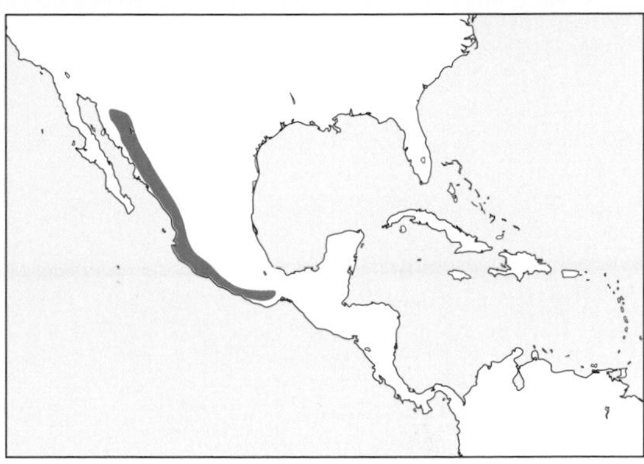

Identification Mostly olive above, greyish when worn. Forehead and crown grey or green, nape barred olive or buff. Ocular area, ear-coverts and lores buff. Chin and throat mottled olive and white. Underparts cream, buff or yellow boldly barred olive, particularly on breast. Uppertail brownish with darker tip, undertail yellow. Wings greenish-bronze, flight feathers darker with some yellowish tones. Iris chestnut. Bill greyish. Legs grey. Sexes differ: male has red malar and some red flecks at sides of crown: female lacks red, having malar mottled dark and pale. Juvenile most like adult male, but often vaguely barred below and malar rufous or grey.

Vocalisations Medium-pitched, steady, repeated, rattling or trilling series of *churr* notes. A sudden, sharp, *kee-ah* and rough, gruff, mewing *growh*.

Drumming Known to drum, but precise details lacking.

Status Poorly known, often inconspicuous and easily overlooked. Few data on population trends, but considered stable overall.

Habitat In N of range mainly damp oak or oak-pine woodlands; in S more tropical evergreen and deciduous forests.

Range Endemic to W Mexico: Pacific slope from S Sonora and Chihuahua to S Oaxaca. Lowlands and mountains, usually between 900–2400m. Resident and sedentary.

Taxonomy and variation Monotypic. Formerly in *Piculus*, but moved to present genus following phylogenetic studies. Variation slight.

Similar species Golden-olive and Bronze-winged Woodpeckers are larger, have red napes and do not overlap in range.

Food and foraging Termites, other invertebrates and berries. Forages at all levels, including on ground.

▼ Adult male Grey-crowned Woodpecker differs from the female in having a bold red malar stripe, and often a few red flecks on the crown. Jalisco, Mexico, March (*Greg R. Homel*).

▼ Adult male Grey-crowned Woodpecker. Within its range along the Pacific slope of western Mexico, this endemic is unmistakable. Barranco Liebre, Mexico, March (*Gary Thoburn*).

▼ Adult female Grey-crowned Woodpecker lacks the red malar stripe and crown markings of the male, and is overall much drabber. Jalisco, Mexico, March (*Larry Sirvio*).

▼ Juvenile male Grey-crowned Woodpecker. Note the first signs of the red malar stripe are apparent. Sonora, Mexico, July (*Dave Krueper*).

158. BRONZE-WINGED WOODPECKER
Colaptes aeruginosus

L 23–24cm

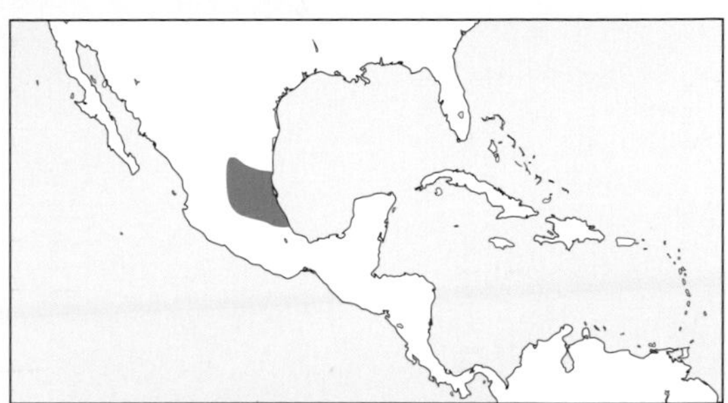

Identification Deep olive-green mantle and back, rump lightly barred. Pale underparts heavily scaled and scalloped olive, darkest on breast, wider and looser on belly, vent and flanks. Green wings edged bronze on flight feathers. Relatively long tail brownish, also with bronze tones. Charcoal-grey forehead and crown. Pale throat streaked pale green. Cream ear-coverts and ocular area, dusky at rear. Iris deep red. Relatively short, stout grey-black bill. Legs greyish. Sexes differ: male has broad red malar and red patch running from above eye to nape; female has red only on nape, lacking red malar. Juvenile less marked below, red malar less distinct on male.

Vocalisations Sharp, nasal, single or repeated *kyow-n* or *chey-eh* notes, recalling Squirrel Cuckoo. A shrill (sometimes more squeaky) series of *weeyk* or *wheeir* notes. Also low-pitched throaty chattering.

Drumming Regularly drums, but details lacking.

Status Locally not uncommon but range-restricted. Data on population size and trends lacking. IUCN conservation category not yet assigned.

Habitat Mainly humid, upland and foothill broad-leaved evergreen forest. Usually at edges and in more open areas with cacti and mesquite. Also frequents plantations.

Range Endemic to NE Mexico: Atlantic slope from C Nuevo Leon and Tamaulipas to C Veracruz. From sea-level to around 2100m. Resident and sedentary.

Taxonomy and variation Monotypic. Formerly considered a race of Golden-olive Woodpecker, but split due to distinct differences in plumage, calls and distribution. Slight individual variation.

Similar species Golden-olive Woodpecker *yucatanensis* race (which also occurs in Mexico and may coincide) is less green above, barred rather than scaled below, shorter-tailed, has different calls and males have more red on crown sides. Smaller Grey-crowned Woodpecker does not overlap.

Food and foraging Diet presumably like that of Golden-olive Woodpecker, but specific information lacking.

► Adult male Bronze-winged Woodpecker. The male mainly differs from the female in having a broad red malar stripe. San Luis Potosi, Mexico, April (*Greg R. Homel*).

▲ Adult female Bronze-winged Woodpecker at the nesting cavity. Note the malar region is speckled grey and white. San Luis Potosi, Mexico, April (*Greg R. Homel*).

◄ A pair of Bronze-winged Woodpeckers change over at the nest; the male is at the cavity entrance, the female outside. San Luis Potosi, Mexico, April (*Greg R. Homel*).

159. CRIMSON-MANTLED WOODPECKER
Colaptes rivolii

L 23–26cm

Identification Striking bright crimson on back, mantle and nape, mottled when worn. Olive rump barred buff, with reddish hue. Tail black. Wings dull red. Yellow from breast to vent, flanks spotted black, chest loosely but boldly scaled black, white and red. Throat black, speckled white. Ear-coverts buff, cream or white. Crown black or red depending on race and sex. Iris chestnut. Bill blackish. Legs grey. Sexes differ: male has red lower cheeks and malar which female lacks, being black. Juvenile brownish-red above; crown and malar black; chin and throat heavily barred black and white.

Vocalisations Calls infrequently. Single squeaky *kik* notes, sometimes up to 6 in series. Strident bursts of harsher *wik* notes. Some racial differences: *brevirostris* makes a rapid, stuttering, tinny *kee-r-r-ker-r-ke-r-r* rattle and rising, high-pitched *ree, ka-wip* and *kre-ep; atriceps* a low-pitched, rolling, falling *churrr-r-r* or *grrr-r-r-l*.

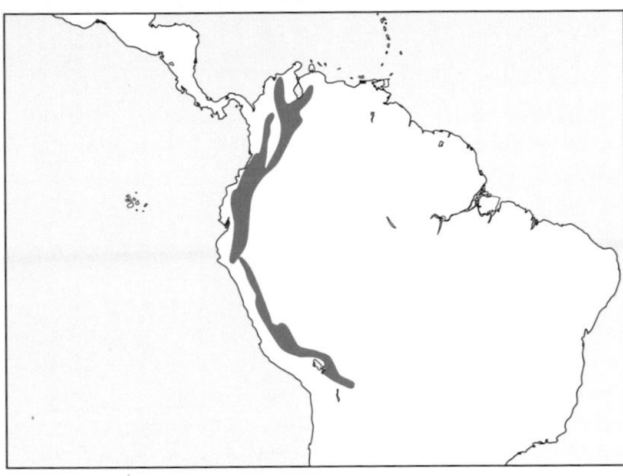

Drumming Occasionally produces soft, subdued rolls of variable speed.

Status Uncommon in Ecuador, locally common in Venezuela, Colombia and Peru. Overall considered stable.

▼ Adult male Crimson-mantled Woodpecker of the nominate race. Although crown colour varies, males of all races have a broad red malar stripe. Caldas, Colombia, May (*Félix Uribe*).

▼ A calling adult male *brevirostris*. This race has brighter red wings than the nominate. Pichincha, Ecuador, June (*Nick Athanas*).

Habitat Humid and wet, tall upland mossy *yungas*, cloud, elfin and dwarf forests. Also in drier areas and degraded forests. Ranges out into treeless bushy *paramo* to forage.

Range South America. Andes from Colombia and Venezuela S to NW Peru on Pacific slope and down E Slope into Bolivia. From 700m, typically between 1500–3700m. Resident and sedentary.

Taxonomy and variation Previously in *Piculus*. Five races: ***rivolii*** (Andes of EC Colombia) male has red crown, female black; ***meridae*** (Andes of NW Venezuela) is deep yellow below, rump and uppertail-coverts blackish, male's chin black, female buff below and chin spotted white; ***quindiuna*** (Andes of NC Colombia) female has some red on crown; ***brevirostris*** (Andes of SW Colombia, Ecuador to C Peru) is pale yellow on belly, wings very red, male with red mid-crown to nape flecked black; ***atriceps*** (Andes of SE Peru and S Bolivia) is distinct, short-billed, bronze above, with minimal red in wings and none on chest, olive ear-coverts, both sexes with black crown.

Similar species None: unmistakable within range.

Food and foraging Forages unobtrusively for ants, beetle larvae, spiders etc, mostly in canopy, probing bromeliads, epiphytes, leaf-clusters and mossy limbs, but also on ground. Some fruit taken. Often in pairs, families and mixed-species flocks.

▼ Adult female *brevirostris*. Females of all races differ from the males in lacking red in the malar stripe. Ecuador, October (*Murray Cooper*).

160. BLACK-NECKED WOODPECKER
Colaptes atricollis

L 24–26cm

Identification Large black bib formed by chin, throat and chest; neck-sides cream or grey finely barred black (despite name, black-throated rather than black-necked). Breast, belly and undertail-coverts whitish, with bold bars and chevrons. Forehead greyish, fore- and mid-crown black, red nape often shaggy. Cheek and ear-coverts buff or cream. Olive-bronze above, also heavily and tightly barred black. Rump paler. Upperwing brownish, barred olive or yellow, underwing yellowish. Tail brown, barred pale. Bill grey. Legs olive-grey. Iris chestnut. Sexes differ: male has red malar flecked black and some red on crown sides and forehead; female has blackish malar and red only on nape. Juveniles duller overall, dusky on face, mid-crown often red; male's malar variably red and black, female's black.

Vocalisations Territorial song a rapid series of loud, strong, trilling *ki-ki-ki* or *di-di-di* notes. Single, sharp (sometimes more squeaky) falling *kee, keer, kew* or *peah* notes repeated after brief pauses. Repeated *wic-wic-wic* and *whi-cop, whi-cop* in disputes.

Drumming Occasionally produces steady, level-pitched rolls, repeated after short pauses and interspersed with calls.

Status Rather uncommon and localised, but overall population considered stable.

Habitat Mainly drier open, scrubby tropical forests; also cloud-forest, gallery forest, wooded river valleys, upland shrub country and desert with columnar cacti, plus cultivated areas with scattered trees and wooded gardens. Plantations and orchards, with native or exotic trees, have become important where native forests have been felled.

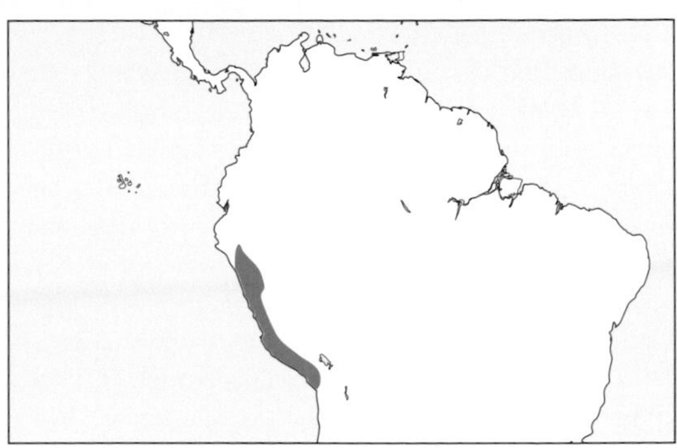

Range South America. Endemic to Andean Peru, between 500–4300m. Resident, but may make seasonal altitudinal movements.

Taxonomy and variation Two races: ***atricollis*** (S Peru: W Andean slope from La Libertad to W Arequipa); and ***peruvianus*** (N Peru: Marañon Valley on E Andean slope), which is less barred below and more barred above, wing-coverts edged pale, overall smaller and shorter-billed than nominate.

Similar species Golden-olive Woodpecker (which may overlap) is smaller, usually plain-backed (but beware *rubripileus* race) with less black on throat.

Food and foraging Mainly ants in all stages. Not as terrestrial as some relatives, though will forage low in bushes, sometimes on the ground.

► Adult male Black-necked Woodpecker has a variable amount of red on the crown and a red malar stripe. This bird is of the race *peruvianus*, Marañón Valley, Peru, November (*Simon Walkley*).

►► Adult female nominate Black-necked Woodpecker differs from the male in having a black forecrown and lacking red in the malar region. Santa Eulalia Valley, Peru, October (*Pete Morris*).

161. SPOT-BREASTED WOODPECKER
Colaptes punctigula

L 18–23cm

Other name Spot-breasted Flicker

Identification Variable in size and plumage, but always barred above and spotted below. Plain cream or white cheek and ear-coverts striking. Bronze, golden or olive above, with barred and scaled black. Underparts olive or yellow spotted black, chest often washed rufous, belly plainer. Forecrown black, mid-crown to nape red. Black and white throat. Green or bronze wings barred black. Uppertail blackish, coverts and outer feathers yellowish. Iris chestnut. Bill blackish. Legs greyish-green. Sexes differ: male has scarlet malar, which female lacks. Juvenile like respective adult (male with red in malar) but greener above, duller below, spotting bolder.

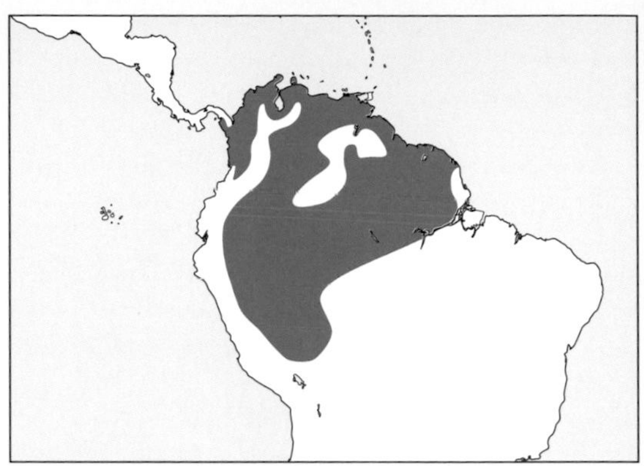

Vocalisations Variable, fast or slow, steady or whinnying series of 8–12 high-pitched whistling or nasal *kee, kah, wee* or *wha* notes, like Great Black Hawk or Solitary Eagle. Mewing, *toowee* and *whi-cop,* recalling Black-necked Woodpecker. Shrill, fast, repeated *peek, wick* or *ka-wick* notes when alarmed, piping *whew* in displays.

Drumming Level rolls of varying length produced, repeated with short pauses between each.

Status Possibly increasing as fairly adaptable and benefits from forest clearance. Often common and conspicuous, perching on dead palms, utility poles and even wires

Habitat Various open, patchy, humid woodlands: rainforest edges, riverine forest, *várzea, llanos,* swamps, mangroves, palm and coffee plantations, wooded savanna, farmland, gardens and even city parks.

Range South America. From Panama through Amazonia to N Bolivia. Mainly lowlands, but to 1600m. Resident, moving into cleared areas.

Taxonomy and variation Six races: ***punctigula*** (the Guianas) is smallest; ***striatigularis*** (WC Colombia) pale green above, rump and breast reddish, heavily spotted, throat with minimal black; ***ujhelyii*** (E Panama, N Colombia) lightly barred above, breast vivid orange-red, much red on crown; ***zuliae*** (NW Venezuela) yellow or orange barred black above, rump buff or yellow with black heart shapes, large but sparse breast spots, throat mostly white; ***punctipectus*** (E Colombia, Venezuela,

◄ Adult male Spot-breasted Woodpecker of race *guttatus*. The male differs from the female in having a broad, bright red malar stripe. Amazonas, Brazil, April (*Marcelo Barreiros*).

except NW) grey or olive above with wide barring, rump buff or yellow, no red below, breast spots small and few, throat mostly black, male's malar tinged black; ***guttatus*** (Amazonian Ecuador, Peru, Bolivia and NW Brazil) dark green above, olive breast heavily spotted, throat mostly black with large white spots, male's malar flecked black, red on crown reduced.

Similar species Green-barred Woodpecker larger, darker, boldly barred below, not spotted. Hardly meets Golden-olive Woodpecker, which is barred below and plain above.

Food and foraging Mainly ants, in all stages. Regularly forages in family groups, rarely with other species. Often in *Cecropia* trees and on ground.

▲ Adult male nominate race. Deforestation may have benefited this species, as it prefers open secondary habitats. French Guiana, December (*Michel Giraud-Audine*).

◄ Adult female *ujhelyii*. Note lack of red malar. This race has orange tones on the chest and breast. Antioquia, Colombia, November (*Félix Uribe*).

162. GREEN-BARRED WOODPECKER
Colaptes melanochloros

L 27–29cm

Other name Green-barred Flicker

Identification Very variable. Upperparts green or yellow barred chocolate. Rump paler. Yellowish-cream below, chest and breast spotted black, belly less so, flanks barred. Wings brown or olive, finely barred pale, underwings buff. Tail black, variably barred yellow. Forehead to mid-crown black, nape red. Ear-coverts cream tinged olive. White throat, streaked black. Iris chestnut. Bill black. Legs grey or green. Sexes differ slightly: male has red malar flecked black; female has black malar flecked pale. Juvenile has bolder, broader barring above and some barring below.

Vocalisations Up to 10 high-pitched, undulating, squeaky, liquid *kwik*, *wik* or *wika* notes, sometimes laughing or bubbling. Also *ker-wick* and *ta-wick*. Repeated, sharp *kip* or *chip* and *peek* notes. Single or double, rapid, nasal, sometimes throaty, falling *tid-urrrr* and harsher *wheeo*. Slower series of 6–7 high-pitched *wirr* notes and strident series of loud piping calls.

Drumming Both sexes produce occasional, medium-paced, level-pitched, short rolls, often interspersed with calls.

Status Widespread and locally common. Overall probably stable.

Habitat Wide range occupied. Humid and dry open woodlands, gallery forest, bamboo, *caatinga* scrub, wooded savanna, pampas and desert, dry upland Andean valley scrub, plantations and parks.

Range South America. Brazil, Paraguay, Uruguay, Argentina and Bolivia. Sea-level to 3000m in Bolivia. Most populations sedentary, though local movements apparently in C Argentina.

Taxonomy and variation Five races differing in size, markings and habitat. Often placed in two groups. Nominate ***melanochloros*** (SE Brazil, SE Paraguay, NE Argentina and Uruguay) and smaller, more yellow, finely spotted ***nattereri*** (NE and C Brazil into E Bolivia: Santa Cruz region) are more arboreal. Three larger, more terrestrial races together sometimes treated as distinct species 'Golden-breasted Woodpecker': ***melanolaimus*** (C and S Bolivia) has golden breast, white belly; ***nigroviridis*** (S Bolivia, W Paraguay, N and E Argentina, W Uruguay) has boldly barred tail, less gold below and is more boldly spotted; ***leucofrenatus*** (NW and WC Argentina S to W Rio Negro) is largest and brownest, golden-orange with heavy black chevrons on breast, barred lower flanks and white rump.

◄ Adult male Green-barred Woodpecker of race *nigroviridis*. Note the hint of red in the malar. Buenos Aires, Argentina, April (*James Lowen*).

Races intergrade. Some individuals plain-backed.

Similar species Spot-breasted Woodpecker much smaller and yellower. Black-necked Woodpecker does not overlap in range.

Food and foraging Invertebrates, mainly ants, in all stages, taken on the ground (often with Campo Flickers) and in bamboo and trees. Also sap, berries and fruit, including cactus.

▼ Adult female; note the black-and-pale malar lacks red. Together with the nominate, this race, *nattereri*, is regarded as being more arboreal than others of this species. Goiás, Brazil, July (*William Price*).

▼ Adult female *leucofrenatus* – one of the so-called 'golden-breasted' group. Santa Rosa, Patagonia, Argentina, January (*Gerhard Rotheneder*).

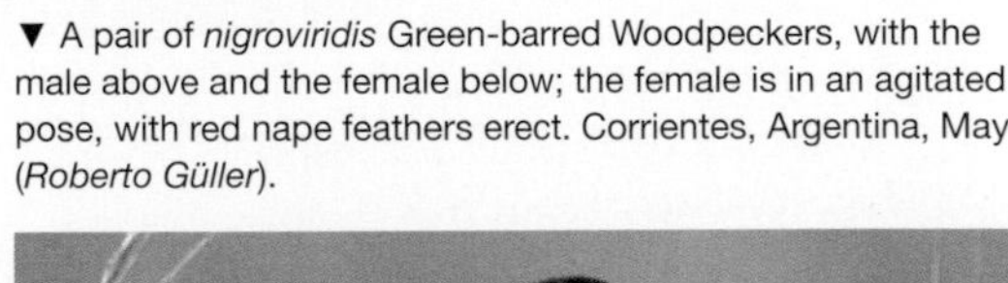

▼ A pair of *nigroviridis* Green-barred Woodpeckers, with the male above and the female below; the female is in an agitated pose, with red nape feathers erect. Corrientes, Argentina, May (*Roberto Güller*).

163. NORTHERN FLICKER
Colaptes auratus

L 30–33cm

Identification Very variable (see below for forms). General characteristics include the following. Tan back barred black. White rump, obvious in flight. Black tail, white on outer feathers. White or buff below, boldly spotted black with large black chest band. Yellow or red underwing, striking in flight. Long, dark, slightly curved bill. Iris chestnut. Legs grey. Sexes differ mainly in malar colour. Juvenile 'yellow-shafted' has red on nape or even crown; both sexes of juvenile 'red-shafted' usually have colour in malar stripe.

Vocalisations Very vocal. A loud, steady, low-pitched, monotone crescendo series *kwik-wik-wik, kick-kick-kick* or *wick-wick-wick* of about 20 seconds. Slower, repeated *wick-a, wick-a, wik-up, wik-up* or *we-cups-we-cups* during displays. Pairs call to each other with a soft *fli-quer* or *flicker.* Also a drawn-out, cackling *pic-pic-pic-pic.* Contact calls include a sharp, clear, high-pitched, falling *keeew* and *klee-yer.* Soft, rolling *wirrr* or *whirrdle* probably produced by wings. Startled birds utter *bwirr* and *ee-ee-ee. Kee-you* or *ki-u* in alarm.

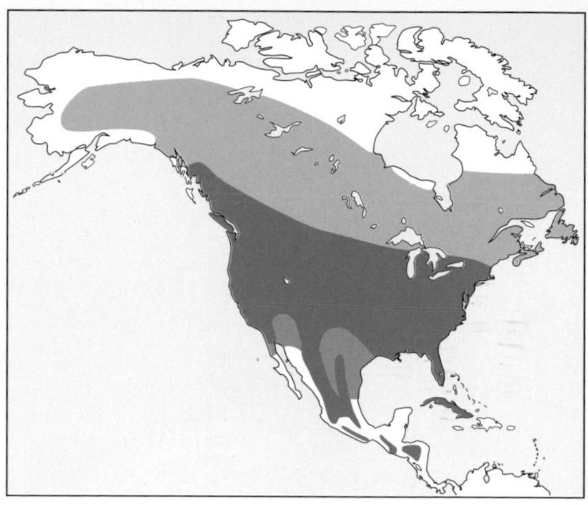

Drumming Both sexes drum. Simple, long, even roll of c.25 strikes (22 per second). In spring, rolls repeated every 10–40 seconds, often interspersed with *kwik* or *wick* calls.

Status Common and widespread, but has decreased locally in USA and threatened by deforestation in Cuba.

Habitat Wide variety of open boreal, temperate and tropical mixed forests. Also savanna, swamps, mangroves, riparian woods, meadows, pastures, arable land, parks, plantations, gardens.

Range North and Central America. Breeds from Alaska and Canada south of tree line through most of USA to Nicaragua. Sedentary on Cuba and Grand Cayman. Northernmost populations migratory, wintering as far south as Mexico. Large passage groups occur along coasts in September-October and late March-April. Some movements also made from mountains to lowlands and Pacific coast. Sea-level to 4000m. 'Yellow-shafted' vagrant to Azores and Denmark.

Taxonomy and variation Taxonomy complex. Some races, differing in size, colour and markings, may warrant consideration as species. Nine races, often placed in four groups. **'Yellow-shafted Flicker'**: ***auratus*** (SE USA), ***luteus*** (C Alaska to S Labrador, Newfoundland, Montana, NE USA). **'Red-shafted Flicker'**: ***cafer*** (S Alaska, British Columbia to N

◄ Adult male *cafer* – this race is in the 'red-shafted' group. Note the red malar stripe (which is cinnamon in the female, and black in male 'yellow-shafted'), and the red on the shafts of the tail feathers. California, October (*Tom Reichner*).

▲ Adult male *gundlachi*, showing the yellow underwings and undertail. Colours vary between regions and races. Grand Cayman, April (*Yves-Jacques Rey-Millet*).

▲ Adult female *gundlachi* lacks the black malar of the male. Grand Cayman, October (*Yves-Jacques Rey-Millet*).

▼ A pair of Northern Flickers in display. These are of race *luteus*, part of the 'yellow-shafted' group. The male (left) has a black malar stripe, which is absent in the female. Note the yellow of the tail-feathers. New York, United States, May (*Tom Vezo*).

California); ***collaris*** (SW USA, NW Baja, NW Mexico); ***mexicanus*** (W Mexico: Durango to San Luis Potosi and Oaxaca); ***nanus*** (W Texas, NE Mexico). '**Guatemalan Flicker**': ***mexicanoides*** (Chiapas, Mexico to Nicaragua). '**Cuban Flicker**': ***chrysocaulosus*** (Cuba); ***gundlachi*** (Grand Cayman). 'Yellow-shafted' resides N and E of a diagonal line from Alaska to Gulf of Mexico; 'red-shafted' to its W and S. The two are not difficult to distinguish, but a stable overlap zone exists from S Alaska and W Canada, along the E Rockies and N Great Plains where hybrid 'orange-shafted' birds may predominate. 'Red-shafted' has pink or red underwing-coverts and tail feather shafts, grey face and throat, brown crown and broad chest band. 'Yellow-shafted' has yellow wing and tail markings, tan face and throat, grey crown, narrower crescent-shaped chest band and red nape patch. Male 'red-shafted' has red malar, female cinnamon; male 'yellow-shafted' has black malar, which female lacks. 'Guatemalan' has orange underwing-coverts and tail feather shafts, orange or rusty crown, grey face, large square chest band, female has cinnamon malar. 'Cuban' has golden underwing-coverts and tail feather shafts, red nape, large chest band; male has black malar, female none.

Similar species Smaller, shorter-winged Gilded Flicker overlaps (and hybridises) with 'red-shafted', males of both having red malar. In Cuba larger Fernandina's Flicker lacks red nape, chest band and white rump.

Food and foraging Omnivorous. Typically forages on ground for ants, also termites, insect larvae, spiders, berries, nuts, fruit, seeds; also forages in trees and bushes and visits feeders. Hawks for winged prey. Often in groups, especially on passage.

164. GILDED FLICKER
Colaptes chrysoides

L 26–30cm

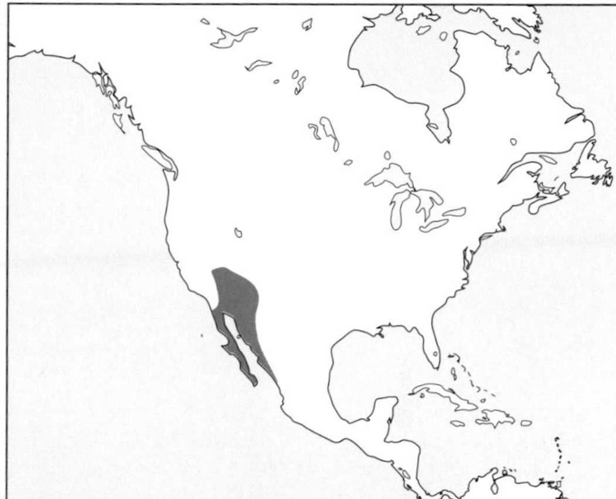

Identification Typical flicker with yellow (gilded) underwings and undertail. Brown crown with cinnamon forehead. Grey face, throat, ear-coverts and neck. Upperparts tan, sparsely barred chocolate. Large black patch across chest forms a squared-off bib. Breast and belly white with bold black spots, more like chevrons on flanks. White rump obvious in flight. Tail brown or black with one third to one half yellow beneath. Long, dark bill. Legs greyish. Iris chestnut. Sexes differ slightly: male has red malar, female lacks red but may have rufous tinge. Juvenile has bolder barring above, larger spots below, smaller bib, duller yellow underwing; juvenile male has slight red malar.
Vocalisations Similar to Northern Flicker, possibly higher-pitched. Thin, squeaky notes, rapid yapping and repeated rolling, throaty call. A sudden, powerful, falling *pe-ah, klee-yer* or *kleer.* Repeated *whit, wik, kik* notes. Soft *wick-a* chatter uttered by pairs and groups.
Drumming Quiet, soft rolls when drumming on saguaros, as loud as other flickers when on cottonwoods trees.
Status Common locally but habitat change in Mexico, where parts of Sonora Desert have been converted to farmland, has meant declines. Gone from much of SE California, declined in parts of Arizona but increasing elsewhere in USA.
Habitat Lowland deserts with saguaro, cacti and yucca (nest-holes usually excavated in saguaro or cottonwoods, later used by owls and other wildlife). Also open scrub and riparian woodlands, especially with cottonwoods and willows. Moves into grassy suburbs and visits feeders.
Range Extreme southern North America. Restricted to NW Mexico, Baja California and very SW USA. Sea-level to 900m. Resident and sedentary.
Taxonomy and variation Formerly considered race of Northern Flicker. Four races: ***chrysoides*** (S Baja California); ***brunnescens*** (C and N Baja California) much like nominate but browner; ***mearnsi*** (extreme SE California, Arizona, extreme NW Mexico) palest overall with cinnamon crown; ***tenebrosus*** (NW Mexico:

► Adult male Gilded Flicker has a distinct red malar stripe, which the female lacks. Nest-holes are typically in a saguaro cactus. This bird is of race *mearnsi*. Arizona, United States, April (*Stan Tekiela*).

Sonora S of previous into N Sinaloa) darkest and most barred, crown brown. Intergrades occur.

Similar species Very like Northern Flicker (hybridises) but smaller and shorter-winged. Most like 'red-shafted' form, but base of tail and underwings yellow (like 'yellow-shafted'), crescents rather than spots on flanks and larger, squarer chest bib.

Food and foraging Rather terrestrial, often foraging in open for invertebrates, particularly ants. Cactus fruit, nectar and nuts also taken.

▲ Adult female *mearnsi*. Note the cinnanmon crown and lack of red malar. Arizona, United States, April (*Stan Tekiela*).

◄ Adult male Gilded Flicker of the nominate race. Note the yellow undertail and black chest patch, which is larger than on the similar Northern Flicker. Baja California, Mexico, April (*Pete Morris*).

165. FERNANDINA'S FLICKER
Colaptes fernandinae

L 30–33cm

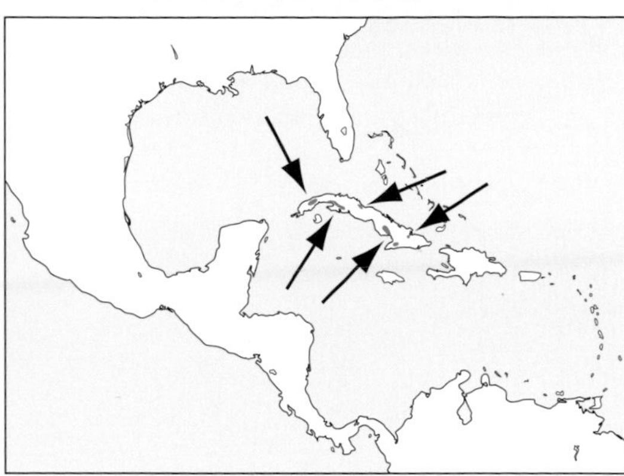

Other name Cuban Flicker (as is, confusingly, Cuban race of Northern Flicker)

Identification Upperparts, wings and long tail yellowish or tan, heavily and finely barred and flecked chocolate. Chest, belly and underwings yellow or buff with broader black barring. Chin and throat heavily streaked black and white. Pale crown and nape finely streaked chocolate, sometimes with orange tones. Ocular area cream or grey, ear-coverts and rear neck-sides cinnamon. Grey orbital ring, iris dark. Long, decurved black bill. Legs greyish. Sexes differ: male has broad black malar; female malar indistinct, greyish mottled white. Juvenile warmer, plainer above, with broader bars below.

Vocalisations Often silent. Series of shrill, sharp *pic-pic-pic* or *wik-wik-wik* notes of variable speed, deeper-pitched than sympatric Northern Flicker, recalling Gundlach's Hawk. A brief, nasal *ch-ch-ch*, a loud, sharp *keer*, a chattering *krrr* (not as harsh as West Indian Woodpecker). Also a falling *peah*.

Drumming Infrequent quiet rolls produced.

Status VU. Rare. Once widespread, but now with

▼ Adult male Fernandina's Flicker has a broad black malar stripe; that of the female is greyish, flecked white. Bermejas, Cuba, April (*William Price*).

a fragmented, declining population estimated at fewer than 900 individuals, and perhaps as low as 400. Main threats are logging and clearance of trees for farming. Since nest trees are often shared with Cuban Parrots, illegal felling by trappers to collect young parrots causes the loss of woodpecker clutches or broods. Conservation work has included educational projects in villages to raise awareness of this problem.

Habitat Wooded savanna, pastures and swamps, palm plantations, open forests and parkland. Scattered trees, especially palms, whether dead or alive, important for nesting.

Range Endemic to Cuba. Localised, core area being Zapata Swamp, Matanzas province. Resident, but has occurred on Grand Bahama.

Taxonomy and variation Monotypic. Variation insignificant.

Similar species Cuban race of Northern Flicker more boldly marked with crimson nape and black chest patch.

Food and foraging Invertebrates supplemented with seeds and berries. Typically forages on bare ground and in leaf-litter.

▼ Adult female. This Cuban endemic is seriously threatened and now very localised. Bermejas, Cuba, April (*William Price*).

166. CHILEAN FLICKER
Colaptes pitius

L 30–33cm

Identification Appears stocky and round-winged. Relatively short bill and short tail. Heavily barred, not brightly coloured, overall grey, black and white, browner when plumage worn. Upperparts and wings greyish-brown, heavily barred buff. Chin and throat buff, with dark spotting. Buffy below, densely barred brown on breast, looser on belly and flanks. Chocolate flight feathers show pale yellow shafts in flight. Underwing yellowish. White rump also obvious in flight. Crown dark grey, forehead and nape paler. Face and ear-coverts buffy. Blackish bill, slightly drooped. Iris yellowish. Legs grey. Sexes differ: male has vague dusky malar, sometimes slightly rufous, nape sometimes tinged red; female has pale malar, never showing red. Juvenile much like adult female, but crown black

► Adult male Chilean Flicker. The sexes are similar but, although variable, males always have a darker malar stripe than the females. Torres del Paine, Chile, February (*Gonzalo Gonzalez*).

with pale feather tips; broader bars above, more spotting below; iris darker, bluish.

Vocalisations Very vocal. Loud, repeated, high-pitched, sharp *pitee-you, pitee-u* or *pit-tweeo* (local names *pitio* and *pitiu*). Of variable speed, faster versions recalling a squeaky wheel. High-pitched *wick* and *week-a* notes in series. Strong, single, double or repeated, whistling *kwee*. Also harsh laughing series of *wheek* notes, louder as it progresses.

Drumming May tap by nest, but not known to drum properly.

Status Often locally common. Few data on numbers and trends, but overall considered stable.

Habitat Fairly wide range of open, dry and damp wooded habitats. These include cool temperate woodlands, especially with southern beech (*Nothofagus*), forest edges, bushy scrub, riverine valleys, cultivated land, plantations, fields with scattered trees and around settlements.

Range South America. Restricted to temperate Andean foothills in C and S Chile and Patagonian SW Argentina. Sea-level to tree line. Resident and essentially sedentary.

Taxonomy and variation Monotypic. Variation slight.

Similar species None within range.

Food and foraging Mainly ants in all stages. Also other insects, scorpions and seeds. Often forages on ground but also in trees, in pairs and raucous family groups.

▲ Adult female; note the lack of colour in the malar stripe. Santa Cruz, Argentina, November (*James Lowen*).

◄ Juvenile Chilean Flickers are very similar; however, the darkish malar stripe on this bird indicates that it is a male. Note the bluish iris and mottled crown Los Glaciares, Patagonia, Argentina, December (*Gerhard Rotheneder*).

167. ANDEAN FLICKER
Colaptes rupicola

L 32–33cm

Identification Long-billed and long-tailed, appearing heavy and round-winged in flight. Crown and nape black. Ear-coverts, chin and throat cream or buff. Boldly barred black or brown and buff or cream above. Black tail finely barred pale on outer feathers, white uppertail-coverts lightly barred chocolate, undertail sides buff. White or buff rump, sometimes faintly barred, obvious in flight. Brownish upperwings subtly barred buff, underwings yellowish with dark trailing edge. Mostly cream or buff below, chest and flanks lightly spotted and flecked black, breast often washed orange. Long, decurved, broad-based black bill. Iris yellow. Legs variably grey, buff or flesh. Sexes differ: male has red (varying according to race) in dark malar; female lacks red and has shorter bill. Juvenile overall duller with buff nape, more barring below and pale blue iris.

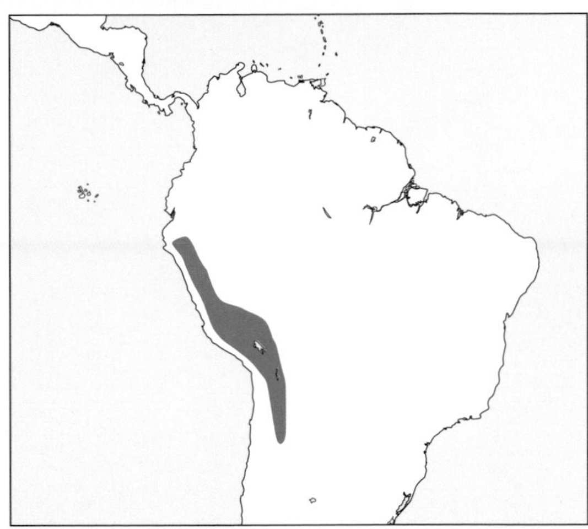

▼ Adult male nominate Andean Flicker. This is the least marked race below, although males have the most red in the malar stripe. Parinacota, Chile, October (*Gonzalo Gonzalez*).

◄ An adult female Andean Flicker takes off from a rock, showing the yellow underwings. This bird is of the nominate race. Lauca, Chile, November (*James Lowen*).

◄ Adult male *puna*. The sexes of this race are similar; both have red on the nape, but males also have some red in the black malar stripe. Huarcapay, Peru, November (*Gerard Gorman*).

Vocalisations Often vocal, families constantly chattering. Various loud, sharp or yapping *peek, peea, kik, kek* and *quoi* contact notes. Whistling *tew-tew-tew,* recalling some *Tringa* sandpipers. Loud, laughing *kwa-kwa-kwa* and *kway-ap-kway-ap* in displays. Trilling or rattling, falling *brrrri-dip* and plaintive *keeoow,* both carrying well in open terrain. Also a *kli-kli-kli* series, rising *oo-eet* and scolding alarm often given in flight.

Drumming Drums very rarely (some may never drum), producing low, level-pitched rolls.

Status Little data on population size and trends. Some local declines, but probably stable overall.

Habitat High Andean treeless, stony, rocky, grassy terrain (*puna* and *paramo*), often by boggy ground, nesting in canyons and outcrops. Occasionally scrub, woodland patches at tree line and plantations.

Range South America. NC Andes, usually between 2000–5000m, sometimes down to 800m. Resident, not entirely sedentary, wandering to lower elevations when snow hinders foraging.

Taxonomy and variation Three races: ***rupicola*** (Bolivia, N Chile, NW Argentina) is palest race, least marked, male has mostly red malar; ***cinereicapillus*** (extreme SE Ecuador, N Peru) largest, darkest, ochre-cinnamon on face and below, chest barred, male with minimal red at rear of black malar; ***puna*** (C and S Peru) very buff, yellowish on rump, spotted below, red on nape, male with partially red malar. Races intergrade.

Similar species None: Chilean Flicker in different habitat.

Food and foraging Insects. Highly terrestrial, foraging in groups on bare ground, sweeping away debris, digging into soil and probing grassy tussocks.

▼ Andean Flickers are highly terrestrial, and are unlikely to be confused with any other woodpecker. This is an adult female of the race *puna*. Cusco, Peru, July (*Carlos Nazario Bocos*).

168. CAMPO FLICKER
Colaptes campestris

L 28–31cm

Identification Striking, mainly black, white and yellow overall. Mantle and back chocolate boldly barred cream or white. White rump finely barred dark, brownish uppertail-coverts barred white. Tail chocolate, central feathers mostly brown, outers barred buff or white. Underwings pale. Throat black or white (see below). Neck and breast yellow, rest of underparts cream or buff finely marked with chocolate bars, spots and chevrons. Crown black. Ocular area greyish, ear-coverts buffish. Lores whitish. Iris chestnut. Long, slightly decurved, grey-black bill. Legs grey, sometimes pinkish. Sexes differ slightly: male has variable amount of red in black malar; female black and white speckled malar. Juvenile has paler yellow neck and breast and darker barring below.

Vocalisations Often noisy. Shrill, single notes include *ee, oo, wik, gwik, kyow* and *pya*. Contact call a low-pitched *wicka-wicka* or *wee-a-wee-a*. Alarm a sharp, whistling *week-week-week* or *keep-keep-keep,* recalling some *Tringa* sandpipers. A harsh *kwih-kya-wi-kya-wi* or *ka-ka-a-a-a-ka-waa.* A loud *kyoo-kyookyoo-kyek-kyek* usually given in flight. Also a liquid bubbling song. Birds indulge in duets of high-pitched *wicwicwic* and lower *wucwucwuc.*

◄ Adult male Campo Flicker of the race *campestroides*. Males of both races mainly differ from the females in having rufous tones in the malar stripe. Corrientes, Argentina, January (*Roberto Güller*).

Drumming May not drum, or perhaps only rarely, but information lacking.

Status Locally common and conspicuous, but ecology little studied. Increasing, as occupying deforested areas in Atlantic Forest and Amazonia and benefiting from woodland clearance for pasture and farmland.

Habitat Open lowland and hill country: savanna, pampas and pastures. Also forest clearings, plantations, cultivated land, wasteland, parkland. Locally in *caatinga*, bushy *cerrado* and wet grasslands in Pantanal and Paraguayan Chaco. Nest-holes are excavated in dead trees, earth banks and termite mounds.

Range South America. East of the Andes, mostly S of the Amazon. Isolated populations N of Amazon in Brazil and Surinam. Resident and essentially sedentary.

Taxonomy and variation Two races: ***campestris*** (S Suriname, SE and E Brazil, Bolivia, C Paraguay) has black throat; ***campestroides*** (S Paraguay, S Brazil, Uruguay, NE Argentina), which has been considered full species 'Field Flicker', has buffish-white throat, is less barred below, male has less red in malar, female usually with white malar spotted black. Races hybridise in Paraguay and S Brazil, offspring with

variable throat colour. Some birds have pale iris.
Similar species None: unmistakable within range.
Food and foraging Mostly ants and termites taken on ground and at their colonies. Opportunistic, taking other insects, some fruit, even nestlings of other birds. A social species, foraging in family groups.

▲ Adult female *campestroides*. This white-throated race has been considered a distinct species (when it is referred to as 'Field Flicker'). Corrientes, Argentina, November (*James Lowen*).

▲► Adult female nominate. Note the black throat, sharply different from that of *campestroides*. Itanhaem, Brazil, April (*Ronald Gruijters*).

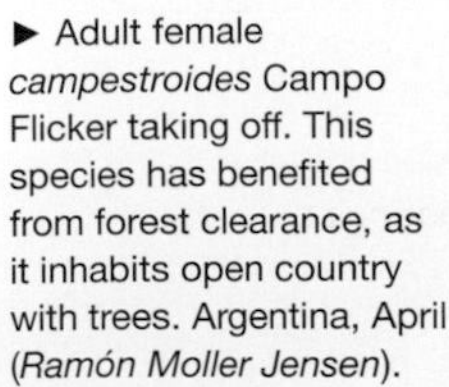

► Adult female *campestroides* Campo Flicker taking off. This species has benefited from forest clearance, as it inhabits open country with trees. Argentina, April (*Ramón Moller Jensen*).

Blond-crested Woodpecker *Celeus flavescens*, adult male. This bird is of the race *ochraceus*. Itanhaem, Brazil, March.

CELEUS

A genus of 11 arboreal species that occur in Central and South America, particularly Amazonian Brazil. They are distinctive, medium to relatively large, several appearing stout and robust, most with rich rufous, brown or cinnamon plumage (Cream-coloured Woodpecker is the exception). Many sport impressive, well-developed bushy crests and pale bills. Most *Celeus* forage in the canopy of humid, lowland forests and regularly eat fruit.

169. CINNAMON WOODPECKER
Celeus loricatus

L 19–23cm

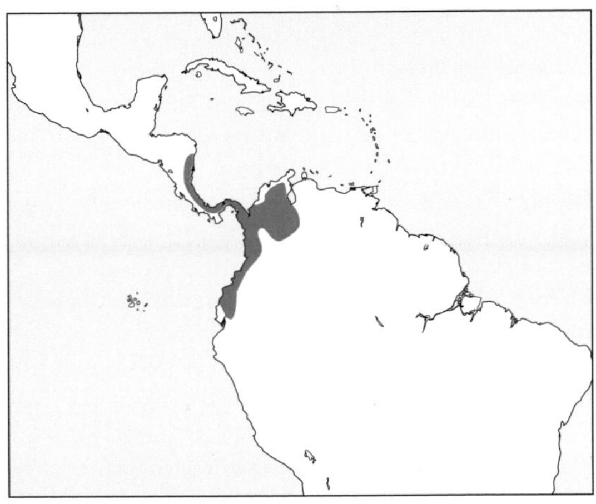

Identification Cinnamon and brown above, variably marked, often sparsely, with black bars and chevrons. Rump paler. Buff, yellow and cinnamon below with heavy or light black chevrons, especially on belly and flanks. Flight feathers chestnut finely or broadly barred black. Upper tail barred buff and black, tip black. Short crest, shaggy nape. Crown, crest and most of head cinnamon-brown. Grey or yellow bill. Iris reddish. Legs grey. Sexes differ: male has red chin, throat, cheek and malar region; female lacks red and has duller bill. Juvenile similar to respective adult but less marked below.

Vocalisations Often quiet. Song a loud, shrill, ringing series of usually four or five *peee-peee-pew-poo-pu* or *wheeet-wheeet-wheeet-it* notes, accelerating but

► Adult male Cinnamon Woodpecker differs from the female in having red over the throat and malar region, and often a paler bill. This is the nominate race. Rio Claro, Colombia, January (*Pete Morris*).

falling in pitch – recalling Black-striped Woodcreeper *Xiphorhynchus lachrymosus*. Sometimes proceeded by *chuweeoo*. Variant, with a more musical ending, is *dwee-dwee-dwe-dwe-it*. Also *phet, phet, phet, phet,* a hard, rattling, chattering *chikikikik* ending in squeaks and *titittit-too* and *chwee-titit*. Series of *splink* contact notes that increases in tempo before weakening.

Drumming Brief, steady, careful, slow rolls.

Status Locally common, but uncommon in Ecuador and Colombia. Overall population considered stable, but some declines noted.

Habitat Tall, lowland, primary rainforest and humid to wet, mature secondary growth. Occasionally in drier forests and partially logged forests.

Range Central and South America. Mostly N of Equator. From Nicaragua south along Caribbean slope to Colombia, down Pacific slope into Ecuador (only *Celeus* on Pacific slope). Mainly lowlands and foothills to 1500m. Resident and sedentary.

Taxonomy and variation Four races with significant racial and individual differences, particularly in extent and intensity of barring, some perhaps warranting species status: ***loricatus*** (W Colombia to S Ecuador) dark and very heavily caled black below; ***diversus*** (E Nicaragua, E Costa Rica, NW Panama) lighter, more cinnamon, less marked above, finely barred below, much red on throat, yellowish bill; ***mentalis*** (rest of Panama, NW Colombia) paler still, cream below, very lightly barred above, crown spotted black, tail evenly barred black and white; ***innotatus*** (N Colombia) most distinct race, head lacks spotting and barring, throat patch smaller, usually cream and cinnamon below with only faint markings, tail with broad white and narrow black bars.

Similar species Chestnut-coloured Woodpecker larger, head pale, darker chestnut below and calls very different. Most like Scale-breasted and Waved Woodpeckers, but does not meet either.

Food and foraging Ants, termites, berries and fruit. Usually in canopy, foraging inconspicuously alone, but also lower down in undergrowth. Rarely joins mixed flocks.

▼ Adult female Cinnamon Woodpecker. Note the bold black chevrons on the underparts of this species. This is the nominate race. Rio Claro, Colombia, March (*Pete Morris*).

170. WAVED WOODPECKER
Celeus undatus

L 22–23cm

Identification Various subtle shades of chestnut, rufous and cinnamon on body, head and paler face. Neck and short shaggy crest and nape (appears hammer-headed) gently streaked blackish. Throat cinnamon or buff, spotted black. Upperparts rufous-cinnamon finely barred black. Rump buff or yellowish with wavy dark barring. Underparts rufous or buff, densely marked, particularly on flanks and belly, with black chevrons and bars. Most of upperwing chestnut barred boldly black; flight feathers black also barred; underwing cinnamon. Uppertail tipped black, under-tail paler. Yellowish bill with bluish base. Legs greyish. Iris reddish. Sexes differ: male has wide red area over malar and cheek; female lacks red. Juvenile less barred.
Vocalisations Sudden, nasal, whistling, rising then falling two-note *kurry-hoo* or *curry-koo,* almost identical to Scale-breasted Woodpecker. Also a loud, harsher version *whick-coer* or *wit-coa* and a metallic *pring-pring.*
Drumming Both sexes drum. Steady, usually quiet, level-pitched rolls, often interspersed with calls.
Status Locally common in the Guianas, Brazil and Venezuela. Population data limited, but possibly decreasing, though seems adaptable.
Habitat Rainforest, riverine forest, mangroves. Occasionally drier forests and wooded savanna.
Range NE South America. Found in Venezuela, the Guianas and Brazil. Mainly lowlands. Sea-level to

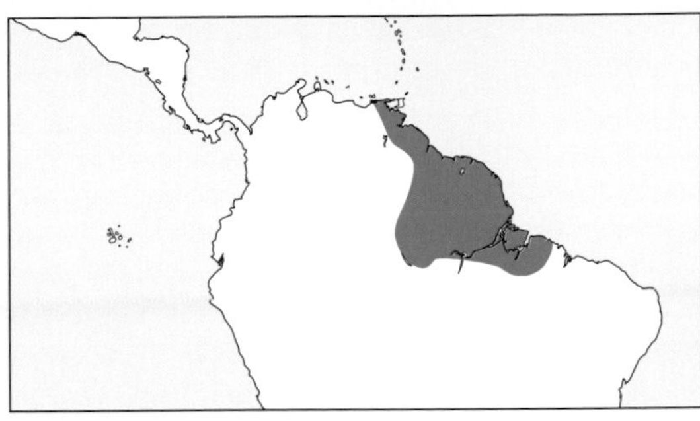

around 1000m. Resident and sedentary.
Taxonomy and variation Three races: ***undatus*** (E Venezuela, the Guianas, NE Brazil: N of Amazon) finely barred overall, head pale; ***amacurensis*** (NE Venezuela: Amacuro Delta) dark, chestnut, with plain crown and crest, rump rufous; ***multifasciatus*** (NE Brazil: S of Amazon) is largest race, pale, rather buff, head and tail usually unmarked, bill dark. Underpart markings black when worn, black with cream edges when fresh, but vary regionally, some nominate birds having almost all-black chest.
Similar species Scale-breasted Woodpecker has unbarred rump and darker head.
Food and foraging Mainly ants and termites. Also fruit, seeds and berries. Usually forages unobtrusively in canopy foliage. Often in mixed-species flocks.

► Adult male Waved Woodpecker has a red cheek, which females lack, but this is not always obvious when birds forage high in cover. This is the nominate race. Las Claritas, Venezuela, March (*Pete Morris*).

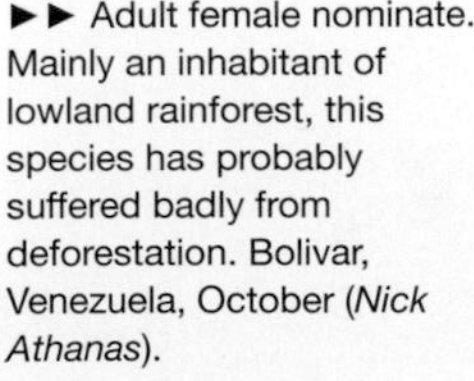

►► Adult female nominate. Mainly an inhabitant of lowland rainforest, this species has probably suffered badly from deforestation. Bolivar, Venezuela, October (*Nick Athanas*).

171. SCALE-BREASTED WOODPECKER
Celeus grammicus

L 22–25cm

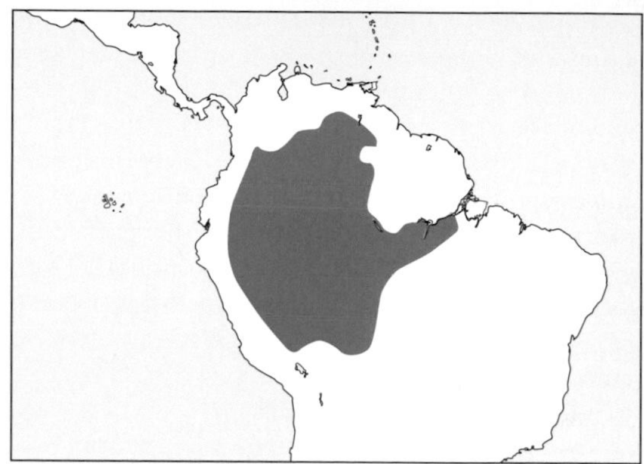

Other name Scaly-breasted Woodpecker

Identification Variably rufous, chestnut and brown overall. Head and short shaggy, pointed crest often slightly streaked black. Upperparts and most of wings barred black, finely or broadly depending on race. Primaries blackish, edged rufous, underwing brown with buffy coverts. Rump, vent and undertail-coverts plain buff, yellow or cinnamon. Uppertail-coverts slightly barred. Paler, tawny or cinnamon, below; breast and belly with black bars and chevrons, flanks variably scaled yellowish or brown. Tail plain chocolate. Bill cream-yellow with bluish or greenish base. Legs grey. Iris red. Sexes differ slightly: male has wide red patch

▼ Adult male nominate Scale-breasted Woodpecker. As is typical for *Celeus* woodpeckers, males have a red cheek, which females lack. Amazonia, Peru, February (*Pete Oxford*).

over malar and lower cheek; female lacks red. Juvenile similar to respective adult, but head darker, browner, and mantle and back more barred.

Vocalisations Common call a sudden, nasal, whistling, rising then falling two-note *kurry-hoo* or *curry-koo* – almost identical to Waved Woodpecker. Also 2–4 sharp, sometimes rasping, metallic *pring* notes, scratchy *reekup* and harsh *doit-gua*.

Drumming Not an avid drummer, both sexes only occasionally producing soft rolls.

Status Fairly common in Peru and Venezuela, rather uncommon in Ecuador and Colombia. Poorly known, population data scant, but probably declining due to Amazonian deforestation.

Habitat Rainforest, *terra firme*, *várzea* and swamps, often at edges and in clearings. Also secondary growth and drier wooded savanna.

Range South America. Occurs in Colombia, S Venezuela, Amazonian Brazil, Ecuador, Peru and N Bolivia. Mostly lowlands, but to over 1000m. Resident and probably sedentary.

Taxonomy and variation Four races: ***grammicus*** (SE Colombia, NE Peru, S Venezuela, W Brazil) is heavily barred; ***verreauxii*** (E Ecuador, NE Peru) only lightly barred below; ***subcervinus*** (W Amazonian Brazil: lower Rio Tapajos to N Mato Grosso) has cinnamon rump and flanks; ***latifasciatus*** (SE Peru, N Bolivia and SW Brazil: upper Rio Madeira) is pale, cinnamon rather than chestnut, especially on head and throat, light buff-brown below, especially from belly to vent. Plumage differs both between and within races. Birds in N usually darker than those from S of Amazon. Some birds have red tips to rump feathers.

Similar species Most like Waved Woodpecker but darker, especially on head, tail unbarred and calls also very similar. Chestnut Woodpecker much larger and lacks scaling.

Food and foraging Ants, other insects, fruit and sap. Forages on trunks, boughs and vines from mid-levels to the canopy. Roves in small family parties and often associates with mixed-species flocks.

◄ Adult male *verrauxii*. Both sexes and all races have a distinctly shaggy crest. Napo, Ecuador, February (*Glenn Bartley*).

▼ Juvenile *subcervinus*. Juvenile Scale-breasted Woodpeckers are less rufous, browner and drabber overall than adults. Mato Grosso, Brazil, July (*Nick Athanas*).

172. CHESTNUT-COLOURED WOODPECKER
Celeus castaneus

L 23–25cm

Identification Mostly rich chestnut-brown, sometimes with burgundy sheen, scalloped with black chevrons and bars. Rump paler, yellower. Flight feathers unmarked, rest of upperwings dotted black, underwing-coverts yellowish. Pale, ochre-cinnamon head, with golden, shaggy, hammer-headed crest that contrasts with darker body. Tail blackish. Iris chestnut, orbital ring bluish-grey. Pale, yellowish bill, bluish-green at base. Legs grey-olive. Sexes differ: male has red cheek and malar area, sometimes up to eye: female lacks red. Juvenile less marked, especially below, duller, darker overall, with dusky patch over malar region.

Vocalisations Falling, piping, whistling *skeew* or *peew,* often followed by 2–4 sharp, nasal *kheeu, keh* or *heh* notes. Also *peew-ekk-ekk, howp* or *howp-rrr* in series and excited, double *wik-kew* notes. Low-pitched, single, squawking *kwaar,* loud, squeaky *pi-chi* or *ki-chi* and sudden *kyow* or *whehoo,* before repeated *heh-heh-heh* mocking notes.

Drumming Produces a series of well-spaced, rapid, soft 1.5-second rolls.

Status Generally uncommon. Overall population considered stable, though limited data. Deforestation a threat though somewhat adaptable.

Habitat Mainly interior of tropical, wet, evergreen lowland forest and thickets. Also tall secondary growth, partially logged forests; in some areas mangroves, coastal scrub, cacao plantations and wooded suburban gardens.

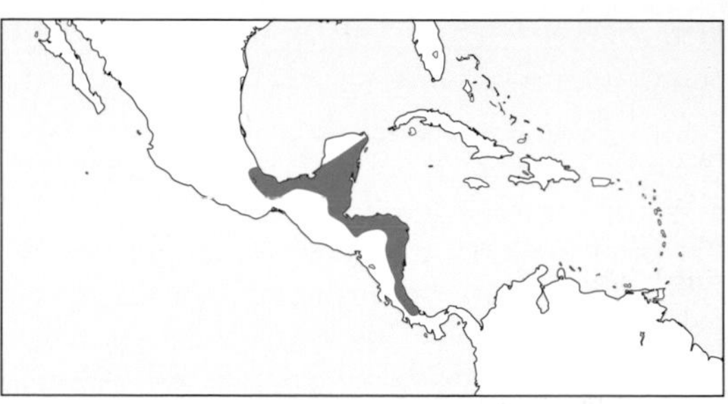

Range Central America. Northernmost *Celeus,* found along Caribbean slope from SW Mexico, Belize, Guatemala, El Salvador, Honduras, Nicaragua, E Costa Rica and W Panama. Sea-level to 1000m. Resident but not totally sedentary, some moving locally to mangroves and plantations in winter.

Taxonomy and variation Monotypic. Some individual variation in extent of underpart markings.

Similar species Cinnamon Woodpecker (sympatric in Honduras, Costa Rica, Panama) has same brownish head colour as upperparts, reddish throat and is more boldly marked black below. Waved and Scale-breasted Woodpeckers do not overlap.

Food and foraging Mainly ants and termites. Also other insects, *Cecropia* fruit, nuts and seeds. Forages alone or in pairs on trunks, boughs, foliage and epiphytes. Often in canopy, but will descend close to ground to follow ant-swarms.

◄◄ Adult male Chestnut-coloured Woodpecker is reddish over the cheek, in the malar region and sometimes around the eye. Heredia, Costa Rica, January (*Dave Hawkins*).

◄ Adult female. The pale head contrasting with the darker body helps separate Chestnut-coloured Woodpecker from the sympatric Cinnamon Woodpecker. Heredia, Costa Rica, February (*Scott Olmstead*).

173. CHESTNUT WOODPECKER
Celeus elegans

L 26–30cm

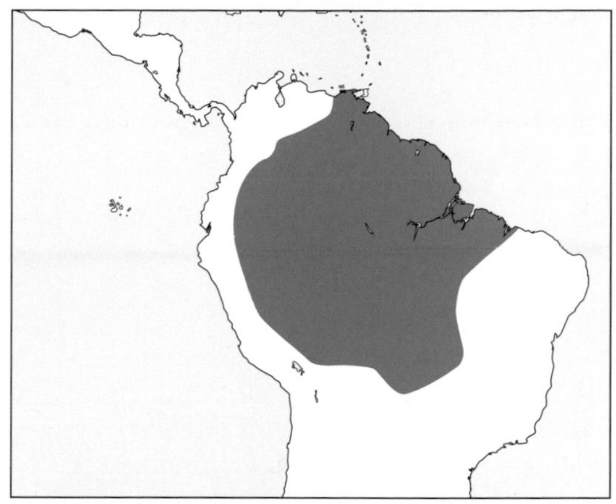

Identification Variable, but mostly chestnut-brown on upperparts, wings, chest, breast, neck and crested head. Paler (cinnamon/buff/golden, depending on race) on belly, flanks, undertail-coverts, uppertail-coverts and rump. Tail blackish. Bill ivory or yellowish with bluish-grey tip. Legs grey. Iris chestnut, orbital ring bluish. Sexes differ slightly: male has large, broad red malar extending over cheek, which female lacks. Juveniles like adults, but mottled below, darker on face.
Vocalisations Falling, piping, musical *weewah-ew-ew-ew-ew-ew*. Mocking, laughing *ha-hahahaha*. Harsh, chattering, yapping *wharrrr-wha-wha-wha* or *whee-jar-ja-ja*. Screeching, rasping *whick-frrr* and *keeeaaa* and repeated, grating *wika-wika* notes when agitated. Also clear, mewing *rrrew-chwee-chwee-chwee* series, nasal *kyeenh* and softer *gwarrrr* notes.
Drumming Both sexes produce solid, loud, regularly repeated rolls, often with long pauses between each. Pitch and speed level; length variable (between 1–2 seconds long).
Status Often uncommon, though fairly common in Colombia, Venezuela, Guyana and Peru. Probably threatened by Amazonian deforestation.
Habitat Various tall, tropical lowland forests: rainforest, gallery forest, humid *terra firme*, *várzea*, mangroves, swamps, wooded savanna, sometimes mature plantations.
Range South America. Occurs in Colombia, Venezuela, Brazil, the Guianas, Ecuador, Bolivia and Peru. Also Trinidad and Tobago. Mainly lowlands, but to around 1000m. Resident and sedentary.
Taxonomy and variation Much variation in plumage. Six races (some possibly distinct species – taxonomy needs review) usually placed in two groups. Long-crested, pale-crowned ***elegans*** group of four: ***elegans*** (French Guiana, N Surinam, NE Brazil: N of Amazon) cinnamon overall, dotted yellow above, gold on crown and crest; ***hellmayri*** (E Venezuela, Guyana, most of Surinam) dark, spotted on wing-coverts and scapulars; ***leotaudi*** (Trinidad) small, paler, rump yellow, crown orange; ***deltanus*** (NE Venezuela: Amacuro Delta) chocolate, crown golden. Short-crested, dark-crowned

► Adult male Chestnut Woodpecker; this race, *leotaudi*, which is endemic to Trinidad, is among those that sport an impressively long, pointed, yellowish crest. Trinidad, October (*Kevin Schafer*).

jumanus group of two: ***jumanus*** (E Colombia, SW Venezuela, N Bolivia, much of Amazonian Brazil) very dark, rump yellow, uppertail-coverts orange, crown and crest chestnut and ***citreopygius*** (E Ecuador, E Peru) darkest race, rump and uppertail-coverts dull orange, crown and crest chocolate. Intergrades occur.

Similar species Other *Celeus* species smaller, more marked and/or much paler.

Food and foraging Omnivorous. Eats fruit and berries, but mainly ants and arboreal termites, breaking into their nests and following swarms. Often in groups, joined by smaller birds, foraging at low and mid levels.

◄ Adult female *leotaudi*. The various races differ in plumage, but all females lack red on the cheek. Trinidad, February (*Neil Bowman*).

▼ Adult male Chestnut Woodpecker of the race *jumanus*; this is one of two distinctive races with a brown and relatively blunt crest. Amazonas, Brazil, May (*Rudimar Narciso Cipriani*).

174. PALE-CRESTED WOODPECKER
Celeus lugubris

L 24–26cm

Identification Crown, bushy crest, face, ear-coverts, nape and throat buff, cream or cinnamon. Dusky-brownish around eye. Mantle and back brown or chestnut, finely barred and scaled buff or cream. Rump cream or cinnamon. Tail chocolate, upper-coverts rufous barred black. Chocolate wings, flight feathers barred rufous. Buff underwing barred brown. Underparts from neck to vent plain brown or chestnut. Leg feathering cream with fine blackish barring. Iris chestnut, orbital ring bluish-grey. Bill grey, lower mandible paler. Legs grey. Sexes differ: male has broad red malar extending onto cheek, sometimes to ocular region; female malar indistinct, dusky merging into orbital area. Juvenile like respective adult, but head darker.

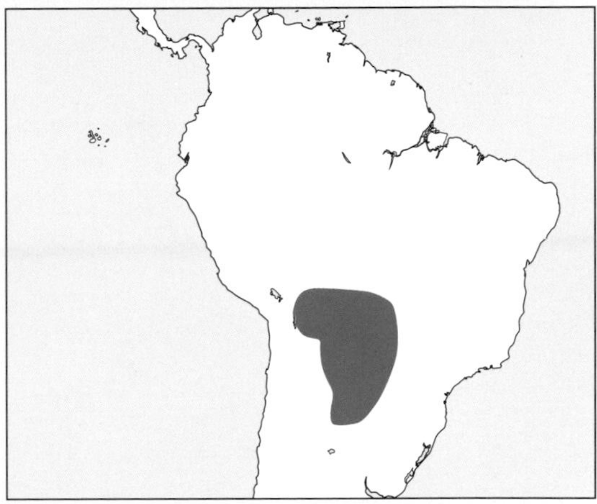

▼ Adult male Pale-crested Woodpecker of the race *kerri*. Males have a broad patch of red over the malar region and cheek. This race is darker than the nominate, with darker brown on the body; compare the 'dirtier' head of this race with that of the bird on p. 374. Rio Clarinhio, Brazil, August (*Jeroen Onrust*).

▲ Adult male nominate. Note the 'clean' head of this race compared to *kerri*. Santa Cruz, Bolivia, November (*Dubi Shapiro*).

Vocalisations Song a pleasant, high-pitched, whistling *wee-wee-week* and *twee-twee-tee*, repeated 3–4 times. A two-note squeak or squawk, yapping calls and 2–5 harsher, rasping notes.

Drumming Not an avid drummer, producing gentle, level-pitched 1–2-second rolls.

Status Locally common to uncommon. Overall population considered stable, though poorly known.

Habitat Dry, open, lowland semi-deciduous woodlands such as savanna and *cerrado*. Also palm groves, gallery forests and seasonally flooded woodlands.

Range South America. Heart of continent in parts of Bolivia, Brazilian Pantanal, and Chaco in Paraguay and NE Argentina. Sea-level to around 800m. Resident and presumably sedentary.

Taxonomy and variation Two races: ***lugubris*** (E Bolivia, SW Brazil: W Mato Grosso) is rufous-brown below, and ***kerri*** (Paraguay, NE Argentina and S Brazil: S Mato Grosso), which is darker, chocolate below with cream areas duller.

Similar species Blond-crested Woodpecker (has been considered conspecific) has darker body, pale wing-barring, yellower head and face, and does not overlap.

Food and foraging Mainly ants and termites, often following swarms, and also other arboreal invertebrates as they are disturbed. Also excavates nest-hole in arboreal ant or termite nests, as well as in trees.

► Adult female *kerri*. The female differs from the male in having a brownish rather than red cheek and malar region. Misiones, Argentina, October (*Roberto Güller*).

175. BLOND-CRESTED WOODPECKER
Celeus flavescens

L 26–29cm

Identification Head seems large. Face, ear-coverts, crown, nape, throat and prominent pointed (spiky when raised) crest cream, yellow or ochre depending on race. Upperparts and wings black, brown or ochre finely barred and scaled buff or yellow, underwing yellower. Plain black or brown below, sometimes slightly barred on flanks and undertail-coverts. Tail black, rump yellow or ochre. Leg feathering buff or ochre, flecked black. Legs bluish-grey. Iris reddish, orbital ring greyish. Bill pale, bluish. Sexes differ: male has broad red area over malar and cheek; female lacks red, having indistinct black malar, sometimes merely a few dark streaks. Juvenile darker on face, crest less prominent.
Vocalisations Usually 2 or 3, but up to 7, clearly-spaced, loud, shrill, piping *week, weep* or *peep* notes, of varying speed and pitch. A falling *weeh-weeh-weeh* and repeated harsh, rasping *wick, wicka* and *wicket* notes.
Drumming Occasional, steady but subdued, level-pitched rolls produced.

▼ Adult male Blond-crested Woodpecker of the nominate race. Males have a bright red cheek and malar patch, while females lack the red. Argentina, October (*Ramón Moller Jensen*).

▼ Adult female nominate. Despite being conspicuous and locally common, the natural history of this bird is largely unknown. Misiones, Argentina, July (*Roberto Güller*).

Status Overall considered stable, though data lacking. Locally often fairly common.

Habitat Rainforest, gallery forest, *cerrado*, *caatinga*, wooded savanna, palm groves, plantations, orchards and well-wooded rural gardens.

Range South America. Parts of Brazil, Argentina and Paraguay. Mostly lowlands, but to 1200m. Resident and sedentary.

Taxonomy and variation Three races currently recognised, though splits likely: ***flavescens*** (Brazil: S Bahia to Rio Grande do Sul, E Paraguay, NE Argentina) is dark, black on body; ***intercedens*** (E Brazil: W Bahia to Minas Gerais) like nominate but browner below, often rufous on wings. Distinctive ***ochraceus*** (E Brazil: Amazonia to E Bahia) has tawny-ochre head and crest, is sooty below, ochre on undertail and above with heavy chocolate bars and scales, male with broad red malar; ongoing study suggests species status as 'Ochre-backed Woodpecker'.

Similar species Pale-crested Woodpecker (sometimes considered conspecific) is paler overall with rufous rather than pale wing-bars, and does not overlap.

Food and foraging Mainly arboreal ants and termites (excavates nesting cavity in ant nests). Also other invertebrates, fruit (visits feeders), berries, sap and seeds – an important pollinator and seed disperser.

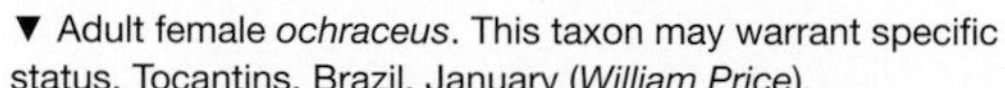

◄ Adult male nominate Blond-crested Woodpecker. Perhaps the most handsome of all the *Celeus*. Itanhaem, Brazil, March (*Ronald Gruijters*).

▼ Adult male *ochraceus*. This race is very different from the nominate, being paler, and buffish-cinnamon or ochre, particularly on the head, mantle and undertail. Tocantins, Brazil, January (*William Price*).

▼ Adult female *ochraceus*. This taxon may warrant specific status. Tocantins, Brazil, January (*William Price*).

176. CREAM-COLOURED WOODPECKER
Celeus flavus

L 24–27cm

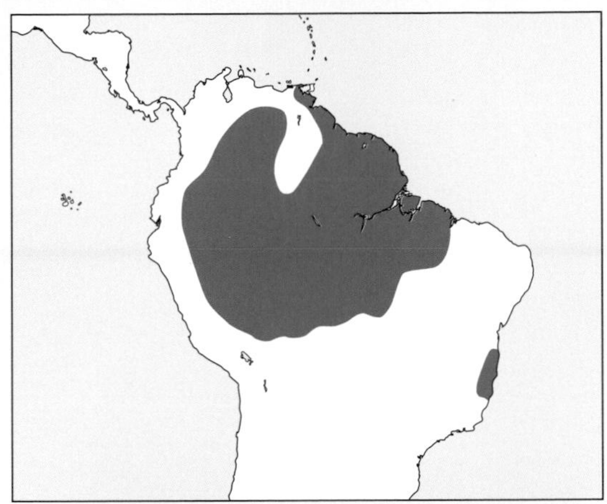

Identification Unmistakable. Crest blunter than on relatives. Mostly cream, buff or yellow, but very variable: some birds bright, some drab, washed-out, ghostly. Generally duskier when plumage worn. Flight feathers brown or chestnut, greater coverts ochre-cinnamon, underwings brown, axillaries buff. Tail black or brown. Iris dark. Bill yellow, tinged blue at base. Legs greyish. Sexes differ: male has broad crimson malar area, often streaked creamy white, female lacks red. Juveniles like respective adults, but not as bright and tertials sometimes barred.

Vocalisations Loud, clear, far-carrying, high-pitched, piping, mocking, sometimes bubbling, usually 4-note, *pee-pee-pee-purr, pew-pew-pew-purr* or *kee-hoo-hoo-hoo* that drops in pitch on final note. When agitated up to 8

► Adult male nominate Cream-coloured Woodpecker. Males differ from females in having a broad red patch in malar region. Napo, Ecuador, January (*Glenn Bartley*).

notes. Sometimes just 3 or 4 sharp *pee* notes uttered. Also, a repeated or single, throaty *wheejah* call. Flight call a harsher, rattling *wick-a, wick-a.*

Drumming Produces quiet rolls of level speed and pitch, often interspersed with calls.

Status Uncommon in Ecuador, Colombia, Venezuela and Surinam, more common in Guyana, French Guiana and Brazil. Race *subflavus* is rare. Overall population probably declining due to Amazonian deforestation.

Habitat Mainly wet or humid lowland forests: rainforest, wooded swamps, *várzea,* mangroves, riverine forest, deciduous woodlands. Also *terra firme* and coffee plantations.

Range South America. From Colombia and Venezuela in the N, S to Bolivia and Brazil; *subflavus* occurs in an isolated population in Bahia and Espirito Santo. Mainly lowlands, but to around 700m. Resident and sedentary.

Taxonomy and variation Four races: ***flavus*** (E Colombia, Ecuador, NE Venezuela, the Guianas, W Brazil, N Bolivia) is generally rufous in wings; ***peruvianus*** (E Peru) browner in wings; ***tectricialis*** (NE Brazil) has brown wing-coverts, less colour on flight feathers; ***subflavus*** (SE Brazil) is largest race, with chocolate markings on breast, mantle and wings. Also individual variation in body and wing colour. Races intergrade, producing intermediates.

Similar species None. Some calls like Chestnut Woodpecker.

Food and foraging Mainly arboreal ants and termites, hacking directly into their nests. Also other insects, seeds and fruit. Forages mostly at high levels, but will drop to ground.

▲ Adult female nominate. Both sexes are visually distinctive, and cannot be mistaken for any other woodpecker. Napo, Ecuador, January (*Glenn Bartley*).

► A pair of nominate Cream-coloured Woodpeckers; the male is below. The preferred rainforest habitat of this species continues to disappear across much of its range. Napo, Ecuador, January (*Glenn Bartley*).

177. RUFOUS-HEADED WOODPECKER
Celeus spectabilis

L 26–27cm

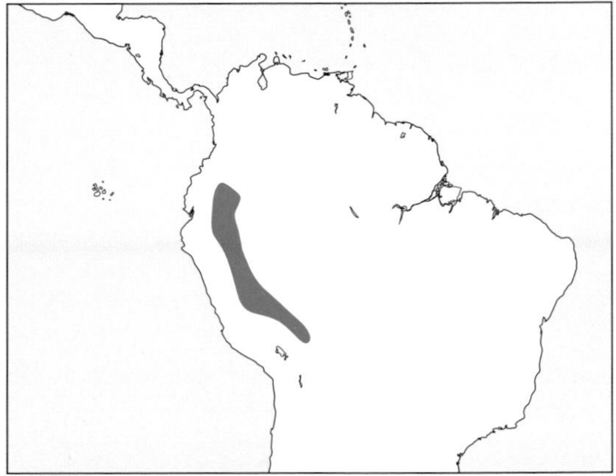

Identification Head, peaked crest, face and throat rich chocolate and chestnut. Shaggy nape mustard. Buff patch on neck-sides runs down to chest-sides. Chest black, breast spotted black. Flanks, belly, undertail-coverts and vent cream or yellow, with bold black bars, scales and chevrons. Mantle and back barred yellow and black, black bars broadest. Lower back to uppertail-coverts cinnamon or buff, tail black. Flight feathers brown or chestnut, coverts black, tertials cinnamon, underwing yellowish. Bill ivory or yellow. Legs grey. Iris dark. Sexes differ: male has broad crimson malar, band over ear-coverts and crest; female lacks red, having plain rufous-brown head. Juveniles essentially like respective adults, though bill darker,

► Adult male Rufous-headed Woodpecker of race *exsul*. Males have a varying amount of red on the crest, over the ear-coverts and in the malar region. Madre de Dios, Peru, September (*Glenn Bartley*).

often dusky or black on face, less black on chest, males with red crest.

Vocalisations Song is a loud series that starts with a screeching, squealing *squeear* or *skweeeak* followed by a mocking, whinnying, bubbling *kloo-kloo-koo* or *kluh-kluh-kluh*. Also mewing, chuckling *wur-hee-hrr-hrr-hrr* and single harsh, parrot-like squawks when agitated and in flight.

Drumming Level, even-pitched rolls, loud when produced on hard, hollow bamboo.

Status Found over relatively large area, but often localised, usually rare or uncommon, while trends and needs largely unknown. Rare in Ecuador, locally more common in Peru and W Brazil. Conservation status needs review.

Habitat Lowland rainforest, floodplain and riverine forest, especially on islands. In south of range spiny bamboo (*Guadua*) stands are important, elsewhere thickets of *Gynerium* cane, with *Heliconia* and *Cecropia* trees, are used. Mainly lowlands, up to 700m.

Range South America. W Amazonia from E Ecuador, E Peru, Bolivia and extreme W of Brazil. Resident and sedentary.

Taxonomy and variation Two races: ***spectabilis*** (E Ecuador, adjacent NE Peru) and ***exsul*** (SE Peru, extreme W Brazil, N Bolivia), which is usually less barred, more scaled and spotted below than nominate. Some females have red on head.

Similar species Ringed Woodpecker darker above and on wings, lighter on head. Formerly conspecific Kaempfer's Woodpecker paler overall with almost unmarked yellow back and plain, unbarred underparts, but does not overlap in range.

Food and foraging Insects, particularly Bamboo Ants. Often forages alone from lower to high levels in wet forest, also dropping onto forest floor and fallen logs.

▼ Adult female *exsul* Rufous-headed Woodpecker. This bird was trapped during research at the Los Amigos Biological Station (CICRA) in Madre de Dios, Peru. March (*Joe Tobias*).

178. KAEMPFER'S WOODPECKER
Celeus obrieni

L 26–28cm

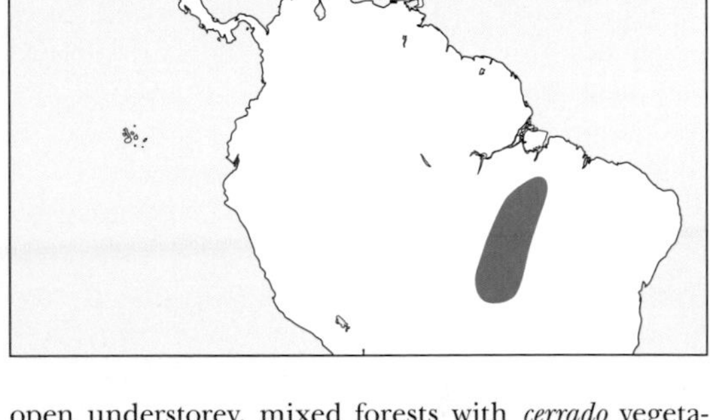

Other names Caatinga Woodpecker, Piaui Woodpecker
Identification Striking rufous head and bushy crest. Black throat, chest and breast, belly plain yellow. Yellow-cream on neck-sides, nape and from mantle to rump. Mantle lightly barred black. Scapulars streaked black, flight feathers rufous or chestnut. Tail black. Short yellow or cream bill. Iris black, orbital ring bluish-grey. Legs grey. Sexes differ: male has broad red malar and variable red streak from behind eye to crest, which female lacks. Juvenile differs mainly in having chocolate head and face rather than rufous, chestnut crest, some black feathering on the head, which can extend onto the throat and chest, and buff mantle that lacks black barring.
Vocalisations Distinctive, laughing, upwardly slurred song, beginning with a shrill squeal or squeak followed by more subdued notes, described as *reeahh-kah-kah-kah-kah* and *squeeah-kluh-kluh-kluh-kluh*. Also brief, harsh, rasping calls.
Drumming Both sexes drum, usually on bamboo. Fast, even-paced 2–3-second rolls, with a 16–20 second gap between each.
Status EN. Rare. Absence of records in the second half of the 20th century suggested extinction. Observations have recently increased, but population still considered small, perhaps a few hundred individuals. Research aims to clarify distribution and population. Threats include clearance and fragmentation of habitat for cultivation and ranching. Little original habitat remains within the range and large stands of forested *cerrado* with patches of bamboo need to be conserved.
Habitat Gallery forests with a closed canopy and semi-open understorey, mixed forests with *cerrado* vegetation, *babaçu* palm forest and particularly dense *Gadua paniculata* bamboo.
Range South America. Endemic to CW Brazil. Mainly in Maranhão, Piauí, Tocantins and Goiás states, in protected areas like Lageado State Park and Indigenous Reserve Craos. Recent records also from Caxias and E Mato Grosso. Site of rediscovery in NE Tocantins was around 400km SE of type specimen locality.
Taxonomy and variation Monotypic. Considered a race of Rufous-headed Woodpecker until 2007, based upon a single female specimen collected in 1926 in NE Brazil. 'Rediscovered' after 80 years and given species status based on geographical isolation, and morphological and molecular distinctness.
Similar species Most like Rufous-headed Woodpecker, though less barred on mantle, back, wings and below.
Food and foraging Feeds mainly on ants (particularly *Camponotus depressus* and *Azteca fasciata*) taken from their colonies by drilling holes in tall, dry bamboo stems.

► Adult male Kaempfer's Woodpecker differs from the female in having a red malar region and a variable amount of red over the ear-coverts. Manahao, Brazil, June (*João Quental*).

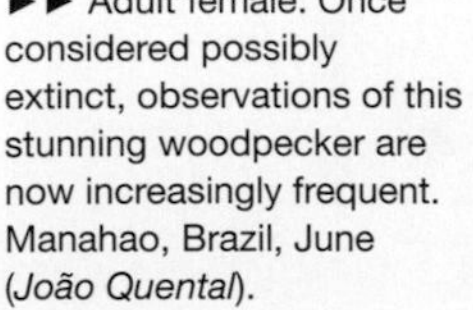

►► Adult female. Once considered possibly extinct, observations of this stunning woodpecker are now increasingly frequent. Manahao, Brazil, June (*João Quental*).

179. RINGED WOODPECKER
Celeus torquatus

L 26–28cm

Identification Crown shaggy and tufted rather than crested. Head, neck, chin and throat cinnamon, sometimes with rufous tones, especially on forehead and nape. Upperparts, wings and tail rich rufous or chestnut with varying amount of black barring or chevrons, depending upon race. Tail tip black. Chest solid black. Breast, belly and ventral area plain cinnamon or barred black and white, depending on race. Long yellowish or greyish bill. Iris chestnut. Legs greyish. Sexes differ: male has broad red patch covering cheek and lower ear-coverts which female lacks. Juvenile similar to adult but with more black barring; juvenile male has only faint red on cheek.

Vocalisations Song a distinctive, far-carrying series of 2–5 loud, even-pitched, carefully spaced, piping *kleee, peee* or *deee* notes, perhaps *kuu-kuu-kuu,* recalling Least Pygmy Owl or perhaps a steam-train whistle. Also a very loud ringing version and faster, yapping variant of 3–5 notes.

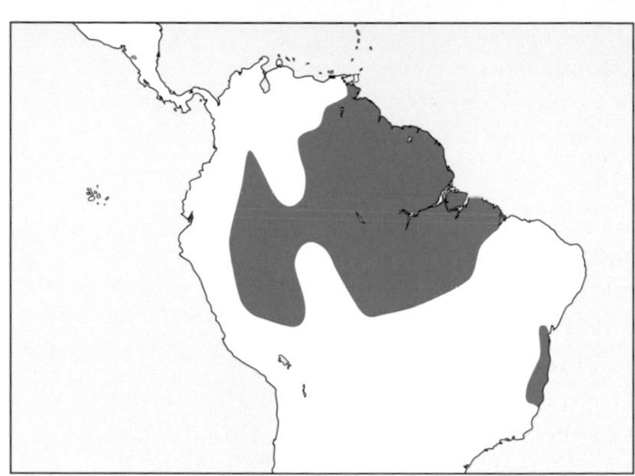

Drumming Rapid, powerful, level-pitched, 1-second rolls produced by both sexes.

Status Varies from locally common to rare across its large range. Overall population considered stable, though often unobtrusive and poorly known. Race

◀ Adult male nominate Ringed Woodpecker. Although the various races differ in plumage, males always have red in the malar region. Pará, Brazil, January (*Nick Athanas*).

tinnunculus now restricted to fragmented forests in E Brazil and endangered.

Habitat Rainforest, gallery forest, *várzea*, *terra firme*, also drier savanna woodlands and advanced secondary growth. In some areas partially logged, degraded forests.

Range South America. Colombia, Venezuela, the Guianas, Bolivia, Ecuador, Peru and Amazonian Brazil. Isolated population in E Brazil. Mostly lowlands. Resident and sedentary.

Taxonomy and variation Four races: ***torquatus*** (E Venezuela, the Guianas, NE Brazil) is distinct with solid black mantle, mostly plain, unmarked chestnut back, rump and uppertail-coverts and unbarred buff or cinnamon below; ***pieteroyensi*** (Belém, Pará, Brazil) differs from nominate by broken neck-ring; ***occidentalis*** (SE Colombia, E Peru, N Bolivia, Brazil: Amazonia and Mato Grosso) has dark, orangy head; ***tinnunculus*** (E Brazil: Bahia and Espirito Santo) is most heavily barred overall with black outer-tail feathers. Last two races both lack black mantle of nominate, have tail, uppertail-coverts and rump heavily barred black, and buff/cream underparts barred and scaled black.

Similar species Similar-sized sympatric Chestnut Woodpecker lacks black chest and barring. Rufous-headed and Kaempfer's Woodpeckers have darker, more rufous heads, and have yellow rather than white or cinnamon below.

Food and foraging Omnivorous. Takes arboreal ants, termites, other invertebrates and seeds, probably some fruit. Occasionally forages in family groups and mixed-species flocks, but usually solitary and unobtrusive.

▲ Adult male *occidentalis*. This race has a richer, more orange head than the nominate. Iquitos, Peru, January (*Pete Morris*).

◄ Adult female *occidentalis*. Females of all races lack red in the malar region and cheek. Manu, Peru, September (*Matthias Dehling*).

Black Woodpecker *Dryocopus martius*, adult male. Skåne, Sweden, June (*Lars Petersson*).

DRYOCOPUS

Of the seven species in this genus, three are found in the Old World and four in the New World. All are large, including some of the biggest woodpeckers on the planet; they are mostly black with red sexual badges and have a flapping, corvid-like flight style. Most are mainly ant-eaters and they are powerful drummers. They are also keystone species: wherever they occur the large cavities they excavate provide homes for many non-excavating birds, mammals and insects. Despite a resemblance to the *Campephilus*, DNA studies suggest the *Dryocopus* are not actually closely related.

180. HELMETED WOODPECKER
Dryocopus galeatus

L 27–30cm

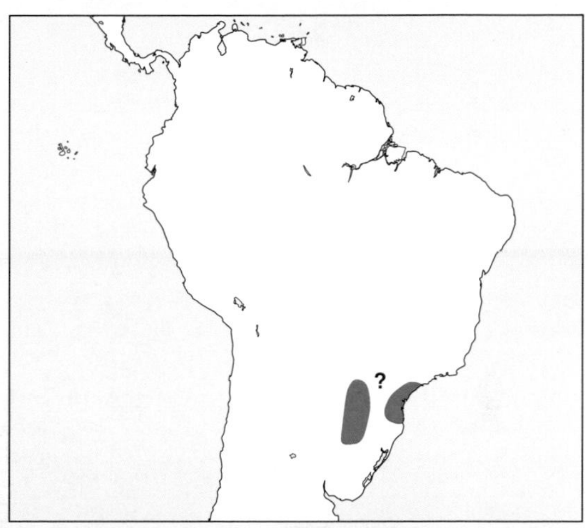

Identification Smallest in genus. Bushy red crown and crest not always helmet-shaped, changing according to posture and mood, sometimes a cone, raised when excited. Mantle, chest and breast black. Belly to vent finely barred black and white or cream. Upperwing black, with cinnamon base to flight feathers. Underwing cinnamon. Lores and throat rusty. Ear-coverts finely barred cinnamon and black. White line from neck to upper flank. Tail mainly black with long, creamy coverts comprising over half of length. Rump and lower back white. Bill greyish. Iris brownish. Sexes differ: male has red malar, rufous cheek and ear-coverts; female has more cinnamon in face. Juvenile browner, less rufous.

Vocalisations Usually quiet outside breeding season. Territorial call a variable, clear, drawn-out, far-carrying

► Adult male Helmeted Woodpecker: a threatened species that sports one of the most impressive crests in the woodpecker world. Paraná, Brazil, August (*Rudimar Narciso Cipriani*).

keer-keer-keer of 3–6 (sometimes more) notes, delivered harshly, stridently or as slower, pleasant whistling. Similar call of Lineated Woodpecker composed of up to 24 notes with less even tempo and pitch over first few notes. Similar call of Blond-crested Woodpecker composed of 3–5 sharper, higher-pitched notes. Gentle, cooing, *tu-tu-u-u-u* or *doo-doo-doo-doo* and intimate *chik* and *che* calls.

Drumming Even-pitched, rapid, 1–1.5-second rolls, with 14–15 second gap between each.

Status VU. One of the rarest Neotropical woodpeckers. Has seriously declined due to habitat loss, and decline expected to continue as occurs only in highly endangered Atlantic Forest. Densities low (perhaps under-recorded) but seemingly absent from large areas of suitable forest. Official estimate of maximum 10,000 pairs probably very optimistic and conservation status may need upgrading.

Habitat Large tracts of well-preserved, humid, lowland and montane mature forest. Also older gallery forest, mixed hardwood stands and forests with *Araucaria* or emergent Paraná pines. Very occasionally in wooded savanna and fragmented, partially logged or burnt forest.

Range South America. Restricted to inland areas of Atlantic Forest in SW Brazil, adjacent E Paraguay and NE Argentina (Misiones). Resident and sedentary.

Taxonomy and variation Monotypic. Variation slight.

Similar species Sympatric Lineated and Robust Woodpeckers similar in being black and white with red crests, but both white in face, not cinnamon. In flight Robust shows cinnamon in wings (though this more spotted than uniform), white underwing-coverts, totally cream-white back and completely red neck. Lineated lacks cinnamon in flight feathers.

Food and foraging Various invertebrates, especially beetle larvae. Usually forages alone, or in loosely associated pairs, at mid-levels in trees. Hacks into timber less than relatives, preferring to probe and strip away bark.

▼ The adult female Helmeted Woodpecker differs from the male mainly in having less red in the face, with the cheek, ear-coverts and throat being cinnamon. Parana, Brazil, October (*Rudimar Narciso Cipriani*).

181. BLACK-BODIED WOODPECKER
Dryocopus schulzi

L 31cm

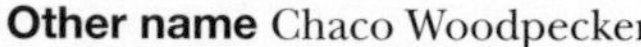

Other name Chaco Woodpecker

Identification Large, but small for genus. Most of upperparts, upperwing and tail plain, glossy black. Brownish when worn. Mostly black below. Underwing-coverts and axillaries white. White flight-feather shafts sometimes visible. Red-crimson crown and prominent, peaked crest. Slight white supercilium. Ear-coverts pale grey. Lores yellow. Bold white moustache runs below ear-coverts to rear neck-sides and onto shoulders. Chin and throat plain grey or white. Bill and legs greyish. Iris chestnut, orbital ring grey. Sexes differ slightly: male has red malar, which female lacks. Juvenile like respective adult but dull black with brownish hue, flanks often barred, forecrown lightly spotted white.

Vocalisations Slow series of *wick-wick-wick* calls. Falling, harsh *kirrrrr* alarm.

Drumming Produces 1-second rolls of 17–18 strikes per second.

Status NT. Locally common, but range-restricted and poorly known. Relatively small population has declined, mainly due to habitat loss, especially in Argentina. Main threats are logging for charcoal and tannins, clearance for agriculture, cattle-ranching, settlements and planting of alien tree species.

Habitat Mainly occurs in arid savanna woodland with acacia, cacti and carob. Also in dry deciduous woodlands in sierras of Córdoba and NE San Luis. Overall needs unclear as also occurs in some subtropical hill forests and even plantations.

Range South America. Mainly in Chaco region of S

Bolivia, SC Paraguay and NC Argentina. Also transitional subtropical forests up to 1500m in Andean foothills of SC Bolivia and NW Argentina. Resident and sedentary. Core populations in two separate areas: Córdoba and San Luis, Argentina, and Paraguayan Chaco.

Taxonomy and variation Monotypic. Some birds, mostly in N, have pale irides, white scapular lines, some white scapular patches and occasionally fine white barring on belly and/or flanks. These features may result from hybridisation with Lineated Woodpecker. Also clinal differences in size, birds in S average slightly smaller.

Similar species Sympatric Cream-backed Woodpecker is also plain black below, but shows prominent cream mantle patch. Close relative Lineated Woodpecker nearer in size but has white scaling and heavy barring below, dark ear-coverts, heavily streaked dark throat, dark bill and different calls.

Food and foraging Diet presumably insectivorous (ants, beetles etc), like relatives, but precise information lacking. Often forages in pairs, sometimes in family parties.

► Adult male Black-bodied Woodpecker has a red malar stripe, which the female lacks. Cordoba, Argentina, June (*Roberto Güller*).

►► Adult female. This threatened species occurs mainly in dry woodlands, which continue to be degraded. Santa Fe, Argentina, September (*Horacio Luna*).

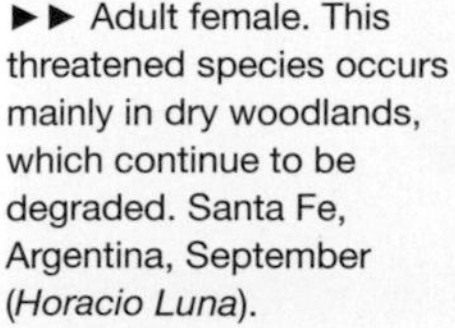

182. LINEATED WOODPECKER
Dryocopus lineatus

L 30–36cm

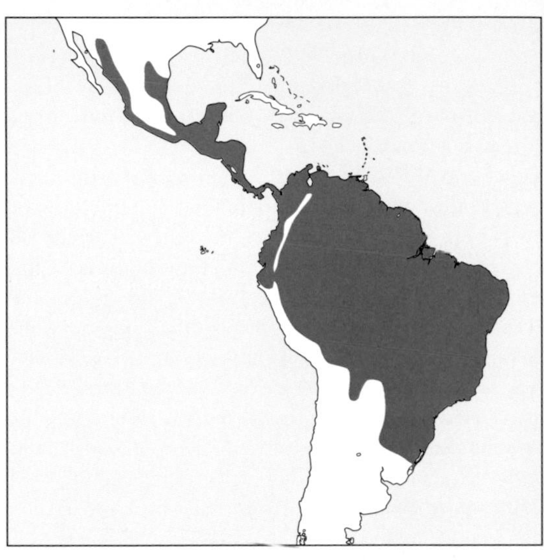

Identification Mostly glossy black. Impressive rounded red crest, tufted or pointed, depending on mood. Lores ochre. White moustache runs to nape and down neck-side to chest. Ear-coverts greyish. Mostly black above with broad white scapular stripes. White throat finely streaked or mottled black. Lower breast, belly, vent and flanks whitish, variably barred or scaled black. Tail and upperwing black, underwing cream or white. Iris cream or yellow, orbital ring brownish. Bill usually greyish, lower mandible paler, tip darker. Legs variably grey, olive or bluish. Sexes differ: male has all-red crown, crest and malar; female red only on nape, hindcrown and crest. Juvenile similar to respective adult but duller, irregularly barred below, flight feathers tipped white, iris grey-brown.

Vocalisations Noisy. Commonly a loud, laughing, slightly rising series of 15–25 *wik* or *yik* notes that increase, then decrease in volume. Sometimes a more

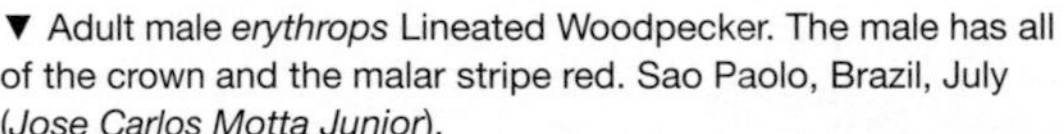

▼ Adult male *erythrops* Lineated Woodpecker. The male has all of the crown and the malar stripe red. Sao Paolo, Brazil, July (*Jose Carlos Motta Junior*).

▼ Adult female Lineated Woodpecker has a black forecrown, and lacks the red malar stripe of the male. This bird is of the race *erythrops*. Itanhaem, Brazil, August (*Ronald Gruijters*).

trilling or bubbling *weep-weep* or *keep-keep*. Also more intense *wuk* notes, loud *kek-krrrrrrrrrrrr*, yelping *ree-ree-ree-ree-ree* and yapping *pi-sha-sha-sha-sha-ah*. Alarms include raucous, rattling *kip-whurrr*, *keep-grrr*, *put-airr*, *pik-urrr*, *ik-rrrr*, *ti-chrr* or *chiurrrr*. Also single, sharp *pik*, *pip* and *chip* notes.

Drumming Both sexes produce powerful, accelerating 1–2-second rolls, 1–3 per minute. Sudden, single raps when alarmed.

Status Widespread. Probably increasing as it inhabits open forests and has benefited from fragmentation resulting from logging. Also moves into areas where dams have produced flooded areas with standing dead trees.

Habitat Variety of open woodland: rainforest, gallery forests, *várzea*, mangroves, drier woodlands, thorn scrub, plantations, wooded pastures, farmland and urban parks where large trees remain.

Range Americas. Mexico to Bolivia and Argentina. Also Trinidad and Tobago. Mainly lowlands but into Andean foothills. Resident and sedentary.

Taxonomy and variation Five races: ***lineatus*** (E Costa Rica, Panama, W Colombia, Venezuela, the Guianas, Trinidad, E Brazil, E Peru, N Paraguay); ***scapularis*** (S Sonora to Oaxaca, W Mexico) is smaller than nominate, pale-billed and usually lacks white stripe above malar; ***similis*** (Tamaulipas, Mexico, to NW Costa Rica) bill grey, buffy below; ***fuscipennis*** (coastal W Ecuador, NW Peru) is relatively small, bill dark, breast and belly sooty, flanks marked brown, vent buff, brownish upperparts and flight feathers; ***erythrops*** (SE Brazil, E Paraguay, NE Argentina) often has darker bill, reduced or absent white scapular stripes, and many in Misiones, Argentina, are rufous below – has been considered a distinct species.

▼ Adult male *similis*. This race is buffy below and grey-billed. Cano Negro, Costa Rica, October (*Dave Hawkins*).

Similar species Differs from sympatric large black, white and red woodpeckers, particularly Black-bodied, Pale-billed, Crimson-crested and Guayaquil, in black throat streaked white, white scapular lines that do not form a V-shape and narrow white stripe across lower face from bill-base that joins neck stripe (rather than a stripe that broadens into a patch as in *Campephilus* females).

Food and foraging Preys on larger ants, especially *Azteca* species, and wood-boring beetle larvae. Also fruits and seeds from palms and *Cecropia*. Often in pairs, sometimes family groups, foraging from canopy to ground and often in isolated stumps or trees in clearings.

◀ Lineated Woodpeckers are sexually dimorphic even before they fledge. A young male is below (note red malar stripe and all-red crown) with a female above (black forecrown and malar stripe). French Guiana, May (*Michel Giraud-Audine*).

183. PILEATED WOODPECKER
Dryocopus pileatus

L 42–48cm

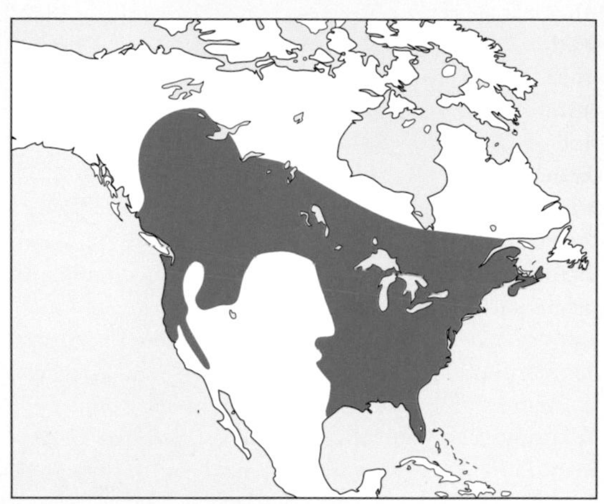

Identification Sooty black body, black and white face with long neck and impressive red crown and crest. Black from nape to tail, browner when worn. White face crossed by black band through eye. Chin and throat white. Upper flanks whitish. White bases to primaries. White wing lining obvious in flight. Broad bill greyish, tip black. Iris yellowish, orbital ring grey or green. Legs bluish-black. Sexes differ: male 10–15% larger, with all-red crown, crest and malar; female red only on hindcrown and crest. Juvenile resembles respective adult, but less glossy with grey chin and throat, blunt crest and dark iris. Juvenile male has less red, sometimes orange, on crown and malar.

Vocalisations Much seasonal variation, but year-round call is a loud, laughing series of deep *kuk* or *wuk* notes

◄ Adult male Pileated Woodpecker of the race *abieticola*. All of the crown and the malar stripe is red; females have a black forecrown and malar stripe. Pend Oreille County, Washington, United States, May (*Gerrit Vyn*).

that rise and fall in volume and frequency. Territorial song a high-pitched, drawn-out *kuk-kuk-keekeekeekeekee-kuk-kuk*. Slower, wilder, series of *wek* notes and low-pitched mewing *waaa* made by pairs. Also *yucka, yucka, yucka* similar to Northern Flicker. Squeaky *waak, woick* or *wok* notes repeated during interactions, shrill *g-waick* notes during disputes. Low, grunting *hn-hn* notes, like Grey Squirrel.

Drumming Both sexes drum all year round, peaking in early spring. Loud, powerful, but fairly slow 1–3-second rolls that accelerate before trailing off, with about 15 strikes per second. In peak periods males produce 1–2 rolls per minute for 2–3 hours.

Status Fairly common in SE USA. Uncommon, more localised, in Great Lakes and Pacific coast regions. After a decline, has recovered in recent decades.

Habitat Mature boreal and temperate coniferous, deciduous and mixed forests. Also swamps, parks, even suburban areas where there are large snags and fallen timber.

Range North America. British Columbia E to Nova Scotia, S to C California and Idaho, through eastern USA to Florida and Texas. Lowlands to around 2300m. Resident and mostly sedentary, though some seasonal altitudinal movements.

Taxonomy and variation Two similar races: ***pileatus*** (SE USA from Kansas to Maryland, Texas and Florida) and ***abieticola*** (remainder of range), which is slightly bigger and longer-billed. Size differences also clinal, northern birds on average larger.

Similar species None within range – Ivory-billed Woodpecker probably extinct.

Food and foraging Preys on carpenter ants, termites, wood-boring beetle larvae and other insects. Occasionally berries, nuts, even carrion, and visits feeders for suet. Forages at all levels, often on stumps and logs.

► Adult female Pileated Woodpecker race *abieticola*. North America's biggest extant woodpecker is making a gradual comeback after a lengthy period of decline. United States, October (*Gerald Marella*).

184. WHITE-BELLIED WOODPECKER
Dryocopus javensis

L 38–48cm

Identification Variable in plumage and size, but all long-billed, long-tailed and mainly glossy black. White or cream belly, variable red on head. In flight white rump and lower back (some races) and pale underwing-coverts obvious. Iris yellowish. Bill grey or black. Legs bluish-grey. Sexes differ: male has red malar, crown and crest; female lacks red malar, forecrown black (but see *richardsi*). Juvenile duller black, iris grey; mirrors respective adult, though young male has crown mottled dark and less red in malar.

Vocalisations Vocal, making various squawks, toots and yaps. Single, brief, metallic *chiank* or *kyank* contact notes, uttered 3–4 times at 2–3 second intervals. Nasal *eeeee-es,* explosive single *kee-er* or *keeee-ah,* more staccato *tut-t-tut-tut-t-tut.* Laughing series of *kiyaar* or *kyah* calls. Long, rapid, rattling *kyek-yek-yek-ek-ek* and *wik-wik-wik,* 3–4 notes per second, falling in volume, usually in flight.

Drumming Both sexes produce powerful, far-carrying, 1–2-second rolls. Variable in speed, usually accelerating before fading.

Status Though widespread, status needs review as population fragmented and several races restricted to islands: *richardsi* gone from Tsushima Island, Japan, and critically endangered in lowland forests on Korean peninsula; Cebu Island endemic *cebuensis* possibly extinct. Local declines often due to heavy logging.

Habitat Varies across range. Mainly primary, damp deciduous forests and jungle. In some areas mixed deciduous-conifer, bamboo stands, plantations, secondary growth, peat-swamps, mangroves, partially logged areas, even gardens. Large trees essential.

Range SE Asia. Parts of India, to S China, Indochina, S to Borneo, Sumatra, Java, Bali, other Indonesian islands and Philippines. Disjunct Korean population. Resident and sedentary.

◄ Adult male *hodgsonii* White-bellied Woodpecker. Although some races differ significantly in plumage, all males have a red malar stripe. Kerala, India, October (*John Holmes*).

Taxonomy and variation Fifteen races differing in size and plumage. Nominate ***javensis*** (S Thailand, peninsular Malaysia, Singapore, Greater Sundas and offshore islands) adults have black rump, juveniles sometimes white; ***hodgsonii*** (continental India) large, bill blackish, underwing-coverts white; ***forresti*** (Burma (Myanmar), SW China) large, throat black; ***richardsi*** (Korean peninsula) large, female lacks red, perhaps a distinct species 'Tristram's Woodpecker'; ***feddeni*** (S Burma (Myanmar), N Thailand, Indochina) white in primaries, crown orange-red; ***parvus*** (Simeulue Island, off Sumatra) smallest race, buff below; ***mindorensis*** (Mindoro: Philippines) throat broadly speckled; ***hargitti*** (Palawan: Philippines) most white and red; ***esthloterus*** (N Luzon: Philippines) has speckled throat; ***confusus*** (C and S Luzon: Philippines) has broadly speckled throat, male has large red malar; ***philippinensis*** (Panay, Negros, Masbate, Guimaras: Philippines) has small white rump, pale lower mandible, male has extensive red malar; ***cebuensis*** (Cebu: Philippines) has small white area on back; ***pectoralis*** (Leyte, Samar, Panaon, Calicoan, Bohol: Philippines) has throat, neck and ear-coverts streaked and speckled black and white, breast flecked or barred pale, flanks boldly barred; ***multilunatus*** (Basilan, Dinagat, Mindanao: Philippines) has broadly speckled throat, breast barred buff, lacks white rump; ***suluensis*** (Sulu Archipelago) is small, throat finely speckled white, minimal or no white on rump. Nominate, *parvus, confusus, cebuensis, pectoralis* and *multilunatus* usually have black rump; *hodgsonii, forresti, richardsi, feddeni, mindorensis, hargitti, philippinensis* and *suluensis* white.

Similar species Black Woodpecker may overlap in North Korea, but easily differentiated by lack of white in plumage.

Food and foraging Forages on both live and dead trees, logs and stumps, mainly for large ants, termites and wood-boring beetle larvae. Some fruits also eaten. Forages at all levels, often on snags, stumps and ground.

▼ Adult male *confusus*. This is one of the races with a solid black chest, with white speckles on the throat. Luzon, Philippines, November (*Con Foley*).

▼ Adult females never have a red malar stripe and are black on the forecrown. This bird is of race *confusus*. Luzon, Philippines, November (*Con Foley*).

◄ Adult female nominate. Within its range, this impressive woodpecker cannot be mistaken for any other species. Southern Thailand, October.

▼◄ Adult male *pectoralis*. This race is heavily speckled white on the face, neck and down to the breast. Bohol, Philippines, May (*Ramon Quisumbing*).

▼ Adult male *feddeni* in flight. Like all large woodpeckers, White-bellied flies with the primaries separated. Northern Cambodia, February (*James Eaton*).

185. ANDAMAN WOODPECKER
Dryocopus hodgei

L 38cm

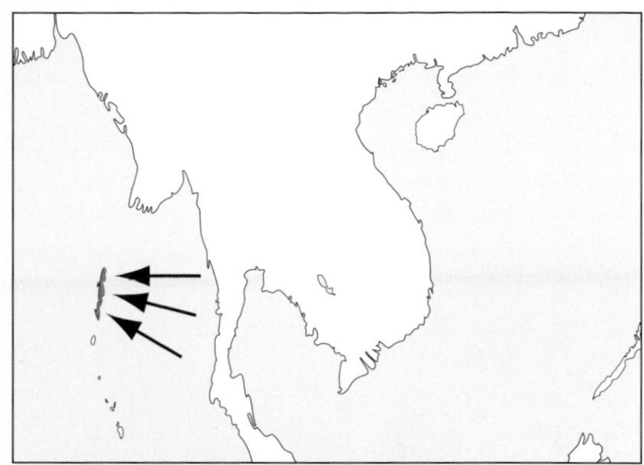

Identification Relatively short-billed, long-tailed and thin-necked. Almost totally glossy black, sometimes sooty or with brownish tones. Pale iris and grey orbital ring prominent in black face. Bill black. Legs grey. Sexes differ: male has red malar and vermillion crown that peaks into a bushy crest at rear; female lacks red malar and has black forecrown with red only on hind-crown and crest. Crest often cone-shaped. Juveniles duller black, red on the head flecked with black and sometimes white feather tips; juvenile male has little or no red in malar.

Vocalisations Often vocal. Repeated, shrill, two-syllable *quee-ee* whistle, like White-bellied Woodpecker

► Adult male Andaman Woodpecker. The male has an all-red crown and crest, and a red malar stripe. Females are black on the forecrown and on the malar stripe. South Andaman Island, India, November (*Niranjan Sant*).

but higher-pitched. Sometimes just a single squeaky *quee* note. Loud, chattering *kuk-kuk-kuk* series, sometimes ending in a whistling *kui*. Also briefer, harder *kek-ek-ek-ek-er* or *kik-kik-kik* and an explosive, inflected *kleeee*.
Drumming Loud, relatively slow, level-pitched 1.5 to 2-second rolls, accelerating slightly before trailing off. Both sexes drum all year round.
Status NT. Locally common, but a range-restricted island endemic with already small population decreasing. Main threat habitat loss and degradation due to a growing human population and associated increase in logging, farming and construction.
Habitat Mainly mature evergreen rainforest. Sometimes more open woods with clumps of tall trees. Rarely in plantations and mangroves.
Range Endemic to Andaman Islands, India, in Bay of Bengal. Sea-level to 350m. Resident and sedentary on larger forested islands.
Taxonomy and variation Monotypic. No variation noted.
Similar species None within range.
Food and foraging Mainly large ants. Often forages in pairs or loose family parties, on snags, stumps and ground.

▼ Adult female Andaman Woodpecker. Endemic to forests on a small group of remote islands where development is ongoing, this species is vulnerable. South Andaman Island, India, November (*Niranjan Sant*).

186. BLACK WOODPECKER

Dryocopus martius

L 45–50cm

Identification On average the largest *Dryocopus* species. Slender neck and pointed hindcrown create hammer-headed look. Mostly glossy black, sometimes with bluish sheen, matt when worn. Primaries of first-winter birds often rusty. Hindcrown and nape shaggy, but not crested. Iris white, cream or yellow, usually with dark mark pointing towards bill. Large dagger-shaped bill, ivory with dark tip and culmen. Legs bluish-grey. Sexes differ: male has all-red crown; female red only on hindcrown and nape. Juvenile like respective adult: male with most of crown red, flecked with dark bases, female with red hindcrown, but often just a few red tips. Plumage sooty, often with brownish tones, iris dark, bill white. Fledgling has wedge-shaped tail, due to central feather pair being short.

Vocalisations Four main calls: seven or more high-pitched, churring *krruc-krruc-krruc* or *kru-kru-kru* notes in flight, sometimes more melodious *krrri-krrri-krrri* or pleasant *pree-pree-pree;* territorial and contact call a far-carrying, plaintive, wailing *kleeeee* or *kleeea* made when perched; a two-syllable *klee-ah, ki-jah* or more hurried *kliiiii-ehh;* laughing, metallic series of 10–20 *kwee, klee* or *quee* notes in spring, in flight or when perched, slower version *kwik-wik-wik-wik* or *kwip-kwip-kwip,* with whooping beginning, increases in tempo and pitch before levelling out. Also short, sharp, two-syllable *ke-jak* or *pee-ack* calls like Eurasian Jackdaw and scolding *kayak-kayak* or *keyak-keyak.*

► Adult male Black Woodpecker. Unlike the female, all of the crown is red. Skåne, Sweden, June (*Lars Petersson*).

Drumming Both sexes drum powerfully, males more often. Usually 2–3-second rolls with 15–20 strikes per second.

Status Often locally common across vast range. Increasing in many areas.

Habitat Varied open, mature wooded habitats depending upon latitude, altitude and local factors. Conifer forests dominate in boreal zone, deciduous in temperate zone. Also riverine forest, parkland, plantations, wooded suburbs, even city parks. Large trees for nesting essential.

Range Eurasia. Much of Europe east to Kamchatka, China and Japan, as far north as tree line. Significant expansion in Europe in recent decades. Resident and mainly sedentary though dispersive movements made.

Taxonomy and variation Two similar races: ***martius*** (most of Eurasian range) and ***khamensis*** (SW China: eastern Qinghai-Tibetan Plateau, Yunnan). Clinal differences in size, N birds larger. Some birds tinged brown.

Similar species Unmistakable. Only other possibly sympatric *Dryocopus* is *richardsi* race of White-bellied Woodpecker in North Korea.

Food and foraging Highly insectivorous. Specialises in ants, especially large carpenter ants (*Camponotus*) in all stages. Also wood-boring beetles and other insects. Forages at all levels, often on stumps, snags and ground.

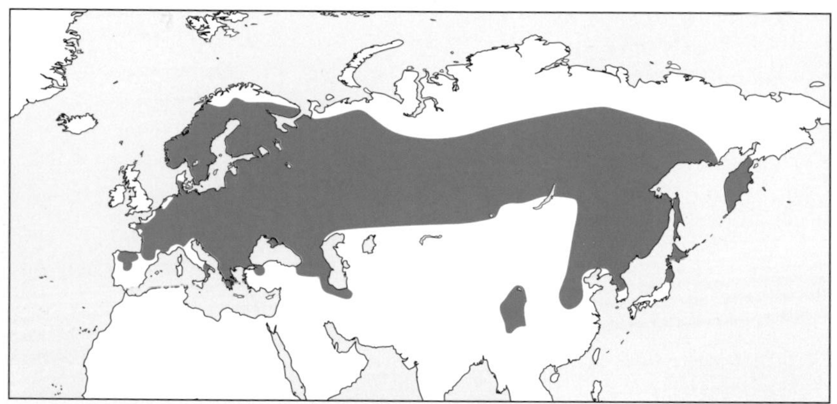

▼◄ Adult male. Black Woodpecker is the most widely distributed *Dryocopus*; it is unlikely to be mistaken for any other Eurasian woodpecker. Hokkaido, Japan, June (*Pete Morris*).

▼ Adult female Black Woodpecker has red only the hindcrown and nape – these red areas are hardly noticeable at all in this pose. Kuusamo, Finland, February (*Oliver Smart*).

CAMPEPHILUS

A New World genus of 11 species, the so-called 'ivory-bills', although three species actually have dark bills. They are large, mainly black and white, often with red heads, some sporting impressive crests. A long fourth toe is typically held pointed to the side and front. DNA studies suggest that the *Campephilus* are not closely related to the visually similar *Dryocopus*, but instead to the *Chrysocolaptes* flamebacks of SE Asia. Most do not drum in the proper sense to proclaim territory, but make distinctive double or triple raps with the bill on trees or logs – the first strike so rapidly followed by the second that it sounds like a single strike and an echo. The ecology of most species has not been studied in depth and sadly two, Imperial and Ivory-billed Woodpeckers, are probably extinct.

Magellanic Woodpecker *Campephilus magellanicus*, adult male. Tierra del Fuego, Argentina, October.

187. POWERFUL WOODPECKER
Campephilus pollens

L 33–37cm

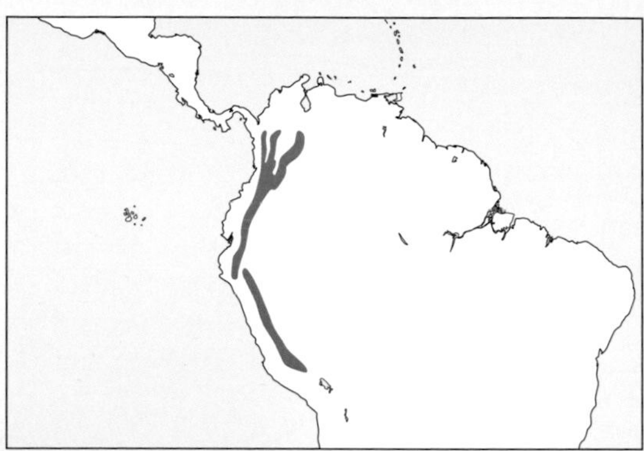

Identification Mostly black. Black face crossed by a wide white stripe which runs from the bill and lores, over the cheek to the rear neck-sides and then onto the scapulars and mantle, forming a V-shape on the back. Upperparts and tail black. White or buff rump obvious in flight. Throat and chest black. Ochre breast and belly with rows of black bars and chevrons. Wings black with white tips on primaries and spots or bars on secondaries. Bill blackish. Iris pink or cream. Legs greyish. Sexes differ: male has red nape, crown and coned crest; female lacks red on head. Juveniles like respective adults, but male has less red on head; both

◄ Adult male Powerful Woodpecker has an impressive red crown and crest. This is the nominate race. Tapichalaca, Ecuador, August (*Francesco Veronesi*).

overall chocolate, greyer below with broader barring, more barred on back and with dark iris.

Vocalisations Limited range of simple calls. Single or repeated *choo* or *tjoo*, more nasal *kee-aah* or *kyaah* and falling, squeaky-toy-like *pee-your, pee-yaw* or *pee-seew*. Loud *udd-daa-da-da*. Mocking, laughing, rapid *kikikikikaw*, often made in flight, falling *kikikiki-keh-keh-keh* and *kek-kek-kek-kek*. Single notes can develop into rattling, chattering or laughing depending upon mood and situation.

Drumming Produces a rapid double rap, but also often 3, sometimes 4–5 strikes, almost forming a proper drum roll.

Status Nowhere common. Poorly known; overall population size unknown, but considered stable. Rare and threatened by deforestation in Venezuela.

Habitat Mature and secondary mountain rainforest and cloud-forest.

Range South America. Confined to high forests in N Andes, either side of the Equator. Usually over 900m, up to 3750m. Resident and sedentary.

Taxonomy and variation Two races: ***pollens*** (Andes in N Colombia, W Venezuela and Ecuador) and ***peruvianus*** (Andes in N Peru), which is cinnamon or buff on lower back and rump and narrowly barred buff on uppertail-coverts.

Similar species Pale lower back and rump separates it from Lineated and Crimson-crested Woodpeckers; black and white neck and scapular lines separates it from Crimson-bellied, though ranges hardly coincide.

Food and foraging Presumably large insects and their larvae, but precise information lacking. Usually forages in pairs on trunks and boughs inside forests from mid to lower levels.

▼ Adult male nominate. This rainforest-dwelling species is under threat from over-logging and habitat degradation. Rio Blanco, Colombia, November (*Francesco Veronesi*).

▼ Female Powerful Woodpecker lacks the red crown and crest of the male. It is still a seriously impressive bird. This is the nominate. Pichincha, Ecuador, February (*Nick Athanas*).

188. CRIMSON-BELLIED WOODPECKER
Campephilus haematogaster

L 33–35cm

Identification Head boldly marked red, buff and black. Body black and red. Red nape and crown, topped by a peaked, blunt crest. Yellow-buff forehead, thin supercilium and ear-coverts, wide black post-ocular stripe. Yellowish moustachial area. Chin and throat black, continuing down onto chest in broken bars. Upperparts and tail black. Lower back and rump red, obvious in flight. Underparts crimson, barred black on lower flanks. Black wings spotted white on flight feathers. Iris reddish; orbital ring grey. Bill and legs grey or black. Sexes differ slightly: male has red neck-sides; female lacks red on neck, and yellow from cheek continues down the neck to the chest sides. Juveniles like respective adults, both duller, browner above, less rufous below.

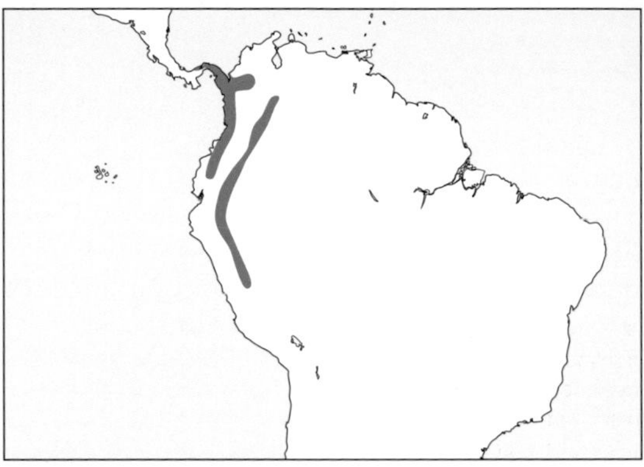

◄ Adult male Crimson-bellied Woodpecker of the nominate race. The sexes are easily confused unless seen well; males have red sides to the neck, females yellowish. San Martin, Peru, November (*Gerard Gorman*).

Vocalisations Rapid, low-pitched *psit-trr-r-r* or *stk-krr-r-r* rattle, sometimes trilling, recalling those of some smaller picids. Loud *st-kr-r-r-r* and falling *kukukukrrr*. Nasal, squeaky, suppressed sneeze-like *ti-sue* or *p-sit* and harsh, sometimes raucous, metallic notes.

Drumming Nominate does triple or more strikes which may develop into a 2-second roll. Solid, heavy, double rap produced by *splendens* race.

Status Nowhere common. Data on numbers and trends lacking, but overall considered stable.

Habitat Interior of rainforest, humid tall lowland and slope forests and *várzea*.

Range South America. NW of continent from Panama to Peru. Lowlands to around 2200m. Resident and sedentary.

Taxonomy and variation Two races: ***haematogaster*** (E Colombia to E Peru) and ***splendens*** (Panama, W Colombia to W Ecuador), which has been considered a distinct species (Splendid Woodpecker), differing from nominate in being less rufous, more barred below, black confined to throat (not running onto chest), and with some red feather tips.

Similar species Red rump, crimson underparts and yellow face separates it from other overlapping large woodpeckers.

Food and foraging Mainly adult and larval large wood-boring beetles. Usually forages alone, sometimes in pairs, low on larger trunks and on snags.

► Adult male Crimson-bellied Woodpecker. This is race *splendens*, which has sometimes been regarded as a distinct species. Chocó, Colombia, June (*Nick Athanas*).

▼ Adult female of the nominate race. Note the neck coloration. The natural history of this stunning rainforest species is largely unknown. Abra Patricia, Peru, July (*Pete Morris*).

189. RED-NECKED WOODPECKER
Campephilus rubricollis

L 30–34cm

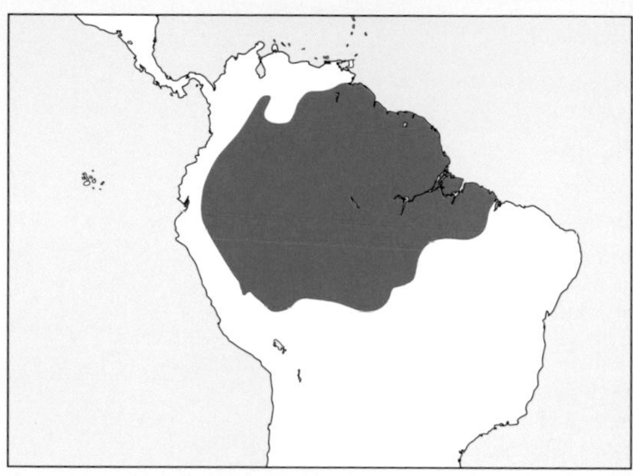

Identification Mainly black and rufous. Scarlet hood covers head, neck, chest and upper mantle. Rear of crown peaked and pointed. Breast, belly and vent plain cinnamon, with some reddish feather tips. Uniform black from back to rump. Upperwings mostly blackish, reddish on flight feathers and underwing obvious in flight. Tail black. Iris white or yellow. Orbital ring grey. Bill pale. Legs greyish. Sexes differ: male has small, often inconspicuous, black and white lateral oval patch below ear-coverts; female has broad white triangle-shaped streak bordered by black running from the bill-base below ear-coverts and over cheek. Juvenile browner on upperparts and wings, more orange below. Juvenile male has cream malar; juvenile female very much like adult female.

Vocalisations Limited repertoire. Single or double soft squeaky mews. Harsh throaty caws and raucous bugle-like contact notes. Commonly, a loud, nasal, sneeze-like *nkaaah, ngkah, kyah* or *khiaaah*. Sudden double *kerra-kerra* or *querra querra* and churring *ca-wa-rr-r*.

◄ Adult male Red-necked Woodpecker of the nominate race. Males have a small black-and-white patch on the cheek on an otherwise all-red head; females have a broad pale streak from the bill to the cheek. Eastern Venezuela, March (*Pete Morris*).

Drumming Solid, rapid, double rap, first strike louder than second. Often repeated after long pauses.

Status Locally fairly common across much of range. Surprisingly little known about its ecology, overall considered stable, but probably affected by deforestation in Amazonia.

Habitat Typically humid forests: rainforest, cloudforest, *terra firme*, *várzea*, swamp and riverine woods. But also drier forest, wooded savanna, secondary growth and parkland with large trees. Where it overlaps with Crimson-crested (e.g. S Venezuela), seems to prefer more closed forest.

Range South America. Resident and sedentary E of Andes in parts of Colombia, Venezuela, the Guianas, Brazil, Ecuador, Bolivia and Peru. Mainly lowlands and hills, but to 1600m in Peru and Bolivia.

Taxonomy and variation Three races: ***rubricollis*** (E Colombia, E Ecuador into Venezuela, the Guianas, N Brazil); ***trachelopyrus*** (NE Peru, N Bolivia, W Brazil south of Amazonia) is largest, blackest above, deepest red below, with large rufous patch on flight feathers; ***olallae*** (Brazil from River Madeira to Pará and Maranhão into Bolivia) intermediate in size and colour tones between above and nominate. Races intergrade.

Similar species Sympatric Crimson-crested Woodpecker also red-hooded but larger, barred below and striped white on neck and back. Uniform plumage separates from Lineated Woodpecker.

Food and foraging Larvae of large beetles and other insects. Often forages within forest in pairs, usually low on large trunks but also high in cover.

▼ Adult female *olallae*. The large cinnamon panel on the flight feathers is typical for this race. Mato Grosso, Brazil, April (*Valdir Hobus*).

190. ROBUST WOODPECKER
Campephilus robustus

L 32–37cm

Identification Mostly black and white with complete red hood. Hindcrown peaked and pointed, but not crested. Buff or cream below, heavily but finely barred black from breast to vent, less barred on belly. Buff or white from mantle (slightly barred black sometimes tinged buff) to rump, very striking in flight. Tail black. Upperwing glossy black with cinnamon barring or spotting on flight feathers, particularly obvious in flight. Underwing brownish with rufous coverts and pale spotting on flight feathers. Large ivory or grey bill. Iris white or yellowish. Legs grey. Sexes differ: male has small black and white lateral oval patch below ear-coverts; female lacks this, having broad, white, triangular black-bordered streak which runs from lores and bill-base over cheek, ending below ear-

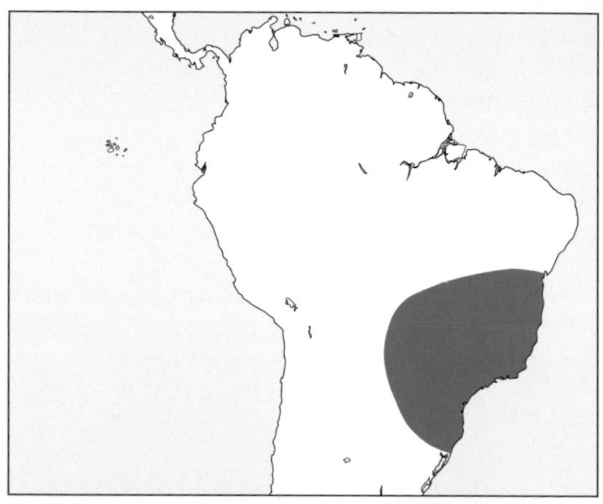

coverts. Juveniles of both sexes more like adult female, with white streak on face, but black plumage browner, less glossy, whiter below; juvenile male may have some red tips on cheek.

Vocalisations Nasal, squeaky toy-like, repeated *pseew*. Single *choo* or *tjoo* notes like suppressed sneezes, sometimes harsher and linked in a raucous series. *Keeew, keee* or *kew* notes uttered both in flight and when settled. *Pso-ko-po-po-po-po-at* also described.

Drumming Solid, abrupt, double rap, repeated after 20–30-second pauses.

Status Often uncommon. Overall population size and trends mostly unknown, but possibly increasing in some areas and also found in regions where logging is ongoing.

Habitat Rainforest and *araucaria* forest. Also clearings and cane-breaks where some large trees (dead or living) remain.

Range South America. Mainly restricted to Atlantic rainforest of SE Brazil, E Paraguay and NE Argentina. Lowlands to around 2200m. Resident and sedentary.

Taxonomy and variation Monotypic. Some clinal differences in size.

Similar species Crimson-crested Woodpecker similar in size, colour and barring below, but has white lines down neck and mantle. Cream-backed Woodpecker male like Robust male in head colour and pattern, but Cream-backed plain below and smaller. Lineated Woodpecker lacks red hood and has white line on neck. Helmeted Woodpecker has contrasting pale rump and back, but mainly all-red head and is much smaller.

Food and foraging Large wood-boring beetles and their larvae, supplemented with some fruit and berries. Usually forages at mid-levels in large trees, dead or alive, seldom on ground.

► Adult female. Although essentially a rainforest species, Robust Woodpecker is seemingly able to adapt to degraded and secondary habitats. Misiones, Argentina, September (*Roberto Güller*).

◄ Adult male Robust Woodpecker. In common with several other *Campephilus* species, males have a small black-and-white patch on the cheek, and females have a pale streak from the bill running below the eye. Itatiaia, Rio de Janeiro, Brazil, July (*Luiz Claudio Marigo*).

191. CRIMSON-CRESTED WOODPECKER

Campephilus melanoleucos

L 34–38cm

Identification Mainly black with prominent, peaked red crest. Throat, neck and chest black. Breast, belly and undertail-coverts white or buff barred black. White line from neck onto mantle and scapulars form V-shape on back. Rest of upperparts, rump and tail black. Upperwing black, primaries tipped white when fresh. Underwing white. Iris yellow; orbital ring grey. Bill ivory or grey, base darker. Legs grey. Sexes differ: male has mostly red head, pale lores, small black and white lateral oval patch below ear-coverts; female has red crest and head sides, black ridge on crown and broad buff or white band, bordered by black from bill across lower cheek to neck. Juveniles of both sexes like adult female but duller, more heavily barred below, supercilium pale.

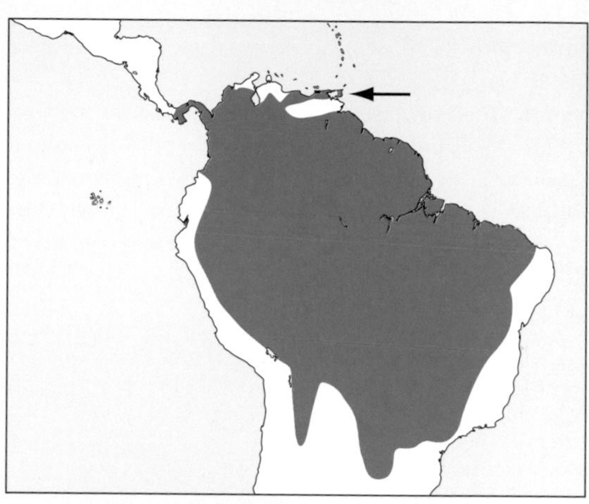

Vocalisations Repeated *queer-queerer* or *kwirr-kwirra,*

◄ Adult male Crimson-crested Woodpecker of the nominate race. The male has a black-and-white patch on the cheek, and a pale loral area. Amazonian Ecuador, October (*Murray Cooper*).

► Adult female nominate. Females differ from the males in having a black ridge to the crown and crest, and a broad whitish band from the bill to the neck. Amazonian Ecuador, October (*Murray Cooper*).

like some tree-frogs. Down-slurred *kiarrah*. Shrill, whistling, repeated *put-put-puttas* when excited. Rapid, chattering *tkep-tkep-tkep*. Sharp, high-pitched *ca* alarm notes, vibrating *chiz-ik* or *chis-sic* in displays. Low *wuk-wuk, wrr-wrr, wunwun* and *uh-uh* intimate calls. Females make gentle *k-da, k-da* begging calls, juveniles *k-arr, k-arr*.

Drumming Both sexes produce 3–5 raps, occasionally 2, and even-pitched abrupt rolls of 5–6 strikes that accelerate then fade. Pairs indulge in rapping duets.

Status Fairly common locally. Considered stable and may benefit from forest fragmentation.

Habitat Upland and lowland forests: rainforest, cloud-forest, *terra firme*, *várzea* and gallery forest. Also more open woodlands, swampy forests, wooded savanna, palm groves, plantations, wooded farmland, urban areas with scattered trees, parks and partially logged areas. Some large trees essential.

Range C and S America. Most widespread *Campephilus*. E of the Andes from Panama to N Argentina. Also Trinidad. Lowlands to over 3000m. Resident and sedentary.

Taxonomy and variation Three races: ***melanoleucos*** (most of range from E Colombia, Ecuador, Venezuela, Trinidad, the Guianas, much of Brazil, Peru, Bolivia, Paraguay, NE Argentina); ***malherbii*** (W Panama to N and C Colombia) often ochre or cinnamon below, bill darker, greyer than nominate; ***cearae*** (E and S Brazil) is smallest race.

Similar species Robust Woodpecker also red-headed but has red neck. Red-necked Woodpecker red-headed but smaller, lacks barring below and white lines on back. Female most like Lineated Woodpecker, both having white line from bill, but Lineated's is narrower and ear-coverts are grey.

Food and foraging Mainly large wood-boring beetle larvae. Also ants, termites, other invertebrates and berries. Often forages in families, young staying with parents for around a year after fledging. Hacks deeply into timber of isolated dead trees and stumps.

▼ Adult male *malherbii*. This race has a darker bill than the nominate. Panama, January (*Robert Scanlon*).

▼ Adult female *malherbii*. This adaptable species has the largest range of the *Campephilus* woodpeckers. Santa Marta Mountains, Colombia, November (*Nick Athanas*).

192. PALE-BILLED WOODPECKER
Campephilus guatemalensis

L 35–38cm

Identification Mostly black and white with scarlet head and bushy, rounded crest. Neck black with white stripes down each side continuing onto black back to form a V-shape on scapulars. Black mantle enclosed by this white shape. Uppertail chocolate, undertail brownish-buff. Black wings tipped white in fresh plumage, underwings pale. Black rump sometimes barred white. Chest black, breast barred black and buff or cream. Long ivory bill, base sometimes bluish. Iris cream or yellow; orbital ring grey or black. Legs grey. Sexes differ: male has all-red head; female red sides to head but forehead, mid-crown and throat blackish, together with orbital ring creating 'goggles'. Juvenile duller, browner, less distinctly barred below; bill and iris darker; head pattern like female, but more orange.

Vocalisations Commonly, a repeated laughing or nervous, chattering *ka-ka-ka-ka-kay-nuk* or *kuh-kuh-kuh-kuh-uh-uh* and fast, squirrel-like clucking *chuk-chuk-chuk*. Series of squeaky, sometimes quacking, *kwirr-a* notes (like some tree-frogs), first two notes clear, subsequent notes merged into giggle or rattle. Also throaty cawing and raucous bugling. Nasal, tooting *kint* like some relatives, and low-pitched, repeated contact *keeu* note. Nestlings utter *kuk-kuk-kuk* calls.

Drumming Sudden, solid, double or triple raps. Usually repeated once or twice per minute. Also drum-like roll of up to 7 rapid strikes.

Status Locally common in Mexico, Belize, Nicaragua and Costa Rica. Considered stable, but range-restricted and abandons heavily logged areas.

Habitat Wet and dry lowland forests. Also upland forests, rainforest, mangroves, plantations, partially cleared forest and suburban areas with large trees.

Range Central America. Pacific (from S Sonora) and Atlantic (from S Tamaulipas) slopes of Mexico and Yucatan Peninsula to Panama. Mainly lowlands but to 2000m. Resident, probably sedentary.

Taxonomy and variation Three races: ***guatemalensis*** (S Mexico, Belize, Guatemala, El Salvador, Honduras, Nicaragua, Costa Rica and W Panama); ***nelsoni*** (W Mexico: S Sonora to Oaxaca) is smallest race, less glossy, browner above, pale areas whiter than nominate, often

► Adult male Pale-billed Woodpecker has an all-red head and throat. This is the nominate race. Heredia, Costa Rica, February (*Dave Hawkins*).

darkly barred on rump; ***regius*** (NE Mexico: Tamaulipas to Veracruz) largest and longest-billed.

Similar species Within range most like similar-sized Lineated Woodpecker, though that species has black and white face and darker bill.

Food and foraging Mainly large wood-boring beetle larvae, especially long-horned beetles. Also ants, sometimes berries and fruit. Often forages in pairs or family groups, usually in canopy on snags on large trees.

► Adult male nominate at the nest-hole. The distinctive pale bill helps separate this species from other sympatric woodpeckers. Tortuguero NP, Costa Rica, February (*Gerard Gorman*).

▼ Adult female differs from the male mainly in having a black centre to the red crown, and a black throat. Sarapiqui, Costa Rica, April (*Glenn Bartley*).

193. GUAYAQUIL WOODPECKER
Campephilus gayaquilensis

L 33–34cm

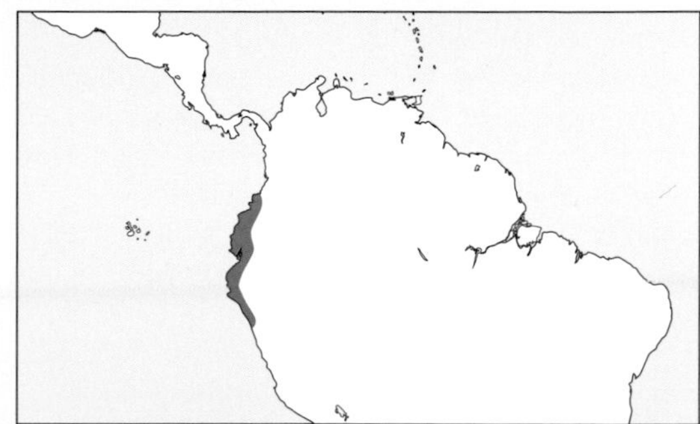

Identification Mostly black tinged brownish. Mainly red head with peaked crown. Chin and throat black with a few red flecks. Broad white line runs through black neck down to scapulars to form V-shape on back. Mantle and tail black, rump and uppertail-coverts barred black and white or buff. Wings chocolate, flight feathers brownish with small ochre or buff patch on inner webs, underwing whitish. Chest to vent barred black and buff. Iris yellow. Bill ivory or grey. Legs greyish. Sexes differ: male has most of head red with black and white patch just below ear-coverts; female lacks this patch, having broad white

► Adult male Guayaquil Woodpecker. The all-red head has a lateral black-and-white oval patch under the ear-coverts. Mindo, Ecuador, September (*Joel N. Rosenthal*).

or cream stripe from lores and bill across lower cheek to merge with white neck line. Both juveniles more like adult females but less barred below.

Vocalisations Rather basic range of chattering and squeaking calls. Commonly, a fast, nervous, squeaky *quick-quick-quickerrrr* and liquid *kwi-kwi-kwe-rrrrrr*.

Drumming Abrupt, 1-second roll of 4–7 strikes. Does not produce true raps, unlike some relatives, though first two strikes are strong, others falling away.

Status NT. Can be locally common and persists in fragmented forests, but uncommon to rare overall. Declining owing to continuing logging and clearance for agriculture and grazing of livestock. Some local populations now isolated in forest pockets.

Habitat Dry deciduous and humid Andean Pacific-slope forests and woods. Also taller, mature secondary growth and mangroves.

Range South America. Restricted to lowlands along W slopes of Andes in SW Colombia, W Ecuador and NW Peru, either side of the Equator. Sea-level to 800m, occasionally to 1800m. Resident and sedentary.

Taxonomy and variation Monotypic. Formerly considered a race of Crimson-crested Woodpecker. Rump sometimes all-black.

Similar species Lineated Woodpecker has less red on face, pale throat and white scapular lines do not form a V-shape. Powerful and Crimson-bellied Woodpeckers both reddish below, but rarely meet, as at higher elevations. Very similar Crimson-crested Woodpecker does not overlap in range.

Food and foraging Diet presumably like that of close relatives (wood-boring beetle larvae, ants, termites), but precise information lacking. Usually forages in pairs, on snags at upper levels and in canopy.

▼ Adult male Guayaquil Woodpecker. This threatened species continues to suffer from logging and the degradation of its woodland habitats. Pichincha, Ecuador, December (*Roger Ahlman*).

▼ Adult female differs from the male in having a broad white band running from the bill across the cheek and onto the neck. Pichincha, Ecuador, December (*Roger Ahlman*).

194. CREAM-BACKED WOODPECKER
Campephilus leucopogon

L 30–34cm

Identification Black, white and red with prominent, peaked crest. Plain black below. Large, distinct, cream or buff patch on mantle and back, sometimes tinged cinnamon. Rest of upperparts to rump black. Upperwing black, flight feathers pale on inner webs. Underwing mostly black with cinnamon or buff bases to flight feathers, pale line over coverts. Relatively short black tail. Throat and neck red. Striking white or yellow iris. Long ivory bill, broad at base. Legs grey. Sexes differ: male has all-red hood, covering short crest, head and neck, except for small black and white lateral oval patch below rear ear-coverts; female has black crown, crest, orbital area, chin and neck, with red only on ear-coverts, throat and nape, and broad black-bordered white or buff streak running from bill base below ear-coverts and over lower cheek. Female's black crest longer, wispier than male's, sometimes curled. Juveniles of both sexes more like adult female, but head more orange; juvenile male has more red than adult female.

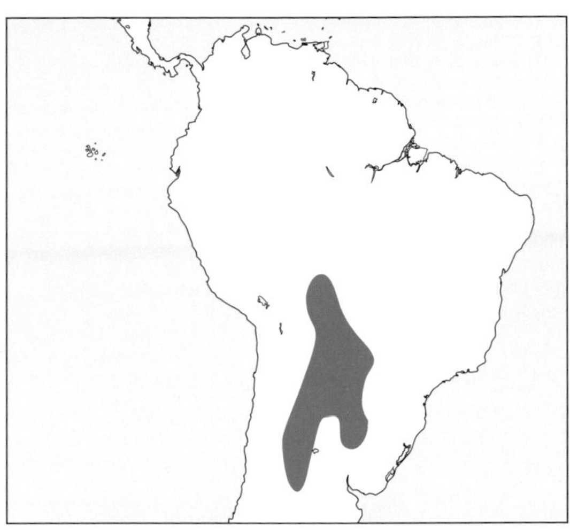

Vocalisations Rather limited range of simple calls. Nasal, squeaky double-notes: *pee-aw, pi-ow, kwee-yaw* or *kwee-or*. These notes often slowly repeated and uttered in a chattering or whimpering series when excited or agitated. Double noted, feeble *psi-ur or tiss-ue* like a suppressed sneeze. A harsh *reurr-reurr-reurr*.

Drumming Simple, solid, abrupt double rap produced.

Status Usually uncommon. Poorly known, though fairly widespread. Habitat change and loss in Chaco region a threat, where clearance for charcoal, cattle-ranching, settlements and planting of alien trees continues.

Habitat Dry, open woodland. Also savanna, pastures, palm groves and farmland with woodland fragments. In some areas upland transitional forest. Avoids thick forest.

Range South America. Restricted to NC Bolivia, W and C Paraguay, NC Argentina, N Uruguay and SE Brazil. Mainly lowlands but to 2500m. Resident and sedentary.

◄ Adult male Cream-backed Woodpecker has a small black-and-white patch below the ear-coverts on an otherwise all-red head. Córdoba, Argentina, November (*Graham Ekins*).

Taxonomy and variation Monotypic. Variation slight.
Similar species Sympatric Black-bodied Woodpecker also red-headed and plain black below, but has white stripe on neck, lacks cream back patch and is smaller.
Food and foraging Mainly large wood-boring beetle larvae. Forages alone, in pairs and in family parties until autumn, at all levels in trees and on stumps and logs.

► The adult female is less red on the head than the male, with the long crest, crown and orbital region being black. There is a white band from the bill to the cheek. Formosa, Argentina, November (*Roberto Güller*).

▼ A pair of Cream-backed Woodpeckers; the male is above, the female below, with crown feathers raised. This *Campephilus* inhabits open woodlands, seldom entering the forests proper. Salta, Argentina, December (*Nick Athanas*).

195. MAGELLANIC WOODPECKER
Campephilus magellanicus

L 36–38cm

Identification Largest woodpecker in South America. Mostly glossy black with bluish sheen. Upperwing black with white stripe formed by tertials and webs of flight feathers. Underwing mostly white, obvious in flight. Iris yellow, orange or pink; orbital ring greyish. Large blackish-grey bill. Legs grey. Sexes very different: male has complete red hood, often with black and white speckles, and pointed, forward-curling crest; female has mostly black head with crimson around bill base, and black, floppy, double-plumed crest that curls in any direction. Juveniles similar to respective adults but duller and differ in head pattern. Recently fledged male has mostly black head with red crest and malar (all-red head acquired after three months). Newly fledged female has smaller, straighter crest than adult.

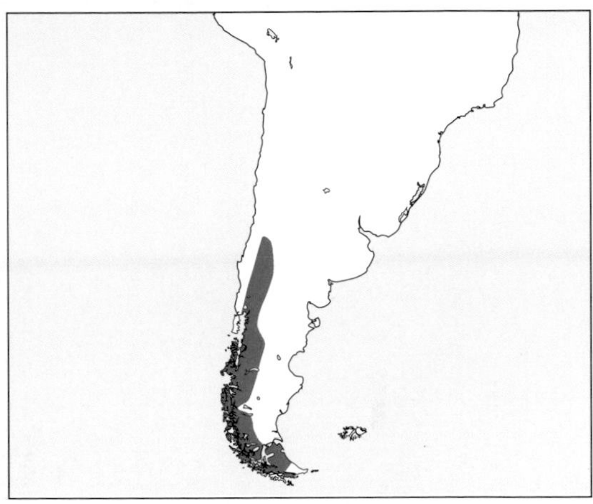

At about six months young largely resemble adults, with exception of black barring on white wing-patches. Sub-adults, and some adults, may also show such barring.

Vocalisations Often vocal, with loud and soft nasal chattering. Various squawks, whines and toots often feeble. Commonly, *pisss-aaah,* like suppressed sneeze, an explosive *pi-caa,* often repeated 5–7 times, and gentle *kwee-oo.* Contact calls include repeated, gargling *prrr-prr-prrr* or *weeerr-weeeeerr.* Descending, cackling, nervous *cray-cra-cra-cra,* usually given in flight or when threatened.

Drumming Produces a loud, far-carrying, solid, rapid double rap, diagnostic within range. Also quiet, brief tapping rolls, produced near nest.

Status Locally common, but overall population probably declining. Certainly endangered in N Chile, due to loss and degradation of mature forests.

Habitat Mainly old-growth, deciduous, temperate forests with large trees, particularly pure southern beech and other *Nothofagus* species, sometimes mixed secondary growth; also feeds in monkey-puzzle trees *Araucaria araucana.* A keystone species in Patagonian forests, numerous non-excavating birds and other wildlife using its cavities.

◄ Adult male Magellanic Woodpecker has an all-crimson hood; this spectacular bird cannot be mistaken for any other species in its range. Tierra del Fuego, Argentina, November (*James Lowen*).

Range South America. Most southerly woodpecker in the world. Endemic to Patagonian forests in Chile and SW Argentina. From San Fernando foothills, Chile, and Neuquén, Argentina, south to Tierra del Fuego and adjacent islands. Sea-level to around 2000m. Resident, but altitudinal movements to avoid deep snow sometimes made.

Taxonomy and variation Monotypic. Variation slight.
Similar species None: unmistakable within range.
Food and foraging Mainly wood-boring beetle larvae, though sap, fruit and small vertebrates also consumed. A social species, clans of 3–5 birds remaining in contact all year (offspring stay with parents for up to four years), foraging close to each other, often on logs and stumps.

◀ Adult male Magellanic Woodpecker. This stunning and iconic species is endemic to mature forests in Patagonia. Torres del Paine NP, Chile, December (*Gerhard Rotheneder*).

▼ A juvenile female; note the dark eye and somewhat stunted crest. Los Glaciares NP, Patagonia, Argentina, December (*Gerhard Rotheneder*).

▼ Adult female Magellanic Woodpecker has a mostly black head with an impressive, long, wispy crest. Torres del Paine NP, Chile, December (*Gerhard Rotheneder*).

◄ Adult male Magellanic Woodpecker. Perhaps the most spectacular of all the extant woodpeckers. Tierra del Fuego, Chile, October.

196. IVORY-BILLED WOODPECKER
Campephilus principalis

L 48–53cm

Identification Huge. Mostly black and white, with impressive curved crest and heavy, dagger-like ivory-white bill. White stripes along neck, mantle and back. White secondaries and inner primaries form broad white trailing edge above and below. Folded wings mostly white. Iris cream. Sexes differ: male with rear of head, nape and pointed crest red; female lacks red. Recently fledged juvenile browner with white tips to outer primaries, stubby black crest, blunt tail and chestnut iris.

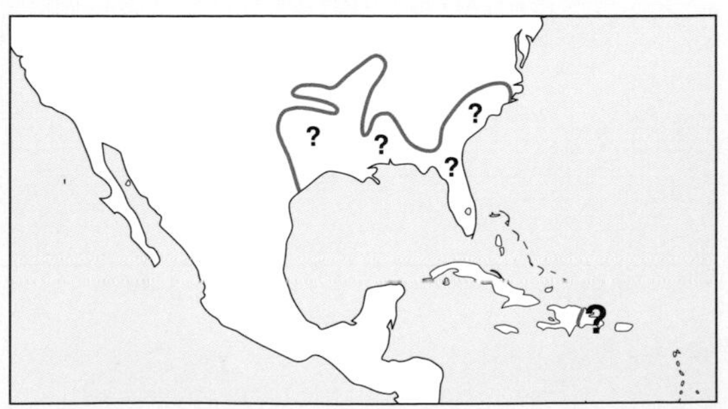

Vocalisations Nasal, repeated alarm note *kent* or *pent* or *yank,* likened to Red-breasted Nuthatch, though more metallic, like a tin trumpet *toot.* Also a prolonged, repeated, up-slurred *kient* or *keent,* a softer *yent-yent* or *key-ennnt, key-ennnt* and intimate *toodle-toodle-toodle.* Single *yap* and double *yap-yap notes. Kak, kak, kak* like alarm of Cooper's Hawk *Accipiter cooperii.*

Contact call a soft *cape-cape-cape.*
Drumming Known to make a loud double rap, first strike followed immediately by second.
Status CR. Probably (but not officially) extinct. Last confirmed sighting in USA in Louisiana in 1944, in Cuba in the Cuchillas del Toa Mts in 1987. Reports from Cuba in the 1990s and, in the USA, in Florida in 2005 and Arkansas in 2004 and 2005, prompted inconclusive searches. Habitat loss, hunting and collecting of trophies and specimens all contributed to its demise.
Habitat In Cuba, lowland hardwood forests and upland pinewoods. In USA, lowland hardwood forested floodplains (bottom-lands), alluvial swamps, hammocks and pinewoods.
Range SE USA and Cuba. In USA originally from Illinois to N Carolina, Oklahoma, Texas and Florida. Formerly most of Cuba, but probably never common. Little suitable forest remains in Cuba: Alejandro de Humboldt NP in the east offers the best hope for the species' survival.
Taxonomy and variation Two races: ***principalis*** (SE USA) and ***bairdii*** (Cuba), which has white neck-stripe beginning closer to the bill than in nominate. Two species possibly involved.
Similar species Pileated Woodpecker, being large and black and white, a possible source of confusion in USA. White on Pileated Woodpecker's wing limited to underwing lining and small primary patch; Ivory-billed's white secondaries and inner primaries form broad white trailing edge above and below. Perched Pileated shows only small white patch on primaries.
Food and foraging Large wood-boring beetle larvae. Some fruit, berries and nuts. Mainly on snags and dead limbs, seldom on ground.

197. IMPERIAL WOODPECKER
Campephilus imperialis

L 56–60cm

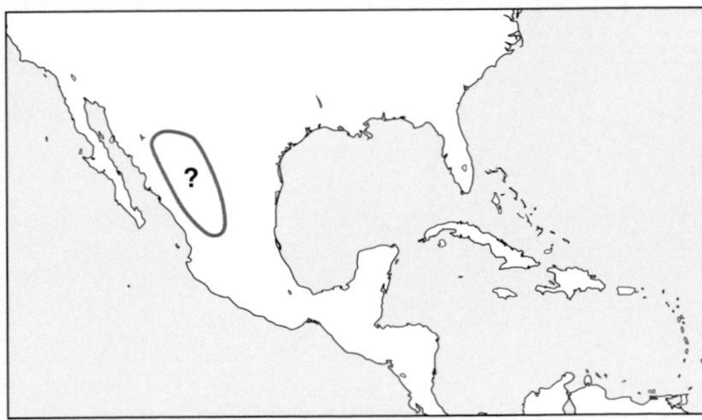

Identification Huge. Largest woodpecker known, 20% larger than Ivory-billed Woodpecker. Mostly glossy black. Prominent white triangular patches on folded wings when perched, broad white trailing edge clear in flight. Bill ivory. Iris yellow. Legs grey. Sexes differ: male with rear of head, nape and crest red; female lacks red, having forward-curling black crest.
Vocalisations Accounts mention 'cackling' sounds and pairs 'chattering' loudly. Nasal 'penny trumpet-like' *keent-keent* notes and tinny, nuthatch-like call, similar to Ivory-billed, also described.
Drumming No information available.
Status CR. Last confirmed record a female filmed in Durango, Mexico, in 1956. This 16mm film is the only known documentation of a living specimen. Around 160 museum specimens are known, most collected between 1890 and 1910. Probably became extinct in the late 20th century, disappearing from Durango by 1960. Reasons cited include logging, clearance of forests, hunting by local people and later collecting for museums and trophies. May have still been common in pine forests in the Sierra Madre in the 19th century. Recent reports include a pair in C Durango in 1993, a male around 20km from this site in 1995, a female in N Sonora in 1993 and an individual in Chihuahua in November 2005. Subsequent searches have failed to confirm its presence and prospects for the survival of the species look bleak.
Habitat Open old-growth upland pine and oak forests with large trees, especially yellow pine species. Records from between 1675–3050m. The filmed bird was in old-growth coniferous forest with abundant large trees and snags at 2700–2900m. Though such habitat remains, probably not enough old-growth remnants are large enough for a breeding territory.
Range Unclear. Probably restricted to the Sierra Madre Occidental in Mexico: Sinaloa, Chihuahua, Durango, Nayarit, Zacatecas, Jalisco and Michoacán.
Taxonomy and variation Monotypic. Some individual differences in size.
Similar species None within range.
Food and foraging Unknown, but presumably large wood-boring beetle larvae, sought by family parties.

Greater Yellownapes *Chrysophlegma flavinucha*. Thailand, October (*Setaphong Tantanawat*).

CHRYSOPHLEGMA

An Old World (SE Asian) genus of three species, all formerly placed in genus *Picus*, but recently reassigned following detailed molecular phylogenetic studies. Further studies may well result in other current *Picus* species, some of which are very similar, being moved to this genus. The *Chrysophlegma* essentially occur in primary forests and are arboreal in habits, seldom visiting the ground. All three have, to varying degrees, yellow napes which are raised in disputes and displays.

198. BANDED WOODPECKER
Chrysophlegma miniaceum

L 25–27cm

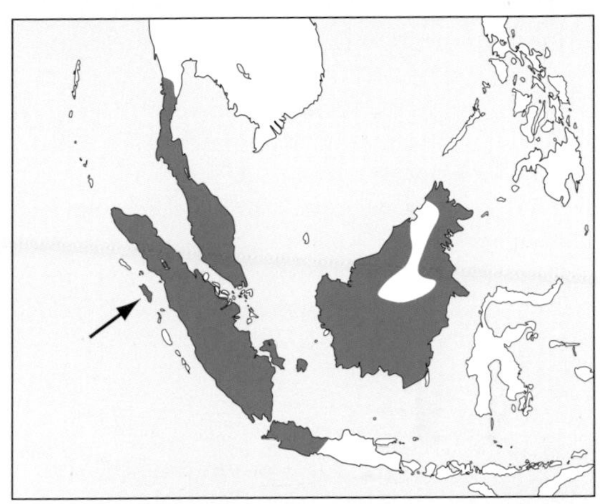

Identification Mostly rufous-brown. Mantle dull olive, subtly barred or scaled buff, yellowish-green on mantle. Rump yellow. Most of head and ear-coverts rufous-brown, finely streaked pale. Neck, chin and throat brown. Shaggy, dull yellow nape. Breast reddish or maroon, barred olive. Belly to vent paler, white or buff heavily barred black-brown, though somewhat diffuse. Uppertail chocolate; coverts olive or brown gently barred buff. Primaries brownish barred pale, secondaries and tertials rufous or greenish, coverts deeper red. Rufous-brown underwing barred buff. Bill dark, lower mandible greyer. Iris chestnut; orbital ring bluish. Legs greenish. Sexes differ slightly: male has reddish face and throat, less rufous when worn; female browner, with face, throat and ear-coverts flecked

► Adult male Banded Woodpecker of the race *malaccense*. The sexes can be hard to separate in the field unless the male's red face and throat can be seen clearly. Singapore, December (*Con Foley*).

white or buff. Juvenile dull brown, underpart barring weak, mantle plain, iris brown; juvenile male red on crown and nape, female red only on nape.

Vocalisations Falling series of up to 7 melancholic *kwee* or *peew* notes. When uttered singly *peew* note usually squeaky, sometimes drawn out. In conflicts, a fast *kwi-wi-ta-wi-kwi*. Single, loud, piercing *keek* or *kee* contact note, recalling Crested Serpent Eagle. Latter notes sometimes threaded into squawking series.

Drumming Drums rarely and weakly. Little information.

Status Locally common to uncommon. Population size and trends mostly unknown, but considered stable. Has adapted to man-made habitats.

Habitat Primary, evergreen dipterocarp rainforest, particularly with epiphytes, vines and rotting timber. Also open secondary forest, mangroves, coastal scrub, rubber plantations, parkland, wooded suburbs and overgrown gardens.

Range SE Asia. From S Burma (Myanmar) through Thai-Malay Peninsula to the Sundas. Mainly lowlands, higher on Java and Borneo. Resident and sedentary.

Taxonomy and variation Four races, differences mainly involving back and rump colour and extent of barring and yellow on nape. Nominate ***miniaceum*** (Java) very barred below, reddish on mantle, minimal yellow; ***perlutum*** (Burma (Myanmar), Peninsular Thailand) green-yellow above, rump bright yellow, narrowly barred below; ***malaccense*** (Peninsular Malaysia, Sumatra, Bangka and Belitung Islands, Borneo) green-bronze scaled mantle, clear yellow nape, broadly barred below; ***niasense*** (Nias Island) most red on face, chest unbarred, nape clear yellow.

Similar species Most like juvenile Crimson-winged Woodpecker, but more barred, browner, red areas duller and less yellow on nape.

Food and foraging Insects, particularly arboreal ants. Often feeds in high cover and on vines, probing moss and epiphytes, sometimes in small parties or mixed-species flocks.

▼ Adult female *malaccense*. Note the white speckling on the face and throat. Singapore, February (*Con Foley*).

▼ Adult male Banded Woodpecker; the widespread race *malaccense* has a greenish-bronze mantle and back. Singapore, February (*Daniel Koh Swee Huat*).

199. CHEQUER-THROATED WOODPECKER
Chrysophlegma mentale

L 26–29cm

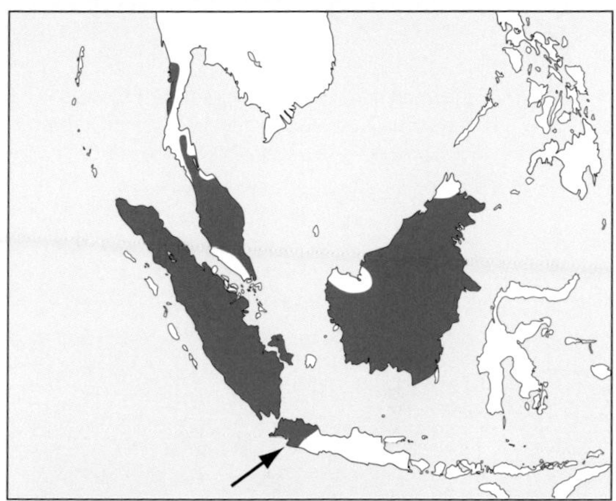

Identification Colourful. Dark olive above. Uppertail black. Crown olive-green, sometimes dotted red. Crested hindcrown and shaggy nape yellow. Ear-coverts olive, flecked rufous. Chin and throat variable black and white. Chest and neck-sides plain chestnut. Dark green below. Most of wings chestnut, primaries barred black or brown. Underwing brownish, coverts dark green, barred cinnamon. Bill dark. Iris chestnut; orbital-ring olive. Legs grey-olive. Sexes differ slightly: male has blackish malar spotted or streaked white; female's malar chestnut, bill shorter. Juvenile duller, darker red in wings, plain rufous below, some with reddish tones on nape.

Vocalisations Crying series of *wi* or *we* notes, lower-pitched than similar call of Greater Yellownape. Harsh, sharp *kyick* alarm note. Single or repeated squeaky *kwee* and *kyew* notes.

Drumming Short, steady, level-pitched rolls of up to 20 strikes. Faster than those of most relatives.

Status Locally often common. Has declined in some areas (e.g. Sundas) due to forest clearance, but seems to have adapted better than close relatives to degraded forests. Now uncommon on Java, lost from Singapore.

Habitat Mainly tall mature evergreen rainforest, typically with moss-clad dipterocarp trees, epiphytes, vines and thick understorey. Sometimes in mangroves, clearings with damp, dense growth and cultivated areas where some large trees remain.

Range SE Asia. From Burma (Myanmar) through Thai-Malay Peninsula to Indonesia. Lowlands to about 2200m. Resident and sedentary.

Taxonomy and variation Two races: ***mentale*** (W Java) female has chestnut throat; ***humii*** (S Burma (Myanmar), S Peninsular Thailand, Malaysia, Sumatra, Borneo) is smaller, lighter green, brighter red in wings, yellower on nape, sometimes with red hue, chin and throat more white than black (opposite on nominate), sometimes barred rather than spotted, female chestnut from neck across cheek, sometimes onto chin, and has black and white throat.

Similar species Differs from smaller Crimson-winged Woodpecker in having marked throat and lacking red

► Adult male Chequer-throated Woodpecker. The sexes are similar; the male has a black-and-white malar stripe, while that of the female is rufous-brown. This is race *humii*. Johor, Malaysia, September (*James Eaton*).

crown and bluish orbital ring. Similar-sized Lesser Yellownape lacks red in wings. Head shape and pattern more like Greater Yellownape, but that species visibly larger and lacks red wings and neck.

Food and foraging Ants, termites, beetle larvae and other insects. Sometimes berries. Probes in dead wood, vines and epiphytes. Often in mixed-species flocks with attendant drongos.

► Adult male of the nominate race. Now confined to western Java, the nominate race is increasingly scarce, having suffered from deforestation. Gede Pangrango, Java, Indonesia, July (*Khaleb Yordan*).

▼ Adult female *humii*. This race is more colourful – a brighter red and yellow – than the nominate. Johor, Malaysia, June (*Con Foley*).

▼ An adult female (left) feeding one of her fledged young. Gede Pangrango, Java, Indonesia, July (*Lars Petersson*).

200. GREATER YELLOWNAPE
Chrysophlegma flavinucha

L 32–35cm

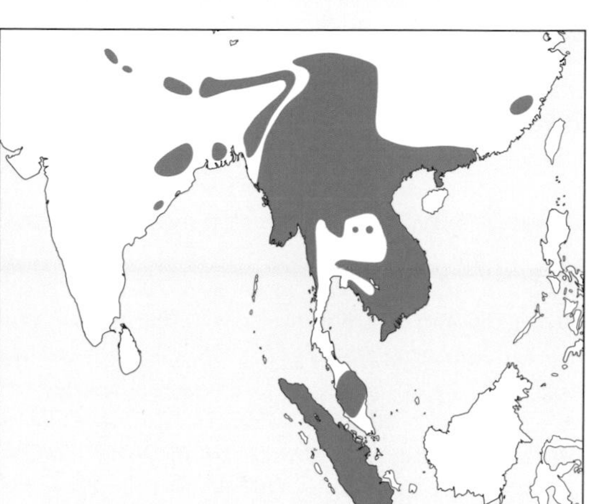

Identification Largest 'yellownape'. Mostly green above, plain green-grey below. Rufous flight feathers barred black. Tail black. Large, bright yellow nape and prominent crest produces (more so on males) triangular head profile. Crown brownish, ear-coverts olive. Flight feathers chestnut, barred black. Dark bill. Iris chestnut, orbital ring greyish-blue. Sexes differ: male has broad cream or yellow throat and lower cheek and malar, sometimes streaked black; female has brown, chestnut or rufous throat and malar streaked white, less yellow on nape. Juvenile male has pale yellow nape, whitish throat spotted black; juvenile female duller green above with rufous throat spotted black.

Vocalisations Single, sharp, metallic *chenk*. Single or double *chup* or *kyup,* sometimes followed by a quick,

▼ Adult male Greater Yellownape of the race *lylei*. Males of all races are generally brighter than the females, with yellow in the throat and/or malar stripe. Kaeng Krachan NP, Thailand, March (*HY Cheng*).

▼ Adult female – note the black-and-white throat – with a juvenile peering from the nest-hole. This is race *lylei*. Thailand, March.

high-pitched staccato series of same notes. Loose series of inflected *kyaar* notes, a similar *kyerrd*, a brief but repeated mocking *keeyuu* and an explosive, loud, musical *kchaer*. More plaintive, falling *pee-u, pee-u* and a long, accelerating *kwee-kwee-kwee*.

Drumming Rarely drums. Subdued, weak but rapid rolls of even tempo, often beginning loudly, before wavering and fading.

Status Locally common. Overall population size and trends unknown, but considered stable, although *ricketti* now rare.

Habitat Varied open mixed deciduous-conifer forest. Often with sal, oak and pine. Also mature parkland, less common in managed forests such as teak plantations.

Range N India, through Nepal, Bangladesh, Bhutan and China to Indochina, Thailand, Peninsular Malaysia and Sumatra. Resident and sedentary.

Taxonomy and variation Nine races differing mainly in extent of yellow on crest and nape. Nominate ***flavinucha*** of N and E India to Burma (Myanmar) is dark olive on breast and neck-sides; ***kumaonense*** (C Himalayas) large, very green above, nape golden; ***ricketti*** (N Vietnam, SE China) very red primaries, very yellow crest; ***pierrei*** (SE Thailand to S Vietnam) yellowish-green above, black streaks on chin; ***styani*** (Hainan Island, adjacent mainland China) crest pale yellow, wing-tips reddish; ***lylei*** (W Thailand, E Burma (Myanmar), S China, N Laos, NW Vietnam) large, prominent yellow crest and throat, dull red crown, white chest streaked black; ***wrayi*** (Peninsular Malaysia) small, dark, throat heavily marked, male with clear yellow malar, small dull yellow crest; ***mystacale*** (N Sumatra) dark breasted, lacks black and white throat; ***korinchi*** (S Sumatra) dark throat, dull brownish-red in wings.

Similar species Lesser Yellownape smaller (if seen together size difference obvious), barred below, lacks black bars on primaries and never has yellow throat.

Food and foraging Mainly ants, termites and beetle larvae. Some seeds and berries. Often forages in pairs, sometimes in vocal family parties, frequently in mixed flocks with babblers and drongos. Forages at most levels.

▲ Adult female *wrayi* Greater Yellownape. The main confusion species, Lesser Yellownape, is smaller and barred on the underparts. Pahang, Malaysia, August (*Daniel Koh Swee Huat*).

◄ A calling juvenile of the nominate race. Juveniles are drabber overall than the adults; juvenile females tend to be reddish on the chin and throat. Uttarakhand, India, May (*Nitin Srinivasamurthy*).

PICUS

An Old World genus of 13 species, ranging over a vast region from Britain, Iberia and N Africa to Japan. Though variable in plumage, most are essentially olive-green, with visual sexual dimorphism reflected in crown or malar colour. Several species are mainly terrestrial foragers that prey on ground-dwelling ants in open areas, though all nest and roost in trees. Recent molecular phylogenetic studies resulted in three species being transferred from this genus to the *Chrysophlegma* and further taxonomic work may well result in the assignment of Lesser Yellownape and Crimson-winged Woodpeckers to that genus too.

Black-headed Woodpecker *Picus erythropygius*, adult female. Huay Kha Kaeng Wildlife Sanctuary, Thailand, November (*Carl-Johan Svensson*).

201. LESSER YELLOWNAPE
Picus chlorolophus

L 25–28cm

Identification Mostly olive-green above with bright yellow shaggy nape, raised and tufted according to mood. Variable red on crown, white post-ocular and moustachial streaks. Green below, finely barred white or grey from breast to vent. Rufous patch on secondaries, primaries plain or barred white (depending on race). Tail black. Upper mandible grey, lower yellowish. Iris chestnut, orbital ring bluish or grey. Sexes differ: male has variable red malar; female less marked on head, with little red on crown (depending upon race) and none in malar. Juvenile resembles respective adult, but duller, breast often spotted or barred; male lacks red malar.

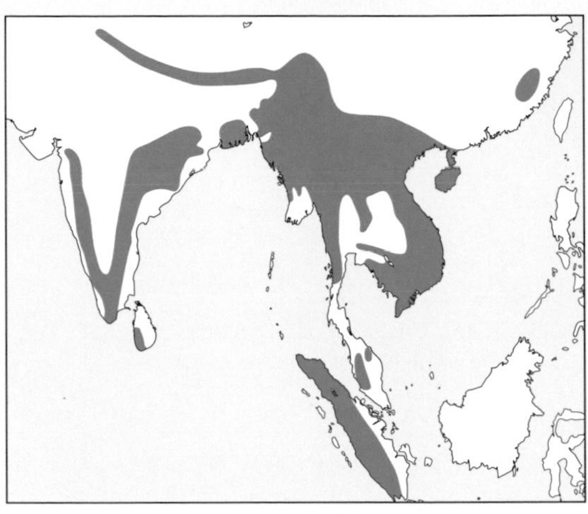

Vocalisations Often vocal, calls varying regionally. Far-carrying, clear, whining, rising *Buteo*-like mewing

▼ Adult male Lesser Yellownape. Head patterns and colours vary between the races, but males always have some red in the malar stripe. This is the race *simlae*. Uttarakhand, India, January (*Harri Taavetti*).

▼ Adult female Lesser Yellownape. The extent of the yellow nape varies greatly; even females of this race, *rodgeri*, have yellow reaching the crest. Pahang, Malaysia, March (*Con Foley*).

kweee-ee, *peee-uu* or *peee-oow*, slowly repeated. Loud, falling, high-pitched *kee* or *kwee* alarms in long series; brief, harsh *chak* and rapid 2–3 note *kyee-kur-kur*.

Drumming Seldom drums. Information lacking.

Status Overall considered stable. Often locally common. No major threats, though small population in SE China is isolated.

Habitat Open, dry or damp, deciduous and evergreen woodlands, bamboo stands, scrub, plantations, parkland, even rural gardens.

Range SE Asia. Parts of Indian subcontinent, Sri Lanka, Burma (Myanmar), China, Indochina, Thai-Malay Peninsula and W Sumatra. Sea-level to around 2000m. Resident and mainly sedentary, although a record from NE Pakistan.

Taxonomy and variation Relationship to the *Chrysophlegma* needs study. Extent of yellow crest and facial patterns vary greatly. Ten races: ***chlorolophus*** (E Nepal, Burma (Myanmar) to N Vietnam); ***simlae*** (N India, C Nepal) is large with white above eye, male with whitish malar, bordered red, below; ***chlorigaster*** (India: W Ghats) is small, dark green, spotted below, rufous in wings, male with red crown, yellow on nape but not usually on crest; ***laotianus*** (N Laos, NE Thailand) crown very red; ***wellsi*** (Sri Lanka) is small, dark green, spotted below, rufous in wings, male has red crown; ***annamensis*** (SE Thailand to S Vietnam) dark above, pale below, much red on crown; ***citrinocristatus*** (N Vietnam, SE China) is dark, barred only on flanks, nape lemon, much red on crown, but minimal in malar; ***longipennis*** (Hainan Island) very green below, heavily barred on flanks; male ***rodgeri*** (W Peninsular Malaysia) has black feather-tips in red crown, crest golden, pale cheek line, darker on neck-sides, dark below narrowly barred pale; ***vanheysti*** (upland Sumatra) very green below, prominent white line over cheek.

Similar species Greater Yellownape larger (when seen together size difference obvious), with much heavier bill, more prominent yellow crest, lacks red on head, unbarred below and flight feathers barred black. Lesser never has yellow throat.

Food and foraging Arboreal ants, beetle larvae and other insects. Some fruit and nectar. Forages at most levels, including on ground, usually probing and gleaning rather than boring into timber. Often in pairs and frequently in roving mixed flocks, especially with drongos, babblers and other woodpeckers, including Greater Yellownape.

▼ Adult female *simlae* Lesser Yellownape. Females may have a prominent white streak across the cheek and red on the crown, but there is never red in the malar region. Uttarakhand, India, January (*Ishmeet Sahni*).

▼ Race *chlorigaster* is spotted below, and males have reduced yellow on the nape, but much red on the crown and in the malar region. Karnataka, India, May (*Nitin Srinivasamurthy*).

202. CRIMSON-WINGED WOODPECKER
Picus puniceus

L 24–28cm

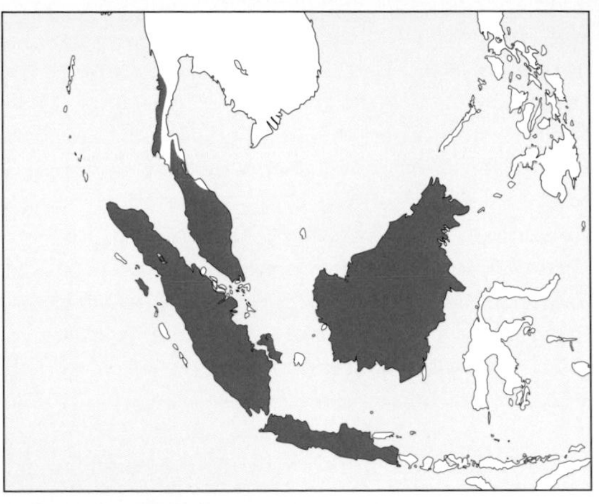

Other name Crimson-winged Yellownape
Identification Brightly coloured. Green-olive body with scarlet wings and crown. Rump light green or yellow depending upon race. Uppertail blackish. Plain green below, flanks sometimes with yellow or white chevrons. Primaries can be blackish, outer webs of secondaries and coverts crimson, tertials green, with some yellow spotting. Underwing brown, buff on coverts and flight feather bases. Ear-coverts and neck-sides green, throat brownish. Red crown with some greenish feather tips, ending in pointed crest and yellow, shaggy nape. Iris reddish. Prominent bluish 'goggles' formed by orbital rings. Lores blackish. Upper mandible grey or brown, lower yellowish. Legs olive. Sexes differ slightly: male has red malar, which

◄ Adult male Crimson-winged Woodpecker of race *observandus*. Males are usually brighter, but the sexes can be difficult to separate unless the male's red malar stripe is seen. Johor, Malaysia, August (*Daniel Koh Swee Huat*).

► Adult female Crimson-winged Woodpecker of the nominate race. This beautiful woodpecker is threatened by deforestation across its range, but the nominate on Java is particularly vulnerable. Java, Indonesia, July (*Lars Petersson*).

female lacks. Female also plainer below, orbital ring often less obvious. Juvenile duller, red on greenish head confined to rear, but more marked with white on neck and below; juvenile male shows variable amounts of red in malar, sometimes none.

Vocalisations Characteristic, squeaky *pee-bee* or *chee-chee* with stressed first syllable and lower-pitched and shorter second. Longer, variable *pee-dee-dee* song of 3–5 notes. Also *tiuik* and quieter, lower-pitched *wee-ek*. Short, sharp *peep*-like notes, 5–7 strung in fast series during disputes, and brief *pi-eew*.

Drumming Brief, weak rolls of about one second.

Status Uncommon. Considered stable, but trends unknown and occurs in several areas where heavy logging continues. Extirpated from Singapore.

Habitat Edges and clearings of evergreen rainforest, also coastal scrub, plantations and gardens near forest, though large trees needed.

Range SE Asia. From S Burma (Myanmar) through Thai-Malay Peninsula to Sundas. Resident and sedentary. Usually lower elevations but to around 1700m on Borneo.

Taxonomy and variation Relationship to genus *Chrysophlegma* needs study. Three races: ***puniceus*** (Java) is largest, darkest race, with brownish throat; ***observandus*** (S Burma (Myanmar), Thai-Malay Peninsula, Sumatra, Bangka Island, Borneo) paler green above, yellower on nape and rump; ***soligae*** (Nias Island, off W Sumatra) is palest, yellowish-green above, including rump, grey or green below and redder crest with less yellow.

Similar species Banded Woodpecker browner, less yellow on head and male lacks red malar. Juvenile more like Banded Woodpecker adult. Chequer-throated Woodpecker similar in colour, but larger, reddish on neck and chest and has olive orbital ring.

Food and foraging Arboreal ants and termites in all stages. Often in pairs and roving mixed-species flocks, especially with malkohas and drongos. Forages mainly in canopy.

203. STREAK-BREASTED WOODPECKER

Picus viridanus

L 30–33cm

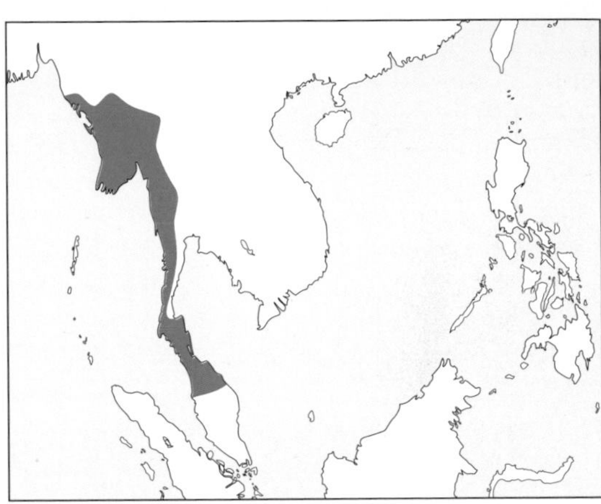

Other names Burmese Woodpecker and confusingly (see *Picus squamatus*) Scaly-bellied Green Woodpecker
Identification Despite English name not streaked below. Buffy breast, belly and flanks heavily marked with dark green scales or chevrons. Mostly plain brown-olive throat, sometimes finely streaked white. Light green gorget. Ear-coverts pale grey with dusky streaks. Neck, mantle and back olive-green, rump yellowish. Olive uppertail-coverts, rest of tail blackish with weak light brown bars. Undertail-coverts white or cream streaked olive. Upperwing olive, finely barred buff or white, black barring on linings. Flight feathers chocolate. Brownish underwing barred white, paler coverts barred olive. Both sexes have weak black malar flecked white, with thin white upper border. Long white supercilium, broadest and edged black above. Greyish bill, lower mandible yellower. Iris reddish. Legs grey. Sexes differ: male has all-red crown and nape; female lacks red, throat less marked. Juveniles of both sexes drabber with more diffuse markings below, flanks more scaled and tail more boldly barred. Juvenile male has variably-sized reddish or orange crown.
Vocalisations Loud, sudden *kirrr* or downwardly slurred *kwirrr* that begins strongly before ending as whirring purr (suggesting Banded Pitta *Pitta guajana*). Short but strident series of clear, sharp *tchew* or *tcheu* notes that can develop into excited rattle, and sharper, squirrel-like *kyup*. Female said to make a subtly different, more prolonged *quierrr*.
Drumming May not drum, or perhaps only rarely, but information lacking.
Status Nowhere common, but not considered threatened. Population size and trends unknown, though has probably declined locally due to logging.
Habitat Varies locally. Mainly lowland, humid, evergreen forest and mangroves. In some areas hill forest edges, drier scrub and older plantations.
Range SE Asia. Confined to relatively limited area, mainly coast and lowlands, from Bangladesh, Sundarbans and Burma (Myanmar) through Thailand

◄ Adult male Streak-breasted Woodpecker has an all-red crown from the lores to the hindneck; females have a black crown. This is the nominate race. Kaeng Krachan, Thailand, February (*Martin Grimm*).

to NW Malaysia. In Malaysia seems to replace Laced Woodpecker from Penang northwards. Resident and sedentary.

Taxonomy and variation Two races: ***viridanus*** (Bangladesh, Burma (Myanmar), SW Thailand) and ***weberi*** (N and C Peninsular Malaysia), which is smaller, darker and more marked on throat and chest than nominate.

Similar species Very like Laced and Streak-throated Woodpeckers. Laced has lighter, plain yellow throat and chest and bolder malar. Streak-throated has less defined malar, streaked chest, darker cheek, bolder white supercilium and distinct yellow rump in flight. These two relatives do not make the *kwirrr* call.

Food and foraging Mainly forages on ground for terrestrial ants.

▼ Adult female nominate Streak-breasted Woodpecker. Care should be taken to avoid mistaking this bird with the very similar (and similarly sized) congener Laced Woodpecker. The finely streaked throat of this species is not visible in this photograph. Kaeng Krachan, Thailand, February (*Martin Grimm*).

204. LACED WOODPECKER
Picus vittatus

L 27–33cm

Identification Plain brownish-green from chin to chest. Breast to vent buff, finely marked with greenish chevrons. Greyish ear-coverts finely streaked black and white. White supercilium, broadest over eye, and almost reaching nape. Lores buff. Both sexes have bold, black malar, sometimes speckled white, bordered above by thin white line. Mostly unmarked above, mantle and back dark green, rump yellowish. Uppertail black with indistinct light barring on outermost feathers, undertail brownish-green, lightly barred. Wings mostly green with chocolate primaries and dark green secondaries finely barred buff. Underwing-coverts buffy, barred brown. Upper mandible greyish, lower yellowish. Iris chestnut, orbital ring pale. Legs greyish. Sexes differ: male has red crown and nape with thin black border; female crown black, chest and throat more olive. Both sexes can appear slightly crested, but male more so. Juvenile overall duller, browner, tail more heavily barred, throat slightly streaked and more scattered scaling below; juvenile male has rufous or orange crown, less extensive than on adult.

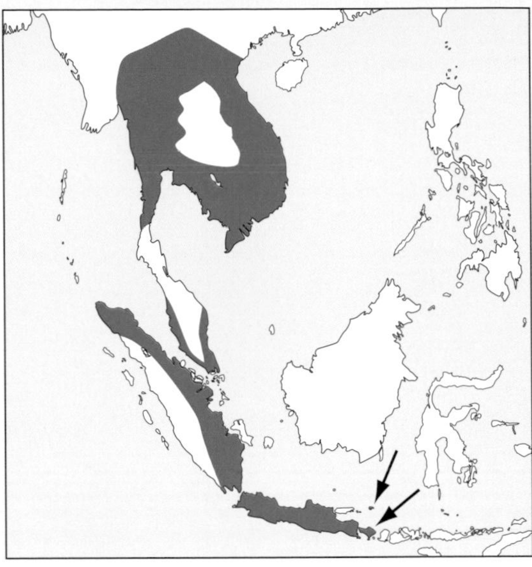

◄ Adult male Laced Woodpecker of the nominate race, feeding a well-grown nestling at the cavity entrance. Singapore, August (*Con Foley*).

Vocalisations Long series of quickly delivered, low-pitched, piping *kew* notes. Single, shrill or squeaky, *kweep, keep* or *kweeck* notes, sometimes two-syllable *keep-ip*. A loud, sharp *yik* and disyllabic *chaakauk*. Rapid *wick-awick-awick* when agitated.

Drumming Occasional brief but steady rolls produced.

Status Locally common in N of range. Overall probably not threatened, although population data lacking. Has declined locally, eg. Sumatra, due to intense logging.

Habitat Various open deciduous and evergreen damp

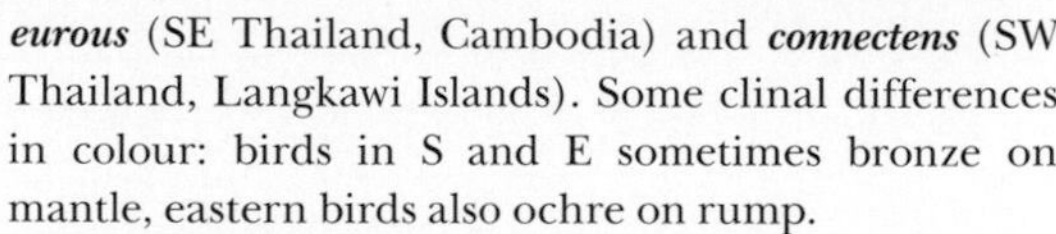

woodlands. In Malaysia particularly mangroves, in Indochina bamboo stands. Also rubber, coconut and palm plantations, sometimes scrub and gardens. Mostly lowlands, especially coastal areas.

Range SE Asia. From S China and Burma (Myanmar) through Indochina and Thai-Malay Peninsula to Singapore. Also Sumatra, Java, Bali and smaller islands. Resident and sedentary.

Taxonomy and variation Four similar races, some disputed: ***vittatus*** (Malaysian Peninsula, Singapore, Sumatra, Java, Bali and Kangean Islands); ***eisenhoferi*** (E Burma (Myanmar), S China, Laos, Vietnam); ***eurous*** (SE Thailand, Cambodia) and ***connectens*** (SW Thailand, Langkawi Islands). Some clinal differences in colour: birds in S and E sometimes bronze on mantle, eastern birds also ochre on rump.

Similar species Similar-sized Streak-breasted Woodpecker has streaked throat and chest (beware juvenile Laced), darker green neck, bolder white supercilium and weaker, paler malar.

Food and foraging Various invertebrates. Forages unobtrusively in understorey, bamboo, on the ground in grass and soil, and in mangroves probes into mud. Also takes some fruit and plant matter.

▼ Adult male at the nest hole. Note the thin black border skirting the striking red of the crown. This is race *connectens*. Thailand, October (*Boonchuay Promjiam*).

▼ Adult female Laced Woodpecker of the nominate race. The plain throat of this species is the best distinction from the very similar Streak-throated Woodpecker. Singapore, September (*Daniel Koh Swee Huat*).

205. STREAK-THROATED WOODPECKER
Picus xanthopygaeus

L 28–30cm

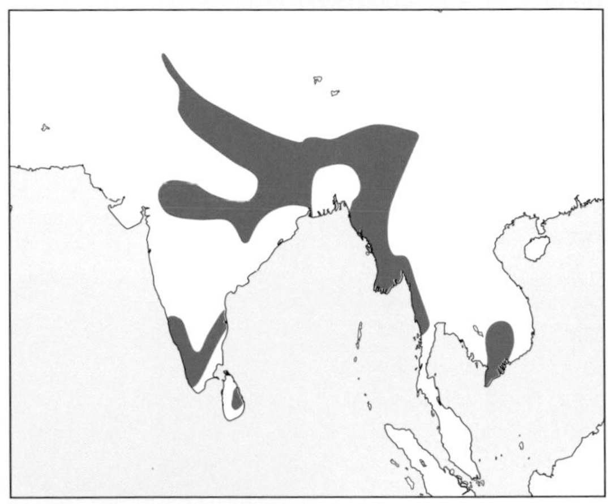

Other name Locally in India Scaly-bellied Woodpecker (but see *Picus squamatus*)

Identification Green or olive above. Densely streaked on pale green throat and chest, tightly scaled olive from white or buff breast to vent. Wings mostly green with black and white barred flight feathers. Yellow rump obvious in flight. Dark tail faintly barred. Dusky ear-coverts and cheeks, subtly streaked. White supercilium broadest above eye. Faint black malar flecked white. Grey upper mandible, lower yellowish. Iris dark or reddish (rarely pale as stated in most literature). Legs grey. Sexes differ: male has complete red crown bordered below by thin black line; female lacks red, crown black streaked grey. Juveniles similar to adults but with all dark bill, more rounded scales below and

◄ Adult male Streak-throated Woodpecker differs from the female in having red on the crown. Haldummulla, Sri Lanka, July (*Kithsiri Gunawarden*).

appear mottled above due to grey bases to mantle and scapular feathers. Juvenile male has some red on black crown, female with less crown streaking.

Vocalisations Limited range of calls, and often silent. Utters clear, sharp, repeated *tchik* and squeakier *quip* or *queemp* notes. Short, penetrating, nasal *kyik* when agitated.

Drumming Drums infrequently. Information scant.

Status Locally common but often rare. Overall population size and trends unknown, but not believed to be declining.

Habitat Open, damp, tropical, broadleaved forest. In Cambodia in dry dipterocarp forests. Also savanna, parkland, bamboo stands and date-palm, tea and rubber plantations.

Range SE Asia. India, Nepal, Bangladesh, Bhutan, Burma (Myanmar), SW China, also Sri Lanka. Local and rare in parts of Indochina and SW Peninsula Thailand. Mainly below 1000m but to 1700m in Himalayas. Resident and sedentary.

Taxonomy and variation Monotypic. Variation slight.

Similar species Streak-breasted Woodpecker lacks significant white supercilium and has plainer throat. Laced Woodpecker has black malar and lacks neck and throat streaking. Larger Scaly-bellied Woodpecker has paler bill and lacks throat and chest streaking.

Food and foraging Forages for ants and termites low on trunks, the ground and among rocks. Also takes nectar and fruit. Sometimes in small family parties and often followed by drongos, bulbuls, babblers and starlings which take the prey it disturbs.

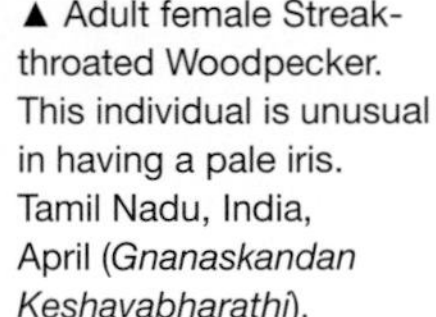

▲ Adult female Streak-throated Woodpecker. This individual is unusual in having a pale iris. Tamil Nadu, India, April (*Gnanaskandan Keshavabharathi*).

◄ Adult male Streak-throated Woodpecker. Note the dense streaking on the underparts. Chitwan, Nepal, January (*Neil Bowman*).

206. SCALY-BELLIED WOODPECKER

Picus squamatus

L 34–35cm

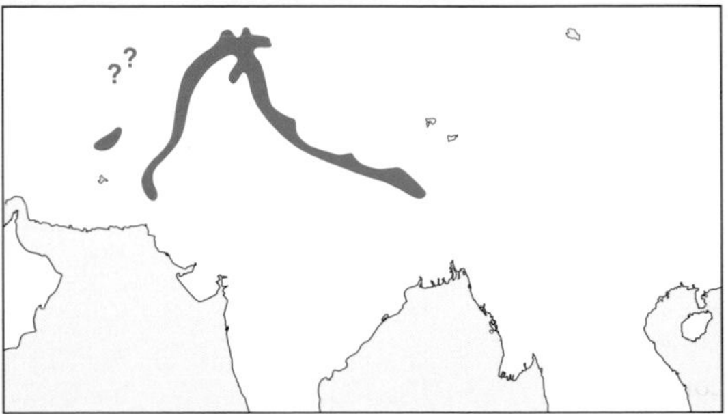

Identification Bulky, largest species in genus. Dark green above. Paler below, buff or greyish, scaled with olive and chocolate chevrons from breast to vent. Chest, cheeks and neck-sides greenish-grey. Ear-coverts dusky. Broad black malar flecked white. Thin black line through eye. Bold white supercilium, bordered above by thin black line, continues to nape. Green tail heavily barred white. Yellowish rump shows well in flight. Flight feathers barred black and white. Upper mandible greyish, lower yellowish. Iris red. Legs grey. Sexes differ: male has all-red crown and nape with crown bordered below by thin black line; female lacks red, crown black streaked grey. Juvenile similar to respective adult but mottled due to grey bases and pale tips to mantle and scapular feathers; also scaled on chest with dark streaking and spotting extending onto throat; iris brown. Juvenile male has red crown streaked or spotted black.

Vocalisations Often vocal with a typical *Picus* laugh, repeated 3–8 times. A rapid *kuik-kuik-kuik* in flight and excitable *kik-kik-kik-eh* like a small falcon. Repeated, melodious *klee-guh-klee-guh* advertising call. Melodic, ringing *pi-coq* or *pee-duck;* far-carrying *pirr;* high-pitched single, nasal *kik or kyik;* single, clear, piping, well-spaced *klu* notes; and disyllabic *kluh-kuk.*

Drumming Soft, even-pitched rolls produced early in breeding season.

Status Common to locally rare. Overall population considered stable and seemingly adaptable. Status in Iran uncertain, perhaps extirpated.

Habitat Open conifer, damp deciduous and mixed montane forests. Also orchards, rural gardens, plantations, juniper scrub with some larger trees, poplar stands and dry, bush-dotted water courses and ravines.

Range Asia. Somewhat fragmented, often localised, occurring mainly in uplands in Turkmenistan, Afghanistan, Pakistan, N India and Nepal; possibly E Iran. Mostly resident though some seasonal altitudinal movements in Himalayas. From 600m to 3700m.

Taxonomy and variation Two races: ***squamatus*** (NE Afghanistan, extreme N India to Darjeeling, Nepal) and ***flavirostris*** (local in Afghanistan, Turkmenistan and W Pakistan), which is paler, brighter yellow than nominate, finer scaled below, face less marked, throat whiter, malar weaker, but more barred on wings and tail.

Similar species Streak-throated Woodpecker smaller with darker bill, scaled chest and throat and lacks white in the tail. Grey-headed Woodpecker smaller and lacks scaled underparts.

Food and foraging Fairly terrestrial, mainly foraging for ants and termites, but also wood-boring beetle larvae and occasionally berries. Forages in loose family groups.

◄◄ Adult male Scaly-bellied Woodpecker of the nominate race. This mainly Himalayan species is noticeably larger than its sympatric *Picus* relatives. Himachal Pradesh, India, January (*Nitin Srinivasamurthy*).

◄ Adult female nominate. Besides lacking red on the crown, the female also has a weaker malar stripe than the male. Himachal Pradesh, India, May (*Szabolcs Kókay*).

207. JAPANESE WOODPECKER

Picus awokera

L 29–30cm

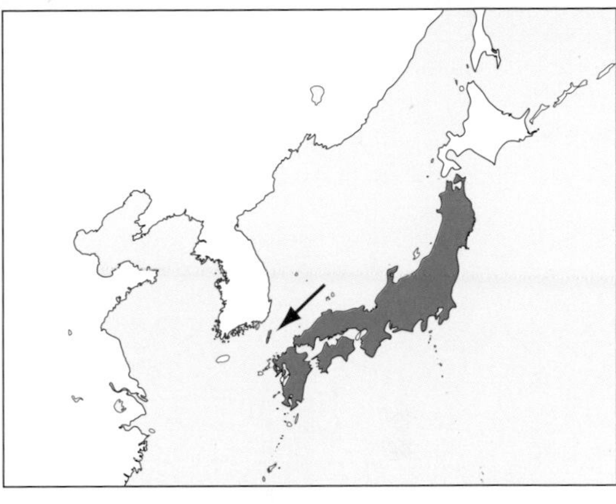

Other name Japanese Green Woodpecker

Identification Olive-green above, rump and uppertail-coverts yellower. Chest and breast grey, buff or green (depending on race), belly white marked with broken black, brown or olive bars and chevrons. Wings bronze or green, flight feathers browner with white bars or spots on inner webs. Underwing paler lightly barred brown. Most of tail green, uppertail brownish. Face, ear-coverts and neck greyish. Chin and throat white. Lores black. Iris chestnut. Bill yellowish with dark tip. Legs bluish-grey. Sexes differ: male has red crown and nape; female crown grey streaked black, red only on nape. Both sexes have black malar with red at its centre, but female has less red. Juvenile duller, more

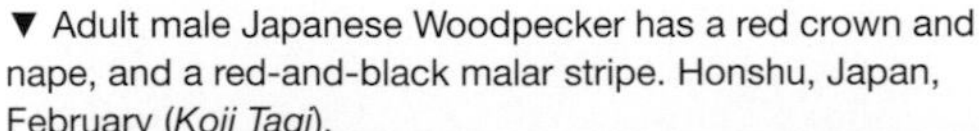

▼ Adult male Japanese Woodpecker has a red crown and nape, and a red-and-black malar stripe. Honshu, Japan, February (*Koji Tagi*).

▼ Adult male. This is the only member of the genus *Picus* in Japan, and hence it is unmistakable. Honshu, Japan, February (*Koji Tagi*).

heavily barred below than adult.

Vocalisations Song a whistling *peoo-peoo, piyoo-piyoo, eoo-eoo* or *ioo-ioo*. Also a whip-lashing *pwip-pwip*, a frog-like *kere-keree* or *ere-erere* and a hard, abrupt *ket-ket*. Contact call, often made in flight, is harsh, downward-slurred, chattering *jerrrerrerr* or *errrerrerr*.

Drumming Fast, long rolls produced, but details lacking.

Status Fairly common locally. Range-restricted, but considered stable with no serious threats apparent.

Habitat Open, damp mixed deciduous and broadleaved evergreen montane woodlands. In some areas also urban parks and gardens.

Range Endemic to Japan. Honshu S to Shikoku, Kyushu, Tanegashima, Yakushima and other nearby smaller islands. Does not occur on Hokkaido. Usually between 300–1400m, but up to 2000m. Resident, some moving to lower elevations in winter.

Taxonomy and variation Three races sometimes claimed: ***awokera*** (Honshu) is largest and palest; ***horii*** (Kyushu, Shikoku) is smaller and darker; southernmost ***takatsukasae*** (Tanegashima, Yakushima) smallest and darkest. These differences are sometimes regarded as clinal and the species monotypic.

Similar species None within range.

Food and foraging Forages less on ground than most other *Picus* species, feeding mainly on arboreal ants, though beetle larvae, other invertebrates and some fruits, seeds and occasionally sap also taken.

► Adult female Japanese Woodpecker has red on the nape only, and less red in the malar region than the male. Honshu, Japan, February (*Tadao Shimba*).

208. EURASIAN GREEN WOODPECKER
Picus viridis

L 31–35cm

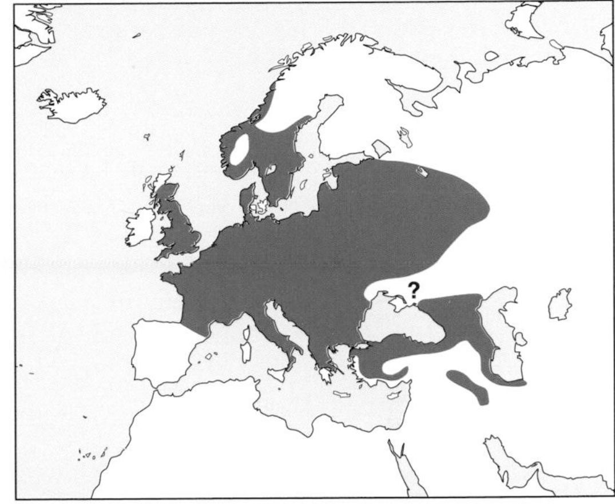

Other names European Green Woodpecker, Green Woodpecker

Identification Looks heavy. Mostly green. Yellowish rump obvious in flight. Red crown and nape often flecked grey. Nominate has black 'Zorro' ocular-mask. Ear-coverts, neck-sides and throat greyish with grey and yellow hues. Off-white below with dark chevrons. Inner tail feathers black, edged green and spotted buff, outers green with dusky barring. Undertail spotted or barred. Blackish primaries dotted white, olive secondaries faintly speckled, greenish underwing gently barred grey. Greyish upper mandible, lower yellowish. Legs grey. Iris white or pink. Sexes differ slightly: male has red-centred black malar, female malar black. Juvenile distinct until first moult in autumn, heavily

► Adult male Eurasian Green Woodpecker has red on the malar stripe; if this is not seen the sexes can be difficult to separate. This is the nominate. Lorraine, France, June (*Michel Poinsignon*).

scaled overall, pale face, underparts mottled black, spotted white above.

Vocalisations Up to 20 loud, laughing *klu* or *plu* notes, accelerating but falling in volume. Females make thinner *pu-pu-pu,* like Grey-headed Woodpecker, though harsher. Crying series of *kjack* and sharp, single or double *kewk or kuk* notes. Rhythmic, high-pitched *kjuck* in flight, clucking *gluk* notes by nest. Alarms include shrieking *kyu-kyu-kyuk* stressed on alternate syllables, often uttered when flushed. Harsh *kek,* recalling Northern Goshawk *Accipiter gentilis.*

Drumming Rarely drums. Rapid but weak rolls sometimes produced.

Status Often common. Local declines mainly due to grassland degradation. Increased in some areas, e.g. Britain.

Habitat Typically, open, drier, deciduous and mixed woodlands, pastures, plantations, orchards, parks, gardens, heaths, grassy dunes. Mature trees and adjacent grasslands needed.

Range Western Palearctic. Mostly confined to Europe, from S Scandinavia to the Mediterranean, E to Iran. Resident and mainly sedentary. Vagrant to Finland, Ireland, Malta.

Taxonomy and variation Three races: ***viridis*** (Britain, continental Europe to Russia); ***karelini*** (Italy, Balkans, Caucasus, Turkmenistan) is duller, duskier than nominate; ***innominatus*** (SW Iran: Zagros Mts) is pale green above, whiter below, more barred tail and may warrant species status as 'Zagros' or 'Mesopotamian' Woodpecker.

Similar species Smaller Grey-headed Woodpecker lacks black mask. Iberian Woodpecker also lacks black mask, has fewer but larger whitish spots on wings, plain undertail-coverts and female has greyish malar. Hybrids in France show variable features, especially shades of black and grey on face.

Food and foraging Most terrestrial European picid, habitually foraging on short grassland, probing for ants (*Formica, Myrmica* and *Lasius* species), collected with long, sticky tongue. Burrows through snow for prey. Also takes other invertebrates and windfall fruit.

▼ Adult nominate pointing skywards. A species that often forages on the ground, these birds are wary of aerial predators. Germany, March (*Ralph Martin*).

▲ Adult nominate female Eurasian Green Woodpecker; note the all-black malar stripe. Hungary, December (*Rudi Petitjean*).

▲► Adult female on a frosty morning. This bird is of the race karelini; it is duller and duskier than the nominate. Tuscany, Italy, November (*Daniele Occhiato*).

► Juveniles are very different from adults. This is a male: note the red malar. Race *karelini*. Tuscany, Italy, July (*Daniele Occhiato*).

209. IBERIAN WOODPECKER
Picus sharpei

L 30–34cm

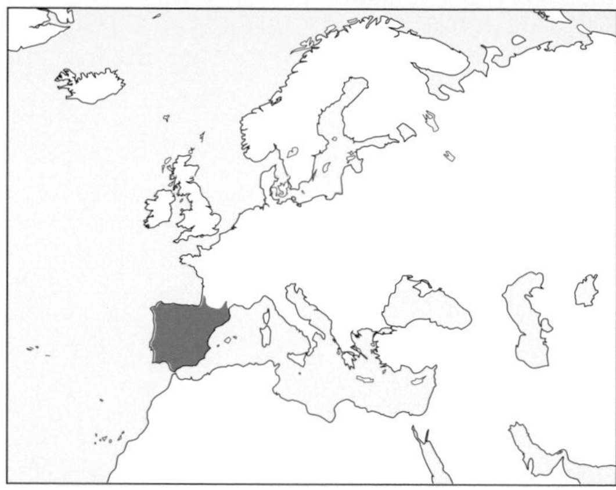

Other name Iberian Green Woodpecker

Identification Mostly green. Yellowish rump and uppertail-coverts obvious in flight. Red crown and nape often flecked grey. Ear-coverts, neck-sides and throat greyish with yellowish hues. Off-white below with dark chevrons, lower flanks barred. Inner tail feathers black, edged green and spotted buff, outers green with dusky barring, undertail-coverts unbarred. Blackish primaries dotted white, olive secondaries faintly speckled. Underwing greenish, gently barred grey. Grey bill, lower mandible base yellowish. Legs grey. Iris white or pink. Sexes differ: male has red malar with thin incomplete black edge; female has greyish malar, crown with some orange and often more grey feather

▼ Adult male Iberian Woodpecker has a mostly red malar stripe, while that of the female is black. Leon, Spain, December (*Carlos Nazario Bocos*).

◄ Adult female Iberian Woodpecker. Note the lack of red in the malar. Cataluña, Spain, June (*Wim de Groot*).

▼ Juvenile female Iberian Woodpecker. Note the grey malar stripe. Segovia, Spain, August (*Juan Matute*).

tips than male. Juvenile darkly spotted below, speckled on mantle. Juvenile malar colour follows adults.

Vocalisations Laughing song is generally faster, higher-pitched, less throaty and harsher than Eurasian Green Woodpecker, but not always different enough to be diagnostic.

Drumming Rarely drums. Rapid but weak roll produced in spring.

Status Locally common and considered stable with no serious threats.

Habitat Open, drier, deciduous and mixed woodlands, pastures, farmland, plantations, orchards, parks, gardens and grassy dunes. Some mature trees, clearings and adjacent grasslands needed. Seems to be more arboreal than Eurasian Green Woodpecker where they meet.

Range Restricted to Spain, Portugal and extreme southern France. From sea-level to around 3000m. Resident and sedentary.

Taxonomy and variation Monotypic. Variation slight. Formerly treated as race of Eurasian Green Woodpecker, but split in 2012 after detailed studies, including in overlap zone in SE France, on plumage, morphology and genetics.

Similar species Eurasian Green Woodpecker has distinct black mask, undertail-coverts marked, male has black malar with red centre (not red with thin black edge) and female has black, not greyish malar. Hybrids of the two in France show variable features, especially shades of black and grey on face. More like Grey-headed and Levaillant's Woodpeckers, but neither occur within range.

Food and foraging Ground-dwelling ants. Also other invertebrates taken on ground or in trees. Some fruit.

210. LEVAILLANT'S WOODPECKER

Picus vaillantii

L 30–32cm

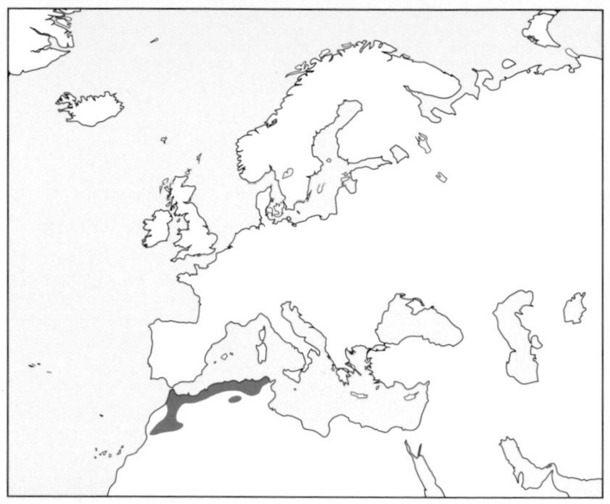

Other name Levaillant's Green Woodpecker

Identification Mostly green above, showing obvious yellowish rump in flight. Pale greenish-grey below, ventral area barred. Wings mostly green, barred black and white on outer webs. Underwing paler, barred brownish. Dark green tail barred black below. Ear-coverts, ocular area and lores greyish. Both sexes have black malar bordered above by a white line. Large grey-blackish bill. Legs greyish. Iris white or pink. Sexes differ slightly: male has complete red crown and nape; female crown mottled grey and black, red only on nape. Juvenile barred, flecked and spotted, underparts marked with chevrons, face mottled, iris darker; juvenile male has less red on crown than adult, female some red on forecrown.

◄ Adult male Levaillant's Woodpecker has an all-red crown; note that both sexes have a black malar stripe. Oued Ourika, Morocco, February (*Steve Blain*).

Vocalisations Song a rapid series of clear, whistling *pee-pee-pee* notes. More musical, higher pitched, less mocking than that of Eurasian Green Woodpecker. In flight a loud *yak-yak-yak* or *ki-yak-ki-yak-kiyak*.

Drumming Drums more than European relatives. An (approx) 2-second roll, with 20–21 strikes per second.

Status Locally often common. Population size and trends unknown but not considered to be declining or seriously threatened.

Habitat Open, drier deciduous woodlands, particularly mature montane forests of pine, larch, evergreen oak and cedar. Also wooded river valleys, walnut, olive and palm groves, parks and even gardens.

Range North Africa. A Maghreb endemic, from NW Morocco through Algeria to W Tunisia, but not continuous. Resident and mainly sedentary though some dispersal after the breeding season. From around 900m to 2000m in the Atlas Mts.

Taxonomy and variation Monotypic. Formerly treated as race of Eurasian Green Woodpecker. No variation noted.

Similar species None within range; only *Picus* in Africa.

Food and foraging Mostly terrestrial ants, but also other invertebrates and fruit.

▲ First-winter male: note the dark iris and grey flecks in crown. Levaillant's Woodpecker. Morocco, April (*Cristian Jensen*).

◄ Adult females are red only on the nape, with the forecrown greyish black. Morocco, March (*John Hawkins*).

211. RED-COLLARED WOODPECKER

Picus rabieri

L 30–32cm

Identification Distinctive 'green' woodpecker, both sexes showing much red on nape and neck. Olive above, rump paler green. Most of tail green, uppertail blackish. Wings green, flight feathers blackish-bronze, webs with white bars or spots, underwing whitish barred grey or brown. Breast pale green; belly and flanks olive with pale scales. Chin and throat streaked whitish. Lores and ear-coverts olive. Iris chestnut, orbital ring pale. Bill grey, paler at base. Legs greenish-grey. Sexes differ: male crimson from forehead to nape, onto neck-sides, chest and malar and has slight white supercilium; female less red, black on forehead and crown, malar indistinct. Juvenile more like adult female, red areas duller, more orange; juvenile male has more orange or red on head and chest.

Vocalisations Single or repeated, loud, throaty but mellow upslurred whistle: easily confused with territorial call of Blue-naped Pitta. Also a short, slightly nasal, nervous, single or repeated note (described as sounding intermediate between the same pitta and a macaque) and a single, loud *keck,* often quickly repeated, sometimes quite squeaky.

Drumming Fairly fast, irregular roll reported, but few details available.

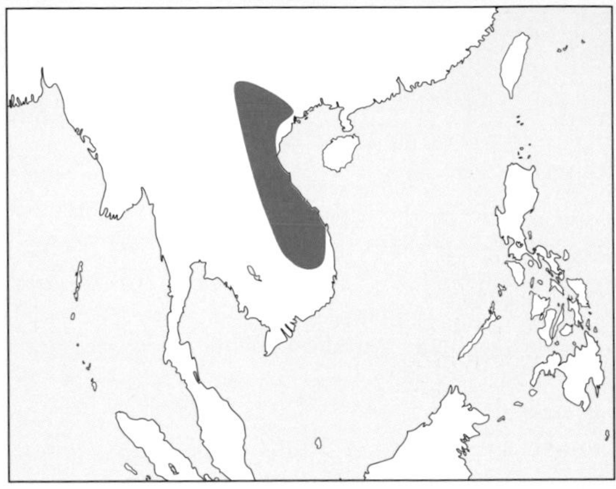

Status NT. Rare to uncommon in Vietnam and Cambodia, locally common in Laos. Little-studied, often remarkably elusive, and information limited for some countries, such as China. Declining due to habitat destruction and clearance of lowland forests for farming.

Habitat Tall evergreen and semi-evergreen forest and secondary growth, also mixed deciduous forest and bamboo. Appears to adapt to disturbed, partially logged forests where a few large tall trees have been left.

Range SE Asia, E of Mekong River. Restricted to Indochina in Laos, Vietnam (from N and E Tonkin S to C Annam) and extreme NE Cambodia. Possibly still in Yunnan, SW China. Core population probably in Laos. Usually below 300m, but to around 1000m. Resident and probably sedentary.

Taxonomy and variation Monotypic. Variation slight.

Similar species On poor views might be mistaken for Bamboo Woodpecker in narrow overlap zone in central-western Laos. Some calls similar to sympatric Laced Woodpecker, but *keck* call not as harsh or explosive.

Food and foraging Mainly ants and presumably other insects. Fairly terrestrial, otherwise foraging low in trees, rarely in upper levels. Often seen in mixed foraging flocks, particularly with babblers, fulvettas, drongos and laughing-thrushes.

◄ Adult male Red-collared Woodpecker. This digiscoped image is one of very few taken of the highly elusive species. Ninh Binh, Vietnam, February (*John Wright*).

212. BLACK-HEADED WOODPECKER
Picus erythropygius

L 31–35cm

Identification Striking. Mostly black head and nape. Chin, throat, chest and neck-sides bright yellow, upper breast more olive, buff or white with faint grey-brown chevrons from mid-breast onto belly, flanks and ventral region. Mantle and back green. Lower back and rump crimson, often obvious. Upper tail blackish, undertail white barred brown. Wings mostly green with primary-coverts and flight feathers black, marked with up to six white bars. Underwing pale. Heavy bill greyish. Legs grey-green. Iris yellowish, orbital ring grey. Sexes differ slightly: male has red patch on mid-crown which female lacks. Juvenile not as bright yellow, underpart markings more diffuse; male has some red on crown but duller and less than on adult male.

Vocalisations Families often very vocal making a fast,

► Adult male Black-headed Woodpecker differs from the female in having a red centre (of variable size) to its black crown. This is race *nigrigenis*. Thailand.

repetitive, undulating, chattering *cha-cha-cha, cha-cha-cha* or *ka-tek-a-tek-a-tek-a-tek-a*. Usually squeaky or bubbling, sometimes harsher, more nasal.

Drumming May not drum, or perhaps only rarely, but information lacking.

Status Generally uncommon. Considered stable, although overall population size and trends unknown.

Habitat Dry deciduous forests, in particular of mature dipterocarp. In some areas in pines and damper forests.

Range SE Asia. Burma (Myanmar), Thailand (except south), Laos, Cambodia and adjacent Vietnam, but not continuous. From lowlands to 1000m. Resident and sedentary.

Taxonomy and variation Two races: ***erythropygius*** (NE Thailand, Laos, Vietnam, Cambodia) and ***nigrigenis*** (Burma (Myanmar), NW Thailand), which has darker bill than nominate. Some birds, of both races, have thin white line from the eye across the ear-coverts. Extent of red crown patch on males varies.

Similar species None: unmistakable.

Food and foraging Forages at all levels from ground to canopy, for ants, termites and other invertebrates. Often in roving, noisy family parties that move from tree to tree. Sometimes in association with other birds, including jays and smaller woodpeckers.

▲ Adult female *nigrigenis*. This gregarious, vocal and colourful woodpecker is unmistakable. Thailand.

► Adult male *nigrigenis* in flight. Note the red rump. Huay Ka Kaeng, Thailand, November (*Carl-Johan Svensson*).

213. GREY-HEADED WOODPECKER
Picus canus

L 26–32cm

Other name Grey-faced Woodpecker (S. Asian races)
Identification Very variable: nominate described. Olive-green above, rump yellowish. Greyish below, chest tinged lime. Tail dark green, dark chevrons on undertail-coverts. Primaries black, sometimes tinged brown, barred or spotted white near tips. Remainder of flight feathers greenish-brown lightly dotted white or buff. Head and shoulders grey, neck darker than face, chin and throat off-white. Fine black malar. Bill greyish, lower mandible base paler. Legs grey. Iris reddish. Sexes differ slightly: male has red forecrown; female lacks red and has slighter malar. Juveniles like respective adults, but rump greener, flanks and wings lightly barred grey-brown, spots on primaries larger, iris usually darker, bill lighter; juvenile male has less red on forecrown than adult.
Vocalisations Plaintive, sometimes vigorous, song of 6–10 piping *poo* or *pew* or harsher *koo* notes that fall in pitch. Rapid, croaky, panicky rattle (like a flameback) and brief *kvik* or *kik* done in flight. Excited, short, metallic *kuk* or *kook,* sometimes in series. *Djack, kjak* and softer *chuck* contact calls. Displaying males utter *witty-witty-witty* whilst head-swaying and bill-pointing.
Drumming Both sexes drum. A rolling, loud burst, often beginning weakly before strengthening, typically lasting 1–2 seconds with 20–40 strikes per second.
Status Overall not uncommon, but has declined locally. Very few recent records of *robinsoni*, and *dedemi* may be Near Threatened.
Habitat Varies considerably across range: old-growth open deciduous, mixed deciduous-conifer, subtropical jungle, parkland, plantations and wooded pastures. In Asia *dedemi* and *robinsoni* occur in montane forests.
Range Eurasia. Continental Europe and Scandinavia to the Far East, isolated populations in Peninsular Malaysia and Sumatra. Sea-level to treeline. Resident and sedentary.
Taxonomy and variation A split into 3 species has recently been proposed: Grey-headed *P. canus* (inc. *jessoensis*), Sumatran *P. dedemi,* and Grey-faced *P. guerini* (all other races). Eleven races are treated here, some differing significantly: nominate ***canus*** (continental Europe, Scandinavia, W Siberia); ***jessoensis*** (E Siberia, Sakhalin, Hokkaido, NE China, Korea) paler, less green than above; ***sanguiniceps*** (NE Pakistan, NW India, W Nepal) black-crowned, male also with red on crown; ***hessei*** (N India, Nepal, Burma (Myanmar), S China, Thailand, Vietnam) black-crowned, golden tones above; ***guerini*** (NC China, C Sichuan to Yangtze River) black-crown streaked grey, green below; ***kogo*** (C China: Shaanxi to Qinghai and N Sichuan) black-crown streaked grey, large, pale green overall; ***sordidior*** (SE Tibet, NE Burma (Myanmar), SW China) black-crowned, large and dark; ***sobrinus*** (SE China, N Vietnam) black-crowned, tinged golden above, greenish below; ***tancolo*** (Hainan, Taiwan) black-

► Adult male Grey-headed Woodpecker of the nominate race. Males have a red patch of variable size on the crown, which females lack. Traisen, Austria, November (*Thomas Hochebner*).

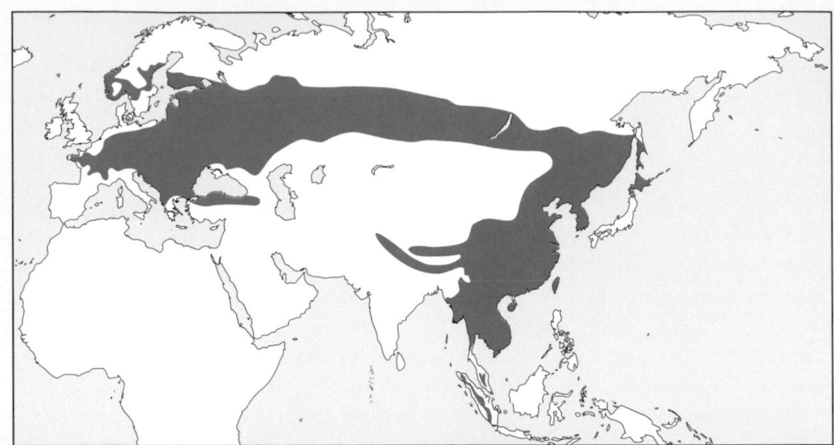

▼ Adult female Grey-headed Woodpecker, nominate race. The crown is all-grey, but otherwise the sexes are very similar. Traisen, Austria, January (*Thomas Hochebner*).

crowned, face dark, bottle green overall, relatively small; ***robinsoni*** (upland Peninsular Malaysia) isolated and rarely seen, mostly dark green contrasting with yellow rump and pale throat; isolated ***dedemi*** (upland Sumatra) distinct, smallest race, very dark, tail black, deep red above, scarlet rump.

Similar species Slimmer, smaller-headed than Eurasian Green Woodpecker, and lacks black mask. In Sumatra beware Maroon Woodpecker, in Indochina Laced and Streak-throated Woodpeckers.

Food and foraging Mainly smaller terrestrial ants, but also termites, arboreal insects, nuts, fruit and berries. Rather opportunistic, sap, suet at feeders and even carrion sometimes taken.

► Adult male *hessei* of the Grey-faced group. This race is black-crowned, the males having a red patch on the forecrown and golden-green on the upperparts and green tones below. Uttarakhand, India, May (*Nitin Srinivasamurthy*).

▼ Adult male of the race *dedemi*, sometimes regarded as a separate monotypic species, Sumatran Woodpecker. This form is the most distinct of all the races (*Chairunas Adha Putra*).

▼► Adult female *sobrinus*, of the grey-faced group. Hunan, China, May (*Julien Thurel*).

DINOPIUM

An Old World genus of five species from the Indian sub-continent and SE Asia. Commonly (along with the *Chrysocolaptes*) called flamebacks or goldenbacks. All the *Dinopium* have black hind-necks, are short billed and stocky. Four species are three-toed, one four-toed. Though not always easy to observe, facial and nape patterns and rump colour are key identification pointers, though actual intensity of the golds, yellows and reds varies individually and can also depend on light conditions.

Black-rumped Flameback *Dinopium benghalense*, adult male. Sri Lanka, October (*Martin B. Withers*).

214. OLIVE-BACKED WOODPECKER
Dinopium rafflesii

L 27–28cm

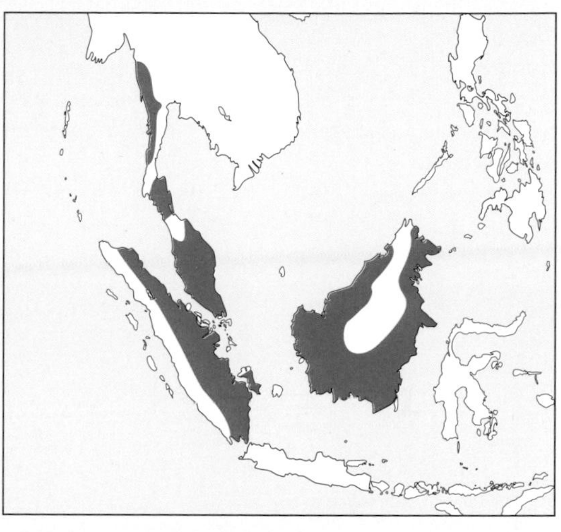

Identification Olive above with bronze sheen in fresh plumage, buff or yellow, sometimes rufous when worn. Rump flushed with either yellow, orange or red. Breast and belly olive, flanks variably spotted white. Lores buff. White face with broad black post-auricular stripe reaches the nape. Lower cheek variably buff, pink or cinnamon. Neck-sides white, nape black. Chin, throat and chest yellowish-green or cinnamon. Uppertail black. Primaries black-brown, secondaries greenish with some white spots, coverts olive with flush of yellow or bronze. Underwing chestnut brown, spotted white. Grey-black bill. Iris reddish. Legs bluish-grey, three-toed. Sexes differ: male has crimson crown and pointed crest, raised during displays; female's black and blunter. Juvenile duller overall with stunted crest; juvenile male has blackish crown with some red on crest and sometimes on forecrown; female like adult female, but crown tinged olive.

Vocalisations Quite vocal. Song a series of carefully delivered, high-pitched, piercing *chak* notes, of varying speed, and sometimes rather whining. Also a fast, excited version of many notes, harsh and grating, mocking or whinnying. Same *chak* note also

► Adult male Olive-backed Woodpecker of the nominate race. This rare woodpecker continues to decline as its forest habit is logged. Perak, Malaysia, January (*Lim Kim Chye*).

uttered singly. Low-pitched, quieter *ch-wee, ch-wee, che-wee* during displays. Soft, steady trilling *ti-i-i-i-i* and squeakier *tiririt.*

Drumming Rapid, level rolls of about 2 seconds, separated by pauses of 10–11 seconds. Also shorter 1-second bursts.

Status NT. Scarce. Probably declining as many forests continue to be logged in its range and, unlike some relatives, seemingly unable to adapt. Extirpated from Singapore.

Habitat Dense primary, humid, lowland, evergreen forest. Also swamp-forest and in some areas mangroves. Seldom in secondary growth or degraded forests. Dead wood needed.

Range SE Asia. Extreme SW Burma (Myanmar) through Thai-Malay Peninsula to E Sumatra and Borneo. Mainly lowlands and hill country, up to 1590m in Borneo. Resident and sedentary.

Taxonomy and variation Two races: ***rafflesii*** (SW Burma (Myanmar), Thai-Malay Peninsula, Sumatra, Bangka) and smaller, slighter-billed ***dulitense*** (Borneo). Some individual variation in colour.

Similar species Within range most like slightly larger Common Flameback, but darker green, plainer below, lacking red rump and having more pointed crest (latter not always obvious on females).

Food and foraging Mainly ants and termites. Forages unobtrusively inside forests (does not often visit clearings), from low to mid-levels, on trunks, logs, stumps and snags.

▼ A pair of nominate Olive-backed Woodpeckers: male on the left, female on the right. Johor, Malaysia, July (*Con Foley*).

215. HIMALAYAN FLAMEBACK
Dinopium shorii

L 30–32cm

Other name Himalayan Goldenback

Identification Appears stout. Face boldly striped black and white: wide white supercilium, bold black post-auricular stripe which reaches nape, black stripe from malar down onto neck-sides and chest. Throat and chest brownish or buffish. Black nape and mantle. Back, scapulars and back olive-green with variable gold, yellow or rufous tones, scarlet lower back and rump. Black upper tail, undertail browner. Whitish belly and flanks marked with bold dark scales and chevrons. Flight feathers brownish, secondaries and coverts golden-olive washed rufous. Brown underwing spotted white. Bill black. Legs olive or brownish. Iris red, brown or gold. Sexes differ: male has red, shaggy crown, bordered by thin black line, peaking at

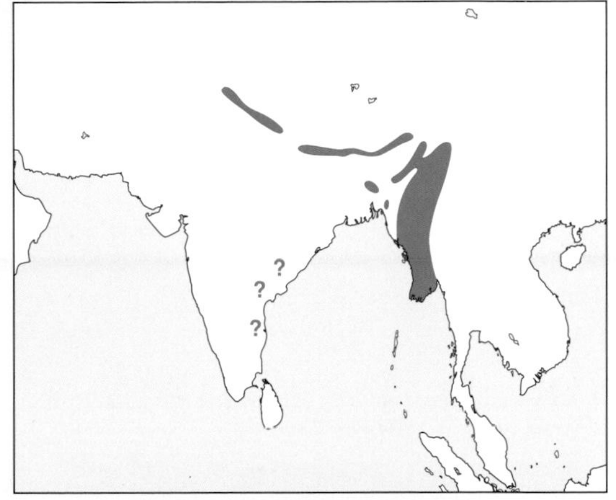

► Adult male Himalayan Flameback, showing his shaggy red crown and crest and pinkish malar region, both of which the females lack. This is the nominate. Uttarakhand, India, April (*Manish Singhal*).

rear into a crest, and pinkish malar enclosed by black; female crown and crest black flecked white, pale malar within two black lines. Juveniles browner, less marked below, with white malar bordered by black like adult female; juvenile male has red only on crest, female crest brownish streaked pale.

Vocalisations Often noisy. Fast, excited series of nasal notes. Also a more intense, metallic *klak-klak-klak* series with notes merging, similar to Greater Flameback but more subdued. Also slow, mocking, yapping notes.

Drumming Reported to drum, but details unavailable.

Status Locally common to scarce. Surprisingly little-studied and probably declining overall due to deforestation.

Habitat Mature, deciduous lowland forest and jungle. Sometimes drier forests, rarely in degraded forest or plantations.

Range SE Asia. India, Nepal, Bangladesh, Bhutan and Burma (Myanmar). Disjunct populations possibly in SE India in Eastern Ghats, Tamil Nadu, Odisha and Andhra Pradesh, and reported from elsewhere in India, but clarification needed. Generally sedentary. Up to around 1220m.

Taxonomy and variation Two races: ***shorii*** (NW India to Bangladesh, possibly further S in Tamil Nadu) and ***anguste*** (NW Burma (Myanmar) and Assam, NE India), which has shorter bill, wing and tail than nominate, but these hard to judge. Female with finer white streaks on crown. Most birds three-toed, although some may show remnant of a fourth.

Similar species Common Flameback smaller, blacker on throat and chest, females whiter on crown, malar not looped. Greater Flameback larger with longer bill, white nape and four toes.

Food and foraging Diet presumably similar to other flamebacks (chiefly insects), but specifics lacking. Often forages in company of other birds including drongos, laughing-thrushes and Greater Flameback.

▼ Adult female nominate. This woodpecker falls between the smaller Common Flameback and larger Greater Flameback in size. Chitwan, Nepal, January (*Neil Bowman*).

216. COMMON FLAMEBACK
Dinopium javanense

L 28–30cm

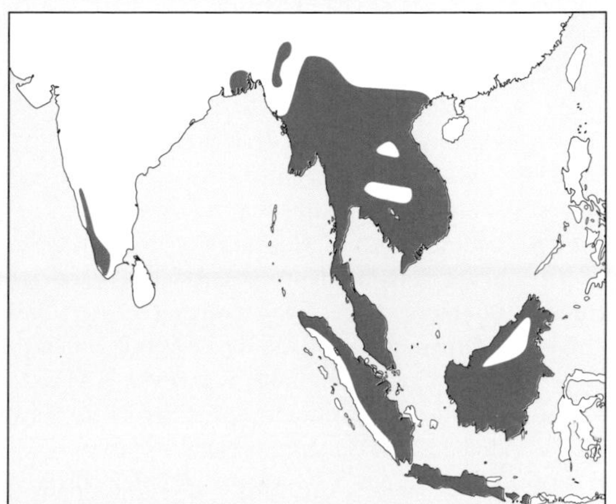

Other names Common Goldenback, Indian Flameback

Identification Appears stocky. Bold black and white striped face formed by white supercilium, black post-auricular stripe, white moustache, thin black sub-moustachial line. Malar tinged rufous or orange. Buff-white throat with gular line of black spots. Nape black, mantle and back olive tinged gold or orange and yellowish feather tips. Lower back and rump scarlet. Uppertail-coverts blackish, undertail brownish tinged yellow. Whitish underparts heavily streaked or spotted black, especially on breast. Belly and flanks barred and scalloped; sometimes up to chest. Flight feathers chocolate with secondaries and tertials greenish-yellow with variable white spotting. Underwing brownish

► Adult male Common Flameback is easily separated from the female by its bright red crown and crest. This is the nominate race. Singapore, December (*HY Cheng*).

spotted white. Black-grey bill shorter in length than head width. Iris chestnut, orbital ring black. Grey-olive legs, three-toed. Sexes differ: male has red crown and peaked crest; female (most races) has black crown and crest flecked white. Juvenile similar to respective adult, though browner below dotted white, iris brownish; juvenile male has black forecrown with red restricted to rear and crest.

Vocalisations Noisy. Loud, high-pitched, rapid, harsh, rattling *churrrrrrr.* Rapid, trilling, whinnying *ka-di-di-di-di.* Nasal *wicka-wick-wicka* during displays. Single or double, piping or squeaking *kow* notes. *Kowp-owp-owp-owp* and tinny *klek-klek-klek* in flight.

Drumming Details scant, but drums said to be less powerful, more rolling than Greater Flameback.

Status Common locally. Has adapted to man-influenced habitats. Population presumed stable.

Habitat Lowland, damp, open evergreen forest and jungle. In some regions coastal; in the Sundas often in more open mangroves; in other regions upland pine forests, woody scrub, plantations. park-like landscapes, even wooded golf courses and settlements.

Range SE Asia. From NE India to S China, through Indochina and Thai-Malay Peninsula to Indonesia. Isolated population in SW India. Resident and sedentary.

Taxonomy and variation Five races: ***javanense*** (Thai-Malay Peninsula, Sumatra, Riau Archipelago, W Java, most of Borneo) rather small, face and throat often buff; ***malabaricum*** (SW India) small, olive above with fine bill and stubby crest; ***intermedium*** (Bangladesh, Assam to C and E Burma (Myanmar), SW China, N Vietnam, N and C Thailand), large, with white throat, reddish-brown forehead and lores; ***raveni*** (NE Borneo, some adjacent islands) throat boldly streaked black, broad supercilium, black malar, heavily scaled buff below; female finely streaked on crown; ***exsul*** (E Java, Bali) has bold, haphazard markings below, female with some orange on hindcrown.

Similar species Most like Himalayan Flameback, though that species slightly larger with bigger bill, paler malar, fulvous wash on chest and less rufous mantle. Olive-backed Woodpecker darker overall, unmarked on throat and underparts. Black-rumped has black rump, white spots on black wing-coverts and four toes. Greater Flameback visibly larger, with longer, stronger bill, white-spotted black nape and mantle, untidy crest and four toes.

Food and foraging Various invertebrates, especially ants, termites, beetle larvae and scorpions. Forages at all levels. Often in pairs and mixed-species flocks, drongos often in attendance.

▼ Adult male *intermedium* probing for insects. This widespread flameback occurs in both mature woodlands and secondary habitats. Kaeng Krachan, Thailand, February (*Neil Bowman*).

▼ Adult female Common Flameback shows no red on the head. This is the nominate race. Negri Sembilan, Malaysia, February (*Liew Weng Keong*).

217. SPOT-THROATED FLAMEBACK
Dinopium everetti

L 28–30cm

Identification Rufous, pinkish or buff on face, throat, neck and chest. Throat dotted grey, chest mottled, breast usually plain brown, belly and flanks with dark bars and chevrons. Narrow white supercilium, broad black post-ocular stripe. Nape and mantle black. Back and wings olive with rufous tones. Lower back and rump crimson. Tail black. Iris dark. Bill grey-black. Legs grey-olive, three-toed. Sexes differ: male has shaggy red crown and crest extending onto head-sides behind ear-coverts, and variable, narrow reddish malar; female has black crown, usually plain, sometimes with a few white flecks, and sometimes red on nape and buff or cream malar. Juvenile similar to respective adult but browner and iris paler.

Vocalisations Long, harsh *churrrrrrr* and rattling *ka-di-di-di-di*. Variable *kowp-owp-owp-owp* in flight. Single or double *kow* notes when perched.

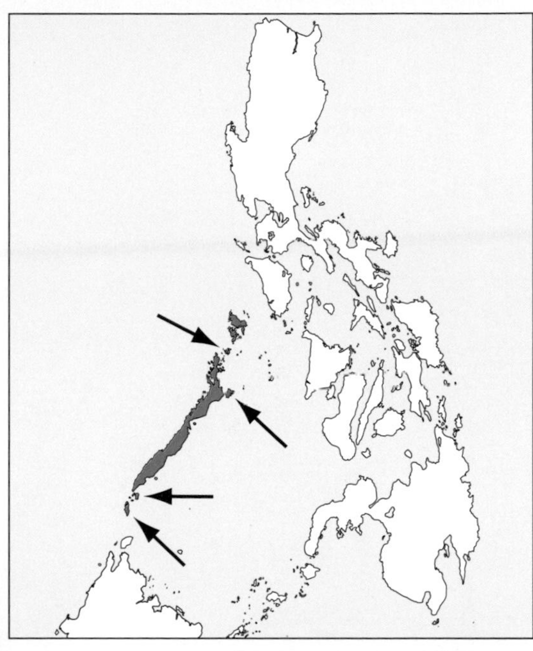

Drumming Apparently drums, presumably similarly to relatives, but details lacking.

Status Localised and uncommon. Poorly known and IUCN conservation category not yet assigned.

Habitat Open forest and jungle, woodlands and coconut plantations.

Range Endemic to SW Philippines: Balabac, Palawan, Busuanga, Culion and Calamian Islands. Resident and sedentary.

Taxonomy and variation Monotypic. Formerly treated as race of Common Flameback. Recently split to species as geographically isolated and differing significantly in plumage. Variation slight.

Similar species Sympatric Red-headed Flameback is visibly larger, with longer, pale bill, striped neck and throat and is four-toed.

Food and foraging Diet presumably similar to relatives (ants, termites, beetle larvae, etc) but specific information lacking. Forages at all levels, often in mixed-species flocks.

◄ Adult male Spot-throated Flameback. All males have a red crown and crest, but the amount of red in the malar region varies. This individual has very little. Palawan, Philippines, February (*Alain Pascua*).

▲ Adult female Spot-throated Flameback lacks the bright red crown and the red in the malar region of the male. Palawan, Philippines, February (*Alain Pascua*).

218. BLACK-RUMPED FLAMEBACK
Dinopium benghalense

L 26–29cm

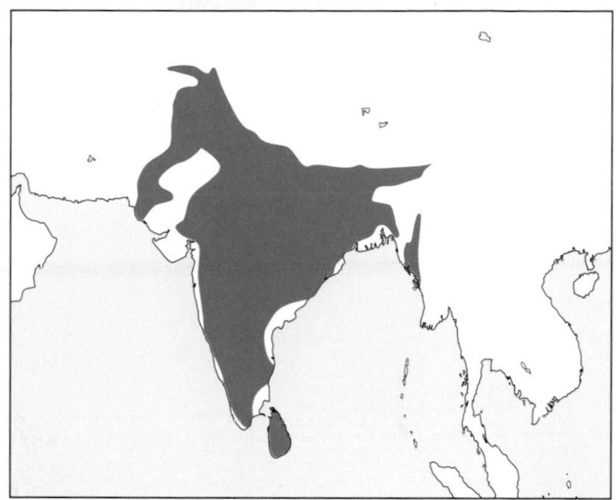

Other names Black-rumped Goldenback, Lesser Goldenback, Lesser Flameback

Identification Plain black nape and upper mantle, back colour varies according to race. Black rump. Dark chevrons, scales and streaks on white underparts. Black throat and post-auricular stripe, though sometimes faint. White supercilium. Mostly olive wings, dotted white on lesser-coverts, primaries barred. Bill blackish. Iris chestnut. Legs grey or green; the only *Dinopium* with four toes. Sexes differ: male has red crown and crest, forecrown streaked black; female has red hindcrown and crest, rest of crown black streaked or spotted white, throat with broader white flecks. Juvenile browner than adult above, greyer below; female usually with plain black forehead, male with red and white spotting on black crown.

Vocalisations Distinctive sharp, strident, whinnying *kyi-kyi-kyi* that begins slow and soft, becomes faster, then falls away. Single *kierk* or *klerk* contact note. Short, strident, slurred *grrrk*. Shrill, nasal, decelerating rattling *woicka-woicka*. Also raucous, harsh laughing.

Drumming Both sexes produce fast 2-second rolls of even tempo, wavering in volume and fading at the end. Several rolls often in quick succession.

Status Common locally. Considered stable, though population data patchy.

Habitat Open, dry or wet tropical forests, wooded cultivated areas, plantations, groves, around settlements. Avoids dense forest.

Range SE Asia. India, Pakistan, Nepal, Bangladesh, Bhutan and Sri Lanka. Resident and sedentary. Mainly low elevations, but to 1700m.

Taxonomy and variation Six races, with upperpart colour varying greatly, N birds usually paler than richer-toned S ones. Extent of white spotting on wing-coverts also variable. Nominate ***benghalense*** (Assam, NE India); ***dilutum*** (Pakistan, W India) pale yellow or golden above and whiter below than nominate; ***tehminae*** (SW India) more buff on belly; ***puncticolle*** (C and S India) golden or orange above and on wings, throat spotted, belly buffy; ***jaffnense*** (N Sri Lanka) very variable with four colour forms (Yellow-backed,

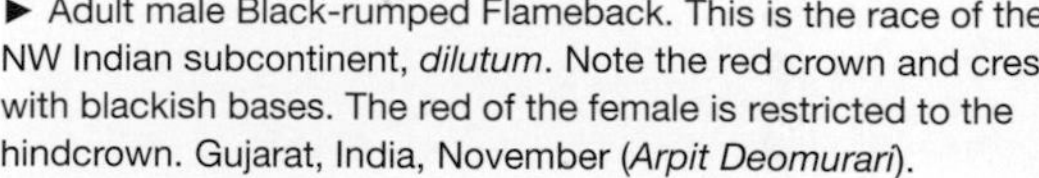

► Adult male Black-rumped Flameback. This is the race of the NW Indian subcontinent, *dilutum*. Note the red crown and crest with blackish bases. The red of the female is restricted to the hindcrown. Gujarat, India, November (*Arpit Deomurari*).

Golden-backed, Orange-backed and Red-backed); ***psarodes*** (C and S Sri Lanka) has crimson mantle, back, coverts and tertials, and black crown and throat.

Similar species Black throat and rump eliminates all other *Dinopium* species. Crimson-backed Flameback in Sri Lanka also red above, though much larger, with long yellowish bill, white-spotted nape and white throat.

Food and foraging Mainly ants, terrestrial and arboreal, in all stages. Also spiders, beetles, some fruit, seeds and nectar. Forages at most levels from canopy to ground, often in pairs and followed by drongos, bulbuls, babblers and starlings.

◄ Adult female of the nominate race. Note lack of red on forecrown. Kolkata, India, January (*Abhishek Das*).

▼◄ Adult male *psarodes*. This race, from central and southern Sri Lanka, is very distinct; it lacks the gold and yellow tones of the mainland races. Katunayake, Sri Lanka, March (*Chris Holtby*).

▼ Adult female *psarodes* differs from the male in much the same way that other races do – it lacks red on the forecrown. Sri Lanka, October (*Uditha Hettige*).

CHRYSOCOLAPTES

Old World (Asian) genus of eight species. Commonly (along with *Dinopium* species) they are called 'flamebacks' and sometimes 'goldenbacks'. Until recently only two species were generally recognised but Greater Flameback recently split into seven species based on geographical isolation and plumage variation. Several species are restricted to islands and endangered. The *Chrysocolaptes* are large, slim and thin-necked with long, impressive bills. Most roost communally with individuals using single roost-holes in a cluster of nearby cavities.

Greater Flameback *Chrysocolaptes guttacristatus*, adult female. Thailand, November.

219. BUFF-SPOTTED FLAMEBACK
Chrysocolaptes lucidus

L 26–29cm

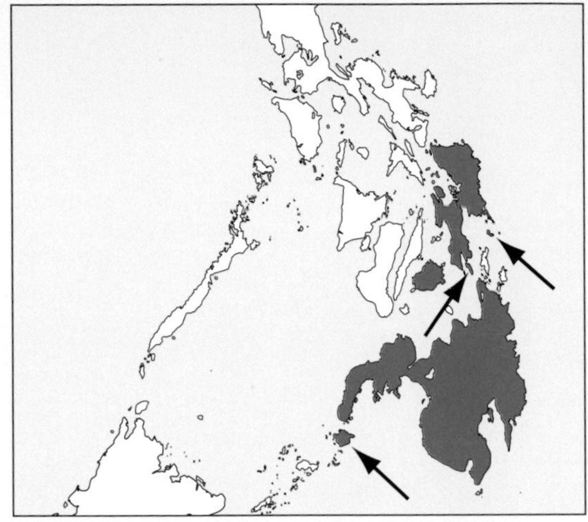

Identification Slender-necked. Large bill as long as head. Bronze above with some gold and red tones. Rump brighter red. Wings brown-olive with blackish flight feathers and white spotting on inner webs. Underparts from throat to vent yellowish or cream, black edges creating bold scaling. Tail blackish. Face and neck rufous and buff flecked black. Iris red, orbital ring purple. Bill pale, often yellow. Legs olive or grey. Sexes differ: male has deep red crown and coned crest; female olive, brown or reddish flecked golden. Juvenile like respective adult but duller, plainer and greener, with brown iris; juvenile male has less red on head than adult male.

Vocalisations Loud, metallic rattles of often four *kik* notes, steady in pitch and tempo. Sometimes a more stuttering *kik-ki-ki-ki*. Also a sharp, piercing *di-di-di-di-di*, recalling a cicada. In flight a rapid, lower pitched *di-i-i-i-t* or a staccato, repeated *tyu-tyu-tyu* with 3–5 notes.

Drumming Produces fast, powerful rolls that usually accelerate before losing speed and volume.

Status Though not uncommon locally, has restricted range on islands where much native forest has been lost. IUCN conservation category not yet assigned.

Habitat Primary and secondary forests, plantations, always with some large trees.

Range Endemic to S and E Philippines: Basilan, Mindanao, Samar, Biliran, Leyte, Calicoan, Bohol, Panaon and Samal. Resident and sedentary.

Taxonomy and variation Three races, formerly included in Greater Flameback: ***lucidus*** (S Philippines: Basilan, Zamboanga Peninsula on Mindanao) has back tinged red, buffy face and belly scalloped black; ***rufopunctatus*** (EC Philippines: Samar, Biliran, Leyte, Calicoan, Bohol, Panaon) has buff face tinged rufous, belly scalloped black, male with pinkish malar and deep red mantle and back, female with black crown dotted pinkish; ***montanus*** (S Philippines: C and E Mindanao, Samal) pure golden above usually lacking reddish hues, female with golden crown.

Similar species None within range.

Food and foraging Presumably various invertebrates and some plant matter, as for relatives, but specific information lacking.

◄◄ Adult male Buff-spotted Flameback has a red crown and crest. The female lacks red, having a variably mottled crown. This is race *montanus*. Mt. Kitanglad, Mindanao, Philippines, January (*Rob Hutchinson*).

◄ Adult female. This bird is of the race *montanus*, which has the most golden-yellow crown of all the races. Mt. Talomo, Mindanao, Philippines, September (*Ramon Quisumbing*).

220. LUZON FLAMEBACK
Chrysocolaptes haematribon

L 26–28cm

Identification Slender-necked with grey-black bill as long as the head. Lores, ear-coverts and neck-sides chocolate. Buff-yellowish malar. Crown bordered by thin black line. White supercilium broken with black, runs to nape. Densely and finely spotted buff on throat and chest, yellowish from breast to vent, vaguely scaled or barred grey. Nape and mantle blackish, red back tinged olive. Wings reddish, flight feathers variably rufous edged crimson, spotted white on inner webs. Tail chocolate. Iris chestnut, orbital ring brown. Legs grey. Sexes differ: male has pale face spotted black, dull red crown and coned crest; female darker on head, crown black boldly dotted white. Juveniles duller, juvenile male with less red in crest.

Vocalisations Fast, broken, staccato series of excited *di-di-di* notes, like relatives. Variable in pitch, but usually level in volume and speed.

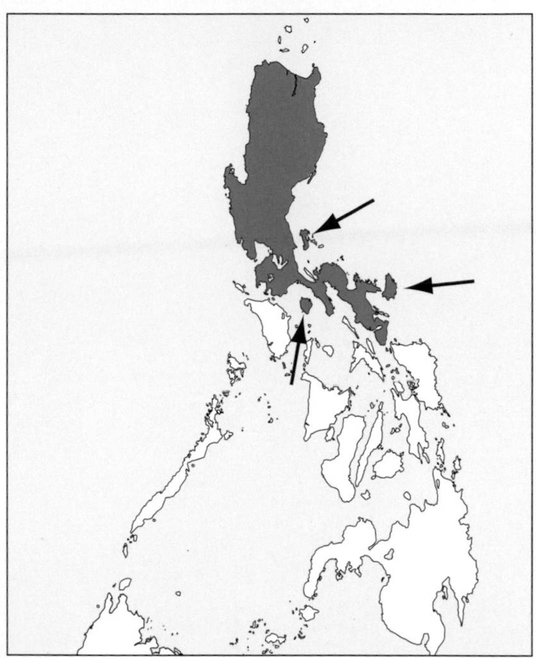

Drumming Presumably similar to other large flamebacks, but specific details unavailable.

Status Not uncommon, but restricted to islands where much native forest has been lost. IUCN conservation category not yet assigned.

Habitat Primary and secondary forests, plantations, always with some large trees.

Range Endemic to N Philippines: Luzon, Polillo, Marinduque and Catanduanes. Resident and sedentary.

Taxonomy and variation Monotypic. Formerly treated as a race of Greater Flameback. Birds on Greater Luzon redder on back, buffy on face and with more diffusely barred belly.

Similar species None within range.

Food and foraging Presumably ants, other invertebrates and some plant matter, as for relatives, but specific information lacking.

► Adult male Luzon Flameback. This stunning woodpecker has a red crown and peaked crest. Zambales, Luzon, Philippines, August (*Adrian Constantino*).

▲ Adult female Luzon Flameback. The female has a black crown, with the rear of the head heavily spotted white. Palay Palay, Luzon, Philippines, June (*Ely Teehankee*).

◄ Adult female Luzon Flameback. A glorious woodpecker of the forests of the northern Philippines. Luzon, Philippines, August (*Adrian Constantino*).

221. YELLOW-FACED FLAMEBACK
Chrysocolaptes xanthocephalus

L 26–28cm

Identification Slender-necked with large pale yellow bill as long as head. Head, face, neck and breast yellowish spotted black. Belly plain yellow. Slight black malar, sometimes with hint of red below. Crimson upperparts and wings, often washed golden. Rump red. Tail black, uppertail-coverts tinged red. Legs flesh-coloured. Iris red. Legs pale grey. Sexes differ: male has scarlet crown and coned crest; female head and crown all yellow, crest sometimes orange or golden.
Vocalisations Fast, trilling, often rather squeaky *di-di-di-di-di*. Series variable in pitch, volume and often broken, like other large flamebacks.
Drumming Presumably similar to relatives, but specific details lacking.
Status Though not uncommon locally, occurs on islands where much native forest has been felled. Poorly known and IUCN conservation category not yet assigned.
Habitat Primary and secondary forests, plantations, always with some large trees.
Range Endemic to west-central Philippine islands of Ticao, Masbate, Panay, Guimaras and Negros. Resident and sedentary.
Taxonomy and variation Monotypic. Formerly treated as race of Greater Flameback.

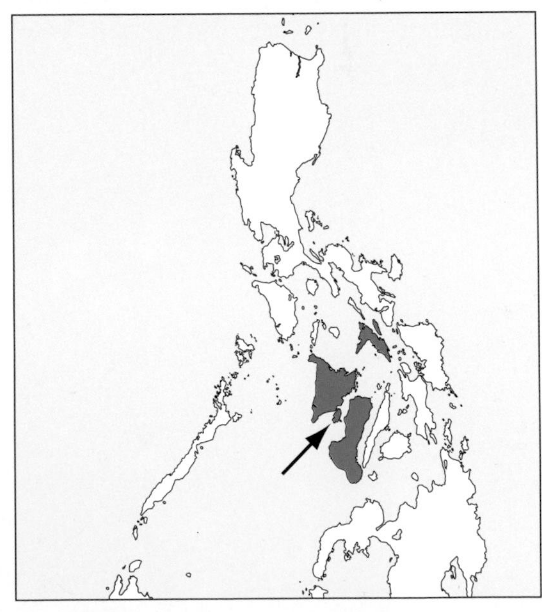

Similar species None within range.
Food and foraging Presumably ants, other invertebrates and some plant matter, as for relatives, but information unavailable.

222. RED-HEADED FLAMEBACK

Chrysocolaptes erythrocephalus

L 26–28cm

Identification Slender-necked with large, pale yellowish bill as long as head. Dark spot or smudge on ear-coverts. Fine dark malar. Chin and throat pinkish. Pale neck striped narrowly black. Back and wings greenish or golden with reddish tones. Red from rump to lower back, slightly barred chocolate. White below, heavily and narrowly striped or scaled black on chest and breast; arrowheads on flanks, less marked on belly. Tail brown. Iris dark red. Legs grey. Sexes differ: male has head and coned crest red; female's crown and crest duller, darker red, flecked pink, olive or golden. Juvenile has less red on head.

Vocalisations Presumably much like those of relatives, but information unavailable.

Drumming Probably similar to other large flamebacks, but specific details lacking.

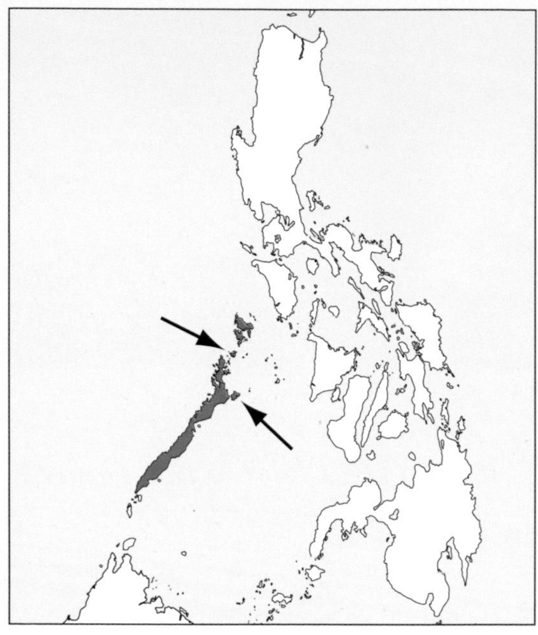

Status Common locally. Restricted to islands where much native forest has been lost. Poorly known and IUCN conservation category not yet assigned.

Habitat Primary and secondary forests, plantations, always with some large trees.

Range Endemic to Palawan and Calamian Islands in W Philippines. Resident and sedentary.

Taxonomy and variation Monotypic. Formerly treated as race of Greater Flameback. Birds on Greater Palawan light green or golden above, buffy face tinged red and belly strongly marked.

Similar species Sympatric Spot-throated Flameback visibly smaller, with short dark bill, black and white striped face, plain black nape and mantle, and three toes.

Food and foraging Presumably ants, other invertebrates and some plant matter, as in other flamebacks, but specific information lacking.

◄ Adult male Red-headed Flameback has a stunning all-red head and peaked crest. Palawan, Philippines, February (*Pete Morris*).

► Adult female differs from the male mainly in having a variably mottled (rather than solid red) crown. Palawan, Philippines, May (*Tonji Ramos*).

▼ A family of Red-headed Flamebacks. This woodpecker is endemic to the western Philippines, where its forest habitats are under heavy logging pressure. Palawan, Philippines, May (*Clemn A. Macasiano Jr*).

223. JAVAN FLAMEBACK
Chrysocolaptes strictus

L 25–28cm

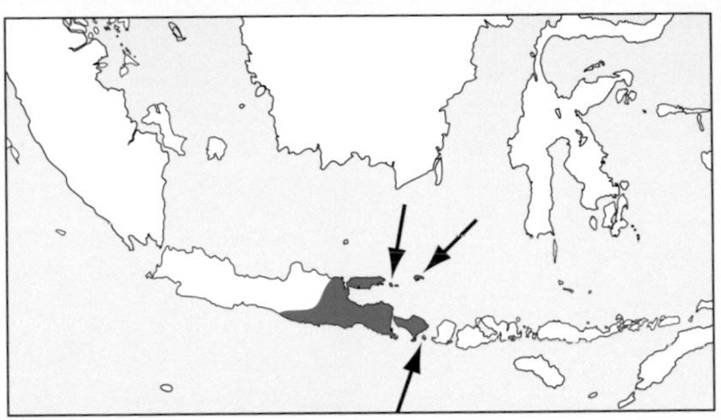

Identification Slender-necked with bill as long as head. Face buff with wide white supercilium and broad chocolate post-ocular stripe over ear-coverts, both of which reach nape. White moustache and malar. Throat buff striped dark. Mantle and back golden, yellow or green with rufous wash. Rump dull red, slightly flecked or barred and relatively small. Underparts heavily spotted, blotched or scaled brown and white. Most of upperwing green, flight feathers browner with large white spots. Tail brownish. Iris brown. Legs grey. Sexes differ: male has orange or red crown and coned crest, usually plain, sometimes slightly marked dark; female has vivid yellow-golden crown with some black flecking.

Vocalisations Fast, excited, trilling, stuttering, often metallic, *di-di-di-di-di* notes in series, given when perched and in flight.

Drumming Rapid loud rolls that accelerate before decelerating and fading reported.

Status Uncommon and threatened, as restricted to islands where much native forest, particularly in lowlands, has been felled. IUCN conservation category not yet assigned.

Habitat Deciduous jungle, primary and secondary forests, coastal woodlands, mangroves, plantations. Some large trees needed.

Range Indonesia. Java, Bali and Kangean Islands. Resident and sedentary.

Taxonomy and variation Two similar races, formerly included in Greater Flameback: ***strictus*** (SW, C and E Java, Bali) and ***kangeanensis*** (Kangean Islands), which is smaller, with redder rump, reduced black facial markings, and narrower, browner markings below.

Similar species Differs from Greater Flameback (which occurs on Java but does not overlap in range) in being slightly smaller, having yellow-green back and wings, duller red rump, faint buff (not white) barring on face and breast, and brown iris. Male Javan differs from male Greater in mostly plain, occasionally darkly barred, golden to orange or yellow crown and crest. Sympatric Common Flameback similar in size, but has black nape, shorter bill, and three toes.

Food and foraging Presumably ants, other invertebrates and some plant matter, but specific information lacking. Pairs often forage close to each other.

◄◄ Adult male Javan Flameback of the nominate race. The female lacks the distinctive red crown and crest of males, with this being yellowish variably marked black. Baluran, Java, Indonesia, May (*Swiss Winnasis*).

◄ Adult male nominate. This range-restricted woodpecker is increasingly rare, inhabiting island forests where heavy logging continues. Baluran, Java, Indonesia, May (*Swiss Winnasis*).

224. GREATER FLAMEBACK
Chrysocolaptes guttacristatus

L 30–33cm

Identification Bulky body, slim neck. Face boldly marked black and white: white supercilium, black post-ocular stripe, ear-coverts and neck-sides, white moustachial stripe, white malar within thin black lines. Throat white with dark gular line. White or buff below, often dull, feathers tipped and edged boldly black, especially on breast, forming large scales. Golden-greenish above, sometimes with rufous tones. Tail black. Crimson rump extends onto lower back. Most of upperwing golden-olive, flight feathers blacker; underwing brown boldly spotted white. Iris pale. Dagger-like grey bill. Legs greyish. Sexes differ: male has striking all-red crown and tufted crest; female has black crown and crest spotted white. Juvenile duller, greyer below, olive above with more rufous tones and dark iris; juvenile male has less red on head than adult, and juvenile female similar to adult.

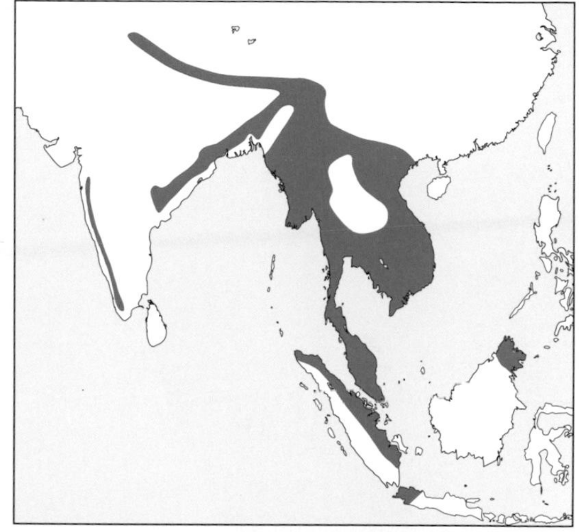

► Adult male Greater Flameback has a striking bright red crown and crest. Note the huge bill. This is the nominate race. Kolkata, India, April (*Abhishek Das*).

Vocalisations Fast, trilling, long or short series of monotone *di-di-di-di-di* notes, also given in flight and in duets. Varies in pitch, often intense, sometimes 'relaxed'. Likened to 'song' of some cicadas. Also single *kick* notes and a loud, trumpeting flight call.

Drumming Powerful, rapid 2–3-second rolls of about 15 strikes per second, often accelerating before fading.

Status Often common locally, but overall declining as native forests across its range are felled. Extirpated from Singapore.

Habitat Deciduous jungle, forest, mangroves, plantations. In all areas some large trees, including standing dead timber, important for foraging and nesting.

Range SE Asia. From India to China, Indochina, Thai-Malay Peninsula and Greater Sundas. Resident and sedentary.

Taxonomy and variation Four races: ***guttacristatus*** (N India, Nepal, Bangladesh, S China, Indochina, Thailand); ***socialis*** (SW India) is olive above, scarlet on rump, smaller, stockier, than nominate and perhaps a distinct species 'Malabar Woodpecker'; ***chersonesus*** (Peninsular Malaysia, Sumatra, NW Java) is smallest race, redder on back, underpart feathers with black centres; ***andrewsi*** (NE Borneo) has chocolate fringes and centres to underpart feathers.

Similar species On poor views Common and Himalayan Flamebacks, but both smaller, with three toes, shorter bill, black nape and malar not split.

Food and foraging Mainly ants, beetles and other invertebrates. Also figs and other fruits. Forages from canopy to trunk in large trees, occasionally on ground, and even hawks for winged-termites. Regularly followed by drongos and other birds though, unlike smaller woodpeckers, often avoids being kleptoparasitised.

▲ Adult female Greater Flameback lacks red on the head, having a white-dotted black crown, and tufted crest. This is race *chersonesus*. Perak, Malaysia, October (*Tan Choo Eng*).

► Adult male *chersonesus* often shows some reddish tones on the mantle and back. Penang, Malaysia, January (*Ingo Waschkies*).

225. CRIMSON-BACKED FLAMEBACK
Chrysocolaptes stricklandi

L 29–30cm

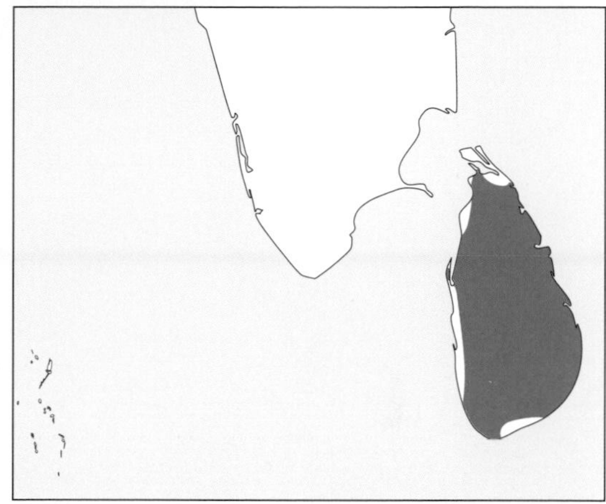

Other names Crimson-backed Woodpecker, Crimson-backed Goldenback, Sri Lankan Flameback

Identification Striking. Distinctive deep red above, rump brighter. Most of wings rich red, primaries browner with white spots. Underwing brown, boldly spotted white. Underparts heavily blotched and scaled chocolate and white, less so on belly. Tail blackish. Much of head, face and slim neck blackish. Narrow, weak supercilium, often mere line of spots. Nape spotted white. White malar enclosed by thin black lines. Throat white with black gular line. Long yellow-cream bill, often greener at base. Iris yellow or white. Legs grey. Sexes differ: male has crimson crown and coned crest; female has black head, heavily dotted white. Juvenile more subdued in colour.

▼ Adult male Crimson-backed Flameback. Note the crimson crown and coned 'crest'. Sinharaja, Sri Lanka, March (*Gehan de Silva Wijeyeratne*).

▲ Adult male Crimson-backed Flameback. This magnificent woodpecker is confined to Sri Lanka. Sinharaja, Sri Lanka, March (*Gehan de Silva Wijeyeratne*).

Vocalisations Rapid, high-pitched, tinny, trilling *kiririri*, sometimes more trumpeting. Also a more whinnying *tree-tree-tree*, both repeated and made when perched and in flight. Some calls suggest those of large cicadas. Also a squeakier single note version.

Drumming Both sexes produce loud, rapid rolls of even tempo that rise slightly and then fade and lose volume. About 20 strikes per second.

Status Not uncommon locally, and quite widespread, but range-restricted and threatened by loss of forest habitat. IUCN conservation category not yet assigned, but classed as NT by the National Red Data List of Sri Lanka.

Habitat Dense, lowland and hill forests, mainly in wet zone but drier areas as well. Also wooded tea estates, coconut groves and plantations.

Range Endemic to Sri Lanka. Resident and sedentary. From sea-level to uplands to around 2100m.

Taxonomy and variation Monotypic. Variation slight.

Similar species Sympatric *psarodes* race of Black-rumped Flameback also crimson-backed, but smaller, dark-billed, dark-eyed, with plain black nape and mantle.

Food and foraging Presumably ants, beetles, other invertebrates and some plant matter, as for relatives, but specific information lacking.

▼ Adult female Crimson-backed Flameback has a black head, dotted white on the crown and crest. Sinharaja, Sri Lanka, February (*Uditha Hettige*).

▼ A pair of Crimson-backed Flamebacks, with the female above and the male below. The birds' much larger size and long pale bill rule out confusion with the sympatric (and also crimson in colour) Black-rumped Flameback race *psarodes*. Horton Plains, Sri Lanka, April (*Uditha Hettige*).

226. WHITE-NAPED WOODPECKER

Chrysocolaptes festivus

L 29cm

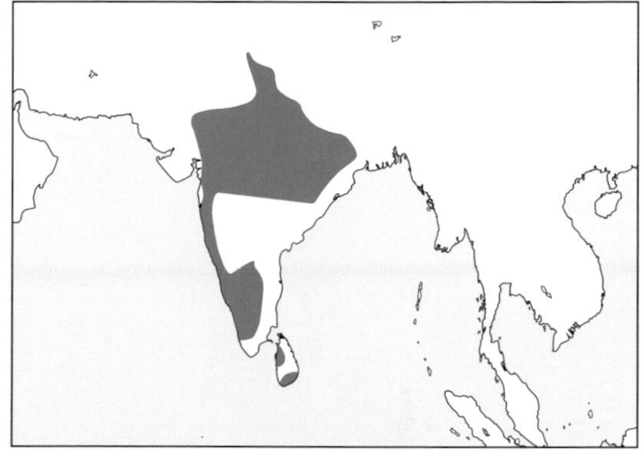

Identification Bold black V-shape formed by scapulars encloses conspicuous white nape and mantle. Head and face striped. Broad white supercilium extends almost as far as nape. Broad black post-ocular stripe crosses ear-coverts and runs down neck-sides to meet scapular stripe. White moustachial stripe, white malar within thin black loop, chin and throat white with black gular line. Forehead black speckled white. Rump black. Tail black. White below, marked with black streaks, arrowheads and chevrons. Wings olive with yellow or green coverts and tertials. Very long dark bill. Iris reddish. Legs grey. Sexes differ: male has crimson crown and peaked crest; female yellow, tinged brown

► Adult male White-naped Woodpecker differs from the female mainly in having a red crown. This is the nominate race. Karnataka, India, February (*Nitin Srinivasamurthy*).

or buff on forecrown and sides. Juveniles have brown iris, black areas browner, sometimes reddish hue on rump; male with buff forehead and orange, pink or golden crown streaked or speckled red, crest blunter; female yellowish crown tinged orange or pink at rear.

Vocalisations High-pitched, trilling, sharp, tinny rattle *kwirri-rr-rr-rr,* squeaky or whinnying, sometimes more raucous and mocking. Also a weak, squeaky *tirrip-tirrip-tirrip* that falls sharply in pitch. Calls might suggest Crested Kingfisher.

Drumming Both sexes drum, but infrequently. Specific details unavailable.

Status Population size and trends largely unknown, though considered stable. Quite widespread, but often very local.

Habitat Dry, open, deciduous, tropical woodlands. Also plantations, coconut groves, cultivated areas and scrub with scattered larger trees.

Range Endemic to Indian subcontinent: most of India, from Uttar Pradesh to W Bengal and Kerala, Nepal and Sri Lanka. Mainly lowlands and hill country, sea-level to around 1000m. Resident and sedentary.

Taxonomy and variation Two races: ***festivus*** (SW Nepal, India) and ***tantus*** (Sri Lanka), which is slightly smaller, darker, more boldly streaked below with wider gular line than mainland birds.

Similar species Might be confused in India with flamebacks, but distinctive black and white back pattern rules all out. Female is only large woodpecker within range with yellow crown.

Food and foraging Ants, wood-boring beetle larvae and other insects. Also fruit and seeds. Usually forages low in trees, sometimes dropping onto barren ground.

▲ Adult female White-naped Woodpecker is unique among sympatric woodpeckers in having a yellow crown. This is the nominate race. Rajasthan, India, January (*Ishmeet Sahni*).

► An adult male of the endemic Sri Lankan race *tantus*. This taxon is uncommon and localised. Sigiriya, Sri Lanka, March (*Uditha Hettige*).

Bamboo Woodpecker, Gecinulus viridis, adult female nominate. Chiang Mai, Thailand, August (*Apisit Wilaijit*).

GECINULUS

An Old World, SE Asian, genus of two three-toed species that occur primarily in forests and jungle with bamboo. Both are rather skulking and little studied, and their taxonomic relationship is unclear: formerly considered conspecific, they possibly hybridise in a narrow zone of overlap in northern Thailand. In addition, the overall taxonomic position of *Gecinulus* within the Picidae remains unresolved.

227. PALE-HEADED WOODPECKER
Gecinulus grantia

L 25–27cm

Identification Compact. Pale golden, buff or green head and neck, face unmarked. Maroon or chestnut mantle and back. Mostly rufous or brownish wings, buff or pinkish barring on primaries more evident in flight. Dusky, brownish-olive underparts. Tail darker brown, edged rufous. Iris reddish. Bluish or yellowish bill, often with green base. Olive legs with three toes. Sexes differ slightly: male has red or pink central crown which female lacks. Most juveniles like adult female, but browner on back and head, darker below and some males may have red or pink on the crown.

Vocalisations Loud, strident, staccato, laughing series with a stressed first note: *yi-wee-wee-wee*. Alarm a loud, cackling, rattling *keriki-keriki-keriki*. Contact call a harsh, nasal series of 4–5 *chaik* notes which becomes faster towards the end. Also a high-pitched, shrill, harsh, repeated *grrit-grrit-grrit...grrit-grrit-grrit*, squeaky *kwee* notes when agitated, and piercing *kweep* notes.

Drumming Loud, fast, brief, even-pitched rolls. Rapid at first before decelerating.

Status Nowhere common and often scarce. Declining due to loss of habitat, particularly bamboo. No recent records from Nepal, in China *viridanus* now rare. Official status may need reassessing.

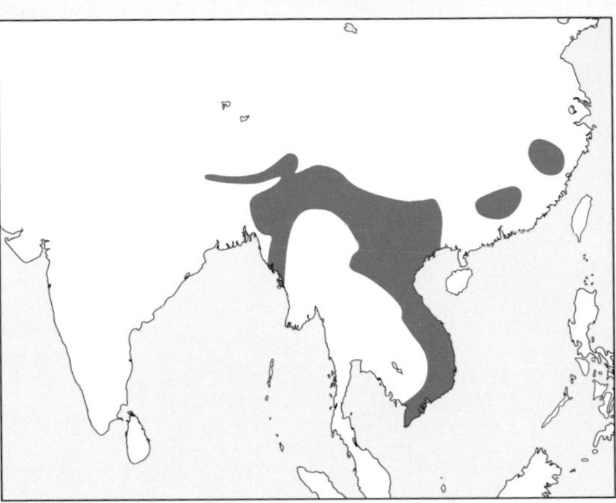

Habitat Mainly bamboo-dominated jungle and thickets. Also wet and dry mixed deciduous forest, degraded stands, scrub and plantations.

Range Himalayas in NE India and Nepal through Bangladesh, Bhutan, Burma (Myanmar), S China, Laos, Vietnam and possibly N Thailand, but not continuous. From sea-level to 1200m. Resident and sedentary.

Taxonomy and variation Four races: ***grantia*** (NE India, E Nepal, W Burma (Myanmar) into W Yunnan, China), male reddish above and on crown; ***indochinensis*** (SW Yunnan, NE Burma (Myanmar), Laos, Cambodia, N Vietnam, perhaps NW Thailand) chestnut above, sooty below, greyer on face, male pinkish on crown; ***viridanus*** (SE China: Fujian and N Guangdong) large, dark, more olive, less rufous, bolder barring on wings and tail; ***poilanei*** (S Vietnam) is poorly known, said to resemble *indochinensis*.

Similar species Most like Bamboo Woodpecker; calls also very similar and to some extent like Bay Woodpecker's.

Food and foraging Insects, especially ants and beetle larvae. Often reveals its presence by noisy foraging on bamboo, though wary and usually hard to approach. Tends to feed low down, but seldom on ground.

◄ Adult female Pale-headed Woodpecker of the race *indochinensis*. This scarce, skulking and often elusive species is declining as its favoured bamboo habitat is degraded. Cambodia, January (*Neil Bowman*).

228. BAMBOO WOODPECKER
Gecinulus viridis

L 25–26cm

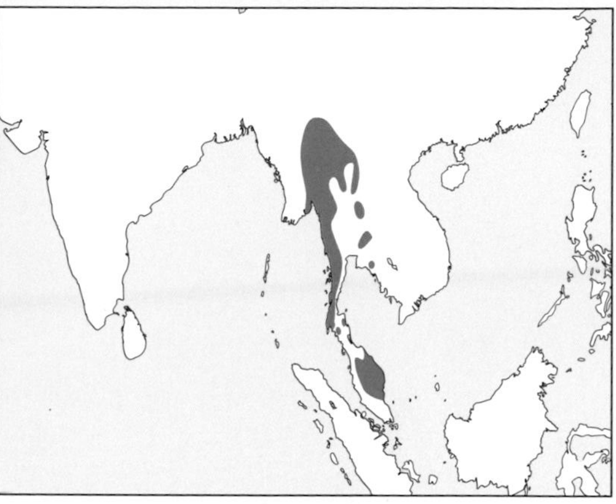

Identification Rather plain greenish-brown, subtly marked. Head lighter than body. Mantle and back dusky-olive with yellow tones. Rump and uppertail-coverts darker with red feather tips. Deep olive-brown below, usually paler on belly and ventral area. Face light greenish-buff, often with golden hue. Chin and throat olive-brownish. Uppertail black-brown edged with olive, undertail brown with amber hue. Most of wings olive with primaries and secondaries darker, browner, with some indistinct buffy bars. Underwing brownish with light green or grey barring and mottling. Relatively fine, conspicuously yellow-cream bill, often greyish-green at base, paler at tip. Iris reddish. Grey-olive legs with three toes. Sexes differ: male has solid red central crown and nape, which is tufted or shaggy and often raised into a crest, and often golden patch on the neck-sides below this; female lacks red, being greenish-yellow on crown, often ochre on nape. Juveniles of both sexes more like adult female, but duller and darker, especially below, and lack yellow tones; juvenile male red only on nape. Juvenile female may lack red on rump.

Vocalisations Not overly vocal. A rather dry cackle of even tempo, which fluctuates in both pitch and volume (not unlike Bay Woodpecker). Song is a quite loud, excited yapping series of *keep-kee-kee-kee.* When interacting makes monotone *kweep, kyeek* or *kweek* notes. Also *wee-a-wee-a-wee-a* and single *bik* contact note.

Drumming Loud rattling controlled 1–1.5-second rolls, rapid at first before decelerating; usually drums on bamboo.

Status LC (Least Concern); despite this categorisation, there is no room for complacency as nowhere abundant, has a fragmented distribution and overall has probably declined. Being dependent on one main habitat type (bamboo) makes the species vulnerable.

Habitat Tropical humid forest and jungle. Strongly attached to mature bamboo stands or large clumps within deciduous forest, also regenerating forests and plantations.

Range From Burma (Myanmar) to Peninsular Malaysia. Mainly lowlands and hill country to 1400m. Resident and sedentary.

Taxonomy and variation Two races: ***viridis*** (E and S Burma (Myanmar), most of Thailand) and ***robinsoni*** (S Thailand and Malaysian Peninsula). Some subtle regional differences. Birds in Malaysia usually darker with very narrow wing barring.

Similar species Most like Pale-headed Woodpecker; calls also very similar. Yellowish bill rules out confusion with other greenish woodpeckers in range.

Food and foraging Mostly ants. As its name suggests, strongly associated with live and dead bamboo for foraging (and nesting) working low down, but seldom on ground. Often in pairs and mixed-species flocks.

◄ Adult male Bamboo Woodpecker. The two races are similar, but *robinsoni* (here) is often darker than the nominate. The female (see the bird on p. 481) is similar to the male but greenish olive on the crown, rather than red. Perak, Malaysia, June (*Lim Swee Yian*).

Bay Woodpecker *Blythipicus pyrrhotis*, adult female. Yunnan, China, May (*Tang Jun*).

BLYTHIPICUS

An Old World genus of two species that inhabit dense, damp forests in SE Asia. The *Blythipicus* are rather unobtrusive forest species, not always easy to observe as they warily creep around in low cover. Both also flick their wings when calling and raise their crown feathers in display.

229. MAROON WOODPECKER
Blythipicus rubiginosus

L 23–24cm

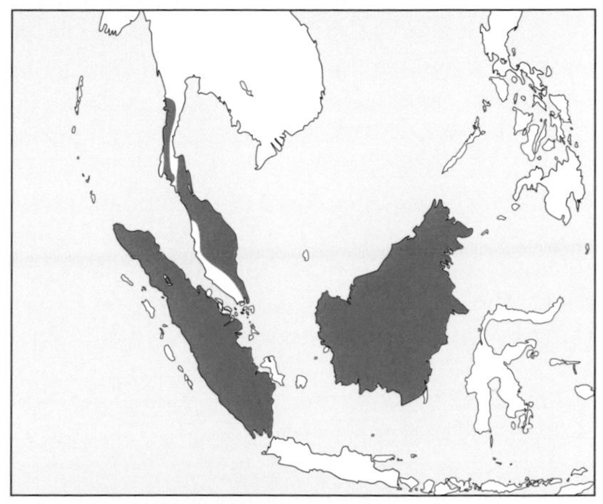

Identification Though not brightly coloured, a handsome woodpecker. Mantle and back plain rich burgundy or maroon. Rump faintly barred paler. Throat greyish, chest to vent dull brown-blackish with some reddish feather tips on breast. Most of head olive-brown with paler feather tips, ear-coverts dusky. Mostly rusty wings with browner coverts, some pale chevrons on tips and faint barring on flight feathers and tertials. Underwing brown. Chocolate tail indistinctly barred pale. Relatively long bill mostly mustard or cream, greener at broad base. Iris chestnut, orbital ring bluish. Legs grey-black. Sexes differ: male has crimson nape that extends to neck-sides and is sometimes rufous on lower cheek; female lacks distinct red, browner overall, sometimes with rufous tinge on neck. Juvenile

► Adult male Maroon Woodpecker; this beautiful woodpecker has red on the nape. The female lacks red, and is drabber overall. Johor, Malaysia, February (*Daniel Koh Swee Huat*).

similar to adult though paler above, often with rufous or orange hue, and darker iris; juveniles of both sexes have some red on crown, and male may show more on nape and neck-sides than adult.

Vocalisations Various metallic, squeaky, single *pit, pick, kik* or *kyuk* notes, when doubled, *kik-ik* or *pick-ik*, second syllable pitched higher than first and inflected upwards. Sometimes these notes are threaded into fast shrill series. Song is up to 14 slowing, high-pitched notes: *keek-eek-eek-eek-eek*. Louder, falling series of 7–11 trilling *chaj* notes and squeakier *keekik* or *chikick* with the second syllable higher-pitched.

Drumming May not drum, or perhaps only rarely, but information lacking.

Status Not uncommon locally, but found in several areas (such as the Sundas), where extensive logging continues and is thus surely affected. Probably extirpated from Singapore.

Habitat Mature closed evergreen rainforest with dense understorey and plenty of rotten timber. Often by watercourses. Also secondary growth, bamboo stands and in some areas rubber and albizia plantations.

Range SE Asia. Rather restricted, from very S of Burma (Myanmar) through Thai-Malay Peninsula and on Sumatra and Borneo. Lowlands and mid-elevations, but on last two islands to 2200m, more common above 1500m and appearing to replace Bay Woodpecker. Resident and sedentary.

Taxonomy and variation Monotypic. Slight regional differences in plumage; birds on Sumatra and Borneo often smaller than on mainland.

Similar species Sympatric Bay Woodpecker is also dark with a pale bill and red nape, but is strongly barred and visibly larger. On poor views perhaps Rufous Woodpecker.

Food and foraging Mainly insect larvae. Feeds rather secretively, low in rainforest understorey, on dead and live trees, snags and stumps, in pairs or alone.

▼ Adult female Maroon Woodpecker. This skulking, easily overlooked forest species is not rare, but it is poorly known. Johor, Malaysia, September (*Con Foley*).

230. BAY WOODPECKER
Blythipicus pyrrhotis

L 27–30cm

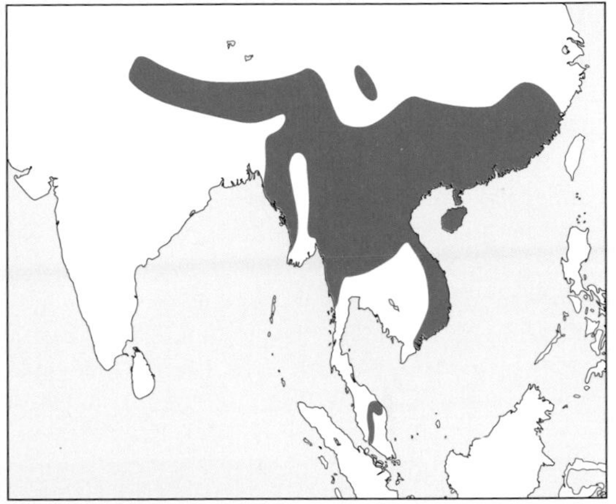

Identification Dark overall with distinct long lemon bill. Chestnut above, barred boldly but variably black and cinnamon. Mostly plain rusty-brown below, flanks faintly barred. Face and nape lighter than body, ear-coverts gently streaked, throat and malar pale. Dusky crown slightly tufted at rear. Rufous tail lightly barred black on upper coverts; undertail cinnamon or reddish, boldly barred black. In flight rufous and black barred wings, particularly underwings, striking. Iris chestnut, orbital ring bluish. Legs grey-olive. Sexes differ: male has variably sized crimson patch on side of lower neck which female lacks. Juvenile duller with heavier barring on mantle, darker below and with pale streaks on dark crown; juvenile male has some red-orange on neck.

► Adult male Bay Woodpecker of the race *cameroni*. The red neck-patch on males of this race can be slight, and the sexes therefore difficult to separate. Pahang, Malaysia, August (*Con Foley*).

Vocalisations Often noisy. A range of nasal, laughing calls include a far-carrying, fairly slow series of 9–13 *pee* notes; a falling, but accelerating, laughing *keek-keek-keek* series and around 20 long harsh *kwaaa* notes; a cackling *kitter-ak-chitter-ak-kitter-ak* or *kecker-rak-kecker-rak* like Striped Squirrel, often done in flight; and a squealing *nyaak, nyaak, nyaak*. Alarm a rapid, rattling series of up to 30 *pit* or *pik* notes, also a chugging, dry *dit-d-d-di-di-di-dit*. In flight also utters a chattering *kerere-kerere-kerere*.

Drumming May not drum, or perhaps only rarely, but information lacking.

Status Uncommon, possibly overlooked. Population data lacking but considered stable, though much forest has been logged within its range.

Habitat Mature and dense evergreen deciduous forest, jungle and bamboo stands. In some areas, eg. E Indochina, occurs in heavily degraded forests.

Range SE Asia. N India, Nepal, Bhutan, Bangladesh and Burma (Myanmar), E to S China, Indochina and parts of Thai-Malay Peninsula. Mainly uplands. Resident but not entirely sedentary – altitudinal movements recorded in Hong Kong.

Taxonomy and variation Five races: ***pyrrhotis*** (Nepal to S China, Laos, N Vietnam, N Thailand); ***sinensis*** (SE China) paler than nominate, with buff streaking on breast, barring above more cinnamon; ***annamensis*** (S Vietnam) very dark, especially below, sometimes sooty, barring above brown, male with minimal red on neck; ***hainanus*** (Hainan Island) relatively small and short-billed; ***cameroni*** (S Thailand, Peninsular Malaysia) also dark with heavily barred flight feathers and very small red patch on males. Intergrades occur.

Similar species Smaller Maroon Woodpecker lacks heavy barring. Overlapping Rufous Woodpecker is superficially similar though smaller and with a short, dark bill.

Food and foraging Insects, particularly ants, termites and beetle larvae. Typically forages low down, on moss-covered trunks, stumps, rotting logs, in tangles of vines, bamboo and leaf litter. Sometimes joins mixed-species foraging flocks.

◄ Adult female Bay Woodpecker. This is another often inconspicuous forest dweller of which very little is known. This is race *sinensis*. Guangdong, China, June (*Samson So*).

REINWARDTIPICUS

A monospecific genus. The large, striking, but poorly known Orange-backed Woodpecker exhibits marked sexual dimorphism in plumage, with the male being brightly coloured and striking, while the female is rather drab and dull. Displays include swaying, wing-flicking, head-bobbing and jerking and raising of the crest.

Orange-backed Woodpecker *Reinwardtipicus validus*, adult male. Malaysia, July (*Yap Kah Hue*).

231. ORANGE-BACKED WOODPECKER
Reinwardtipicus validus

L 30cm

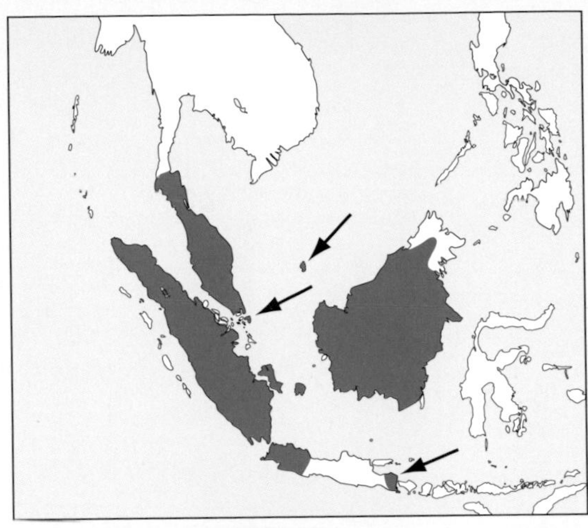

Identification Thin serpentine neck, chunky body. Black upperwings barred with three to five bold orange-chestnut bars; underwings blackish, barred cinnamon or buff. Relatively short black tail. Long, slightly curved bill broad at base with a sharp chisel-tip. Upper mandible dark with buff or yellow base, lower mandible yellow. Iris reddish. Legs grey or flesh. Sexes very different: male much more colourful with complete red crown that peaks in rounded or coned crest, a mostly gold or orange face, golden-rufous malar area, pale nape, ochre mantle, orange back and blood-orange rump sometimes with yellowish tones. Chest to belly rufous, flanks, lower belly and vent tinged yellowish-green. Female lacks bright colours, being mostly black and grey above, grey-brown below, greyish on head, crest and over ear-coverts and flushed

pink on neck-sides; bill often greyer than male's. Juvenile resembles adult female, though male may have some red on crown and ochre on rump.

Vocalisations Often vocal. Range of loud, yapping or squeaky calls include repetitive *wicka-wicka* and *cha-cha;* a faster, powerful *wheet-wheet-wheet-wheow, polleet-polleet-polleet* and *toweetit-toweetit;* and a fast trilling *ki-i-i-i-i* and slower *kit, kit, kit, kit-it* series that ends sharply on a double note. Single sharp *pit* notes are linked into a rapid rattling series that serves as an alarm.

Drumming Produces a level roll of less than 1 second.

Status Generally uncommon. Widespread but scarce in Borneo and occurs in areas (such as the Sundas) where heavy logging continues. Extirpated from Singapore. Population size and trends unknown, but considered stable.

Habitat Typically primary lowland evergreen rainforest. In some areas drier forest, secondary forest, shrub woodland, clearings and clear-cuts with isolated dead trees, and older plantations.

Range SE Asia. From S Thailand to Sumatra, Java, Borneo and some smaller Indonesian islands. Mainly lowlands, including coastal areas, though occasionally at higher elevations in Java and Borneo, eg. 2250m on Mt Kinabalu. Resident and sedentary.

Taxonomy and variation Two races: ***validus*** (Java) and ***xanthopygius*** (extreme S Thailand, Peninsular Malaysia to the Riau Archipelago, Sumatra, Bangka Island, Natuna Island, Borneo). Differences inconsistent, though male *xanthopygius* tends to have less red and more orange on back and rump than nominate.

Similar species None: unmistakable within range.

Food and foraging Ants, termites, beetle larvae and other invertebrates. Forages at all levels, from canopy to fallen logs, in noisy family groups and mixed-species flocks, especially with malkohas and drongos.

► Although not well-marked, female Orange-backed Woodpeckers are nevertheless unmistakable within the species' range due to its structure 'jizz'. This is the race *xanthopygius*. Selangor, Malaysia, July (*Yap Kah Hue*).

◄◄ Adult male Orange-backed Woodpecker is brightly coloured; it is very different from the rather plain female. This is race *xanthopygius*. Johor, Malaysia, December (*Daniel Koh Swee Huat*).

◄ The *xanthopygius* race of Orange-backed Woodpecker is more widespread than the nominate, with the latter found only on Java. Johor, Malaysia, May (*Daniel Koh Swee Huat*).

Rufous Woodpecker *Micropternus brachyurus*, adult male. Singapore, August (*Daniel Koh Swee Huat*).

MICROPTERNUS

A monospecific genus of SE Asia. Rufous Woodpecker was formerly placed in *Celeus* and was the sole member of that genus outside the Americas. Though it does visually resemble some *Celeus* species, molecular studies have revealed that it is not closely related.

232. RUFOUS WOODPECKER
Micropternus brachyurus

L 25cm

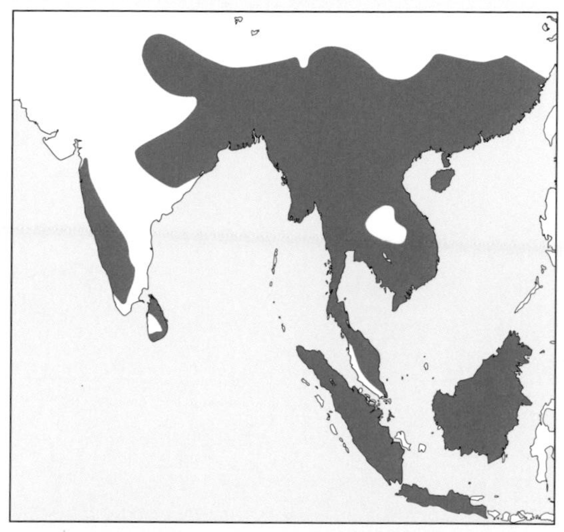

Identification Various shades of brown overall, including on short, shaggy crest. Most are barred black above and on wings and tail. Less barred, sometimes plain, below. Pale throat streaked dark. Iris chestnut. Stout, dark bill. Legs grey-black. Sexes differ slightly: male has weak reddish mark on cheeks, behind and/or below eye (depending upon race), which female lacks. Juvenile similar to respective adult.

Vocalisations Up to 16 *kweek* or *kweep* notes, descending in pitch but accelerating. A faster, high-pitched series of 3–5 sharp, nasal *keenk-keenk-keenk*. *Whi-chi* or *wee-chee* in conflicts. Irregular, falling, laughing *tu-wic, tu-wic, tu-wic.*

Drumming Both sexes produce distinctive, diagnostic, knocking rolls of up to 5 seconds, which decelerate before grinding to a halt: *dddd-d-d-d-dt.* Has been compared to stalling engine or misfiring motorbike.

Status Locally often common, but probably declining where heavy logging continues.

Habitat Fairly open, tropical, deciduous, evergreen and peat-swamp forest and jungle. Locally scrub, mangroves, coastal woods, bamboo, plantations and gardens. Generally at lower elevations, but up to around 1700m.

Range Asia. From N India, Nepal, Bangladesh, Bhutan and Burma (Myanmar) into S China, Indochina and Thai-Malay Peninsula. Also Sri Lanka, Sumatra, Java and Borneo. Resident and sedentary.

Taxonomy and variation Ten races: ***brachyurus*** (Java) relatively small, long-tailed; ***humei*** (NW India, W Nepal) large, throat pale, head grey; ***jerdonii*** (C and SW India, Sri Lanka) scaled on throat, dark, rich chestnut overall; ***phaioceps*** (C Nepal, NE India, SE Tibet, SW China, Burma (Myanmar), NE Thailand) large, dark chestnut, usually lighter on head; ***fokiensis*** (S and SE China, N Vietnam) most distinct race, head cream or buff, crown, nape and throat often ochre, dusky below, wide black barring above; ***holroydi*** (Hainan Island, China) small, long-tailed, very dark; ***annamensis*** (Laos, Cambodia, S Vietnam) small and dark, especially on head; ***squamigularis*** (SW Thailand into Malaysia) small, pale, throat heavily marked, belly with bold barring or

► Adult male Rufous Woodpecker of the race *phaioceps*. The red mark behind the eye that separates males from females can be very faint, as on this individual. Kolkata, India, April (*Abhishek Das*).

chevrons, males with tiny red mark below eye; ***badius*** (Sumatra and nearby islands) like previous but belly less barred; ***badiosus*** (Borneo, Natuna Islands) long-billed, blackish tail barred rufous, back plain, belly lightly barred, throat scaled. Also much individual variation, some having rufous rather than black barring.

Similar species Bay Woodpecker also mainly brown, but much larger and has long, pale bill.

Food and foraging Has close relationship with arboreal *Crematogaster* ants, feeding upon them and excavating its nesting cavity in their hive-like nests. The ants do not abandon their nest when the woodpecker hacks into it and seemingly do no harm to adult woodpeckers and rarely attack their eggs or young. These ants are common in shade-coffee plantations in India where they are considered pests because they protect and support mealy bugs; as an ant predator, Rufous Woodpecker is gradually being seen as a natural pest-controller. Often joined by other insectivorous birds when opening ant nests. Also forages at all levels in trees and on logs, stumps, even dung, for other invertebrates.

◄ Adult male *jerdonii*; the red cheek patch is very faint. This race is usually a very dark brown overall. Karnataka, India, May (*Nitin Srinivasamurthy*).

▼ Adult male *fokiensis*. This taxon has the palest head of all the races, and hence the male's red patch is more obvious. Fujian, China, July (*Koel Ko*).

▼ A pair of *fokiensis* Rufous Woodpeckers. The male is on the left, the female to the right. Note the cinnamon tones on the nape, chest and wings. Fujian, China, July (*Koel Ko*).

Buff-rumped Woodpecker *Meiglyptes tristis*, adult male. Thailand, October.

MEIGLYPTES

An Old World genus of three species, all resident in SE Asian forests. They are small, short-tailed and large-headed, with crests or tufts that are raised in alarm and displays. They are agile gleaners rather than borers, and participate in mixed-species foraging flocks, often with babblers, monarch flycatchers and leafbirds.

233. BUFF-RUMPED WOODPECKER
Meiglyptes tristis

L 16–18cm

Identification Smallest in genus. Distinctive, short-tailed, dumpy. Subtle dark and pale vermiculations over much of plumage. Large head with crest; just a tuft when relaxed, bushy when raised. Plain buff around bill base and eye, sometimes extending into a supercilium. Orbital ring buff. Nape and neck grey or brown. Depending upon race, upperparts and upperwings finely barred black and buff or white, flight feathers with larger, bolder pale bars. Throat and chest also finely barred; breast, belly and flanks barred or plain. Uppertail barred, rump and lower back plain buff-cream. Fine black bill, curved on culmen. Iris blackish. Legs grey. Sexes differ slightly: male has small, often indistinct reddish malar which female lacks. Juvenile similar to adult female, though duller, less barred, black areas browner and barring above bolder.

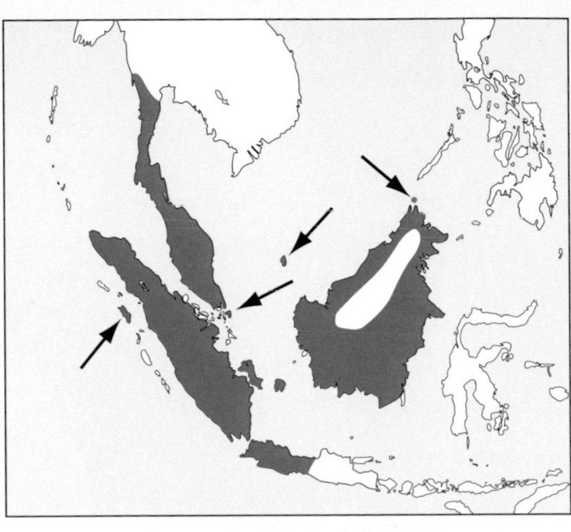

▼ Adult male Buff-rumped Woodpecker differs from the female in having a small red malar streak. This is race *grammithorax*. Johor, Malaysia, May (*Con Foley*).

▼ Adult male *grammithorax*. This race occurs over most of the range, with the nominate occurring on Java. Johor, Malaysia, June (*Daniel Koh Swee Huat*).

Vocalisations Trilling, quivering but soft, high-pitched *drrrrrrr,* lasting about two seconds. Also a fast *ki-i-i-i-i-i-i* trill. Single or double *pit* or *chit* contact notes, sometimes in series, also done in flight. Drawn-out *peee* alarm call. Agitated *wicka-wicka* calls when in dispute.

Drumming Rapid 1–3-second rolls with around 15 strikes per second. Variable, weak or strong, level or falling.

Status However, nominate on Java in grave danger as much of the island's lowland forest has been felled; *grammithorax* extirpated from Singapore, but fairly common elsewhere.

Habitat Primary and secondary open tropical forests, including swamp and heath forests with clearings and edge habitats, sometimes drier forests. Seems to have adapted to man-made habitats like older rubber, cocoa and albizia plantations, orchards and gardens in some areas.

Range SE Asia. Extreme south of Burma (Myanmar) to Java, Sumatra, Borneo and some smaller islands. Lowlands to about 1100m. Resident and sedentary.

Taxonomy and variation Two distinct races: ***tristis*** (Java) is pied above, rather plain, uniform below with pale throat that contrasts with dark chest; ***grammithorax*** (S Burma (Myanmar), Thai-Malay Peninsula, Sumatra, Borneo and some adjacent islands) has finely barred throat, is barred buff below, male has more red in malar.

Similar species Other *Meiglyptes* both larger and less marked. Some calls like Grey-and-buff Woodpecker.

Food and foraging Mainly small arboreal ants and termites. Pairs or family parties forage unobtrusively on saplings, foliage and bamboo leaves. Will join mixed-species flocks.

▲ Adult female *grammithorax* Buff-rumped Woodpecker. The female lacks the red malar streak of the male; otherwise the sexes are alike. Johor, Malaysia, May (*Con Foley*).

▼ Buff-rumped Woodpeckers are fairly social, with birds often foraging together in parties and in 'bird-waves' with other species. Johor, Malaysia, June (*Daniel Koh Swee Huat*).

234. BLACK-AND-BUFF WOODPECKER
Meiglyptes jugularis

L 17–20cm

Identification Compact, short-tailed. Pied body. Most of head black with some fine buff barring. Lores buffish. Hindcrown peaked into bushy crest. Mantle and nape white or cream. Back black, occasionally barred buff. Uppertail black, rump cream or white. Black throat mottled or barred buff. Breast and belly chocolate. Flanks lightly barred white. Outer scapulars white, cream or buff. Most of upperwing black with cream-tipped coverts, flight feathers finely barred cream, white or buff. Underwing mostly sooty, coverts cream. Relatively long black bill, curved on culmen. Iris brown. Legs greyish-blue. Sexes differ slightly: male has weak red malar patch, often just a few faint tips; female lacks red. Juvenile like adult but more obviously barred on head and overall duller.

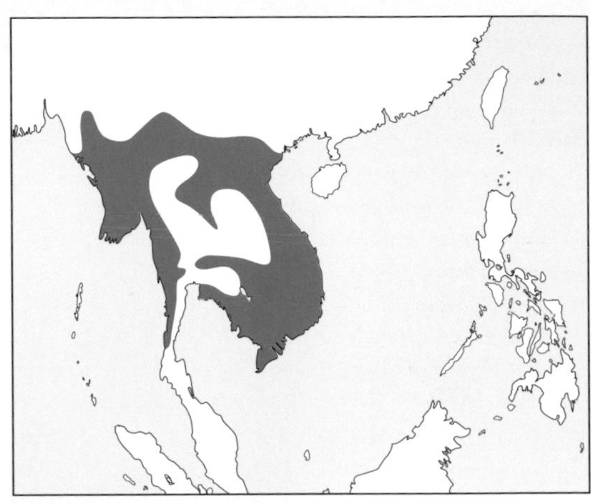

◄ Adult male Black-and-buff Woodpecker. The sexes are very similar, although males have a faint red area by the lower bill-base that females lack. Thailand, October (*Boonchuay Promjian*).

Vocalisations Song a high-pitched, shrill trilling *titti-tititit*, repeated after short pauses. Also a nasal *ki-yew* and *tititi-week-week-week*.

Drumming Occasional quiet but rapid low-pitched bursts of even tempo.

Status Rare to fairly common locally. Overall population size and trends unknown, but considered stable.

Habitat Humid, tropical, evergreen, tall lowland forest. Sometimes in bamboo stands and fragmented, degraded forests. Avoids dense forests, preferring edges and more open areas.

Range SE Asia. Most northerly distributed *Meiglyptes*, occurring in Burma (Myanmar), parts of Thailand, Cambodia, Laos and Vietnam. Mainly lowlands, rarely over 1000m. Resident and sedentary.

Taxonomy and variation Monotypic. Variation slight. Some birds very buff.

Similar species Most like sympatric Heart-spotted Woodpecker in shape, pied pattern and calls, but that species visibly smaller with black nape and pale throat. Male Heart-spotted never has red malar, female has white forecrown.

Food and foraging Arboreal ants and termites. A nimble forager, hanging below twigs and foliage when gleaning prey. Often in canopy, unobtrusive and does not seem to join mixed-species flocks as regularly as relatives.

▼ Adult female. This individual is particularly buffy, rather than white, on the chest, neck and wings. Thailand, October.

235. BUFF-NECKED WOODPECKER
Meiglyptes tukki

L 21–22cm

Identification Appears dumpy. Chocolate overall with heavily barred body. Head plain brown, sometimes with rufous tinge on forehead. Nape slightly tufted, shaggy. Prominent buff or yellow patch on rear neck-sides below ear-coverts. Chin and throat gently barred chocolate and buff. Chest chocolate; rest of underparts brown, narrowly barred buff or yellow, bars often widest on flanks, more diffuse on belly. Brown above from mantle to tail-coverts, finely barred buff. Flight feathers darker, finely barred pale, wing-coverts sometimes edged rufous. Stout bill clearly curved on culmen. Upper mandible black, lower paler. Iris chestnut. Legs greyish-green. Sexes differ: male has red malar, which female lacks, and neck-patch yellower and larger. Juvenile has broader buff barring and less

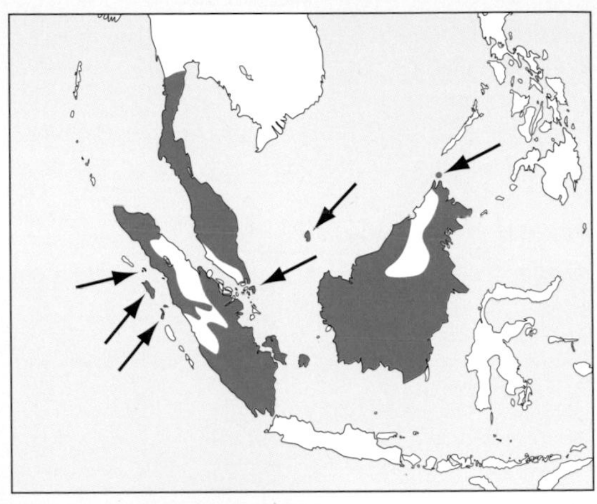

◄ Adult male Buff-necked Woodpecker has a short, broad, red malar stripe, and a larger area of buff on the neck than the female. This is the nominate race. Johor, Malaysia, July (*Con Foley*).

defined, darker, throat patch; juvenile male has some red in malar and sometimes red feather-tips on crown.

Vocalisations High-pitched, slow but strong, trilling *kirr-r-r* that often decelerates at end. Single *pee* and *dwit* notes. Fast series of shrill *ki-ti* and *ti-ti* notes when excited. Repetitive *wick-wick-wick* when agitated.

Drumming Both sexes produce solid 1–3 second rolls of varying tempo and cadence. Up to 60 strikes per roll.

Status NT. Fairly common locally, but declining overall due to continued large-scale clearance of forests, particularly in the Sundas. Extirpated from Singapore.

Habitat Mainly mature lowland evergreen rainforest with thickets, dense understorey and rotting timber. Also taller secondary, peat-swamp and heath forests, mangroves and older plantations.

Range SE Asia. Extreme S of Burma (Myanmar) to Borneo, Sumatra and smaller islands. Mainly lowlands, but to 1225m. Resident and sedentary.

Taxonomy and variation Five similar races: ***tukki*** (S Burma (Myanmar), Thai-Malay Peninsula, Sumatra and some adjacent islands, N Borneo); ***infuscatus*** (Nias, off NW Sumatra) has weak, often indistinct barring, dark crown and shorter wings; ***batu*** (Batu, off W Sumatra) darker overall with more distinct black breast, blackish crown; ***pulonis*** (Banggi, off N Borneo) very brown with pale throat and longest bill of all; ***percnerpes*** (S Borneo) more rufous-brown and heavily barred. Some island populations show slight differences in plumage from mainland birds but variation within these populations also exists.

Similar species Lack of developed crest helps separate from other small woodpeckers in its range. Some calls like those of Buff-rumped Woodpecker.

Food and foraging Often in pairs which restlessly forage together at lower levels on trunks and in bushes for smaller arboreal ants and termites. Also joins mixed-species flocks.

► Adult female. Mainly found in lowland rainforest, Buff-necked Woodpecker is threatened by intensive logging. This is the nominate race. Johor, Malaysia, October (*Yap Kah Hue*).

Male Great Slaty Woodpecker *Mulleripicus pulverulentus*. Johor, Malaysia, August (*Con Foley*).

MULLERIPICUS

An Old World, SE Asian, genus of four large species with slim necks. Recent molecular phylogenic studies suggest a close relationship to the Old World *Dryoco* (probably more closely related to them than ar the New World *Dryocopus*). In common with most other big woodpeckers, the do not fly in an undulating fashion, but rather flap like crows or hornbills.

236. ASHY WOODPECKER
Mulleripicus fulvus

L 39–40cm

Other name Celebes Woodpecker

Identification Slim, long-tailed, long-billed. Mantle and back grey to sooty. Upper tail brownish or dusky, tail-coverts grey. Wings dark grey to sooty. Underparts variably cream, cinnamon or ochre, often with greyish hue on breast and flanks and sometimes a rufous tinge. Ventral area tan with yellowish tones. Grey nape speckled white. Throat and fore-neck light grey or buff, also lightly spotted white and this can create an overall mottled appearance. Bill black. Iris cream or white, orbital ring blackish. Legs greyish. Sexes differ: male has variable amount of red on head and face, depending upon race; female lacks red, being grey, finely spotted white. Juvenile duller, more spotted, both sexes with some red on face.

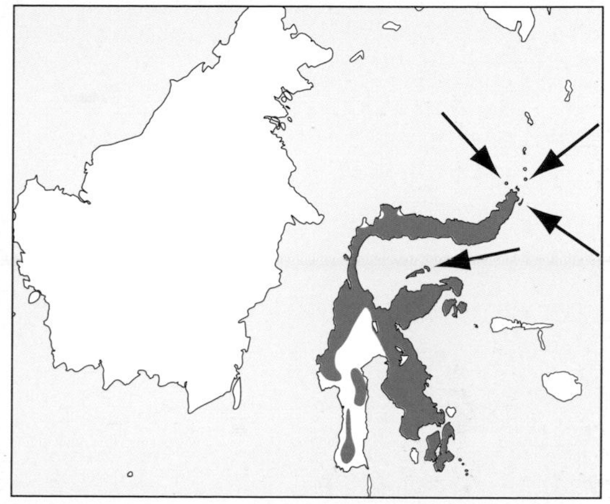

► Adult male Ashy Woodpecker nominate race. The male of this race has red restricted to the front of the face and crown. Northern Sulawesi, Indonesia, August (*Stijn de Win*).

Vocalisations Often vocal. Gentle series of *twee-twee-twee* notes, sometimes bubbling, sometimes trilling. Rapid, but subdued, mocking series of *hew-hew* or *tuk-tuk* notes. Also 6–8 faster but weak, throaty *kikiki* notes lasting just over a second. Longer variant begins rapidly before slowing, each note distinct.

Drumming Slow 2-second rolls of clearly separated, knocking strikes.

Status Locally not uncommon. Poorly known, but overall considered stable. Fairly widespread, but scattered across various islands, some suffering from serious deforestation.

Habitat Typically tall, closed, primary and secondary tropical forest, in hills and lowlands. Also partially cleared areas, forest clumps in savanna, mangroves and coconut groves.

Range Endemic to Sulawesi (Indonesia), and some adjacent islands. Lowlands to 2200m. Resident, probably sedentary.

Taxonomy and variation Two races: ***fulvus*** (N Sulawesi, Bangka, Lembeh, Manterawu and Togian islands) male has red restricted to lores, fore- to mid-crown, cheek and hindneck grey speckled white; ***wallacei*** (C, E and S Sulawesi, Muna and Butung islands) paler, shorter-billed, longer-winged and longer-tailed than nominate, male with more and brighter red on head, covering crown and ear-coverts.

Similar species None within range.

Food and foraging Invertebrates, especially arboreal termites. Often forages in pairs or family parties on larger tree trunks.

▲ Adult female Ashy Woodpecker lacks red on the head. Both sexes are unmistakable, as no other large woodpeckers occur within this bird's range. This is the nominate. Northern Sulawesi, Indonesia, October (*Stijn de Win*).

► Juvenile male of the nominate race. Northern Sulawesi, Indonesia, October (*Ingo Waschkies*).

237. NORTHERN SOOTY WOODPECKER
Mulleripicus funebris

L 30cm

Identification From afar often seems totally grey or black except for conspicuous pale eye and bill. On close views glossy bluish-black upperparts and sooty underparts apparent. Neck, and especially throat, finely speckled white. Long, narrow, slightly curved, ivory or yellowish bill, dark at base and on culmen. Iris yellowish. Legs grey-brown. Sexes differ: male is red or burgundy on forecrown, forehead, lores, cheek, ear-coverts and malar region, with black speckling; female lacks red, these areas being black speckled white (though speckles often indistinct). Juvenile similar to respective adult, but browner, lacking gloss and with larger pale spotting.

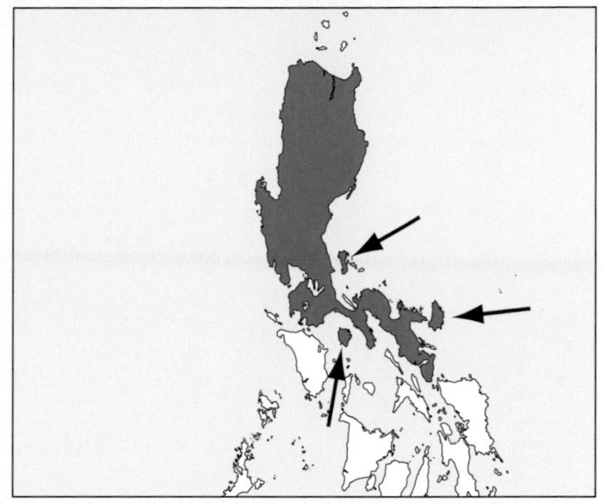

Vocalisations Quite vocal, foraging pairs calling to keep in contact. Most common call a repeated, loud,

► Adult male Northern Sooty Woodpecker differs from the female mainly in having red on the face, although this is not always obvious. Luzon, Philippines, November (*Con Foley*).

shrill, piping *chil-lel-lel-lel-lel,* lasting around a second, and likened to a referee's whistle.

Drumming Solid, powerful, variable, but usually accelerating 1–2-second rolls of at least 20 strikes.

Status IUCN conservation category not yet assigned. Was listed as LC when lumped with Southern Sooty Woodpecker, but little studied and status needs reassessing. Population size and trends unknown and occurs on islands where much native forest has been logged. Rarer than Southern Sooty Woodpecker.

Habitat Various humid lowland and upland forests, particularly evergreen stands. In some places in secondary growth, montane oak-pine forests and occasionally plantations.

Range Endemic to N Philippines. Usually below 500m. Resident, probably sedentary.

Taxonomy and variation Formerly lumped with Southern Sooty Woodpecker, but recently split due to differences in plumage, morphology and calls. Three similar races: ***funebris*** (C and S Luzon, Catanduanes, Marinduque)*;* ***mayri*** (N Luzon); and ***parkesi*** (Polillo). Males of latter have less red on head than nominate. All birds browner in worn plumage.

Similar species None. Southern Sooty Woodpecker does not overlap in range.

Food and foraging Presumably arboreal insects, but precise information lacking. Often inconspicuous, foraging alone, sometimes in pairs, at all levels, but usually high, in both live and dead trees.

▲ Adult female lacks red; it often appears to be almost totally black. This is the nominate race. Luzon, Philippines, April (*Arnel Ceriola*).

► A pair of nominate Northern Sooty Woodpeckers, with the female higher on the tree. Both sexes have white speckles on the head. Luzon, Philippines, December (*Michael Anton*).

238. SOUTHERN SOOTY WOODPECKER
Mulleripicus fuliginosus

L 30cm

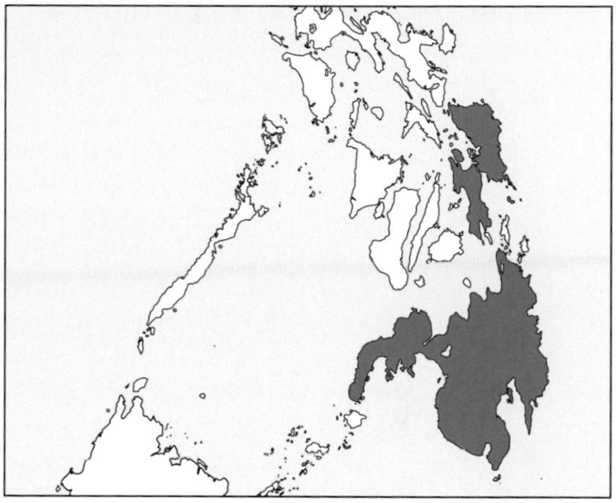

Other name Tweeddale's Woodpecker

Identification Smaller, shorter-tailed, thicker-billed and paler overall than Northern Sooty Woodpecker. Smoky-grey above, pale grey below. Head speckled white (though speckles often hard to see), with larger white spots and flecks on chin, throat, neck and hindcrown. Long, narrow, slightly curved, grey, ivory or yellowish bill, dark at base and on culmen. Iris yellowish. Legs grey-brown. Sexes differ: male has broad but variably sized red malar flecked black; female lacks red. Juvenile similar to respective adult but browner, lacking gloss and with larger pale spotting.

Vocalisations Surprisingly soft and thin whistles. Uttered singly, doubled or strung into a loose faster series. Does not seem to make loud ringing call of Northern Sooty Woodpecker.

Drumming Solid, powerful, variable, but usually accelerating rolls, but specific details unavailable.

Status IUCN conservation category not yet assigned. Was LC when lumped with Northern Sooty Woodpecker, but status needs reassessing. Little studied and range-restricted, occurring on islands where much native forest has been logged.

Habitat Various humid lowland and upland forests, particularly evergreen stands. In some places in secondary growth, montane oak-pine forests and occasionally plantations.

Range Endemic to islands of Samar, Leyte and Mindanao in S and E Philippines. Usually below 1000m but to 1350m. Resident, probably sedentary.

Taxonomy and variation Monotypic. Formerly lumped with Northern Sooty Woodpecker. Slight individual variation.

Similar species None: Northern Sooty Woodpecker does not overlap in range.

Food and foraging Presumably arboreal invertebrates, but poorly known and information lacking.

► Adult male Southern Sooty Woodpecker has a deep red malar region, which the females lack. Samar, Philippines, March (*Rob Hutchnson*).

►► Adult female Southern Sooty Woodpecker. Although a large and not inconspicuous woodpecker, very little is known about its natural history. Samar, Philippines, March (*Rob Hutchnson*).

239. GREAT SLATY WOODPECKER
Mulleripicus pulverulentus

L 45–51cm

Identification Huge, probably the biggest living picid. Reptilian jizz arising from thin serpentine neck, round head and long tail. Almost totally grey, sometimes with bluish tinge. Ear-coverts and neck speckled white. Underparts paler than upperparts; tail and wings darkest. Breast faintly dotted and flecked pale. Throat and upper neck cream or golden. Long, robust bill, lower mandible greyish or yellowish; upper mandible grey, culmen and tip darker. Iris brownish, orbital ring grey. Legs bluish-grey. Sexes differ slightly: male has reddish or pink patch in malar area and pinkish tips to throat feathers: female lacks pink or red. Juvenile overall drabber, browner, particularly above, more spotted on breast, with white throat and faint pale scaling on crown; juvenile male has red malar, sometimes red on crown and rufous flecks on forecrown.

Vocalisations Often vocal, not necessarily loud. Common call 2–5 whinnying, yodelling *woik* or *wuk* notes, first pitched high, later lower. Sometimes rather bubbling, trembling, uttered quickly: *woi-kwoi-kwoi-kwoik*. Described as 'goat-like bleating' but usually harsher. Also softer, mewing and squeaky contact calls *wick*, *whu-ick* and *fu-eek* and a single *dwot*. More aggressive *ta-whit* or *dew-it* calls during encounters.

Drumming May not drum, or perhaps very rarely. Old reports from India mention drumming, but firm evidence lacking.

Status VU. Conservation status up-listed in 2010 after drastic declines due to deforestation became evident. Once common in primary lowland forests, now under pressure. Estimates of extent of decline range from 30–70% over past 20 years.

◄ A Great Slaty Woodpecker family, with the male to the left, the female above and a juvenile below. The sexes are similar, and unless the male's pink malar patch can be seen they can be difficult to separate. These birds are of the nominate race. Pahang, Malaysian Peninsula, June (*Rosmadi Hassan*).

Habitat Mature tropical and subtropical evergreen forest and jungle with clearings. Sal and teak forests often favoured. Also visits adjacent secondary forest, swamps, mangroves and parkland where large, scattered trees present. Extensive forests essential.

Range SE Asia. From the Himalayas to Greater Sundas and Philippines. Mainly lowlands, but to 2000m in Himalayan foothills. Resident but roves over large territory.

Taxonomy and variation Two similar races that intergrade on Thai-Malay Peninsula: ***pulverulentus*** (S Malaysian Peninsula, E Sumatra, Riau Archipelago, W Java, Borneo, Natunas Island, W Philippines: Balabac and Palawan) is darker grey than ***harterti*** (N India, Nepal, Burma (Myanmar), SW China, Indochina, Thailand, N Malaysia). Individual variation in amount of red on males.

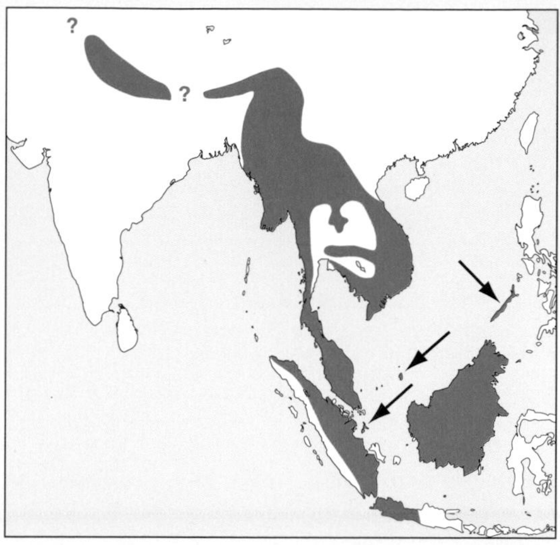

Similar species None: unmistakable. A family in processional flight more likely to be confused with hornbills than other woodpeckers.

Food and foraging Ants, wood-boring beetles and other insects. Forages in tall trees in family groups. Two morphological features exceptional among woodpeckers are close-cropped neck feathering, especially close to the bill base, and fine powder-down covering the plumage. These possibly provide protection from sticky resin and honey found at nests of stingless bees, another common prey.

► This adult female is of the northern race, *harterti*. Bardiya National Park, Nepal, October (*Patrice Correia*).

BIBLIOGRAPHY

Note: For reasons of space (with the exception of a few classic and essential works) only literature from post-2002 is listed. Literature from before this date is well covered in the two recent standard texts on woodpeckers, namely Winkler, Christie & Nurney (1995) and *Handbook of the Birds of the World Volume 7* (2002).

Aghanajafizadeh, S., F. Heydari, G. Naderi & M.R. Hemami (2011): Nesting hole site selection by the Syrian Woodpecker, *Dendrocopos syriacus*, in Yazd province, Iran. *Zool. Middle East* 53: 3–6.

Alder, D. & S. Marsden (2010): Characteristics of feeding-site selection by breeding Green Woodpeckers *Picus viridis* in a UK agricultural landscape. *Bird Study* 57: 100–107.

Alexander M.P. & K.J. Burns (2006): Intraspecific Phylogeography and Adaptive Divergence in the White-headed Woodpecker. *The Condor* 108: 489–508.

Anderson, J. & D. Berhane (2011): Recent observations of Abyssinian endemic bird species in Eritrea. *Bull. ABC.* 18: 31–39.

Angehr, G. R. & R. Dean (2010): *The Birds of Panama: A Field Guide.* Zona Tropical, Comstock Pub. Associates.

Arsenault, D.P., P. Villard, M.A. Peacock & S. St.Jeor (2008): Dispersal and genetic variation in an endemic island woodpecker, the Guadeloupe Woodpecker (*Melanerpes herminieri*). *J. Carib. Ornithol.* 21:1–6.

Ash, J. & J. Atkins (2009): *Birds of Ethiopia and Eritrea: An Atlas of Distribution.* Helm, London.

Atterberry-Jones, M.R. & B.D. Peer (2010): Cooperative breeding by Red-headed Woodpeckers. *Wilson Journal of Ornithology* 122: 160–162.

Aye, R., M. Schweizer & T. Roth (2012): *Birds of Central Asia.* Helm, London.

Backhouse, F. (2005): *Woodpeckers of North America.* Richmond Hill, Ont: Firefly Books.

Bailey, T.N. (2008): Sap Feeding on Birch Trees by American Three-toed Woodpeckers. *Western Birds,* 39: 171–175.

Banks, R.C., C. Cicero, J.L. Dunn, A.W. Kratter, H. Ouellet, P.C. Rasmussen, J.V. Remsen, J.A. Rising & D.F. Stotz (2000): Forty-Second Supplement to the American Ornithologists' Union Check-List of North American Birds. *The Auk* 117: 847–858.

Barnes, K. N. (2000): *The Eskom Red Data Book of birds of South Africa, Lesotho and Swaziland.* BirdLife South Africa, Johannesburg.

Barnett, J.M. (2003): On the migratory status of the Patagonian population of the Striped Woodpecker *Picoides lignarius. Bull. B.O.C.* 123: 130–135.

Benz, B.W., M.B. Robbins & A.T. Peterson (2006): Evolutionary history of woodpeckers and allies (Aves: Picidae): placing key taxa on the phylogenetic tree. *Molecular Phylogenetics and Evolution* 40: 389–399.

Benz, B.W. & M. B. Robbins (2011): Molecular phylogenetics, vocalizations, and species limits in *Celeus* woodpeckers (Aves: Picidae). *Mol. Phylogenet Evol.* 61(1): 29–44.

Bird, J.P., J.M. Buchanan, A.C. Lees, R.P. Clay, P.F. Develey, I. Yépez & S.H.M. Butchart (2012): Integrating spatially explicit habitat projections into extinction risk assessments: a reassessment of Amazonian avifauna incorporating projected deforestation. *Diversity and Distributions* 18: 273–281.

Bodrati, A. & K. Cockle (2006): Habitat, Distribution, and Conservation of Atlantic Forest Birds in Argentina: Notes on Nine Rare or Threatened Species. *Ornithologia Neotropical* 17: 243–258.

Bohórquez, C.I. (2003): Mixed-species bird flocks in a montane cloud forest of Colombia. *Ornitologia Neotropical* 14: 67–78.

Borrow, N. & R. Demey (2010): *Birds of Western Africa.* Helm, London.

Brook, B.W., N.S. Sodhi & P.K.L. Ng (2003): Catastrophic extinctions follow deforestation in Singapore. *Nature* 424: 420–423.

Brambilla, M., E. Bassi, V. Bergero, F. Casale, M. Chemollo, R. Falco, V. Longoni, F. Saporetti & S. Vitulano (2013): Modelling distribution and potential overlap between Boreal Owl *Aegolius funereus* and Black Woodpecker *Dryocopus martius*: implications for management and monitoring plans. *Bird Conservation International. First View Issue:* 1–10.

Brazil, M. A. (2009): *Birds of East Asia.* Helm, London.

Bruggeman, D.J., T. Wiegand & N. Fernandez (2010): The relative effects of habitat loss and fragmentation on population genetic variation in the red-cockaded woodpecker (*Picoides borealis*). *Molecular Ecology* 19: 3679–3691.

Brummelhaus, J., M.S. Bohn & M. Petry (2012): Effect of urbanization on bird community in riparian environments in Caí River, Rio Grande do Sul, Brazil. *Biotemas* 25: 81–96.

Buchanan, J. B., R. E. Rogers, D. J. Pierce & J. E. Jacobson (2003): Nest-site habitat use by White-headed Woodpeckers in the eastern Cascade Mts, Washington. *Northwestern Naturalist* 84:119–128.

Buckingham, M. A. (2011): The avian communities of Iguazu National Park. (Doctoral dissertation, Stephen F. Austin State University).

Bull, E.L. & J.A. Jackson (2011): Pileated Woodpecker (*Dryocopus pileatus*). *The Birds of North America Online* (A. Poole, Ed.). Ithaca: Cornell Lab of Ornithology.

Burton, K.M., D. Uribe & R.E. Webster (2013): First record of Yellow-bellied Sapsucker *Sphyrapicus varius* from the Andes. *Cotinga* 35: 107.

Charif, R. A., K.A. Cortopassi, K.M. Fristrup, H.K. Figueroa, K.V. Rosenberg & J.W. Fitzpatrick (2005): *Status of recent acoustic research for Ivory-billed Woodpecker.* Abstracts of the U.S. American Ornithologists' Meeting, University of California, Santa Barbara, August 23–27.

Charman, E. C., K.W. Smith, D.J. Gruar, S. Dodd, & P.V. Grice (2010): Characteristics of woods used recently and historically by Lesser Spotted Woodpeckers *Dendrocopos minor* in England. *Ibis* 152: 543–555.

Charman, E.C., K.W. Smith, S. Dodd, D.J. Gruar & I.A. Dillon (2012): Pre breeding foraging and nest site habitat selection by Lesser Spotted Woodpeckers *Dendrocopos minor* in mature woodland blocks in England. *Ornis Fennica* 89: 182–196.

Charman, E. C., K. W. Smith, I. A., Dillon, S. Dodd, D.J. Gruar, A. Cristinacce, P.V. Grice & R. D. Gregory (2012): Drivers of low breeding success in the Lesser Spotted Woodpecker *Dendrocopos minor* in England: testing hypotheses for the decline. *Bird Study* 59: 1–11.

Chazarreta, M. L., V. S. Ojeda & A. Trejo (2011): Division of labour in parental care in the Magellanic Woodpecker *Campephilus magellanicus*. *J. Ornithol.* 152: 231–242.

Chazarreta, M. L., V. S. Ojeda & M. Lammertink (2012): Morphological and foraging behavioral differences between sexes of the Magellanic Woodpecker *(Campephilus magellanicus)*. *Ornitologia Neotropical* 23: 529–544.

Clements, J. F. (2007): *The Clements checklist of the birds of the World*, 6th Edition. Cornell, Ithaca, New York.

Cockle, K.L. (2010): Interspecific Cavity-sharing Between a Helmeted Woodpecker (*Dryocopus galeatus*) and Two White-eyed Parakeets (*Aratinga leucophthalma*). *Wilson Journal of Ornithology* 122: 803–806.

Cockle, K. L., K. Martin & T. Wesolowski (2011): Woodpeckers, decay, and the future of cavity-nesting vertebrate communities worldwide. *Frontiers in Ecology and the Environment* 9: 377–382.

Cockle, K. L. & J. I Areta (2013): Specialization on Bamboo by Neotropical Birds. *The Condor* 115: 217–220.

Collins, M. D. (2011): Putative audio recordings of the Ivory-billed Woodpecker (*Campephilus principalis*). *Journal of the Acoustical Society of America*, 129: 1626–1630.

Collar, N, J. (2011): Species limits in some Philippine birds including the Greater Flameback *Chrysocolaptes lucidus*. *Forktail* 27: 29–38.

Conner, R. N., D. C. Rudolph & J. R. Walters (2001): *The Red-cockaded Woodpecker: surviving in a fire-maintained ecosystem.* University of Texas Press, Austin, Texas.

Cooke, H.A. & S.J. Hannon (2012): Nest-site selection by old boreal forest cavity excavators as a basis for structural retention guidelines in spatially-aggregated harvests. *Forest Ecology and Management* 269: 37–51.

Cordeiro, N. J. & M. Githiru (2000): Conservation evaluation for birds of *Brachylaena* woodland and mixed dry forest in north-east Tanzania. *Bird Conservation International* 10: 47–65.

Costa, R. & S.J. Daniels. (Eds.) (2004): *Red-cockaded Woodpecker: road to recovery.* Hancock House Publishers. Blaine, Washington, USA.

Coudrain, V., R. Arlettaz & M. Schaub (2010): Food or nesting place? Identifying factors limiting Wryneck populations. *J. Ornithol.* 151: 867–880.

Cox, A.S. & D.C. Kesler (2012): Reevaluating the Cost of Natal Dispersal: Post-Fledging Survival of Red-Bellied Woodpeckers. *The Condor* 114: 341–347.

Cuervo, A.M., F.G. Stiles, C.D. Cadena, J.L. Toro & G.A. Londoño (2003): New and noteworthy bird records from the northern sector of the Western Andes of Colombia. *Bull. BOC.* 123: 7–24.

Czeszczewik D. & W. Walankiewicz (2006): Logging and distribution of the white-backed woodpecker *Dendrocopos leucotos* in the Bialowieza Forest. *Ann. Zool. Fennici* 43: 221–227.

Dalsgaard, B. (2011). Nectar-feeding and pollination by the Cuban Green Woodpecker (*Xiphidiopicus percussus*) in the West Indies. *Ornitologia Neotropical* 22: 447–451.

da Silva, M., J.B. Irusta, M.C. Rodrigues & B.R. de Albuquerque Franca (2012): Population density and home range of the Ochraceous Piculet (*Picumnus limae*) in Northeast Brazil. *Ornitologia Neotropical* 23: 43–50.

de Pietri, V. L., A. L. Manegold, Costeur & G. May (2011): A new species of woodpecker (Aves; Picidae) from the early Miocene of Saulcet (Allier, France). *Swiss Journal of Palaeontology* 130: 307–314.

de Sousa Azevedo, L., A. Aleixo, M. P. D. Santos, I. Sampaio, H. Schneider, M. Vallinoto, & P. S. do Rêgo (2013): New molecular evidence supports the species status of Kaempfer's Woodpecker (Aves, Picidae). *Genetics & Molecular Biology* 36: 192–200.

del-Rio, G., L. F. Silveira, V. Cavarzere & M.A. Rêgo (2013): A taxonomic review of the Golden-green Woodpecker, *Piculus chrysochloros* (Aves: Picidae) reveals the existence of six valid taxa. *Zootaxa* 3626: 531–542.

Dias, R. I., D. Goedert & R. H. Macedo (2009): Abnormal iris coloration in the Campo Flicker, *Colaptes campestris*: pigmentary color production error? *Rev.Bras.Orn* 17:152–154.

Dickinson, E. C. (ed.). (2003): *The Howard and Moore complete checklist of the birds of the World.* 3rd edition. Helm, London.

Donatelli, R.J. (2012): Cranial Osteology of Meiglyptini (Aves: *Piciformes*: *Picidae*), *Anatomy Research International.*

Dornas, T., G.A. Leite, R. T. Pinheiro & M.A. Crozariol (2011): Primeiro registro do criticamente ameacado pica-pau-do-parnaíba *Celeus obrieni* no Estado do Mato Grosso (Brasil) e comentários sobre distribuicão geográfica e conservacão. *Cotinga* 33: 140–143.

Downing, C. (2005): New distributional information for some Colombian birds, with a new species for South America. *Cotinga* 24: 13–15.

Drever, M.C., K.E. Aitken, A.R. Norris & K. Martin (2008): Woodpeckers as reliable indicators of bird richness, forest health and harvest. *Biol. Conserv.* 141:624–34.

Dudley, J.G., V.A. Saab & J.P. Hollenbeck (2012): Foraging-Habitat Selection of Black-Backed Woodpeckers in Forest Burns of Southwestern Idaho. *The Condor* 114: 348–357.

Eberhardt, L.S. & D.C. McCool (2006): The secret lives of sapsuckers. *Living Bird* 25 34–38.

Ericson, P. G. P. (2012): Evolution of terrestrial birds in three continents: biogeography and parallel radiations. *Journal of Biogeography* 39: 813–824.

Fayt, P., M.M. Machmer & C. Steeger (2005): Regulation of Spruce Bark Beetles by Woodpeckers: A Literature Review. *Forest Ecology and Management* 206: 1–14.

Fitzpatrick, J. W., M. Lammertink, M. D. Luneau Jr., T. W. Gallagher, B. R. Harrison, G. M. Sparling, K. V. Rosenberg, R. W. Rohrbaugh, E. C. H. Swarthout, P. H. Wrege, S. B. Swarthout, M. S. Dantzker, R. A. Charif, T. R. Barksdale, J. V. Remsen, Jr., S. D. Simon, & D. Zollner (2005): Ivory-billed woodpecker (*Campephilus principalis*) persists in continental North America. *Science* 308: 1460–1462.

Fleischer, R. C., J.J. Kirchman, J.P. Dumbacher, L. Bevier, C. Dove, N. C. Rotzel, S.V. Edwards, M. Lammertink, K.J. Miglia & W.S. Moore (2006): Mid-Pleistocene divergence of Cuban and North American ivory-billed woodpeckers. *Biology letters* 2: 466–469.

Flockhart D. T. T. & K. L. Wiebe (2009): Absence of reproductive consequences of hybridization in the Northern Flicker (Colaptes auratus) hybrid zone. *The Auk* 126: 351–358.

Franzreb, K.E. (2010): Red-cockaded Woodpecker Male/Female Foraging Differences in Young Forest Stands. *Wilson Journal of Ornithology*, 122: 244–258.

Frei, B., J.W. Fyles & J.J. Nocera (2013): Maladaptive Habitat Use of a North American Woodpecker in Population Decline. *Ethology* 119: 377–388.

Froemming, S. (2006): Traditional use of the Andean flicker (*Colaptes rupicola*) as a galactagogue in the Peruvian Andes. *Journal of Ethnobiology and Ethnomedicine* 2:23.

Fuchs, J., J. I. Ohlson, P. G. P. Ericson, & E. Pasquet (2006): Molecular phylogeny and biogeographic history of the Piculets (Piciformes: Picumninae). *J. Avian Biol.* 37: 487–496.

Fuchs, J., P. G. Ericson, & E. Pasquet (2008): Mitochondrial phylogeographic structure of the white-browed Piculet (*Sasia ochracea*): cryptic genetic differentiation and endemism in Indochina. *Journal of Biogeography* 35: 565–575.

Fuchs, J., J-M. Pons, P.G.P. Ericson, C.Bonillo, A.Couloux & E. Pasquet (2008): Molecular support for a rapid cladogenesis of the woodpecker clade Malarpicini, with further insights into the genus Picus (Piciformes: Picinae). *Molecular Phylogenetics and Evolution* 48: 34–46.

Gagne C., L. Imbeau & P. Drapeau (2007): Anthropogenic edges: Their influence on the American three-toed woodpecker (Picoides dorsalis) foraging behaviour in managed boreal forests of Quebec. *Forest Ecology and Management,* 252: 191–200.

Garcia-del-Rey E, G.Delgado, J. Gonzales & M. Wink (2007): Canary Island great spotted woodpecker (*Dendrocopos major*) has distinct mtDNA. *Journal of Ornithology* 148: 531–536.

Garcia-del-Rey, E., J.M. Fernández-Palacios & P.G. Muñoz (2009): Intra-annual variation in habitat choice by an endemic woodpecker: Implications for forest management and conservation. *Acta Oecologica* 35: 685–690.

Garcia-Trejo, E.A., A.E. Monteros, M. Coro Arizmendi & A.G. Navarro-Sigüenza (2009): Molecular Systematics of the Red-bellied and Golden-fronted Woodpeckers. *The Condor* 111: 442–452.

Garmendia A., S. Carcamo & O. Schwendtner (2006): Forest management considerations for conservation of Black Woodpecker *Dryocopus martius* and White-backed Woodpecker *Dendrocopos leucotos* populations in Quinto Real (Spanish Western Pyrenees). *Biodivers. Conserv.* 15: 1399–1415.

Garrett, K.L. (2005): San Diego County Bird Atlas. *Wilson Bulletin* 117: 206–207.

Garrigues, R. (2007): *Field Guide to the The Birds of Costa Rica.* Helm, London.

Geiser, S., R. Arlettaz & M. Schaub (2008): Impact of weather variation on feeding behaviour, nestling growth and brood survival in wrynecks *Jynx torquilla. J. Ornithol.* 149: 597–606.

Gentry, D.J. & K.T. Vierling (2007): Old burns as source habitats for Lewis's Woodpeckers in the Black Hills of S Dakota. *The Condor* 109: 122–131.

Gill, F and D Donsker (Eds.) (2013): IOC World Bird Names (v3.3). Available at http://www.worldbirdnames.org

Ginsberg P.A. (2012): First documented mainland South American record of Yellow-breasted Sapsucker *Sphyrapicus varius. Cotinga* 34: 160–161.

Gleffe, J.D., J.A. Collazo, M.J. Groom & L. Miranda-Castro (2006): Avian reproduction and the conservation value of shaded coffee plantations. *Ornitología Neotropical* 17: 271–282.

Gohli, J., J. E.Røer, V. Selås, I. Stenberg & T. Lislevand (2011): Migrating Lesser Spotted Woodpeckers *Dendrocopos minor* along the coast of southern Norway: where do they come from? *Ornis Fennica* 88: 121–128.

Gorman, G. (2004): Three-toed Woodpecker – species, races and clines. *Birding World* 17: 209–220.

Gorman, G. (2004): *Woodpeckers of Europe. A study of the European Picidae.* Bruce Coleman, Chalfont St. Peter, UK.

Gorman, G. (2011): Marks on the iris of the Black Woodpecker. *British Birds* 104: 95–96.

Gorman, G. (2011): *The Black Woodpecker: a monograph on* Dryocopus martius. Lynx Edicions, Barcelona.

Gorman, G. (2011): In Search of Malaysia's Woodpeckers. *Suara Enggang* 19: 20–24.

Gotelli, N. J., A. Chao, R.K. Colwell, W.H. Hwang & G.R. Graves (2012): Specimen-Based Modeling, Stopping Rules, and the Extinction of the Ivory-Billed Woodpecker. *Conservation Biology* 26: 47–56.

Grangé, J-L. (2008): Le Pic de Sharpe *Picus viridis sharpei* dans les Pyrénées occidentales. *Le Casseur d'Os* 8: 84–97.

Grangé, J.-L. & F. Vuilleumier (2009): Le Pic à dos blanc *Dendrocopos leucotos*: deux scénarios pour expliquer l'histoire de son peuplement dans le sud de l'Europe et analyse des rapports taxonomiques entre les sous-espèces *lilfordi* et *leucotos. Nos Oiseaux* 56: 195–222.

Greeney, H. F., J. Simbaña & L.A. Salazar-V (2010): First description of the eggs and nestlings of Powerful Woodpecker (*Campephilus pollens*). *Boletín SAO* 20(1): 5–11.

Grimmett, R., C. Inskipp & T. Inskipp. (2011): *Birds of the Indian Subcontinent.* Helm. London.

Grivet, D., P.E. Smouse & V.L. Sork (2005): A novel approach to an old problem: tracking dispersed seeds. *Molecular Ecology* 14: 3585–3595.

Gussoni, C.O A., A.C. Guaraldo & Y.T. Lopes (2009): Nest description and parental care of Scaled Piculet (*Picumnus albosquamatus*) and Little Woodpecker (*Veniliornis passerinus*). *Rev.Bras.Orn.* 17:141–143.

Gyug, L.W. (2009): Classification of Williamson's Sapsucker calls. *British Columbia Birds* 19: 16–23.

Gyug, L.W., C. Steeger & I. Ohanjanian (2009): Characteristics and densities of Williamson's Sapsucker nest trees in British Columbia. *Canadian Journal of Forest Research* 39: 2319–2331.

Haynes-Sutton, A., A. Downer, R. Sutton & Y-J. Rey-Millet (2009): *A Photographic Guide to the Birds of Jamaica.* Helm, London.

Hazler, K.R., D.E.W. Drumtra, M.R. Marshall, R.J. Cooper & P.B. Hamel (2004): Common, but Commonly Overlooked: Red-bellied Woodpeckers as Songbird Nest Predators. *Southeastern Naturalist* 3: 467–474.

Hewett Ragheb, E. L. & J. R. Walters (2011): Favouritism or intra-brood competition? Access to food and the benefits of philopatry for red-cockaded woodpeckers. *Anim Behav.* 82: 329–338.

Hidasi, J., L. G. A. Mendonça, & D. Blamires, D. (2008): Primeiro registro documentado de Celeus obrieni (Picidae) para o estado de Goiás, Brasil. *Ararajuba* 16: 373–375.

Hill, G.E., D.J. Mennill, B.W. Rolek, T.L. Hicks & K.A. Swiston (2006): Evidence suggesting that Ivory-billed Woodpeckers (*Campephilus principalis*) exist in Florida. *Avian Conservation and Ecology – Écologie et conservation des oiseaux* 1:2.

Hilty, S.L. (2003): *Birds of Venezuela.* Helm, London.

Hockey, P.A.R., W.R.J. Dean & P.G. Ryan (eds.) (2005): *Robert's Birds of Southern Africa,* 7th Edition. John Voelcker Bird Book Fund, Cape Town.

Hollenbeck, J. P., V.A. Saab, & R.W. Frenzel (2011): Habitat suitability and nest survival of white headed woodpeckers in unburned forests of Oregon. *The Journal of Wildlife Management* 75: 1061–1071.

Honey-Escandón, M., B.E. Hernández-Baños, A.G. Navarro-Sigüenza, H. Benítez-Díaz & A.T. Peterson (2008): Phylogeographic patterns of differentiation in the Acorn Woodpecker. *Wilson Journal of Ornithology* 120: 478–493.

Hoyt, J.S. & S.J. Hannon (2002): Habitat associations of black-backed and three-toed woodpeckers in the boreal forest of Alberta. *Canadian Journal of Forest Research* 32: 1881–1888.

Husak, M.S. & T.C. Maxwell (2000): A review of 20th century range expansion and population trends of the golden-fronted woodpecker (*Melanerpes aurifrons*): historical and ecological perspectives. *Texas Journal of Science* 52: 275–284.

Hutto, R.L. & S.M. Gallo (2006): The Effects of Postfire Salvage Logging on Cavity-Nesting Birds. *The Condor* 108: 817–831.

Indrawan, M., S. Somadikarta, J. Supriatna, M. D. Bruce, S. Djanubudima & G, Djanubudima (2006): The birds of the Togian islands, C Sulawesi, Indonesia. *Forktail* 22: 7–22.

Isenmann, P. & A. Moali (2000): *Birds of Algeria.* Oiseaux d'Algérie. Société d'Etudes Ornithologiques de France, Paris.

IUCN (2011): IUCN Red List of Threatened Species: www.iucn-redlist.org

Jackson, J. A (2006): *In Search of the Ivory-billed Woodpecker.* Smithsonian Books/Collins, New York.

Jaramillo, A. (2003): Field Guide to the Birds of Chile. Helm, London.

Jennings, M C. (2010): Atlas of the Breeding Birds of Arabia Vol 25 *Fauna of Arabia.*

Jeyarajasingam, A. & A. Pearson (2012): *A Field Guide to the Birds of Peninsular Malaysia & Singapore.* Oxford University Press, Oxford.

Jogahara, T., G. Ogura, T. Sasaki, K. Takehara, & Y. Kawashima (2003): Food habits of cats (*Felis catus*) in forests and villages and their impacts on native animals in the Yambaru area, northern part of Okinawa Island, Japan. *Honyurui Kagaku (Mammalian Science)* 43:29–37 (Japanese with English abstract).

Johansson, U. S., & Ericson, P. G. (2003): Molecular support for a sister group relationship between Pici and Galbulae (Piciformes *sensu* Wetmore 1960). *Journal of Avian Biology 34:* 185–197.

Joy, J.B. (2000): Characteristics of nest cavities and nest trees of the Red-breasted Sapsucker in coastal montane forests. *Journal of Field Ornithology* 71: 525–530.

Kajtoch, Ł., T. Figarski & J. Pełka (2013): The role of forest structural elements in determining the occurrence of two specialist woodpecker species in the Carpathians, Poland. *Ornis Fennica* 90: 23–40.

Kappes, J. J. & K. E. Sieving (2011): Resin-Barrier Maintenance as a Mechanism of Differential Predation Among Occupants of Red-Cockaded Woodpecker Cavities. *The Condor* 113: 362–371.

Keith, A.R., J.W. Wiley, S.C. Latta, & J.A. Ottenwalder (2003): *The birds of Hispaniola: Haiti and the Dominican Republic.* British Ornithologists' Union, Tring, UK.

Kennedy, R. S., P.C. Gonzales, E.C. Dickinson, H.C. Miranda & T.H. Fisher (2000): A guide to the birds of the Philippines. Oxford University Press, Oxford, UK.

Kesler, D.C. & J.R. Walters (2012): Social composition of destination territories and matrix habitat affect red-cockaded woodpecker dispersal. *The Journal of Wildlife Management* 76: 1028–1035.

Khan, M. Z. & J. R. Walters (2002): Effects of helpers on breeder survival in the Red-cockaded woodpecker (*Picoides borealis*). *Behavioral Ecology and Sociobiology* 51:336–344.

Khan, M.M.H. (2005): Species diversity, relative abundance and habitat use of the birds in the Sundarbans East Wildlife Sanctuary, Bangladesh. *Forktail* 21: 79–86.

Khanaposhtani, M. G., M.S. Najafabadi, M. Kaboli, A. Farashi & D. Spiering (2012): Habitat requirements of the Black Woodpecker, *Dryocopus martius*, in Hyrcanian forests, Iran: (Aves: Picidae). *Zoology in the Middle East* 55: 19–25.

King, R. S., K.E. Brashear & M. Reiman (2007): Red-Headed Woodpecker Nest-Habitat Thresholds in Restored Savannas. *Journal of Wildlife Management,* 71: 30–35.

Klicka, J., G.M. Spellman, K. Winker, V. Chua & B.T. Smith (2011): A Phylogeographic and Population Genetic Analysis of a Widespread, Sedentary North American Bird: The Hairy Woodpecker (*Picoides villosus*). *The Auk* 128: 346–362.

Koenig, W.D. (2003): European Starlings and Their Effect on Native Cavity-Nesting Birds. *Conservation Biology,* 17: 1134–1140.

Koenig, W.D., J.P. McEntee & E.L. Walters (2008): Acorn harvesting by acorn woodpeckers: annual variation and comparison with genetic estimates. *Evolutionary Ecology Research* 10: 811–822.

Koenig, W.D., E.L. Walters & J. Haydock (2009): Helpers and egg investment in the cooperatively breeding acorn woodpecker: testing the concealed helper effects hypothesis. *Behavioral Ecology and Sociobiology* 63: 1659–1665.

Koenig, W.D. & E.L. Walters (2012): Brooding, provisioning, and compensatory care in the cooperatively breeding acorn woodpecker. *Behavioral Ecology* 23: 181–190.

Koenig, W. D., A. M. Liebhold, D. N. Bonter, W. M. Hochachka & J. L. Dickinson (2013): Effects of the emerald ash borer invasion on four species of birds. *Biological Invasions* 15: 1–9.

Kossenko, S.M. & E.Y. Kaygorodova (2001): Effect of habitat fragmentation on distribution, density, and breeding performance of the Middle Spotted Woodpecker *Dendrocopos medius* in Nerussa-Desna woodland. *Entomological Review* 81: 1S161–S166.

Kostecke, R.M. (2008): Population Trends of Breeding Birds on the Edwards Plateau, Texas: Local Versus Regional Patterns. *Southwestern Naturalist,* 53: 466–471.

Kotagama, S.W. & E. Goodale (2004): The composition and spatial organization of mixed-species flocks in a Sri Lankan rainforest. *Forktail* 20: 63–70.

Kotaka, N. & S. Matsuoka (2002): Secondary users of Great Spotted Woodpecker (*Dendrocopos major*) nest cavities in urban and suburban forests in Sapporo City, northern Japan. *Ornithol Sci.* 1: 117–122.

Kozma, J. M. (2010): Characteristics of trees used by White-headed Woodpeckers for sap feeding in Washington. *Northwestern Naturalist* 91 :81–86.

Kozma, J. M. & A.J. Kroll (2012): Woodpecker nest survival in burned and unburned managed ponderosa pine forests of the northwestern United States. *The Condor* 114: 173–184.

Kumar, R., G. Shahabuddin & A. Kumar (2011): How good are managed forests at conserving native woodpecker communities? A study in sub-Himalayan dipterocarp forests of northwest India. *Biol. Conserv.* 144: 1876–1884.

Lammertink, M. (2004): Grouping and cooperative breeding in the Great Slaty Woodpecker. *The Condor* 106: 309–319.

Lammertink, M. (2004): A Multiple-Site Comparison of Woodpecker Communities in Bornean Lowland and Hill Forests. *Conserv. Biol.* 18: 746–757.

Lammertink, M. (2011): Group roosting in the Grey-and-buff Woodpecker *Hemicircus concretus* involving large numbers of shallow cavities. *Forktail* 27: 74–77.

Lammertink, M., Prawiradilagac, D.M., Setiorini, U., Nainge, T.Z., Duckworth, J.W. & Menkena S.B.J. (2009): Global population decline of the Great Slaty Woodpecker (*Mulleripicus pulverulentus*). *Biol. Conserv.* 142: 166–179.

Lammertink, M., A. Bodrati & R.E. Santos (2011): Helmeted Woodpecker *Dryocopus galeatus:* a little-known Atlantic forest endemic. *Neotropical Birding* 8: 45–51.

Lammertink, M., T.W. Gallagher, K.V. Rosenberg, J.W. Fitzpatrick, E. Liner, J. Rojas-Tome & P. Escalante (2011): Film documentation of the probably extinct Imperial Woodpecker (*Campephilus imperialis*). *The Auk* 128: (4): 671–677.

Latta, S., J. Wiley, C. Rimmer, H.A. Raffaele, A.R. Keith, K. McFarland & E. Fernandez (2006): *The Birds of the Dominican Republic & Haiti.* Helm, London.

Lee, W-S., T-H. Koo & J-Y. Park (2000): A field guide to the birds of Korea. LG Evergreen Foundation.

Lees, A.C. & C.A. Peres (2008): Avian life-history determinants of local extinction risk in a hyper-fragmented neotropical forest landscape. *Animal Conservation* 11: 128–137.

Lees, A. C., N.G. de Moura, A. Santana, A. Aleixo, J. Barlow, E. Berenguer, J. Ferreira & T.A. Gardner (2012): Paragominas: a quantitative baseline inventory of an eastern Amazonian avifauna. *Rev.Bras.Orn.* 20: 93–118.

Lees, A.C., I. Thompson & N. G. Moura (In review): Reentrâncias Paraenses; an inventory of a forgotten Amazonian avifauna. Boletim do Museu Paraense Emílio Goeldi: *Ciências Naturais.*

Leite, G.A., D.G. Marcelino & R.T. Pinheiro (2010): First description of the juvenile plumage of the critically endangered Kaempfer's Woodpecker (*Celeus obrieni*) of Central Brazil. *Orn. Neotrop.* 21: 453–456.

Leite, G. A., R. T. Pinheiro, D. G. Marcelino, J. E. C. Figueira & J. H. C. Delabie (2013): Foraging Behavior of Kaempfer's Woodpecker (*Celeus obrieni*), a Bamboo Specialist. *The Condor* 115: 221–229.

Leniowski, K. & E. W grzyn (2013): The carotenoid-based red cap of the Middle Spotted Woodpecker *Dendrocopos medius* reflects individual quality and territory size. *Ibis.* doi: 10.1111/ibi.12050

Leonard, D. & J. Heath (2010): Foraging strategies are related to skull morphology and life history traits of *Melanerpes* woodpeckers. *Journal of Ornithology* 151: 771–777.

Li, M. H., K. Välimäki, M. Piha, T. Pakkala & J. Merilä (2009): Extrapair paternity and maternity in the three-toed woodpecker, *Picoides tridactylus*: insights from microsatellite-based parentage analysis. *PloS one* 4: e7895.

Long, A. (2011): Orientation of Sap Wells Excavated by Yellow-bellied Sapsuckers. *Wilson Journal of Ornithology* 123: 164–167.

Losin N., C.H. Floyd, T.E. Schweitzer & S.J. Keller (2006): Relationship between aspen heartwood rot and the location of cavity excavation by a primary cavity-nester, the Red-naped Sapsucker. *The Condor* 108: 706–710.

Luna, J.C., T. Ellery, K. Knudsen & M. McMullen (2011): First confirmed records of Yellow-bellied Sapsucker *Sphyrapicus varius* for Colombia and South America. *Conserv. Colombiana* 15: 29–30.

Macchi, L., P. G. Blendinger & M. G. Núñez Montellano (2011): Spatial analysis of sap consumption by birds in the Chaco dry forests from Argentina. *Emu* 111: 212–216.

Madhav, N. V., & J. R. Victor (2010): Wryneck *Jynx torquilla* feeding on bird in Sundarbans, W Bengal, India. *Indian BIRDS* 7 (2): 48.

Mahood, S.P. & J.A. Eaton (2012): The vocalisations of Red-collared Woodpecker *Picus rabieri. Forktail* 28: 167–169.

Manegold, A & A. Louchart (2012): Biogeographic and Paleoenvironmental Implications of a New Woodpecker Species (Aves, Picidae) from the Early Pliocene of South Africa. *Journal of Vertebrate Paleontology* 32: 926–938.

Manegold, A. & T. Töpfer (2013): The systematic position of *Hemicircus* and the stepwise evolution of adaptations for drilling, tapping and climbing up in true woodpeckers (Picinae, Picidae). *Journal of Zoological Systematics and Evolutionary Research* 51: 72–82.

Mann, C.F. (2008): *The birds of Borneo.* British Ornithologists' Union/British Ornithologists' Club Checklist Series No. 23. BOU, Peterborough, UK.

Martínez, D. & G. González (2004): Las aves de Chile. Nueva guía de campo. Ediciones del Naturalista, Santiago de Chile.

Mattsson, B. J., R. S. Mordecai, M. J. Conroy, J. T. Peterson, R. J. Cooper & H. Christensen (2008): Evaluating the small population paradigm for rare large-bodied woodpeckers, with implications for the Ivory-billed Woodpecker. *Avian Conservation & Ecology* 3:5.

Mayr, G. & R. Gregorová (2012): A tiny stem group representative of Pici (Aves, Piciformes) from the early Oligocene of the Czech Republic. *Paläontologische Zeitschrift* 86: 333–343.

Mazgajski, T.D. & L. Rejt (2006): The effect of forest patch size on the breeding biology of the great spotted woodpecker *Dendrocopos major. Ann Zool Fennici* 43: 211–220.

McDevitt AD, L. Kajtoch, T.D. Mazgajski, R.F. Carden, I. Coscia, C. Osthoff, R.H. Commbes & F. Wilson (2011): The origins of Great Spotted Woodpeckers *Dendrocopos major* colonizing Ireland revealed by mitochondrial DNA. *Bird Study* 58: 361–364.

Melletti, M. & V. Penteriani (2003): Nesting and feeding tree selection in the endangered White-backed Woodpecker, *Dendrocopos leucotos lilfordi. Wilson Bull.* 115: 299–306.

Mendel, Z., Y. Golan & Z. Madar (1984): Natural control of the eucalyptus borer, *Phoracantha semipunctata* (F.) (Coleoptera: Cerambycidae); by the Syrian woodpecker. *Bull. Ent. Res.* 74:121–127.

Mendenhall, M. (2005): Old friend missing – species profile: Imperial Woodpecker. *Birder's World* 19: 35–39.

Mermod, M., T. S. Reichlin, R. Arlettaz & M. Schaub (2009): The importance of ant-rich habitats for the persistence of the Wryneck *Jynx torquilla* on farmland. *Ibis* 151(4):731–742.

Mikusinski, G. (2006): Woodpeckers: distribution, conservation, and research in a global perspective. *Annales Zoologici Fennici* 43: 86–95.

Monahan, W.B. & W.D. Koenig (2006): Estimating the potential effects of sudden oak death on oak-dependent birds., *Biological Conservation* 127: 146–157.

Moore W.S., A.C. Weibel & A. Agius (2006): Mitochondrial DNA phylogeny of the woodpecker genus *Veniliornis* (Picidae, Picinae) and related genera implies convergent evolution of plumage patterns. *Biol. J. Linn. Soc.* 87(4): 611–624.

Moore, W.S., L. C. Overton & K. J. Miglia (2011): Mitochondrial DNA based phylogeny of the woodpecker genera *Colaptes* and *Piculus*, and implications for the history of woodpecker diversification in South America. *Molecular Phylogenetics & Evolution* 58: 76–84.

Montellano, M.G.N., P.G. Blendinger & L. Macchi (2013): Sap Consumption by the White-Fronted Woodpecker and its Role in Avian Assemblage Structure in Dry Forests. *The Condor* 115: 93–101.

Morrissey, C. A., P. L. Dods, & J. E. Elliott (2008): Pesticide Treatments Affect Mountain Pine Beetle Abundance and Woodpecker Foraging Behaviour. *Ecological Applications*, 18:172–184.

Moskwik, M., T. Thom, L.M. Barnhill, C. Watson, J. Koches, J. Kilgo, B. Hulslander, C. Degarady & G. Peters (2013): Search Efforts for Ivory-Billed Woodpecker in South Carolina. *Southeastern Naturalist* 12: 73–84.

Müller, J., J. Pöllath, R. Moshammer & B. Schröder (2009): Predicting the occurrence of Middle Spotted Woodpecker *Dendrocopos medius* on a regional scale, using forest inventory data. *Forest Ecology and Management* 257: 502–509.

Myers, S. (2009): *Birds of Borneo: Brunei, Sabah, Sarawak and Kalimantan.* Princeton University Press.

Nappi, A., P. Drapeau, J-F. Giroux, J-P. L. Savard, & F. Moore (2003): Snag use by foraging Black-backed Woodpeckers (*Picoides arcticus*) in a recently burned eastern boreal forest. *The Auk* 120: 505–511.

Nappi, A. & P. Drapeau (2003): Reproductive success of the black-backed woodpecker (*Picoides arcticus*) in burned boreal forests: are burns source habitats? *Biological Conservation* 142: 1381–1391.

Nemesio, A., J.A. Jackson & M. Rodrigues (2005): Ivory-billed Woodpecker supposed rediscovery: science or politics? *Atualidades Ornitológicas,* 128: 26.

Newlon K.R. & V.A. Saab (2011): Nest-site selection and nest survival of Lewis's Woodpecker in aspen riparian woodlands. *The Condor* 113: 183–193.

Nielsen-Pincus, N. & E.O. Garton (2007): Responses of cavity-nesting birds to changes in available habitat reveal underlying determinants of nest selection. *Northwestern Naturalist* 88: 135–146.

Nikiforov, M. (2003): Distribution trends of breeding bird species in Belarus under conditions of global climate change. *Acta Zoologica Lituanica* 13: 255–262.

Oatley, T. B. (1997): Ground Woodpecker *Geocolaptes olivaceus.* In: *The atlas of southern African birds.* Vol. 1: Non-passerines. Harrison, J.A., Allan, D.G., Underhill, L.G., Herremans, M., Tree, A.J., Parker, V. & Brown, C.J. (Eds.); 736–737. BirdLife South Africa, Johannesburg.

Oatley, T. B. (2003): Going to Ground. The life of a terrestrial woodpecker. *Africa – Birds & Birding* 8:5: 29–33.

Oda, J., J. Sakamoto & K. Sakano (2006): Mechanical evaluation of the skeletal structure and tissue of the woodpecker and its shock absorbing system. *JSME International Journal Series A* 49: 390–396.

Odion, D.C. & C.T Hanson (2013): Projecting Impacts of Fire Management on a Biodiversity Indicator in the Sierra Nevada and Cascades, USA: The Black-Backed Woodpecker. *Open Forest Science Journal* 6: 14–23.

Ojeda, V. S. (2003): Magellanic Woodpecker frugivory and predation on a lizard. *Wilson Bulletin* 115: 208–210.

Ojeda, V. S. (2004): Breeding biology and social behaviour of Magellanic Woodpeckers (*Campephilus magellanicus*) in Argentine Patagonia. *Eur. J. Wildl. Res.* 50: 18–24.

Olioso G., & J.-M. Pons (2011): Variation géographique du plumage des Pics verts du Languedoc-Roussillon. [Variation of the plumage of Green Woodpeckers *Picus v.viridis* and *P. v.sharpei* in Languedoc-Roussillon (Southern France).] *Ornithos* 18 (2): 73–83.

Overton, L. C. & D.D. Rhoads (2006): Molecular phylogenetic relationships of *Xiphidiopicus percussus, Melanerpes* and *Sphyrapicus* (Aves: Picidae) based on cytochrome *b* sequence. *Molecular phylogenetics and evolution* 41: 288–294.

Pacheco, J.F. & E. Maciel (2009): Um registro recente e documentado de *Celeus obrieni* (Piciformes: Picidae) para o estado de Goiás. *Atualidades Ornitológicas* 150: 14.

Paclik, M., J. Misik & K. Weidinger (2009): Nest predation and nest defence in European and North American woodpeckers: a review. *Ann. Zool. Fennici* 46: 361–379.

Paguntalan, L.M.J. & P.G. Jakosalem (2008): Significant records of birds in forests on Cebu island, C Philippines. *Forktail* 24: 48–56.

Pasinelli, G. (2006): Population biology of European woodpecker species: a review. *Ann. Zool. Fennici* 43: 96–111.

Pasinelli, G. (2007): Nest site selection in middle and great spotted woodpeckers *Dendrocopos medius & D. major*: implications for forest management and conservation. *Vert. Cons.& Bio.* 16: 1283–1298.

Pechacek, P. & W. d'Oleire-Oltmanns (2004): Habitat use of the three toed woodpecker in central Europe during the breeding period. *Biological Conservation* 116: 333–341.

Pechacek, P., K.G. Michalek, H. Winkler & D. Blomqvist (2006): Classical polyandry found in the three-toed woodpecker *Picoides tridactylus. J Ornithol.* 147:112–114.

Pecho, J.O., O. Gonzalez, E. Perez, M. Tenorio & Q. Whaley (2010): El Pájaro Carpintero Peruano *Colaptes atricollis* en la agricultura tradicional de la región de Ica, Perú: primeras observaciones de anidación y el desarrollo de polluelos. *Cotinga* 32: 8–11.

Perktas, U., G.F. Barrowclough. & J.G. Groth (2011): Phylogeography and species limits in the green woodpecker complex (Aves: Picidae): multiple Pleistocene refugia and range expansion across Europe and the Near East. *Bio. Journ. Linn. Soc.* 104: 710–723.

Perktas, U., & E. Quintero (2012): A wide geographical survey of mitochondrial DNA variation in the great spotted woodpecker complex, *Dendrocopos major* (Aves: Picidae). *Bio. Journ. Linn. Soc.* 108: 173–188.

Piana, R., F. Angulo, E. Ormaeche. & C. Mendoza (2006): Two new

species for Peru: Lemon-rumped Tanager *Ramphocelus icteronotus* and

Black-cheeked Woodpecker *Melanerpes pucherani. Cotinga* 25: 78–79.

Pichorim, M. (2006): Reproduction of the Mottled Piculet in southern Brazil. *J.Field Ornithol.* 77 (3): 244–249.

Pinheiro, R.T. & T. Dornas (2008): New records and distribution of Kaempfer's Woodpecker *Celeus obrieni. Rev.Bras.Orn.*16: 167–169.

Pinheiro, R.T. & T. Dornas, G.A. Leite, M.A. Crozariol, D. Gomes Marcelino & A. Grassi Correa (2012): Novos registros do pica-pau-do-parnaiba *Celeus obrieni* e status conservacao no Estado de Goiás, Brasil. *Rev.Bras.Orn.* 20: 59–64.

Pizo M.A. (2004): Frugivory and habitat use by fruit-eating birds in a fragmented landscape of southeast Brazil. *Ornitol. Neotrop.* 15:117–126.

Pons, J.-M., G. Olioso, C. Cruaud & J. Fuchs (2011): Phylogeography of the Eurasian green woodpecker (*Picus viridis*). *Journal of Biogeography* 38: 311–325.

Porter, R. & S. Aspinall (2010): *Birds of the Middle East.* Helm, London.

Portier, B. (2008): First confirmed record of Cardinal Woodpecker *Dendropicos fuscescens* for Niger. *Bull. ABC* 15: 93–94.

Ouellet-Lapointe, U., P. Drapeau, P. Cadieux & L. Imbeau (2012): Woodpecker Excavations Suitability for and Occupancy by Cavity Users in the Boreal Mixedwood Forest of Eastern Canada. *Ecoscience* 19: 391–397.

Rasmussen, P. C. & J. C. Anderton (2005): *Birds of South Asia: The Ripley Guide.* Vols 1 & 2. Smithsonian Institution and Lynx Edicions, Washington, D.C. & Barcelona.

Reading, R., S. Harris & A. Braunlich (2011): Rufous-bellied Woodpecker *Dendrocopos hyperythrus*: first record for Mongolia. *BirdingAsia* 15: 104–105.

Redman, N., T. Stevenson & J. Fanshawe (2011): *Birds of the Horn of Africa: Ethiopia, Eritrea, Djibouti, Somalia, and Socotra.* Helm, London.

Rêgo, M.A., S. Dantas, E. Guilherme & P. Martuscelli (2009): First records of Fine-barred Piculet *Picumnus subtilis* from Acre, western Amazonia, Brazil. *Bull.Brit.Orn.Club* 129: 182–185.

Rêgo, M. A. (2011). *Taxonomia do complexo Picumnus exilis (Aves: Picidae).* Dissertação de Mestrado, Instituto de Biociências, Universidade de São Paulo, São Paulo.

Rehnus, M., J-P. Sorg & G. Pasinelli (2011): Habitat and cavity tree selection by White-winged Woodpeckers *Dendrocopos leucopterus* in the walnut-fruit forests of Kyrgyzstan. *Acta Ornithologica* 46: 80–92.

Remsen, J. V., Jr., C. D. Cadena, A. Jaramillo, M. Nores, J. F. Pacheco, J. Pérez-Emán, M. B. Robbins, F. G. Stiles, D. F. Stotz, and K. J. Zimmer (2013): *A classification of the bird species of South America.* American Ornithologists' Union. http://www.museum.lsu.edu/~Remsen/SACCBaseline.html

Restall, R., C. Rodner, & M. Lentino (2006): *Birds of Northern South America: An Identification Guide.* Vols.1 & 2. Helm, London.

Ridgely, R.S. (2010): Species Accounts. In Birds of Brazil: the Pantanal and Cerrado of Central Brazil, by J.A.Gwynne *et al.* Cornell University Press.

Rimmer, C.C., J. Klavins, J.A. Gerwin, J.E. Goetz & E.M. Fernandez (2006): Ornithological Field Investigations in Macaya Biosphere Reserve, Haiti, 2–10 February 2006. *Unpublished report.* Vermont Institute of Natural Science, Woodstock, VT.

Roberge, J.-M., P. Angelstam & M.-A. Villard (2008): Specialised woodpeckers and naturalness in hemiboreal forests – deriving quantitative targets for conservation planning. *Biological Conservation* 141: 997–1012.

Roberge, J-M., G. Mikusinski & S. Svensson (2008): The white-backed woodpecker: Umbrella species for forest conservation planning ? *Biodivers. Conserv.*17: 2479–2494.

Robles, H., C. Ciudad, R. Vera, P. P. Olea & E. Matthysen (2008): Demographic Responses of Middle Spotted Woodpeckers (*Dendrocopos medius*) to Habitat Fragmentation. *The Auk* 125: 131–139.

Robles, H. & C. Ciudad (2012): Influence of Habitat Quality, Population Size, Patch Size, and Connectivity on Patch-Occupancy Dynamics of the Middle Spotted Woodpecker. *Conservation Biology* 26: 284–293.

Robson, C. R. (2011): *A Field Guide to the Birds of South-East Asia.* New Holland, London.

Rocca, M. A., M. Sazima & I. Sazima (2006): Woody woodpecker enjoys soft drinks: the blond-crested woodpecker seeks nectar and pollinates canopy plants in south-eastern Brazil. *Biota Neotropica* 6: 1–9.

Rocca, M. A. & M. Sazima (2008):Ornithophilous canopy species in the Atlantic rain forest of southeastern Brazil. *Journal of Field Ornithology*, 79: 130–137.

Rodewald, P.G., M.J. Santiago & A.D. Rodewald (2005): Habitat use of breeding red-headed woodpeckers on golf courses in Ohio. *Wildlife Society Bulletin* 33: 448–453.

Rodriguez Mata, J.R., F. Erize & M. Rumboll (2006): *A field guide to the birds of South America. Non-Passerines: from rheas to woodpeckers.* Collins, London.

Rojas-Soto, O.R., M. Westberg, A.G. Navarro-Sigüenza & R.M. Zink (2010): Genetic and ecological differentiation in the endemic avifauna of Tiburón Island. *Journal of Avian Biology*, 41: 398–406.

Romero, J. L. & J. Perez (2008): Two cooperative breeding cases in Lesser Spotted Woodpecker *Dendrocopos minor. J Ornithol.* 149: 67–74.

Romero, J. L., S. Mucke & J. Perez (2010): A male destroying an egg in a cooperative breeding attempt in Lesser Spotted Woodpecker *Dendrocopos minor. J Ornithol.* 151: 805–809.

Rosas-Espinoza, V.C., E. Maya-Elizarraras, O.F.R. Bustos & F.M. Huerta-Martinez (2008): Diet of Acorn Woodpeckers at La Primavera Forest, Jalisco, Mexico. *Wilson Journal of Ornithology* 120: 494–498.

Rossmanith, E. V. Grimm, N. Blaum & F. Jeltsch (2006): Behavioural flexibility in the mating system buffers population extinction: lessons from the lesser spotted woodpecker (*Picoides minor*). *J. Anim. Ecol.* 75: 540–548.

Round, P.D., J.M. Hobday, R. Kanjanavanit & J.S. Steward (2012): A nesting pair of *Gecinulus* woodpeckers in a likely zone of intergradation between Pale-headed Woodpecker *G.grantia* and Bamboo Woodpecker *G.viridis. Forktail* 28: 113–120.

Sandoval, L. & G. Barrantes (2009): Relationship between species richness of excavator birds and cavity–adopters in seven tropical forests in Costa Rica. *Wilson Journal of Ornithology.* 121:75–81.

Santharam, V. (2003): Distribution, ecology and conservation of the White-bellied Woodpecker *Dryocopus javensis* in the Western Ghats, India. *Forktail* 19: 31–38.

Santharam, V. (2003): Foraging associations and interactions in woodpeckers. *J. Bombay Nat. Hist. Soc.* 100: 627–628.

Santharam, V. (2004): Duetting calls of the Heart-spotted Woodpecker *Hemicircus canente*. *J. Bombay Nat. Hist. Soc.* 101:157–158.

Santharam, V. (2004): Woodpecker holes used for nesting by secondary cavity-nesters in the Western Ghats, India. *J. Bombay Nat. Hist. Soc.* 101: 158–159.

Santos, M.P.D. & M.F de Vasconcelos (2007): Range extension for Kaempfer's Woodpecker *Celeus obrieni* in Brazil, with the first male specimen. *Bull. British Ornith. Club* 127: 249–252.

Savignac, C. & C.S. Machtans (2006): Habitat requirements of the Yellow-bellied Sapsucker, *Sphyrapicus varius*, in boreal mixedwood forests of northwestern Canada. *Canadian Journal of Zoology* 84: 1230–1239.

Schlatter, R. P. (2005): Magellanic Woodpecker (*Campephilus magellanicus*) sap feeding and its role in the Tierra del Fuego forest bird assemblage. *J. Ornithol.* 146: 188–190.

Schroeder, E. L., C.W. Boal & S.N. Glasscock (2013): Nestling Diets and Provisioning Rates of Sympatric Golden-fronted and Ladder-backed Woodpeckers. *The Wilson Journal of Ornithology* 125: 188–192.

Schulenberg, T. S., D. F. Stotz, D. F. Lane, J. P. O'Neill & T. P. Parker. (2007): *Birds of Peru*. Princeton Univ. Press, Princeton, NJ.

Seavy, N. E., R.D. Burnett & P.J. Taille (2012): Black-backed woodpecker nest-tree preference in burned forests of the Sierra Nevada, California. *Wildlife Society Bulletin* 36: 722–728.

Sedano, R., M. Reyes-Gutiérrez & D. Fajardo (2008): Description of nesting, foraging behavior, and vocalizations of the Grayish Piculet (*Picumnus granadensis*) *Ornitología Colombiana* 6:5–14. (In Spanish).

Seneviratne, S.S., D.P.L. Toews, A. Brelsford & D.E. Irwin (2012): Concordance of genetic and phenotypic characters across a sapsucker hybrid zone. *Journal of Avian Biology*, 43: 119–130.

Servin, J., S. Lyndaker Lindsey & B.A. Loiselle (2001): Pileated Woodpecker Scavenges on a Carcass in Missouri. *Wilson Bull.* 113: 249–250.

Short, L. (1982): *Woodpeckers of the World*. Delaware Museum of Natural History. Greenville, Delaware.

Shunk, S. A. (2005): Sphyrapicus Anxiety. Identifying Hybrid Sapsuckers. *Birding* 37: 289–298.

Sibley, D. A. (2000): *The Sibley Guide to Birds*. Alfred A. Knopf, New York.

Sibley, D. A., L. R. Bevier, M.A. Patten & C. S. Elphick (2007): Ivory-billed or Pileated Woodpecker? *Science* 315: 1496–1497.

Sigel, B. J., T. W. Sherry & B. E. Young (2006): Avian community response to lowland tropical rainforest isolation: 40 years of change at La Selva Biological Station, Costa Rica. *Conservation Biology* 20: 111–121.

Silveira, L. F., F. Olmos & A. Long (2003): Birds in Atlantic Forest fragments in Alagoas, northeastern Brazil. *Cotinga* 20: 32–46.

Smart, L. S., J.J. Swenson, N.L. Christensen & J.O. Sexton (2012): Three-dimensional characterization of pine forest type and red-cockaded woodpecker habitat by small-footprint, discrete-return lidar. *Forest Ecology and Management* 281: 100–110.

Snyder, N. F. R., D. E. Brown & K. B. Clark (2009): *The Travails of Two Woodpeckers: Ivory-bills and Imperials*. University of New Mexico Press. Albuquerque.

Solow, A., W. Smith, M. Burgman, T. Rout, B. Wintle & D. Roberts (2012): Uncertain Sightings and the Extinction of the Ivory-Billed Woodpecker. *Conservation Biology* 26: 180–184.

Sreekar, R (2011): Figs in the diet of Greater Golden-backed Woodpecker *Chrysocolaptes lucidus*. *Indian BIRDS* 7: 147.

Strange, M (2012): *A Photographic Guide to the Birds of Indonesia*. Tuttle Publishing, Singapore.

Styring, A. R. & K. Ickes (2001): Woodpecker participation in mixed-species flocks in Peninsular Malaysia. *Wilson Bulletin* 113: 342–345.

Styring, A. R. & K. Ickes (2001): Interactions between the Greater Racket-tailed Drongo *Dicrurus paradiseus* and woodpeckers in a lowland Malaysian rainforest. *Forktail* 17: 119–120.

Styring, A. R. & K. Ickes (2001): Woodpecker abundance in a logged (40 years ago) vs. unlogged lowland dipterocarp forest in Peninsular Malaysia. *Journal of Tropical Ecology* 17: 261–268.

Styring, A. R. & M. Zakaria (2004): Foraging ecology of woodpeckers in lowland Malaysian rain forests. *Journal of Tropical Ecology* 20: 487–494.

Styring, A. R. & M. Zakaria (2004): Selective logging and woodpeckers in Malaysia: the relationship between resource availability and woodpecker abundance. *Journal of Tropical Ecology* 20: 495–504.

Styring, A. R., & M. Z. B. Hussin (2004). Effects of logging on woodpeckers in a Malaysian rain forest: the relationship between resource availability and woodpecker abundance. *Journal of Tropical Ecology 20:* 495–504.

Tarboton, W. R. (1997): Family Picidae: woodpeckers. In: *The atlas of southern African birds. Vol. 1: Non-passerines*. Harrison, J.A., Allan, D.G., Underhill, L.G., Herremans, M., Tree, A.J., Parker, V. & Brown, C.J. (Eds.); 738–752. BirdLife South Africa, Johannesburg.

Thévenot, M., R. Vernon & P. Bergier (2003): *The Birds of Morocco – BOU Checklist N°20*. British Ornithologists Union, Tring, UK.

Tobias, J.A., N. Seddon, C.N. Spottiswoode, J.D. Pilgrim, L.D.C. Fishpool & N.J. Collar (2010): Quantitative criteria for species delimitation. *Ibis* 152: 724–746.

Tøttrup, A. P., F. P. Jensen & K.D. Christensen (2005): The avifauna of two woodlands in southeast Tanzania. *Scopus* 25: 23–36.

Townsend Peterson, A. (2006): Taxonomy *is* important in conservation: a preliminary reassessment of Philippine species-level bird taxonomy. *Bird Conserv. International* 16: 155–173.

Tozer, D.C., E. Nol & D.M. Burke (2011): Quality of mature aspen and maple forests for breeding Yellow-bellied Sapsuckers (*Sphyrapicus varius*). *Canadian Journal of Zoology* 89: 148–160.

Tremain, S.B., K.A. Swiston & D.J. Mennill (2008): Seasonal variation in acoustic signals of Pileated Woodpeckers. *Wilson Journal of Ornithology* 120: 499–504.

Tremblay, J.A., J.Ibarzabal & J-PL. Savard (2010): Foraging ecology of black-backed woodpeckers (*Picoides arcticus*) in unburned eastern boreal forest stands. *Can. J. For. Res.* 40: 991–999.

Tubelis, D. P. (2007): Fruit consumption by *Colaptes campestris* (Aves, Picidae) at Emas National Park, Brazil. *Biotemas* 20: 131–133.

Turner, K (2011): Der Mythos vom Trommeln des Mittelspechts *Dendrocopos medius*. *Limicola* 25: 37–53. (German with English summary).

USDI (2003): *Recovery plan for the Red-cockaded Woodpecker (Picoides borealis)*: second revision. U.S. Department of Interior Fish and Wildlife Service, Atlanta, Georgia, USA.

van Wijk, R. E., M. Schaub, D. Tolkmitt, D. Becker & S. Hahn (2013): Short-distance migration of Wrynecks *Jynx torquilla* from Central European populations. *Ibis.* doi: 10.1111/ibi.12083.

van Perlo, B. (2009): *A Field Guide to the Birds of Brazil.* Oxford University Press, New York.

Varner J.M., J.S. Kush & R.S. Meldahl (2006): Characteristics of Sap Trees Used by Overwintering *Sphyrapicus varius* (Yellow-bellied Sapsuckers) in an Old-growth Pine Forest. *Southeastern Naturalist* 5: 127–134.

Vergara, P. & R. P. Schlatter (2004): Magellanic woodpecker (*Campephilus magellanicus*) abundance and foraging in Tierra del Fuego, Chile. *J. Ornithol.* 145: 343–351.

Vickery, P. D., H. E. Casañas & A. S. Di Giacomo (2003): Effects of altitude on the distribution of Nearctic and resident grassland birds in Córdoba province, Argentina. *Journal of Field Ornithology* 74: 172–178.

Vierling, K.T., D.J. Gentry & A.M. Haines (2009): Nest Niche Partitioning of Lewis's and Red-headed Woodpeckers in Burned Pine Forests. *Wilson Journal of Ornithology* 121: 89–96.

Villard, P., P. Feldmann, A. Ferchal & C. Pavis (2010): Population size and habitat associations of the endemic Guadeloupe Woodpecker. *Journal of Field Ornithology* 81: 278–286.

Virkkala, R. (2006): Why study woodpeckers? The significance of woodpeckers in forest ecosystems. *Ann. Zool. Fennici* 43: 82–85.

Vishnudas, C. K. (2008): Crematogaster ants in shaded coffee plantations: a critical food source for Rufous Woodpecker *Micropternus brachyurus* and other forest birds. *Indian Birds* 4:9–11.

Vivero Pol, J. L. (2001): *A guide to endemic birds of Ethiopia and Eritrea.* Shama Books, Addis Ababa, Ethiopia.

Walters, E.L., E.H. Miller & P.E. Lowther (2002): Red-naped Sapsucker (*Sphyrapicus nuchalis*). *The Birds of North America Online* (A. Poole, Ed.). Ithaca: Cornell Lab of Ornithology.

Walters, E.L., E.H. Miller & P.E. Lowther (2002): Red-breasted Sapsucker (*Sphyrapicus ruber*). *The Birds of North America Online* (A. Poole, Ed.). Ithaca: Cornell Lab of Ornithology.

Wang, L., J. T. M. Cheung, F. Pu, D. Li, M. Zhang & Y. Fan (2011): Why do woodpeckers resist head impact injury: a biomechanical investigation. *PloS one, 6:* e26490.

Warakagoda, D. & U. Sirivardana (2009): *The avifauna of Sri Lanka: an overview of the current status. Taprobanica* 1: 28–35.

Warakagoda, D., C. Inskipp, T. Inskipp & R. Grimmett (2012): Birds of Sri Lanka. Helm, London.

Webb, D.M. (2002): Morphological and molecular evolution of the order Piciformes with emphasis on the woodpeckers of the world (subfamily Picinae). *ETD Collection for Wayne State University.*

Webb, D.M. & W. S. Moore (2005): A phylogenetic analysis of woodpeckers and their allies using 12S, Cyt b and COI nucleotide sequences (Class Aves: Order Piciformes). *Mol. Phylogenet. Evol.* 36: 233–248.

Weibel, A.C. & W.S. Moore (2005): Plumage convergence in *Picoides* woodpeckers based on a molecular phylogeny, with emphasis on convergence in Downy and Hairy Woodpeckers. *The Condor* 107: 797–809.

Weisshaupt, N., R. Arlettaz, T. S. Reichlin, A. Tagmann-Ioset & M. Schaub (2011): Habitat selection by foraging Wrynecks *Jynx torquilla* during the Breeding season: identifying the optimal habitat profile. *Bird Study* 58: 111–119.

Wesolowski, T. (2011): "Lifespan" of woodpecker-made holes in a primeval temperate forest: A thirty year study. *Forest Ecology and Management, 262:* 1846–1852.

Whittaker, A.,A. Aleixo & F. Poletto (2008): Corrections and additions to an annotated checklist of birds of the upper rio Urucu, Amazonas, Brazil. *Bull. B.O.C.* 128: 114–125.

Wiebe, K. L. (2002): First Reported Case of Classical Polyandry in a North American Woodpecker, the Northern Flicker. *Wilson Bulletin* 114 (3): 401–403.

Wiebe, K.L. & G.R. Bortolotti (2001): Variation in colour within a population of Northern Flickers: a new perspective on an old hybrid zone. *Can.J. Zool.* 79: 1046–1052.

Wiebe, K. L. & H. Gerstmar (2010): Influence of spring temperatures and individual traits on reproductive timing and success in a migratory woodpecker. *The Auk* 127:917–925.

Wiebe, K. L., W. D. Koenig & K. Martin (2007): Costs and benefits of nest reuse versus excavation in cavity-nesting birds. *Ann. Zool. Fennici* 44: 209–217.

Wiebe, K.L. & W.S. Moore (2008): Northern Flicker (*Colaptes auratus*), *The Birds of North America Online* (A. Poole, Ed.). Ithaca: Cornell Lab of Ornithology.

Winkler, H., D.A. Christie & D. Nurney (1995): *Woodpeckers: a guide to the woodpeckers, piculets and wrynecks of the world.* Pica Press, Robertsbridge, UK.

Winkler, H. & D. A. Christie (2002): Family Picidae (woodpeckers). Pp. 296–555 in del Hoyo, J., A. Ellliot & J. Sargatal, (Eds.): *Handbook of the birds of the World,* 7. Jacamars to Woodpeckers. Lynx Edicions, Barcelona.

Winkler, H., N. Kotaka, A. Gamauf, F. Nittinger & E. Haring (2005): On the phylogenetic position of the Okinawa woodpecker (*Sapheopipo noguchii*). *J. Ornithol.* 146: 103–110.

Yoon, S-H., & S. Park (2011): A mechanical analysis of woodpecker drumming and its application to shock-absorbing systems. *Bioinspir. Biomim.* 6.

Zahner, V., L. Sikora & G. Pasinelli (2012): Heart rot as a key factor for cavity tree selection in the black woodpecker. *Forest Ecology & Management* 271: 98–193.

Zhu, X., D.S. Srivastava, J.N. Smith & K. Martin (2012): Habitat Selection and Reproductive Success of Lewis's Woodpecker (*Melanerpes lewis*) at its Northern Limit. *PloS one* 7(9): e44346.

Zink, R.M., S.V. Drovetski & S. Rohwer (2002): Phylogeographic patterns in the great spotted woodpecker *Dendrocopos major* across Eurasia. *Journal of Avian Biology* 33: 175–178.

Zink, R.M., S, Rohwer, S.V. Drovetski, R.C. Blackwell-Rago & S.L. Farrell (2002): Holarctic phylogeography and species limits of Three-toed Woodpeckers. *The Condor* 104: 167–170.

Zyskowski, K., M. B. Robbins, A. T. Peterson, K. S. Bostwick, R. P. Clay, & L. A. Amarilla (2003): Avifauna of the Northern Paraguayan Chaco. *Ornitologia Neotropical* 14: 247–262.

PHOTOGRAPHIC CREDITS

Front cover: top – adult male Iberian Woodpecker *Picus sharpei* (*Carlos Nazario Bocos*); bottom left – adult female Northern Flicker *Colaptes auratus* (*teekaygee*); bottom centre – adult male Pale-crested Woodpecker *Celeus lugubris* (*Dubi Shapiro*); bottom right – adult female White-browed Piculet *Sasia ochracea* (*Boonchuay Promjiam*). Back cover – adult female Great Spotted Woodpecker *Dendrocopos major* (*Bildagentur Zoonar GmbH*).

Copyright information for the photographs in this book; t = top, b = bottom, l = left, r = right.

Abhishek Das 466t, 475, 493; **Adam Riley/Rockjumper Bird Tours** 86r, 200l, 264b, 308l, 338br; **Adam Scott Kennedy/www.rawnaturephoto.com** 185t, 215l; **Adrian Constantino** 469, 471; **Alain Pascua** 223, 463, 464; **Alex Lees** 330l, 330r; **Amanda Lahaie** 292; **Amano Samarpan** 203, 204, 227r, 228t, 243t, 259b; **Amit Bandekar** 41; **Anatoliy Lukich** 1, 336–362 h; **Andrea Ferreira** 66, 326; **Andy & Gill Swash/worldwildlifeimages.com** 44t, 78, 79t; **Anselmo d'Affonseca** 56, 57t, 64l, 64r; **Anthony Levesque** 107l, 107r; **Apisit Wilaijit** 481, 482–483 h; **A. P. Leventis** 182l, 194l, 194r, 207b, 216, 333t; **Arijit Banerjee** 236b; **Arnel Ceriola** 506; **Arpit Deomurari** 242; 465; **Ariadne Van Zandbergen/FLPA** 193; **assoonas** 495; **Benito Hernández Leyva/www.birdingoaxaca.com** 134, 135b; **Bill Baston/FLPA** 167; **Bim Quemado** 224; **Bob Steele** 271, 272; **Bookchuay Promjian** 88, 89–92h, 93, 437l, 496–500h, 498, 499; **Callan Cohen/www.birdingafrica.com** 191; **Carl-Johan Svensson** 429, 452b; **Carlo Benitez Gomez** 16b; **Carlos Naza Bocos** 337br, 361, 446; **Catherine Chatham** 182r; **Chairunas Adha Putra** 455bl; **Chien Lee/Minden Pictures/FLPA** 91; **Chris Holtby** 466bl; **Chris Li** 92; **Christopher Borges** 331l; **Cláudio Timm** 81t, 300r, 301t, 301b; **Claus Meyer/Minden Pictures** 325; **Clemn A. Macasiano Jr** 222, 473b; **Cristian Jensen/Audouin Birding Tours** 449t; **Con Foley** 243b, 393l, 393r, 423, 424l, 426l, 430r, 437, 458, 486, 487, 496l, 497t, 500, 502, 505; **Dan Polley** 147; **Daniel Koh Swee Huat** 226l, 424r, 428t, 432, 437r, 485, 490l, 490r, 492, 496r, 497b; **Daniel Martínez A.** 337t; **Daniele Occhiato**/www.pbase.com/dophoto 445tr, 445b; **Dario Lins** 333b; **Dario Sanches** 316l; **Dave Hawkins Photography, Nashville, TN USA/www.studiohawkins.com** 16t, 84, 111t, 112, 113, 124, 125l, 142, 143l, 144, 145t, 145b, 270, 149t, 273b, 276, 277t, 277b, 370l, 389t, 411; **Dave Krueper** 340br; **Dave Semler and Marsha Steffen** 196; **David Beadle** 197t; **David Kjaer/naturepl.com** 251r; **David Jirovsky** 266; **David Monticelli** 201l, 211; **David Seibel/BirdsInFocus.com** 319; **David Tipling/FLPA** 29; **Dax Roman** 30bl, 94, 95, 95h, 96t, 96b, 128, 129t, 129bl, 129br; **Dolly Bhardwaj** 241bl; **Dominic Mitchell** 135t; **Double Brow Imagery** 154–160h, 158; **Doug Wechsler/VIREO** 90; **Dubi Shapiro** 127t, 205tl, 374r; **Duncan Butchart** 169br; **Dušan Brinkhuizen** 20b, 323, 329r; **Elizabeth Barrett/animalphotos.me** 267tr; **Ely Teehankee** 470; **Ernst Albegger** 137, 364; **Eyal Bartov** 174, 178t, 262; **feathercollector** 385–397 h; 490h; **Félix Uribe** 122l, 122r, 123, 309l, 309r, 343l, 347b; **Fernando Urbina Torres** 278; **Flávio Cruvinel Brandão** 72, 74; **Florian Andronache** 16, 36–38h; **FloridaStock** 103–150h; **Francesco Veronesi** 249, 400, 401l; **Fredrik Sahlin** 51t; **Gabriel Leite** 327; **Gary Thoburn** 13, 234l, 340t; **Gary Upfold** 39t, 39b; **Gaurav Sharma** 43t; **Gehan de Silva Wijeyeratne** 468–479 h, 477, 478t; **Gerald Marella/Shutterstock** 275, 391; **Gerard Gorman** 28, 40, 46, 62, 63, 152t, 157b, 162, 163h, 164, 186, 205tr, 295b, 312l, 321l, 321r, 360b, 403t, 412t; **Gérard Soury/Biosphoto/FLPA** 143r; **Gerhard Rotheneder** 349bl, 358b, 418l, 418r, 419; **Gerrit Vyn/naturepl.com** 390; **Ghulam Rasool** 2614l; **Ginger Livingston Sanders** 281; **Glenn Bartley/www.glennbartley.com** 68l, 68r, 69tr, 69b, 75, 106, 138b, 269, 283, 289, 290, 291, 292t, 294, 369l, 377, 378t, 378b, 379, 412b; **Gnanaskandan Keshavabharathi** 25bl, 26b, 439t; **Gonzalo Gonzalez** 304t, 306, 307, 357, 359; **Graham Ekins** 195r, 302l, 302c, 415; **Greg Lavaty** 298, 299t; **Greg R. Homel - Natural Elements Productions** 18t, 19, 34, 132, 133t, 136, 146l, 282r, 317, 339, 341, 343t, 343b; **Guillaume Passavy** 189; **Gwo-Chiang Yang** 232t; **Hanne & Jens Eriksen** 244, 245t, 245b; **Harri Taavetti/FLPA** 286, 288, 430l; **Herbert Brehm/Naturepl.com** 293; **Horacio Luna** 387r; **Hugh Chittenden** 35, 38; HY Cheng 225l, 427l, 461; **Ian Merrill** 154, 190; **Ignacio Yufera/FLPA** 23t; **ImageBroker/Imagebroker/FLPA** 37bl, 165; **Ingo Waschkies** 101tl, 169t, 214, 219, 226r, 231, 240, 476b, 504b; **Ishmeet Sahni** 241t, 259t, 431, 480l; **Jaap van der Waarde** 185b; **James Eaton/Birdtour Asia** 27t, 218, 246, 247tr, 254br, 267tl, 348, 394br, 425, 503–508 h; **James Lowen/jameslowen.com** 304b, 305r, 358t, 360t, 363tl, 417; **Jan Axel Cubilla** 328r; **Javier Hernandez Ramos** 108; **J. Dunning/VIREO** 47, 59t; **Jean-Lou Zimmerman/Biosphoto/FLPA** 37br; **Jean-Louis Rousselle** 58, 59b, 308r; **Jean Mayet/Biosphoto/FLPA** 103; **Jim Burns/www.jimburnsphotos.com** 318; **Jeroen Onrust** 373; **Jitendra Bhatia** 241br; **Joab Souza** 41–87h; **Joao Quental** 81b, 299b, 316r, 331r, 381l, 381r; **Joe Fuhrman** 82l, 82r; **Joe Tobias** 380; **Joel N. Rosenthal** 83l, 83r, 413; **Johanna van de Woestijne** 26tl, 31br, 161; **John & Jemi Holmes** 42b, 109; **John Hawkins/FLPA** 449b; **John Holmes/FLPA** 12, 100, 247tl, 392; **John Wright** 450; **Jonathan Martinez** 247b; **José Ardaiz** 254bl; **Jose Carlos Motta Junior** 104t, 388l; **Juan Matute/vultour**

447b; **Judd Patterson/BirdsInFocus.com** 141tl, 279r; **Julien Thurel** 455 br; **Jürgen Rekkers** 120; **Kazuyasu Kisaichi** 234r; **Kenji Takehara** 255, 256, 257t, 257b; **Kevin Schafer/Minden Pictures/FLPA** 371; **Khaleb Yordan** 426tr; **Kithsiri Gunawarden** 438; **Koel Ko** 493h, 494bl, 494br; Koji Tagi 441l, 441r; **Kristian Svensson/www.flickr.com/photos/macronyx** 209l, 217b, 221l, 273t; **Larry Sirvio** 340bl; **Lars Petersson/www.larsfoto.se** 69tl, 89l, 89r, 117b, 181, 183l, 201r, 206, 207t, 209r, 217t, 238r, 312r, 314, 315t, 324, 384, 397, 426br, 430–453h, 433; **Laura Stafford** 141b; **Lee Mott** 261; **Lesley van Loo** 149b; **liewwk@www.liewwkphoto.com** 462r; **Lim Kim Chye** 457; **Lim Swee Yian** 483; **Lloyd Spitalnik/lloydspitalnikphotos.com** 111b; **Luiz Claudio Marigo** 406; **Malcolm Schuyl/FLPA** 140, 141tr; **Manish Singhal** 459; **Marcelo Barreiros** 45, 60, 61, 116tr, 346; **Martin Goodey** 166, 198, 210; **Martin Willis/Minden Pictures/FLPA** 168; **Martin B Withers/FLPA** 172l, 456; **Martin Grimm** 434, 435; **Martin Hale** 232b; **Matteo Photos** 219–265h; **Matthias Dehling** 200r, 383b; **Maxime Dechelle** 14, 49, 315b; **Michael Anton** 506b; **Michel Giraud-Audine** 48, 115, 300l, 347t, 389b; **Michel Poinsignon/naturepl.com** 443; **Mike Barth** 184; **Mike Danzenbaker/Agami.nl** 153; **Mircea Bezergheanu** 269–291h; **Mladen Vasilev** 20t; **Mohd Rosmadi bin Hassan/madibirder.blogspot.com** 508; **Murray Cooper/FLPA** 295t, 344, 408, 409; **NaturePixel** 2-3; **Neil Bowman** 482; **Neil Bowman/FLPA** 37t, 172, 220, 225r, 227l, 264t, 372t, 439b, 460, 462l; **Niall Perrins/www.niall.co.za** 166–188h, 170, 171b, 173r, 199t, 202l; **Nick Athanas/tropicalbirding.com** 43r, 46b, 54, 55, 57b, 65, 73, 79b, 119t, 125r, 127b, 133b, 284, 294–316h, 297, 311, 313l, 313r, 337bl, 343, 367r, 369r, 382, 401r, 402, 410r, 416b; **Niels Poul Dreyer** 53; **Nigel Voaden** 176br; **Nik Borrow** 171t, 178b, 197t, 202r, 208l, 208r; **Niranjan Sant** 237, 395, 396; **Nitin Srinivasamurthy** 428b, 431r, 440l, 455t, 479, 494t; **Noel Ureña/www.costaricabirdingtours.com** 26tr, 85tr, 85b, 121; **Oliver Smart** 398; **Otto Samwald** 30, 285, 286l; **panda3800** 394t, 451, 452t; **Patrice Correia/Biosphoto/FLPA** 509; **Paul Bannick/PaulBannick.com** 279l, 280; **Paul Noakes** 213t, 287r; **Pete Oxford/naturepl.com** 368; **Pete Morris** 23b, 24t, 32, 50, 77, 86l, 87l, 87r, 163, 254tl, 254tr, 354b, 345r, 322t, 322b, 365, 366, 367l, 383t, 398l, 403b, 404, 472; **Peter Hawrylyshy** 296; **Priscilla Burcher** 114b; **Raj Kamal Phukan** 235; **Ralph Martin** 444; **Ram Mallya** 25t, 97, 98–100h, 101tr; **Ramón Moller Jensen** 27b, 67b, 104b, 303, 363b, 375l; **Ramon Quisumbing** 394bl, 468r; **Richard Tipton** 146r, 268, 282l; **Rob Gipman** 195l; **Rob Hutchinson/Birdtour Asia** 221r, 468l, 507l, 507r; **Rob McKay** 335; **Robert Scanlon** 138t, 310, 338bl, 410l; **Robert Wienand** 177t, 215r; **Roberto Güller** 67t, 118, 119b, 126,302r, 305l, 336, 349br, 362, 374l, 375r, 387l, 407, 417t; **Roger Ahlman/www.pbase.com/ahlman** 400–420 h, 414l, 414r; **Roger Tidman/FLPA** 334; **Rolf Nussbaumer/Imagebroker** 155, 159; **Roman Teteruk** 36; **Ronnie Potgieter** 180; **Ronald Gruijters** 22, 25br, 70, 71t, 71b, 363tr, 376t, 388r; **Rudi Petitjean** 233, 251l, 445tl; **Rudimar Narciso Cipriani** 372b, 385, 386; **S & D & K Maslowski/FLPA** 110, 114t; **Samson So** 488; **Santiago Carvalho** 80; **Saturnino Llactahuaman Lastra** 76; **Scott Olmstead** 370r; **Setaphong Tantanawat** 422; **Seyed Bubak Musavi** 260r; **Shivashankar** 101b; **Simon Walkley** 345l; **Soumyajit Nandy** 258; **Stacey Ann Alberts** 176bl; **Stan Tekiela/Naturesmartimages.com** 21tl, 21tr, 21bl, 21br, 353, 354t; **Stephen Shunk/Paradise Birding** 290r; **Steve Bird** 318–332h, 320r; **Steve Blain** 448; **Steve Byland** 160; **Steve Garvie** 177, 188; **Steve Gettle/Minden Pictures** 148; **Stijn de Win** 503, 504t; **Stubblefield Photography** 399; **Super Prin** 423–427 h, 427r; **Swiss Winnasis** 474l, 474r; **Szabolcs Kókay** 440r; **Tadao Shimba** 230t, 230b, 265, 442; **Tan Choo Eng** 476t; **Tang Jun** 484, 485–487 h; **Thomas Hochebner** 31t, 250, 252, 453, 454; **Tokio Sugiyama** 229; **Tom Middleton** 274; **Tom Reichner/Shutterstock** 105; 163; **Tom Vezo/Minden Pictures/FLPA** 352b; **Tomi Muukkonen** 253; **Tonji Ramos** 473t; **Tony Hamblin/FLPA** 267b; **Tony Morris** 51b; **Trevor Ellery** 328l; **Uditha Hettige** 228l, 228r, 466br, 475bl, 475br, 480r; **Uku Paal** 23b; **Un-hoi Jung** 18b; **Valdir Hobus** 43l, 44b, 365–382 h, 405; **Vaughan & Sveta Ashby/Birdfinders** 109, 116tl, 117, 183r, 187, 212, 213b, 238l, 239, 263, 320l, 329l; **Vijay Anand Ismavel** 236t; **Vincent Grafhorst/Minden Pictures/FLPA** 169bl; **Warwick Tarboton** 175, 179, 191h, 192t, 192b, 194–216h, 199b, 205b; **William Price** 349t, 355, 356, 376bl, 376br; **Wim de Groot** 52, 85tl, 102, 139, 447t; **Yap Kah Hue** 98, 99, 489, 491, 501; **Yves-Jacques Rey-Millet** 130, 131, 150, 151, 152b, 156, 157t, 351, 352t.

INDEX

A

B

C

D

E

I

J

K

L

M

N

O

P

Q

R

S

T

U

V

W

X

Y

Z